The Book of
Alternative Photographic Processes

Second Edition

Christopher James, *Kafka-Man*, Venice, 1987 –
Diana plastic toy camera negative—palladium print
(Courtesy of the author)

Christopher James

DELMAR
CENGAGE Learning

Australia • Brazil • Japan • Korea • Mexico • Singapore • Spain • United Kingdom • United States

CENGAGE Learning

The Book of Alternative Photographic Processes, Second Edition
Christopher James

Vice President, Technology and Trades ABU: David Garza

Director of Learning Solutions: Sandy Clark

Managing Editor: Larry Main

Senior Acquisitions Editor: James Gish

Product Manager: Nicole Calisi

Editorial Assistant: Sarah Timm

Marketing Director: Deborah Yarnell

Marketing Specialist: Jonathan Sheehan

Production Manager: Stacy Masucci

Content Project Manager: Andrea Majot

Technology Project Manager: Chris Catalina

Art Director: Bruce Bond

Cover Designer: Dutton and Sherman Design

Cover Photo: Christopher James

For product information and technology assistance, contact us at
Cengage Learning Customer & Sales Support, 1-800-354-9706
For permission to use material from this text or product,
submit all requests online at **www.cengage.com/permissions**
Further permissions questions can be emailed to
permissionrequest@cengage.com

ExamView® and ExamView Pro® are registered trademarks of FSCreations, Inc. Windows is a registered trademark of the Microsoft Corporation used herein under license. Macintosh and Power Macintosh are registered trademarks of Apple Computer, Inc. Used herein under license.
© 2007 Cengage Learning. All Rights Reserved. Cengage Learning WebTutor™ is a trademark of Cengage Learning.

Library of Congress Control Number: 2007942016

ISBN-13: 978-1-4180-7372-5

ISBN-10: 1-4180-7372-5

Delmar
Executive Woods
5 Maxwell Drive
Clifton Park, NY 12065
USA

Cengage Learning is a leading provider of customized learning solutions with office locations around the globe, including Singapore, the United Kingdom, Australia, Mexico, Brazil, and Japan. Locate your local office at **www.cengage.com/global**

Cengage Learning products are represented in Canada by Nelson Education, Ltd.

To learn more about Delmar, visit **www.cengage.com/delmar**

Purchase any of our products at your local bookstore or at our preferred online store **www.cengagebrain.com**

Notice to the Reader
Publisher does not warrant or guarantee any of the products described herein or perform any independent analysis in connection with any of the product information contained herein. Publisher does not assume, and expressly disclaims, any obligation to obtain and include information other than that provided to it by the manufacturer. The reader is expressly warned to consider and adopt all safety precautions that might be indicated by the activities described herein and to avoid all potential hazards. By following the instructions contained herein, the reader willingly assumes all risks in connection with such instructions. The publisher makes no representations or warranties of any kind, including but not limited to, the warranties of fitness for particular purpose or merchantability, nor are any such representations implied with respect to the material set forth herein, and the publisher takes no responsibility with respect to such material. The publisher shall not be liable for any special, consequential, or exemplary damages resulting, in whole or part, from the readers' use of, or reliance upon, this material.

Printed in the United States of America
3 4 5 6 7 17 16 15 14 13

CONTENTS

CHAPTER 1
The Pinhole: Making Pictures with a Box of Air

CHAPTER 2
The Salted Paper Process

CHAPTER 3
The Calotype Process & the Art of Fixing Shadows

CHAPTER 4
The Negative: Alternative Process Options

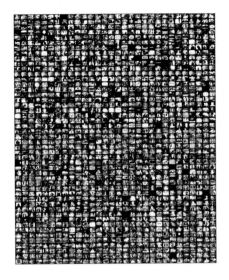

CHAPTER 5
The Digital Options: An Odd History, Workflows for Negatives, & the Digital Arts

CHAPTER 6
The Anthotype & Chlorophyll Process: The Art of Printing with Flowers and Vegetation

CHAPTER 7
The Cyanotype Process

CHAPTER 8
Cyanotype: Variations & Adaptations

CHAPTER 9
The Argyrotype Process

CHAPTER 10
The Van Dyke, B-V-D, & Brownprint

CHAPTER 11
The Kallitype Process

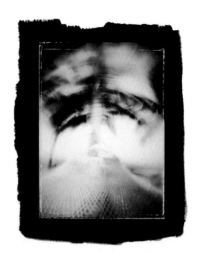

CHAPTER 12
The New Chrysotype Process

CHAPTER 13
The Platinum/Palladium Process

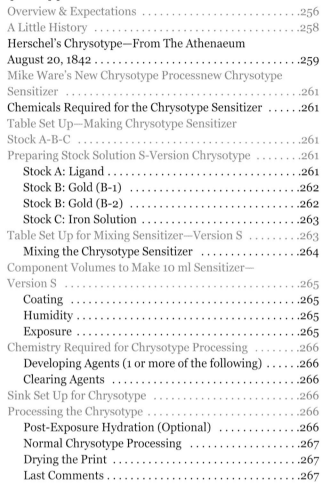

CHAPTER 14
The Ziatype Process

CHAPTER 15
Paper and Alternative Substrates: History, Considerations, Preparation, & Sizing

CHAPTER 17
Dichromate Options: The Chromatype, the Dusting-On Process, Alternative Surfaces for Gum, 3-D Gum Bichromate

CHAPTER 18
The Carbon Print Process

CHAPTER 19
POP: Printing Out Paper

CHAPTER 20
Tintypes & Hand Applied Emulsions

CHAPTER 21
The Albumen Process

CHAPTER 22
Wet Collodion & Gelatin Dry Plate Emulsion

CHAPTER 23
Light Marking: Photographic Alternatives

APPENDIX A
Safety Considerations and Data for Chemicals Used in This Book

APPENDIX B
Small Volume Conversion Table

APPENDIX C
Light & Exposure Options

APPENDIX D
An Alternative Process Working Space

ACKNOWLEDGMENTS

I can't imagine successfully completing a project of this magnitude without the generous collaboration, knowledge, and wisdom of my friends, fellow artists, and family, and with that in mind I'll happily use this space to express my respect and esteem.

First off, I'll make a deep bow of gratitude to my wonderful core group of proofreaders. They are, by unanimous consensus, the very best in the world of alternative process photography and I am honored to call them friends. I am ever grateful for their time and demanding editing. Thank you Mike Ware, France Scully Osterman, Mark Osterman, Judy Seigel, and Dick Sullivan. A special thank you to my colleague, Margot Kelley, for line editing all 1000 pages of my first draft.

Equally sincere thanks to my expert proofreaders: Dan Burkholder, John Paul Caponigro, Dan Estabrook, Sandy King, Allyson Fauver, Jo Babcock, Stephen Livick, Lyle Rexer, John Stilgoe, Cig Harvey, Joy Goldkind, Howard

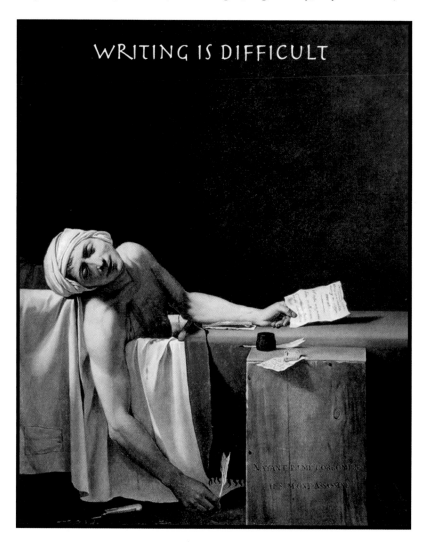

**Christopher James, *Writing is Difficult*, 2007—
appropriated image & text**

Efner, Craig Barber, Brenton Hamilton, Ben Sloat, xtine Burrough, Linda Stemer, Jonathan Bakos, Sandra C. Davis, Marissa Molinaro, Lisa Elmaleh, Rachel Woodburn, Zernike Au, Larry Schaaf, Kevin Sullivan, and Joyce Tennyson.

Thank you to David Stinchcomb, Scott McMahon, Amy Sue Greenleaf, Zoe Zimmerman, Tony Gonzalez, and Galina Manikova for their patience and their process collaboration during the first drafts. Thank you to Joe Boyle for his great illustrations. Thank you, for the second time: Dick Sullivan for all of your input with the carbon process and for letting me play in your great carbon facility in Santa Fe. Thank you, also for the second time, France Scully Osterman, and Mark Osterman, for the weeks you invested in experimenting, proofing, and writing; truly, the wet collodion, albumen, salted paper, and gelatin dry plate topics have never had such intense scrutiny and care.

Anyone who has ever done a project even half this size knows how important it is to have your editor, production team, and publisher believing in what you are creating. I was lucky with the first edition and am lucky again. Thank you to my editor, Jim Gish, Larry Main, Andrew Crouth, Nicole Calisi, Sarah Timm, Andrea Majot, Anne Majusiak (a superb picture researcher if you are seeking one), and Tom Schin, who thought this subject was a good idea seven years ago.

Thanks as well to: Dan Steinhardt at Epson for his support and generosity, John Zokowski of Butler–Dearden Paper, Dave Shafer at Digital Art Supplies, and Shin Koike and Steve Vallario at Pictorico/Mitsubishi Imaging. Thanks to Nicole Miller at The Haines Gallery, Carolyn Francis at Gagoshian Gallery, and Val Bitici at Pace-MacGill Gallery. Thank you to Linda Briscoe Meyer at The Ransom Center/U. of Texas. Thank you to Terry Keeney, former Dean at The Art Institute of Boston, for encouraging me to finally take a sabbatical to write this book. Thanks to my assistant Lisa Ward, and my faculty, for holding down the fort while I took a semester away. None of them ever thought I would ever do such a thing.

Thanks to all of the artists who allowed me to reproduce their excellent work in this book. Your generosity, support, and enthusiasm were outstanding and perfect on every level imaginable.

A heartfelt thanks to my mother and father, Edie and George, for supporting my dreams of being an artist. Thanks to my uncle, Michael James, for showing me, what it meant to be an artist. Have I forgotten anyone? Oh yeah! Just kidding! Most importantly, I thank my wife, Rebecca Welsh, for her perpetually zany sense of humor, love, patience, and support. It was wonderful staying home in the studio, with you and Felix, while I wrote this book. I've never had so much fun!

INTRODUCTION - PART I

This new edition of *The Book of Alternative Photographic Processes* represents a significant part of my evolution as an artist and teacher of artists. For the last three decades, I've been modifying, editing, and adding to this body of knowledge. Before the publication of the first edition, the information was copied and handed out, in chapters, to my students as working notes. The content now represents what we learned together; pertinent and peculiar observations, techniques, anecdotes, and a good dose of interesting history. There are also a lot historical rumors, to enhance the connections between past and contemporary processes and the real people that were involved with them. My intention has always been to entertain and educate, to create a definitive alternative process resource, abundant with images, interesting to read, and user friendly, to guide and entice creativity. I wanted to encourage my students to let their interdisciplinary associations out to play. To paraphrase Mark Twain: it hardly matters when your technique is great if your imagination is out of focus.

Once again, I've organized this book to meet the needs of several different audiences. For teachers, the book is designed to be flexible and compatible with individual teaching styles. I have done my best to make the contents interesting, clear, and accessible to high school and college age students, and to professional artists. A significant number of the illustrations in this book were made by students, and their images are easily integrated with the work of the seasoned professional. This comparative forum helps establish expectations and demystifies the genre.

For the student, this edition is designed as a comprehensive, inspirational and technical resource, addressing historical, procedural, and interdisciplinary connections from the beginnings of photography to its present. The word "student" implies someone in a class, but in truth we are all forever students. This book is a guide for photographers and artists of all abilities and levels. It is increasingly clear that nearly all graphic disciplines, and individual intentions, can be accommodated by the integration of alternative processes into those respective mediums. In essence, the marriage of 19th and 20th century handcraft, science, and romanticism, with 21st-century technologies and concepts.

New to this edition is the following: a complete re-write, hundreds of new images, many new process chapters, coating table and sink set-ups to enhance the learning process, condensed chapters that mirror changes in the media, and a new section that deals with alternative photographic ideas as well as process. It is called Light Marking and the end of that chapter is the beginning chapter of my next book.

I've made every effort to avoid a dogmatic or pedagogical (a favorite word of academics and one I truly dislike) model and I've written the text as though you were sitting next to me. Success in alternative processes blossoms from a willingness to enjoy image-making for the pleasure of the process rather than the product. These processes tend to be mercurial and full of surprises. We learn to enjoy their quirks and see them as opportunities! Much of what the reader discovers will emerge as a result of play. If you don't embrace the play, you probably won't learn a lot.

If you take a moment to consider the things that you do best in your life, you will come to the reasonable conclusion that your unique talents are ones that you taught yourself. This is the truth of how the animal kingdom learns; it is called *play*. It is play that has guided my teaching. It is play that delights the mind and propels the process of teaching yourself just for the joy of it. And that joy is the philosophy of this book.

Christopher James, *Niépce Grab Shot at le Gras,* **2007**

INTRODUCTION - PART II: AN ALLEGORY

Update From Pictureville: 2007

About the time that I wrote the introduction to the first edition of this book, there was a dynamic, and metaphorical, image-making community I called Pictureville. Pictureville consisted of several quite compatible neighborhoods, each with a different approach to decoration, structure, content, and expression, but universally committed to similar ways of seeing and being. They were, in ways that their aesthetic and political leaders would never comprehend, bipartisan and appreciative of the differences between them. They were, in a charming way, compatible.

One of the neighborhoods in Pictureville was committed to tradition and was quite pragmatic in regards to its syntax and philosophical convictions. Sure, there was a lot of political yammering about content and context, but in the end the intentions were compatible, that is, until the emperor's new photographers moved in and began talking about pictures that no one else could see.

This traditionalist neighborhood was split into two parts, based on stylistic beliefs, and was referred to as Upper and Lower Normal. All of the dwellings had white walls, but you always knew which neighborhood you were in by whether there were mirrors, or windows, in the window frames. Both Upper and Lower Normal were constantly damp and smelled like used Rapid Fixer, reminding me of the stench coming from the sidewalk vents in front of the Ferranti-Dege camera store in Harvard Square. I had grown up in this neighborhood, loved it dearly, and the smell, although unpleasant, was comforting and reassuring. People in this community wore analog watches with hands on them.

Pictureville also had a modern digital neighborhood that seemed to have materialized out of thin air. One day the birds were singing and the wind was making those romantic wind noises in the trees; the next, it was all paved, cabled, and wired. There had been rumors that a development like this was coming, but no one had expected it to develop as quickly as it had. Those who had just moved in called this new part of town "The Future."

In The Future, all of the dwellings were in perpetual states of renovation even those that had just been built. Apple wood and adobe were the accepted building materials and the neighborhood was always crowded with visiting, and very young, specialists brought in to assist in the repairs, upgrades, and reconstruction projects. You had no choice really upgrades were required if you wanted to live in The Future. People in this community had watches with digits that blinked. This fact led one of the residents from Upper Normal, on Bath Road, I believe, to ask how the children in this neighborhood would ever learn the meaning of clockwise and counterclockwise.

The oldest section in Pictureville was Alternative Town. This section was populated by a snappy, but friendly, group of "old salts." The structures in this part of Pictureville were made of paper, tin, egg whites, iron, silver, and, in the most elegant part of town, noble metals such as gold, platinum, and palladium. Oddly, most of the dwellings featured dark outlined edges that appeared to be unconcerned with staying in the lines of the house construction.

The inhabitants of this neighborhood enjoyed the eclectic nature of nature and seemed most comfortable mixing, and appropriating, the visual elements of both their neighbors, and the other neighborhoods of Pictureville. The people in this community didn't wear watches but some had sundials on the front lawn.

It seemed that it happened without warning. The residents of the Upper and Lower Normal neighborhoods began to have trouble finding building materials to fix their homes. This, because more and more of the traditionalist building suppliers had stopped producing those materials in favor of those better suited to The Future, the modern, digitally dedicated, neighborhood.

At the same time, the traditionalists were rapidly being seduced by the alluring songs of the Sirens, the digital daughters of Achelous whose singing had lured many an "old salt" onto the proverbial rocks. Their tunes were seductive and it wasn't long before the traditionalists were convinced that the loss of their old materials wasn't that tragic. Who, they asked, wouldn't jump at the chance to trade in their stinky labs for the antiseptic cleanliness of the desktop and the pure dependable beauty of binary code strings over delicate negative films?

And here we are. Pictureville is different now. The smelly neighborhood that I grew up in is shrinking rapidly and getting quainter by the minute. The digital neighborhood is looking a lot like Las Vegas or Los Angeles or Mexico City and the like, when one flies over them at night searching for a place to land. You know what I mean: the neighborhood is so big now that you'll never be able to find its true center.

Oddly enough, Alternative Town is also growing. Once it was clear that only two neighborhoods might survive in Pictureville, many inhabitants from the Upper and Lower Normal communities began to move in. They also began making their own materials and adapting their unique traditions, in a very anti-iconoclastic way, to the cherished parts of Alternative Town and appropriating the useful elements they had found in The Future. For many, the health and well-being of Alternative Town was nothing less than a battle for the very soul of Pictureville. (I hear bagpipes.)

Reality is not as dire as this allegory. True, all the cherished family albums recently burned onto CDs are doomed. All it will take is a decent solar storm, like the one that occurred in 1859, and 17 hours and 40 minutes later it's likely that every hard drive on the receiving end of that solar flare will have instantly become a good doorstop. As I tell my students, if you have an image that means a lot to your family, it would be an excellent idea to make a version of it using an alternative process with a noble metal.

Another thing I tell my students . . . the future of photography is in its past.

© Christopher James, 2007

www.christopherjames-studio.com

The Book of
Alternative Photographic Processes
Second Edition

Christopher James, *Rockets*, Mexico, 1992

The Pinhole: Making Pictures with a Box of Air

OVERVIEW AND EXPECTATIONS

Because this is the first chapter, it is the best time to introduce you to my book's personality and to offer you a pretty honest idea of what you can expect on your way through it. Most people consider my writing style to be conversational and anti-academic-speak . . . I flinch when I hear academics using the words *paradigm* (pair-o-dimes) or *pedagogy* (pet-a-doggie) . . . so I will do my very best to keep it that way.

In this chapter you'll get a compressed overview of some early photographic history and the myriad scientific, social, cultural, and artistic connections that revolved around the camera obscura and pinhole camera. This is the first of the "*A Little History*" sections, and although it may appear to be extensive, it is this prehistory that sets the stage for a great deal of what follows in the book. You'll find *A Little History* beginning nearly every chapter, and I have made an effort to fill it with salient historical references as well as the odd, ironic, and silly things that permeate most human endeavors.

You'll also get a little science that briefly explains how the pinhole camera works and instructions on how to make one. You'll learn how to test your pinhole camera and how to use it. Also included are easy solutions for those of you who are "*handmade impaired*," which direct you to resources, images, and Internet sites for more information on this wonderful and idiosyncratic way of making images.

As in every chapter in the book, you will get an abundant number of historical—and contemporary—images to make the visual connections and to inspire you to make your own contributions to this history.

Figure 1–1

Christopher James, *Kassi, San Pancho, Mexico*, 2007

There is a beautiful beach on the Pacific Coast of Mexico, about 80 miles north of Puerto Vallarta, where our friends Jeff and his dog Kassi spend their winters. Kassi has ambitions regarding the circus. I made this image of her practicing on Polaroid Type 55 P/N film using a Zero Image 4" × 5" pinhole camera with a zone plate.

(Courtesy of the author)

A LITTLE HISTORY

The Conception and Connections

First the rumors: It is reported that the earliest writing regarding the camera obscura ("*dark room*" in Latin) occurred in the 5th century BCE (*Before Common Era*) diaries of Chinese philosopher Mo Tzu. In his journals, Mo Tzu contemplated the effects and nature of light and the reflection presented by an inverted image when light, and the image carried in it, passed through a small hole and landed upon an opposing flat surface. Mo Tzu also advocated a philosophy that was based on the principle of loving everything . . . a 5th century BCE hippie. Just for the record . . . Mo Tzu, in many writings about pinhole history, is incorrectly identified with the philosopher Lao Tzu (Ti).

Much later, somewhere in the vicinity of 350 BCE, Aristotle (384–322 BCE) witnessed corresponding phenomena during an eclipse and included the concept of a camera obscura in his syllabus and curriculum. Evidently the next time someone thought the optical magic of the camera obscura was worthy of investigation was nearly 1,300 years later when the renowned Arabian mathematician and physicist, Ibn al-Haitam, c. 965–1040, used a pinhole aperture, as had his hero Aristotle, to view an eclipse.

Ibn al-Haitam (also known as Ibn al-Haytham, al-Hazen, al-Basri and al-Misri) was a big fan of the third of the Big-Three Greek philosophers (Socrates, Plato and Aristotle), and it was Aristotle's writing that persuaded al-Haitam to abandon his dedicated religious studies in order to adopt a life in pursuit of scientific truth. Al-Haitam is reputed to have penned nearly 100 separate works (of which only 52 are known today) explaining diverse inquiries into such subjects as optics, the linearity of light, and the squaring of a circle.

In his experiments with candles and paper screens having small apertures, he described the linear propagation of light and how a light-image, traveling through his tiny paper apertures, became more focused as the aperture was made smaller . . . like going from f. 1.5 to f. 64. Al-Haitam expressed his amazement over this observation in his book, *On the Form of an Eclipse,*

in 1038. The dissemination of this work may have led to the following story regarding the practical applications of the camera obscura.

A thousand years ago (more or less), nomadic tribes in the deserts of the Middle East were fully aware of the light (*fotizo*) writing (*graphi*) image. In the beginning, so the story goes, these wanderers would rest during the intense heat of the day and travel at night when the conditions were less difficult for man and beast. In their tents, protected from the sun, they could rest and gaze out of their tent openings scanning the horizon for possible problems, relatives perhaps, who might come from that general direction. Occasionally, they would take a glance at a shimmering, upside down "*shadow picture*" of the view from the other direction . . . the one behind the tent. This image was projected upon the solid wall of the tent. To make this inverted image, they would poke a small hole (*the aperture*) into the wall of the tent that was at their back. The landscape of that view, illuminated by the intense reflections of sun and sand, would, as in a camera, flip and project an upside-down version of that scene on the tent wall opposite the hole. Lots of holes, lots of views, as long as the tent was dark, and the resting nomads could relax knowing that they were alone and free of company. Thus, the basic principles of photographic optics were exploited for purely practical reasons. Perhaps this was the knowledge that launched al-Haitam's inspiration.

Officially, however, academic historians give the credit to the remarkable Greek mentor-philosopher, Aristotle, who noticed that light rays converged in order to pass through small holes that had been punched out of opaque objects. Aristotle also noted that these same light rays diverged on the back-side of the opaque plane in exactly the same way they went through the front in straight lines. As a result, the image illuminated was seen upside down and in proportion to the original. Aristotle's experiments also demonstrated that the shape and proportions of the camera obscura, such as the focal length (distance from the aperture to the wall of the camera opposite the aperture) had a direct relationship to how the image was seen on the final projection surface. What Aristotle could never figure out, however, is why the image from a geometrically squared aperture would result in a circular image. In any event,

Figure 1–2

Joe Boyle, *Finger Puppeteer in Camera Obscura Tent*

My illustrator, Joe Boyle, is a graduate of The Art Institute of Boston at Lesley University. Now with his own business, I hired Joe to do the icons and drawing in this book. This is one we came up with after discussing how you might pass the time in a camera obscura tent . . . making up finger puppet stories seemed like a good idea.

(Courtesy of the artist)

there was no concept of saving the image; it was just interesting to look at and trace.

In the early 1400s two Italian gentlemen had a significant influence on the way artists would observe and record three-dimensional objects and space on a flat two-dimensional plane, such as paper, canvas, or a wall destined to become a fresco. In the first decade of that century, Italian architect, Filippo Brunelleschi (1377–1446), was a prominent exponent of one-point perspective which seemed suddenly to be everywhere in Europe. Brunelleschi's odd, photographically rendered architectural tracings from the camera obscura solidly support this historical impression. Brunelleschi, by the way, won a major architectural competition to design the prominent dome of Florence's Santo Maria del Fiore. Coincidentally, the famed Italian astronomer, Paolo Toscanelli (1397–1482), installed a bronze plate, with a pinhole aperture, in a window of Santa Maria del Fiore, and on sunny days a projected image of the sun can be clearly seen on the floor of the church, as a notation of time. A wonderful book on Brunelleschi and his dome written by Ross King is well worth reading (*Brunelleschi's Dome: How a Renaissance Genius Reinvented Architecture*).

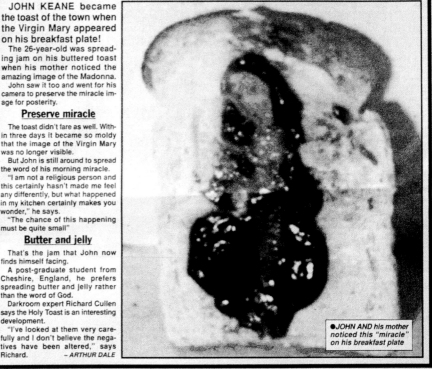

VIRGIN MARY APPEARS ON A SLICE OF TOAST

JOHN KEANE became the toast of the town when the Virgin Mary appeared on his breakfast plate!

The 26-year-old was spreading jam on his buttered toast when his mother noticed the amazing image of the Madonna.

John saw it too and went for his camera to preserve the miracle image for posterity.

Preserve miracle

The toast didn't fare as well. Within three days it became so moldy that the image of the Virgin Mary was no longer visible.

But John is still around to spread the word of his morning miracle.

"I am not a religious person and this certainly hasn't made me feel any differently, but what happened in my kitchen certainly makes you wonder," he says.

"The chance of this happening must be quite small"

Butter and jelly

That's the jam that John now finds himself facing.

A post-graduate student from Cheshire, England, he prefers spreading butter and jelly rather than the word of God.

Darkroom expert Richard Cullen says the Holy Toast is an interesting development.

"I've looked at them very carefully and I don't believe the negatives have been altered," says Richard. — ARTHUR DALE

●JOHN AND his mother noticed this "miracle" on his breakfast plate

Figure 1–3

Touch This Miracle Photo and Be Cured

I am addicted to Weekly World News and recommend to anyone teaching art history that it is a fine idea to pepper your lectures with Weekly World News pages, as they really are an invigorating remedy for the standard "art in the dark" class experience. *(Courtesy of Weekly World News / American Media Inc.)*

The second gentleman was Leon Battista Alberti (1404–1472), literally the "point-man" for the illumination of Renaissance artistic theory. In his 1435 treatise, *de Pictura*, "On Painting" (dedicated to Brunelleschi by the way), Alberti—dashing eternal prototype of the universal Renaissance Man—described how the perspective idea worked, illustrating the concept of the theoretical, and real, window of the camera obscura and what possibilities that optical instrument offered to the artist on its glass-tracing surface. Alberti called the drawings that came from his own camera obscura "miracles."

In 1490, Leonardo da Vinci (1452–1519) supposedly made the first recorded drawing of a camera obscura and its operation in his *Codex Atlanticus* (1478–1518 c.). He was presumably aware of how an artist could use this contraption in order to chronicle real-life by drawing the image projected by the camera obscura. However, because da Vinci wrote with his less-dominant hand, and backwards, it took about 300 years before anyone managed to decode his inspirations and confer proper credit for them. When his thoughts were finally deciphered, it turned out that his words were as beautiful as his paintings and works in marble. He wrote of the camera obscura,

> *"Who would believe that so small a space could contain the image of all the universe? O mighty process!"*

Shortly thereafter, in 1558, Giambattista della Porta (c. 1535–1615) began writing about the focusing abilities of differently shaped pieces of glass in what would eventually become his published, four-volume *Magiae Naturalis*; a major work that he began at the age of 15! There was a problem with the della Porta attribution . . . no one was ever able to verify that the idea was originally his. This is due to della Porta's politically inspired habit of assigning credit for his discoveries to others who were more socially or politically powerful. For his work on the telescope he gave credit to Frederico Cesi, the president and founder of the Academy of Lynxes, an association for the advancement of science, to which both he and Galileo belonged.

The first person actually credited with placing a lens for focusing on a camera obscura was the infamous mathematician, Girolamo Cardano (1501–1576), in 1550. Cardano was a brilliant individual but, like many special people who fail to fit into the "normal" mold, he had a reckless weakness for gambling and socially questionable nightlife activities. His extensive analysis of the "theory of probability" greatly assisted his gambling addiction but got him into an incredible amount of trouble with his family and associates.

Cardano's brainstorm of placing a lens on the camera obscura was described quite clearly in 1568 by the Venetian, Daniele Barbaro (1513–1570), in his book, *La prattica della perspettiva*. Here Barbaro wrote of "*the magic, clouds, water twinkling and flying birds,*" and noticed that one could actually record this magical life by means of tracing, as long as the user moved the tracing paper towards, and away from, the lens in order to achieve focus. Other historical accounts give credit for the first lens, in 1583, to Giovanni Benedetti, curtly describing his invention as a "*solid hunk of non-moveable glass*" on the camera obscura.

Honestly, giving credit for the idea of moveable lens focus is pretty difficult because no one really knows the exact facts of the matter. This is also true when attempting to attribute first discovery of other related inventions partly because, as the axiom goes, the "winners" write the history. A good example of this, if I may offer a short detour, is the invention of the telescope, the microscope, and Heliocentric Theory.

Connections

Credit for the telescope had been demanded by several gentlemen, including Hans Lippershey (1570–1619), an eyeglass maker in Holland who, in 1608, came up with the idea of a telescope by watching two children play with discarded convex and concave glass lenses on the floor of his optical shop. Coincidentally, Jacob Metius of

Figure 1–4
Leonardo da Vinci (1452–1519), *Self Portrait*
(Courtesy, Biblioteca Reale, Turin, Italy)

Belgium filed for his own patent rights to the telescope. Although Metius's extensive work with convex and concave optics was well known, his proprietary rights over Lippershey could not be established, and, for political and financial reasons, Metius decreed that all his notes and tools be destroyed upon his death.

A parallel anecdote from 1609 described a tale in which Galileo Galilei (1564–1642) got wind of Lippershey's optical invention while Hans was on his way to Italy to present a show & tell and hopefully sell his new telescope to the Venetians . . . who were always enthusiastic about owning great art and ideas. According to this tale, Galileo quickly reasoned that his appropriation of Lippershey's wonderful idea

Figure 1–5

Reinerus Gemma-Frisius, *Solar Eclipse, 1544—*
Camera Obscura

Reinerus Gemma-Frisius witnessed an eclipse of the
sun at Louvain on January 24, 1544. In his book, *De
Radio Astronomica et Geometrica*, 1545, Gemma-
Frisius used this illustration to document that event.
According to John H. Hammond's book, *The Camera
Obscura, A Chronicle*, it is considered to be the first
published illustration of a camera obscura . . ."

might be a perfect way to extricate himself from the
chronic state of debt, which was an irksome distraction to his existence as an intellectual. Within days,
Galileo constructed a telescope, presumably using
della Porta's *Magiae Naturalis* book on *Refraction* as
a guide, and beat Lippershey to Venice; this deception
proved to be both that historically, and personally, a
lousy idea. Here's why . . .

Galileo was an ardent disciple of Polish astronomer
Nicolaus Copernicus's (1473–1543), who had developed a
Heliocentric Theory (*helio* meaning *sun* and *centric*
meaning *center*) declaring the sun, and not the earth, at
the center of all planetary movement in the universe.
While not at all radical now, Copernican theory was
absolutely counter to the ancient and accepted theological

view of the Greek astronomer Ptolemy (127–151) that
placed the earth at the center of the universe.

Ptolemy had created a system where all heavenly
bodies could be tracked through an indecipherable application of cycles. Better still, Ptolemy had actually determined the latitude and longitude of all 1,022 stars in the
sky. That's correct . . . all one thousand and twenty-two of
them. It is interesting to note that Copernicus's idea
about the heavens was originally that of Aristarchus of
Samos (310–230 BCE), who had attempted to figure out
the distances between the sun, moon, and earth with his
good friend Eratosthenes of Cyrene (276–195 BCE).

In 1632, the Catholic Church decreed that it had had
enough of this Copernican nonsense and reacted rather
petulantly when Galileo aimed his telescope at the heavens

and publicly proclaimed, approximately 2,000 years after Aristarchus and Eratosthenes, and 118 years after Copernicus, that the earth did indeed move around the sun.

As they say, "Heaven Forbid" . . . and the church, never an institution to adapt quickly to scientific revelations concerning the heavens, officially proclaimed Galileo's announcement as heresy, threw him in the holy jail, and remained adamant that he was guilty as sin, until 1992, three hundred and sixty years later, when it decided to forgive and forget. As an aside, Galileo is often given credit, along with Anton van Leeuwenhoek (1632–1723) and Robert Hooke (1635–1703), for inventing the microscope.

Leeuwenhoek constructed and used single-lens microscopes and made the landmark discovery of bacteria by bravely examining plaque in the mouth of an old man who, in his entire life, had never cleaned his teeth. Also, Hooke constructed a lens that he called a "compound" microscope, and in 1665, wrote *Micrographia*, one of the most influential biology texts in history. None of these distinguished scientists was, in fact, responsible for the microscope. The actual inventors were the father and son collaborators Hans and Zacharias Jansen, of Middleburg, Holland, who, in 1595, crafted a small, working instrument that they christened "The Royal Jansen."

With the advent of the telescope, and the ability to craft and work glass into tools of magnification, scientists placed multiple, and multiply shaped, lenses on their small camera obscura holes. They then noticed that, depending on the focal length (the distance between the aperture and the plane where the image landed, the image distance), they could focus and alter the effects of the image.

In 1604, mathematician and father of modern optics, Johannes Kepler (1571–1630), worked out a formal relationship between mirrors, lenses, and vision. Five years later, in 1609, Kepler wrote a book titled *Astronomia nova* that had a profound influence on the way scientists thought about light; he was the first to describe the "ray theory of light" to explain vision and what our eyes are able to see. One of the strongest reactions to Kepler's work, was seen in the writings of Isaac Newton (1643–1727) who, in 1675, demonstrated with a prism that white light wasn't really white at all . . . that

Figure 1–6

John A. Whipple (1822–1891), *The Moon,* **1852**

This image is reputed to be the first daguerreotype of the moon although there is some evidence that Jean Claudet made the first in 1845. He was also the first to produce images of stars other than the sun (*Vega and the double star Castor and Pollux*). This image was exposed at the 15-inch refractor of the Harvard College Observatory, Cambridge, Massachusetts, and February 26, 1852. Prints were made with Whipple's glass plate, albumen sensitized, *Cyrstalotype Process,* and glued into the world's first photography magazine, *The Photographic Art-Journal,* 1853.
(Courtesy of Harvard College Observatory, Cambridge, Massachusetts)

it was actually an entire spectrum of colors. Kepler, by the way, is credited with being first to use the words "camera obscura."

The evolution of these early cameras, which worked nicely as drawing aids for painters, is fairly well documented. But for the advent of photography itself, some chemical discoveries also had to happen. In 1727, Johann Heinrich Schulze discovered the darkening effects of light on silver salts when he mixed silver-contaminated nitric acid with chalk, creating silver carbonate that reacted to sunlight by turning the compound a dark violet. A short time later, Swedish chemist Carl Wilhelm Scheele published the book, *Chemical Observations and*

Figure 1–7
Edyta Wypierowska, from
Still Life II Series, 2004–2005—pinhole
This graphic tableau, still life,
construction was created using a
pinhole camera.
(Courtesy of the artist)

Experiments on Air and Fire. He described how the blue-violet end of the spectrum had a noticeable impact on a compound of silver and chlorine (*silver chloride*) through the chemical act of reduction, i.e., salt to metal. (More on Schulze, and the related work of Scheele, in the salted paper chapter.)

The camera obscura, however, was still going strong. Count Francesco Algorotti suggested in his book *Essays on Painting* (1764) that many Italian painters were presumably using the "contrivance"—for how else to explain the realism of their drawings. This realism was especially demanded for portraiture, and in 1786, the camera obscura took its turn at providing the wished-for reproducible reality, through the invention of the *Physionotrace* by Frenchman Gilles-Louis Chrétien (1754–1811). If you wanted to stretch an association, you could say that the Physionotrace heralded the beginning of modern art. They didn't know it yet, but painters around the world were about to be set free from the task of forever painting the likenesses of those who could afford it. A photographic likeness, however, was required to guarantee the change.

Then something really important happened. In London, on the 5th of November, 1794, Mrs. Elizabeth Fulhame self-published a book modestly titled, *An Essay on Combustion, with a View to a new Art of Dyeing And Painting, wherein the Phlogistic and Antiphlogistic Hypotheses are Proved Erroneous*. This grandiose title described a tedious series of experiments that began in the summer of 1780, because Mrs. Fulhame wanted to devise a way of staining fabric for her dresses with heavy metals such as silver and gold. She hypothesized that this might be possible with the influence of water and light, and her research led her to conclude that water played the major role in catalytic reactions as both the *reducing* and *oxidizing* agent. She also noted that after those reactions had occurred, the water was always restored to its original state.

More than one photographic historian has suggested that Elizabeth Fulhame's great achievement, the discovery of *Catalysis*, was the beginning of photography as an art based on scientific and chemical principles. Elizabeth Fulhame's social position as the well-to-do and charming wife of Dr. Fulhame, and her status as an amateur scientist, resulted in her thesis being ignored except for Count Rumford, by the scientific and academic community. This quasi-official reaction didn't seem to temper her zeal or curiosity. In a response she wrote, "*. . . censure is perhaps inevitable; for some are so ignorant at the sight of any thing, that bears a semblance of learning, in whatever shape it may appear; and should the spectre appear in the shape of a woman, the pangs which they suffer, are truly dismal.*"

What Happened . . . Niépce

In 1816, Nicéphore Niépce (1765–1833) attempted the second "camera obscura-based" images by making salted paper (silver chloride) negatives . . . Thomas Wedgwood had made the first silver chloride images using a microscope in 1802 and by contact printing objects. These first experiments by Niépce and his brother Claude, using a camera obscura, were designed to be used with a hot air, engine-powered, lithography press that the brothers had designed together. Their first results yielded negative images that Niépce was only partially able to preserve. In 1817, he turned his attention to *guaiacum*, a resin produced by a small evergreen in tropical America, that would change color and harden (become insoluble) upon exposure to sunlight. Still frustrated at not being able to capture an image using a camera obscura, he began investigating the possibility of using bitumen of Judea which exhibited similar light sensitive attributes.

As an aside: By 1819, Niépce was busy working on a way to save his images using a very stinky Dippel's Oil (a.k.a., pyridine or bone oil . . . *oil from the bones of animals*) and oil of lavender (*today sold as an oil to instill feelings of love and peace*). Curiously and concurrently, on the 8th of January, 1819, in the *Edinburgh Philosophical Journal*, Sir John Herschel (1792–1871) wrote, "*Muriate of silver (silver chloride), newly precipitated, dissolves in this salt (referring to hyposulphite of soda—discovered by Chaussier in 1799) almost as readily as sugar in water.*" Herschel's discovery was the foundation for his

Figure 1–8

Joseph Nicéphore Niépce, *Cardinal d'Amboise,* **1827—Heliograph**
Although Niépce had made salted images using a camera obscura as early as 1816, he was unable to preserve them. In 1817, he turned his attention to *guaiacum*, a resin produced by a small evergreen in tropical America, that would change color and harden upon exposure to sunlight. Niépce also began experimenting with bitumen of Judea, and by 1822 he had successfully produced a copy of an engraving. Niépce applied varnish to an etching, making the paper support translucent. Once the paper had dried, he placed it in direct contact with a pewter, copper, or tin plate coated with a thin layer of bitumen of Judea. The plate was then exposed to direct sunlight in contact with the varnished engraving and subsequently immersed in a bath of oil of lavender, thinned with a white kerosene solvent, that dissolved the unhardened / unexposed bitumen of Judea.
(Courtesy of The National Media Museum/Science & Society Picture Library (also the new repository for the collection of the Royal Photographic Society), London)

announcement in 1839, twenty years later, that he could fix a *photograph* . . . a word he is given credit for coining.

By 1822 Niépce had successfully produced a copy of an engraving by exposing a glass plate coated with bitumen of Judea hat he had placed in contact with an engraving on paper. Bitumen of Judea is a photosensitive agent (*light hardens it*) that is natural asphalt, like tar. Known since antiquity, it was gathered from the Dead Sea (*also known as Asphalite Lake*) where it floated, naturally, to the surface from the seabed. The Egyptians used this unique material to embalm the dead before entombment and as a caulking for waterproofing ships. It was also employed as a weatherproof construction material for the tiles and terraces of Babylon. By the 19th century, the process for extracting bituminous tar from rock was well known, and it was this generic material that Niépce used, not the exotic type from the Dead Sea.

In 1824, Niépce put a lithographic stone, coated with bitumen of Judea, inside his camera obscura, and after a rather lengthy exposure, made the very first "fixed" continuous tone image . . . a landscape. Unfortunately, this image was immediately lost when Niépce attempted to etch the stone for lithographic printing.

The first successful positive photographic image was made by coating a pewter (also silver-coated copper) plate with the light-sensitive asphalt dissolved in lavender oil (also called *spike*). The asphalt layer would, upon exposure to UV sunlight, become less soluble. This is essentially a polymer process similar to the one that occurs in the gum bichromate process when a dichromate is added to a solution of gum Arabic, water, and paint, and is then exposed to ultraviolet (UV) light.

Niépce applied varnish to an etching, making the paper support translucent. Once the oiled paper had dried, he placed it in direct contact with a pewter, copper, or tin plate coated with a thin layer of bitumen of Judea, which he gently heated to cure the coating. The plate was then exposed to direct sunlight in contact with the varnished engraving for 4–5 hours and subsequently immersed in a bath of oil of lavender thinned with a white kerosene (known in Europe as *paraffin*) solvent. The bitumen that had been protected from light under the lines of the engraving then dissolved, revealing the unexposed metal. The resulting plate was a negative version of the engraving, but one that could be etched with a Dutch Mordant* to produce positive prints on a press. He called the process Heliography and he called the images he made "*retinas*."

🐝 **Note: Dutch Mordant is a metal-dissolving solution used prior to etching with nitric acid in printmaking for cutting into metal plates. Its recipe is: 1 liter Water, 125 ml hydrochloric acid, 25 g potassium chlorate and 25 g sodium chloride. Hydrochloric acid mixed with potassium chlorate makes a highly toxic chlorine gas. It is safer to make your Dutch Mordant with ferric chloride, i.e., a stock solution of 2 parts water to 1 part ferric chloride. Please consult an expert printmaker for advice and safety concerns before attempting to make a Dutch Mordant solution.**

Making a Heliograph with a Camera Obscura: A Quick Explanation

Step 1 Make an approximately 5%–10% solution. Dissolve powdered Judea bitumen in oil of lavender until it is the consistency of syrup. This doesn't work well for the first week or so after it's made. Howard Efner, who does a good deal of experimenting with Dick Sullivan in Santa Fe, reports using a 2.5% to 5% stock solution of asphalt in xylene. You can substitute xylol for the xylene, and this product is fairly simple to find in most hardware stores. If the coating is too thick, you'll get flaking during development. The 5% solution is easier to prepare.

- 5 g asphaltum
- 100 ml xylene

Store solution in a dark glass bottle for a week, and decant through a filter before using.

Step 2 Meticulously clean a metal or glass plate and rinse it with paint thinner and allow it to dry.

Step 3 Using a pipette, or eye dropper, take several ml of your 5% stock solution and dilute it with an equal volume of xylene or xylol . . . this will give you a 2.5% solution. Warm your substrate (glass, tin, copper, etc.) and pour on the solution, moving the plate around until the excess has flowed off. Then let it dry flat or, as in wet collodion, heat the bottom of the substrate and let the solution evaporate more quickly. By hot drying the plate you will end up with a dark cherry red-colored, and glossy, plate. If you are using a silver plate, the color will be yellow.

🐚 **Note: According to Mark Osterman, at Eastman House, the original technique for thick coatings used in the acid-etched plates was with a pencil . . . also known at that time as a small paintbrush. The asphalt was painted on in thin overlapping stripes, which evened out when the plate was heated. The technique for applying thin coats for direct positives was with a leather dauber . . . like those used to apply ink to type in the old days . . . the collodion technique is not good for this process.**

Step 4 Load this plate into a view camera and expose it to a subject illuminated by UV light for about 8–10 hours. If you are in a hurry you can make a contact positive in a mechanical UV exposing box. A UV box exposure will take 1–4 hours. It is important to remember that heat will harden the asphalt, so you need a combination of the brightest light with the least amount of heat.

Step 5 After the exposure, you won't see much of anything. Have faith.

Step 6 Immerse the plate in a glass, metal, or enamel tray of kerosene with a little oil of lavender and the unexposed/unhardened bitumen of Judea will dissolve and fall off the plate. You may also use an alternative developer consisting of 25 ml xylene and 75 ml naphtha (also known as paint thinner or mineral spirits). A 100 ml mix will be adequate for developing an 8 × 10. The more dissolved asphalt in the solvent, the more control you will have over your development. To remove all of the softened asphalt you will need to very gently wash the plate in water. Be careful not to add too much xylene to the solvent mixture as that may dissolve the image.

Step 7 The image you will see will be a negative.

Step 8 One way that Niépce made positives was to underexpose the plate that had been coated with a matte (or waxed) varnish. If the asphalt coating was thin enough, you may look at the plate at a low angle, and in dim light, you see a positive. This is what you see when you under expose or underdevelop film and hold it up against a dark background.

Step 9 The other way of getting to a positive is to use a highly polished silver plate as a substrate. This technique requires a thicker coating and careful development to create a relief image. Once the exposure has been completed, *and this may take days*, develop the plate and place it in a closed box with crystals of iodine. Within a short time, the fumes will penetrate the asphalt layer in proportion to the exposure in the camera obscura. For a line-art image, the silver portions of the plate unprotected by the varnish will be iodized, creating a *silver-iodide* compound. When the varnish is removed with a solvent, the silver iodide will blacken when exposed to light . . . creating a positive image.

By 1826, Niépce began exposing a scene directly in the camera and created what is considered to be the first photographic image: *View From the Window at Gras, 1826*. In 1827, Niépce took his discovery to England with the ambition of presenting it to the Royal Society and getting a little credit for his years of dedicated work. Niépce, however, was unwilling to reveal all of his formulas and technique, and this proved to be a significant stumbling block, as that documentation was a requirement of the Royal Society for acceptance. Niépce returned to France convinced that the English were inept.

Meanwhile, that same year, Niépce and Louis Jacques Mandé Daguerre (1787–1851) were introduced to one another by an optician named Charles Chevalier. (In some historical accounts, an engraver named Lemaitre initiated their introduction.) Daguerre was widely known as an engaging entrepreneur and the proprietor of the famous Parisian Diorama, a spectacularly lit, theater-like experience likely based on Robert Barker's *Panorama* from 1794.

In December of 1827, Niépce was called to England to attend to his brother Claude who had become quite ill. Niépce's travel plans went badly and so he took the

Figure 1–9

Joseph Nicéphore Niépce ((1765-1833), *"Point de Vue du Gras"/View of the Window & Courtyard at le Gras,* **1826—heliograph**

This image is, by almost unanimous agreement, the first camera-generated photographic image ever made.

(Courtesy of The Gernsheim Collection, Ransom Center, U. of Texas-Austin, Texas)

opportunity to arrange a meeting with Daguerre. Some accounts place the meeting in Paris while other versions put them in a carriage or coach. In any event, the two men got along well. Niépce was transfixed by Daguerre's theatrical Diorama and very much interested in his interest in capturing the effects of that theater with a camera obscura. Daguerre had tried saving an image within a camera obscura with a plate coated with phosphorescent powders. He did indeed manage to record a light-induced image, but it lasted a very short time, slowly fading from sight, as he was unable to fix it. Essentially, each of the men had interests and abilities that greatly impressed the other and they agreed to exchange letters. By 1829, after much correspondence, Niépce suggested a partnership in order to finish his work on the Heliograph. By 1832, a year before Niépce died, they worked together at Niépce's estate at Gras inventing a new process called the Physautotype.

The Physautotype

The Physautotype (*fizz–auto-type—from the Greek meaning "a copy of nature herself"*) can be explained simply. Niépce and Daguerre evaporated oil of lavender or colophony (a.k.a., rosin) by heating it until they could harvest the dry and brittle residue that was the byproduct of the evaporation. This was the most difficult part of the process. The byproduct was a dark brown, tar-like substance that was both hard and brittle. By dissolving a small chunk of this substance in alcohol, and then pouring it over a highly polished silver plate, a uniform

photosensitive, super-fine, powdery white residue would remain on the plate's surface when the alcohol evaporated. The plate was then loaded into a camera obscura and exposed to bright sunlight for . . . well, a very long time. I have heard reports of a few hours for the exposure while others have recommended going on a vacation after beginning the exposure. After exposure, the plate was placed upside down in a tray filled with white petroleum (kerosene). Smaller plates can be developed face up, and if you can't easily acquire kerosene, paint thinner can be used as a substitute. The kerosene fumes made the unexposed areas of the white residue turn clear. The process delivered direct positive images as the white residue remained where it was hardened by light. Depending on how you look at the plate, it can be seen as both a positive and a negative image . . . nearly identical visually to a daguerreotype.

After Niépce died in 1833, his son Isadore succeeded him as a partner in the business. Isadore was a pleasant fellow but he did not have his father's abilities and was unable to produce results from the processes that his father had developed . . . both alone and in his partnership. Daguerre, feeling very much on his own since Niépce was gone, went to work and found significant ways to improve on the Physautotype method. He sensitized silver plates with iodine and exposed them in a camera long enough to print out negative images that could be made positive by wiping the plate and reexposing.

By 1837, he had gone well beyond those techniques and had worked out a way to create a latent image made

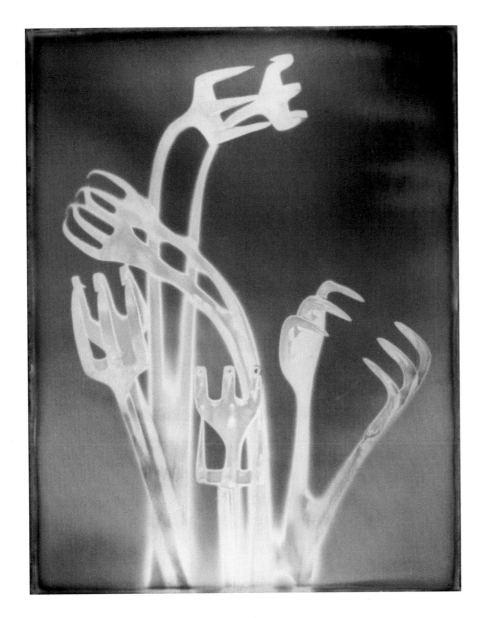

Figure 1–10
Mark Kessell, *Florilegium #1397*, 2006—daguerreotype
Between 1768 and 1771, the naturalist Joseph Banks accompanied Captain James Cook on a voyage of discovery to Australia, seeking, at each landfall, plants never before seen by European eyes. He called the collected drawings of these wonders "Florilegium." Mark wrote that it was the beauty, the menace, and the exquisite engineering of these quasi-biological forms, and their visual ambiguity, that attracted him. Mark's most recent works are 11 × 14 daguerreotypes of surgical instruments that he uses as a source to create large-scale digital prints. The daguerreotypes are not the final work.
(Courtesy of the artist)

visible via the fumes of mercury. Daguerre preserved the image with sodium chloride . . . later with sodium thiosulfate, something Sir John Herschel had discovered much earlier but did not announce until 1839. He now possessed a complete process that could render photographic images in minutes. Daguerre had, by then, decided that the invention of "photography" (Herschel's word) was solely his and began referring to his images as *Daguerreotypes*.

Curiosity Cabinets

Daguerre's first truly successful images depicted small tableaus, or curiosity cabinets (*a.k.a., wunderkammern and wunderkabinette*) of plaster casts and other odd things he had in the studio. These images were titled *Intérieur d'un Cabinet Curiosité*. The curiosity cabinet

played a significant role in society between the 16th and 18th centuries, and its popularity and importance played a major role in the formal establishment of the public museum.

These cabinets were filled with marvelous objects of all types intended to stimulate conversation and thought. Each object, natural or man-made, related to another. Once interpreted, the riddle of their meaning would be revealed to those who could solve the puzzle of the associations. The cabinets were for both entertainment and educational. In a very real way, the curiosity cabinet is a perfect metaphor for the era, akin to the camera obscura (with its interior filled with light curiosities) in its merger of nature, culture, and science.

Figure 1–11
Jerry Spagnoli,
***11:58 pm–12:02 am, Times
Square***, 1999–2000
This half-plate daguerreotype
was made by Jerry as a part of
his project, *The Last Great
Daguerreotype Survey of the
20th Century.* The scene
depicts the 4 minutes of exposure needed to make the plate
as the century changed. The
text, you may notice, reads
backwards because that is
how the daguerreotype
records life.
(Courtesy of the artist)

On the 7th of January 1839, the well-connected French physicist and director of the Paris Observatory, Dominique François Arago, presented Daguerre's work to the Academy of Sciences, and in September 1839, Daguerre demonstrated the process in public for the first time.

How a Daguerreotype Was Made Prior to 1841

First, it is very important that you do not perform this procedure without some expert advice and training in the daguerreotype process. Heating mercury for daguerreotype development is very hazardous business, and the resulting fumes can be lethal to your being. Here's how it is done, with just enough information to explain it but not enough to actually do it.

◆ Prepare a sheet of copper that has been electroplated with a coating of metallic silver (*The Sheffield Process*), and buff it to a fine sheen. This, according to those who make daguerreotypes, is the most difficult part of the process.

◆ Place the metal plate in a light-tight box (called an iodizing box) that contains iodine. In the box the iodine fumes will react with the silver, creating a light-sensitive silver iodide coated plate. The plate will turn several colors during this iodizing stage from straw yellow to deep yellow, rose, blue, and green. Deep yellow, tinged with rose was a typical fuming state of iodine-only daguerreotypes.

◆ Under the illumination of candlelight, load the sensitized plate into a camera and expose it to a subject in bright sunlight. Mark Osterman recommends a starting point of 1 minute of exposure for every f. number, i.e., f. 8 = 8 minutes of exposure in full sun. Less exposure if you're shooting architecture and more exposure if you're shooting trees and foliage.

◆ Next, develop the plate in a box with the fumes of mercury that has been heated to 140° F. During this stage, the mercury will merge (*amalgamate*) with the silver iodide that has been exposed to light.

◆ Finally, the plate is washed with a diluted solution of sodium thiosulfate (originally sodium chloride; *Daguerre's manual, 1839*) and washed with water. The shadows of the image are highly reflective polished silver, and the highlights are a white amalgam that scatters light, created by the mercury's effect upon the silver during development. Once dried, it is permanent.

Figure 1–12

Hippolyte Bayard (1801–1887), *Self Portrait as a Drowned Man,* **1840**

This direct positive, silver chloride sensitized print was created as a reaction to Daguerre's accreditation as the inventor of photography in 1839. Bayard had actually shown his photographic images to Dominique Arago three months before the Daguerre/Niépce invention was announced by Arago. Bayard, a clerk in the French Ministry, was given a small pension to keep his invention to himself as too many important people had a vested interest in Daguerre's success. This image can probably be considered the first political protest photograph. *(Courtesy of Societe Francais de la Photographie)*

It is interesting to note that commerce and marketing began to influence truth at this point. Arago was doing such a spectacular job promoting Daguerre that he blatantly ignored the fact that there was physical proof that Daguerre was not the first person to produce a photographic image. Francis Bauer had informed the press that Daguerre's invention was identical to Niépce's in February 1839 and that he personally had actual images (possibly Physautotypes) that had been given to him by Niépce.

A clerk in the French Ministry of Finance, Hippolyte Bayard (1801–1887), had shown his own photographic images to Arago on the 20th of May 1839, three months before the announcement of the daguerreotype. After Arago announced Daguerre's genius, Bayard reacted to the news by making a self-portrait showing himself as a drowned man and expressing in sarcastic sentiments his feelings that the government had given Daguerre everything . . . that being the case, the wretch had drowned himself and here was the proof.

NOTE: I'm going to jump ahead a bit here in the history but will be returning to this period of time between 1840 and 1900 in subsequent chapters.

By the late 1800s, the medium had literally exploded into the public consciousness. Following a rapid, often overwhelming, series of photographically related processes and discoveries, the pinhole camera had come into its own. As photographic sensitizers and emulsions became more sensitive, photographers around the world were using both lensless, and lens-equipped, cameras to make images of everything from Egyptian archeology to romantic Pictorialist expressions.

As the 19th century came to an end, commercial enterprise entered the fray and pinhole cameras, such as the "Ready Fotografer" and the "Glen Pinhole Camera" were manufactured and sold worldwide. The Ready Fotografer, according to Jo Babcock, was ahead of its time and marketed as a disposable camera that was preloaded with a single glass plate. After exposing the plate, the shooter could then process the plate using the chemistry listed on the

Figure 1–13

Portrait of Blind Man Holding a Cat,
Unidentified Photographer, c. 1850
daguerreotype—6.7 × 5.2 cm., 1/6 plate
I love this daguerreotype and thought,
when I first saw it, that it could so easily be
used for a contemporary album illustration
for a metal band called Headless Cat.
(Courtesy George Eastman House, Museum
Purchase: ex-collection Zelda P. Mackay)

camera or simply drop the camera off for processing in San Francisco at J. M. Howe's at 6 Eddy Street.

These inexpensive cameras came with such extras as glass plates, foil lenses, chemistry and printing frames. All at once, there was a great flurry of activity, as artists and scientists attempted to capture the "fairy pictures" that Talbot had described, the ones that had scooted by their eyes in the camera obscura. Finally, after 2,300 years, everyone was interested. Still, for my historical betting dollar, it was the nomad in the tent who did it first.

A LITTLE SCIENCE

The Thumbnail Principle

To comprehend how a pinhole camera works, take a piece of paper and poke a small hole in its center with the tip of a sharp pencil. Then, hold the paper as close to your favorite eye as possible and look through the hole. To give yourself something to look at, keep your eye right up next to the hole and hold your thumb, and attached thumbnail, an inch or two away from the hole. Notice how you can see your thumbnail really clearly and much closer than you could possibly do with the naked eye. Notice as well that the background is also in clear focus. Pull the paper away, and your eyesight goes back to being less than perfect. What you just experienced was infinity as it applies to depth of field. It is one of the principle characteristics of pinhole photography.

Tech Support

🖤 **Note: Focal length is simply the distance from the lens to the film when focused at infinity. However, since the pinhole camera does not have an actual lens and is always dealing** with infinity, this term may be more accurate if described as image distance to the far subject. I suspect that everyone reading this book understands focal length easily as the term describing the lens/hole to the film plane, so I'll use the term focal length.

A pinhole camera creates an image that varies in size and viewpoint according to the distance between the aperture hole and the surface the image falls upon, be it a sensitized film, paper or wall. If the pinhole is close to the end surface, it will yield a wide-angle image. If the distance is further away, it will provide an image that is normal to telephoto. This distance is called focal length (see note above). If you take a subject and photograph it at the same distance with cameras of various focal lengths, you will find that the longer focal length magnifies the subject, bringing it closer, while the shorter focal length interprets the subject at a smaller size. There is a difference, however . . . with a longer focal length the image size increases but less of the subject or scene is covered. With a camera that has a shorter focal length, the image size decreases but the coverage area covered increases.

The "focal length" of a pinhole camera is calibrated in the same manner as in a traditional "*grown up*" camera: 25 mm = 1". A 3" focal length will cover a 4" × 5" piece of film while a camera with a 6" focal length will cover an 8" × 10" piece of film. If your focal length is too short then you will make circular pictures just like George Eastman did in his first, flexible film, roll camera in 1888. This information changes when you do away with the flat film plane and start bending the film or paper inside the camera. If your pinhole aperture is small enough, almost every nonmoving subject that you point your camera at will be pretty sharp; remember the trick with your thumb and the hole in the paper. In the end, there is no limit to what form your images can take and how you can alter the concept of the pinhole camera.

Generally, the sharpness of an image will become more acute as the pinhole becomes smaller. If however, the hole is too small, this gradual increase in definition will eventually deteriorate, due to diffraction (the spreading of light at the edges of an opaque

Figure 1–14

Rachel Woodburn, *Surface, 2006*—kallitype/pinhole negative
This piece was made by Arizona artist Rachel Woodburn during one of my alternative process workshops in 2006. The image of her niece was made with a pinhole camera and then rendered as a gold, borax-toned kallitype, using a 50% sodium acetate/50% ammonium citrate developer that we were experimenting with to find a way to eliminate buff-colored tonalities in the highlight areas.
(Courtesy of the artist)

object). There are specific proportions considered ideal for particular aperture-to-plate distances. People who take great pleasure in being exact with numerical definitions have worked out these mathematical proportions and the results of their work can be found in many pinhole texts. Basically, a pinhole of 1/64 diameter is quite adequate for focal lengths up to 6 inches. Using the same focal length, a smaller diameter, 1/100 for instance, will provide a nice life-size ratio for making detailed pinhole images of close-up objects using the same focal length.

Exposure time is dependent on how bright it is outside, the size of your pinhole, and the focal length of your camera. This is referred to as the f-value. An f-value is figured with the following equation: Let's say that you have a focal length of 6 inches, and a pin-hole diameter of 1/64, and you want to know the *f*-value. Simply multiply the focal length (6") by the "reciprocal" of the diameter of the pinhole (*the bottom of the fraction*) (64) and you will come up with a *f*-value of *f* 384. Simple, huh? . . .

No? OK, let's try saying the same thing in a different way. Exposure time is dependent on the size of your pinhole and the focal length of your camera. This combination is referred to as the *f*-value. A *f*-value is figured with the following ratio.

$$f = \frac{\text{Focal length}}{\text{Aperture diameter}}$$

If your focal length is 6″, and your pinhole diameter is 1/64, and you want to know the *f*-value . . . dropping those numbers into the ratio we get this:

$$f = \frac{6}{(1/64)}$$

Algebra decrees that dividing by a fraction is the same as multiplying by the fraction's reciprocal, and the reciprocal of 1/64 is . . . ta-dah . . . 64. So simply multiplying the focal length (distance from film plane to lens) 6" × the reciprocal (64) you will arrive at the correct *f*-value of *f* 384. The exposure time is proportional to the square of the *f*-value. This is the Official End of the Math Section.

Of course, available light will also play a large role in determining exposure, and extensive testing of your camera, and the film and or paper used within it will provide a matrix for subsequent use. There are formulas for determining the exact exposure times for pinhole exposures, but I have found that the variables of the handmade pinhole camera are significant enough to call for individual testing of one's camera rather than a carved-in-stone standard.

Eric Renner and Nancy Spencer, of The Pinhole Resource, estimate that there have been more than fifty separate charted formulas defining workable pinhole diameter/focal length perfection. These formulas come with complex mathematical equations that define what happens to your image when numbers are assigned to

Figure 1–15

Eric Renner & Nancy Spencer, *Moonrise Over Manifest Destiny,* **"on deaf ears"** *series,* **2001–2006**

The pinhole images in "on deaf ears" are a collaboration between Eric Renner and Nancy Spencer… the operators of Pinhole Resource. Sixteen years ago, they began constructing assemblages, many of which dealt with social issues of human rights, religion, sexuality, and stereotypes. In the summer of 2001, they began photographing segments of their assemblages with a pinhole camera, realizing there was the possibility of an altered context in making 2-D images of 3-D dimensional assemblages. The pinhole images make use of color shifts due to long 6- to 8-minute exposures, vignetting, and altered perspectives enhanced by the wide-angle pinhole camera.
(Courtesy of the artists)

the diameter of the aperture, the wavelength of the light, and the focal length of the camera. The gist of this is that you can spend all your time doing scientific testing and seeking pinhole perfection, or you can deal with the fact that you are taking pictures with a box of air and a hole. You can make one in a few minutes, and if it doesn't work, go and make a new one. Get out of the studio, build or purchase a pinhole camera, and go make pictures. If your camera isn't providing you with the sharpness, or romanticism, that you want, then modify it until it does.

Figure 1–16

Pinky Bass, *Elizabeth Turk Two-Tasseled Pinhole Camera Bra*, **1989**

Pinky Bass made this amazing two-tasseled pinhole camera bra for Elizabeth Turk, who teaches alt processes at SCAD (Atlanta College of Art) and who is also in this book. I'm sure there's a story behind this innovative clothing option, but I don't know it.

(Courtesy of the artist)

HOW TO MAKE A PINHOLE CAMERA

The Basic Materials

Great pinhole cameras have been made from containers as small as a thimble to as large as an airplane hanger. I've seen cameras made out of a person's mouth, bedrooms, trucks, and vans. Because you can use literally anything as the primary form for a pinhole camera, describing how to make one doesn't really address all of the concerns that may arise in production. You'll have to keep your sense of humor and invention and do a lot of testing as you go. Here is a really simple set of instructions for making your own pinhole camera.

◆ You will need a can of black matte spray paint. To make sure that your container doesn't have a lot of light bouncing around inside it during lengthy exposures, spray the interior of the camera with at least two or three coats. You can also use extra-plush black velvet if you want absolutely no reflection of any kind during the exposure.

◆ You'll also want a nice piece of thin metal to make your pinhole. Tin foil, metal flashing material, brass shims, a cut-up soda can... anything thin and sturdy that you can punch a needle hole through for your aperture. K & S Engineering Co., Chicago, IL, makes a wide assortment of brass, aluminum and copper shims that are excellent for pinhole aperture plates. The ideal shim stock can be found in 0.001" or 0.002" thickness, and you can get the stock at most well-equipped hardware stores in the painting and door hardware sections. You can also buy your pinhole premade, either as a straight aperture or on sheet film as a zone plate lens.

Figure 1–17
Danuta Gibka, *Dana & Artur, 1999*— pinhole
I was introduced to Dana's work via a show of Polish pinhole photographers that had been organized by Jesseca Ferguson and Bonnie Robinson at The Art Institute of Boston. In a recent e-mail, discussing this image of Dana and her husband Artur, she wrote, "*Desire to meet, and nothing else . . . Turning into passion . . . Head over heels . . .*

Opening up for something, what is not me, what is the world, another man . . . The process of seeking myself doesn't end though . . . Each picture is a trial of finding one's own identity."
(Courtesy of the artist)

Zone Plate

In the simplest sense . . . a zone plate is a series of concentric rings, like a graphic target. These rings alternate, from the center to the outside of the circle, between opaque and clear like an archery target without colors . . . just alternating rings of black and white. The zone plate can be of any number of zones (*a zone is a circle, black or transparent*); the greater number of zones, the fuzzier the images and the faster the exposure time.

The zone plate is different from the conventional pinhole in that it is not a single "pin" hole but a group of concentric bands that allow light to make your exposure.

This means that your exposures are much shorter, i.e., a pinhole exposure of 30 seconds in bright sun and shade would probably be a 5-second exposure with a zone plate. This also means that you have the option of shooting hand-held pinhole . . . which is a lot of fun.

The images made with a zone plate are "Pictorialist" and romantic. The zone plate delivers a soft, infrared-like, glowing image, and this glow takes place adjacent to subject edges where there is significant contrast. This allows the image to escape the syrupy, greeting card look that permeates the card racks in drugstores and features visual sentiments of long walks on the beach, conversations by an open fire, puppies, and fuzzy kittens.

The best way to have this experience is to go to www.zeroimage.com and take a look at their deluxe 4 × 5 that has a turret giving you the option of shooting the pinhole or zone plate with a single camera. They also market zone plates that are simple pieces of film with the zone plate concentric circles. You can also go to www. pinholeresource.com (Eric Renner's site) and get soup-to-nuts pinhole stuff. They sell zone plate turrets as well as pinhole lens-cover caps for your new digital cameras.

◆ Add to your list a pair of scissors or shears that can cut a thin metal shim, and a sturdy sewing needle . . . a #18 works well. Also, a piece of sandpaper for metal, needle-nose pliers for pushing the sewing needle through the metal, a simple ruler, a Sharpie, emery cloth for a really smooth finish, and a timing device to time your exposures. You may want some paint or decoration for your camera to make friends envious and to inspire children.

◆ If you are not using Polaroid Type 55 Positive/Negative film (see the Negative chapter), you'll need a darkroom for loading and unloading your film or paper and for processing. If you are going to load your camera with photographic paper, you will want resin-coated paper without the manufacturer's logo on the back. RC paper is thin and lacks paper fibers to make your image fuzzier than it will be anyway. If you are going to load with film, I recommend that you begin with large sheets of ortho film, as it's slow and forgiving. Again, please see the Negative chapter for additional information.

Not too long ago there was a type of photographic paper made by several companies that permitted the option of making positive color prints from positive transparency films. This paper could be loaded directly into a pinhole camera, exposed, and processed with the correct Ilfachrome or Cibachrome chemistry, and when it was done, you had a color positive print. An example is in the late 70's work of Willie Anne Wright who is well-known for her "Beach Series" using 8" × 10" and 11" × 14" wooden boxes fitted with slots for film holders at different focal lengths. Color balance was corrected with an 85 B glass filter behind the pinhole aperture, and her exposures were between 3 and 5 minutes long. Another artist, who used this paper in combination with his trailer pinhole camera, was my friend Chris Pinchbeck.

Figure 1–18
Lesley Krane, *Self Portrait (grapes)*, 1991
4" × 5" chromogenic pinhole
(Courtesy of the artist)

In case you were curious, alternative process exposures in pinholes can be done, but you need the patience of a hero, because the sensitizers are so slow. You also need a terrific sense of humor. Mark Osterman, at Eastman House, has done daguerreotypes and collodion plates using a pinhole camera and wrote that as long as the distance to the subject as not too great, and the subject was illuminated with bright sunlight, it was possible. It would be difficult to use a pinhole with albumen, salted paper, or any process that prints out that has an excess of silver, as this would reduce back to a metallic state over time.

Simple Pinhole Construction

Select a container and think about what kind of image you want to create. Wide angle, telephoto, macro, multiple lens, long and narrow, short and wide, mural size, button size . . . you decide. It might be a fine idea to make several cameras so that you can shoot the same thing

Figure 1–19

Willie Anne Wright, *Group at Nag's Head*—**1980s (Cibachrome pinhole)**

I first saw Willie Anne Wright's pinhole/Cibachrome work I was an artist represented by the Witkin Gallery (NYC). The images in this series are one-of-a-kind Cibachrome direct positives. The camera had a single focal length, multiple slots for the film holders, and was 16" × 20" in size. Willie Anne used an 85B filter to compensate for a big color shift and because Cibachrome was created for use with tungsten light and she was shooting in daylight. Unfortunately, Cibachrome is no longer available.

(Courtesy of the artist)

with all of them and see the difference. Begin by measuring your distance between the film plane and the aperture, and determine what your coverage is going to be. The shorter the focal length, the wider the angle of view . . . see above. A good way to see how much coverage you're going to get is to place a mark at the rear of the top-middle edge of your camera, on the film plane of the camera, and draw straight lines to the front left and right corners. If you follow those lines out to the horizon, you will see what your coverage area will be.

Spray several coats of matte black spray paint, or black velvet for the deluxe version, into the inside of your constructed "camera." Note: If you are using a bread truck or your apartment, this may not be a good idea, and you will have to figure out another solution, i.e., black paper or fabric. Then, draw an "X" from corner to corner to show you where the exact middle of your camera is. This will be, if you are feeling conservative, where your pinhole aperture will go. Take your matt knife and cut a small hole in the camera where your piece of brass shim metal will be placed. Scribe an "X" to show you the center, and very gently push your needle through the material. If you are using tin foil, you are pretty much done, but you have a very fragile aperture that can easily be damaged. If you are using a brass shim, then you will want to complete the following steps.

Figure 1–20

Chris Pinchbeck, *White Sands National Monument, New Mexico*, 1999

Chris Pinchbeck uses a trailer as his pinhole camera and exposes direct positive Type R Cibachrome prints. This image is 30" × 75".

(Courtesy of the artist)

Figure 1–21

Philippe Moroux, *le jour de l'éclipse #1 (Etretat-Normandy, France)*

This extraordinary pinhole camera image by Netherlands photographer, Philippe Moroux, was made on the day of a solar eclipse. Philippe used a hand-made pinhole camera, fitted with a Polaroid back to accommodate 4" × 5" Type 55 Positive/Negative film. He then made multiple exposures, prewashed the negatives in the sea, and later translated them into prints that are Van Dyke variants utilizing silver nitrate, silver oxide, and sulfamic acid.

(Courtesy of the artist)

Figure 1–22
Pinky Bass, *Body Nostalgia 1*
Pinky Bass made this compelling image with a homemade pinhole that she named *Bible with Two Points of View Pinhole Camera*. The image is a 40" × 32" toned silver gelatin print.
(Courtesy of the artist)

As soon as the needle begins to protrude through the other side of the shim, stop pushing and turn the metal piece over. Gently push the needle back through the same hole and twirl it as you go in much the same manner as an acupuncturist does when inserting needles into a body. Go back to the front side and repeat the penetrating twirl until you have a nice hole.

Then, take a piece of fine emery cloth, silicon, or carborundum paper and gently massage both sides to remove any irregularities or burrs. When the hole is smooth, gently push your needle back through it to clear out any metal dust. Check your perfection with a magni-fying loop. Remember, a small hole with rough edges will result in light being diffracted and a blurry image. The Golden Rule of Pinhole: fuzzy holes make fuzzy pictures.

Putting the Camera Together

Now it is time to put the newly made pinhole aperture into the camera and to create a shutter, *also known as a piece of black tape over the hole*. First, take your foil or shim with the pinhole, and tape it inside your camera, being sure the pinhole is centered over the small hole you cut out. Make sure that the seal around the aperture plane is perfect and light tight.

Figure 1–23

Mary Mayer, *Great Picture Project, Hangar Interior*, 2006

On July 12, 2006, Jerry Burchfield, Mark Chamberlain, Jacques Garnier, Robert Johnson, Douglas McCulloh, and Clayton Spada hosted a reception where they unveiled the world's largest photograph... inside the world's largest camera. Mary Mayer, an MFA student at The Art Institute of Boston and human firecracker, was one of the volunteers and made this picture of the camera.

(Courtesy of the artist)

To make a shutter, take an inch or two of the black tape and stick two pieces of the tape together (sticky side to sticky side), leaving one of the ends longer than the other. You are going to want to put your shutter somewhere during the exposure, and the best way to manage this is by leaving a sticky end tab on the shutter so that it can adhere to your camera when shooting. When it is time to expose, simply grab the pull-tab, uncover the pinhole, stick the shutter somewhere on the camera, say the magic words, "al-Hazan," and wait. At the conclusion of the shot, cover up the hole again, being positive that the tape is making a tight seal with the pinhole to avoid stray light.

You may wish to construct a system for easily inserting your film or paper into the camera. The easiest solution is to tape the film or RC paper to the side of the camera opposite the aperture hole. A better solution requiring a little more time, but worth the effort, is to make a channel setup so that you can slide your film or RC paper along permanent tracks. This is similar to a paper easel or 4" × 5" film holder channel system. In fact, you might want to consider taking a 4" × 5" film holder and making it a permanent part of your camera. If you intend to use different size films and papers in your camera then you must either build different format channel systems or make cameras specifically for the size film or paper you intend to use. Don't forget the information about focal length and image size. Now, figure out a way to be sure that your camera is light tight and that it is easily disassembled for the next loading of light-sensitive material. It is now time to test your creation.

THE GREAT PICTURE PROJECT

Now, if you take the instructions above and apply them to an airplane hangar you will get The Great Picture Project concept. In the summer of 2006, Jerry Burchfield, Mark Chamberlain, Jacques Garnier, Robert Johnson, Douglas McCulloh, and Clayton Spada set up shop at the former Marine Corps Air Station El Toro in Irvine, California. Their intention was to transform a giant airplane hangar into the largest "functioning" camera in the history of mankind. These artists are members of The Legacy Project, which has been documenting the transformation of the El Toro Air Station into The Orange County Great Park since 2002.

On July 12, 2006, Jerry, Mark, Jacques, Robert, Douglas, and Clayton hosted a reception where they unveiled the world's largest photograph . . . inside the world's largest camera. Their photograph measured 31 feet 7 inches × 111 feet, covered a total of 3,505 square feet, and showed a panoramic view of a portion of the former Marine Corps Air Station El Toro that is destined to become the heart of the Orange County Great Park.

The Great Picture was produced over a two-month period with the assistance of hundreds of individuals, businesses, and sponsors. To give you a sense of it . . . here are some of the specifics of the project. Really, no different than a Quaker Oats pinhole camera . . . only a lot bigger.

Great Picture Fact Sheet

◆ Camera size: 45 feet high × 80 feet deep × 160 feet wide

◆ Final size with rigging: 31 feet 7 inches × 111 feet, 3,505 sq. feet in total

◆ Image size: 28 feet × 108 feet, 3,024 square feet in a single, seamless piece of fabric

◆ Photograph type: black & white negative image with a gelatin sizing and a hand-coated silver gelatin emulsion

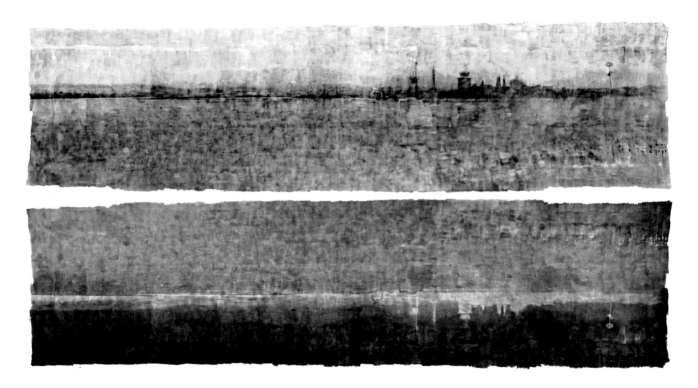

Figure 1–24

Great Picture Project, el Toro Air force Base, Positive and Negative—2006

Camera size: 45' H × 80' D × 160' W. • Final size with rigging: 31 feet 7 inches × 111 feet, 3,505 sq. feet. • Image size: 28' × 108', 3,024 sq. feet in a single, seamless piece of fabric. • Photograph type: B & W negative image with a hand-coated silver gelatin emulsion. • Subjects depicted in the photograph: the MCAS El Toro control tower, twin runways, and heart of the future Orange County Great Park, with a backdrop of the San Joaquin Hills and the Laguna Wilderness. Location: former Marine Corps Air Station El Toro, Irvine, CA.

(Courtesy of the artists)

- Subjects depicted in the photograph: the MCAS El Toro control tower, twin runways, and heart of the future Orange County Great Park, with a backdrop of the San Joaquin Hills and the Laguna Wilderness. Location: former Marine Corps Air Station El Toro, Irvine, CA.

- Camera location: Building #115, a former fighter plane hangar that served as a helicopter hangar for the Sea Elk squadron during its final days.

- Materials used to darken the airplane hangar to make it into a camera:

  24,000 square feet of 6-mil black viscine

  200 large cans of spray foam gap filler

  8,000 feet of two-inch wide black gorilla tape

  40 cans of black spray paint

- Fabric base of the photograph: single seamless piece of unbleached muslin specially ordered from Germany with a total weight (fabric and rigging) of 1,200 pounds, which probably qualifies as the world's heaviest photograph.

- Aperture size: one-quarter inch (6mm) pinhole—no lens or optics were used. Aperture height: 15 feet.

- Date of emulsion coating: July 7, 2006

- Emulsion: 20 gallons of Liquid Light—a silver gelatin B&W sensitizer that was hand-painted onto the fabric under safelight illumination

- Date of exposure: July 8, 2006 at 11 a.m.

- Exposure time: 35 minutes

- Date of development: July 8, 2006

- Developing materials:

  600 gallons traditional B&W developer

  1,200 gallons fixer

- Developing "tray": eight-mil vinyl pool liner— 114 feet × 35 feet × 6 inches

- Sanctioned by the Guinness Book of Records as the World's Largest Camera

- Sanctioned by the Guinness Book of Records as the World's Largest Photograph

TESTING YOUR CAMERA

Load up the camera in the darkroom with either film or satin-finish RC paper. It is faster to test paper, so that should be your medium for the light-tight test. Remember that if you are using paper, the shiny or emulsion side faces the lens just like in printing. If you are using film, hold the film so that your right index finger is on the upper right-hand corner notch code of the film. The emulsion side is now facing you. This side faces the aperture and the scene in front of the camera. Load the film sheet in total darkness. Back to the test:

- Place a piece of paper, or film, on each wall of the inside surfaces of the camera.

- Close up the camera in the darkroom and don't forget to put your shutter (tape) over the lens.

- Go outdoors and place the camera in direct sunlight for 15 to 20 minutes but **DO NOT REMOVE THE SHUTTER**. Every so often, move the camera so that a different side faces the sun.

- Go back into the darkroom and process the piece of paper or film and see how you did.

If all of the pieces of paper or film are unexposed, then you have made a fine camera and you are ready to make pictures. If some or all of your paper has gray or dark exposed light leaks showing, you will have to figure out where the leaks are and fix the camera with more paint or tape. It is important to understand how the image is coming into the camera. If you have a light leak showing on the top-left corner of your paper test, your problem is located in the lower right hand corner of your camera. Continue the testing process until the light leaks are gone . . . and keep your sense of humor.

Finding the Correct Exposure

It would be numbing to try and provide you with a mathematical set of calibrations to guarantee a perfect exposure with your pinhole. There are simply too many variables to make sane recommendations. The time of year and day, the "real" size of your pinhole, the temperature, the atmosphere . . . nearly anything could make a difference. The wisest procedure, with a new

Figure 1–25

Martin Novak, *Doppelgänger—Pieta, 2003*—Holga pinhole & gum bichromate print

Martin wrote, "When I found pinhole camera photography I was surprised by how such basic photographic equipment could be so effective, as well as having so many creative options. When working with pinhole cameras, the most enjoyable element for me is its unpredictability. In the photographs I explored the relationships between individual and selves. My pinhole images express differing kinds of inner dialogs that I may have, or have just imagined, within myself. All the double exposed images are created on a single piece of film in the camera using time lapse (each photo is about a 10 minute exposure). I take several exposures while changing the placement of the figures 2 or 3 times during exposure. I only have a general idea of what the image is going to come out like, but I am never sure until I process the negatives."
(Courtesy of the artist)

pinhole, or a change in season, is to work intuitively or take the time to make a series of exposure tests using film (Polaroid or conventional sheet film) or RC photographic paper. Begin making exposures, in bright sun, with a good intuitive guess (which is how I've made every pinhole exposure I've ever done). Process the material and go from there. With a preconstructed Leonardo, Zero Image, or Lensless Camera Mfg. Co. pinhole and Polaroid Type 55 P/N (*positive/negative*) film with a 4" × 5" Polaroid back, you can begin with a 1–3 second exposure on a sunny day with a zone plate lens or an 8–10 second exposure with a regular pinhole. Pay attention to the cleared negative rather than the positive . . . you do not want a good positive print with Type 55. You are going for the negative, which needs density. See the Negative chapter please.

Pinhole Camera Aperture Exposure Table

Calculating specific exposures for your handmade pinhole camera is complicated due to the variables of homemade construction. The Lensless Camera Mfg. Co., however, has created the following table of apertures and *f*-stops for their products. The film format of the camera is irrelevant, because only the working aperture and focal length determine the *f*-stop.

Most modern light meters will help you in determining the correct exposure of your pinhole camera. However, I am going to dispense with the mathematical formulas in this edition (I have not met a single person who has bothered to use them, as most prefer the seat-of-the-pants approach to pinhole photography) and give you some simple advice. Go to one of the dedicated Web sites mentioned in this chapter and in the resource

Focal length	Pinhole diameter		*f*-stop
	(1000 ths)	(Fractions)	
675mm/27"	0.0156"	1/64	*f*/2000
450mm/18"	0.0156"	1/64	*f*/1200
300mm/12"	0.0156"	1/64	*f*/840
225mm/9"	0.0156"	1/64	*f*/630
200mm/8"	0.0156"	1/64	*f*/560
150mm/6"	0.0156"	1/64	*f*/420
100mm/4"	0.0156"	1/64	*f*/280
75mm/3"	0.013"	1/77	*f*/230
50mm/2"	0.013"	1/77	*f*/154
Calculation by The Lensless Camera Mfg. Co., Santa Barbara, CA.			

Figure 1–26
Nancy Spencer, *Marlene & Mark #2*
Nancy Spencer is one of the leading figures in the alternative photography world and specializes in the art and science of the pinhole camera. She and her husband, Eric Renner, operate Pinhole Resource.
(Courtesy of the artist)

Appendix and buy an inexpensive exposure calculator that forces you to spin a dial to find out the exposure. The other option is to guess at the exposure. I realize this isn't very scientific but it is a lot more fun . . . like opening a present when you see what happened.

Making Pictures

Select a subject, or create one. Most of the time people photograph things that don't move because of the lengthy exposures. However, many pinhole photographers love the ghostly quality of movement in their images. Leaves blowing in the wind, moving water, parts of bodies, blinking eyes in a portrait . . . are all wonderful in the light movement tracks they deposit on the film plane. Position the camera so it will not move, and untape the shutter. Check your watch and count each second during the exposure . . . *"one Ansel Adams, two*

Ansel Adam, three Ansel Adams" . . . keep notes on each shot and begin to calibrate how your camera works.

When your exposure is complete, go back into the darkroom, remove the paper or film from the camera and process it. If you want to process everything at once, later in the day, you must keep the material in a light-tight box. In the field, you can use a changing bag to remove, load, and store your exposed and unexposed light-sensitive materials. After processing, you will probably want to make a print. If you are using film, then the contact process is as simple as making a contact sheet. If you are using RC paper and printing through it as a paper negative, there are a few ways to make the print. If you are shooting digi<ental pinhole then make a negative on Pictorico OHP ink-jet film. If you are shooting Polaroid Type 55, or photo paper, or other types of film, then scan those as well and enlarge

Figure 1–27
Joe Boyle, *Illustration of Pinhole Camera and Type 55 Polaroid Pull Process Technique*
(*Courtesy of the artist*)

your negatives on Pictorico OHP or some other comparable clear inkjet material. Please refer to the digital and negative chapters for recommendations. Personally, I like to shoot Type 55, rinse it clear in a hypo clearing agent like Perma Wash or sodium sulfite, give it a water rinse, dry it on a clothesline, and make a contact print with the process I intend to use with the negative.

Closing Pinhole Thoughts

If your ambitions for pinhole photography exceed this set of instructions, then you are in good company. Many artists have taken the pinhole concept and built their entire creative process around it. Included in this group are a lot of people whose work illustrates this chapter. I love their attitude about making images . . . one that has defined my own over the last several decades.

There are many artists whose imaginative variations of the pinhole camera are often as vital as the work that comes from them. The primary connections here are the marriage of the syntax they decide to work with and the context of their ideas and intentions. Chris Pinchbeck used a trailer as his pinhole camera and drove around the country shooting giant Ilfochrome landscapes. One of my former workshop students, Pinky Bass, a great artist and inspiration to all who know her, seems to make cameras for the occasion. Emily Hartzell, a former student of mine at Harvard, turned her New York apartment into a pinhole. Another workshop participant, Frank Varney, built a panorama pinhole specifically to record the geysers of Yellowstone National Park. Jo Babcock turned a VW van into a pinhole camera in 1973, and another VW van into a pinhole- and lens-equipped camera obscura in 1989 to produce 40" × 50" paper negatives, and then made an Airstream motor home into a camera in 1990.

Philippe Moroux makes beautiful Kallitypes with negatives from his pinhole cameras. His interpretations of the coast of Normandy during a full solar eclipse are amazing. Eric Renner and Nancy Spencer are the preeminent pinhole authorities, and their Pinhole Resource

Figure 1–28
Marilyn Ruseckas, *July 1980—* **35 mm pinhole camera & infrared film**
A former student of mine, Marilyn Ruseckas, is an accomplished fine artist and world-class bike racer (on the racing circuit she is referred to as the *Beast From The East*). For this image, Marilyn removed the lens from her 35 mm camera, created a pinhole with a metal plate over the space where the lens used to be and poked a pinhole in it. She then loaded her camera with infrared film and made beautiful images that would have inspired any Photo Secessionist.
(*Courtesy of the artist*)

enterprise has inspired countless numbers of people to embark on a pinhole adventure. Check out their life-mask pinhole camera results at the end of this chapter.

Another former student of mine, Marilyn Ruseckas, is an accomplished artist. For this image, (Figure 1-28) she removed the lens from her 35mm camera and replaced it with a metal shim with a pinhole aperture. She then loaded her camera (in the dark) with infrared film and made beautiful images that would have inspired any Pictorialist. There is simply no end to it . . . in pinhole photography, if it can be imagined, it is possible. Just ask the guys who accomplished the Great Picture Project.

To begin your love affair with pinhole cameras, you should really make one first. Once you have done the "rustic" thing, I suggest that you consider purchasing a hand-built camera from one of several outstanding pinhole camera makers. I have terrific cameras from the Lensless Camera Mfg. Co., Leonardo cameras from Eric Renner & Nancy Spencer's Pinhole Resource, and Zernike Au's entire Zero Image product line (see the resource section in the Appendices). I've used all of them for decades, lent them to hundreds of students, taken them on trips around the world, and have never had a single problem . . . after all, what could go wrong with a box of air with a hole in it? Bottom line . . . pinhole photography has an incredibly rich history and is the foundation of the entire medium of photography. It is also a great deal of fun . . . my advice to you is to go have some.

Figure 1–29
Eric Renner & Nancy Spencer, *Evolushin, "on deaf ears" series*, 2001–2006—Type C pinhole from 4 × 5 negative
This is another wonderful image from the "on deaf ears" series begun 16 years ago as a collaboration between Eric Renner and Nancy Spencer. Their assemblages have been greatly influenced by passages in *The Women's Encyclopedia of Myths and Secrets* by Barbara Walker and by relevant and related social issues. On a lighter note, they also made assemblages dealing with Mickey Mouse, Elvis, Marilyn, and their own relationship. *(Courtesy of the artists)*

The Salted Paper Process

OVERVIEW & EXPECTATIONS

The Salted Paper, and the calotype chapter that preceded it, share a homologous history, largely because the inspiration behind both processes was William Henry Fox Talbot (1800–1877). He was also the person who took 200 years of assorted scientific clues regarding light, metal, salt, and the camera obscura and solved a significant portion of the puzzle. For that reason, the two chapters share a combined narrative and they are written with the intention that you will connect them as a single account in the development of salted paper photography.

This chapter will feature "a little history" of the investigations of chemists and scientists who preceded Talbot, including Schulze, Hellot, Scheele, Wedgwood, and Davy. William Henry Fox Talbot, however, plays the leading role in this account of the development of the salted paper process, as he did in devising the *art of fixing shadows* through photogenic drawings and the calotype process . . . the first chemically developed latent image and the first light-sensitive, silver-based, negative to positive paper imaging system. This set the stage for the future of photography, in which the negative could be used as a matrix to reproduce an image multiple times. The chapter will also illustrate how Talbot's discovery, and work, fit into the context of photography's beginning and its future impact upon world cultures.

The chemistry and formulas for salted paper will be revealed and you will learn variations of sizing and salting formulas. Also described are variations of silver nitrate sensitizing formulas, application techniques, and guidelines for how the prepared paper is exposed and processed. You will also learn a number of toning options along with fixing and final washing considerations. My advice to you, should you want to get a good idea of the path Fox Talbot explored, is to go back a chapter and begin by learning how to make a calotype.

Figure 2–1
France Scully Osterman, *Light Pours In*, 2002—waxed salt print from 8 × 10 collodion negative
France Scully Osterman is a charter member of the antiquarian avant-garde. Each year I invite her to Boston to dazzle my alternative process students at The Art Institute of Boston, and she, along with her husband Mark, are among the elite when it comes to the antique processes of salt, albumen, wet collodion, and gelatin dry plate emulsions.
(Courtesy of the artist and The Howard Greenberg Gallery)

A LITTLE HISTORY

Fox Talbot Gets Married

The salted paper process owes its existence to several hundred years of very clever men and women studying the surprising, and assorted, relationships between light and chemistry. The actual process, and concept, made its unique debut in the imagination of William Henry Fox Talbot while he was on his honeymoon in 1833. Talbot, his new bride, Constance, and his new toy, a *camera lucida*, traveled to Lake Como, Italy, to celebrate the beginning of their life together. While attempting to make a decent drawing of the lake (*which is truly beautiful and well worth the effort of attempting a drawing*) with his *camera lucida* (Fig 2–2), Talbot confronted, head-on, his utter lack of talent for rendering. At this point, he considered the possibility of how charming it might be to permanently capture the images he was seeing in a more perfect manner and to return home and impress his friends and neighbors. When the honeymoon concluded, Talbot, his new bride, and the useless *camera lucida* returned to England and he set to work on a solution for his inspiration . . . a burning desire for vacation pics. In 1834 he came up with the beginnings of a significant discovery.

William Hyde Wollaston's Camera Lucida

In 1806, William Hyde Wollaston (1766–1828) invented the *camera lucida*, a drawing and tracing instrument welcomed by many English gentlemen and women who were not only expected to be scholars and intellectuals but also to possess the skill to render an object with a pencil in a lifelike manner . . . something Talbot could not do very well even with the aid of the *camera lucida*. It should be noted that Sir John Herschel was quite good with the device . . . very good, actually.

A *camera lucida* is composed of a series of interrelated parts including an eye-level glass prism held by a rod and connected to a drawing surface. All the operator had to do was look through the prism, and the image before the "artist" was visible at both eye and drawing board levels simultaneously. The operator's task at that point was to "*trace*" the projected image on the drawing board to achieve a realistic graphic interpretation of the subject. Unfortunately, or perhaps fortunately, the device was not an easy one for Talbot to use, and it was his difficulty mastering it that drove him to seek a way to make his holiday images in another, and more perfect, way.

But First . . . Schulze, Scheele, Wedgwood & Davy

But first . . . in 1802, 31 years before Constance and William went on their honeymoon, Thomas Wedgwood and his friend, Sir Humphry Davy, made what may have been the first silver sensitized *photogram*. Wedgwood, as mentioned in an earlier chapter, was familiar with the scientific investigations of Johann Heinrich Schulze (1687–1744) who, in 1725, accidentally discovered the darkening effects of light on silver when he mixed silver contaminated nitric acid with chalk (*calcium carbonate*), creating silver carbonate. He was attempting to make a phosphorescent compound associated with the study of alchemy and called "aluminous stone" or Baldewein's Phosphor. Curious about why his results turned a deep violet when exposed to sunlight; eventually he figured out that it was caused by contamination of the acid solution by silver.

Schulze was aware that the silver nitrate in his lab had turned dark in its glass bottle . . . except for where the bottle's label on the jar covered the chemical. This prompted Schulze to conduct experiments on the light-sensitive properties of silver salts. He did this by first filling up jars with a mixture of silver nitrate and chalk. He then got to work cutting out, and adhering (with beeswax), paper alphabet letters to the outside of the silver nitrate jars. Regarding his investigations he wrote, "*. . . I often wrote names and whole sentences on paper and carefully cut away the inked parts with a sharp knife. Thus I struck the paper thus perforated on the glass with wax. It was not long before the sun's rays, where they hit the glass through the cut-out parts of the paper, wrote each word or sentence on the chalk precipitate so exactly and distinctly that many who were curious about the experiment but ignorant of its nature took occasion to attribute the thing to some sort of trick.*"

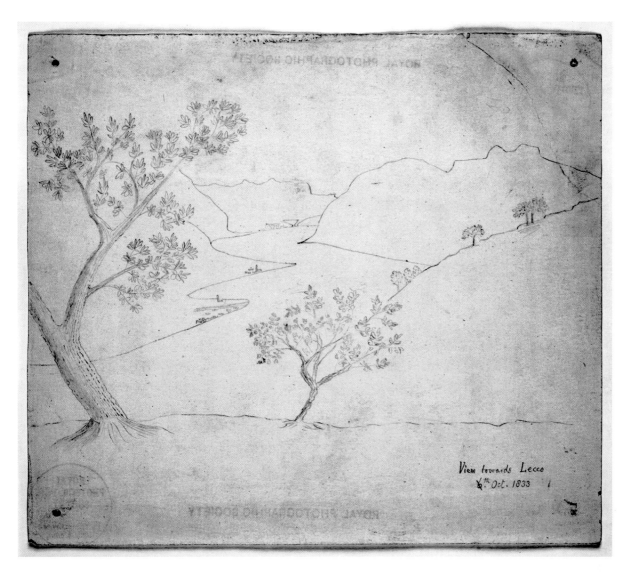

Figure 2–2

William Henry Fox Talbot, *Camera Lucida Drawing, Italy,* **1833**

Talbot, like most English gentleman, was expected to be as accomplished at drawing as he was at science, botany, poetry, and music. Sadly, Talbot's skill with a camera lucida left much to be desired in his efforts to make vacation pics to show his friends. It was precisely Talbot's difficulty mastering the device that drove him to seek an alternative to make the same representational images in another, and more perfect, way.

(Courtesy of The National Media Museum / Science & Society Picture Library—also the new repository for the collection of the Royal Photographic Society, London)

A very interesting side note regarding Schulze's experiments and silver nitrate's sensitivity using letter stencils: In 1737, a French chemist, Jean Hellot (1685–1766) recommended the use of a dilute silver nitrate solution as an invisible ink that could be utilized by spies in the course of their espionage. According to Hellot, the message to be delivered by the spy would be written using silver nitrate. Later, having reached the intended eyes, the message could be made legible by exposing it to sunlight whereupon the color of the secret message would turn purple, then brown, and finally black.

A short time later, Swedish chemist (pharmacist) Carl Wilhelm Scheele (1742–1786), published a book entitled *Chemical Observations and Experiments on Air and Fire* (1777). In it, Scheele worked with his newfound knowledge of how the blue-violet end of the spectrum had a noticeable impact on a compound of silver and chlorine (*silver chloride*) through the chemical act of salt to metal reduction. Scheele's findings were later confirmed by Jean Senebier (1742–1809), who reconfirmed the sensitivity of silver chloride to blue-violet rays, noting that darkening took a scant 15 seconds versus the 20 minutes it would take to achieve the same effect if the rays were solely from the red end of the spectrum.

Just for your interest, in a publication titled, *Mémoires physico-chimiques sur l'influence de la lumière solaire* (Genève 1782, vol. III), Senebier's experiments are described; they reveal muriate of silver's (*silver chloride*) sensitivity to the various bands of the light spectrum. Times required to darken muriate of silver by the rays of the sun: red = 20 min., orange = 12 min., yellow = 5 min. & 30 sec., green = 37 sec., blue = 29 seconds, violet = 15 seconds. This knowledge had a significant impact on Sir Humphry Davy when he and Thomas Wedgwood began experimenting with silver nitrate on white leather 20 years later.

Scheele eventually gave up his occupation as a pharmacist for the rarified life of a university professor so that he could dedicate himself to revelation and discovery. Among the gems . . . an observation that silver chloride could be dissolved by ammonia but that darkened (exposed) metallic silver was impervious to it. This employed knowledge allowed him to preserve his experiments with exposed silver chloride, on sheets of paper, by bathing them in an ammonia bath . . . a method of fixing/clearing the print that was ignored for years! Armed with the knowledge of Senebier's and Scheele's work (with the exception of overlooking Scheele's ammonia fixing bath), Wedgwood and Davy commenced coating paper, glass, and bleached white leather with silver nitrate solutions and laying stencils and other object on these surfaces in sunlight.

You may recall from an earlier "A Little History" segment how, in 1793, Davy had been told by Joseph Priestly about some experiments being conducted by Elizabeth Fulhame and how those efforts eventually became the foundation of her 1794 self-published book, *An Essay on Combustion, with a View to a new Art of Dying And Painting, wherein the Phlogistic and Antiphlogistic Hypotheses are Proved Erroneous.* In this early research, Fulhame had been seeking a way to impregnate, and stain, fabrics with precious metals such as gold. She hypothesized that this might be possible

with the influence of water and light and her research brought her to the conclusion that water played the major role in catalytic reactions as both the *reducing* and *oxidizing* agent. She also noted that following those actions the water was always restored to its original state. Fulhame suggested that if one were to take advantage of the phenomena of silver and light interaction, this might be employed by cartographers as a technique to create maps. My assumption is that Davy, being a very intelligent and curious scientist, put all of these influences together when he went into collaboration with Wedgwood.

During the photogram exposures made by Davy and Wedgwood, the silver salt sensitizer turned a gray, purple brown (*the same colors that Talbot achieved in his photogenic drawings preserved with salt water*), and, eventually, black in the areas open to exposure. Their "Sunprints" required only a simple water wash to remain visible and were successful enough that Wedgwood and Davy formalized their discovery . . . which of course exposed the paradox that the light that they needed to make an image would also destroy that image if it could not be stabilized. Undeterred, Wedgwood and Davy exhibited their stenciled photograms by candlelight, thus permitting their work to be acknowledged. Although there is evidence that a few of these prints were still visible into the late 1800s there are none, that I am aware of, in existence today. Eventually, Wedgwood and Davy published their discoveries in a manuscript titled *An Account of a method of Copying paintings Upon Glass and Making Profiles by the Agency of Light Upon Nitrate of Silver* (1802).

By the early 1840s, amateur artists and chemists were employing photogram techniques with simultaneous creative and practical scientific intentions. Notable projects underway during this period were Sir John Herschel's Anthotypes created with the juices of flowers and sunlight; Anna Atkins's cyanotype studies of algae (*a process that she presumably learned from Herschel who lived down the road, and who had invented the process*); Mongo Ponton's work with potassium dichromate as a light sensitizing solution for his "*shadowgraphs*" (which would lead to the gum bichromate process); and William Henry Fox Talbot's efforts with his photogenic drawings

Figure 2–3
William Henry Fox Talbot, _Photogenic Drawing,_ 1839
Talbot coated a piece of writing paper
with a solution of sodium chloride. The
salted paper was then dried and recoated
with a second solution of silver nitrate.
This sequence was sometimes repeated.
The result was a sensitized silver chloride
paper that was noticeably faster in its
light sensitivity than silver nitrate by itself.
Talbot then contact printed a selection of
found objects and exposed the paper and
objects to sunlight until an image
appeared, as in a photogram. The print
was "fixed" initially in a strong solution of
sodium chloride or potassium iodide.
Talbot called his representational creations _photogenic drawings._
_(Courtesy of The National Media
Museum / Science & Society Picture
Library—also the new repository for the
collection of the Royal Photographic
Society, London)_

and, later, calotype paper negatives. And after that short history excursion we are now back to Talbot's significant discovery in 1834.

In January of that year, Talbot began to experiment with the ideas and inspirations generated on his honeymoon trip to Lake Como. Using his knowledge of past silver salt experimentations, he proceeded to create precise photogram "tracings" of flowers, leaves, feathers and lace on salted and silver nitrate sensitized stationary. He called his discovery "_the art of photogenic drawing._"

In Talbot's earliest photogenic drawing exercises, he coated a fine piece of gelatin-sized stationery in a weak solution of common table salt _(sodium chloride)._ The paper that Talbot used was typical of the majority of quality stationery manufactured in the 1800s and intentionally sized and infused with gelatin, and/or other natural organic binders such as albumen (_egg whites_) and whey (_a high protein by-product of cheese making_), in order to enhance the sheet strength of the paper. English made papers were traditionally surface sized with gelatin, whereas French papermakers employed starch for the same purpose.

After the salted stationery had dried, Talbot applied a second coating of a 6%–8% silver nitrate solution . . . or stronger. This idea wasn't a completely serendipitous inspiration, as we have seen there is evidence of a fairly well-worn path leading to the moment. When the silver nitrate coating had dried, a light-sensitive compound of silver chloride had precipitated within the fibers of the paper. What Talbot was to surmise later was that the silver chloride will provide only a wispy rendition without the impurities within the paper to absorb the chlorine formed during the compounding of silver and sodium chloride. It is the excess of silver nitrate that facilitates the reaction.

These _Sciagraphs,_ or _Photogenic Drawings,_ that Talbot made during his experiments were semi-preserved with a bath of saturated salted water, although, as Talbot noted, "_we shall find that its_ [regarding his exposed paper] _sensibility is greatly diminished, and, in some cases, seems quite extinct._" Talbot went on to write that if that same piece of paper was then to be washed with an additional coating of silver nitrate, it would become sensitive once again—indeed, even more sensitive than the first time. Excited by the idea of creating an even faster exposure, Talbot noted that the proportions of salt and silver were critical and that in some cases the silver chloride was _disposed to darken of itself_ without any

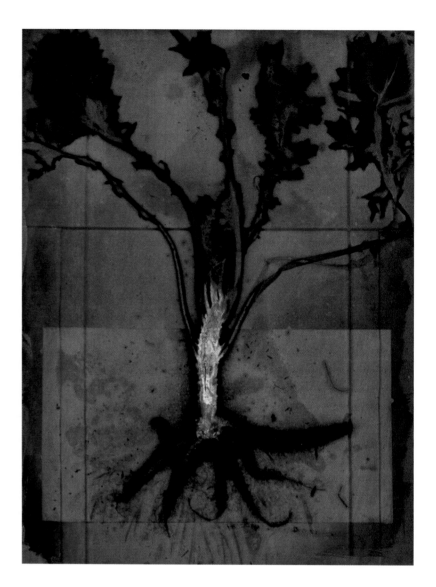

Figure 2–4

Carol Panaro-Smith & James Hajicek, *Earth Vegetation - 2*, 2005

Carol Panaro-Smith & James Hajicek have been making photogenic drawings in collaboration for many years. Using their secret variations of Talbot's formulas they select organic matter from the earth and sea and contact print on their prepared papers. This organic material withers under the intense heat and light of the Arizona sun as it completes its final act of participation in the creation of its own image.

exposure to light at all. Eventually, he got to the point where he could alternate between percentages, and numbers, of washes of salt and silver nitrate to the critical point where the paper would be ideal for rapid exposure in the camera obscura.

His method of selecting which piece of sensitized paper to use was an interesting one. He would prepare several large sheets in the manner described, cut off small samples, and number both. He would then lay the test samples out in a line in very diffused light for 15 minutes. The sample paper that showed the greatest tendency to change, under the influence of that low light, was the winner of the test, and Talbot would proceed to use its larger companion sheet (the one with the corresponding number) for his camera obscura exposure.

It is interesting to point out several things at this juncture in the process. First, in Talbot's initial attempts

to "fix" his *photogenic drawings,* he used Scheele's ammonia fixing bath from 1777 but with, as he wrote, "*imperfect success.*" Talbot then recalled a remark by Sir Humphry Davy in which Davy indicated that his experiments with the iodide of silver (*actually a sub-iodide*) showed that chemical to be more sensitive than silver chloride in producing a light-sensitive reaction.

During a subsequent residence in Geneva, in 1834, Talbot tried working with Davy's information and discovered that in his own experiments the opposite was true and that Davy's silver iodide formula was not sensitive to light in the least. Talbot immediately began to use this knowledge as a way to *fix,* and stabilize, his silver chloride photogenic drawing images by dipping them in a very dilute bath of iodide of potassium. In this way, an iodide of silver was formed, making a fixing bath that would render the print, "*absolutely unalterable by sunshine.*"

Figure 2–5

Charles *Négre—The Vampire (Henri Le Secq) at Notre Dame Cathedral,* 1853—salted paper print from a paper negative

This view is from the balustrade above the grand Galerie of Notre Dame Cathedral (beautiful view of Paris and a way to work off some calories). The gentleman in the photograph is the artist's good friend, Henri Le Secq. Négre was one of the first generation of painters-turned-photographers and was an advocate of photography being a powerful medium not only for the recording of life detail but also for expressing that life.

(Courtesy of The national Gallery of Canada)

During the *"brilliant summer of 1835,"* Talbot returned to his original goal of making pictures in camera and created the first camera-made paper negative that could be used to generate multiple positive photographic prints. (See Fig. 3-5, *Latticed Window at Lacock Abbey (with the Camera Obscura, August 1835).* Following his discovery, Talbot wrote a charming description of this experience in his 1839 paper to the Royal Society, "Some Account of the Art of Photogenic Drawing." He wrote, *"In the summer of 1835 I made in this way a great number of representations of my house in the country . . . and this*

building I believe to be the first that was ever yet known to have drawn its own picture."

The year 1839 was a big one for photography and the first months were really chaotic. On the 7th of January, Daguerre's "invention" of photography was delivered, to the Academie des Sciences in Paris by Daguerre's friend, Dominique François Arago. Talbot immediately wrote a letter to Arago, not realizing that the two techniques were quite different, informing him that it was he, not Daguerre, who had invented this image-making process.

You may recall that the French Ministry of Finance clerk, Hippolyte Bayard, had shown his own invention of photography, direct positive images on sensitized paper, to the same Monsieur Arago just three months earlier. But Arago had already invested too much of his reputation in Daguerre, so Bayard was told to be quiet and was subsequently ignored. On the 25th of that same month, Michael Faraday (1791–1867), the discoverer of *electromagnetism*, showed Talbot's work to the members of the Royal Institution. On the 31st, Talbot unveiled his salted paper "photogenic drawings" to the Royal Society in London and read from his paper "Some Account of the Art of Photogenic Drawing or the Process by Which Natural Objects may be Made to Delineate Themselves Without the Aid of an Artist's Pencil."

Mr. Talbot's Ferns Are Fixed by Mr. Herschel

Talbot's friend, Sir John Herschel, became very interested in all of this commotion and wrote a letter to Talbot using the word *"photography"* for the very first time. Then, on the 1st of February, Talbot dropped in on Herschel for tea and learned of Herschel's knowledge of the fixing abilities of sodium hyposulphite of soda (*sodium thiosulfate*), a fact that Herschel had actually realized some 20 years earlier.

In a letter written by Maggie Herschel to her son, Alexander Herschel, in February 1872, she wrote. *"I remember very well the visit . . . to Slough of Mr Fox Talbot, who came to shew [sic] to Herschel his beautiful little picture of ferns and Laces taken by his new process—when something was said about the difficulty of fixing the pictures. Herschel said, 'let me have this one for a few minutes,' and after a short time he returned to give the picture to Mr. Talbot saying,*

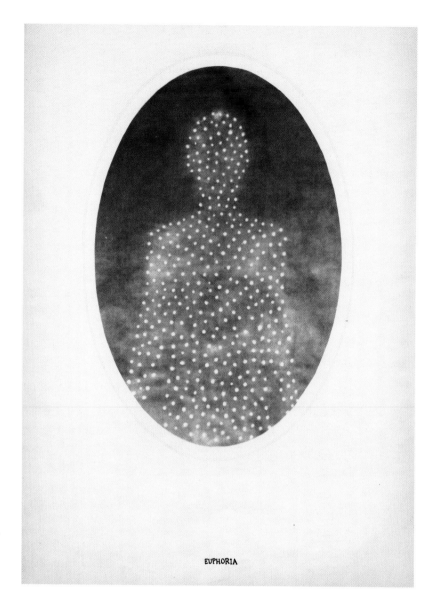

Figure 2–6
Dan Estabrook, *#9, Euphoria*, 2004—salt and ink
Dan is a former student of mine from Harvard and, curiously, still one of my favorite artists. This salted paper print is one of a series he calls Nine Symptoms.
(Courtesy of the artist)

EUPHORIA

"I think that you will find that fixed"—this was the beginning of hyposulphate of soda fixing."

With Herschel's consent, Talbot described this last piece of the photographic puzzle. When Daguerre heard the news, he immediately embraced the chemical for use in his own work, thus solving one of his biggest problems. On February 8, 1841, Talbot placed a restrictive patent on his calotype discovery, nearly putting the brakes on the new "photographic" medium.

The effects of Talbot's patent were relatively short lived; however, due to the enthusiasm of other scientists for making pictures and to the advent of Blanquart-Evrard's albumen technique and its integration with Frederick Scott Archer's wet-collodion glass plate negative process in 1851. It is interesting to note that Talbot eventually realized that

he had not perfected an art form but had certainly commenced one, and it is Talbot's salted paper process that led directly to our modern silver halide based photography.

GELATIN SALTING, CHEMISTRY & FORMULAS

In 1835, Fox Talbot had no need to size his papers with gelatin because the fine stationery of that time was manufactured with gelatin and other organic binders in the rag fibers. In my workshops and classes, I have found that a simple gelatin sizing is an easy way to enhance the quality, contrast and tonalities of the salted image. This may be less than a pure approach to the process but it beats being frustrated by the inevitable dry-down that occurs in salted paper. Don't size automatically. Try many different kinds of papers and you may get lucky. If not, and it is more and more likely that that will be the case, try gelatin sizing with one of the salting formulas that follow and evaluate your degree of success. If you run into a problem, there's more than a good chance it can be fixed with attention to detail and simple gelatin sizing. In the salted paper process, the paper is initially coated with a gelatin or starch, and salt (*sodium chloride*) solution. Here are several formulas, and we'll begin with my favorite.

TABLE & SINK SET UP FOR GELATIN SALTING PAPER

Gelatin Salting #1

(*Yields a reddish-purple salt print without toning*)

  8 g gelatin
      (*Knox gelatin from the grocery is OK / photo grade is better, i.e. Maco—LPE410 or Bostick & Sullivan's photo grade*)
 18 g sodium citrate
 20 g ammonium chloride
1 liter (1000 ml) of distilled water
Electric kettle for heating water
Several clean plastic beakers
Clean trays for salt soaking the paper: 1 large and 1 small
Clothesline for hanging salted paper
Zip Lock bag for paper storage

I use this sizing formula almost exclusively and find it especially successful when used with classes or workshops with a large number of people. Remember this important rule of gelatin sizing . . . keep your gelatin warm at all times.

Gelatin Salting #2

(*Yields a blue-purple salt print without toning*)

  8 g gelatin (*Knox gelatin from the grocery is OK / photo grade is better, i.e., Maco—LPE410 or Bostick & Sullivan's photo grade*)
 18 g sodium citrate
 20 g sodium chloride
1 liter (1000 ml) of distilled water

Electric kettle for heating water
Several clean plastic beakers
Clean trays for salt soaking the paper: 1 large and 1 small
Clothesline for hanging salted paper
Zip Lock bag for storage

Contrast Control in Sizing for Gelatin Salting #1 & #2

Employing a slightly weaker salting solution can increase contrast. Increasing the amount of sodium citrate in your gelatin/starch sizing solution will reduce contrast, whereas decreasing the amount of sodium citrate, or eliminating it altogether, will increase the contrast. Make adjustment in very small increments.

Gelatin Salting Step Sequence

Step 1 Begin by soaking the gelatin, in a clean plastic beaker, in half of the water at room temperature for 15 to 20 minutes. This period of time is referred to as the "bloom" time. The bloom number of your gelatin will inform you as to its hardness. Knox gelatin has a low bloom number and is considered "soft." Photo grade gelatin has a higher bloom number and is harder.

        After the bloom, add the remaining 500 ml of distilled water and heat the solution to 100° F. I find that the easiest method of doing this is to create a double-boiler like system where you have a very clean plastic beaker to hold your sizing solution and this is set into a larger container holding water warm enough to maintain a 100° constant temperature.

Step 2 When the gelatin and water mix is at temperature, slowly add the sodium citrate and ammonium chloride and stir slowly into solution.

Step 3 Prepare a "double-boiler" tray set up where a smaller tray (large enough for your paper) is filled with the warm gelatin and salts . . . see each formula for specifics. This smaller tray is set into a larger tray filled with very hot water. The smaller tray floats on the hot water in the larger tray keeping the gelatin warm during the sizing. If the gelatin cools, it hardens . . . just like a gelatin dessert.

Figure 2–7
Niles Lund, *Portrait of*
Christopher, **2004—salt print**
Niles took a workshop with
me at The Maine Media
Workshops and brought along
his view camera with a motor-
ized focal plane shutter. I used
Nile's negative of me for a
salted paper print demo.
(Courtesy of the artist/author)

The purpose of the gelatin sizing is to prevent the silver nitrate from sinking too deeply into the paper. As well, it helps eliminate a muddy looking image after dry down. The primary difference between Gelatin formula #1 and #2 is an ammonium chloride/sodium chloride swap. The use of ammonium chloride will result in a little better contrast and a reddish-purple tonality. If, on the other hand, you wish to lessen the contrast, or want a print that is blue-purple, then you should consider the Gelatin Salting Emulsion #2 with sodium chloride formula.

Step 4 Gently feed your paper, a sheet at a time, into the tray of warmed gelatin salted solution. I like to put about 10 sheets of paper into the gelatin at a time and slowly sort through the stack being sure to immerse each sheet completely.

Step 5 After 3 to 5 minutes, remove the paper from the warm gelatin solution and hang each sheet on a line, with clothespins, to dry. After the first minute or so, flip the papers upside down on the line to prevent the gelatin from hardening on the lower half of the hanging paper. This will help ensure an even coverage. When the paper is dry, flatten it in a dry mount press at a low temperature, raising and lowering the platen so as not to burn the gelatin. If you don't have a dry mount press, don't worry about it.

Fauver's Gelatin Salting Formula

20 g	citric acid
20 g	Kosher salt (*Sodium Chloride—Morton's Kosher*)
4 g	Knox gelatin (or photo grade gelatin)
1000 ml	distilled water

Figure 2–8
Allyson Fauver, *Salt #10*, 2005
Allyson comes to my workshops simply to make better salted paper prints than I do in my demonstrations. Her sentences are far too long to quote and utilize in this space well. This is one of her salted paper images, unfixed, stabilized with Kosher salt, forced to a solarized state via reexposure, and then toned in a variety of toners.
(Courtesy of the artist)

This formula is one used by Allyson Fauver, who is one of the best salted paper printers I know. Allyson's images are known for the brilliantly deep reds she achieves and by her traditional use of salt as a fixing bath. Notice that there is no sodium citrate in her formula. Begin by making sure everything you will be using . . . beakers, stirrers, trays, etc. are meticulously clean.

Step 1 In a 1000 ml beaker, sprinkle the gelatin into 200 ml of cold distilled water and let it stand for 15 minutes.

Step 2 Dissolve the sodium chloride (Kosher Salt) and citric acid in 700 ml of distilled water that you have heated to a 100° F constant temperature

Step 3 Pour the sodium chloride/citric acid solution into the gelatin solution, and add hot (distilled) water to make a total volume of 1000 ml. Place the beaker, double boiler style, in a larger beaker of hot water and stir well until the gelatin is fully dissolved.

Step 4 Continue the gelatin salting sequence as detailed above.

Allyson's Deep Red

Allyson's deep red coloration is due to her post-exposure work on the print. She washes her images in a 3% salted bath (a 30 g of Kosher salt to 1000 ml of distilled water solution) for 5–6 minutes. This bath changes the color of the print to a dark red/brownish orange.

Next, the wet print is then reexposed to UV light. As the print is unfixed at this point, the new salt bath essentially washes the print in a new and different silver chloride/salt solution, and this second exposure brings out lavender in the highlights and results, after drying, in a deep rust red/lavender duo-toned print. The older the sodium chloride salt rinse bath, the more dramatic the color shift to lavender. The print is then washed in running water for 15 minutes and hung to dry in a dark environment. After drying, if you hot press the paper, the color will darken additionally.

Allyson doesn't mention these variations to her technique, but I'll toss them in here as I think it may help make the print more stable. While you are experimenting, try adding 10 g of citric acid to the sensitizer solution. This will lower the pH and this step is often a benefit. Also after washing, try toning your print for 30 minutes in a gold/borax toner. Finally, in answer to the obvious question of why she hasn't included a fixing step in her process . . . it's quite simple. Fox Talbot's earliest salted paper prints were unfixed, and the technique that Allyson is using is a form of tribute to the mystique and alchemy of the work that could only be appreciated by candlelight. Her prints, as were Talbot's, are stabilized, but unfixed. "They are, she writes, by their nature and my intent, changeable. Ephemeral, both physically, and emotionally. A reflection of our own beauty, fragility, and mystery."

TABLE SET UP FOR SENSITIZING SALTED PAPER

- Clean dark brown glass bottle for silver nitrate solution. (*See below for several sensitizer formulas that will be suitable for your printing needs.*)
- Clean paper for the table surface
- Salted & labeled paper for coating (see instructions in text for salting)
- New hake brush (labeled Salted Paper)
- Clean distilled water in a beaker

- Clean beaker for silver nitrate sensitizer coating
- Pencil
- Hair dryer
- Contact printing frame
- Negative for contact printing

Silver Nitrate Sensitizing Salted Paper

When your salted paper has dried sufficiently, it is time to sensitize it with a solution of silver nitrate. Up to this point, the completion of the salting stage, your paper has not been light-sensitive. The coating of silver nitrate will change this situation and it is necessary to conduct this next stage of your salted paper preparation under a very low light level.

Begin by preparing the silver nitrate solution and be very careful with this chemical. I'm going to give you three different silver nitrate formulas. The first is a simple and basic one that you use directly. The other uses citric acid as a preservative and extends the time that you can use the paper should you not be printing immediately. In any case, both standard formulas will do the job. The third formula is one that I use at high altitude. *Before you begin, be sure to read this:*

Silver Nitrate: *Read This*

Note: Silver nitrate appears as a colorless and odorless crystal and discolors on exposure to light. Silver nitrate is highly corrosive. Silver nitrate can cause severe skin and eye problems and is particularly destructive to mucous membranes and the upper respiratory tract. It is the primary silver salt found in photographic emulsions, alternative processes (i.e., van dyke, salted paper, etc.), and intensifiers. Silver nitrate will discolor your skin as it binds with the proteins in the epidermal layer of it . . . the stain will go away. It may cause blindness if it gets into your eyes and it is caustic so do not touch your face when working with it. If you get silver nitrate on your skin you may experience redness, pain, and burning. Upon exposure, wash the area well with repeated rinses of water. Rubbing the area of exposure with

sodium chloride (table salt) will help lessen damage to a degree and will also help with stain removal. If you get silver nitrate in your eyes immediately flush with copious amounts of water and continue flushing while medical attention is summoned.

Black silver nitrate stains on counters can be eliminated by washing the stained area with a solution of 2 teaspoons of sodium bisulfite in a quart of water. Be cautious of the sulfur dioxide gas that will be created by this act of cleansing. Silver nitrate is a very strong oxidizer. It will combust and forms an explosive precipitate if allowed to come into contact with any ammonia compounds, i.e., ammonium hydroxide (the strong concentration of ammonia used in mordançage). Never mix silver nitrate with metals such as aluminum or zinc. Use all safety precautions especially by wearing gloves and goggles or safety glasses when working with this chemical.

That said, I have discolored my skin for a few decades now without pain, burning, or any other negative effects. Students, no matter how careful they are, and unless they decide to wear nitrile gloves, inevitably get a brown spot or two from silver nitrate solution on their fingers during coating and so far, not a single person has been damaged in any way. Just be aware that silver nitrate can be dangerous if you don't respect it.

Here's another bit of silver nitrate information you might want to keep in mind . . . silver nitrate isn't very light-sensitive all by itself, but as soon as it gets together with an organic binder such as dust, gelatin, starch, and the like, it becomes light-sensitive.

Standard 10% Silver Nitrate Sensitizer Formula

This traditional formula makes a 10% sensitizer solution. Add the 10 g of silver nitrate to the 100 ml of warmed distilled water and stir gently with a nonmetallic stirrer until it is dissolved into solution. You can make any concentration that you like and many salted paper printers prefer a less aggressive concentration of 6% with which they double coat their paper.

    10 g   silver nitrate
  100 ml   of distilled water

Standard 10% Silver Nitrate & Citric Acid Sensitizer Formula:

I prefer this solution formula to the standard mix above, especially if I am experiencing highlight problems or do not intend to print immediately . . . the citric acid makes the solution more acidic, lowers the pH of the sensitizer, and acts as a preservative. Mix the 10 g of silver nitrate into the 50 ml of warm distilled water and carefully pour the solution into a clean dark glass container with a plastic cap. Then mix 5 g of citric acid into the remaining 50 ml of warm distilled water and add it to the silver nitrate solution in the dark glass container.

  100 ml   of distilled water
    10 g   of silver nitrate
     5 g   citric acid (*this lowers the pH and makes it more acidic*)

High-Altitude/No Humidity 20% Salted Paper Sensitizer Formula:

This formula is an option if you happen to be working in Aspen, Santa Fe, or Machu Picchu. Interestingly enough, I've started to use this mix at all altitudes and like it a lot . . . as long as your coating to exposure time is very short. Notice that the citric acid is also in this sensitizer mix, lowering the pH and extending the time I can have before exposure.

  100 ml   of distilled water
    20 g   of silver nitrate
     5 g   citric acid

Mix the 10 g of silver nitrate into the 50 ml of warm distilled water and carefully pour the solution into a clean dark glass container.

Then mix 5 g of citric acid into the remaining 50 ml of warm distilled water and add it to the silver nitrate solution in the dark glass container.

Sensitizing Considerations

As a rule, try to use the freshly sensitized paper as soon as you can. Salted paper dislikes humidity, and in humid conditions the paper will begin to discolor in a few hours. If this is the environment you are printing in, try using the silver nitrate #2 formula due to the addition of citric acid. In dry, dark, and cool conditions, the addition of the citric acid may preserve the sensitized paper for a day or two.

Be careful not to apply heat (*when blow-drying*) to the newly sensitized paper because that temperature change will cause a loss of sensitivity. If you do use a hairdryer, be sure that it is set on a cool setting and blow on the backside of the coated paper for the majority of the drying time, making sure that your paper is totally dry before exposing. Blow-drying on the backside of the coated paper also helps draw the sensitizer into the paper's fibers. Moisture in the paper will cause staining and generally poor quality, so you might want to consider having a dry mount press, set at a low temperature, nearby for removing any residual moisture immediately prior to printing. If using a press, make sure that the time the platen and the paper are together is very brief. Open and close the press rapidly and you'll see the moisture escape out of the back of the press.

If you see a speckled print, with black or brown spots, reminding you of Niépce's view from the window at Gras perhaps, you could be experiencing a variety of maladies. The most common are . . . the paper is contaminated in some way; the paper is the wrong one for the process; the silver nitrate application brush has been compromised and not thoroughly washed between coatings; the silver nitrate (if you are dipping the brush) has gone bad due to this contamination; or the paper was moist when you exposed it; you are not using distilled water; kosher salt hasn't been added to the first wash bath, and so forth . . . this list can get quite lengthy.

Very often, the problem is simply related to the brush not being cleaned well. What has happened is that the brush has picked up salted gelatin and dust from repeated applications of silver nitrate sensitizer when brushing across the paper's surface. Then, when a second coating is performed, and the brush is dipped again into the silver nitrate, the solution becomes contaminated. My best advice is to use a shot glass with a drop

count (approximately 22 drops for a 4×5 inch negative) of fresh silver nitrate for each print. You could also use a glass coating rod (refer to Chapter 13 for the technique) or new foam brush for each new application.

If you are having problems, change one thing at a time. My first move would be to remix the silver nitrate solution, adding the citric acid, and try again. My second change would be to go to the drop count in the shot glass versus the dipping of the brush into a beaker of silver nitrate. Third, I would change papers. Fourth, I would make absolutely sure that my paper was bone dry before exposing and I would do almost my entire exposure in open shade to cut down on building up heat (resulting in moisture) in the contact frame.

Contrast Enhancement

One of the easiest methods of affecting the contrast of your salted paper print is to alter the initial wash-development bath. To increase the contrast, as well as to change the color of the image to a reddish brown, simply add 3–5 drops of a 10% potassium dichromate solution (*100 g potassium dichromate to a liter of distilled water*) to 1000 ml of distilled water. Then heat this solution in a microwave oven in a plastic beaker or use a double boiler like tray setup. The warmer the solution, the stronger the change to contrast and color, and the less likely you will experience salted paper speckling.

You can also increase the contrast of your print by adding a drop or two of a 1% to 5% solution of potassium dichromate solution to every 28 ml of the sensitizer. This will also result in a color change to reddish brown that is similar to the gold/borax toner described later. (*A 5% solution is made by dissolving 5 g of potassium dichromate in 100 ml of distilled water.*) If you elect to add some potassium dichromate to the solution, warm it up first so that it will incorporate with the silver nitrate more efficiently. This will also help reduce the "speckling" that occasionally shows up on the print when a dichromate is added.

This last technique, of adding to the sensitizer, is more aggressive than adding potassium dichromate to your wash-development, and I would recommend other approaches to contrast adjustments before this one. A simple solution is to simply perform your entire exposure

Figure 2–9

Margaret Adams, *Dress, 2000*—salt print diptych and salt print with potassium dichromate added

Margaret is a former workshop student of mine is now teaching alternative processes at The Corcoran College of Art & Design. She did a good deal of salt testing for me in the first edition and this is one of her images that illustrates the difference between a straight salted paper print and one made with potassium dichromate added to the sensitizer.

(Courtesy of the artist)

in the shade and then have your first wash be a 5-minute one in distilled water with no salt added. The next adjustment I would consider would be making a new digital negative with adequate contrast for the process.

COATING SALTED PAPER

I have often taught this process using a common beaker of silver nitrate and having the students lightly dip a clean brush into it and proceed to coat their paper. Most of the time, this method is perfectly fine, but occasionally there are contamination problems. As mentioned above, the easiest fix for this issue is to make an individual drop

count in a shot glass for each print that you do. Consult the Platinum/Palladium and Ziatype chapters for drop count charts and technique.

If you are going to dip a brush, it is less expensive, in the long run, to use a new, and fresh, foam brush for coating each print . . . seriously. This lesson has taken me a long time to learn but it is good advice. As much as I love the romantic look of the hake brush strokes, the frequency of contamination, even when you are meticulously clean in your working process, is nearly unavoidable with salted paper.

A third method of coating is the traditional floating of the salted paper on a volume of silver nitrate in a tray. If you opt for this technique, consider using a Pyrex baking dish, as it is easy to clean. The traditional method is to float the paper in the silver nitrate solution for 15 to 30 seconds, being sure not to get any emulsion on the "back" of the

SHORTNESS OF BREATH

Figure 2–10
Dan Estabrook, #1. Shortness of Breath (Nine Symptoms series)—salted paper
This is another salted paper print from Dan's Nine Symptoms portfolio.
(Courtesy of the artist)

paper. The easiest way to *float* successfully is to bend up the 4 side edges on your paper (*just like in albumen coating*) so that you create a little origami like "serving tray." The folded edges of the "serving tray" can be trimmed off after the process is complete and this almost eliminates the problem of getting silver nitrate on the back of the paper.

Coating is performed in very subdued light. Sensitize the sized paper by floating, brushing (foam brush), or glass rod coating, applying 1 to 2 coats of your silver nitrate solution. If you are double coating, dry thoroughly between coats. The more silver nitrate in the formula, as Talbot discovered, the more sensitive the solution. This means that you can increase the silver nitrate amount in the previous silver nitrate formulas to make a more light-sensitive solution. However, this doesn't mean loading up

on a big concentration in one coating. Multiple low concentration coatings work better.

If floating is too difficult for you, I suggest using a new cheap foam brush or glass rod method. Always mark the front of your coated paper with an "S" (*for silver or sensitized*) because the formula tends to be quite difficult to see in low light conditions. In both brush and rod coating, allow your newly sensitized paper to sit still in the dark for a few minutes before drying or hanging it up.

Be sure to use distilled water because normal tap water will almost always cause one problem or another due to the mineral concentration or the pipes that the water flows through. If you use a hake brush to coat, then be sure to wash it with distilled water between applications.

PAPER: PRINTING SALTED PAPER

For the salted paper process, I recommend using a quality 100% rag paper with a smooth surface such as Bergger's Cot 320, Crane's Platinotype, Arches' Platine, Crane's Kid Finish, Arches Acquarelle, Arches Grain Satine, or Bienfang 360. Another paper that has come to my attention lately is called Weston Diploma Parchment and it is available through the Butler & Dearden Paper Service in Boylston, Massachusetts. You will, of course, determine which is best for you according to the intentions of your image.

When using a lighter weight paper you will generally experience a salted paper image that exhibits a greater degree of clarity and tonal resonance. The reason for this is that the process is going to be taking place on a gelatin sized paper and the best results will come from a delicate technique with a delicate application and restrained printing.

As a place to start, your negative should be high in contrast with a D-max in the 1.5 to 2.0 neighborhood. This is a moderately dense and contrasty negative that would generally be suitable for a conventional silver paper of grade 0. When making negatives for the salted paper process, try to make the best negative possible and then overdevelop it by 50%. If you are going to be making a digital negative, then seek a curve profile that increases the contrast and density.

Exposure Times

Once you are ready to expose your sensitized paper, place your negative, and bone-dry sensitized paper in a hinged, contact printing frame so that the light will penetrate the glass, right-reading negative, and sensitized paper in that order. Go outside and place your printing frame in light shade but not directly facing the sunlight. You will notice that the paper begins to darken immediately and subsequently eases off. In my experience, sunlight will expose an average negative well in 6–12 minutes but will likely block shadow details in the darkest values. A UV exposure unit will provide a good exposure in 7–12 minutes. Again, the darkest shadows

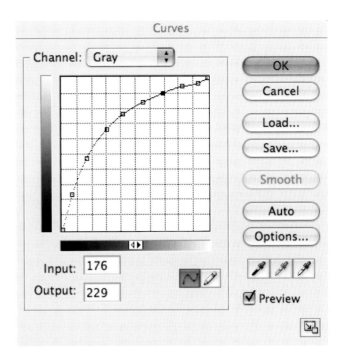

Figure 2–11

Salted Paper Curve Profile Example

This curve adjustment screen illustrates how a salted paper custom curve profile, one suited to the specific process, would look after loading it. Please refer to the Digital Options chapter for details.

will tend to block unless you filter the exposure with a translucent sheet such as Pictorico OHP. My recommendation for the best exposure strategy is to use a combination of sun and shade for 6–12 minutes. Do the majority of your exposure in the shade and then hit it with some direct sunlight at the end of the exposure to intensify the darks in the image. This technique will yield the best contrast potential with the best density and detail in the shadows.

As mentioned, it is generally best to face your contact printing frame away from the direct sun, or keep it in the shade, so that you can better control your exposure and contrast. Negatives low in density or contrast should be printed in this manner for greater contrast. Contrast can also be slightly increased by placing a sheet of tissue or vellum over the glass during exposure to slow the pace of the exposure. I will add here that printing salted paper in cold weather, or in a cold and dry environment, is difficult. Although this is a bit of an irritation if you live in places where there is an actual winter, it does open up the possibility of one benefit . . . storing sensitized paper in the freezer, where it will stay viable for about a week if you're fortunate.

Examine the progress of the exposure at different times during the printing in the same manner you would with other printing-out processes when using a contact-printing frame. Look at your paper in a very low light area so as not to fog the image. The printed-out image should be allowed to go quite deep: highlights should appear much denser than you will want in the final image and shadows will become almost a metallic bronze color. You may lose a minimum of 2 to 4 steps on a calibrated gray scale step tablet after all of the processing has been completed, but there are some things that you can do at this stage to reduce that depreciation.

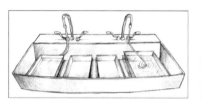

SINK SET UP FOR SALTED PAPER

Tray 1   3% salting bath Mix: 30 g of Kosher salt to 1 liter of distilled water. Add 1% citric acid (10 g) to the salted bath liter. Agitate for about 5 minutes.

Tray 2   **Optional** **Toning Baths:** Toning must be done BEFORE fixing the print. Toning baths will alter the image color and often aid in the archival properties of the print. Please refer to the text for specific salted paper toner formulas and times.

Tray 3   **10% Sodium Thiosulfate fixing bath:** Mix: 100 g sodium thiosulfate to 1 liter distilled water and 2 ml household strength ammonia

Tray 3   **Optional: Sel d'or Toner/Fixer Monobath Formula:** Mix: 500 ml water to 75 g sodium thiosulfate, 1-teaspoon bicarbonate of soda and 3 grains of gold chloride (*Use a 30 ml Stock Solution*)*

Tray 4   **Hypo Clearing Bath:** Mix: 1% solution of sodium sulfite (10 g to 1000 ml water)

Tray 5   **Final wash** for 20–30 minutes

PROCESSING SALTED PAPER

Salt Wash Bath

This first bath in the processing sequence consists of a slightly acidic salt bath whose purpose is to precipitate the free (or excess) silver by producing silver chloride. If you have no salt in this bath you will not be removing the free silver and this will create problems with toning, as the gold will not adhere to the silver unless the free silver nitrate has been eliminated. Following your exposure, immerse your print in this bath of salted water that has been made slightly acidic, lowering its pH, with the addition of citric acid.

    10 g   citric acid
    30 g   kosher salt
 1000 ml   distilled water

Immerse your print in this solution under low to moderate light, and agitate slowly for about 5 minutes.

Following this step, move your print to a tray filled with fresh water and gently agitate. Repeat the fresh water exchange with a separate tray of fresh water 2 to 3 times and then move on to the normal washing stage that follows. One more thing . . . If you forget to remove your print from the salted bath, you will notice that your print will begin to fade a bit. The stronger the salt solution, the more fade you'll see. This could be a way to clear your highlights in a desperate situation.

Washing the Print

After the prewash salt bath, immerse your print for 15 minutes in clean running water, making exchanges on a regular basis. This bath clears out the remaining free, unexposed, silver. If you do not wash the print well, subsequent toning and fixing will not work adequately and your final image may be flat and muddy in appearance. You will also notice a host of salted paper problems with one of the most common being little dark spots.

Continue to rinse the print until all of the milkiness in the water has disappeared. If you have a black plastic tray, this will help. The paper is still slightly sensitive to UV light, so be careful. Also, do not be shocked by the color of the image when it is placed in the water wash. It

---

* Stock Gold Solution for Sel d'or Toner/Fixer Mix: 154 ml distilled water to 1 g gold chloride (1 gram = 15.43 grains)

Figure 2–12
Christopher James, *Sarah, Maine*—2000—gold toned salted paper print
This gold-toned, salted paper, print of Sarah was generated from a Polaroid Type 55 P/N film and a pinhole camera. Following the completed salt process, I enhanced the darks with a very short gum bichromate exposure using a mix of gum Arabic, 13% potassium dichromate, and black and red watercolor pigment in registration with the salted paper print.
(Courtesy of the author)

will shift toward red and the print will lighten considerably. Hot water will also accelerate the highlight clearing and may result in a more reddish brown shift if your water is alkaline.

SALTED PAPER TONING FORMULAS: PRIOR TO FIX

If you go directly to the fixer after the wash stage your print will be reddish-brown. A toning step is not necessary if this is a color decision that you've made for your image.

Toning the print following the wash cycles, and prior to the fixing bath, allows you to select from a palette of colors that range from red to purple to blue-brown and smokey-black. Toning will also increase the longevity of your image. The following toning formulas are for you to experiment with and will provide you with an assortment of tonalities, hues, and contrasts. The first toner example is made with gold chloride and borax, and it yields a warm reddish color. The ammonium thiocyanate toner will yield a more blue shift in the highlights and mid tones but depending upon time, will often leave your reds alone. The Gold 231 will often result in a smokey-black with highlight shifts to cool rather than the original warmth. Each toner will react differently depending upon freshness and intensity of the toner, the paper you are toning, temperature of the toner, success of your washing cycles, and a host of other alt pro gremlins that may decide to visit your print. Experiment and do not invest even a portion of your self worth in the success of the toner. Have fun with it and see what happens.

Gold-Borax Toner (*warm/reddish color*)

800 ml   distilled water at 100°
   6 g   borax
  12 ml   1% gold chloride solution

Dissolve the borax in the distilled water and add the prepared 1% gold chloride to the solution. Gold chloride in a premixed state can be purchased from most chemical suppliers. Toning will take 15–30 minutes depending on the tone you are seeking. Generally, the color of the image becomes cooler the longer you have the print immersed in the solution. Keep in mind that a dry print looks cooler than a wet print. Prepare this toning solution at least an hour before use and work with it at room temperature. If you find the toning less than active, add or replenish the toner with additional gold chloride solution. One way to be economical about gold chloride is to trim off any parts of your paper that you will eventually over-mat. This will cause less of the gold to be absorbed by the paper. For a black tonality, check out the gold-borax combination with platinum toner in this section. Note that this formula is very similar to the gold-borax albumen toner except that it is half as concentrated.

If you are seeking a deep burgundy color, then try the gold borax toner for 30 minutes followed, after a rinse, by the 30-minute gold ammonium thiocyanate toner.

Gold-Ammonium Thiocyanate Toner: Standard Salt

(*Blue/gray tonality*)
800 ml   distilled water
  25 g   ammonium thiocyanate
   2 g   tartaric acid
   5 g   sodium chloride
  20 ml   1 % gold chloride
Distilled water to make 1 liter (1000 ml)

Tone in the same manner as you do with the gold-borax formula. This toner will give you much colder values and an immersion of 6–15 minutes in a fresh ammonium

thiocyanate toning bath will yield blue-gray tonalities. This toner does not keep well so only mix the amount that you intend to use during a single working session . . . about 8 prints. If you use a thiocyanate toner, be aware that the sodium thiosulfate fixing bath may precipitate sulfur. If this is a problem, and you will know it by the aroma, you can easily fix the problem by adding 5 g of sodium sulfite to the sodium thiosulfate fixer formula and replace the fixer every 4 to 5 prints.

Gold-thiocyanate toner is particularly compatible with platinum toner and a range of colors, from warm red to slate gray to sepia, can be achieved by adjusting the times of the salt print in each toner and in the sequence they are used.

Gold-Ammonium Thiocyanate Toner II: POP Formula (Bostick & Sullivan Premixed Solution A & B)

(*Blue/gray tonality*)
Stock Solution A
  10 g   ammonium thiocyanate
500 ml   distilled water at 120°F

Combine the ingredients into a uniform solution, store in a clean plastic or glass bottle, and allow the solution to sit for 8-12 hours before use.

Stock Solution B
   1 g   gold chloride
500 ml   of distilled water at 70°F

To use: Mix 50 ml of Stock A with 50 ml of Stock B and 900 ml of distilled water. The toner is good for about 8 prints before it begins to wear out. When you need to replenish the solution simply keep what is in your toning tray and add 50 ml Stock A and 50 ml Stock B to it. The toning time is subjective and usually between 10 and 30 minutes. The longer you tone, the cooler the mid tones and highlights.

Gold-Sodium Acetate Toner (*sepia to deep burgundy*)

800 ml   distilled water at 95°F to 100°F
  20 g   sodium acetate
  20 ml   1% gold chloride solution (*order it prepared; see resources*)
Distilled water to make 1 liter (1000 ml)

Figure 2–13

Mark Osterman, *Catching Blanks*,—waxed salt print from 8 × 10 collodion negative (Confidence Series)
There are quite a few of Mark Osterman's images in this book because he is simply one of the best practitioners of the genre. This is a waxed salted paper print made from one of his wet collodion glass plate negatives.
(Courtesy of the artist and The Howard Greenberg Gallery)

This toner, like the others, is used prior to the fixing bath. Begin by immersing the print in the distilled water prewash and salt prewash baths. Prepare your toner and see that its temperature is in the 65°F to 75°F range. Place your print in the toner and inspect it closely for the changes. Do not over-tone the print with the gold-acetate toner or you will get an overall yellow cast. It is a decent idea to do a test print for a few minutes and see if you like it. Gold acetate toning can be employed in a double toning sequence with the gold borax toner to get a black tonality. Be sure to wash the print well between the two toners if you are performing the split. After toning, rinse and continue the process with the fixer and final wash.

Palladium Toner (*reddish-brown to slate gray*)

450 ml distilled water
2.5 ml sodium chloropalladite (15% solution)
2.5 g sodium chloride (sea salt)
2.5 g citric acid
Distilled water to make a solution of 500 ml

This palladium toner will alter a salted silver nitrate sensitizer (*with a little potassium dichromate for a contrast boost*) from a traditional reddish-brown salt print to a slate gray. It's quite nice but different from its companion toner (platinum). The sodium chloropalladite can be ordered in a prepared state and can also be used for your palladium printing.

Begin your toning process by prewashing your print in the recommended salt prewashes and then rinse the print in running water for 15 minutes. After the wash, immerse the print in the palladium toner until you are pleased with the results. After toning, continue the process with the fixer and final wash stages.

Platinum Toners (*warm sepia/reddish-brown/yellow/gray*)

I'll give you two options for salted paper platinum toning. The first is a traditional salted paper platinum formula. The second is a similarly constructed formula but one that is designed to work with printing-out process papers; you'll find it repeated in the POP chapter Platinum toner is a little more expensive due to the cost of the potassium chloroplatinite (20% solution) but like the palladium, it can also be used for platinum printing or as an additive for palladium printing. Some very nice tonalities can be realized by two-stage toning combinations such as platinum toner and gold-thiocyanate toner. I'll provide you with the POP platinum-gold-thiocyanate formula as well. Gold-thiocyanate toner is particularly compatible with platinum toner and a range of colors, from warm red to slate gray to sepia, can be achieved by adjusting the times of the print in each toner and in the sequence that they are used. As with all toning, in every process, experimentation will often yield some lovely results . . . and then drive you crazy when you try to repeat the color on a different day.

Platinum Toner #1

450 ml	distilled water
1.5 ml	potassium chloroplatinite (*20% solution premix*)
2.5 g	citric acid
2.5 g	sodium chloride (sea salt)

Distilled water to make 500 ml

Begin your toning process by prewashing your print in the distilled water and salt prewash baths and then rinse the print for 15 minutes in fresh running water. After the wash, immerse the print in the platinum toner until you

Figure 2–14
Jesseca Ferguson, *Finis*, 2003 salted paper print & collage
This is a nice example, by Boston artist, Jesseca Ferguson, of combining media. In this case a salted paper print with collage.
(Courtesy of the artist)

are pleased with the results. After toning continue with the fixer and final wash stages.

POP Platinum Toner #2 (neutral black-sepia)

Bostick & Sullivan makes a prepared POP platinum toner using potassium chloroplatinite #3. The kit includes:

10 g	citric acid
10 ml	potassium chloroplatinite #3 (20%)
1	empty 1000 ml plastic container for storage of the solution

To make the platinum toning solution, measure out 10 g of the citric acid on a gram scale and dissolve it in 1000 ml of room-temperature distilled water. This will result in a 1% solution of citric acid.

To the citric acid solution, add 7 to 15 drops of the potassium chloroplatinite #3. The more drops added to the citric acid solution, the faster the toning and the faster you will run out of this very precious mix. You may wish to add fewer drops to allow time to subjectively inspect your toning progress. *Platinum toner does not have to be discarded after use it simply wears out.* If you feel that its effectiveness and speed are not what they used to be, then simply add 5–10 more drops of the potassium chloroplatinite #3.

To use: It's best to overexpose your salt print by 15%. Go through the prewash and salted prewash bath sequence and then rinse your print in fresh water for 15 minutes. Then, place the print in a clean tray and immediately pour the platinum toner over its entire surface. Agitate the tray continuously during the toning process. The toner will make itself evident first in the deeper shadow areas of the print and then work its way through the sequential tonal stages from dark to light. A short toning time will result in a warmer print and a longer toning period will yield blacks and a cooler image. When you are content with the coloration, rinse the print for 5 minutes and proceed to the fixing stage.

POP Platinum-Gold-Thiocyanate Split Toner

After your prewash sequence, you can achieve a wonderful gold-platinum split toned POP print by partially gold toning the print (*a short toning time in the gold-thiocyanate toner*), rinsing the print for 5 minutes, and then immersing the print in the platinum toner until you like what you see. The darker values will be purple-sepia in the shadows following the gold toner, whereas the highlights and lighter mid-tones will tone a cool-blue-black in the platinum. Always be sure to first tone with the gold because the citric acid in the platinum toner will be unkind to the gold toner.

Black-Gray Toning

Add 3 drops of a warm 5% potassium dichromate solution to every 28 ml of the silver nitrate sensitizer; coat and expose the print in a normal manner. Following exposure, proceed through the distilled and salted water prewash sequence. This salted prewash is quite necessary here, so don't overlook it. Then, tone the print in the gold-borax toner for 5 minutes and wash it in clear running water for 15 minutes. Following the wash, tone the print in the platinum toner for 5 to 15 minutes followed by a wash of 30 minutes. Rinse the print in fresh water for 10 minutes and then move on to the fix and final wash.

FIXING THE SALTED PAPER PRINT

Standard 10% Sodium Thiosulfate Fixing Bath for Salted paper

Prepare two separate fixing trays and into each one add a liter of 10% sodium thiosulfate fix solution detailed below. Fix prints, untoned or toned, for 30 to 60 seconds in each bath. Do not over-fix.

```
1 liter   distilled water (1000 ml)*
 100 g    sodium thiosulfate
   2 g    sodium bicarbonate OR 2 ml of ammonia*
```

You may go directly to the fixer after the toning and your image will become lighter the longer it stays in the solution. *Do not over-fix the print and certainly for no longer than a minute.*

SEL D'OR TONER/FIXER MONOBATH FOR SALT

Sel d'or Toner/Fixer Monobath

Several years after the daguerreotype process was announced, a French physicist by the name of Hippolyte Fizeau introduced an important process change, called sel d'or (salt of gold), that gave Daguerreotypists a way to intensify and tone their work. Sometime between 1847 and 1855 the technique was applied to paper prints, i.e., calotype, salted paper, albumen, etc.

For many years, in the mid-19th century, sel d'or gold toning was commonly incorporated into the albumen and salted paper processes. Although it was quite difficult to predict whether the technique would improve, or fade, the print, the single bath toner/fixer was widely practiced. When an albumen or salted paper print

---

* Be sure to use only distilled water for your fixing bath to avoid bleaching down the road.

was immersed in the sel d'or toner/fixer monobath the image color would lighten (orange-brown) and then reconstitute itself to either a cool sienna, purple, or blue-black. The final image color is based upon the depth of the printing, the toning formula, and the length of time the print is in the toning solution. It is recommended that you print deeply if you intend to use this technique.

The sel d'or toner is a toning-fixing monobath and is constituted by mixing a solution of gold chloride into a solution of sodium thiosulfate and a little bicarbonate of soda, to make the solution a bit to alkaline. Using it allows the photographer to tone and fix their print in a single bath. Again, it is unpredictable, and the following formula is more "kitchen-sink" than lab. Toning-fixing time is approximately 4 minutes following the wash stage.

Sel d'or Toner/Fixer Formula

500 ml	water
75 g	sodium thiosulfate
1	teaspoon bicarbonate of soda
3	grains of gold chloride (use a 30 ml stock solution)*

Stock Gold Solution for Sel d'or toner / fixer

154 ml	distilled water
1 g	gold chloride (1 gram = 15.43 grains)

Take your 1-gram ampule (*a sealed glass capsule containing a liquid*) of gold chloride and drop it into a bottle containing 154 ml distilled water. (*Leave the glass ampule there.*) Because 1 gram equals 15.4 grains, and you mixed this amount with 154 ml distilled water. Every time you need 1 grain of gold chloride for a formula, all you need do is add 10 ml of the gold stock solution.

1% SODIUM SULFITE CLEARING BATH OPTION

Use a 1% solution of sodium sulfite following the fixer to shorten your final washing time. To make it, add 10 g of sodium sulfite to each 1000 ml of distilled water.

FINAL WASH & COMMENT

If you can possibly do this it is a good idea to do your final wash, or at least the beginning minutes of your final wash, with distilled water. Wash your images for 20 to 30 minutes after the fixing stage. You can reduce this time if you elect to use the sodium sulfite mix above. Be very, very careful not to rub the print surface during the wash because the delicacy of the process depends on the surface of the print as well as the rendering of the negative. Following the "dry-down," you will notice that your image has darkened and that some of your contrast has been lost. I often force dry a print to see an approximation of what I will have at the end of the process.

Salted paper, like Van Dyke, has always been labeled as an unreliable process that will eventually fade and break your heart. This is true if you have casual lab skills or if you have been subjected to misinformation when learning the techniques. Most of the time, however, it is simply a matter of working clean and paying attention to the process. Salt prints will fade if there is residual thiosulfate left in the paper. Another reason that early salt prints faded was that they were rinsed and fixed in non-distilled water. As far back as the beginning of this process, it was known that even small amounts of muriatic acid (hydrochloric acid) in well water reacts with simple nitrates and will cause your print to bleach out.

One other element to help ensure the longevity of your salted paper print is to tone it with one of the gold toners . . . this works well as long as you have maintained decent work habits during the process. Salted paper printing is a lot of fun to do but it is loaded with little traps that will drive you nuts if you're not paying attention. Whatever you do, please approach this process, and all of the others that are in the book, with a sense of adventure and don't take the success of your work too seriously while you're learning. Remember, every living creature learns through the process of play . . . so please have fun with the process.

---

* The addition of either the sodium bicarbonate or ammonia makes the solution slightly alkaline. This will reduce the *bleaching* effect of the fixer but will not affect the color or contrast of the image.

Figure 2–15

Rebecca Welsh, *Sunrise, Grand Canyon #2,* 1995—salted paper print

New Hampshire fiber artist, photographer, conservationist, and tactical arts range officer made this image at the edge of the Grand Canyon at sunrise. In addition to being talented in a plethora of disciplines, she is also a legendary beauty . . . and my wife.
(Courtesy of the artist)

The Calotype Process & the Art of Fixing Shadows

OVERVIEW & EXPECTATIONS

This chapter, and the Salted Paper chapter, Chapter 2, share the same history, and this is because the primary force and inspiration behind both processes was William Henry Fox Talbot. For that reason, the two chapters will share a combined history, and they are written with the intention that you will connect them as a single account in the development of salted paper photography.

In this chapter, I will show you how to make a calotype paper negative that can be utilized for subsequent contact printing with Talbot's salted paper process . . . or, for that matter, almost any other contact process you might care to attempt. I will tell you how Talbot made his calotypes and what level of contemporary knowledge has proven useful over the past century in efforts to improve upon his process. Chief among these changes is the elimination of gallic acid from Talbot's original developer formula.

The calotype was among the first silver-based negative techniques that could be utilized as a matrix to reproduce an image multiple times. (Talbot's photogenic drawing negatives also worked well in this regard.) This made it quite different from the daguerreotype, which was a one-of-a-kind technique. Unfortunately, the quality comparisons between the two processes were unarguably in favor of the daguerreotype in terms of clarity and fidelity to the image's subject. It is significant that the calotype negative demonstrated the first example of a latent image and, more importantly, inspired further development of salted paper printing. This, in turn, evolved as a block in the foundation of the albumen process that, when used with a wet-collodion glass plate negative, offered the clarity of the daguerreotype and reproduction ability of the calotype. The calotype technique is arguably a much more complicated process to perform than the daguerreotype. There are so many variables, so many ways to get lost in the proverbial weeds, that this may not be the process for the impatient. The technique is overly sensitive to almost everything including water types and temperatures, ambient heat, cold, and relative humidity, type of paper being used, chemistry . . . and so on. If, however, you want to go exploring with the earliest photographic techniques, you will be amazed and discover how lovely a paper negative can be.

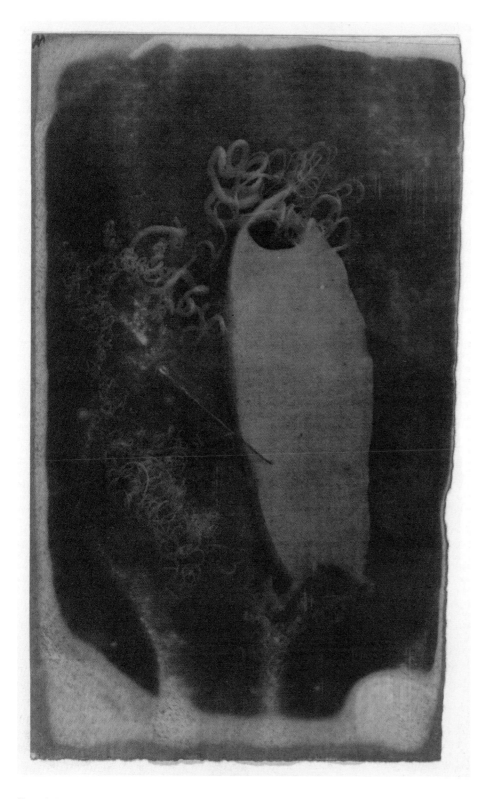

Figure 3–1

Shark Egg Case, 1840–1845, Plate #9, camera-less salted paper print

This piece is from a personal album of British watercolorist Henry Bright (1814–1873), and it illustrates the photogram form of a shark's egg case (Scyliohinidae family of sharks). Unlike other photogram materials, such as leaves, feathers and lace, the 3-D nature of the egg case allowed light to pass over, and around, the parts of the egg case giving the impression of fluidity and water.

(Courtesy The Metropolitan Museum of Art, Gilman Collection, Gift of the Howard Gilman Foundation, 2005, Image © The Metropolitan Museum of Art)

A LITTLE HISTORY

The predecessor of the calotype, *photogenic drawing* in 1835, was documented, and submitted, by Talbot in two separate letters to The Royal Society. The first and most well-known reading was modestly titled *Some Account of the Art of Photogenic Drawing or the Process by which Natural Objects May Be Made to Delineate Themselves without the Aid of an Artist's Pencil* and was delivered on January 31, 1839. This was Talbot's attempt, having heard about Daguerre's announcement on the 7th of that month, to be recognized as the sole inventor of *photography* . . . a word that had not yet been introduced by Sir John Herschel. A clarification letter was delivered the following month, on February 20, which actually described how to perform the process. Three days later, it was published in the *Literary Gazette* and was officially "in play" as a technique for the public . . . without a patent restriction of any kind.

On September 23, 1840, so the legend goes, Talbot made the discovery that changed everything. While resensitizing a piece of previously exposed salted paper, one that had failed to come forth as an image, Talbot poured a solution of gallic acid and silver nitrate (*gallo-nitrate of silver*) over the paper and was privileged to see the very first chemical development of a latent image on paper. Talbot named his new technique calotype (from the Greek words *kalos* and *tupos* meaning beautiful/print). On June 10, 1841, Talbot sent a communication to The Royal Society entitled *The Process of Calotype Photogenic Drawing*, in which he described his calotype technique in full and simultaneously revealed a latent image that could be developed with chemistry . . . and the earliest known photographic negative on paper. It should be pointed out that the daguerreotype also involved the development of a latent image, as did Niépce's asphalt and colophony processes.

In Talbot's calotype process, he coated sheet of stationery paper with silver nitrate solution. The paper was dried under low light and when nearly dry, dipped into, or

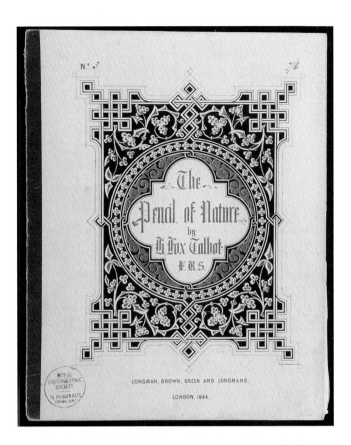

Figure 3–2

***The Pencil of Nature*, Issue #3, 1844**

In the spring of 1844, Longman, Brown, Green & Longmans (London) published the first installment of Talbot's *The Pencil of Nature*. It was published in an edition of a few hundred copies and available only via subscription, which fell off rapidly due to production difficulties. The historians of photography often give credit to Talbot for publishing the first photographically illustrated book. In fact, *Pencil* was second to Anna Atkins, who published the first volumes of her *British Algae: Cyanotype Impressions* in October 1843. *(Courtesy of The National Media Museum/Science & Society Picture Library—also the new repository for the collection of the Royal Photographic Society, London)*

brushed with, a solution of potassium iodide for 2–3 minutes. This newly iodized paper must then be washed well in water in order to remove the newly made potassium nitrate. This newly iodized paper should be a soft "primrose yellow" now and can be subjected to low light without harm. The iodized paper is then allowed to dry.

Note: One of the potentially biggest problems that you will have making calotypes will be not properly washing out the potassium nitrate that is formed after the silver nitrate-coated paper is dipped into the potassium iodide, making the iodized paper.

Figure 3–3
William Henry Fox Talbot—*Botanical Specimen*, 1835—Plate #1 camera-less salted paper print
This is a very early example of Talbot's experiments with salted paper. The lilac tonalities are a result of trying to stabilize the print with baths of sodium chloride.
(Courtesy The Metropolitan Museum of Art, Gilman Collection, Gift of the Howard Gilman Foundation, 2005, Image © The Metropolitan Museum of Art)

The "stock" iodized paper is now going to be made light-sensitive via a second washing of silver solution containing a restrainer . . . acetic or citric acid. The restrainer (the acetic or citric acid) in the sensitizer must be strong enough to hold back spontaneous development of nonimage silver. The volume of this restrainer should be increased when the ambient temperature is high, as in a summertime lab situation.

A solution of gallo-nitrate of silver (*silver nitrate, acetic acid and gallic acid*) was mixed just prior to use, and the recently iodized stock paper was painted upon using a soft brush and then rinsed briefly in fresh water. Talbot had originally included gallic acid in the sensitizer (what he called gallo-nitrate of silver) . . . but quickly removed that from the formula . . . as did everyone else using Talbot's instructions, because it caused fog, called *browning* in calotype circles.

The sensitized paper could then be dried and kept for several hours or used immediately in a damp state. The paper's sensitivity was far greater than Talbot had expected, and he noted that all work had to be performed under candlelight at considerable distance. His in-camera exposure time, using his "mousetrap" cameras (a name his patient wife, Constance, had given to the Joseph Foden's camera constructions) was comparatively rapid. Following exposure, there was only an invisible latent image on the paper.

Once the exposure was completed, the paper was taken into a very low light-level environment and once again washed with the same gallo-nitrate of silver solution used to sensitize the original iodized paper. The gallic acid is the developer. The acetic acid is the restrainer, added to hold back the fog/browning of nonimage development. The silver in the solution "feeds" the physical development of the image.

The solution, in this case, had been warmed prior to the wash. In seconds, the exposed portions of the image were revealed by a darkening action created by the gallo-nitrate of silver. As in a normal negative, the unexposed portions of the paper remained white. Talbot noted that repeated washings of a weak image, in fresh gallo-nitrate of silver solution, would result in an even stronger development within 1–2 minutes.

The developed calotypes were washed in fresh water and then fixed in a solution of bromide of potassium, or sodium thiosulfate, for 1–2 minutes, washed in water, and then dried. In the fixing instructions, I am recommending a traditional sodium thiosulfate fixing bath for convenience and efficiency. If the calotype is not fixed and washed well, it will demonstrate a yellow tint due to the lasting presence of silver iodide in the paper. After the paper had dried, Talbot occasionally waxed the calotype,

either entirely or in selected areas, to enhance its transparency and utilized it as a contact negative with a new,
and similarly, sensitized piece of paper. He also applied
ink or graphite to selected areas of the calotype to hold
back transmission of light through the paper. Talbot
called the results of this process *Calotype Pictures.*

After a few improvements, some admirers of the
process changed the name of it to the Talbotype, although
Talbot modestly persisted with his original calotype label.
On February 8, 1841, he placed a rather restrictive patent
on his "beautiful print" discovery that nearly stopped the
new medium in its proverbial tracks. Talbot was tena-
cious about protecting his patent, perhaps due to a failing
family fortune, and unless aspiring amateurs paid him an
annual fee of about £2, the fledgling image-makers would
invariably find themselves in court facing Talbot and an
irksome lawsuit over a process that neither the lawyers
nor the judges could comprehend.

The calotype was a refinement of Talbot's earlier
investigations with his photogenic drawing technique,
which were essentially salted silver paper photograms

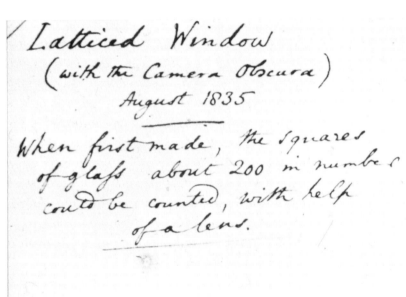

Figure 3–5

William Henry Fox Talbot (1800–1877), The Latticed Window at Lacock Abbey (Talbot's home), 1835

The first photographic negative (photogenic drawing) ever made. Talbot wrote of this negative, "I obtained (with his mousetrap camera) very perfect, but
extremely small, pictures (negatives); such as without great stretch of the imagination might be supposed to be the work of some Lilliputian artist."
*(Courtesy of The National Media Museum/Science & Society Picture Library—also the new repository for the collection of the Royal Photographic
Society, London)*

Figure 3–6

Talbot Establishment, 1845—Talbot right, Henneman left
In 1844, in hopes of fame and fortune, Talbot (on the right) went into a salted paper photographic printing business for the public with his former valet, Nicholas Henneman (on the left), in the town of Reading, England.
(Courtesy of The National Media Museum/Science & Society Picture Library—also the new repository for the collection of the Royal Photographic Society, London)

that had been slightly stabilized with immersion into solutions of sodium chloride, potassium iodide, or potassium bromide. The new and improved process featured a far more sensitive chemistry, and refined result, due to its unique latent (*unseen until processed*) image that was *physically developed* in chemistry.

In 1844, Talbot established the Reading Establishment with his former valet, Nicholas Henneman, to produce editions of calotype images necessary for his forthcoming book, *The Pencil of Nature*. This was the *second* photographically illustrated book in history; Anna Atkins's book of cyanotype photograms (*British Algae: Cyanotype Impressions*, October 1843) was the very first, traditional accounts to the contrary not withstanding. It was the custom at the Reading Establishment to fix all prints with a bath of sodium thiosulfate (*the fixer we use today for practically all alt pro silver work*), but the prescribed washing times were often woefully inadequate . . . leading to an excess of thiosulfate, which would, over time, produce the yellow evidence of silver sulfide and subsequent fading.

Talbot summed up his contributions to the medium well when he wrote,

> "*. . . I do not profess to have perfected an art but to have commenced one, the limits of which it is not possible at present exactly to ascertain. I only claim to have based this art on a secure foundation.*"

In spite of the restrictive patent that Talbot placed on his process, his calotype was never competitive commercially, as was ruefully discovered by Talbot and Henneman during their salted paper printing business in Reading, England.

Around 1843, something very interesting happened to the new medium of photography. A portrait painter by the name of David Octavius Hill (1802–1870) entered into a business partnership with scientist Robert Adamson (1821–1848). Hill had accepted a daunting commission to paint a group portrait of the 400-plus people who had recently founded the Free Church of Scotland. Because it wasn't practical to paint hundreds of people from life, Hill adopted Talbot's calotype negative to salt print process as a means of recording each person's portrait. These he would use as a visual guide for his massive painting of the founders of the Free Church of Scotland.

To accomplish the task, Hill secured the services of Robert Adamson as his technical expert for the project. Because both were from Scotland, they were geographically free of the patent restrictions that Talbot had placed on his Calotype process and between 1843 and 1847 they made nearly 2,000 images. (*Adamson died in 1848 at the age of 27.*) What was really unprecedented about their collaborative work was its artistic scope. As a result of Hill's obsession with making photographic images that

Figure 3–7

David Octavius Hill & Robert Adamson, *The Rev. Thomas Henshaw Jones*, 1843/1848—salted paper print from calotype negative

The painter David Octavius Hill had accepted a commission to paint a group portrait of the over 400 people who had recently founded the Free Church of Scotland. Hill turned to the Calotype as a means of recording each person's likeness and secured the services of Adamson as his technical support. Between 1843 and 1847 they made nearly 2,000 images. What was really unprecedented about their collaborative work was the artistic scope of it and Hill's obsession with making images that recorded the subjectively true essence of the subjects. They had introduced the concept of artistic "*intent*" in harmony with the new science of photography.

(Courtesy of The George Eastman House/International Museum of Photography)

recorded the *true* essence of the subjects, he and Adamson were, in my opinion, the first individuals to introduce the concept of artistic *intention* in harmony with the new science of photography.

In 1844, one of the amateur photographers who began working with Talbot's calotype process was a French cloth merchant by the name of Louis-Désiré Blanquart-Evrard (1802–1872). It is said, in some academic circles, that Blanquart-Evrard appropriated Talbot's method without acknowledgment and subsequently claimed it as his own process. While this may not seem surprising, considering the impact of influences, his work with the calotype led directly to his development of the albumen process, in 1850, that would eventually evolve into the internationally accepted standard for making photographic prints for decades to come. In 1847, Blanquart-Evrard wrote a letter to the French

Academy of Sciences describing several modifications that he had made to Talbot's calotype process; in doing so, he had made the technique both efficient and greatly improved. These claims are still being bandied about.

Rather than coating the surface of the paper, Blanquart-Evrard bathed the paper in two separate immersions, allowing the sensitizer to penetrate the fibers of the paper more deeply than it could with simple buckle brush application. This resulted in the paper being many times more sensitive than Talbot's, and thus able to yield a wider array of intermediate tonalities. Predictably, this news irritated Talbot . . . especially since Blanquart-Evrard never mentioned his name in his letter to the French Academy. He then formally complained that Blanquart-Evrard was a "pirate," and the French Academy, in a very diplomatic move, said that the two processes were identical but then went ahead and published Blanquart-Evrard's work as a means of undermining

Talbot's patent in France. Blanquart-Evrard's success likely resulted in the process becoming more popular and inspired him to begin developing a unique version of the technique that utilized gelatin as sizing, albumen emulsion, and chlorine, iodine, and bromine in combination with silver nitrate as sensitizer ingredients.

A few years later, Blanquart-Evrard's albumen printing technique was coupled with Frederick Scott Archer's wet-collodion glass plate negative process (1851). This new combination was considered the first true, repeatable, paper-based imaging system that employed an original negative. More importantly, not only did Archer's wet-collodion technique describe a photographed scene with the clarity of a daguerreotype, but also it could be reproduced via the Blanquart-Evrard's calotype/albumen technique; these attributes immediately made Talbot and Daguerre's nearly obsolete. In 1851, Blanquart-Evrard, who by this point was being referred to as the "Gutenberg of Photography," opened a printing business for his new and improved process in Lille, France. He employed up to 40 girls to make prints (and to work on his farm when business was slow).

Figure 3–8
Louis-Pierre Théophile Dubois de Nehaut—*Another Impossible Task, #67*, 1854—salted paper print from a glass negative
(Courtesy The Metropolitan Museum of Art, Gilman Collection, Gift of the Howard Gilman Foundation, 2005, Image © The Metropolitan Museum of Art)

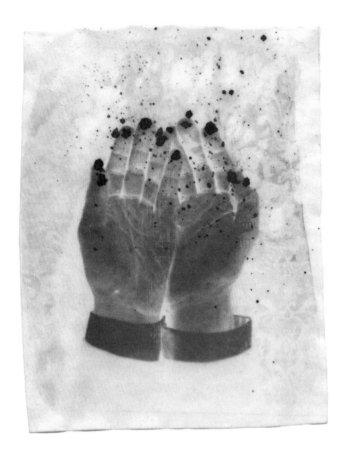

Figure 3–9

Dan Estabrook, *Black Hands*, 2002—pencil and silver on waxed calotype negative

This is another excellent example from my former student, Dan Estabrook; using antiquarian processes to metaphorically express contemporary feelings . . . maybe.

(Courtesy of the artist)

Talbot wasn't finished trying to protect his patent. In 1854, he filed yet another lawsuit against photographer by the name of Laroche (W. H. Silvestor), claiming that Archer's use of pyrogallic acid, as a wet-plate developer, was the same as his calotype's use of gallo-nitrate of silver and that the similarity infringed on his calotype patent. Due to the technical complexity of the subject matter, the judge and jury were once again entirely mystified by the entire argument and eventually ruled that the defendant, Mr. Silvestor Laroche, was not guilty of anything that anyone could comprehend. At this point, Talbot saw the writing on the wall and moved on.

Students are always enthusiastically willing to experience the unpredictability of making a calotype negative simply because the process is so straightforward. The term *calotype* technically refers to the procedure in which the intended final product is a paper negative. The same steps can be repeated using the calotype negative to create a positive print on calotype paper. In almost every positive print version of Talbot's process, the positive was either a photogenic drawing print or a salted paper print made from a calotype negative.

W. H. Fox Talbot & Contemporary Table Set Up for Iodized Calotype Paper Negatives, c. 1840:

*Note: **1 gram = 15.43 grains/1 fluid oz. (USA) = 29.57 ml/1 fluid oz. (GB) = 28.41 ml***

- A fine-quality, 100% cotton stationery stock
- Silver nitrate solution:
  - ***Fox Talbot Mix***: *100 grains into 6 oz. of dist. water*
  - ***Contemporary Mix***: *7.5% solution: 7.5 grams to each 100 ml of distilled water*
- Potassium iodide solution:
  - ***Fox Talbot Mix***: *500 grains into 16 oz of dist. water*
  - ***Contemporary Mix***: *5.5% solution: 5.5 grams into each 100 ml of distilled water*
- A sheet of glass or clean board for coating
- A clean tray: for immersion
- A line for drying
- Hake or new foam brush
- Several zipper-style bags for storage

The first stage in Fox Talbot's calotype negative process is to iodize the stationery paper, in candlelight, first with the silver nitrate solution and then followed by the potassium iodide. First, mark one side of the paper to indicate which side you intend to make your image upon . . . silver nitrate is a clear solution, and there will be no indication between front and back if you don't make the mark.

Step 1 Begin by making a 7.5% solution of silver nitrate (*7.5 g of silver nitrate in each 100 ml of distilled water*), and stir it well until the silver nitrate has completely dissolved; 200 to 300 ml will be adequate for your needs. Store the mixed solution in an amber glass bottle. Be very safety-conscious when using silver nitrate. Wear gloves and safety glasses when mixing and never, ever, touch your eyes while working with the chemistry.

Step 2 Next, make a separate 5.5% solution of potassium iodide (for example, 5.5 g potassium iodide in each 100 ml of distilled water), and store it in an amber glass bottle.

Step 3 Select a nice piece of smooth rag writing paper (*Cranes Kid Finish is a good one except for the watermark**) that does not contain a watermark in the area where the image will be printed. Clearly mark the paper with a penciled notation on one side, because this will be the surface you will sensitize. Then cut the paper so that it will slide into a 4" × 5" film holder for the eventual exposure.

Step 4 Using a hake brush, coat only the marked side of the paper with your prepared 7.5% silver nitrate solution, and set it aside to begin drying. When the paper is still damp but shows no standing puddles of silver nitrate, immerse it in the solution of potassium iodide.

Step 5 Allow the paper to be submerged in the potassium iodide for 2–3 minutes so that the silver nitrate and potassium iodide convert to silver iodide. The paper will change color from the original white to a primrose yellow. Remove the paper, place it in a clean tray, and gently wash it in distilled water for an hour or two, with multiple changes of water, and hang it up to dry. You have now created iodized paper.

You can store the iodized paper in an acid-free box (see Appendices) or a zipper-style bag, for an unlimited amount of time, but it's best not to wait more than 24 hours, as browning may occur. I recall reading a letter, some years ago, which obliquely suggested that contrast could be increased by hanging the iodized paper in bright sunlight for a few hours. The reasoning behind this technique is that the silver iodide has an excess of iodide and is therefore insensitive to light.

Sensitizing Calotype Paper with Gallo-Nitrate of Silver for In-Camera Exposure

The sensitizing portion of the calotype process should be conducted under very low light conditions; Talbot used a candle but you may use a red safelight or a bug light . . . just avoid the blue end of the spectrum. The sensitizer is made up of four components that, when combined, Talbot called gallo-nitrate of silver. It consists of a silver nitrate, acetic acid, gallic acid, and distilled water. Only make as much sensitizing solution as you intend to use at any given time. This chemistry has an extremely short life once in solution. This is especially true for gallic acid, which you should avoid using anyway. As mentioned earlier, Talbot, and other calotypists, dropped the gallic acid from the formula, as it created many more problems than it solved.

Part A

- Part A-1 is a 11.4% solution of silver nitrate made by dissolving 11.4 g of silver nitrate into 100 ml of distilled water.

- Talbot's Original Formula: 100 grains of silver nitrate dissolved in 2 oz. of distilled water

- Part A-2 is made by adding 5.5 ml of 33% acetic acid to 28 ml of Part A.

- Talbot's Original Formula: The volume of A-2 acetic acid is 1/6 the volume of Part A and is added to Part A to make the complete Part A mix. The acetic acid in the silver sensitizer can be increased to prevent fogging . . . the silver and acid restrainer should be added to the developer as needed and little by little as you develop the image.

---

* A note regarding the paper: It is important that the paper you select is thin, as it's going to be a negative when the process is complete.

Part B: (Optional)

Note: Although gallic acid, Part B, was originally in Talbot's process, it was soon realized that the chemical was unnecessary and actually very problematic, as the gallic acid oxidized rapidly and was responsible for a premature browning (fogging) of the image. I've included it here for informational purposes, but if you simply eliminate it from your workflow, your calotypes will be more successful. If you want to stay pure in your calotype process, you might consider exchanging pyrogallic acid for the gallic acid, as it works a bit better.

◆ Part B is a saturated solution* of gallic acid and is made by dissolving 1.1 g of crystallized gallic acid (pale, white-yellow crystal) in 100 ml of cold distilled water. Consider using pyrogallic acid instead of gallic acid.

Sensitizing the Paper

Using a plastic dropper, you can now create the gallo-nitrate of silver sensitizer by combining 6 drops of Part A and 6 drops of Part B (optional, see above) to every 8 ml of distilled water. This volume will easily cover an 8.5" × 11" piece of writing paper; a new batch must be made for each new piece of paper that you coat. If you find that the concentration is too weak, simply reduce the amount of water in the sensitizer. The sensitizer is applied to the surface of the iodized paper, marked with a pencil, with either a fresh hake brush or a "Buckle Brush," a thin test tube with a wad of cotton ball stuffed into the end. The advantage of the Buckle Brush is that you can have a "new" brush for every stage of the process by simply replacing the cotton ball. Once the paper is coated, blot it quickly with even pressure and let it sit for 1–2 minutes in the darkened room.

If you opt to try the gallic acid in the formula, be aware that it oxidizes very rapidly, and this oxidation results in muddy imagery. Talbot would occasionally develop his calotypes face down in a puddle of developer applied to a level sheet of glass in an effort to prevent air from reaching the paper during development.

Wet or Dry Paper Option

Talbot's original workflow called for the paper to be dipped into water following the sensitizer, then blotted and dried. He said that when the paper was dry, it was fit to use and could now be called Calotype Paper. If the paper had been kept in the dark, then Talbot claimed it could be used in-camera for up to 3 months with no appreciable difference in its quality or ability to record an image using the camera obscura. His caveat was that this wasn't always the case and that using it immediately after drying was the better option. If one were to use the paper directly after blotting, the paper could be used in-camera in a moist state. Printing when the paper is moist may indeed lessen the chances of fog/browning of the paper.

Calotype Exposure

Talbot exposed his first photogenic drawings in the tiny mousetrap cameras. In later work with calotype, he used larger cameras and sensitized papers in either a dry or moist state and a "sandwich" of an absolutely clean glass plate (in front) and a warmed piece of slate or metal (in back) to hold the paper flat. The warmed plate accelerated the exposure. You can use your 4" × 5" film holder. To avoid the problem of having the dark slide harming the damp paper as it is pulled out and reinserted, during the exposure stages you might want to just load the holder while still in the darkroom and place it in the camera prior to each exposure. See the Scully & Osterman plate-holder conversion in Figure 22–8.

This is going to be a situation in which you will need to customize your exposures to various influences such as where you live, the amount of heat present at that time of year (*heat is not beneficial to calotypes*), how strong your sensitizer is, the time of day when you are making pictures (there is more UV light in the middle of the day

---

* A saturated solution is one in which the chemical is added to distilled water until no more of the chemical can be dissolved into solution. Talbot's original formula called for a saturated solution in the same manner as above but without specifying the amounts.

Figure 3–10
William Henry Fox Talbot, *Constance and Daughters*, 19 April 1842—salted paper
This curious salted paper print, from a calotype negative, is one of several group portraits Talbot created between 1840 and 1843. On September 23, 1840, while resensitizing a piece of previously exposed salted paper, one that had failed render an image, Talbot poured a resensitizing solution of gallo-nitrate of silver over the paper, to and saw that he had created the first chemical development of a latent image on paper. Talbot named his new technique calotype (from the Greek words *kalos* and *tupos*, meaning beautiful/print). On June 10th, 1841, Talbot presented his discovery to The Royal Society in a paper titled "The Process of Calotype Photogenic Drawing," in which he revealed how a latent image could be developed with chemistry. For the first time, any number of prints could be made of a single image from a negative. *(Courtesy of The National Media Museum/Science & Society Picture Library—also the new repository for the collection of the Royal Photographic Society, London)*

and this will require less exposure than early or late in the day), and how fast your camera lens is.

If you are making pinhole calotype negatives, then you must have infinite patience and optimism. To start, try an exposure in the vicinity of f/2 or f/4.5 for 30–40 seconds. A bright sunny day at f/8 will be around 2 minutes. If you are using a lens that is not very fast your exposure may be as long as 5 minutes. Talbot, in his 1841 reading of *Calotype Photogenic Drawing*, claimed that with his process you could lay a leaf upon a sheet of gallo-nitrate of silver-sensitized paper under the light of a full moon and make a contact photogram exposure in 15 minutes!

One thing to keep in the back of your mind about exposure times . . . an excess of gallic acid reduces the sensitivity of the paper. Talbot used to resensitize his papers until just before the paper would spontaneously expose. As well, you might want to increase the percentage of silver nitrate in the formula as that may help as well. Overexposure will often result in a visible image when the paper is removed from the camera. Dilute your developer and silver or add more restrainer prior to developing overexposed negatives.

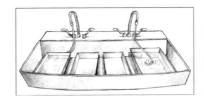

SINK SET UP FOR CALOTYPE: DEVELOPMENT & FIXING

- ◆ Solution A (aceto-nitrate of silver)
- ◆ Solution B (OPTIONAL: saturated Gallic Acid solution)
- ◆ 10% sodium thiosulfate fixing bath
- ◆ Distilled water
- ◆ Sea salt
- ◆ A tray and a sheet of glass larger than the tray
- ◆ A glass/plastic beaker for warming the developing solution
- ◆ *Talbot's Original Formula Mix: potassium bromide* Buckle Brush (glass tube and cotton balls)

Development of the Calotype (Negative)

You will need to work in a room that either has a safelight, a candle, or a bug light, as this paper, when coated, will be sensitive to blue light. You will also want to be wearing latex or Nitrile examination gloves.

Figure 3–11

George School, Mark Osterman, 1996, waxed calotype negative using Talbot's formula, 6" × 8", 1996 and George School, gold toned albumen print from waxed calotype negative, 2002

The definition of a calotype has been used to describe both negative and positive prints. This has often resulted in confusion of the true definition because a calotype in specific terminology is a latent image made with silver iodide paper and made visible through a development process . . . it is *developed out* with chemistry. Talbot did make some developed out positive prints from his developed out paper negatives and these would also be called calotypes. However, almost all of the final images were salted paper prints *printed out* using the silver chloride process. During the 19th century, a calotype negative was used to make a photogenic drawing (stabilized with salt), a salted paper, and an albumen print (fixed with hypo).

(Courtesy Scully & Osterman Studio)

Mix up a developer solution that is made up of a warm solution of equal portions of Part A (acetic acid and silver nitrate = aceto-nitrate of silver) and Optional Part B (gallic acid). You will need about 10 ml of each (or 20 ml of aceto nitrate of silver) part to develop a sheet of writing paper. This is gallo-nitrate of silver.

Note: Again, just in case I haven't been entirely clear, you can omit the gallic acid from this step and go entirely with aceto-nitrate of silver. I include the gallic acid part for historical purposes only. You may increase the acetic acid restrainer in this step, a little bit at a time, to prevent fogging . . . if needed.

Remove the exposed paper from the film holder (in the safely lit area), and you will notice that there will be a slight whisper of an image or nothing at all. Lay the exposed paper on the warmed glass clean surface, and gently brush on a light coating of the mixed solution of the developer with a *new* buckle brush.

Talbot would warm his paper at this point to help bring out the image, but using a hairdryer will *not* be a great idea because it will dry out the paper too quickly. Instead, fill a tray with hot water, and place a larger piece of thick glass over it. The back of the tray will warm up, and you can use the surface to heat the paper. Warming the paper creates darker values in the negative. It should be noted that heat speeds up a chemical process and promotes fog and browning in calotypes. For this reason, it might be best to forget the warming of the paper or developing surface when first beginning to do calotypes. The development will take longer, up to an hour, but you will avoid the fog.

The success of making good calotypes is based on your ability to manage the following three components and by evaluating the negative as development progresses. To continue development, you will need three things:

1. Energy from the initial exposure in the camera (can't do anything about that once it's established)

2. An active reduction agent a.k.a. developer (which can be renewed as needed)

3. Free silver to build up density (which can be added as needed)

Optional: Once the image has come up, recoat the paper with a Part B (gallic acid) solution to intensify the blacks. When you are satisfied, immerse the developed paper in distilled water for a minute or two. If the gallic acid is warm, the effect will be stronger and more rapid.

An aside regarding gallo-nitrate of silver: Lesser amounts of gallo-nitrate of silver result in a greater darkening effect. It is also noticed that the biggest change in the values, when applying the gallo-nitrate of silver, occurs when the paper is nearly dry . . . be patient.

You will know the negative is ready when you hold the paper up to strong light and you can see distinctive contrast between dark and light values. Rinse the developed negative in fresh water for a few minutes, to remove any free silver or developing agent, before fixing.

Fixing, Washing, Waxing, and Printing the Calotype

Talbot's original formula called for a first rinse in water followed by an immersion in *bromide of potassium* (100 grains of this salt dissolved in 10 oz. of water). He also used solutions of hyposulfite of soda (sodium thiosulfate) to fix his image.

Contemporary Fix

We will use the sodium thiosulfate (regular alt pro silver fixer) at a 10% dilution of 100 g of sodium thiosulfate to every 1,000 ml of water. Immerse the print in the fixer for approximately 4–5 minutes or longer. Do not stop this fixing step until all of the yellow tint has been cleared from the paper. If you see any yellow in your paper, it indicates that there is still silver iodide in the paper.

Talbot had a dramatic solution to this yellow staining problem. He would make a solution of hyposulfite of soda dissolved in about 10 times its weight of water and heat it to a boiling point. He would then immerse the print in the hot solution for 10 minutes, causing the paper to become white and transparent. Make up two separate trays and fix the negative in each tray for ½ the time. Change the fixer every few pieces of paper.

Wash the fixed print in softly running water for 20–30 minutes, and then lay it on a clean screen to dry.

Postdevelopment and Fixing Table Setup:

- Dorland's Art Wax, or simple beeswax
- Hair dryer
- Vegetable oil
- Paper towels

Waxing the Calotype (Negative)

Once your calotype is dry, you can wax it in order to make a more translucent negative for contact printing. Talbot's waxing method called for beeswax and a hot iron. I have used Dorland's Art Wax, a soft transparent wax that can be applied with your finger, with success. Once the calotype negative is waxed you can use it as a contact negative for a compatible process such as salted paper, cyanotype, or albumen, or you can repeat this procedure and contact print the calotype negative with a newly sensitized calotype paper to obtain a positive calotype. You might also want to try an older waxing technique that calls for waxing the back of the calotype negative and mounting it on a piece of white or black paper for an unusual effect.

The easiest way to accomplish this task is to use Dorland's Art Wax. Once the paper is dry, gently rub in the Dorland's Art Wax with your fingers. Move in delicate circular motions and evenly cover the entire negative image area. Be sure that there is no excess wax, and then take a hair dryer and blow hot air over the surface of the print until the wax melts and dries in the paper's fibers. Rewax if you wish, and repeat the heat and drying pattern.

Another method that works well is to turn the paper over on a clean surface of absorbent paper towels and rub in vegetable oil until the paper is translucent. The oil will always be a part the paper and may, if the weather is warm enough, become a part of your salted paper positive. You may need to use a sheet of acetate between the calotype negative and the sensitized salted paper print.

Wax is not always mandatory. Hill & Adamson hardly ever waxed their work and if your stationery is thin enough you may not have to, either. Both Talbot and Hill & Adamson used a writing paper called Whatman's Turkey Mill.

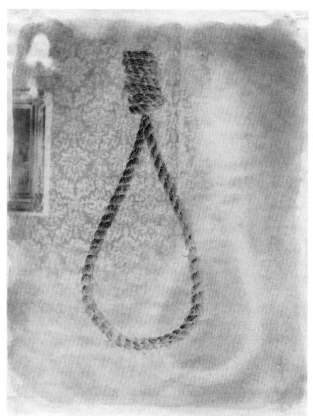

Figure 3–12

Dan Estabrook, *Noose, Drawn*, 2001—calotype negative and salted paper print
Here is another image combination from Dan Estabrook illustrating a calotype negative and the salted paper print created using it.
(Courtesy of the artist)

Restoring a Calotype Negative after It Fades

As Talbot discovered, if you don't perform the calotype process perfectly, i.e., removing all of the yellow from the paper negative in the fixing stage, your calotype will begin to fade after it has been used to make a few salted paper prints. This is how to restore it.

Immerse your calotype in a warm solution of gallo-nitrate of silver (or aceto-nitrate of silver) for several minutes or until you see a noticeable change in the dark areas of the negative. Talbot wrote that very often this technique revealed portions of the image that had not been obvious in the original calotype and had, indeed, been lying in the paper as a latent image.

LAST COMMENTS

A Simple Test of Your Formula's Sensitivity

This comes from Mark Osterman: The best way to test a calotype formula is to sensitize a piece of paper and then expose it with a large coin lying in the center. Begin to develop the outer edges of the sheet to maximum density. If you can do this without generating a stain under the area where the coin covered the sheet then you should be fine.

Paper

You will need a thin and high-quality stationery stock to be successful. Unfortunately, many nice writing papers have a maker's watermark stamped, inevitably, somewhere in your image area. If this doesn't trouble you, then Crane's Kid Finish is a nice paper. We tried Buxton and Weston Parchment, but nothing works as well as a difficult-to-find French paper called Crobb d'art. Next time you're in Paris, hunt for it. In the meantime, you'll need to test a lot of paper before finding one that suits you. I will recommend considering gelatin sizing the paper you select. We found that sizing helped a lot with image clarity. See the chapters on Salted Paper (Chapter 2) and Paper (Chapter 15) for instructions.

Contamination

Contamination is your biggest enemy. Keep everything as clean as you possibly can, and do not overlook anything. If you brush coat, consider using foam brushes and retiring them after the coating.

Heat

Hot weather is a problem. If you are working in high ambient temperature, then think about increasing the volume of your restrainer (acetic acid) in the developing solution. In fact, if you see fogging (browning), one of the first steps that you might want to consider is adding extra drops of acetic to your sensitizer and developer.

Gallic Acid

As mentioned more than a few times in this chapter, gallic acid often causes more problems than it's worth. For this reason, Talbot stopped using it almost immediately and stuck with the aceto nitrate of silver, A-1 and A-2, alone. If you want to use a formula close to Talbot's original, consider substituting pyrogallic acid for the gallic acid. Don't forget that gallic acid oxidizes very quickly, and this will lead to browning or fog during an extended development.

Patience

Calotype printing may be the most difficult alternative process to do well, as the variables are many, and any misstep can spell disaster. I've never made a good one. Please be patient, and do not expect miracles when you first begin to work in this process. All of my expert alt pro friends, who are familiar with this technique, insist that there is no other that is as confounding and mercurial. Only Dan Estabrook and Mark Osterman seem to have negotiated the maze. Patience, my friends, patience.

The Negative: Alternative Process Options

OVERVIEW & EXPECTATIONS

In this chapter, I will start you off with a little magical realism . . . an excerpt from 1760 . . . from Tiphaigne de la Roche's (1729–1774) *Giphantie*. In his poetic vision, you will see a conception of modern photography nearly 80 years before it was officially described to the respective scientific societies in France and England. Also presented in this chapter is a little history of curious individual and scientific connections regarding the conception, and evolution, of the photographic negative.

A good deal has changed in the world of photography since the first edition of this book in 2001. The biggest change is the very real reduction of "traditional" photographic materials. A small alert notice has been accompanying quite a few traditional films and papers from traditional manufacturers . . . and this has been really upsetting for some. One such recently received notice read: ***NOTICE OF DISCONTINUANCE—Digital techniques have substantially decreased the demand for Commercial Internegative Film, Therefore, this film will be discontinued when inventories run out.*** Honestly, though, this inevitable change to the medium has actually opened the doors of alternative process possibility for many others. I cannot recall a time when this genre has been so popular.

In this edition, there are far fewer films to discuss, including those lovely single stage duplicating films such as my long-gone favorite, Kodak SO-132. We will discuss a small selection of multistage negative to positive films that are still being produced and how to process them so that they can be controlled for your alternative process needs. One such technique is Dave Soemarko's contemporary LC-1 and LC-1B process for creating continuous tone negatives with litho film. As well, we'll deal with simple solutions for shooting negatives for contact printing. You do not have to hunt around in this chapter for information on working in digital formats, because most of that information will be in the Digital Options chapter.

For those who are well free of the darkroom, perhaps have never even been in one, and are not quite equipped to deal with the nuances of the digital world, I will deal with making negatives from photogram materials, using acrylic lifts, transparent films generated on a copy

Figure 4–1

Christopher James, Rachel w/ Wings, Maine, 1995

This piece was made during a workshop cyanotype on fabric mural project. I made the image with a Lensless Camera Co. pinhole camera fitted with a Polaroid 4" × 5" back and Polaroid Type 55, Positive/Negative Film. The Type 55 negative was then used to demonstrate the palladium process.

(Courtesy of the author)

machine or ink-jet printer, digital waxed & oiled transparent calotype-like paper negatives (*see the calotype chapter*), pinhole camera generated paper and film negatives, Polaroid Type 55 Positive/Negative film, cliché verre negatives on glass, acetate, or plastic, and more.

I'll briefly describe a workflow for giving your digital negatives a pyro like tonality so that you have a much greater chance of success with simple print outs on acetate ink jet films like Pictorico OHP. Don't worry, I'll deal with this information in more detail in specific chapters where it will make sense, i.e., Grayscale to C-M-Y-K negatives for gum printing will be covered in the Gum Bichromate chapter. If you are "white lab coat"–impaired, then you will appreciate that I have done my best to make this chapter uncomplicated. There are plenty of books on the market that revel in their technicalities; see the bibliography in this book's resource section.

There are a few reasons that I am going to take a different tack and make this chapter simple. First, as in the digital section of this book, specific references to products will likely not be relevant in a year or two due to the speed of change in photography. Secondly, the purpose of a negative is to give you the first stage of the necessary things you'll need to make an alternative process print. For me, and this has always been my philosophy of teaching, you need to fall in love before you learn to kiss well . . . and falling in love should be easy.

A LITTLE HISTORY

Imaginative intellectuals, artists, and writers throughout history have been seduced by the romantic concept of a mirror that forever captures the image that it reflects . . . like Narcissus' image in the water. The Roman poet, Publius Papinius Statius (40–96 AD) expressed this sentiment within his five-volume epic *Silvae,* but one of the most notable examples of these published premonitions is found in Tiphaigne de la Roche's, *Giphantie,* written in 1760. In the following excerpt from that writing, de la

Roche describes the imminent discovery of photography, and an important part of the daguerreotype . . . 80 years before the process was publicly announced.

A Vision from 1760

That window, that vast horizon, those black clouds, that raging sea, are all but a picture. You know that the rays of light, reflected from different bodies, form a picture, and paint the image reflected on all polished surfaces, for instance, on the retina of the eye, on water, and on glass. The elementary spirits have sought to fix these fleeting images; they have composed a subtle matter, very viscous and quick to harden and dry, by means of which a picture is formed in the twinkling of an eye. They coat a piece of glass with this matter, and hold it in front of the objects they wish to paint. The first effect of this canvas is similar to that of a mirror; one sees there all objects near and far, the image of which light can transmit. But what a glass cannot do, the canvas by means of its viscous matter, retains the images. The mirror represents the objects faithfully but retains them not; our canvas shows them with the same exactness and retains them all. This impression of the image is instantaneous, and the canvas is immediately carried away into some dark place. An hour later the impression is dry, and you have a picture the more valuable in that it cannot be imitated by art or destroyed by time. . . . The correctness of the drawing, the truth of the expression, the stronger or weaker strokes, the gradation of shades, the rules of perspective, all these we leave to nature, who with a sure and never erring hand, draws upon our canvasses images which deceive the eye.

—Charles Francois Tiphaigne de la Roche,
Giphantie, *Paris, 1760*

Angelo Sala to George Eastman

In 1614, Angelo Sala, an Italian Calvinist who had left Italy to avoid religious persecution, and who is credited with discovering that St. John's Wort could make

Figure 4–2
Christopher James, *Double Strike/Atlantic,* **1981**
A small gift from the picture spirits. The negative was shot with a modified Diana plastic camera.
(Courtesy of the author)

depressed people feel better, documented his experiments in which he noticed that silver nitrate inexplicably turned darker when exposed to sunlight. He also observed that it would stain paper black if placed in contact upon a sheet of it.

Shortly thereafter, in 1664, the Irish scientist, Robert Boyle (1627–1691), noted the influence of light on gold chloride when the gold chloride had come into contact with his skin . . . resulting in a purple discoloration. He also observed that the silver chloride compound he was working with also reacted to light by turning from light to dark. Boyle, unfortunately, thought that the foul air in his lab had caused the reaction and didn't pursue an alternative explanation, that ultraviolet (UV) light was responsible for the change. Boyle, by the way, was the gentleman who created Boyle's Law (1662), the most important physical law of SCUBA diving: *as ambient pressure increases: volume decreases, and vice versa.*

Robert Boyle was also a founder of the Royal Society, where Talbot eventually had his (forgive me) "day in the sun" describing his practical photographic discoveries, which ironically included the sensitivity of silver chloride to UV light.

The story goes that in the latter part of the 1700s, Josiah Wedgwood (1730–1795) and his son Thomas (1771–1805) were asked by Ekaterina the Great of Russia (1729–1796) to produce a porcelain service with her likeness on it in the Wedgwood porcelain factory. Sounds like a simple request, except that photography hadn't been invented yet. Josiah Wedgwood was certainly the guy to ask, however, as he had industrialized the ceramics industry. As a side note, Charles Darwin was Josiah's grandson. One other odd connection: Josiah hired the assistant of Joseph Priestly (the gentleman who discovered carbon dioxide to make soda water, and co-discovered, oxygen) to teach his son Thomas chemistry at home.

Figure 4–3
William Henry Fox Talbot, *Photogenic Drawing of Feathers Lace & Leaves*, 1839
Silver iodide sensitized writing paper *"photogram."*
(Courtesy of The Gernsheim Collection, Ransom Center, University of Texas-Austin)

Sun printed.

In 1802, Thomas Wedgwood, Josiah's son, and his good friend Sir Humphry Davy (1778–1829) made what might have been the first *photogram*. Wedgwood was familiar with the work of Heinrich Schulze and Carl Wilhelm Scheele's experiments, with the light-sensitive properties of silver salts, in which alphabet letters were cut from paper, arranged into words, and wrapped around the jars of silver nitrate impregnated gypsum. With this knowledge, Wedgwood and Davy commenced coating paper, glass, and white leather with silver nitrate solutions and laying stencils on these surfaces in sunlight. During the exposures, the silver salt sensitizer turned gray, purple brown, and, eventually, black.

By the mid-1800s, artists were employing photogram techniques with both creative, and practical scientific, intentions. Notable at this time were Herschel's flower extract Anthotypes; Anna Atkins's cyanotype studies of algae; the Scotsman Mongo Ponton's potassium dichromate *"shadowgraphs"*; and William Henry Fox Talbot (1800–1877), who was making *photogenic* drawings on salted paper.

In March 1851, Frederick Scott Archer (1813–1857) changed the landscape of photography forever. Prior to 1851, providing you didn't want your images to be botanical studies rendered in cyanotype blue, the principle photographic options available were the daguerreotype and the waxed or oiled paper-negative Talbotype/calotype. The daguerreotype was known for its precious detail and elegant presentation, the exceedingly long time it took to make exposures, and the fact that it was a one-of-a-kind product. The calotype image existed on paper and was reproducible, but the image quality was inferior because of the contact paper negative required to make a print. Light had to pass through the paper negative's fibers to

Figure 4–4
Francis Frith, Interior of the Hall of Columns, Luxor, Egypt, 1857–1860
Between 1856 and 1860, Frith made several adventurous expeditions to the Middle East, including one cover a distance of 1,500 miles up the Nile River. Working with the wet collodion process, in a portable darkroom, Frith endured temperatures of over 120°F and the associated problems of sand, dust, and flies settling into his freshly poured, and very tacky, collodion.
(Courtesy of George Eastman House/The International Museum of Photography)

make a positive print. The desirable solution to this limited menu would be a single imaging system that could be simultaneously reproducible, finely detailed, and fast enough to consider recording actual life.

In 1845–1846, Christian Frederick Schönbein (1799–1868) discovered nitrated cotton (*guncotton*) by commingling cotton fibers in a mixture of sulfuric and nitric acids. Ironically, in 1847, a young medical student in Boston by the name of John Parker Maynard formulated a durable, skin-like, medical dressing from the guncotton dissolved in ether and alcohol called *collodion* that could be used to treat wounds from Schönbein's explosives. In 1850, Gustave Le Gray proposed the idea that Parker's collodion solution could be applied to photographic purposes because it was the near-perfect vehicle for holding a light-sensitive solution on glass.

Shortly after this revelation, in March 1851, Frederick Scott Archer described an application of salted collodion on sheets of glass for the purpose of making glass plate negatives. Archer detailed a process in which potassium iodide was combined with a solution of diluted collodion, applied to a glass plate, which was then immersed in a silver nitrate bath resulting in a light-sensitive layer of silver iodide.

This sensitized glass plate was then exposed in a camera immediately after being withdrawn from the silver nitrate, developed in a solution of pyrogallic acid, and fixed in a mild sodium thiosulfate fixing bath. The advantages were immediately evident. The process provided a sharp and reproducible glass negative and was far more sensitive, especially in its wet state, permitting exposure times in seconds rather than minutes. This exposure speed allowed the subject of a portrait to exhibit a bit

Figure 4–5

Fred Church, *George Eastman Aboard the*
***S.S. Gallia with a Kodak #2*, 1890**

The beauty of George Eastman's Kodak system was that it eliminated the psychological barriers of the technical and allowed the amateur to make photographs without the need of chemistry or darkroom. Eastman's motto, *"You press the button, we do the rest,"* transformed photography by establishing a comprehensive photo-finishing industry that was accessible to everyone.

(Courtesy of the George Eastman House/The International Museum of Photography)

of candid behavior. It was also democratically priced, being a fraction of the cost of the daguerreotype. Incidentally, shortly after Archer published his experiments, enterprising photographers realized that an underexposed wet collodion negative, when laid on a dark background and viewed in reflective light, would appear as a positive. This visual phenomenon led directly to the even more democratically available ambrotype and tintype processes.

In 1871, an Englishman by the name of Dr. Richard Leach Maddox (1816–1902) produced the first successful silver bromide dry plate emulsion. With this process, it was possible to make a negative on a glass plate at any time and not just when the plate was wet with the sensitized collodion emulsion. Most importantly, this meant that it was no longer necessary to take your darkroom with you when you went out to make some pictures. Maddox's

achievement, free to the world, like Archer's wet collodion, was described in an issue of the *British Almanac*, and one of its readers was a young man named George Eastman (1854–1932), whose occupation at the time was coating and developing wet plate collodion glass plates.

George Eastman had a revelation. He theorized that if photographers could be guided to a dry plate system of making photographic negatives, then their cameras could be smaller and processing negatives would be less cumbersome and complicated. He also surmised that image development could wait until the end of the shooting experience rather than having to be done immediately following the exposure. He set to work on the inspiration in 1877 and in 1879 was granted a patent for his dry plate system. This was followed, in 1884–1885, by his brilliant idea of creating the world's first commercially produced flexible roll film system.

In this discovery, Eastman utilized very thin and flexible celluloid as the substrate for his emulsion. Celluloid was invented in 1861 and originally consisted of pyroxlene (aka gun cotton) with naphtha, amyl acetate, oil, and camphor. As had been the case with the majority of photographic discoveries, the original seed for the idea belonged to another. The concept of using celluloid as a support for a sensitized emulsion had first occurred to a gentleman by the name of John Carbutt, a man most remembered for his stereographs made while in the employ of the Union Pacific Railroad (*Glimpses of the Great West—1864–1867*).

In 1888, Eastman began to manufacture the Kodak 1A camera, loaded it with a roll of flexible film able to record 100 images, and sold it for under $25.00. The owner of the camera would shoot the film, send the camera back to Kodak, in Rochester, New York, with the exposed film still inside. In a very Netflix kind of idea, the photographer would get a freshly loaded camera (*not necessarily the same one that was sent in with the exposed film*) and two circle-shaped images of each exposure. The beauty of Eastman's Kodak system was that it eliminated the psychological barriers of the complex photographic system and allowed the amateur to make photographs without the need for technical instruction, chemistry, or darkroom. Eastman's idea revolutionized the medium of photography by creating a complete photo-finishing industry that was defined by its advertising motto, "You press the button, we do the rest."

As an aside, there is good story that the word "Kodak" was invented by a group of linguists and language experts at the request of George Eastman. Legend has it that Eastman wanted a name for his company that had no meaning, or similar spelling, in any language on earth. The one that the language experts came up with was *Kodak*.

In the early 1900s, the photogram re-emerged. Christian Schad used torn paper as a photogram source to make negative images. Schad, a principal member of the Cubist movement (*inspired by Paul Cézanne and adapted by Pablo Picasso and Georges Braque*), used photography to address the same issues being explored in contemporary Cubist painting: to illustrate the emotional force of three-dimensional objects, seen two-dimensionally, at once, from

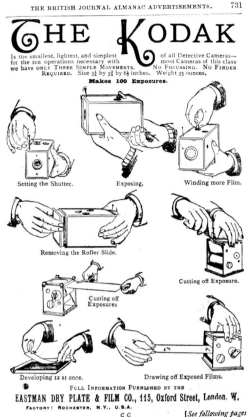

Figure 4–6

Advertisement for the Kodak #1, **British Journal Photo Almanac, 1890**
(Courtesy of George Eastman House/The International Museum of Photography)

many vantage points of place and time. Examples of the graphic power of a photogram can be seen in the work of Lucia and Laslo Moholy-Nagy, Alexander Rodchenko, Georgy Kepes, and Man Ray.

A GOOD MOMENT TO EXPLAIN A FEW THINGS

Let me try to make this simple because it is as important to understand tonal values when making either a traditional or a digital negative. If you are standing on a white sand beach in the moonlight, and the lunar light is illuminating your body, the odds are excellent that there is a shadow of you nearby. That shadow, against a field of white sand is the equivalent of a negative of you in the moonlight and the best way to describe it is to begin with the concept of a photogram.

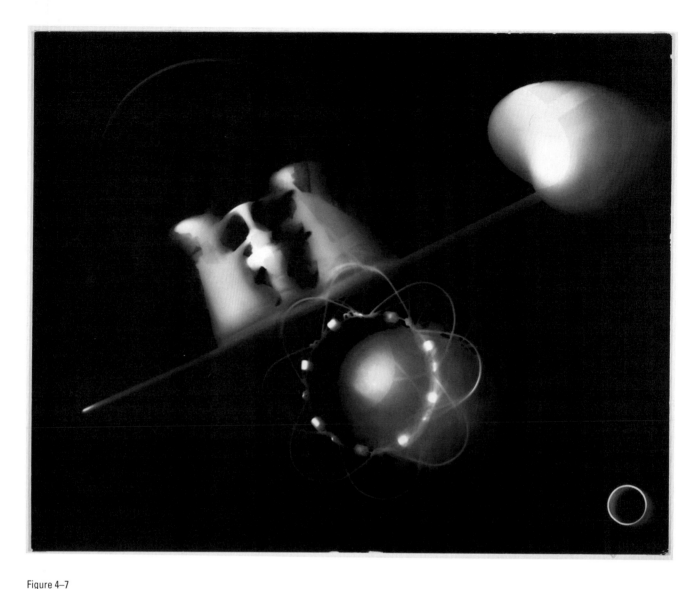

Figure 4–7

Man Ray (Emmanuel Radnitsky) (1890–1976), *Rayograph,* **1950**

Man Ray moved to New York City with his family and was soon exposed to modern art through Alfred Steiglitz's 291 Gallery. He became friends with Marcel Duchamp and Francis Picabia and together they formed the New York Dada movement. Ray preferred the tools of science and machine to make his art, working extensively with the cliché verre negative and the photograms that he called Rayographs.

(Courtesy of George Eastman House/The International Museum of Photography)

The term *photogram* is used to describe a direct shadow pattern . . . the result of exposing a layer, or layers, of transparent, translucent, or opaque objects directly upon a photosensitive receptor . . . a sensitizer, or a sensitized emulsion, on a substrate of some type. The effect is like a negative in that the degrees of transparency in the layers allow light to pass through to a sensitized emulsion according to their respective densities. The most transparent objects allow the greatest exposure whereas the least transparent prevent exposure. A photogram on paper is different from a negative because it is a one-of-a-kind image.

This is pretty elementary, but all negatives have visible zones of film density that describe the amount of silver that has been exposed and developed on the film. Clear or thin areas of the negative have the least exposed and developed silver and are primarily dependent on development. Dark and dense areas of the film have a great deal of exposed and developed silver and are most dependent on exposure. The center of this equation is an 18% gray (*average film density of around 0.745*) that is relative to any exposure made according to a light meter's normal 18% gray, Zone 5, recommendation.

The recommended development times given to films are important to you in that the longer the film is developed, the greater the contrast for that particular film. When your film is being processed and being "pushed" beyond a normal development time, the areas that have received the least exposure (*your shadows*) will not darken to the same degree as the more exposed areas (*your highlights*). Up to a point, the extended development's effect on the highlight areas of the negative will create an ever-increasing comparative contrast, with the shadow areas.

A basic rule of thumb: For more contrast in your negatives, underexpose and overdevelop (*push*) the film. Pushing the film means to develop the film so that the contrast is greater than it would be if the film were to be processed for a normal time. For less contrast, overexpose and under develop (*pull*) the film. Pulling basically means to develop film so that the contrast is reduced relative to what the contrast would be if the film were developed for a normal time. After development, the resulting negative will exhibit a menu of tonal values that many large format photographers refer to as zones. In a negative, these zones are given calibrated values with numbers that can be applied to the lightest low-density shadows (*low density equals degrees of transparency*) and the darkest high-density highlights of the negative. When all of these assigned values and numbers are stirred together you begin to encounter assorted theories about the *Zone System* . . . just thank your lucky stars, we will not go into it in this book.

Just for your information, the ability of the normal photographic paper to render highlight densities is maximized in the vicinity of a 1.2 average density range reading in the negative. In platinum/palladium printing, for instance, the process has the ability to render a much greater range of densities in the negative; thus, the compelling need to have a negative to match the almost linear curve of a perfect platinum negative. It is possible for the Pt/Pd processes to render highlight densities in the negative beyond a densitometer reading of 2.0.

What Does Negative Density Range Mean?

Let's say that when you're reading the directions for platinum/palladium and you come across some information that asks you to try working with a negative that

has a negative density range of **1.5**. The majority of readers will say, "O.K." and read on hoping for the best . . . unless that number is one that they have looked into before or if they have a little experience with densitometers and parametric curves.

- The number **1.5** comes from measuring the value for the thinnest shadow with detail with a densitometer and giving it a number. Let's say that the number you calibrate with the densitometer is **0.35.**

- Next, you will measure the value for the densest highlight with detail. Let's say that this new number has a value **1.85.**

- To find the density range of this negative all that you have to do is subtract the thinnest shadow number from the densest highlight number. In this convenient example, you will come up with the number that was recommended to you for the process. (**1.85 minus 0.35 = 1.5**)

When working in non-silver and alternative processes, it is necessary to create a negative, or a positive, that will match the size of your finished print; one that can be contact printed in direct sun or with an ultraviolet (UV) mechanical light source. Most photographic artists have an occasional desire to make big and impressive images. Being able to produce an enlarged duplicate negative is one of the only ways that you can carry around a small camera and eventually make large enough negatives for alternative contact printing. For all but the most dedicated large format photographers, this is a true bonus.

Another reason for enlarging your negatives is that in the real world your original negative will not have the correct tonal values for a particular process. For instance, negative made for platinum/palladium printing will make you smile if they exhibit a healthy contrast and a negative density range of 1.5 to 1.7; appropriate for printing in a traditional wet darkroom on a silver gelatin paper with a grade of 0. In another example, gum bichromate prints may require a C-M-Y-K negative set of the same image with each having a different density range. Making an enlarged duplicate negative is an option for some ambitious "gumists," while others will simply alter their exposure times or pigment to sensitizer ratios. *Please refer to the Digital chapter for a complete workflow showing you how to easily take a C-M-Y-K negative set for gum bichromate printing.*

As a final thought in this section, in alternative process contact printing, burning and dodging are not practical techniques (*although it's a lot of fun to try*) and making adjustments during the inter-positive phase (*step #1 of a two-step process*) will yield corrections that you might make during a normal paper exposure.

So how do you make a negative for contact printing? It used to be a relatively simple idea. You could either shoot your contact negatives to scale in whatever size camera you were using or you could shoot small and make an enlarged duplicate negative using a host of films and film types. Duplicating could be accomplished as a single stage event, going negative to negative, using a film such as Kodak's SO-132 or SO-339, or you could use a multi-stage negative to inter-positive process to negative with a film such as a two-step Ortho or Arista's Premium Halftone Supreme (APHS). In a multistage duplication process using lith film, you can increase the density range in the inter-positive step and go for the contrast in the negative step. Refer to Dave Soemarko's LC-1 and LC-1B system for long tonal scale lith film inter-positives and negatives later in this chapter.

A great many of these films are gone now but several remain and are still worth writing about . . . if only for the quaint historical reference it will lend to this chapter. In the next segment I'll go over the few multi-stage films still available and discuss how to think of making negatives in different ways.

NEGATIVE PRODUCTION OPTIONS

Commercial Labs: Service Bureaus

If you need perfection, can't do it yourself, or can't afford the materials or time, or don't have the right high-end equipment; you might consider hiring a commercial lab, or service bureau, to make a negative for you. The best way to find one is not to use the Yellow Pages but to ask friends, associates, and those in the business of servicing clients with perfect images. It is important that you hire a service bureau that is familiar with the needs of alternative process artists. That said, this is hardly ever successful or satisfying as an experience and I would implore you to teach yourself how to make your own negatives rather than rely on the chance abilities of another. I don't mean to be sour about this but I've never had a service bureau make a negative, or follow my instructions, to a degree of satisfaction that I am comfortable with.

On the bright side of this discussion, there are people like Kevin Sullivan, of Bostick & Sullivan (the same people who retail alternative process chemistry), who are now expanding their business to include producing negatives for alternative process printing.

The Copy Machine

Most commercial copy services are capable of producing an enlarged duplicate film of whatever flat 2-D source you give to them. The quality is always inferior but that particular look may be exactly what you are searching for. There is no question that there is a funky-ness to copy machine negatives that is truly original and beautiful to a particular eye. Check out your local library as well because they often have a machine that will produce a crude, medium-size transparency . . . the kind used in overhead projectors in school systems that have not moved on to Keynote and Powerpoint presentations.

The Desktop Printer

Desktop scanners and printers are so sophisticated now that there really is no drop off in quality between what you can generate at home and what you can pay an arm and a leg for at a service bureau . . . really. Printers and scanners are more sophisticated and affordable all of the time. And why shouldn't they be considering the cost of premium inks? If you actually priced out ink by the ml it would probably cost about $11,000 a gallon. No matter, it's only money, and it's our art were talking about here.

This afternoon, while I'm writing this, I'm printing a Piezo-generated print on an Epson 1280 using pigment-based inks from MIS Supply and ink-jet compatible Kozo-Shi rice paper from Digital Art Supplies. On another printer, an Epson 2400 with the new Ultrachrome K3 ink sets (yes, I know this may sound out of date a few years from now), I'm printing a digital negative on Pictorico OHP ink-jet film and applying a faux

Figure 4–8

Christopher James, *Mona & The Whale, 2001*—copy machine, digital negative, Pt & gum
This is an example of playing around with a photocopier. The detail of da Vinci's *Mona Lisa* was placed upon a photocopy machine and when the exposure light went in one direction, Mona and the art history textbook went in another, resulting in the moving impression. The laser copy print was then photographed, and an enlarged negative was made on S0-332 (no longer available) direct duplicating film. The enlarged negative could then be used for any contact process.
(Courtesy of the author)

Pyro color layer that will filter UV light like a Pyro developed negative. It's all pretty amazing, considering how fast this technology has evolved.

I'm not going to go into making digital negatives in this chapter, as there is a good deal of information and I want to keep it all in one place. Please refer to Chapter 5, Digital Options, for specifics and recommended workflows.

ACRYLIC LIFT TRANSPARENCIES FROM PRINTED SOURCES

To make an unusual positive or negative, which is a lot of fun on many levels, try this technique. The materials you'll need to do it will be a bottle of acrylic gloss medium, a little dishwashing soap, a tray with warm water, and a stack-o-magazines for inspiration. The process is simple and flexible. You can use the acrylic positives directly as a contact source and get a negative print. You can also use it as a tintype or ambrotype "positive/negative" to produce a positive piece or you can scan it and make a digital negative from the scanned positive acrylic lift. You can also do many of them and then combine them together for multiple image montages.

You'll be appropriating magazine reproductions printed on "*clay-coated*" paper (*high quality inks and paper stock, i.e.,* Vanity Fair, New York Times Magazine, Vogue, *etc.*) and utilizing them as conventional images, distorted images, montage and/or collage sources. Clay coating, in this sense, defines an ink-printed page where a fine mist of clay dust, or talc, is sprayed on freshly printed sheets of paper as it runs through the presses, to prevent the freshly printed paper from sticking together. Another image source that is less common but one that allows you to use your own images is the laser transfer copy print. When making copies, ask that your black & white images be copied in color formatting because this will give you

Figure 4–9

Bina Altera, *13th Hour Montage*—**1996**

This is a nice example of Bina Altera's emulsion lift montages that are always dense with graphic complexity and surprises.

(Courtesy of the artist)

additional layers, beyond a single black, of thermographic dyes to transfer. You can make lifts from these in much the same manner.

Basic Materials for Acrylic Lifts

- High-quality printed magazines (*Time*, *Vogue*, *Esquire*, etc.)
- Acrylic Gloss/Gel Medium
- A clean and dry coating surface (Masonite or Plexiglas®, sheet)
- Brush (foam or watercolor type)
- Hot water in a tray with a little detergent
- Hairdryer

The Technique

With a foam brush, apply an even and thin coat of acrylic gloss medium over the magazine image you wish to make an acrylic lift from. Brush the first coat in a single direction and dry it completely with a hair dryer. Then recoat the image in the opposite direction with the acrylic gloss medium. Repeat this sequence until you have 4 to 6 thin coats.

Applying thick coatings, or continuing to coat once the acrylic medium has begun to "set up" will result in a milky translucent image so work quickly and do not brush to make it smooth . . . it will get smooth on its own. Once you have successfully completed these multiple coatings it will be time to separate the ink graphic from the paper support by immersing the coated image in a tray of hot and soapy water. This will eventually cause the paper support to break down and will leave you with the ink image supported in the flexible and transparent acrylic skin. If you get impatient, you can gently rub the paper support with your fingertips. The positive acrylic image will appear cloudy at first but will dry clear if you haven't over brushed in the coating steps.

Once you have removed all of the paper from the image, the acrylic "image-skin" can be applied directly to paper, wood, or glass with a thin acrylic medium or diluted glue wash. You can nail it, staple it, or tack it. It can also be used as a contact positive for any alternative process. The image can be cut, stretched, montaged, collaged, digitized, and remade on acetate, and played with as you see fit.

As you might expect, the *positive* acrylic image, printed as a contact film, will yield a *negative* print. To make a positive print image it is necessary to make a film inter-negative in the darkroom with one of the few films still being made for that purpose but I again urge you to learn how to work in the "dry darkroom" and do the negative digitally. Simply scan the acrylic lift, work on it in Photoshop, invert it, and print it out on Pictorico OHP. You may also try contact printing the acrylic lift onto an RC paper and using the negative RC paper print as a paper negative.

Figure 4–10

Christopher James, *Acrylic Lift & Cyanotype with Sodium Carbonate & Tannic Acid Toning*

This pair of images shows an example of an acrylic lift and the use of that lift as a contact film in the cyanotype process. The cyanotype, following its final wash, was toned with alternating baths of sodium carbonate and tannic acid.

(Courtesy of the author)

POLAROID TYPE 55 POSITIVE/NEGATIVE FILM

If you want to have a really great time making photographs, let me recommend that you treat yourself to a box of Polaroid Type 55 Positive/Negative 4 × 5 instant film. This ingenious film can be shot in either a conventional 4 × 5 camera or in a pinhole camera that accepts a 4 × 5 Polaroid back. There are several manufacturers of pinhole cameras and they all make a pretty nice camera for a very reasonable price. I've been using a Lensless Camera Co wide-angle model for decades and it has gone around the world a few times with no appreciable damage. I generally pack toiletries in it when traveling and a lunch when out shooting . . . it is, after all, a box of air with a pinhole drilled into it. There is, however, one manufacturer that stands apart in the world of pinhole camera construction, and that is Mr. Zernike Au and his Zero Image pinhole camera line. Zernike's cameras are works of art, made of teak with brass fittings, they come in all formats from

35 mm to 4 × 5, have an array of custom add-ons that can be ordered and even have brass name plates and serial numbers. Please see the Resource section in the Appendices for information.

Polaroid Type 55 P/N yields both a positive print and a negative. It is important to remember, when working with Type 55, that you need to make a choice between creating a great negative for alternative process contact printing or making a nice positive print. It is rare to have both the negative and the positive come out well simultaneously. My advice is to use the positive as a way of evaluating the composition and context of your image and to focus all of your attention on making the best negative for the process you are intending to use it for. This will mean that you are trying to make a thin and washed-out positive print that you will be reluctant to show anyone. However, the negative half of the film packet will be the positive's opposite and will exhibit rich and tonally appropriate qualities for the processes that you will be using the negative with.

Figure 4–11

Jo Babcock—*VW Van Camera*—George Eastman House

San Francisco photographer Jo Babcock has made a career out of constructing pinhole cameras out of an object and then making a related pinhole photograph with it. This portrait of the George Eastman House is one of his most notable combinations.

(Courtesy of Jon Zax for Jo's VW Van Camera & Jo Babcock for Eastman House)

Type 55 film negatives can be cleared successfully in standard hypo clearing baths, such as Perma Wash, or in a simple sodium sulfite bath. The negatives clear quickly and can be washed for permanence in minutes. When I work with Type 55 away from the studio, I fill a plastic food storage container with hypo clearing bath for transporting the negatives and wait until I return to the studio to rinse and hang to dry.

In workshops near the ocean, seawater (*not gathered from the edges of breaking surf where sand is likely to be in the solution*) is also a successful clearing bath but the negatives surely will require a clean water wash later on. Be cautious of the fragile Type 55 negative. Be sure to remove the metal strip and developer pod before placing it in the clearing agent. As an added note, when working away from the studio, please bring along a trash bag to throw away all of the Pola-Trash that is left once you have gone through all of Polaroid's packaging and packets. Also, be very careful when you separate all of the pieces that make up the pod, positive, negative, and protective outer layers. It is very easy to rip or scar the negative at this stage. Finally, Type 55 P/N is the best film to use in a workshop, or class environment, due to its ability to allow instantaneous adjustments to exposure evaluations and instant gratification for the student. The negatives are actually better than satisfactory for any

process you will be engaged in and the very nature of the film's immediacy greatly accelerates a learning curve for anyone learning to shoot contact negatives for alternative process printing.

A QUICK TIP OF THE HAT TO IN-CAMERA FILMS

Shooting large format negatives in camera is still one of the best options for generating the perfect negative. As I mentioned in the earlier edition of this book, digital technology would soon challenge conventional film as a preferred negative source. Well, that day has come earlier than I had imagined . . . and it isn't a bad change at all. In the meantime, conventional black & white films are still being made and used by those hearty folk who are hanging on to the romance of the wet darkroom. Kodak, Ilford, and Agfa are still producing excellent black & white films in a relatively solid menu of sizes, and these can be, as always, manipulated to your specifications through exposure and development.

Conventional standards for exposure and processing in silver gelatin printing are often lacking when applied to many alternative processes. There are few commercial films that are truly ideal for many alternative applications. There are few films in which the full value range in highlights to shadows with detail are explored to the extremes that are possible with a delicate process like platinum/palladium. This single subject, that of film and its relationship to image-making, could easily take an entire book, as you will discover if you go looking for one on the topic. I personally don't have the deep interest, page space, or time to devote to this topic and so I will offer some resources. Fair warning: It is easy to get drawn into the realm of compulsive technique in this genre. The history of alternative process is full of individuals who made stunningly beautiful prints that were, in the end, devoid of life, imagination, and inspiration.

Some Fine Sources for More On This Subject

See Appendix G for additional information on these recommended texts.

- Dick Arentz, *Platinum & Palladium Printing: Second Edition*
- Dan Burkholder, *Making Digital Negatives for Contact Printing*
- Phil Davis, *Beyond the Zone System Handbook*
- David Fokos, *How to Make Digital Negative for Black and White Fine-Art Photographs*
- Dick Sullivan and Carl Weese, *The New Platinum Print*

One last recommendation, which may prove extremely useful years from now, is to look at Mark Osterman's dry plate emulsion contribution in this book. Mark, looking to the future, rather than at the past, which is his forte, has been developing a workflow for coating hand-made emulsions on glass plates that will be used in camera. The first results of this new work look extraordinarily good and I hope that you will try the technique.

A FEW INTERESTING NEGATIVE OPTIONS

The Cliché-Verre

Cliché-verre (*in French, "cliché" means negative in relation to photography and "verre" means glass*) is a term describing a handmade negative on a transparent base of glass or acetate. It is usually created by applying liquid resists, such as paint, syrup, asphaltum, varnish, oils, or

Figure 4–12

Jean Babtiste Camille Corot—*Corot par lui-meme (Self Portrait)* 1858
Corot, a well-known painter, etched into the emulsion of completely exposed, glass albumen plates, and used them as negatives for photographic prints of his drawings.
(Courtesy of Detroit Arts Institute Museum)

ink, to a transparent substrate such as glass or Plexiglas. The painted glass is then printed as is, or reduced via etching, by a contact printing method or projected to a light-sensitive emulsion whereupon the painted areas filter the light to make an image. The degrees of transparency (zones of density) in the various resists allow light to pass through according to density; less resist equals more exposure and vice versa.

The cliché-verre was reinvented by Adalbert Cuvelier in 1853 and used by artists to make reproducible plates for their drawings. Among the most notable of those artists was Jean Baptiste Camille Corot (1796–1875), who used completely exposed and sensitized glass plates as a transparent etching base/negatives for making paper prints of his drawings.

In the 19th century, artists who were disciples of the "Barbizon School" of landscape painting, coated sheets of glass with hard and soft etching grounds (similar to asphaltum or pitch) or with black soot by burning a tallow candle underneath the glass. In either case, the dark opaque coating was then scratched and drawn into with traditional etching tools, brushes, and fingers. The result was essentially a graphic line art negative with the remaining ground/soot functioning as a light-resistant mask. The etched and scratched lines in the ground allowed light to pass to a bichromated colloidal emulsion underneath the plate as a way of making an image on paper. For a quick idea of how this works, take a piece of glass or acetate sheet film and play on it with paint, inks and resists. Then, with a pin, nail, razor blade, comb, etching needle, or pencil, scratch away at the resist. When you're done, use the resulting image as a contact negative with a conventional silver gelatin paper and you'll get the idea immediately.

You can also make a camera obscura–like drawing by directing an image from a slide projector or enlarger to a prepared coated glass plate, acetate, or sheet of vellum. In the projected light, trace your image by following, or abstracting, the lines and forms being projected. When you're done drawing, you have options. Among them, contact printing the new plate to a piece of silver gelatin enlarging paper or using it as a contact negative in any alternative process. Additionally, this technique is a terrific way to include text in your imagery. Simply create the text in your computer, print it out on acetate, and use it as a cliché -verre layer during your exposures.

The Paper Negative

It is possible to use a paper negative for contact printing but fine detail should not be one of your high priorities. Paper negatives are the result of loading conventional printing papers into a pinhole, or any other type of camera. These paper negatives, if exposed on an RC paper, for instance, will often produce excellent images when contact printed with an alternative process or with another piece of conventional printing paper.

When using a paper negative with an alternative process you must be prepared for fairly long exposure times. Successful images are generally quite soft due to the fuzziness of the final print. Be sure that there is no writing on the back of the RC paper negative or those logos will become part of your image. Knowing that, consider writing on the back of the RC paper negative to include script in your image. Remember to pay attention to the way your type will read when you're loading your contact frame.

Should you wish to approximate Talbot's calotype paper negative experiments, consider making a paper negative (*from a film positive*) on a piece of writing paper or vellum and then soaking the paper negative in olive oil and wiping it dry. The olive oil will make the paper far more translucent and will give you a better shot at a readable and successful final image. You may also wish to consider using an inkjet paper negatives by "inverting" your image and using the paper print as your negative. Again, consider oiling the inkjet print but be sure you are making the print with ink that is moisture resistant like Epson's Ks Ultrachrome inks. One last idea that has its roots in the history of the medium is to wax your paper negative before printing. There are a lot of old cut and paste, graphic design, wax machines laying about these days due to the fact that there are no designers cutting and pasting with real pieces of paper anymore. Run your paper negative through the hot wax and rollers and it will be a bit more translucent.

Projection

The use of light projection, either through a positive or negative transparency is another option when dealing with film as the primary force in a final image. I think of both variations as "alternative" image making, adhering to my long belief that any creative process that makes use of light, to leave its mark and intention, can be thought of as photography.

Negative (or positive) projections can be used in installations and performances. A negative projection from a slide projector can be a timesaving tool in printing large images coated with hand applied liquid emulsions. Superimposing these negative projections, in conjunction with other media, can also allow for the creation of entirely new perspectives of content and intention (*see Charlene Knowlton's piece,* Triptych, *1984*). Although *positive* transparency projection is not a negative source, in the

Figure 4–13
Tim Butler, *Family Farm Project*
This image is from Tim Butler's series on the demise of the family farm in America. To make the image, Tim rigged up a projector that was powered by a car battery.
(Courtesy of the artist)

way that we have previously been dealing with film, it offers a wide range of possibilities to the alternative artist. One of the most intriguing uses is the work of my former workshop student, Tim Butler, who photographed the family farm during the day and returned at night to project those images upon the structures of that farm. In this manner, the work became a performance/installation piece as well as a conventional printed image when the evidence of the performance was presented in that manner.

A FEW SINGLE STAGE DUPLICATING FILMS

My favorite single stage, negative-to-negative, duplicating film, Kodak's SO-132, is gone. So is Kodak Precision Line Film LPD7. Agfa's Scala, a very nice black & white positive slide film, that requires custom processing, is still being produced and Agfa recently posted, contrary to all of the rumors, *"We are pleased to announce that processing services for Agfa Scala Black & White Slide Film will continue to be available for many years to come."*

That said, there are a still a few choices in the single stage arena. Kodak still produces Kodak Aerographic Direct Duplicating Film 2422, as well as SO-192 and SO-187. These, however, are aerial films and they are expensive and generally are difficult to obtain . . . as is the case with many Special Order—SO films. If you are feeling adventurous, here are a few to play with.

Kodak Aerographic Direct Duplicating Film 2422: This blue sensitive film provides extremely fine-grain, medium contrast, and is used for high-quality, one-step, duplication of negatives or positives. Although this film requires a high-intensity light source (like the sun, perhaps?), it basically behaves like SO-132. I mention it here as a film that might work very well with sunlight in a contact printing situation . . . or in a pinhole camera. Students of mine have purchased this film by the roll in 9.5" × 250' lengths for that purpose, with the success edge going to the pinhole option.

Kodak High-Resolution Aerial Duplicating Films SO-192 and SO-187 are black & white negative aerial duplicating films. As in the 2422 film, these products have blue-sensitive, hardened emulsions and are extremely fine grain with very high resolving power. They are manufactured, and intended, for use as a second-generation positive and a third-generation negative. Their primary function is to duplicate very fine-grain, high-definition aerial negatives. These films differ only in the thickness of their base and the 187 type may have sufficient dimensional stability to meet requirements for use as aerial duplicate negative in place of glass plates. I cannot guarantee this, but Kodak made the claim.

These aerial films generally require specific chemistry and a Versamat high-speed processor. However, you can improvise with a Jobo or Lomo system and if you're really good, with a tray. Here's how Kodak phrases it: Kodak High Resolution Aerial Duplicating Film SO-192, and Kodak High Resolution Aerial Duplicating Film SO-187, can be processed in the Kodak Versamat Film Processor, Model 11, or 1140, with Kodak Versamat 885 Chemicals, or Kodak Versamat 641 Chemicals. Mechanized processing in roller-transport processors offers the advantages of uniform treatment of all portions of the roll.

I know that it's possible, if you are cutting your stock (red safelight safe) down and using single sheets, to use tray processing in common developers such as Kodak Developer D-19 or Kodak Developer DK-50. My students have used D-76 with interesting results.

Just in case you happen to locate some frozen Kodak SO-132, here is how you use it. A film such as Kodak's SO-132 (*in the past known as Kodak 4168 and Kodak SO-339, just in case you run across this in someone's freezer*) is a simple, orthochromatic sensitive, long tonal range film that is used like a conventional printing paper. When it was being manufactured, it priced out at about $4.00 a sheet in an 8" × 10" format.

SO-132 provided a quick and painless *direct duplication* from an original small negative to an enlarged negative that could be used directly for contact printing. It was quite convenient because you could work with it under normal safelight conditions and develop it in standard paper, or film, chemistry such as Dektol, D-19, D-76, Xtol, and the like. It was also relatively fast and allowed you to get on with your alternative printing without a great deal of technical meandering.

The curious thing about this, and other single-stage films, is that they react in an opposite manner from typical enlarger and paper chemistry. Burning negative information on single-stage films will result in thinner values in the finished film, while dodging will result in denser values. It does take getting used to.

An average negative with a normal tonal scale will require an exposure time of between 1 and 1.5 minutes with the aperture nearly wide open. Development type is a personal choice, but using 1:2 Dektol (paper chemistry) takes 3 to 4 minutes. Exposing this film without burning or dodging will result in a negative that closely approximates, or improves, your original. To achieve an adequate maximum density with this film, essential for many alternative processes, it is necessary to develop the film aggressively. A few artists use an undiluted high contrast developer like D-19 (72 °F) for about 8 minutes. Others simply stay with their traditional paper developers and expose their original negatives with that chemistry in mind. It is possible to play with the contrast potential of SO-132 by using a more concentrated developer than you would normally use for a paper set-up. Conversely, you can decrease the aggressiveness by mixing both film and paper developers.

One last thing, just in case you are lucky enough to find some: During tray development, under safelight conditions, you will see your negative come up in the developer in much the same manner that it does with a paper print. This is due to a light opaque coating on the film that will disappear when you place the film sheet into the fixing bath.

A FEW MULTI-STAGE DUPLICATING FILMS

Because there are only a few exotic single-stage duplicating films still being produced that are suitable for conventional alternative process contact printing, you are left with the options of either shooting large format film in-camera, making very tiny prints the size of your non–large camera negative, or using a multi-stage duplicating film. In the latter case, it is necessary to make an inter-positive before making the final negative . . . thus, multi-stage. Duplicating films provide excellent resolution and are often more appropriate as a film source when you are looking for either a highly graphic representation/translation, or when you want to extend the tonal range, of an existing black & white negative. Many practitioners feel that these films are highly flexible and allow you to alter the original negative's contrast, shadow, and highlight details with no appreciable loss of negative integrity.

When making an inter-positive it is recommended that you work to ensure that all of your negative's information is translated. It is not as important for you to think about contrast in this stage, as it is to think about a fully realized exposure. Contrast can be addressed later in the final (second) inter-positive to negative stage with a more aggressive development. Here are a few of the films that are still available to you.

Figure 4–14

Binh Danh, *The Leaf Effect: Study for Metamorphosis #2*, 2006—Chlorophyll print, butterfly specimen and resin

Binh Danh makes his images directly printing directly on plant leaves through the natural process of photosynthesis. By placing a negative in contact with a living leaf and then exposing it to sunlight for several weeks, the image literally becomes part of the leaf. Danh then permanently "fixes" the image by casting it in resin.

(Courtesy of the artist and Haines Gallery, San Francisco)

Maco Genius Print Film

With a name like this, how could anyone resist? Maco Genius Print Film is a high silver content, chlorobromide, orthochromatic emulsion coated on a clear 170-micron polyester base. It was designed as a replacement for Agfa's Gevatone N31P and is excellent for creating enlarged negatives (in a two-step process) for contact printing. Today, this film is used by an awful lot of alternative process photographers the world over and is regarded as the best of the options. Maco, by the way, is the same company that took over Cachet who made the very best hand applied liquid emulsions, which we will deal with later on in the book.

Maco Genius Print Film is a halftone film, and has a robust, dimensionally stable, and archivally sound film base. It is well suited for processes such as Platinum Palladium, Ziatype, Kallitype, and Bromoil. Although Maco says it is a good film for gum bichromate negatives, you are much better served doing C-M-Y-K negatives digitally.

Maco also recommends this film for use within a pinhole camera. Think about it . . . if it is a two-stage film then it stands to reason that shooting it in a pinhole camera will yield a negative in-camera . . . a very large black & white transparency with a clear base.

This film can be processed in all types of black & white developers; however, the specific type of developer exerts a more pronounced influence on the characteristics of the film than it does with other films. *A manufacturer's warning: When using this transparent photographic material on the baseboard of the enlarger, a black card-board must be put under the MACO GENIUS PRINT film to avoid the reflection which softens the gradation.* Knowing this, it will be mandatory for you to coat the inside of your pinhole camera with a black, and nonreflective, material.

Maco Genius Film has an ISO rating of 25. Varying the concentration of the developer can control the

ISO range. For example using Dektol in a stock solution increases the contrast. Further dilution reduces the contrast. Experimenting with different dilutions and developing times will produce the desired results. Develop at least two minutes with all developers regardless of dilutions.

The Genius Print Film emulsion is relatively fast. Use a standard step wedge to determine exposure times. Put a black card under the film to avoid bounce back through the transparent substrate. When processing this film under a safelight, be sure that the red safelight is at least 5 feet from your trays.

Do not bother with a stop bath, but do rinse the film between the developer and the fixer. Fixing the film is a little tricky but you can do it. Place the exposed film in a rapid/high speed fixer and count the seconds between the immersion and when you see the film clear. Multiply that time by 3, and that will be your fixing time. On larger sheets of film, change the fixer for every sheet of film. Use a fixer-clearing bath and wash for 5 minutes in 68°F water.

Arista APHS Premium Halftone Supreme Ortho Litho

Arista APHS Premium Halftone Supreme Ortho Litho film is a high-end quality graphic arts film that is a replacement for Kodak Kodalith Type III Ortho Litho film. When developed in standard A/B Lith film developer, this film will yield high contrast (black & white only) results as well as excellent halftones when exposed on a copy camera with a line screen. It is a higher resolution film with greater silver content than Arista APH film.

Arista APHS film is also used by many photographers for use in creating highlight masks for fine art printing and for creating enlarged duplicating negatives for alternative process contact printing. Continuous-tone results can be achieved by using a dilute working solution of standard paper developer. Dektol 1:7 is a popular dilution to achieve continuous tone results. Your individual optimal dilution and developing time will vary based on your desired results.

Arista APHS film can be used under red safelight darkroom conditions and also in pinhole cameras for a direct negative.

Arista Premium Halftone Supreme (APHS) can be processed using Dave Soemarko's LC-1 development

formula for a long and linear tonal scale. This film, using the LC-1 system, appears to be quite satisfactory for most alternative processes. This processing option will be detailed later in the chapter.

Arista Premium Halftone (APH)

A two-step lith film for inter-positive to negative production that can be used very successfully with Soemarko's LC-1B low contrast developer formula. It is less expensive than the APHS version and reportedly yields better results when used with the Soemarko's LC-1B formula.

Ilford Ortho Plus

This is good quality, two-step, continuous tone (or high contrast) film with fine grain. This film is a student favorite because of its low cost, quality, and simplicity. In the "*positive*" first-stage Ilford Ortho Plus should be exposed for highlights and developed for shadows and a conventional paper developer, for 2 to 4 minutes, will be adequate. In the second stage "*negative*," you will be exposing for shadow details and developing for highlights. If your shadow density looks good but the highlights lack substance, increase the type or strength of your developer, and vice versa. This film behaves like FP4 without the red sensation and can be developed under safelight conditions. Ilford Ortho Plus comes in sheet sizes from 4×5 to 10×12 and can be developed in ID-11 normally for 6 minutes or 11 minutes for high contrast. You may also use Microphen, which can be developed at 4 minutes for normal development or 7 minutes for high contrast.

Bergger Blue Sensitive Sheet Film BPFB-18

Bergger Blue Sensitive Sheet Film BPFB-18 is a blue-sensitive film of moderately high contrast. It is generally utilized used for copying continuous-tone B&W images and for making graphic highlight masks. The Bergger BPFB-18 is primarily useful for the production of inter-positives and second stage duplicate negatives from original B&W negatives. This two-step duplicating process allows great control over the quality of the final negative and permits the making of either same-sized duplicates via contact printing or with an enlarger. BPFB can be used under red safelight conditions and in your pinhole cameras for a direct negative film. You'll have to run test for exposures in the pinhole as the exposure will be subject to your focal range, light availability, and pinhole size. Bergger indicates that for copy work of documents, using two 1000w Xenon lamps at a distance of 1 meter, or two 45 A arc lamps, should be adequate.

Any good, standard continuous tone film developer, in tray, machine, or tank, can be used to develop BPFB-18. After development, the use of an acid stop bath is recommended, as it will help preserve the fixer. Minimum fixing time in a fresh fixer should be 7 minutes for a normal fixer, and 5 minutes in a rapid fixer.

Kodak 4135 Gravure Positive

This is a standard graphic arts film available through commercial graphic supply houses in a variety of sizes including rolls.

Kodak Commercial Ortho Type 3 Film

This is the most commonly found sheet film used for two-step negative duplication in a class darkroom situation. The first stage yields an inter-positive and the second stage contact with the inter-positive, yields a negative. It is easy to find and is relatively inexpensive but known for its extremely high contrast when processed in special Ortho A-B Developer. You can make a more continuous tonal scale by altering the developer. *For Example, 1/3 Ortho AB, 1/3 HC-110 dilution B or D-76 1:3 and Dektol 2:1*). The Kodak Commercial Ortho Type film is fragile and fogs easily under bright safelights. It also is prone to pinholes and must be handled with great care. Honestly, this would be the last on my list of recommended multi-stage films.

EXPOSURE & DEVELOPMENT

Negative Density Ranges

For each alternative process, slightly different negative requirements will yield the best results. Platinum and palladium negatives, for instance, enjoy a very long sloping tonal scale between shadows and highlight density. The ideal negative here is one with healthy contrast in the neighborhood of a 1.5 to 1.7 density range (DR). In general, the following combinations of paper grades and density ranges offer a good starting place. A negative density range of 1.5 is best printed on a grade 0 paper. A DR of

1.3 on a grade 1; and a DR of 1.1 on a grade 2; a DR of .90 on a grade 3; a DR of .70 on a grade 4; and a DR of .60 (or less) on a high-contrast grade 5. As always, any of these approximate recommendations will only be relevant depending on what you intend to make with your negatives, and exposure of both inter-positive and negative stages should be adjusted to the intentions of the artist.

In multiple stage duplication, the films listed can be processed in Ortho (*high contrast*) developers for a high contrast look or in a variety of film and/or paper developers for more continuous tonalities and a longer tonal scale. If you are chemically astute, you may modify existing developers or make up your own. Many of the Ortho-type films can be processed in film developers such as HC-110 dilution B or D-76, for 4 to 5 minutes by itself, or in combination with conventional paper developers. Freestyle Sales sells a solution called Clayton Extended Plus Developer that can be used for either films or papers. Clayton Extended Plus can be quite successful in giving a longer tonal scale with Ortho type films through dilution strengths in the 1:15 range. It is essential that you experiment with many different combinations of film and developer and ask other artists for their personal recommendations and preferences.

Pyro

If you are extremely compulsive about your negatives, you can become a disciple of the "Cult of Pyro." By joining, you will become a "pyro-maniac" and may indulge yourself in the wondrous world of Pyro developers.

Essentially, Pyro chemistry provides the user with a very long tonal scale negative that is a favorite of platinum—palladium printers. When an exposed piece of film is developed in one of the Pyro formulas, the negative's sensitive silver halide reduction to a metallic state is not all that is taking place. The silver being reduced to its metallic state not only forms a negative but also delivers a greenish-yellow, sometimes tan, stain that functions like a sunscreen or tanning agent, hardening the gelatin into a microscopic bas-relief. This yellow-green Pyro stain works as a filter to UV light and allows films like high contrast lith to yield a long, and very smooth tonal gradation curve. For more on the complicated subject of Pyro . . . and to join the "cult," I suggest investigating Gordon Hutchings, *The Book of Pyro*, published by Bitter Dog Press.

Figure 4–15
Charmaine Craig, 1990
Charmaine Craig created this work, a family portrait, when she was a student of mine at Harvard University. She wrote, "*This piece is intended to evoke my relationship with my mother, who, in Burma of the 1960s, was a beauty queen, an actress, and a leader of the Karen people in their struggle to survive the military dictatorship.*" (Courtesy of the artist)

Dave Soemarko's LC-1 and LC-1B Low Contrast Developer Formulas for Lith Film

First off, it's not a simple task to place density and adjust for the contrast when making an enlarged duplicate inter-positive on a high contrast film. The traditional controls of exposure, development time, and developer dilution fall shorter still when the requirement is placed on an inherently high contrast product such as a lith film.

Traditionally, an artist who wanted a continuous tone lith film would attempt to trick the film into providing a longer tonal scale by processing it in a diluted Dektol paper developer in the 1:4 to 1:10 range. Others would make esoteric mixtures of both paper and film developers in an effort to control the tonal scale and still be able to use this inexpensive film. Everyone encountered the same problems.

♦ High-contrast (high-density) and loss of highlight and/or shadow separation (low density).

♦ Inconsistent densities between the test strips and the final positive and negative film

♦ An uneven or mottled appearance throughout the tonal scale

♦ The need to constantly refresh the developer to maintain consistency

Dave Soemarko's self-assigned task was to develop a working technique in which he could fully control the inter-positive in making an enlarged duplicate negative. The beauty of Soemarko's formula is that it allows the artist to get that low-contrast inter-positive needed for the final negative step in an orderly and consistent manner. His LC-1 inter-positive technique also allows you to use lith film and develop it so that it has a very long tonal scale from toe to shoulder.

Being able to use lith film is a bonus because it comes in a wide array of sheet sizes and rolls, and it is also affordable, even on a student's budget. The film in the first test is Arista Premium Halftone Supreme (APHS), which is readily available. In a more recent test, Soemarko worked with Arista Premium Halftone (APH), which is less expensive than APHS but yields similar (some think better) results. The APH test is described at the conclusion of this section.

Dave goes into a lot of detail in Judy Seigel's *Post-Factory Photography Journal* describing his entire investigation and how he arrived at his formulas. If you're interested in seeing how his mind works, I refer to that specific issue, #2. Following is a description of the salient points of the process. LC-1 is made from 2 stock solutions and water and is manipulated to suit the particular stage of the process you're dealing with, inter-positive or negative.

The Standard LC-1 Formula

Stock A

750 ml	Distilled water (125° F)
3.0 g	Metol
60 g	Sodium sulfite
3.0 g	Hydroquinone

Distilled cold water to make 1 liter

Stock B

10 g	Sodium bisulfite

Distilled cold water to make 1 liter

Once the separate stock solutions have been made, they are mixed together in equal or unequal amounts and diluted with additional water to make a 10-part formula. An example of this would be a 2:1:7 formula: 2 parts of Stock A —1 part of Stock B—7 parts water.

In a developer with a stronger alkalinity such as Dektol, which contains sodium carbonate, the processing speed is faster. The contrast of values is greater and this combination results in accelerated exhaustion of the developer, which, in turn, leads to uneven development.

With Soemarko's LC-1 formula and a mix of the preceding 2:1:7 solution, Dave made multiple tests with the same exposure and development and found that each negative was nearly identical to the other. There was no mottling, or uneven values, proving that the development was well controlled. He presoaked his film for 3 minutes and processed for 5 to7 minutes and achieved a gradation of 21 steps. The inter-positive was low in contrast indicating that he could place all of the tonal separation in the original negative into the inter-positive and go for the higher contrast positive in the negative stage

by extending his development time. This low contrast of the inter-positives is a great help in avoiding compressed values when making the negative.

For a second example with the same negative, Dave changed his formula to 2:2:6, a proportional mix that indicated an increase in the sodium bisulfite portion of the formula. Because sodium bisulfite is an acid, the contrast is reduced. In his test, the inter-positive development was slower and the toe to shoulder curve was nearly linear. If you find unevenness in your developed film, simply add more of the Stock A to your 10-part formula. Density will increase with this change. If you wish to maintain the same low contrast, you will need to add more of Stock B.

The Rule: *The more acid, or bisulfite, in the formula, the less active the developer, and the less contrast in the film. The reverse of this rule is also true.*

An example of this showing a modification to the 10-part formula is indicated in the following way. You have a formula of 2:2:6 giving you the right contrast but showing unevenness in the film. You would want to compensate for this and so you would change the formula to 4:4:2. This new proportion eliminates the unevenness but may give you too much contrast for the inter-positive. An additional modification to a 4:5:1 formula, with a little extra bisulfite, makes a less active developer and reduces the contrast formula, providing the correct results. For almost any inter-positive on lith film, a formula of 2:1:7 or 2:2:6 is going to give you good results with a 5-minute development. Many users find that a formula dilution of 2:3:5 will give a linear response for a longer exposure range, which can be very useful for in-camera use of lith film.

The principle is the same for making both the inter-positive and the final negative. In the inter-positive, a low-density range is sought as a way of adjusting the overall density levels of the negative and having both the top and bottom end of the scale usable.

In the final inter-positive negative stage, the tonal range is attached to the process and you would likely want to use a formula indicating a stronger developer or a LC-1 formula of 2:0:8 with a 6-minute development.

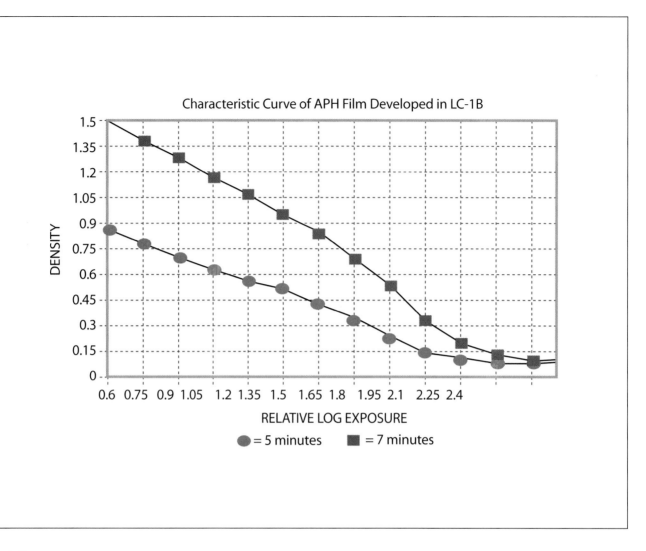

Figure 4–16
Soemarko APH Curve LC-1B Chart

The two-stock LC-1 formula is particularly useful if you are testing a different high-contrast lith film. Once you have worked out the combination and dilution that works best for your film type, it is simple to combine the Stock A and B parts and then dilute them with water before use. Combining Stocks A and B makes the solution less alkaline and extends its storage life.

Figure 4–16 shows the characteristic curves for APH lith film developed with the LC-1B formula at 68° F with continuous agitation for 5 and 7 minutes development times. Note that the film can be developed for linear characteristics or the more typical S-curve characteristic. By closely monitoring the exposure and development, you are able to place the tonalities in the negative to the desired section of the characteristic curve.

Soemarko's LC-1-B Low-Contrast, Formula for APH Film for both Inter-Positive and Negative Production

750 ml	Distilled water (125° F)
4 g	Metol
80 g	Sodium sulfite
4 g	Hydroquinone
20 g	Sodium bisulfite

Distilled cold water to make 1 liter of stock solution

To use: Dilute between 1:5 and 1:10. Develop film between 5 and 10 minutes at 75° F. The LC-1B is similar to an LC-1 dilution of 2:3:5 but with more sulfite and bisulfite added in proportion.

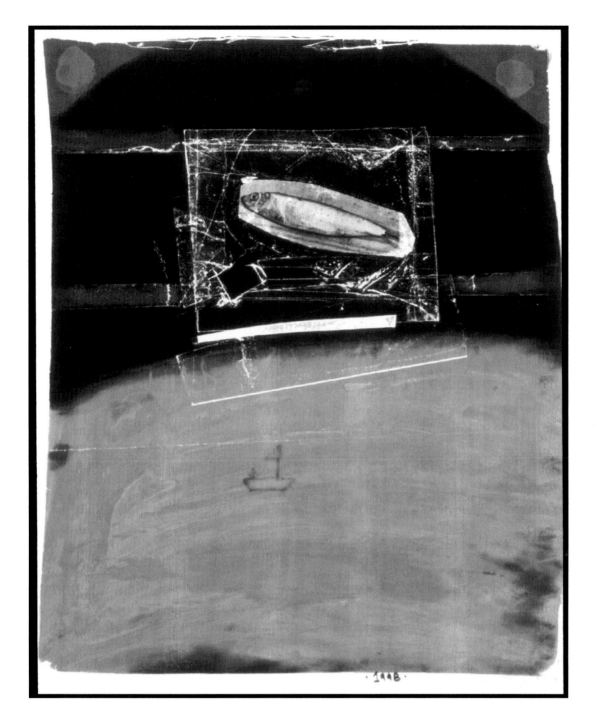

Figure 4–17

Pablo Ortiz Monasterio, *Comida*, 1998—film montage with toners

I first saw *Comida* during Pablo's visiting artist lecture at The Art Institute of Boston. It was a bit of a surprise as my knowledge of his work was limited to his prodigious documentary projects in Mexico City. *Comida* was created by making a montage of film and incorporating toners in post-print work.

(Courtesy of the author)

The Digital Options: An Odd History, Workflows for Negatives & the Digital Arts

OVERVIEW & EXPECTATIONS

I've learned a lot. In 2001, in the Overview and Expectations portion of this chapter I wrote, *"I am a relative neophyte tourist to this new planet in the universe of art. In fact, until eight years ago I had resolutely expressed a nagging distrust of the computer, not only as an art-making tool, but also as a device that you would consider letting into the house. Then I realized I couldn't communicate with my friends if I didn't have e-mail and now I am convinced that the photography programs of the near future will be obsolete if their labs are not digitally integrated."*

So much else has changed since then. In the past few years I have taken to carrying my life around on a laptop. All of my files from The Art Institute of Boston are in my computer instead of taking up space in my office. I conduct my business life on line, my images are all catalogued, and when I lecture my presentations are made with a digital projector, all of my music comes from iTunes, and the only person I send an actual letter to, one with a stamp on it, is to George Tice who has managed to avoid using e-mail.

At The Art Institute of Boston, I add digital offerings to the curriculum each semester and the number of students with outstanding Photoshop skills increases with each incoming class. Most of our students, as is the case everywhere I suspect, are now actively creating work digitally in black & white and color, using inter-disciplinary mixes of still and moving imagery programs, and making negatives on ceramic-coated acetates for alternative process printing. Our color facility, with its large format RA-4, 4 minute dry-to-dry, print processor, is now the romantic "wet lab" and I can count on two hands the number of students working full time in the gang black and white labs.

As much as I have become dependent on the digital world, I am aware, as I wrote in the allegorical introduction to this book, that it would take just one decent solar storm, like the one in 1859, and 17 hours and 40 minutes later, odds are, every hard drive on the receiving end of that solar flare would instantly become a fine door-stop.

Figure 5–1

Christopher James, *Niépce Grab Shot at Le Gras*, 2007—40 × 60 pigment on rag

I was putting together a presentation for one of my classes and decided that it might be interesting to produce a conceptual example of the "first and the most recent" photograph made . . . in this case Niépce's view through his studio window at le Gras in 1826 (acknowledged as the first photograph) and my appropriation of it at 5 pixels per inch and printed digitally.

(Courtesy of the author and GEH/International Museum of Photography)

It's true, I have embraced the "dry darkroom" of digital and have become quite expert at printing beautiful Piezo prints, using pigment-based inks on rag stock, and making really serviceable alternative process negatives on ceramic-dust-coated ink jet film. However, and here is where I might become provocative, I am disturbed by what I'll call "the mushy democracy" of digital imaging. As we all become as "good" as our software and hardware, I believe we are heading backwards as a medium . . . to the days of the salon, when being "good" at making the print was all that was necessary to be a "good" photographic artist.

That said, I am also seeing a resurgent passion for the alternative process image and am observing students use their digital imaging skills to produce powerful visual statements where context, syntax, and content are in harmony with their handmade print intentions. They are using its best, and distinctive, qualities to produce negatives and prints that are as unique as any created in any discipline. This is good.

There are many digital artists whose work I greatly admire. Some create from their camera-initiated images, while others appropriate, and re-create, from the inspirations they discover in life. Then there are many, like myself, who love the handmade photographic image but realize that many of the technical tar pits, the laborious tasks that consume creative time and energy, could be filled in with the assistance of digital technology, i.e., CMYK separations for gum bichromate.

Figure 5–2 A & B

Jerry Uelsmann, *Water Angel*, 1992 & *Threshold*, 1999

Jerry Uelsmann's working style can be compared to that of a concertmaster thoroughly engaged in the music he is conducting. Water Angel is a perfect example of his ability to create multiple layers of imagery on a single sheet of photographic paper with multiple enlargers and negatives. In a recent email to me, Jerry wrote, "*I'm still in the dark. . . . room! The water angel image has only been done as a silver gelatin print . . . I assume after I go to the great darkroom in the sky it might be done in ink jet.*" To make a point about the process of the artist, I asked Jerry to make a piece using Photoshop and was not the least bit surprised that the image he made continued to exemplify his personal vision.

(Courtesy of the artist)

Figure 5–3
Matt Belanger, *Google Search for Weapons of Mass Destruction*, 2005
Art Institute of Boston graduate, Matt Belanger, made this timely and metaphorically dense.
(Courtesy of the artist)

These separations, which once took an exceedingly long time in the lab, can now be accomplished with several clicks of the mouse in Photoshop, and printed out, at very high resolution, on acetate ink jet film. It is significant that the first edition detailed a 26-step sequence for making CMYK ink jet separations for gum bichromate contact negatives. In this new edition I can tell you how to do the same thing in a few very simple steps . . . changing the mode to CMYK and clicking > Channels.

Additionally, near-monthly advances in printing technology now permit digital film reproduction capable of exceeding the parameters of the traditional negative. I can also mimic pyro-developed film tonalities with color layers and assign functioning "curves" for individual alternative processes.

I have done my best to make these topics understandable and to refrain from the usual maze and avalanche of digital tech-talk. If I have learned one thing from the first edition's version of this chapter, it is to be very concise about "why" you are using digital technologies for negatives and prints and to discuss specific software as little as possible. I will not spend a lot of time on specific programs because their life span is so brief . . . on average about 18 months before you must buy a new version. In an alternative process book it is a more than a bit

ironic to be concerned with being out of date before the book comes out. Besides, there are a host of books now on the market now that deal with digital photography more thoroughly than I could hope to do in this book . . . I'll tell you which ones I think are best.

During my brief history of learning, and teaching, in the digital world I have discovered that most writers, and teachers, assume far too much prior knowledge on the part of readers and students. Just a single missing piece of the puzzle in getting from point A to point B in a digital workflow nearly eliminates the possibility of the student ever getting to point B. Sophisticated software programs, as you well know, are quite content to sit on your monitor screen forever, mocking your ignorance, until you provide the correct "*noun*" to go with the correct "*verb*" to complete a digital action. This is the sort of thing that causes rational, and intelligent, people to have irrational and pointless conversations with their computers.

With that in mind, I have attempted to make this chapter, not just entertaining, but also as simple as possible . . . and nearly devoid of information that could make it be obsolete in a few months. You will find some pretty interesting history of how digital technology arrived in our lives, an explanation of what a digital negative is and how to make one easily without melting your brain, and I'll also discuss alternative-process Curves, color layers, and give a quick lesson in making CMYK and CMY gum separations. I'll conclude the chapter with an editorial of my view on the state of the digital arts and digital criticism. If you are less than comfortable traveling in the digital world, this chapter should make you feel better about the trip.

A LITTLE HISTORY

The Loom, The Digesting Mechanical Duck & Sketchpad

In 1984, about a year after Apple had introduced *Lisa*, its first interactive computer-operating system, I was watching a loom weaver in Benares (*Varanasi*), India, create a tapestry that he would likely make repeatedly throughout his life. A thick stack of linked and battered cards, with an abstract pattern of punched holes, provided the answer to the question . . . "How does the color and design of a fabric remain the same from generation to generation?" These cards were similar to those found in the early room-sized computers, the ones with the typed warning: *Do not fold, spindle or mutilate.*

The well-worn cards were integrated into the operation of the weaver's loom and they determined which *shed* would rise in a particular pattern sequence and which wouldn't. The shed's position controlled which of the vertical warp strands of the rug in progress were back or forward in relation to the horizontal *weft* thread strands that the weaver was sliding his or her shuttle through. These rows of fibers, stacked one upon the other, produced the patterns and colors within the fabric.

The action was essentially a binary on/off system.

The evolution of the computer is as complex as the computer itself but several individuals particularly important in its development. We'll begin with Jacques de Vaucanson (1709–1782), whose creative genius was legendary in Europe in the 1700s. Vaucanson was known for his *automatons*, fiendishly complicated mechanical

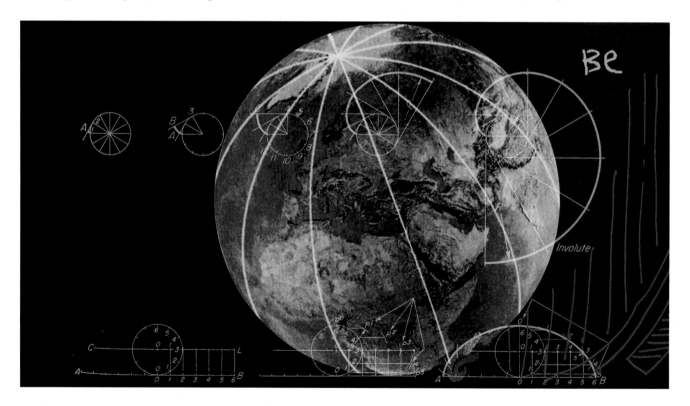

Figure 5–4
John Marshall (*from the book Blasted Bits,* 1997)
A double page spread from John Marshall's inkjet on paper book "*Blasted Bits.*"
(Courtesy of the artist)

Figure 5–5
Christopher James, *Loom*, Benares, India, 1985
In 1984 I was watching a loom weaver in Benares (*Varanasi*), India, create a tapestry that he would likely make repeatedly throughout his life. A thick stack of linked and battered cards, with an abstract pattern of punched holes, provided the answer to the question . . . "How does the color and design of a fabric remain the same from generation to generation?" These cards were similar to those found in the early room-sized computers . . . the ones with the typed warning: *Do not fold, spindle or mutilate.*
(Courtesy of the author)

devices that mimicked actual life. He referred to his art form as *anatomie mouvante* or "moving anatomy" and, among his creations, besides a life-size tambourine and a flute-playing shepherd, was an extraordinary device he called the *Digesting Duck*. Vaucanson's duck consisted of over 1000 intricate parts and was able to wag its tail, eat a fish, digest it, and eventually excrete it in the same manner as a real duck. This feat was accomplished through a digestive tract made of a rubber material called *caoutchouc* that Vaucanson himself had actually discovered in South America in 1731.

Vaucanson then made a machine to manufacture the digestive tubing for his ducks. As an aside, if you're interested in how this idea might play out in a science fiction novel, pick up a copy of Phillip Dick's, *Do Androids Dream of Electric Sheep*, the inspiration for director Ridley Scott's magnificent film, *Blade Runner (1982)*.

Vaucanson's genius was well regarded and Philibert Orry, the general finance comptroller, asked him if he might be able to apply his odd intellectual abilities in service of the troubled French silk industry. In response, Vaucanson revolutionized the making of all fabrics by inventing the first automated loom (1740–1745) and then improving on it by controlling the automation of the system (1750). This enhanced machine was, coincidentally, regulated by a system of those punch cards I mentioned earlier, making it possible to repeat designs through a form of automation rather than remembrance. As a bonus, anyone could learn to use it without a great deal of training.

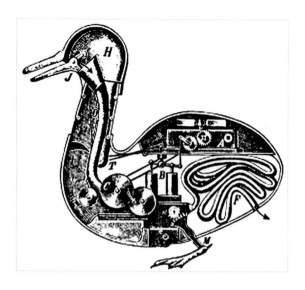

Figure 5–6
Vaucanson's Duck, c.1730

Vaucanson was the inventor of the first automated loom in 1745 but he was better known for his *anatomie mouvante*. Among his creations, besides a life-size tambourine and a flute-playing shepherd, was an extraordinary device he called the *Digesting Duck*. Vaucanson's duck consisted of over 1000 intricate parts and was able to wag its tail, eat a fish, digest it, and eventually poop on the lawn just like a real duck. This feat was accomplished through a digestive tract made of a rubber material called *caoutchouc* that Vaucanson himself had actually discovered in South America in 1731.

Jacquard's Loom

A bit later, in 1801, Joseph-Marie Jacquard (1752–1834) enhanced the concept and created a simplified automatic loom, inspired in part by earlier inventions by the Frenchmen Basile Bouchon (1725), Jean Falcon (1728) and Jacques Vaucanson. This concept totally remodeled the weaving industry through a *linked* sequence of punch cards. In Jacquard's loom, each hole in the punch cards corresponded to a hook called a "*bolus.*" This bolus hook raised or lowered a harness that directed and supported the warp thread so that the weft would lie above or below it. This alternating sequence allowed the pattern to be realized in the final fabric design.

Although Jacquard actually invented his loom in 1790, he kept it hidden due to the social turmoil of the French Revolution (1788–1804). When things quieted down a little, Jacquard was asked to demonstrate his machine to the French government. Seeing the value in mass standardization with the new loom, the government gave Jacquard a healthy annual stipend and declared that his invention was now public property. Unfortunately for Jacquard, his loom was so efficient and simple to use that it resulted in his looms, and his person, being beaten up by angry traditional silk weavers. The Jacquard loom was the punch-card loom design that I observed in India.

Mr. Babbage Lived On Cabbage

Jacquard's innovations led to the steam-driven punch-card systems of Charles Babbage's (1791–1871) *Difference* and *Analytical* Engine calculators. Babbage was a devilishly complicated man who immersed himself in invention, philosophy, politics, statistical analysis, and industry. In a curious merging of coincidences . . . he was also Sir John Herschel's roommate when they were young students at Cambridge.

His inventions, and creations, included the cow-catcher adaptation to the front of railroad steam locomotives, uniform postal rates with the British "Penny Post," occulting illumination in lighthouses, a submarine, colored lighting for the theater, the ophthalmoscope, and his never constructed, but infamous, Analytical Engine—the very first computer. The English humorist E. Clerihew Bentley (1875–1956), the inventor of the "clerihew," an irregular form of humorous biographical verse, composed this little piece in Babbage's honor:

> *Mr. Babbage*
> *Lived entirely on cabbage*
> *He used his head, rather than his thumbs*
> *In inventing his machine for doing sums*

Babbage would have been a strange person to have as a neighbor. He was, as Max Byrd wrote in his book, *Shooting the Sun* (2004), "*one of those irascible and colorful eccentrics that the damp, un-weeded, garden of England seems to throw up in endless profusion.*"

Babbage was enthralled by fire and once had himself baked in an oven, set at over 250°F . . . apparently without appreciable harm to his person. Babbage detested music as well. His public condemnation of that form of expression, coupled with his curmudgeonly and incessantly cranky behavior incited his

Figure 5–11

Ben Sloat, *Gerontion, 2006*

Ben teaches digital media for me at The Art Institute of Boston and is one of the new generation of artists utilizing their critical studies skills to create powerful visual statements. Gerontion is derived from a T.S. Eliot poem of the same name. Playing with religious imagery as well as with photographic portraiture, this piece references a variety of arts, including Renaissance painting, contemporary photography, & vintage Japanese prints.

(Courtesy of the artist)

D-max (maximum density) of the negative, you can provide yourself with a negative that is far easier to print in an alternative process. Add to that negative a color layer that mimics the UV screening pyro tint and you have greatly improved your chances for a good printing experience. This control well exceeds the speed limits one can master in a traditional darkroom environment, which remains dependent on how well everything went during the original shoot. Essentially, there are three steps to a fine digital negative.

Step 1 Start with an image that is digital to begin with, i.e., a RAW file from a digital camera, or one that is made into a digital file through a scanning process. This scanning stage can be done professionally at your local camera store as they are now in the business of digital photography, instead of film processing. There are also a lot of transparencies out there that need to be scanned and placed on a CD. This is an inexpensive and very good option most of the time. You can pay more at a service bureau but the quality, due to the sophistication of the equipment everyone has, will be comparable. A service bureau would be advisable if you intend to make a mural and need quality that exceeds anything you can afford to do at home or can have done at the local camera shop. Another option is to buy your own scanner and do it yourself. Today's home scanning units are elegantly simple, affordable, and first rate. However, you need to be aware that a flatbed scanner is not the ideal piece of equipment for scanning negatives . . . especially if the unit does not have film holders or rear light projection designed specifically for negatives.

Step 2 Once you have the file in hand, it's time to put it into Photoshop, and begin to create an ideal negative (*where you simply invert the image from the positive on the monitor*) for the particular process you intend. This may require loading a specific curve profile for each individual. These curves are readily available on the Internet and many paper and ink manufacturers have them available as free downloads from their web sites. Most people I know are happy making their own, but if that idea makes your brain itch you can also find sample curves on Malin Fabbri's excellent alternative process web site: www.alternativephotography.com

Figure 5–12

David Stinchcomb, *Bandalier*, 2006—Ziatype and reversed negative with color layer

Oklahoma photographer, David Stinchcomb, generated this great Ziatype from his digital negative that was given a color layer to enhance the tonalities in the print.

(Courtesy of the artist)

Step 3 Output the work to provide a contact negative for printing. This output can be done quite simply, and very well, with Pictorico OHP film and a decent quality ink-jet printer with water-resistant inks. Again, you can add color masks to your new negative to make printing with a UV light source even better than you might imagine. I'll chart out the step-by-step workflow for this later in the chapter.

In the past, output of this order had to be delegated to service bureaus, which had the right (and expensive) hardware, but relatively little experience in generating contact negatives for alternative process printing. Few service bureaus were accustomed to working with individual artists, or in black and white, so you had to go to them with low expectations and a clear concept of what you wanted. In my experience this hardly ever worked out well.

In the first edition, I wrote, *"In the near future, high-quality digital negatives will probably be quite inexpensive and easily done at home, manipulated in a Photoshop program and printed out as film on a home printer at ridiculously high dpi."*

Here we are a few years later and many of us are easily generating our negatives at home for about the same cost as making a print on a piece of quality rag stock. Almost everything else I wrote about your specific digital needs in the first edition has become irrelevant, so I'm not going to make that mistake again . . . we're going to keep this simple. Here are a few simple basic needs, before we get into digital negative production.

Some Basic Tech Needs

You will need a computer with a large hard drive for software applications and storage. The monitor for this computer should be large enough for you to see what you're doing and of sufficient quality to render a calibrated screen faithfully. Consider a hard drive with 100GB to be adequate. You will also need a minimum of 1GB of RAM (Random Access Memory) to work on large files, especially those with many layers in 16-bit mode, although 2GB would be best. The bottom line regarding RAM is to have as much as possible. A good rule of thumb: allocate enough RAM to accommodate 4 times the file size. Obviously, file size is dictated by the physical size of the image. Other factors include whether it's a 8 or 16 bit per channel file, the number of layers, masks, alpha channels, how complex the image is, and a host of other things you will learn as you go. Photoshop will use as much RAM as you dedicate to an image while you're working on it and then it will begin using free hard drive space. If you make a 16-bit scan of a 6 × 4.5 negative, at 2500 ppi, the file size will be around 321 MB. Photoshop will need close to 1.3 GB to edit this file. You get the concept here . . . load up on the RAM when you buy a computer.

Both Apple/Mac and Windows allow a nice workflow with Photoshop, but my preference, and that of most everyone I know making digital imagery, is a Mac platform. I'm not as fussy as a lot of my contemporaries, and find that my laptop is perfect for almost every task I ask it to perform as long as I don't attempt to be fast with a finger-pad in humid weather. I recommend having an attached mouse for any delicate work. I realize that a laptop's not the ideal for image editing and color calibration, but my needs are generally monochromatic, or focused upon generating digital negatives for alternative contact printing. My brother-in-law, Rick Mandelkorn, is an amazing architectural photographer and his clients are as demanding as he is . . . he needs large and perfect computers, monitors, and printers . . . I do not. Don't buy what you don't need.

This is serious. You need a back-up hard drive for storing all your images. You must have one of these and it should be large enough to store an unlimited number of images in various stages of completion. It is critical that you get on a schedule for backing up. When I'm working daily, I back up daily. Otherwise, I back up every Sunday morning while having coffee, playing vicious backgammon games with my wife, and reading the newspaper. All you need to do is lose your hard drive once (yes, I have) and you'll never be without a back up drive again . . . you just have to remember to use it.

Right now I have a 100-gigabyte CMS ABS portable hard drive that lives in a safety deposit box, a 100 gigabyte LaCie Rugged drive that bangs around in my studio, and a mini 12 gigabyte Memorex personal drive that I use to back up while I'm working. The CMS drive is lightweight, very portable, can be partitioned for multiple computer back-ups, and can serve

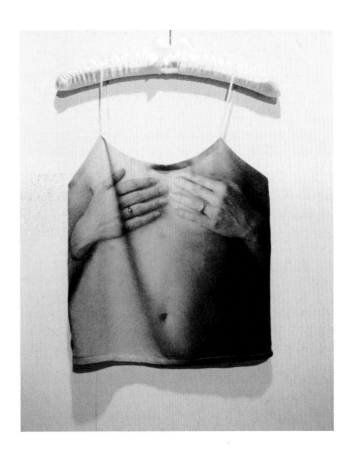

Figure 5–13

Nancy Breslin, *Modesty*, 2005—ink-jet on silk
Modesty began with digital shots of Nancy's back and of her hands over her chest. She used Photoshop to change the images so the whole camisole would "read" as a 3-d torso, and then printed the two images on silk from Color Textiles (17" wide roll silk, which comes backed with paper so it will run through my Epson 4800 printer). After printing, the paper was removed and the silk was briefly soaked in water with a little fabric softener, and then dried. She then cut the pattern using one of her camisoles as a template, sewed it together, and used thin ribbon for straps.
(Courtesy of the artist)

as a start-up drive should you crash your entire system. It's relatively inexpensive and reliable and their customer service is personal. You might ask, why can't I just back up on CDs? You can, but if you need to do an edit, unless you are using a RW (rewrite) CD, you'll have to download your CD's content, make your edit, and burn a new CD. This is politely referred to as a royal pain in the expense.

You will need a good printer. I won't waste a lot of time being diplomatic here. I have used Epson printers for years and have zero complaints or problems with them . . . as long as you use them on a regular basis. The new upscale home lab printer, the Epson 2400, with its K3 Ultrachrome ink sets, superior profiles, and print management system, is about as perfect as you can get for the investment. I have no doubt that within a short period, in fact by the time you read this, the perfect desktop compatible 2400 will have been replaced by newer Epson printer that will be even better.

Other issues to consider: The environment you work in, the paper that you use for proofing and final prints, your color calibration tools and software, the esoteric profiles for specific third party papers, and the economical bulk ink feed systems found in many dedicated digital imaging texts and on the Internet.

Basic Math and Reading Recommendations:

The image you scan into Photoshop will be made up of pixels rather than grains of silver. In order to achieve a continuous tonal range in the final negative, the tonal scale, from black to white, is assigned hundreds of separate levels of pixels and tonalities. Each one of the pixels and levels consists of distinct triggers, and each trigger is either *on* or *off/black* or *white*. When the triggers are activated, each pixel will have an impressive number of separate on or off switches that will determine whether an *on* or *off* switch will print a black or a white dot. That means that each separate pixel is capable, in black and white, of looking like gray when next to another pixel. There is no actual gray dot; just the illusion of gray dots due to the relationship of black and white dots.

Note: In RGB (red-green-blue) mode the pixel is generated by a numeric value (0–255) indicating a level of brightness for the red, green, and blue components. A pixel with a numeric value of 255–255–0 would have fully saturated red and green values but no blue values (in this case, yellow would be the resulting color). This is an entirely different discussion.

If your intention is to enlarge that 4" × 5" negative to a 16" × 20" negative, you will have to scan your original negative at 4 times your intended printer resolution. A 4" × 5" black and white negative scanned at 1200 ppi for printing a 16" × 20" at 300 ppi (pixels per inch) image is mathematically figured out like this:

♦ 4" (*neg. dimension*) × 4 = 16" (*new neg. size*) × 300 ppi = 4800 pixels

♦ 5" (*neg. dimension*) × 4 = 20" (*new neg. size*) × 300 ppi = 6000 pixels

♦ 4800 × 6000 = 28,800,000 pixels (*16" × 20" negative*)

One of the constraints when working with alternative printing processes is that the print cannot be larger than the negative, because the prints are made by contact. If a larger print is desired, then you need to make a larger negative. This is accomplished by creating a copy negative in the darkroom (now a small problem, as many of the films that were exceptionally good for this task are no longer made) or by producing a digital negative on a computer using digital imaging software.

Adobe Photoshop is the industry standard for this task and essential to your knowledge base. Face it, if you are going to function as a visual artist you will need to know how to manage this software program. As I'm writing this, Photoshop CS3 has just been released and I've been able to work with it several times. Once I can afford a copy, I will likely be as happy with it, as I have been with every Photoshop program since the beginning. Learn Photoshop software.

An understanding of resolution is important. You will also need to clearly comprehend the relationship between a negative's density and Photoshop's histogram for that negative. The histogram is a graphic representation of the density range within a negative and is essentially a densitometric map of the image. Photoshop's *Levels* and *Curves* commands can alter the histogram to change the appearance of your image. It's important to have a working knowledge of those commands as well. That's about it. Oh . . . and be very conservative about your enthusiasm for using any of the filters. It's too easy and contributes heavily to the mushy democracy concept . . . you do not want your work to look like everyone else's work.

Figure 5–14

Allen Meier, *AIB Thesis*, 2006—digital

Before moving to digital imaging to create his work, Allen spent his time in the woods constructing elaborate sets of found nature to make his tribal-based self-portraits. Recent work incorporates the respect for reality with the magic realism tools found in his digital toolbox.

(Courtesy of the artist)

There are many excellent books written about how to make your way in the world with Adobe Photoshop by your side. Many of these books give good, solid, basic information on these and other digital topics and I absolutely recommend that you purchase one and use it. In particular, study the chapters relating to resolution, the histogram, levels, and curves. As well, I recommend buying only what you can comprehend so that you don't get overly frustrated. Among my favorites as the best of what is available now:

◆ **George DeWolfe**, George DeWolfe's *Fine Digital Photography Workshop*, McGraw-Hill Osborne Media; 1st edition, 2006). *This book is excellent and written by a master printer. It is recommended for advanced intermediate and higher readers.*

◆ **Dick Arentz**, *Platinum & Palladium Printing: 2nd Edition*, Focal Press, Elsevier, 2005. *This is a wonderful book and absolutely thorough on all levels. I mention it in this chapter because of Mark Nelson's digital negative section in the appendix.*

◆ **Mike Wooldridge, Linda Wooldridge**, Teach Yourself Visually Photoshop CS2 (Paperback), 2005. *This book is recommended for the beginner and is outstanding in that it shows you the way with pictures. In other words, it shows you in step sequences the way your screen should look when you're doing things correctly.*

◆ **John Paul Caponigro**, *Adobe Photoshop Master Class: John Paul Caponigro, 2nd Edition*, Adobe Press; 2 edition (February 14, 2003). *John Paul's book is about as thorough as you can get and highly readable.*

Figure 5–15
Olivia Parker, *Game Edge*, 1995
This image is a representation of Olivia Parker's
digital work in color.
(Courtesy of the artist)

◆ **Dan Burkholder**, *Making Digital Negatives for Contact Printing* (2nd ed.), Bladed Iris Press. *This book is written for people with knowledge and patience. It eliminates a tremendous amount of guesswork and gives recipes for the successful creation of digital negatives. Dan's process is excellent for those with a sound knowledge base.*

◆ **Steve Weinrebe**, *Adobe Photoshop & the Art of Photography*, Thomson Delmar Learning (2008). This is a new addition to the library of digital books that approach the art of digital printing with more than technique and software in mind. Two of the things I like best about this book are the interviews with people who really practice the art of digital imaging, in their work and life, and the abundance of informative illustrations.

MAKING ALTERNATIVE PROCESS NEGATIVES WITH INK-JET COMPATIBLE FILMS

The Pictorico OHP Solution

In the first edition I went into a lengthy discussion of what you needed to make a decent digital negative, what you had to spend to get the right equipment to do it, and all of the myriad steps you had to take to get from where you were to where you wanted to go . . . out in the sun with your new contact negative to make a new print. Not this time around . . . My intent is to simplify this process so that you can achieve a decent level of success quickly and easily.

First, you need a digital file shot in camera . . . preferably a RAW file (and no, I'm not getting into that in this book) or a scan of a negative, transparency, or an existing opaque object, or an image made on the scanner itself. Keep in mind; a large final print requires starting with a large digital file with a great deal of digital information.

You will need to get this digital information into Photoshop and save it as a tiff, psd (Photoshop), jpg, or fractal file. Do not place a lot of reliance upon jpg files as they tend to deteriorate each, and every, time you save one. The jpg format is best for small, 72–150 ppi, files you would use for such activities as *posting* an image to a web site or attaching one to an email. For making a negative you will use for an alternative process contact you will want a file that is a minimum of 300 ppi in resolution. I generally scan all of my original film negatives at 4000 ppi and work from there. Keep this in mind; if you need to increase the size of your image file in Photoshop, that act is called *interpolation.** If you want to go larger and smaller at will, without being visually penalized, invest in a software program that can convert your pixels to fractals. Google this wish, or purchase a software program called Genuine Fractals, to get the full story. Remember . . . *The scan is the essential element in deciphering and determining the final output size of the digital file.* To that end, I will recommend another book to you . . . *Start With a Scan* (2nd Edition), by Janet Ashford and John Odum.

The new digital file that you've created can then be fine-tuned as a positive . . . Clean it up with your spot healing brush and cloning tools, adjust your levels and curves, and generally get the image to a state on the screen where you are satisfied with it. Then you may assign a custom curve profile and *invert* the image to get to a negative state. This inverted negative file can be further enhanced with the addition of a color layer, easily printed on a sheet of Pictorico OHP film and successfully employed as a contact negative in any contact print-based alternative process. Let's begin with a simple exercise in taking a black and white image and converting it into a decent digital contact negative.

CREATING COLOR LAYERS ON INK-JET CONTACT NEGATIVES

Creating a UV Filter Color Layers for Contact Negatives

Pictorico OHP comes in two forms, one is the basic sheet film, which is relatively clear, like acetate, and holds a respectable amount of ink. There is new Pictorico OHP film called Ultra Premium, which has a slight white cast, comes on a roll, and accepts a bit more ink than the normal OHP. I prefer the newer version of OHP (Ultra) as it permits single sheets of film to make a negative rather than printing more than one (regular OHP) . . . one at 100% opacity, and another at anywhere from 40%—to 80% opacity and then registering those for your contact negative. Pictorico OHP is coated with a fine layer of ceramic dust that allows

a formidable amount of ink to be printed on it without streaking or settling on the film as a puddle.

The following is a simple workflow for assigning a color to Pictorico OHP film, via a color layer. This is a variation of several similar digital negative workflows, some of them far more complicated and profound in their approach to this topic than what you are about to learn. If you follow these steps, your negative will print as a reddish-yellow. It has been known for a very long time that these are colors block UV light and will assist your ability to attain a longer tonal scale in your final printed image versus printing with a monochromatic negative. This workflow was fine-tuned by my friend, David Stinchcomb. It works well for many processes and is surprisingly simple and easy to learn.

Before creating the color mask you may want to make some quick adjustments to the Adobe Photoshop Color Management Settings, found in the Edit Dialogue menu. David recommends the following action before making negatives. You must be in the RGB mode with color management turned off. (If Color Management isn't turned off, Photoshop will do strange things to the color mask.) The easiest way to do this is to go into Photoshop's "edit color" settings and, under working spaces, choose Colormatch RGB. Then go down to "color management policies" and make sure they are all turned off. Then save the settings under a title that you will recognize for future use with digital negatives . . . you can load this setting every time you make digital negatives.

If changing your Photoshop Color Management settings is a little too much adjusting for you, then don't worry too much about it. I keep my settings simple with Adobe RGB (1998) and let Photoshop determine the colors. Everyone works a bit differently, depending on his or her process and intentions. What works for you is what you should be doing.

A Quick Word on How Custom Curve Profiles Change Things

OK . . . I promised myself that I would avoid a digital dialogue that was too technical and compulsive because it just isn't the way I work in alternative processes. Besides,

---

* Interpolation is a term you often see "wish-listed" for high-end scanners. The promotional literature will generally tell you that the scanner has an optical resolution of a higher dpi of so and so. Interpolation is where the software does a slick thing and invents pixels for you. This is the opposite of optical resolution that actually describes the real pixels.

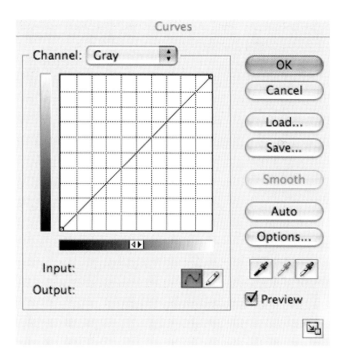

Figure 5–16
Curve Adjustment Dialogue Box
The Curves adjustment box is pretty simple. It's set up like a grid . . . when you open it, you will see a straight line running diagonally from the lower left corner to the upper right corner. The lower point on the line on the grid represents the dark end of the image. The higher point on the line on the grid represents the light end of the image.

as I've written earlier, there are plenty of books that will be delighted to show you all of the shiny bells and whistles dwelling in the realm of digital imaging. The following is a short explanation about Custom Curve profiles and the Curve adjustment dialogue box in Photoshop. The Curves adjustment dialogue box, found in the Menu > Image > Adjustments sequence, is one of the three most useful tools in Photoshop . . . especially if you intend to make your contact negatives digitally in Photoshop and print them out on Pictorico OHP.

The Curves adjustment box is pretty simple. It's set up like a grid . . . when you open it, you will see a straight line running diagonally from the lower left corner to the upper right corner. The lower point on the line on the grid represents the dark end of the image. The higher point on the line on the grid represents the light end of the image.

I'll try and make this as basic as possible. If you take the top right corner point of the diagonal line and make the diagonal steeper by moving the point to the left, you will increase image contrast by making the highest values whiter. If you take that same point and move it

Figure 5–17
Christopher James, *Pilar*, Mexico, 2005—pinhole on Type 55 Polaroid
This is a pinhole of my friend Pilar, one of the all-time best cooks in Mexico. *(Courtesy of the artist)*

down, you will make the line less steep, and simultaneously decrease image contrast. Best advice . . . be conservative when moving the line.

You can place, and lock, any point on the diagonal Curve adjustment line by simply clicking on any point along the line. By doing so, you prevent any tonality changes in the image that you are not initiating. The other way to lock in a point on the line is to place your curser (it looks like an eye dropper when the Curves box is open) on any value in your image that you want to change or preserve. Then simply press the > Apple—Command button and > click . . . this action will lock that point on the line. Here's how it might work . . . If you place, and lock, a point on the middle of the diagonal line and draw it up towards the top left corner, making a bow-shaped arc, you will increase the overall luminosity in all values except for extreme white and black ends, where the line is locked automatically. If you drag the locked point in the other direction, the opposite happens and luminosity decreases uniformly across the image.

If you want to make a digital negative that is customized for the process you are going to print with that negative, the easiest thing to do is load a Custom Curve profile. These profiles are available all over the Internet and are easy to find. This is a good way to begin learning how to work with custom curve profiles and it will give you an understanding of how to eventually begin making your own specifically for the process you are creating the negative for. To sum up, if you go to Curves and click Load, and you have one of these profiles on your hard drive, you can click on it and that profile will automatically load and change your Curve Dialogue Box. You may want to add a color layer (see below), but essentially that's all there is to it.

COLOR LAYER & CURVE WORKFLOW
For Pictorico OHP Ink Jet Film

In this example, you are starting with a black & white (grayscale) file and your intention is to prepare it for contact printing with a Pt Pd digital contact negative. You will be assigning a Custom Curve Profile to the image and then laying a color layer on the image to assist in enhancing the quality of the image.

Step 1 Open up your image in Photoshop and work with it until it meets your expectations and intentions.

Step 2 If you are in Grayscale, go to > Image, then to > Mode, and click > RGB

Step 3 Go to >Image, to >Adjustments, to >Curves and click >Load *

Step 4 Find the correct Curve Profile, in your Curve Profile Folder, for the process you will be working in, and click > Load to apply the curve * *

Step 5 Go to > Image, to > Adjustments, and click > Invert to make the negative

Step 6 Select > Layer from the menu

Step 7 Choose > New Fill Layer—and click > Solid Color

Step 8 Name this new Layer if you feel like it

Step 9 In the Mode box select > Color

Step 10 Keep the Opacity at 100%

Step 11 Click > OK

Step 12 You are now in the Color Picker window

Step 13 Look for the C-M-Y-K boxes in the lower right quadrant of that window

Step 14 Change the following CMYK numbers to: **C**-0, **M**-55, **Y**-55, **K**-0

Step 15 You will now be looking at a deep orange red version of your file.

Step 16 Go to > Image, to > Rotate Canvas, and > Flip your image horizontally * * *

Step 17 Print the file on Pictorico OHP at Highest Quality

Step 18 Let the Pictorico dry thoroughly before using. If it gets scratched . . . make another one. This is the beauty of making digital negatives . . . if it gets destroyed, it's easy to make a new one.

---

* With CS3, the Curves dialog box has witnessed its first major overhaul in 17 years. The Load button is gone. Instead, look for the "Load Preset" in the dialog box's pull-down menu for CS3. There may be a few other changes in how CS3 makes this Color Layer & Curve workflow work, but I suspect it will not be that complicated to figure out once CS3 is the standard.

** It's necessary to do this step before you invert the image. The reason is that it has a different effect on the tonal scale if you apply the curve to the positive as opposed to applying it to the negative.

*** This is the reason for Step P . . . you can take it or leave it . . . it's up to you. If you treat your sheet of Pictorico as a sheet of "real" film, you will notice that when you look at film that the image is reversed when you are looking at it from the emulsion side. Now, with Pictorico, or any other digitally printed film or acetate, the image is printed on the "emulsion" side of the film. Basically this means that when you go to make a contact print with an alternative process you will want your emulsion layer to be in contact with your sensitizer . . . the old law of the darkroom—emulsion to emulsion—make sense?

If you print Pictorico as though you were printing a digital print then the ink (emulsion) will be on the top of the film. When you put it in contact with the sensitized paper there will be an ever so slight difference, of the Pictorico film's width, between the emulsion and the paper. If, however, you reverse the image, you can lay the Pictorico emulsion directly on the sensitized paper. Granted, there are only a few processes, such as glossy albumen, when this careful planning for maximum sharpness will make a difference. I add it here because I know that some of you are really fussy and compulsive about your processes.

*** (Part 2) This is also an important step to keep in mind, as other forms of contact printing with digital materials—such as printing iron-on transfers—will necessitate flipping the image horizontally. To make your life easier, some printer dialog windows have a check box for flipping the image horizontally.

Grayscale to RGB

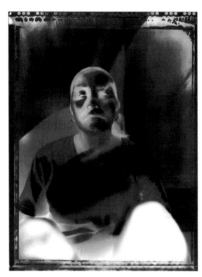

Ziatype Custom Curve Profile

Positive with Custom Curve Applied

Inverted w/ Custom Curve

Inverted w/ Color Layer Applied

Flipped For Contact Printing

Figure 5–18

Christopher James, *Pilar*, Mexico, 2005—Ziatype adjustment curve & color layer

This sequence illustrates the steps I would make taking my negative of Pilar from a grayscale, through the adjustment curve profile for Ziatype, and through the inverted step and color layer application.

(Courtesy of the artist)

MAKING DIGITAL SEPARATIONS FOR GUM BICHROMATE

Simple Workflows

🐢 **Note: I am including this information in both the Gum Bichromate and Digital Options chapters, as the information is important and I want to be sure you see it where it is relevant. In the gum chapter, I will add illustrations to show you what the changes actually look like.**

Gum bichromate artists have always had to accomplish a few tedious tasks before getting to the fun parts of the process with all the colors, multiple pass strategy, and creativity. Along with paper sizing, making CMYK (Cyan, Magenta, Yellow, & Black) negative separations was one of my least favorite things to do for a day in the studio. In the beginning you could shoot the separations in camera or move to the darkroom with an existing negative, and do your separations there with various film types, filters, and projection. Then along came digital imaging and Adobe Photoshop.

In the first edition of this book, I was all impressed with Photoshop v.5 and by the fact that I could make CMYK separations from a black and white source with only 26 primary steps . . . I called it the "speedy, non-fussy version." Now I'm using Photoshop CS2. Next month I'll probably be using Photoshop CS3. No matter, the fact is that with CS 2 or 3 I can now tell you how to go from a black and white (Grayscale) source to CMYK, or from a RGB source to CMY or Grayscale in a flash. Best of all, it really is speedy and simple . . . even for the technical neophyte.

These sequences are a good start. They are not the last word in making digital separations on Pictorico OHP film, going from Grayscale to CMYK, or RGB to CMY, nor is it inflexible. For instance . . . if you flip and exchange, Step E with Step C your separation negatives will look different. These particular workflows are ones that I worked out via e-mail exchanges with my friend, David Stinchcomb, in Oklahoma, Tony Gonzalez in New York, and xtine Burrough in California. Their brains don't melt when they think about things digital and they have been a great help in getting this information into a simple and easy to follow workflow. As with any alternative syntax, in any medium, individuals will adjust the steps in any process to suit their individual needs. Again, these are only workflow recommendations, but they work and they will certainly get you started.

One other thing to consider, the separations I am offering here are simple workflows that are designed for those who just want an easy way to generate their digital negatives. If you are really serious about perfection, and knowing everything there is to know about this subject, then you will want to consider graduating to advanced techniques, such as those developed by Dan Burkholder or Mark Nelson. Dan's web site (www.danburkholder.com) and book are amazingly complete and he has custom profiles and instructions for just about everything you will need.

GRAYSCALE TO C-M-Y-K GUM SEPARATION NEGATIVES

In this example, you start with a black & white (grayscale) file and your intention is to convert it into a set of CMYK negatives for use in gum bichromate printing. Again, I will duplicate this information in the gum bichromate chapter and will include illustrations.

Step 1 Open up your image file and work on it in Photoshop until you are satisfied with the image on the monitor. Save it with a label to indicate the particular set of CMYK negatives that you are making.

Step 2 Go to > Menu Bar, then to > Image, then to > Mode, then click > CMYK

Step 3 Go to > Image, to > Adjustments, to > Curves, and click > Load

Step 4 Find your > Gum Curve (the acv file) and > click Load.*

---

* Free Curve Profiles
The current and simple solution for getting a free Curve Profile for gum bichromate printing is to go to Malin Fabbri's excellent alternative process web site:
www.alternativephotography.com

Figure 5–19

Dan Burkholder, *Flatiron in Spring*, New York, 1997

Dan writes, "I print this as Pigment-Over-Platinum in which I combine digitally applied color pigments with hand-coated platinum. This image works beautifully for the POP process with the transition from the subtle color to the rich platinum blacks being particularly enchanting (for me anyway). This image is printed as a 9' × 13.5" print on Bergger Cot320 paper. In gallery talks and other presentations I describe this as my "homage to Steichen" image. I was trying to capture the same luxurious aquamarine color he used in his gum-over-platinum image.

(Courtesy of the artist)

Step 5 Go to > Image, then to > Adjustments, and click > Invert

Note: You have an option at this point in the process. Some gum printers want a set of negatives that are really "punchy" and have a good deal of contrast. If you are one of these gummists, then this is where you will go to > Image, then to > adjustment and click > Auto Levels. If you are seeking a more true to life CMYK interpretation of an actual color set, then you might want to skip this step. Try it both ways and see what you like. At some point in the process you will be adjusting levels, and by doing so, the contrast levels of your negatives. **Depending on the type of negative separation set you want, contrasty, or sort of true to life, you can adjust now or after you make the separation set.**

Step 6 Next, go to the palette that is probably on your screen, indicating Layers, Channels, and Paths. Click > Channels, and using the tiny arrow on the top right corner of the palette, click > Split Channels. Presto! . . . Photoshop will automatically create 4 separate, and distinct, B & W negatives for you. These are your CMYK separations.

Step 7 For each of these negatives . . . Go to > File and to > Save As. Title your negative to whatever you

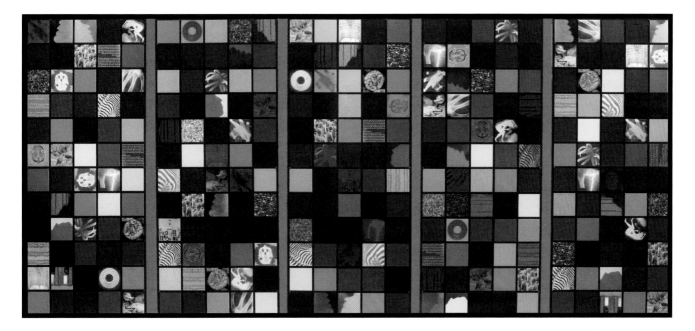

Figure 5–20

Yvette Drury Dubinsky, _Macro-Array_, 2006—cyanotype, VDB, & digital

Yvette's 5' × 12' collage, made for the Cortex biotechnology research building lobby, is taken from the readout of a micro-array . . . a platform for measuring gene activity in cells at a given time or situation. The colors are actually grey scale light intensities converted artificially to a color scale where red indicates an increase of gene activity and green shows lowered activity when comparing two cell types. The intermediate (other) colors show lesser degrees of heightened or lowered activity. Black shows unchanged genetic activity or genes showing no activity or such low activity that they cannot be measured by this technique. Dubinsky has scanned cyanotype and van dyke photograms, digitized them, and changed the colors of the original prints to the colors of an imagined micro-array.

(Courtesy of the artist)

need to name the file in order to remember it. I name my sets by the title of the image and what color negative I will be applying when gum printing. i.e., Cyan., Magenta, Yellow, or Black.

Step 8 Go to > Image, then to > Adjustments, and > click Levels and adjust them manually . . . bringing the left and right adjustment markers to the extreme ends of the Levels histogram. Do this step for each of your separations. Keep in mind that you are making a unique set of negatives here and that you can adjust the contrast of these negatives using Levels or Curves to suit your needs or the type of color you are using. This will make sense once you begin doing the actual gum printing.

Step 9 Go to > Image, to > Canvas Size, and give yourself a little white, black, or gray border to use for registration marks, pin holes, or other miscellaneous marks that will be your guide for gum registration. You can apply registration marks automatically with your printer in > Print With Preview . . . See Below.

Step 10 Print out the CMYK negative separations using Pictorico OHP ink-jet film.

R-G-B TO C-M-Y/GRAYSCALE GUM SEPARATION NEGATIVES

Note: In this example, you are starting with a color file, perhaps R-G-B, and your intention is to convert it into a set of C-M-Y grayscale negatives that you can use in your gum bichromate printing.

Step 1 Open up your image file and work on it in Photoshop until you are happy and content with your image. Save it with a label to indicate that it is specifically for the particular set of CMYK negatives you are making.

Step 2 Go to > Image on the Menu Bar, then to > Mode . . . then click > Multichannel

Step 3 Next, go to the palette, that is probably on your screen, indicating, "Layers," "Channels," and "Paths." Click >Channels and using the tiny arrow on the top right corner of the palette, in this box, click > Split Channels. You will automatically create 3 separate and distinct B & W positives for your CMY separations. Execute the following steps for each of the CMY files.

Step 4 Go to > Image, to > Adjustments, and click > Auto Levels. Or click > Levels instead and adjust your negative manually to your own taste. At some point in the process you will be adjusting levels, and by doing so, the contrast levels of your negatives. Depending on the type of negative separation set you want, contrasty, or sort of true to life, you can adjust now . . . or after you make your separation set.

Step 5 Go to > Image, to > Adjustments, and click > Invert

Step 6 Go to > Image, to > Adjustments, to Curves, and click > Load

Step 7 Find your Gum Curve and click > Load.

Step 8 Go to > Image, to > Canvas Size, and give yourself a white, or black, border to use for registration marks, pinholes, or other miscellaneous notes.

Figure 5–21

Jim Hughes, *Malabe Cheese Factory*, Brooklyn, NY—Alps dye-sublimation printer

Jim was the editor of *Camera 35* and *Camera Arts* magazines and the author of many notable books including the definitive biography of W. Eugene Smith. Long before most photographers, Jim entered into the digital arena and began creating with Photoshop and an Alps dye-sublimation printer. *(Courtesy of the artist)*

Figure 5–22
John Paul Caponigro, *Oriens*, 1999
John Paul is one of the primary leaders of the
digital photography revolution and is well
known for his masterful prints and his editions
of Adobe Photoshop Master Class.
(Courtesy of the artist)

Step 9 Go to > File and to > Save As and title your negative to whatever you need to name the file in
order to remember it. I label mine by the title of
the image and what color negative I will be
applying when gum printing.

Step 10 Check your levels one last time and proceed to
print out the negative separations using Pictorico
OHP ink-jet film.

THE DIGITAL ARTS:
A SECOND EDITION EDITORIAL

The digital arts may always be a weird sort of "waiting-
room" where the thrills and options of the new tools are
not enough, or perhaps all too much, for the work to be
respected as a legitimate art. The reality of everyone
needing to have the latest and greatest upgrades, every
18 months creates a difficult environment. That, plus the
fact that the medium becomes more and more homoge-
nized, is in part responsible for the current "mushy
democracy" of digital imaging. Setting that aside for the
moment, I continue to see three separate and evolving
digital art forms.

The Print: Graham Nash,
Mac Holbert, & Epson

First, much credit for the very concept that ink jet
syntax could be considered as an archival and unique
system of making art goes to Graham Nash and Mac
Holbert of Nash Editions. In the late 1980s, Nash
and Holbert wrote image management software and
applied it to the creation of large-scale digital images

using an Iris 3074 printer and archival rag papers. This was the beginning of the mind-set that began to let photographers think about the concept of the dry darkroom.

Of all the printer manufacturers, one jumped into the concept without looking back . . . Epson. Epson cannot be given enough credit for their commitment to the photographic arts, and for utilizing the resource of grateful artists and photographers in the development of its product line. Epson has also shown an amazing ability to consistently improve on its printers, profiles, and pigment-based ink sets while maintaining a business model geared to professionals and students alike. Although Hewlett-Packard and Canon have joined the parade, Epson continues to lead it.

Images produced as prints are generated from original film, or digital files, and manipulated digitally to become printed, 2-D images. The latest home-based Epson 2400 (or whatever Epson version is newest by the time you read this), in concert with their Ultrachrome K3 ink sets, has set a standard for excellence that may continue to separate it from the competition. Included in this digital stew are the individual pioneers whose ways of modifying and working with digital printing technology have, in a very real way, induced such larger entities as Epson and Hewlett-Packard to put so much effort into mass-market technology. These pioneers include such landmark figures in the digital evolution revolution, as Gary Rogers, Jon Cone, John Paul Caponigro, Stephen Johnson, Graham Nash, Mac Holbert, Pedro Meyer, George DeWolfe, Dan Burkholder, and Mark Nelson.

Photographic prints made with pigment-based, light-fast, water-resistant inks on rag papers can accurately be described as "archival," with a life span of well beyond our own, depending upon the support and the conditions that the print exists in. This form of realized, and printed, digital artistry is most similar to photography and printmaking. As a result of the almost unbelievable improvements in the physical materials, very few practitioners, museums, critics, or collectors harbor reservations about this form of printmaking.

THE SIGNAL: INFORMATION & PERFORMANCE

The second form to be considered in the digital arts is the *signal* . . . the free transmission of electronic information and the World Wide Web itself. In this new cosmos, the artist works independently as a solo act or forms a collaborative creative relationship with others (who might not be aware of the collaboration) to express and influence thought and perception. I see this genre as being broken into two separate parts; the signal itself and the influence of the communication via that signal.

The Signal: Information

On a basic level, it is the signal that carries the information that is critical to the expression. This transmission got its start in the mid-1800s through the inspiration of Alexander Bain's crude facsimile machine that was improved upon in 1860 by Giovanni Casselli, an Italian priest, who invented a working machine he called the Pantelegraph.

To use a Pantelegraph, the operator would draw, or write, with fatty ink on a sheet of tin. The sheet was then placed on a plate that was charged with electric current and, in contact with a transmitter, connected to a telegraph wire. A stylus would pass over the ink and the electric current, unable to penetrate to the charged electronic plate through the fatty ink drawing areas, *would transmit what could not be transmitted* (the fatty ink) to the other end of the telegraph line where the image was received on a chemically treated paper . . . thus making an electronic picture of the thing itself.

Perhaps the first artist to think about rendering a photographic image using electronic code was William Larson. He reasoned that the FAX machine, using the Fax machine's ability to translate images from sounds over a telephone line, produced images in values of gray. More importantly, according to William, "*it transformed the image into a mediated electronic state where it was compatible with other electronically encoded information.*"

When Larson began this work, he considered how photography might be used within an electronic system

TRANSMISSION NO.6 (Received 8:24 PM) TRANSMITTED 8:24 PM   Nov.18 1976   (AUTHORS VOICE) 8:03PM   TRANSMISSION NO.3 (ADULT MALE)
TRANSMISSION NO.2 (ADULT FEMALE STANDING) 8:09PM

Figure 5–23

William Larson, _FAX 1_, 11-18-76

William began working with the FAX back in 1969 recognizing its ability to render a photographic image (in electronic code) suitable for transmission by telephone. In essence, it transformed the image into sound by assigning a different audio tone to the various gray values of the photograph. Perhaps, more profoundly, it transformed the image into a mediated electronic state where it was compatible with other electronically encoded information.

(Courtesy of the artist)

able to translate everything it was given into a FAX code . . . from a song to a picture in a family album . . . and how visually this was, in essence, a montage of signals re-constructed as a whole. By using the FAX technology of 1969, Larson may have made the first electronically montaged photographs intended to be seen, and considered, in the same way as a traditional photograph.

The Signal: Performance

The second aspect of the signal is, I believe, the most vital force of today's efforts in the digital arts. Within the last decade, digital performance has evolved into a major artistic movement, not dissimilar to the Happening movement of the late '60s and early '70s. A wonderful example would be James Downey's 2001 Internet campaign to have as many people as possible direct their personal red laser pointers at the moon at the same moment . . . in order to change the color of the moon. No, it didn't work, but was in the same event category as New York City radio host Jean Shepherd's 1965 box kite flying event in Central Park in conjunction with the transmission of pictures from Mars.

Another work in this genre would be Mike Parr's performance, _Malevich_, at Artspace (University of Western Sydney) in 2001. Regarded as one of Australia's most important artists, Parr nailed his arm to a wall, had his eyes taped over, deprived himself of food (except for

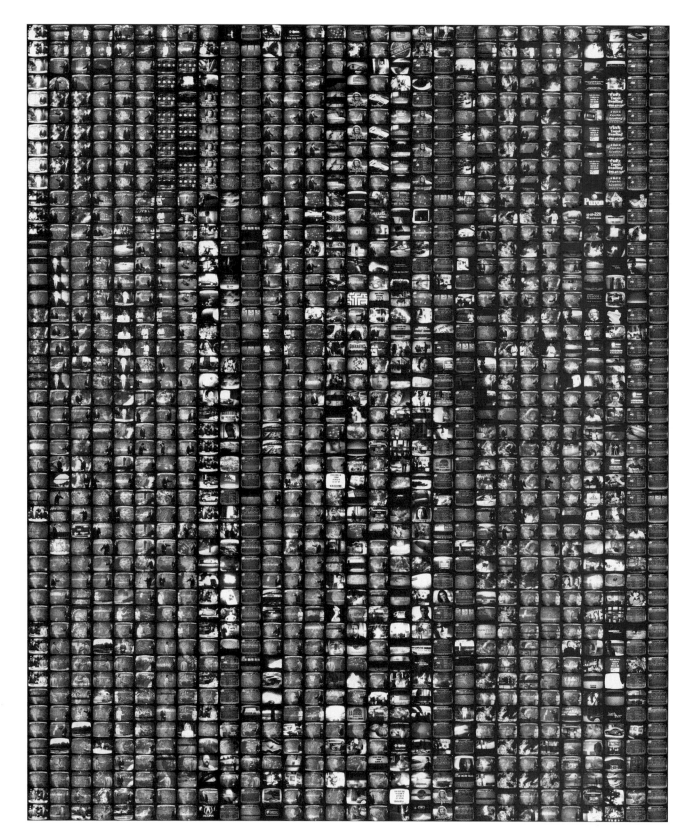

Figure 5–24

Matt Belanger, *Weather Channel*, 06-22-99

This is one of Matt's large-scale TV pieces digitally documenting popular culture and the graphic ordered relationships of television programming . . . in this case, The Weather Channel.

(Courtesy of the artist)

Figure 5–25
Nam June Paik, *TV Buddha*, 1974
Nam June Paik was a primary force in Fluxus, a 60's international collaborative network of artists, including Nam June Paik, John Cage, Alan Kaprow, & Charlotte Moorman. Fluxus was known for its dedication to the integration of disciplines and the concept that a performance required an audience to complete the piece. In one of my favorite Paik works, *TV Buddha*, a statue of Buddha contemplates a TV with an image of Buddha contemplating the TV . . . permitting the audience to connect to this perfect "oneness." *(Courtesy Nam June Paik Foundation/Paik Studios, Inc)*

water) and featured all the suffering and humiliation that one would expect from seeing a person nailed to a wall for an extended period of time. The performance was broadcast over the Internet with more than a quarter million hits in the first 24 hours. Parr performed another work the following year titled Close the Concentration Camps (Australia) where he had his lips sewn together in solidarity with the prisoners being held in Australia's detention centers. These performances bring to mind Chris Burden who, in 1971, performed the piece *Shoot* in F Space (Santa Ana, California) where he had himself shot in the arm by an assistant. This event became famous via word of mouth. Given the power of the Internet to create a world stage in an instant, or a theater as in the case of YouTube, it is mind boggling to consider the impact of Burden's performances had he had the web to work with. As one of my artist friends said of these examples, "Some people would chew off their leg to "make it" in the art world." In other words, don't try anything like this at home as the "buzz" is brief and the art marginal.

Digital performances require the strengths, and the limitations, of the medium's transmissions to be effective, seen, and appreciated. Sometimes it's really funny. Sometimes its sole intention is to promote social and political change and to disturb cultural lethargy. Sometimes it is just publicity. In almost every case that I am aware of, the piece is created for the art of the performance and the power of the idea that is communicated. Financial gain and reward often has nothing to do with it and that's what makes this part of the genre so alive and powerful . . . and democratic.

The Eye of the Monitor

The third digital art form is the advent of the unblinking monitor as the piece itself. In this case, the monitor is both the equipment needed (the tool) and the display (the art), and the making of the image on the computer screen, or screens (as in a modular construction), requires the computer's optical and programmable nature to be used in the translation of the work of art.

This idea got its spark decades ago with the Fluxus (*meaning flow*) movement in the early 1960s. Fluxus, an international collaborative network of important artists, including Nam June Paik, John Cage, Alan Kaprow, Charlotte Moorman, and George Maciunas, was highly regarded for its dedication to the integration and blending of all disciplines. One of the principles of Fluxus was that a performance required an audience to complete the piece and the late Nam June Paik may be considered the "godfather" of what is presently active in this room of the digital arts mansion. Some examples . . .

In one of my favorite Nam June Paik works, *TV Buddha*, a statue of Buddha contemplates a TV with an image of Buddha contemplating the TV . . . permitting the audience to make the connection of this perfect "oneness." In another piece, Paik incorporated the projection of a clear film leader with the 10-9-8-7, etc. sequence of numbers that you used to see just prior to the beginning of a film. When the film leader got to #1 . . . it simply began again, forcing the audience to re-new their anticipation for the film that would never begin.

In 1969, Paik collaborated with classical cellist, Charlotte Moorman, in a work titled *V Bra for Living Sculpture, 1969,* that featured miniature TV monitors in Moorman's bra, broadcasting the sights and sounds of Moorman playing her cello. Earlier, in 1967, they had collaborated on a piece called Opera Sextronique in which Moorman had played her cello topless . . . which resulted in her arrest for indecent exposure. In these pieces, and in Paik's other major works, the monitor functions as the visual source, the narrator, one of the actors, and the director of the event.

Today, the monitor plays the role similar to the one that flew over the nighttime city in Ridley Scott's *Blade Runner*. The monitor is a force field of digital information, designed to direct, influence, coerce and seduce. Consider JumboTrons in football stadiums, Times Square in Manhattan, and the Ginza shopping district in Tokyo. In recent years, these large digital screens have been used to bring digital art to the public and galleries in Cambridge, Massachusetts (Lumen Eclipse) and Toronto, Canada are leading this movement. Then there is the concept of what the "screen" is and what it suggests about the image, or artist, or mass that is projected upon it. An example would be Doug Aitken's 8-channel video piece projected onto the side of the new Museum of Modern Art in February 2007. Did projecting it on MOMA instantly make it art rather than information? All of these are simple references to the power of the screen and what will eventually, in my mind, replace static public advertising, propaganda, and public art display.

Figure 5–26

Doug Prince, *Construction-007,* **2002—digital**

Doug's explorations of photographic media have driven his interest in digital image making. One natural direction in this digital evolution has been to extend the way he assembled images in the photo-sculptures. Constructing a single image from discrete elements on layers of film. This is very similar to building images with layers in Photoshop, using physical space in the first and virtual space in the second.

(Courtesy of the artist)

DIGITAL CRITICISM

The Art

As has been the case for a while now, the primary dilemma for critics (and presumably a huge relief to the rest of the art world) is that there is no great mass of formal academic and critical evaluation for determining the merits of any of this new digital work . . . or, more importantly, of the process or actual systems that render it. There is a growing tendency to apply post-modernistic theory and dialogue to digitally generated, expression but I've yet to hear anyone do it successfully in public without eyes rolling up to the heavens. In the genre of the digital arts, it should be difficult to fully comprehend, appreciate, and evaluate the art without a discussion of that art's syntax . . . the technological components and processes that facilitate the delivery of that art. Think of it as the critique of a jockey absent discussion of the merits of the horse. Digital syntax clearly exceeds the issue of what type of brush a painter uses to render a stroke of paint, as the technology is a true collaborator in the art making.

Clearly, it is not polite to digital artists to apply traditional, critical, and conceptual theory to the various forms of digital expression. What is, after all, the criterion? Where is the traditional atelier, as in painting, that the confused digital artist can return to for re-evaluation, guidance, and mentoring, in order to return to the roots of the process? Where will this work fit in the history of human expression and when will the machine be as relevant as the artist using it is . . . as, say, in horse or stock car racing? These are a few of the questions now evolving from the marriage of digital imaging and artistic expression and ones which will find, trust me, their own perfect and unique answers as time passes. One thing is certain . . . as in every new form of creative expression, there are people who will determine the marketplace and there will be people who find they can make a living by becoming an arbiter of what is, and is not, art in that genre.

The primary hurdle to forming a legitimate critical base is more obvious now than it was five years ago. The sheer speed of the changes in the digital arts makes the formation of a "new" theoretical or critical structure very difficult. As the technology surges ahead, the speed of the processor jousts with the possible speed of the human mind. It will be interesting to see how to place the old square pegs of classical art criticism into the round holes that are being rapidly drilled by the digital arts.

Here's a decent example. In April 2002, Matthew Mirapaul wrote a piece for the *New York Times* about the New York artist Mark Napier, who was attempting to carve out new territory for himself and his art. Mr. Napier, an accomplished digital artist whose work had been shown in both the Whitney and Guggenheim Museums, decided that the Internet was not a gallery and that he still had to make a living. The article went on to describe Mr. Napier's solution to the problem, and the fact that he had succeeded in selling three $1,000 "shares" in his new work,

Figure 5–27

Doug Prince, *Floating Rose*, 1978—Plexiglas boxed images
I first saw Doug's box constructions in Lee Witkin's gallery decades ago. His photo-sculptures are three-dimensional images, constructed of plastics and film, approximately 5 × 5 × 2.5 inches in dimension. The images are printed on graphic arts film, which is supported between panels of clear plastic at various depths within the box structure. The boxes are then viewed by transmitted light from the rear of the sculpture.
(Courtesy of the artist)

called The Waiting Room. It turned out that The Waiting Room was an interactive, animated, painting installed in a private chat-room gallery in a secret place on the Internet. If you wanted to play with or look at, the work . . . you had to invest and sure enough . . . as in the fable of the "emperor's new clothes," and the zeitgeist-shaping, performance work of the 1970s, some people actually did.

For their money, "the investors" received the chance to play with Mr. Napier's software that generated swirling sights and sounds against a very arty black background . . . with each shape and form linked to a specific hum, beep, or chirp.

Mathew Mirapaul wrote, "*Mr. Napier hopes to sell as many as 50 shares in The Waiting Room, an approach that emphasizes the work's participatory nature. When multiple owners (investors) view it online at the same time, they can produce shapes that complement—or obliterate—those made by others* (apparently the other

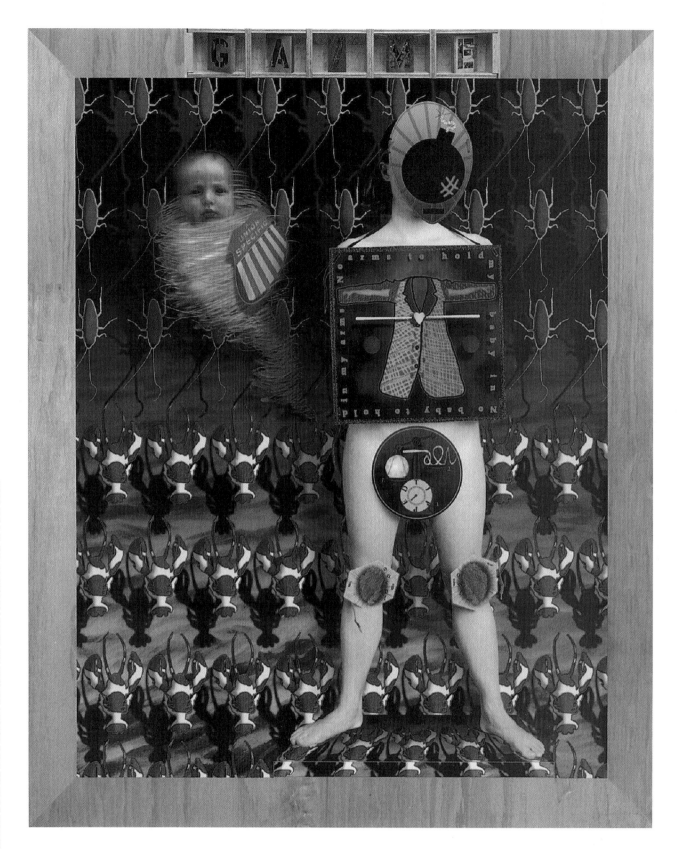

Figure 5–28

Steve Bliss, *GA/ME*

If ever an artist created work that was a mirror reflection of their personality, it is Steve Bliss. He was making strong digital imagery when 500k was considered a very big file.

(Courtesy of the artist)

two investors). *The work is the visual equivalent of an Internet chat room with "conversations" occurring in geometric shapes instead of words."*

The article continued by stating that the key investment points were that the shareholders could visit "their" art anytime they were on line, that they would be receiving a real Certificate of Authenticity and a CD-ROM that contained the software . . . sort of like going to the theater and getting a T-Shirt for *Cats."* The work's value, says the author, *"resides not in its keepsakes but in the experience it provides for the viewer."*

Says Mr. Napier, *"Once you forget that there's a computer mediating this, it is just as physically there in the space as a canvas. It's just a question of shifting an art culture that for centuries has been immersed in the collectible object."*

Figure 5–29
Willey Miller, *Your Rent is Past Due, Art-Boy*, 1997
(Courtesy of the artist)

This reminds me of another good anecdote from the Manhattan art scene. There was this artist (who shall go unnamed) in New York who announced to a number of important collectors that he was going to be producing a very important work and that all they had

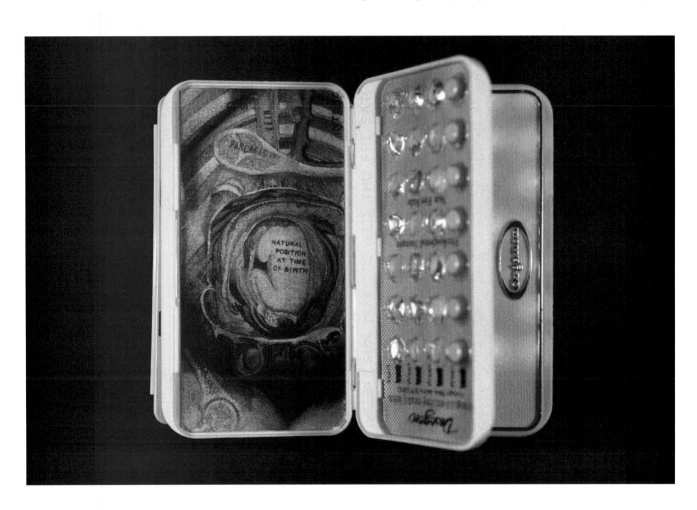

Figure 5–30
Colleen Mullins, *Miscarriage*, 1996
A sculptural work incorporating birth control pill boxes, French ribbon, and digital laser writer prints.
(Courtesy of the artist)

to do to own and collect this important work was to write him a large check. Of course they did, whereupon the artist endorsed the checks and cashed them. Later, when one of the collectors inquired as to when he might be receiving his important work of art the artist asked if the bank had returned to the collector the signed, and cancelled, check . . . which was, of course, the work of art.

Another good example might be the ability of the computer to challenge a sacrosanct discipline . . . such as sculpture. A few years ago, I saw an example of an artist who had her body scanned by an extraordinary laser device that was able to record every nuance, tiny hair, and goose bump of her physical self. The scanner then relayed this information to a computer-controlled casting machine that proceeded to scale, proportion, carve, and duplicate her body in Lucite. Most would agree that evaluating her sculpture from a traditional perspective would be impossible without recognizing the role of the machine in its creation. In truth, the present forms of digitally based aesthetic are experiencing philosophical growing pains not very different from those that photography suffered at its inception.

An illustration of this parallel might be made still more apparent if we consider a few sentiments from the perpetually cranky nineteenth century poet and critic, Charles Baudelaire. In fairness to the argument, I'll point out that Baudelaire was a man of deep moods and unrelenting despair, whose poetry centered on the inseparable connection between beauty and the inevitable corruption of that beauty.

In any event, when Baudelaire described his first impressions of photography he wrote about it in less than glowing terms, implying that society was squalid and narcissistic in its rush to gaze on trivial images of itself rendered on scraps of metal. He also wrote, in a critique of an exhibition in 1859, "*If photography is allowed to supplement art in some of its functions, it will soon have supplanted or corrupted it altogether . . . .*" This is a disposition that has its twin in statements now uttered by many traditional artists and critics speaking about the brave new world of the digital arts. However, unlike a few years ago, these voices become fainter with each passing year. As the beauty of the "science" becomes obvious, and as the digital foundation becomes more a part of our everyday lives, the skeptics are finding it easier to become converts.

Figure 5–31

John Paul Caponigro, *reflection i 5*—adagio—1998

John Paul Caponigro is one of today's outstanding digital artists, authors, and teachers, and he has had a significant role in legitimizing the tools of digital imaging as an artist's instrument and resource.

(Courtesy of the artist)

The Anthotype & Chlorophyll Process: The Art of Printing with Flowers and Vegetation

OVERVIEW & EXPECTATIONS

This chapter is going to be rather short, as the Anthotype process is a profoundly simple method of making images and the fact that I only know of a handful of people, besides myself, that actually practice the process. This is not because it isn't fun or easy to do. . . it is. As well, it is, without a doubt, the most organic, low impact, and environmentally pleasant process in all of the arts. The problem is that the images need to be handled in a very specific manner after they are created if they are to be preserved well. Lately, I've taken to making them, scanning them into Photoshop, and re-printing them on an Epson 2400 with a lovely Japanese rice paper. You should try it.

That said, in this chapter, I will provide you with a little history of the Anthotype, discuss flowers, the color of light, complimentary colors, absorption and reflection, and then tell you what materials you will need and the procedures necessary for you to make your own Anthotypes. I will also tell you about a beautiful technique used by Vietnamese-born artist Binh Danh, and how he makes provocative and poetic images on leaves using the process of photosynthesis.

Figure 6–1

Linda Wilson, *Strawberry - Puppeteer*, 2006—Anthotype

Linda's print is an example of the Anthotype process utilizing strawberries. The image was created from a found illustration, scanned, printed out, drawn on, re-scanned, and the positive printed out on ink-jet film. To get the color, the berries were slowly boiled to evaporate some of the water… resulting in richer color. The berry juice was applied to watercolor paper and then combined, along with the transparency, between sheets of glass sealed together with duct tape. The image was placed outside, weather permitting, for a few weeks of exposure.

(Courtesy of the artist)

A LITTLE HISTORY

Sir John Herschel's Garden

The Anthotype is a quaint and charming process, developed by Sir John Herschel in the early 1840s, that employed nothing but the natural color of flowers, a little alcohol, and sunlight. . . as I've written in the past, the primary ingredients necessary for a romantic vacation.

A decade earlier, in 1832, Herschel conducted several experiments in which he filled glass tubes with a solution called platinate of lime (*also known as calcium chloroplatinite*). He described his experimentation in a paper entitled *"On the Action of Light in Determining the precipitation of Muriate of Platinum by Lime-Water,"* in July of that year. Within the text of this paper, he discussed the *"remarkable action"* confined to the violet end of the spectrum and how he had made a solution out of red rose leaves and then acidified them with a small amount of sulphuric acid (in order to better release the colors of the flower petals). He then filled the glass tubes with the liquid. He went on to describe how the tincture of red from the rose colored solution had prevented the platinum of lime-water from being completely influenced by UV light. Although Herschel made no mention of this in 1832, it suggests two possible avenues for future investigation: the selective filtering of light for purposes of manipulating exposures of light sensitive materials such as silver, and the use of the natural pigments of flowers to make images via the concept of bleaching those colors with sunlight.

Herschel conducted his first plant dye photographic experiments by analyzing the light sensitivity of natural vegetable and plant pigments. He knew that artists had long sought out the minerals found in nature for their paints and dyes because those pigments were not as fugitive as the flavonoids (plant pigmentation) commonly found in plants and vegetation.

Herschel combined this with his knowledge of how specifically colored objects reflected light of the same hue (*hue. . . meaning a color observed as a result of its dominant wavelength in the spectrum*) all the while absorbing the wavelengths from all other hues. One more piece of this puzzle that Herschel understood was that while a color was reflecting its own color; its pigments could be bleached by the colors of its compliment.

How a color is absorbed determines how the eye observes that color. The color most significantly absorbed is the compliment of that color. A material that absorbs the color blue does not look blue, as the colors that are not absorbed are the colors that we can see. Again, the observed color is the compliment of the absorbed color. As an example. . . potassium and ammonium dichromate (a common sensitizing chemical used in gum bichromate printing) is a brilliant red orange to our eyes because these chemicals absorb their color compliment—blue light. As well, an orange-yellow sensitizer will be bleached more aggressively by blue light rays while transmitting orange-yellow light rays. Blue pigments are bleached by red-orange and yellow rays while purple and pink pigments are bleached by green and yellow rays. OK . . . enough of that.

The word Anthotype is from the Greek word *anthos* for flower. In Herschel's quest to explore the new science of *photography*, a word that he made up by the way, he distilled his current knowledge of light, color, and botany and set to work on a practical process of making images with natural flower pigmentation. Here's how he described it in his paper to the Royal Society in 1842, *On the Action of Rays . . . In operating on the colours of flowers I have usually proceeded as follows:—the petals of the fresh flowers, or rather such parts of them as possessed a uniform tint, were crushed to a pulp in a marble mortar, either alone, or with addition of alcohol, and the juice expressed by squeezing the pulp in a clean linen or cotton cloth. It was then spread on paper with a flat brush, and dried in the air without artificial heat, or at the most with a gentle warmth which rises in the ascending current of air from the Arnott stove."*

Herschel used a positive engraving that he had waxed or oiled for translucency as his "negative." Reasoning that the rays of the sun would act on the flower juice coated paper in the areas of the engraving that were least blocked with ink . . . essentially duplicating the engraving via the bleaching action of the sun.

Figure 6–2

Herschel, *Anthotype Portrait #10*—1840

The word Anthotype is from the Greek word *anthos* for flower. In Herschel's quest to explore the new science of *photography,* a word that he coined, he distilled his current knowledge of light, color, and botany and set to work on a practical process of making images with natural flower pigmentation as early as 1836. Herschel understood that while a color was reflecting it's own color; its pigments could be bleached by the colors of its compliment. This image is from an engraving of Mrs. Leicester Stanhope, using the juices of Red Double Stock, one that he used for many of his photographic experiments.

Courtesy of The Gernsheim Collection, Ransom Center, U. of Texas-Austin, TX

In its simplest explanation, the Anthotype is a process that uses the natural pigments of berries, leaves, and flowers for its coloration. Often the colors of flowers used do not end up as the color on the paper and this is due to the way certain flowers react to UV rays and to the acidity or alkalinity of the solution coated on the support paper. These plant specimens are ground into a soupy pulp, mixed with a little denatured alcohol, and strained through cheesecloth to get a liquid "sensitizer." This liquefied solution is then coated on the back side of a damp piece of paper, dried, placed in contact with a film positive, or oiled/waxed paper copy, or photogram material, and placed in sunlight. . . often for a very long time. The average exposure in nice summer weather is totally dependent on the freshness of the flower petals, the individual dye potency of the flower, the intensity of sunlight, the paper used, and whether an acid or an alkali has modified the solution. Generally speaking, the exposure can be as short as several hours with yellow japonica, or beet root, or several weeks with a plant that is less sensitive. . . you'll need to open your contact frame and check it every few hours . . . or days.

In researching for this book I found an interesting Anthotype-related fact. There was a tradition in France, going back to the early 1700s, in which stencils were arranged on fruit. Once the stencils were secure, the fruit was exposed to sunlight. The sunlight would bleach, or ripen, the areas of the fruit's skin into decorative patterns that were, I would suspect, employed to make a table display more impressive. Hippolyte Bayard, a clerk in the French Ministry of Finance in the 1830s, and one of the true inventors of photography, had a father who would create these patterns on a regular basis. That decorative exercise had a profound effect on Bayard's life as an artist and inventor.

TABLE SET UP FOR ANTHOTYPE

◆ Fresh and young flower petals, stalks or leaves—or—dehydrated versions of this same vegetable and plant matter

◆ A blender or mortar and pestle for crushing and blending the flowers

◆ Simple denatured alcohol

◆ Acetic acid or vinegar

◆ Cheesecloth for straining the flower juices

◆ Foam brushes for coating

◆ Water and a clean sponge

◆ Paper for coating: COT 320, Crane's Platinotype, Buxton, etc.

◆ A contact printing frame

◆ A pencil

◆ A film positive or photogram materials

◆ Paper towels

THE WORKING PROCESS

Go to the garden, or market, and collect the flower petals and berries, that you want to use for your color. Herschel, and his colleague Mary Somerville, knew that the freshest flowers yielded the best color so look for new vegetation and petals. You can dehydrate these petals or go directly to making a solution. The best vegetation, i.e., the most sensitive plants and fruits include: frozen blueberries, raspberries, strawberries, pokeberries, beets, turmeric, Yellow Japonica (*most sensitive to bleaching*), Iris, Red Poppies (*Herschel's favorite*), spinach, Marigold, Double Purple Groundsel, Red Dahlia, and most blue flowers. Use your imagination and whatever is in the garden, woods, or market.

A mortar and pestle, or an electric blender, is required for grinding the vegetable matter into pulp if you use fresh flowers. If you elect to dehydrate your vegetation first, which often yields a much greater color concentration in the final image; you will need a blender to chop the dehydrated flowers into little pieces before adding alcohol. The mortar and pestle is the romantic way to accomplish the task of grinding up your vegetation. However, if you are feeling practical, and less romantic, you can use an electric blender, which is quite efficient.

The next step in the process is to add a splash of denatured alcohol to this pulp and re-blend it until it has a nice smooth "soupy" texture. If you want to try and enhancing the color of the final image you may experiment with acidifying this soupy mix with a little acetic acid or vinegar. Mary Somerville's Anthotype experimentations, which she continued after Herschel left photography to pursue other areas of scientific study, noted that, *"the action of rays of mean refrangibility (meaning. . . the ability to refract light) on vegetables was much increased by the addition of a little sulfuric acid."* Essentially, all you need to do is get your solution to a pH 3 and you will have done what is necessary to achieve

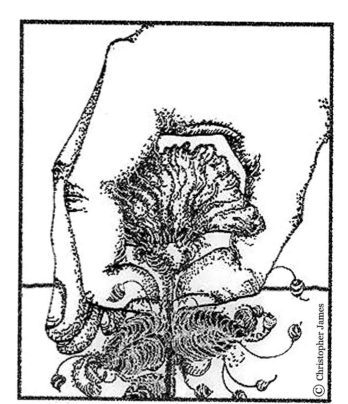

Sir John Herschel's actual fingers selecting an odd flower for his newest anthotype - c. 1840

Figure 6–3

Christopher James, *Sir John Herschel Selecting an Odd Flower for an Anthotype—1840*

(Courtesy of the author)

Figure 6–4

Dan Estabrook, *Anthotype Dressing Gown in Pokeberry*—1999

This anthotype is another example of Dan's forays into the world of the technically obscure. Dan made a positive film of the dress, mixed up an anthotype "sensitizer" with Pokeberries and alcohol, placed the positive in a contact frame with paper coated with the extracted juices, and exposed it to the sun for several days. Pokeberries make a relatively fast exposure while other types of flower extracts may take weeks to render a satisfactory image.

(Courtesy of the artist)

this effect. Now, slowly pour the pulp solution into the cheesecloth. Gather in the corners so that the pulp is secure in the bottom of the cloth, twist it shut, and squeeze all of the pulp juice into a new container.

You will need a good piece of paper and I will recommend that it be something along the lines of Cranes Platinotype or Cot 320. You will also need a clean foam brush for coating and a positive selection of photogram materials or positive film. Producing this positive in a pinhole camera is simple as is creating it in Photoshop and printing out the acetate positive on a piece of Pictorico OHP. *The following type is in bold face because it is disheartening to wait 3 weeks to look at a print only to find out you should have read the text more closely.* **A positive film will give a positive image whereas a negative film will give a negative image.** This is due to the fact that the sun is going to

cause reduction and bleaching rather than a darkening exposure. Using a positive film, the shadow areas are dark and will prevent, to a degree, the bleaching effect of sunlight in the print. This means that the berry/flower color is unchanged. The highlights are clear in the film positive and this permits the sun to do its bleaching thing on the flower juice coating. I suggest high contrast positives to begin learning the process.

Next, dampen the rear of the paper with a wet sponge. Do this until the paper is wet but not dripping and then flip it over and tack it to a board for coating. It is important to coat the juice on damp paper to avoid brushstrokes in the final image. Saturate the paper. When the coating is bone dry, place your film positive on the paper and lock it into a hinged contact frame and expose it to sunlight for as long as it takes to make the image. Depending on the flower/fruit it could be several hours to several weeks. When the exposure is done, that's the conclusion of the process. There is no wash out or development. What you see is what you get so this is, in a very real way, a POP (printing-out-paper) process.

Some flowers and berries yield colors that are different than you would expect. Frozen whole blueberries make a rather nice purple Barney the Dinosaur-like colored image. Fresh Blueberries are a disappointment. Pokeberries work well and result in a purple/raspberry image. Raspberries work pretty well while blackberries and frozen strawberries are image dependable. Generally, natural blue pigments tend to be the fastest in terms of printing time but are difficult to preserve. Extended exposure will cause fading, especially in the reds, but the positive side to this problem is that the highlights will bleach to white. Clove Carnations and Red Damask yield a slate blue. The Sparaxis perennial, a yellow/purple spotted deciduous herb from South Africa, yields a dull olive green while a rose colored Tulip delivers a blue-green. Nasturtium gives a brilliant green, Red Poppies provide a solid blue, and Lavender stalks and flowers give a nice green that will shift to a yellow if the solution is acidified. Beets, when acidified, produce a very nice rose. Bev Conway uses boiled and reduced onionskin and coats it on ink-jet paper to produce her images. Experiment to your heart's content and you will eventually find what you want.

Bev Conway's Onion Skin Anthotype Recipe

6–10 Large Yellow Onions
2 cups of water

Step 1 Peel off, and use, only the brown outer skin of the onion. You will have about 3–4 cups of brown skins.

Step 2 Bring 2 cups of water to a boil and add the onionskins until the liquid is deep orange brown color.

Step 3 Remove all of the onion parts and save the liquid.

Note: No alcohol is used in this Anthotype process to break the color down, as it has already been broken down via the boiling.

Note: The best paper for this onion juice is the ink-jet friendly, 100% cotton rag, Epson Smooth Fine Art paper.

Step 4 Follow the basic Anthotype instructions in the earlier part of this chapter and get set up for your exposure. Total exposure duration in the summer. . . about one month. In Bev's print (Fig. 6–5), part of her exposure time was in Santa Fe. The remainder was in New Hampshire.

Figure 6–5

Bev Conway, *Onionskin Anthotype of Nahanni*, 2005

The exposure of this onionskin anthotype is a bit tricky to calculate. The image was printed during June/July and the total exposure was probably about a month. Every day the contact frame was placed in the sun. The exposure continued in Santa Fe when Bev took the contact frame to a workshop she was attending. She continued to check on the exposure until she thought it was done.

(Courtesy of the artist)

Figure 6–6
Binh Danh, *Wandering Souls*, **2003**
Danh invented a unique process for printing photographs (digitally rendered into negatives) onto the surface of leaves by exploiting the natural process of photosynthesis. The leaves, still living, are pressed between glass plates with the negative and exposed to sunlight from a week to several months. Coined "chlorophyll prints" by the artist, the fragile works are then encapsulated and made permanent through casting them in solid blocks of resin.
(Courtesy of the artist and Haines Gallery, San Francisco)

Other ideas to consider might include mixing different flowers together to create different values and hues. Try mixing the pulp and dehydrating it and then figuring out a system of re-hydration that will give you the best coloration. You might also consider taking a particularly powerful color, such as beets or blueberries, and adding a dichromate to them and using that mix as your color for gum bichromate printing on a sized paper. This obliterates the simplicity of the Anthotype process but it might be a new addition to your gum printing menu.

Here's the rub. . . Unfortunately, there are only a few historical Anthotype images left to look at, due to the fact that the process was not really popular. . . probably the instant gratification factor and the fact that they must be stored in the dark, like a Mark Rothko painting, or else it will fade. Dan Estabrook's "Pokeberry Dressing Gown" (Fig. 6–4) is almost gone 5 years after he sent it to me. Herschel's Anthotypes can be found in the archives of the Harry Ransom Research Center at University of Texas,

Austin and the Museum of the History of Science at Oxford. For those of you who absolutely need to know if it works, it does, and there are actually a few contemporary artists who are making images using the technique. The Anthotype is an easy, intellectually painless, a very inexpensive process to prepare for. . . and an interesting way to tie up a contact printer for a few weeks. It is not a procedure for anyone who absolutely must have a finished print immediately. It is, however, a charming idea and eccentric enough to capture the attention of most alternative children.

THE CHLOROPHYLL PROCESS: BINH DANH'S PHOTOSYNTHESIS ART

In 2002, I was enlightened by an NPR story being broadcast on Ketzel Levine's Talking Plants show. The program was about a young Vietnamese-born man by the name of Binh Danh who was, at that time, a graduate student at Stanford University and in control of a beautifully organic process that featured images on plant leaves. I was taken by the fact that this was a technique reflected in history by the fruit stencils done in 1700's France and that had so influenced Hippolyte Bayard as a child. The difference, though, was significant in that the work Binh Danh was creating powerful, political, and symbolic imagery in ways that greatly exceeded the decorative stencils of an earlier era.

As Ketzel Levine said in the NPR piece, "*When Binh Danh prints pictures on leaves, something inexplicable happens. His small, green canvases expand beyond measure with both the seen and the unseen. The serenity of the Buddha on a circular nasturtium suggests a primordial, benevolent world; armed soldiers in camouflage, crouched in calla lily foliage, appear to be both predator and prey; and a young Vietnamese boy, held in the fingered palm of a philodendron, aches with human vulnerability.*"

Photosynthesis

Binh's chlorophyll prints represent his personal belief in the inter-connectivity between man and the natural world and the process is itself a mirror of that belief as the principle force in the making of the imagery is photosynthesis.

The concept of photosynthesis entered the public consciousness as a result of the early scientific investigations of Jean Senebier (1742–1809) exploring the influence of light on vegetation. Senebier's work, utilizing previous conclusions and speculations from the studies by Malpighi, Hales, Bonnet, Priestly, and Ingenhousz, clearly demonstrated the phenomena of photosynthesis: the process by which the green parts of plants utilize light energy to produce carbohydrates and how "*fixed air*" (carbon dioxide) was converted to "*pure air*" (oxygen) in a light-dependent process. Senebier demonstrated that it was the light of sunlight, and not its heat, that was necessary for photosynthesis to occur.

In our contemporary understanding of photosynthesis, we know it as the process by which plants use the energy from sunlight to produce sugars which *cellular respiration* (*the transfer of energy from plant molecules*) converts into ATP (adenosine triphosphate) the fuel used by all living things on earth. Photosynthesis takes place in plants as carbon dioxide, water, and light energy is converted to sugars and oxygen and is directly connected to the green chlorophyll pigment in plants. In this process, plants use water and release oxygen . . . and basically keep us breathing and eating. Keep this in mind if you ever have a doubt about the threat of global warming and the importance of green things.

Binh's process is pretty basic and it is this simplicity of his syntax, concept, and intent that is so powerful in his work. He begins by selecting a leaf—often from his mother's garden. To prevent it from dehydrating and losing its color and elasticity, he fills a small bag with water and secures it to the stem of the leaf. He then places the leaf on a felt covered board and places a negative directly upon the leaf. He lays a large sheet of heavy glass over the negatives and leaf, clips the glass and the support board together, and places the set up in the sun.

Binh will check on the print's progress from time to time and the process can take anywhere from days to weeks. Most of the time, he is dissatisfied with the results but when it works he will take the leaf and "fix" it by casting the leaf, like a biological sample for scientific study, in a block of clear casting resin such as made by the Fiber Glast Company. It is not the process that makes his imagery work. . . it is the poetry and power of his message.

Figure 6–7

Binh Danh, *The Leaf Effect, Study for Transmission #3*, 2006

Born in Vietnam in 1977, Binh Danh immigrated to the United States with his family when he was a young child. Images from the Vietnam War are prevalent in his work, providing a unique connection between process and subject matter. As he explains, "This process deals with the idea of elemental transmigration: the decomposition and composition of matter into other forms. The images of war are part of the leaves, and live inside and outside of them. The leaves express the continuum of the war. They contain the residue of the Vietnam War: bombs, blood, sweat, tears, and metals." *(Courtesy of the artist and Haines Gallery, San Francisco)*

The Cyanotype Process

OVERVIEW & EXPECTATIONS

The cyanotype, or *Ferro-Prussiate Process*, is often the first process that any of us learn in alternative process photography. This is the process that sinks the "hook" into us and makes us fall in love with the possibilities of image making. One of the primary reasons for this is the absolute simplicity of the nearly fail-safe technique and chemistry and the likelihood that you will make a successful print within a very short time.

In this chapter, the cyanotype process begins with a little history to show you where it all came from, including introducing you to the first woman photographer, Anna Atkins. You'll learn about the chemistry and how to prepare and use it as a UV light-sensitized solution and how to adjust the cyanotype formula for specific corrections. Also included is a discussion about substrates, sizing, coating, light sources, exposure, and development in water or acids for additional control. This chapter also deals with accelerated oxidation, highlight clearing, trouble-shooting, and many toning options for the cyanotype . . . in the event that the color blue just doesn't seem like the right one for the subject in your print.

It will also prepare you for the following chapter, Cyanotype Variations, where you will learn about inter-media applications, cyanotype on fabrics and optional mural materials, cyanotype on glass, Mike Ware's New Cyanotype process, and combination processes with cyanotype.

Figure 7–1
Christopher James, *Foot of the Pyramid*, 1994—toned cyanotype
(Courtesy of the author)

A LITTLE HISTORY

The cyanotype was the first simple, fully realized, and practical non-silver iron process. Discovered by Sir John Herschel (1792–1871) in 1842, a mere three years after the "official" announcement of the discovery of photography, the cyanotype provided permanent images in an elegant assortment of blue values. Herschel is the same gentleman who coined the words "*positive and negative*," "*photograph*," and "*snapshot*."

Like many educated and erudite gentlemen of his era, Herschel was involved in a great many activities in a universe of disciplines as diverse as science, the arts, literature, travel, and virtually any activity that would make him an interesting dinner companion. Among his photographic discoveries, Herschel developed the Argentotype, in which iron salts (*ferric citrate*) were used to precipitate silver under the influence of light and were subsequently developed in silver nitrate. He also developed a charming and odd technique described in the Anthotype chapter, that involves crushed flower petals, a little alcohol, and a 2- to 3-week exposure in sunlight . . . coincidently, the three key ingredients for a nice vacation.

Herschel was a gentleman scientist and, as was the norm within his social circle, his investigations primarily revolved around the concept of experimentation for its own sake, rather than for practical applications. Between 1839 and 1842 he conducted hundreds of separate experiments on the light-sensitivity of silver salts, metals, and vegetation. A goodly portion of this experimentation was dedicated to the idea of making colored photographic images, and in that quest, to finding highly colored dye extracts of flowers from his garden that might show evidence of being light-sensitive.

Another portion of his experimentation was an investigation of potassium ferricyanide. This aspect of his work was greatly augmented by Dr. Alfred Smee's work in electro-chemistry, that led him to a refined variation of potassium ferricyanide that he was generous enough

Figure 7–2

Julia Margaret Cameron, *Sir John Herschel, 1867*—albumen print
Julia Margaret Cameron began her career as a photographer in 1849 shortly after returning to England from India. Her work centered upon the ideals, and allegories, investigated by the Pre-Raphaelites; a group of artists who despised industrialization and yearned for the return of mythic heroes and romanticism. Her style, represented by this portrait of Herschel, is an example of the principal innovation she brought to the medium; the close and uncompromising psychology of the subject before her camera.
(Courtesy The Metropolitan Museum of Art, Gilman Collection, Gift of the Howard Gilman Foundation, 2005, Image © The Metropolitan Museum of Art)

to share with Herschel in 1842. Smee, in his early 20s at the time, responded to a request from the 50-year-old Herschel for "*deeply-coloured salts*" that might be bleached by light. In reply, Smee sent along the bright red potassium ferricyanide as well as a brand new chemical substance called ammonio-citrate of iron that had only recently become available to chemists and physicians as a prescription option for their patients who were in need of an iron tonic to stimulate their energy and to remedy certain gastrointestinal maladies.

Working with Smee's chemistry, Herschel discovered that the ammonio-citrate of iron (ferric ammonium citrate) chemistry was quite sensitive to sunlight and that exposure to ultra violet rays would change the salt of the iron from ferric to a ferrous. When a solution of ferric ammonium citrate and potassium ferricyanide (the two primary chemicals in the cyanotype process) is combined, coated on a paper, and exposed to light, it is reduced to ferrous ammonium citrate and potassium ferricyanide, which then forms ferric ferricyanide . . . the insoluble Prussian blue.

Herschel's Original Cyanotype Formula

Solution A

   20   parts ammonio-citrate of iron (ferric ammonium citrate)
   100 parts water

Solution B

   16   parts potassium ferricyanide
   100 parts Water

Mix equal volumes of A and B for sensitizer.

The Cyanotype was popular for a short time and experimented with by many, thanks to a commercially produced Ferro Prussiate Cyanotype paper. The first commercial use of the cyanotype was initiated in 1876 at the Philadelphia Centennial Exposition and this industrial application heralded the adoption of the process for schematic blueprint drawings used by engineers and builders for the next century. An odd historical tidbit concerning the cyanotype involved Lt. Col. Baden-Powell, founder of Scouting For Boys, a.k.a. The Boy Scouts. Apparently, Baden-Powell ordered the cyanotype process used to make stamps and money during the siege of Mafeking in the Boer War between Great Britain and the Transvaal (1899–1902). In a small demonstration of self-importance he ordered that his own likeness grace the center portrait oval on the currency . . . normally reserved for the portrait of Her Majesty Queen Victoria.

Anna Atkins: The First Woman Photographer

Anna Atkins (1799–1871) is referred to sparingly by traditional photo historians; she made beautiful cyanotype images of algae, ferns, feathers, and waterweeds. The Atkins and Herschel families resided only 30 miles apart in Kent, England, and her botanist father, John George Children, and Herschel were friends. John Children was a

Figure 7–3

Francis Schanberger, _Ginko Photogram Coat_, 2005—cyanotype

Francis Schanberger's working method is a synthesis of past and present, memory and imagination. He carries an old wooden tripod, a view camera, a lab coat, and his cyanotypes pay homage to nineteenth-century naturalists Herschel and Atkins. Francis once worked in a cell biology lab where it was considered bad form to wear one's lab coat out of doors. Francis imagines himself an anachronistic scientist alter ego. His doppelganger always wears a lab coat outdoors, his laboratory is nature, and his body's senses are just the instruments to divine its wonders.

(Courtesy of the artist)

member of the Royal Society, and when his friend Herschel announced his discovery of the cyanotype (1842), Children quickly passed the news on to his daughter Anna. Although there is no conclusive evidence that Herschel was Atkins's mentor, it is more than probable that she learned the cyanotype process in the Herschel household. If not fact, then at least it's a romantic concept.

Anna Atkins made thirteen known versions of her work titled _British Algae: Cyanotype Impressions (1843–1853)_. In October 1843 she began publishing folios of her photogenic (photogram) drawings. In 1850, she began to publish more comprehensive collections of her work, completing a three-volume anthology in 1853. These books, containing hundreds of handmade images, were the very first published works to utilize a photographic system for scientific investigation and illustration. Although Atkins published in 1843, Talbot's Pencil of Nature (1844–1846) is generally considered by historians as the first to have achieved this important milestone.

🐚 **Note: Sir John Herschel was the former owner of a copy of this manuscript that now resides in the archives of the New York Public Library. The specifics:** *British Algae: Cyanotype Impressions—Part I.* **This manuscript was published in October 1843, has 231 photographs, and was dedicated to her father, John George Children. It is in the Spencer Collection—1843 93–440 and can be seen online at the New York Public Library web site.** *Other examples of Atkins's work can be found at the Harry Ransom Humanities Research Center at the University of Texas, the Getty Museum, and public, institutional, and private collections in the United Kingdom and the United States. The work also exists in printed form: Aperture published Larry Schaaf's book, Sun Gardens: Victorian Photograms by Anna Atkins, 1985. Schaaf's beautiful book is out of print, but an Internet search at www.bookfind.com or Andrew Cahan, http://www.cahanbook.com, will likely lead to a copy.*

HOW CYANOTYPE WORKS

Cyanotype is an ultraviolet (UV)-sensitive contact printing process that requires, as do most all alternative photographic processes, a negative the same size as the final print. Of course you can use transparent, translucent, or opaque objects to make cyanotype photograms, as Atkins did.

The blue color of the cyanotype print is the result of the reaction of ferrous ions from the photo reduction of ferric ammonium citrate in combination with potassium ferricyanide. The cyanotype image is highly stable, but can be degraded by something alkaline, such as sodium carbonate or perspiration. It will also fade, like most

Figure 7–4

Anna Atkins, *Lycopodium Flagellatum,* **1843—cyanotype**

From the very first published volumes, illustrated with photographic images, *British Algae: Cyanotype Impressions* (1843–1853). Anna Atkins, the first woman photographer, created this 3-volume anthology over a period of 10 years. There are few known examples but one of the manuscripts that is available was published in October 1843, has 231 photographs, and was dedicated to her father, John George Children. It is in the Spencer Collection—(1843 93-440) and can be seen online at the New York Public Library web site.

(Courtesy of The Gernsheim Collection, Ransom Center, University of Texas-Austin, TX)

things, if exposed to strong direct sunlight over a period of time. Should you experience this fading, your image can generally be restored to its original blue intensity by storing it in a dark environment for a few days.

Contrary to some teaching, the cyanotype print can be controlled in process to yield wonderful and technically exquisite images. The prints can also be toned in a wide variety of ways to provide alternatives to the color blue. Many of these toner options are described later in the toning cyanotype section of this chapter. Cyanotypes are also employed successfully as first impressions in the gum bichromate or Blue-Van-Dyke processes and can also be used to delicately intensify shadow details in platinum or palladium printing.

Figure 7–5
Edward Steichen, *Moonrise—Mamaroneck*, New York, 1904—Pt & Cyanotype
Please refer to Fig 13-25 for information regarding the record auction price of $2,928,000.00 set by a print made with this same negative.
(Courtesy of New York, Museum of Modern Art (MoMA)—Platinum and cyanotype print—gift of the photographer)

THE CHEMISTRY

Cyanotype Sensitizing Formula

There are two principal chemicals that constitute a traditional cyanotype formula and these are mixed together in equal parts to create a working sensitizing solution that will be applied to paper with a hake, or foam, brush. They are: Part A—*ferric ammonium citrate* and Part B—*potassium ferricyanide*. Neither of these chemicals poses a serious health risk unless you are one of the very few people who have an allergic reaction to the chemistry. Ferric ammonium citrate is often found in iron and vitamin supplements and is mostly annoying if it becomes humidified and sticky. Potassium ferricyanide is a stable compound that only becomes a risk if heated beyond 300°F or combined with an acid, neither of which you will be doing.

Part A—Ferric Ammonium Citrate (green type)

In the green powdered state, ferric ammonium citrate (*ammonio-citrate of iron*) is a light-sensitive compound that changes from a *ferric* to *ferrous* state when subjected to ultraviolet (UV) light. Once mixed into solution, it is subject to mold growth after a relatively short storage period.

This moldy state is not detrimental to your cyanotype ambitions and can be avoided by adding a drop or two of formalin (formaldehyde), or a crystal of thymol, to the solution. If mold does appear, it is easily strained off by decanting the solution through a coffee filter. In extreme cases, the mold can be simply skimmed off the top of the solution with a pair of chopsticks. In any event, this mold growth is not something that should cause you to lose any sleep. In hot and humid weather, try not to let the chemical sit out in the open too long before mixing it into solution.

Part B—Potassium Ferricyanide

Potassium ferricyanide is the other half of the formula and is responsible for the blue color when combined with the *ferrous* ammonium citrate. If the chemical is in good condition it should be a nice orange red color, sometimes referred to as "ruby red." If it is in bad condition, you'll see yellow lumps and should avoid using it. Potassium ferricyanide is not particularly toxic because the cyanide group is bound to the iron atom and is not free to behave as a poison. The cyanide part of this chemical can be released as a hydrogen cyanide gas if it is subjected to a strong acid . . . which is something you will not do. Be diligent about avoiding acid contact. You will most likely use everything you mix, but in the event that you need to dispose of this chemical, you should adhere to the following: small portions of potassium ferricyanide should be diluted with excessive amounts of water and flushed. The chemical should never be thrown in the trash in a dry, ruby red, state as in some conditions it may become combustible.

Making the Sensitizing Solution

You will need a non-metallic mixing beaker and two dark glass or dark plastic 500 ml to 1000 ml containers for the mixed solutions. The easiest way to introduce yourself to the process is to purchase a pre-measured dry or wet pack Cyanotype Kit from a supplier such as Photographer's Formulary or Bostick and Sullivan. Honestly, though, the formula for this process is so elementary it is perfect to do while simultaneously teaching yourself to use a gram scale. Best place to get a digital gram scale is to go to an auction site, such as eBay, and search for a small digital jeweler's scale. They are very inexpensive, portable, and totally simple to use.

If you are frugal and intend to do large pieces or a great many prints, keep in mind that kits from any source cost as much as a virtual lifetime supply of cyanotype chemistry made from raw chemicals. Both of the suppliers mentioned above will sell the raw chemistry. After buying the chemistry in bulk, all you will need is that gram scale and some basic lab equipment. The following is a classic cyanotype sensitizer that, with the exception of Dr. Ware's New Cyanotype, is essentially identical to the vast majority of published cyanotype formulas.

Standard Cyanotype Sensitizing Formula

Stock Solution A

400 ml	water (68°F)
100 g	ferric ammonium citrate (green type)

Add water to make a total solution of 500 ml

Stock Solution B

400 ml	water (68°F)
40 g	potassium ferricyanide

Add water to make a total solution of 500 ml

Parts A and B can be separately mixed in normal ambient light and will work best after a ripening period of 24 hours. The Part A and B cyanotype solutions, if stored separately in dark glass or opaque plastic containers, with a good seal, will keep indefinitely. When mixed together, their usable life is relatively brief. In hot and humid conditions a few days would be stretching it. In ideal cool and dry conditions, several weeks. The sensitizer is so simple to prepare that there really isn't a good argument for having a combined A and B solution always at the ready.

Another Cyanotype Sensitizing Formula: (*Dick Sullivan's Mix*)

Stock Solution A

400 ml	water (68°F)
100 g	ferric ammonium citrate (green type)
2 g	oxalic acid

Add water to make a total solution of 500 ml

Stock Solution B

400 ml	water (68°F)
40 g	potassium ferricyanide
2 g	oxalic acid
0.8 g	ammonium dichromate

Add water to make a total solution of 500 ml

The oxalic acid in this formula assists in keeping highlights clean and bright. The ammonium dichromate has a similar role in the formula but be careful as ammonium dichromate, no matter how little is added to the mix, will have an impact on your tonal gradations. See instructions above and use equal parts A & B stock for sensitizer.

Standard Working Solution

Mix equal parts of Stock A and Stock B, i.e., 25 ml of Stock A mixed with 25 ml of Stock B to make a 50 ml working sensitizer solution. A healthy sensitizer will be clear yellow-green color. This is also the color that your dried paper or fabric should be just prior to printing. If, after using good chemistry, you see blue or blue-gray at the dry stage, it is likely that your paper or fabric has been fogged or the humidity has affected the sensitizer.

A Very Brief Word about Non-Standard Mixes

It is an acceptable idea to alter the chemical composition of the cyanotype formula in order to achieve variations in

Figure 7–6
Christopher James, *Self Portrait with Pinhole, Maine*—1994

density, and a few beginning options are discussed below. I have found that greatly increasing the percentage proportions of both the potassium ferricyanide and ferric ammonium citrate to water will result in an increase in the density of the blue. This solution may solve the chronic fading problem that has plagued cyanotype on cotton fabrics in the last few years because the quality of cotton has been compromised by additives in manufacturing. If, however, only ferric ammonium citrate is increased, you will often experience a "bleeding" of the shadows, whereas an increase in only potassium ferricyanide will result in a print with reduced density in those same values. This last observation is dependent on the type of paper you are using.

Low-Contrast/High-Contrast Solutions and Controls

Contrast control in cyanotype is, as in almost every alternative process, a case of controlling the values within your contact negative. That said, it is common to experience a fairly significant loss of tonal gradation during the washing, ton-

ing, and drying stages, and the following suggestions are options you might take if your image was made from a negative that was less than perfect for the process and is therefore exhibiting problems of too high or too low contrast.

A simple solution to reduce contrast is to dilute the standard working sensitizer solution with a small percentage of water. As you dilute the sensitizer, the gradations in the cyanotype print become softer . . . like adding water to soup. You may also create a lower contrast image by developing the image in a white vinegar concentration (described later in this chapter). Another method of controlling contrast is pre-coating your paper with one of a variety of weak acid solutions, such as 1% oxalic acid or 1% glacial acetic acid.

In most cases, depending on the paper you are using, as well as on pre-coating and drying, an acid bath will intensify darks and extend the visible tonal range. Be aware that regardless of the increase in density, this technique will often flatten the mid-range values and take the thrill out of the highlights. You can also achieve lower contrast appearance in your image by using the sun as your UV source. Cyanotype exposed by sunlight tends to provide a longer tonal range than does a mechanical UV light and thus creates a lower contrast image by a light to dark association. This observation changes when exposures are made with color layered digital negatives, different intensity light boxes, open shade exposures, and a host of other factors.

Adding a 1% Dichromate to the Sensitizer for Contrast

A higher-contrast solution can be mixed by adding 4 to 6 drops of a 1% solution of potassium dichromate to every 2 to 4 ml of the standard A & B sensitizer mix. This modest addition to the sensitizer will often let you print a poorly defined negative but it may also degrade a portion of the middle tonal values and highlights, i.e., a far shorter value scale. To make a 1% solution, mix 1g of potassium dichromate with 100 ml of distilled water.

0.2% Potassium Ferricyanide First Bath for Contrast

Another solution to achieving greater contrast following exposure is to immerse your exposed cyanotype print in a 0.2% potassium ferricyanide first water development bath in place of a plain water development bath. This bath is made by mixing 2 g of potassium ferricyanide in 1000 ml of water.

A similar contrast boost effect can be realized by adding a few drops of an ammonium, or potassium, dichromate solution to the initial water development bath. These percentages can range from 1% to 10% and the exact amount that may be effective will depend on the strength of the percentage that you elect to use and the state of flatness in your print . . . you decide.

🐢 **Note: Dichromates are carcinogenic and you must take precautions when working with it. Please consult the chemical section for recommendations if you are unfamiliar with them.**

Begin testing by making a batch of identical exposures through a Stouffer T2115, or equivalent, step-graded transparent scale. Process the first print in plain water as a control. Then make a specific dilute ammonium, or potassium, dichromate solution and add 10 to 15 drops to a liter of water and process a second test print. Write down the information, add either more ammonium dichromate or water, and make a third test. Proceed with the testing until you have established a set of working parameters that you can use effectively.

Double Coating to Increase Density

Contrast can also be managed in other ways. If you let a first coating of sensitizer dry thoroughly and then recoat it with a second application of sensitizer you will notice a remarkable increase in the density of the darker values . . . depending on the paper. Image density in the darker values is intensified well enough to merit this option when you are experiencing problems. Double coating will often mean that your standard exposure time will be different than if you use a single coating . . . generally longer. The best option is to make a great negative that is well-matched to the process.

Coating on Gum Sized Paper to Increase Density

Another option that you might find interesting is to make a cyanotype on a piece of paper that has been "sized" and prepared for gum bichromate printing, i.e., gelatin hardened with glyoxal. (*See Chapter 15, Paper*). Of course, this advice is dependent upon what kind of paper you are working with.

THE NEGATIVE

The cyanotype is a contact printing process . . . like a photogram. I have had success with a wide assortment of negative types and can usually get a good-looking print by adjusting the way I work to fit the negative's potential. This is one of the primary reasons that the process is such a great one to begin learning alternative techniques with, because success comes quickly, even for the rookie. I really do not have a specific general recommendation for a cyanotype negative. I've heard a lot of theories that recommend using a negative that would print well on a paper grade of 0 to 1 (*indicating a fairly contrasty negative density range of about 1.1 to 1.5*) and that this particular type will do well with a standard A & B sensitizing formula. This is true, but the same success can come from negatives that do not specifically meet this recommendation. My best advice is to make a nice negative and learn the process with it. And, just a quick reference back to the digital and negative chapters . . . the "less than fussy" personality of cyanotype makes this a great process for learning to produce digital negatives.

PAPER & FABRIC SUBSTRATES

Almost any type of paper or fabric can be used in the cyanotype process. This is, of course, dependent on what type of statement you are going to make or what your intentions are with the print before, and after, it has completed its cyanotype journey, i.e., cyanotypes in combinations with gum bichromate, collage, painting, paper sculpture, clothing, etc. Those options will determine which surface will be appropriate. Generally speaking, the best paper to use for a single image will be a quality hot or cold press paper like Arches Platine, Fabriano Artistico, Lana Aquarelle, Weston Parchment, Cot 320, Saunders Waterford, Somerset Book, Crane's Platinotype, or any decent watercolor paper. Watercolor papers of all sorts tend to work, but they work with very different degrees of success. Be prepared to experiment. Also try newsprint, paper bags, and any other paper

surface that won't break apart in water. Try colored papers for alternative toned highlights. Or, tone a watercolor paper with vegetable dyes, teas, or coffee before making your cyanotype.

The papers mentioned are neutral pH (*in the middle of being acidic or alkaline and therefore considered a good bet for an archival rating*) and already have a good sizing built into them during manufacturing. This indicates that they are specifically made to withstand the rigors of extended immersion times in liquids.

Other paper options, some of them esoteric, that withstand the rigors of wet processing are those such as the 22" × 30" Gampi Torinoko and Hahnemühle etching paper that you can purchase by the roll. There are a wide variety of rice papers available at well stocked art supply stores, though I would recommend buying small pieces to test before committing to large amounts. One paper that is fun to work with is a roll paper, 18" × 50', that is simply labeled Oriental Rice Paper for Sumi. The paper is tenaciously strong in water almost to the point of being like fabric. Generally, sizing beyond the manufacturer's own process is unnecessary for cyanotype and will only be relevant if you intend to extend your ideas with other processes, such as gum bichromate. With cyanotype, whether you size or not is really dependent upon the

Figure 7–7
Laurie Snyder, *Sun & Pressure*, 1992
This is a fine example of Laurie Snyder's work in the genre of artist's books. The piece is 15" × 24" when opened and consists of 27 double-page spreads of ink monotypes with cyanotype. It is quarter bound in linen and hand-made flax paper.
(Courtesy of the artist)

original attributes of the paper you buy and what your intentions are. If you feel sizing is called for, you can simplify your life by adding a ml or two of liquid gum Arabic to each 40 to 60 ml of the cyanotype A and B sensitizer mix. This will help suspend the coating on the paper's surface. Here is a list of a few papers that work well with this process.

- Arches Platine—moderate smoothness, can be delicate, nice finish

- Arches hot press watercolor—take your pick for weight

- Arches Aquarelle—best for gum/cyanotype combination printing

- Bergger COT-320—a beautiful hot press finish paper for most processes, a bit precious cost wise

- Buxton from Ruscombe Mills—one of the very best papers for cyan

- Cranes AS 8111—lightweight, kid finish, stationary

- Cranes Platinotype—one of the very best!—smooth gradations, holds up well in water, hot press, works well with many processes

- Fabriano Artistico—hot press, works well, rather thick with great surface

- Hahnemühle Photo rag ink-jet paper & printmaking paper

- Kozo rice paper—made from mulberries. This is a delicate & translucent paper with a great wet strength. Dry thoroughly to 'rest' the paper before toning.

- Stonehenge HP 245gsm

- Strathmore Bristol—very smooth surface—BUT . . . tends to break down in long wet immersions due to the layering found in Bristol

- Weston Parchment from Butler & Dearden

Hint: *If you are going to use a delicate paper, then you should make a lifting device out of plastic screening for raising and lowering your print in the trays. Cut a length of plastic screening and staple it to 2 wooden dowels at either end. You'll be raising and lowering the screening by holding onto the dowels which will drape over the edges of the tray.*

Figure 7–8

Sarah Van Keuren, *Seth Holding Wreath*, 1996—cyanotype & gum
University of the Arts professor Sarah is one of the leading alternative process artist/teachers working today. This is an example of her combination cyanotype and gum printing.
(Courtesy of the artist)

TABLE SET UP FOR CYANOTYPE

- Cyanotype sensitizer A & B: ferric ammonium citrate and potassium ferricyanide stock A & B

- Plastic beaker or paper cup for sensitizer

- Clean paper for the table surface coating area

- Rag paper for coating

- New hake brush (labeled Cyanotype)

- Clean distilled water in a beaker

- Pencil

- Hair dryer

- Contact printing frame
- Negative or photogram materials for contact printing

COATING

There are several ways to coat your paper or fabric. A total immersion technique is the best method for fabrics but uses an awful lot of sensitizer. If you're mixing from bulk chemistry this will be of little concern to you as it is so economical. Spraying, with a garden type misting bottle, or a cleaned Windex bottle, is a suitable application technique for large paper sheets. I think the best method for paper under 16" x 20" is to coat with a *hake* brush or inexpensive foam applicator. Both brushes are made without metal *ferrules* (the metallic section that holds the brush hairs to the handle), which may cause problems in a few of the more sensitive alternative processes should metal come into contact with your sensitizer chemistry. To be fair, I've never seen this problem and actually heard of a teacher who coated with a steel wool pad to see if it were true. Apparently everything worked out fine.

I like to coat in regular ambient level room light, or if I'm trying to make a lab a bit less uptight, under a few strands of non-blinking Christmas tree lights. Apply your sensitizer quickly and evenly using a *gentle* vertical, and then horizontal, stroking technique . . . and be wary of leaving puddles of sensitizer on the paper's surface which will wash off in development. Single coats work quite well if you get the right degree of saturation. The quality and thickness of your paper will determine the degree and amount of sensitizer your paper can accept. If your prints are consistently thin, even following extensive exposures, try a second coat once the first one is completely dry. As a rule, most quality artist's papers will only require a single coating but a double coating will yield denser blues.

Hake Brush and Super Glue

Japanese hake, or Chinese jaiban, brushes are made of wood and stitched hairs. They are desirable for alternative process coating due to their lack of metal ferrule and aesthetically organic look and feel. The absence of a metal ferrule is important, because it is often detrimental for any metal to come into contact with an alternative emulsion. The only problem with these lovely brushes is their tendency to shed hairs during the coating. A solution to this shedding is simple. Take your hake brush and run a single bead of Super Glue®, along the hairs where they come into contact with the wood handle. Repeat this step along the opposite side and be careful not to use too much glue. Do not smooth the glue with your finger or you will have "hake finger."

Drying the Paper

Once the paper has been coated well, dry it quickly in low light with a hair dryer or in semi-darkness if you are hanging it on a line or pinning it to a wall. *Be careful of staining the floor and walls.* You will not make people happy if you drip cyanotype sensitizer on anything. You may use a hairdryer on a cool setting to speed up the process. When using a hairdryer, avoid excessive heat and focus on the back of the paper rather than the coated front. This draws the sensitizer into the paper rather than drying it on the surface of the paper.

Be sure that the paper is "bone" dry because any moisture left in the paper will become an instant developer during your exposure (*remember, this is a water development technique*) and your print's detail and clarity will be compromised with fog. Do not use a clothes dryer for drying a coated fabric. The heat will be detrimental and the possibilities of staining future loads of laundry are quite real . . . which will, like dripping sensitizer, make you very unpopular with people who live with you.

A coated, dry, and ready to print cyanotype will be a light green-yellow color . . . known as chartreuse. If your sensitized paper, or material, is blue, rather than chartreuse, prior to printing then you likely have a moisture or chemical problem.

Occasionally you will see a mottling (an uneven coating) on the surface of the support, especially with fabrics. This problem is often no longer evident after exposure and development. Try not to touch the print surface before exposure because the oils and moisture in your fingertips are alkaline and may alter the chemical coating in those spots.

Figure 7–9

Betty Hahn, *Iris Variation #6, 1985*

This piece of Betty Hahn's has always been a favorite example to show students how powerful the cyanotype process can be when mixed with other media . . . in this case watercolor.

(Courtesy of the artist)

LIGHT & EXPOSURE

A Few Words About the Sun

Unless you are totally compulsive about controlling every aspect of alternative process exposures . . . a futile ideal . . . I want to mention the sun as the best light source you can use for contact printing. Unless you are working in a cold and dark climate most of the year, in which case you might think about becoming a poet, the sun provides the most efficient, and least expensive, means of exposing your contact negatives in printing frames. However, and I need to write this, very serious (or cold climate based) alternative process printers swear by a UV exposure unit because they feel it provides a consistent and controllable light source year round.

Why is sun best? It's free, really bright, and nothing can come close to the good feeling of multi-tasking while part of what you're doing is taking place outdoors in nice weather. Secondly, in the summer your exposure times are short and pleasant and it is easy for you to monitor your progress. Outside, the light is bright enough to read the exposure of your edges and their density. Simple observations of the changes will give you a lot of information as alternative process exposures are often best determined by this evaluation method rather than by a set time. When you think that you are close to being done, it is a simple matter of picking up the frame and moving into a shaded area to check on the details of shadows and highlights. This is especially true with any printing out processes such as POP, salt, Argyrotype, and Ziatype.

Of course there are variables with the sun that you will not find with a UV printer unit. The time of year, time of day, humidity level outside, and overall atmospheric conditions will all have something to do with your exposure. A misty and foggy day that makes you squint your eyes will often be an ideal one to print. Printing on a winter's day in New Hampshire, where I have my studio, will often be frustrating due to the low position of the sun and the dryness of the air but the other nine months of the year are great. Use the winter to enrich your life with other interests or make or buy a UV exposure unit (see Appendices). I think the best home unit to buy is made by Jon Edwards at Edwards Engineered products (www.eepjon.com). You can also buy plans if you are unusually handy. Do not waste your time with filtered "black-light" tubes like the ones that make Jimi Hendrix posters come to life because they are very inefficient exposure sources. You may, however, successfully use an unfiltered, UV tube. Another option might be a 1000-Watt BLB Metal Halide Light.

Another Kind of Sun: The 1000-Watt BLB Metal Halide Light

If you really want to simplify the whole process then you can purchase a 1000-Watt metal halide light source . . . called BLB, or black light blue. These light sources are strong, full range, effective, reasonably priced, dependable, long-lived, quick (average exposure for cyanotype is 8 minutes) and make excellent prints.

An example that has received praise would be the 1000-Watt Metal Halide Maximizer Grow Light System from www.hydroponics.net. The set up includes a bulb, ballast, reflector and socket assembly. The Maximizer reflector is constructed of brushed aluminum with a bright white finish on the inside. The reflector measures 21" long × 17" wide × 7-1/2" tall. The Maximizer reflector has a unique adjustable light pattern to customize the spread of light and the average exposure time will be 8–12 minutes. The one possible drawback will be the D.E.A. surveillance helicopters over your working space as they are primed to seek out high-efficiency grow lights and people who experiment with illegal indoor agriculture.

Metal halides emulate mid-day summer sunlight and contain all the wavelengths of the visible spectrum. To plants this means quality simulated sunlight and photosynthesis at a level much higher than that which fluorescent lamps can achieve. The unit runs about $250. And is more than adequate for your UV needs.

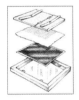

EXPOSING THE CYANOTYPE

When your coated and sensitized paper or fabric is completely dry, place your negative in contact with the coated emulsion and double check to see that it will read correctly when it is completed. The negative that you use will work very well if it has an average negative density range of 1.1 to 1.5.

Be aware that you will be losing a considerable amount of density in the wash and development stages so it is somewhat important that your highlights are able to print. Next, load the negative and coated paper into your contact frame so that the negative is next to the glass of the contact printer and the coated paper is behind the negative. Be sure that the hinge part of the frame back straddles the negative/coated area so that you can undo one side of the frame, during exposure if you wish to check on your progress without losing registration.

The most common problem in cyanotype printing is underexposure, where the highlights and middle values wash out in the water development. It is not a question of whether they will wash out but *to what degree.*

Depending on your negative, you will have a short or a long exposure with denser negatives obviously taking more time than thinner ones. In summer sunlight, at mid-day, an exposure might last anywhere from 10 to 20 minutes. If it is early or late in the day, be prepared for a lengthy exposure that might take as long as 45 minutes. This last sentence is a good argument for having a UV printer but that option lacks romance. It is generally a good idea to make a test print.

Testing Your Exposure Visually

There are several ways to test your exposure while you're making a print. When I am teaching a workshop class how to make cyanotype murals in the sun, I often use the students as photogram objects on a gigantic piece of sensitized fabric. During the exposure I periodically lift a shoe, or an arm, to check on the comparative densities. Checking under fingers doesn't do much for you in humid and hot weather as the sweat from the fingers pre-develops the material. By looking at the unexposed areas under an opaque object I am able to see what the base sensitizer (that chartreuse color) is doing in comparison to the open exposure areas with nothing blocking the sunlight. I am looking for the uncovered areas to turn a silvery gray.

In a contact printing frame, I often place a small opaque object on the glass so that it covers a separate swatch of emulsion that I have added to the bottom of the paper during coating. By quickly lifting the opaque object I can determine where the exposure is and how long I have before the processing begins. As you will discover, overexposing a cyanotype is a difficult thing to do.

A test strip can be easily made by coating a piece of paper with the sensitizer, drying it completely, and placing a negative in contact with the emulsion. Put the sensitized paper and negative in your contact frame and lay a series of opaque strips over the coated test piece. These strips will be removed, one at a time, at predetermined intervals and then processed for the information. You can also use a transparent step wedge for this task but I feel the negative's information from the test is often more important than how many gradations you might achieve with it. When the test exposure is done, process it in tap water until the whites have cleared and there is no evidence of yellow in the wash water. Then, quickly blow-dry the strip and you'll get a rough idea of approximately what the best exposure will be. Be aware that cyanotype print values will darken over a period of 24 hours as the print oxidizes. You can accelerate this oxidization by immersing the washed print in a weak solution of hydrogen peroxide.

Cyanotype is a printing-out process, so you can examine your exposure as you go, providing you are using a hinged contact printing frame. I generally like to see, in a predevelopment examination of the exposure, highlight detail that is a great deal denser than I would be happy with in a finished print. Occasionally I want my deepest shadow areas to have a nearly solarized look (*the density has begun to reverse itself and is transforming to a lighter, almost metallic negative gray*).

In particular, I watch the outside-coated borders that are wide open to all of the exposure. More often than not, the best cyanotypes will be realized when the outside borders have reversed themselves to a silvery-gray. Another "in general" piece of information is that thicker papers, and double coatings, often take a bit longer to expose than do thinner papers and single coatings. Always write down your exposure time on the paper so that you can evaluate your progress over the course of a printing session.

Split Exposure to Increase Shadow Details

One more thing about exposure . . . Judy Seigel has suggested a technique in which the cyanotype exposure is halted halfway through what has been previously determined to be the correct exposure. The Printing frame is placed in a low-light level environment and, after 5–10 minutes, the exposure is resumed. She reports that this interrupted printing results in noticeably better shadow details and separation without losing highlight or D-max integrity. Judy's suggestions are always worthwhile and this may be another good control option to use. Mike Ware suggests that this technique may allow for a greater degree of print-out, which may be slow to build, and therefore more self-masking.

Figure 7–10

Brenton Hamilton, *Gardener,* **2004-05**

Maine artist, Brenton Hamilton, has an unusual exposure unit . . . the back of his pick-up truck. Brenton, one of the best alt pro teachers around, and he creates negatives that are quite dense and that are made with paper masks, post-its, and frisket film. In pleasant weather, he takes his loaded contact frame for a ride and makes exposures lasting 8–12 hours. The Cyanotypes are nearly black when fully processed. The final steps consist of 5 to 8 conventional gum bichromate passes, quite a bit of free hand drawing, and occasional gold leafing.

(Courtesy of the artist)

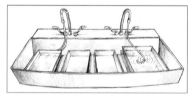

SINK SET UP FOR CYANOTYPE

Tray 1 Initial wash development/running water

Tray 2 Hydrogen Peroxide 3% (a splash) in a liter of water for instant oxidation, dry-down, and "wow-factor."

Tray 3 Final wash—running water

DEVELOPMENT: WATER OR ACID

Traditionally, the cyanotype is developed out in a water bath. This is the least complicated step possible and is the preferred development by most everyone who works with the process. The one shortcoming of water development, if your negative isn't perfect, may be a moderately limited tonal scale. Of course, your tonal scale is dependent on more than your water development but there are solutions to a restricted range of tonalities that go beyond your negative.

An alternative development process, one that often produces a longer tonal scale, involves using dilute acidic solutions made up of water and distilled white vinegar. Other acids that work well would include acetic acid, citric acid, or nitric acid (which works best of all). The nice part of this alternative is that the tonal range will be extended without having to lengthen the exposure. The downside is that by trading for a longer tonal scale you will often lose on the highlight to shadow contrast in the print. You might think of an acid or vinegar development bath as one that turns the cyanotype into a soft graded paper.

The simplest solution to begin experimenting with would be household white vinegar: generally the equivalent of a 5% concentration of acetic acid. White vinegar can be used straight from the bottle or diluted with water for more flexibility. In its pure state, it is worth about 2 to 4 levels on a step table. Here are a few signs to look for if you decide to use vinegar as a development option.

◆ **White vinegar out of the bottle**: A significant increase in the range of values (2 to 4 steps) but a relative decrease in the contrast. This might be a good formula for negatives that are hopelessly too high-key. A hydrogen peroxide "oxidation-hit" will have little effect on this straight vinegar-developed print.

◆ **Vinegar and water 1:1**: Some of the image's highlight crispness begins to return without a loss in the step table. Accelerated oxidation with hydrogen peroxide has a negligible effect in deepening the blue in the print.

◆ **Vinegar and water 1:3**: A 2 to 3-step increase in mid-tone values, better highlight detail and the hydrogen peroxide oxidation adds a little intensification to the blue.

◆ **Vinegar and water 1:5**: Still a pretty decent range in the additional steps and the highlights are better. Decent D-max (*maximum density*) equal to the other prints in the test sequence and the hydrogen peroxide has a modest effect.

◆ **Citric Acid**: A 1% solution of citric acid, 10 g per liter of water, will behave like a 1:2 water to vinegar concentration. Be careful; if you don't remove every trace of the acid from your print it will fade. Be sure to wash your print thoroughly.

If you are using Mike Ware's New Cyanotype Process, explained later, the effects of vinegar development are less distinct. However, that fact is somewhat irrelevant if you are using Ware's formula, which has a longer and

Figure 7–11

Vincent Carney, *Graffiti* I

Vincent scans his negatives into Photoshop to enlarge the image size and adjust the image contrast for the cyanotype process. He then prints out a new negative onto Pictorico OHP. The prints were made with Ware's new cyanotype formula, developed in a 10% citric acid solution, and printed on handmade paper.

(Courtesy of the artist)

similar tonal scale and a softer look to the overall image. Mike's process does employ an acid development that softens contrast.

Acid Post-Development Bath for Additional Tonal Range

Another option for additional tonal range when developing cyanotypes is the technique of rinsing your cyanotype print in a mild acid bath following the regular water development. Adding this acid bath step will often result in an intensification of the darker values while reducing the lighter ones. Traditional manuals, such as the *Kodak Encyclopedia of Practical Photography*, suggest a post-development bath of 4 to 5 drops of hydrochloric acid per 1000 ml of water for a few minutes. I have also heard of cyanotype artists who use weak solutions of citric acid, both chemical and natural, in this step. For fun, try squeezing a few lemons into a water bath and note the effect. You will likely see a bit of clearing and a marginal intensification of darker values.

WASHING

After exposure and development, wash your developed cyanotype print in running water for 5 to 15 minutes or until the highlights have cleared to white. You should no longer see any yellow-green coloration in the water. Pay attention to your washing times. Shorter washing times will leave ferric salts in the paper. Too long a washing time will cause both fading, through a pigmentation loss, and a noticeable decrease in highlight detail.

THE BIG THRILL: IMMEDIATE OXIDATION AND GRATIFICATION

If you need instant gratification, and we all do from time to time, try this. After the first wash, remove the print from the water and add a splash of drugstore grade, 3%, hydrogen peroxide to the water bath. This is the same solution that you put on cuts to prevent infections. It is not the solution that beauty salons use to turn hair different colors. That is a 33% solution and not something to which you would want to subject your new cyanotype print to.

After you add a splash of hydrogen peroxide to your tray of water, about a liter will do, re-immerse the print and watch the blues turn an immediate, and intense, deep blue. This action causes the highlights to appear super white because of their new-found relationship to the suddenly very enhanced and dark blues. This intensification "trick" is everyone's favorite. Really, though, all that is happening is that you are accelerating the oxidization of the iron in the print that will happen naturally without your help the final densities will be the same. Hydrogen peroxide can be used immediately after the yellow has been washed out of the print. You can mix it casually and without fear; after all, this solution is used to clean wounds and as a mouthwash. Don't forget the washing stage after being thrilled.

CLEARING HIGHLIGHTS

A 1%—5% Oxalic Acid Bath for Clearing Highlights and Stains

Immersing a completed cyanotype print in a 1%–5% solution of oxalic acid can aid in clearing white highlights in your print if that is a problem that needs to be corrected. To make a 5% solution, mix 5 grams of oxalic acid with 100 ml of water. This solution is particularly successful for spotting blue stains out of highlight areas. *Take all necessary precautions when using oxalic acid because it is toxic.*

Sodium Carbonate Bath for Reducing Density

If you find that you have significantly over-exposed your cyanotype, a difficult thing to do most of the time, you may want to try this last gasp remedy as a fix. Take 1000 ml of water and add a "pinch" of sodium carbonate and stir thoroughly. Immerse your wet, over-exposed cyanotype into the solution and agitate gently for a few seconds. Then move to a clean water tray and wait for the results. If nothing happens, repeat the process but leave the print in the sodium carbonate a little longer. Eventually, your print will begin bleaching. Sometimes a lovely yellow split tone will form between the highlights and the shadows. Watch out for the first signs of yellow. Too strong a concentration or too long in the sodium carbonate solution will have a serious bleaching effect. If you

Figure 7–12

Brooke Williams, *Self With Family, Jamaica, 1987*—Cyanotype

Brooke made this mural piece while a student of mine at Harvard (she's in the upper left panel.) The work documents a personal and family experience while visiting Jamaica. The text around the outside of the 6 panels is printed on acetate, used as a negative, and contains quotations from Brooke's journals and the writing of Marcus Garvey.

(Courtesy of the artist)

feel you went too far with this idea, you can consult the toning section for techniques on where to go next. Tannic acid would be a likely option. If you opt to do nothing at all with your over-exposed print, save it and try a Blue-Van-Dyke print or print a gum bichromate print on top of it . . . or simply throw it out and do a new one.

Cyanotype Fading

Some papers that you might consider for your cyanotype work, which includes nearly every variety you can imagine, are buffered with a mild base or alkali such as chalk/calcium carbonate. (*See Chemistry Appendix A.*) This is not unusual for any material that may end up being considered as archival. On occasion, the manufacturer of

the paper does not provide this information so you may be inclined, especially if the print is going to be collected, to test the pH of the paper yourself . . . as any alkali will cause a cyanotype to fade. You can buy an inexpensive pH-testing pen, like a highlight marker, from Light Impressions, Talas, or similar store.

TONING THE CYANOTYPE

There will be times when you simply do not want a blue image but still want to use the cyanotype technique due to its flexibility and simplicity. The following are some formulas for changing the color of cyanotypes once they have completed the final wash. In general, it is a good

Figure 7–13
**Lucy Soutter, *Harvard Diptych*, 1990—
cyanotype**
This is a cyanotype diptych that Lucy
made while a student of mine at Harvard.
(Courtesy of the artist)

Figure 7–14
**Alexander Hartray, *The Kiss*, 1986—
tannic acid toned cyanotype**
Alex made this image, while a graduate
student at Harvard, by creating a large
inter-negative on a piece of graphic arts
film and contact printing it on a cyanotype sensitized sheet of printmaking
paper. The print color is due to a post
print toning sequence of sodium carbonate and tannic acid.
(Courtesy of the artist)

idea to overexpose your prints if you intend to tone them. Many of the following formulas utilize sodium carbonate or ammonia, which tend to reduce print density if the solutions are too strong.

Note: These toning suggestions are essentially variations on the theme of alkaline hydrolysis of the Prussian blue followed by the formation of ferric tannate or gallate that forms the new color palette. They are interesting to play with and modify and they almost always lead to prints that look better wet than when dry.

A word of encouragement . . . many times the formulas will not work as you want them to due to water types, contamination, time of year, etc. Take these formulas with a large grain of salt and adapt them to your own aesthetic. Very often, during workshops, I will simply pour and sprinkle formulas together to reinforce the idea that the results from these toning suggestions are not set in stone, either alone, or in combination with other toners. Besides, what have you got to lose? The process is simple, inexpensive, and accidents often become individual and unique techniques.

There is the issue of permanence to consider. The cyanotype, in a pure Prussian-blue state and handled correctly, is very permanent and one of the most stable alternative processes. Toning changes the chemical composition of the cyanotype image and it is occasionally questionable if all of these formulas can be described as "permanent" after the fact. I have found virtually no deterioration in the images I toned with tannic acid over 20 years ago. This is not the case with images done during group toning demonstrations, where inadequate washing times between steps are often the rule . . . especially with sodium carbonate.

It is a good idea to *dry* your cyanotype prints before toning them and to let them oxidize for a day or so. After they have been dried, you should re-wet them to tone. This soaking stage will allow the toning solutions to cover and penetrate the paper's fibers more completely and makes for a smoother-looking tonality in the print. The formulas given are equivalent in ratios and you may

Figure 7–15
Grace Huang, *Portrait of Stefanie, 1989*
Grace Huang made this portrait of Stefanie London in cyanotype and then split toned it with a very dilute toning bath of sodium carbonate, creating the blue yellow split.
(Courtesy of the artist)

feel free to modify the amounts in order to adequately cover the size of your prints.

Removing Blue: Getting Yellow

Many chemicals will alter the intensity of the blue, and change the values of the whites in your cyanotypes. As previously mentioned, hydrogen peroxide, oxalic acid, and sodium carbonate will all cause the blues to change, as will solutions of chlorine bleach, sodium sulfate, sodium silicate, tri-sodium phosphate, sprays of bathroom cleaner, and commercial laundry soaps. You may elect to apply these selectively with a paintbrush or make up diluted baths to alter entire prints.

For example, to make a yellow and white print, make a solution of trisodium phosphate in a ratio of 1 tablespoon to every quart of water. Dissolve the trisodium phosphate in hot water in a plastic tub or tray, and immerse the over-exposed cyanotype in the solution until it fades to yellow. Rinse the print with running water for 30 minutes, or, if using fabrics, run the fabric through a cold wash cycle without soap. The resulting image will be permanent.

Yellow/Blue Split Tones

This is a very simple adaptation of the above and seems to work best in the city where there is a good deal of iron in the water supply. Allow the exposed and washed print to age for a day or two. Re-wet the print and immerse it in a hydrogen peroxide bath followed by a 20-minute rinse. Then place the print in a very weak solution of sodium carbonate (*a pinch between thumb and forefinger to a 1000 ml of water*). Immediately transfer it to a fresh water bath to observe the changes. Allow the changes to occur in the wash water rather than the sodium carbonate to achieve the split. After you are satisfied, wash the print well for 20 minutes.

Basic Tea Toner

Buy some basic and inexpensive household tea (*tannic acid*) and make a very strong solution in hot water. Immerse your print in it until you have the desired tonality. Using a solution of tea as a toner is a nice way to have the print's highlights exhibit a pleasant tan color while the blue takes on a slightly warmer hue. If you don't want any blue, just go through the yellow toning stage with trisodium phosphate and then move on to the tea toning. Using green and herbal teas without tannic acid in them does not work as well. However, if you boil onionskins, and reduce the liquid a bit, and then soak the cyanotype for a while in the solution you can get a lovely bronzing effect.

Brown Toning #1

Part A:

12 ml   non-detergent, household strength, ammonia added to 1000 ml of water (*you may have to modify this percentage as the effect will be dependent upon your exposure*)

Part B:

60 g   tannic acid added and mixed well and added to 500 ml of water

Tannic acid mixing takes a little patience because it does not dissolve readily in water. Break up the clumps and keep stirring until the chemical is in solution. It smells like instant iced tea mix so it isn't an unpleasant task. Immerse the washed and wet print in Part A until it starts to exhibit signs of fading to pale. Rinse the print for 15 minutes. Then, transfer the print to Part B for the conversion to brown. In all of the toning formulas, too short a rinsing time between stages is the primary culprit in the discoloration of highlights and paper-base white.

Black Toning # 1

The success of this toner is not guaranteed. Sometimes it rocks, sometimes it doesn't. Immerse the print in a solution of Dektol. The stronger the Dektol solution the more intense the goldenrod color that will present itself to you. When the blue is almost entirely bleached out, rinse the print for several minutes in water and then immerse it in a solution of tannic acid mixed to 50 g per 1000 ml of water. You should see a smoky black color within 5 minutes. Wash the toned print for 20 minutes.

Eggplant/Red/Black Tones

Age your cyanotype print for 24 hours and re-wet before beginning the toning sequence. Use the Black toning #1 procedure and after the final wash immerse the print in the strong Dektol solution again. For reddish tones, wash in a light sodium carbonate bath (a pinch to a liter of water). I've made violet by making an ammonia bath solution consisting of 250 ml ammonia to 1000 ml water. Play around with this and see what happens.

Black Toning #2

Part A:

6 drops   concentrated nitric acid * added to 1 liter water

Part B:

55 g   sodium carbonate added to 640 ml water

Part C:

55 g   gallic acid added to 640 ml water

Begin by immersing the washed and wet cyanotype print into Part A (nitric acid) for 2 minutes. Be careful; use tongs or nitrile gloves.

Figure 7–16

Amanda Bross, *What to Wear*, 2001—cyanotype and Van Dyke

Amanda, a graduate of AIB, made this whimsical sculptural piece by contact printing medium format negatives and making prints in cyan and Van Dyke. These were stitched together and given tiny hangers to hang . . . presumably in tiny closets.

(Courtesy of the artist)

Then rinse the print for 10 minutes in running water and transfer it to Part B and leave it in this sodium carbonate solution until it disappears and then reappears as a very light orange image.

Then, rinse the print for 10 minutes and transfer it into Part C where the black tones should become evident. Finally, wash the print for at least 15—20 minutes. Your tones may be in the gray to black area depending upon the initial density of the exposure. Print accordingly.

Nitric Acid*

Concentrated nitric acid is not a chemical to take lightly. This is evident as soon as you take the plastic top off the bottle and see the white vapors rising toward the ceiling. Please do not be casual with this chemical. Be sure to read about it in the chemical section in the Chemical section, Appendix A, and wear proper protective lab gloves and a mask when working with nitric acid. When toning, you can always work with a larger volume of more dilute acid for safety.

Blue/Gray Split Toning

Age your cyanotype print for 24 hours and re-wet before beginning the toning sequence. Mix a solution of 6 drops of nitric acid in 1000 ml water and immerse your print in it for 2 minutes. Then, wash the print for 10 minutes. Next, immerse the print in a weak (*a pinch to 1000 ml of water*) sodium carbonate solution until a yellow split occurs, and then wash the print for 10 minutes. Mix up a tannic acid solution of 50 g to 1000 ml water and immerse the print in it until a blue/gray split appears. Finally, wash the print well for 15 to 20 minutes.

Rose Toning

Follow the directions for the blue/gray toning. After the last step in that sequence, immerse the print in a light sodium carbonate solution (a pinch to 1000 ml of water) until rose colored and then wash the print for 20 minutes.

Green Toning

Age your cyanotype print for 24 hours and re-wet before beginning the toning sequence. This toner is a bit complicated if you don't have proper ventilation and I wouldn't recommend attempting it unless you can tone outdoors or under a chemical lab hood. The reason is the Sulfuric Acid. Once I was attempting to show this toner to my class at Harvard and neglected to notice that it was a full strength solution . . . a lazy mistake that essentially ended class for the day due to the fumes. In any event, here's a pretty interesting formula for green tones.

Prepare a 1% solution of sulfuric acid. Photographer's Formulary has a 48% solution that they can ship but you're going to need a DEA Form filled out and submitted before getting the stuff. Best bet is to be in a university setting and to make friends with the science and chemistry people. While you're there, use their chemical hood. To make a 1% solution you need to add 1 ml of the concentrated acid to every 100 ml of distilled water. **Note: although this rule doesn't apply to all acids, it is better to be safe than sorry so REMEMBER: always add an acid to water . . .** not the other way around, or it may splatter upon contact. You're going to need at least 500 ml to immerse the print. Again, you can always work with a larger volume of a more dilute stock acid for more safety. When your acid bath is prepared, immerse your print until you like the color you see. A caveat . . . this toner doesn't always work and I can't explain the reason since I don't particularly enjoy working with sulfuric acid. Wash afterwards for 20 minutes.

Eggplant Black #1

In the first tray, stir a pinch of sodium carbonate into liter of water. Be aware of how much sodium carbonate you use as very light dilutions are best and where the bleaching effect is slower rather than immediate. Attention to this will help with possible staining in the highlights later. Try a test piece of cyanotype. If it

Figure 7–17

Grace Huang, *Thesis*, 1989—sodium carbonate and tannic toned cyanotype *(Courtesy of the artist)*

bleaches too quickly, then add water to the solution to dilute it.

For the second tray, mix 10 tablespoons tannic acid into a quart of water and stir for a while. This tannic mix may be much stronger than you need to get the job done but it works for me. If you find it is too strong, and you see evidence of staining, add water to the solution. You might also try a bath of oxalic acid after you wash the print for a while.

Dry your prints for a day or two and re-wet them in a water bath. Begin by immersing your wet print into the first tray of sodium carbonate for a very brief time. The sodium carbonate decomposes the iron blue quite quickly so watch it closely. I like to slip the print into this solution and immediately remove it to a water bath for the bleaching effect to take place. Generally, this stage is pretty flexible and the less iron blue that decomposes, the greater the possibility of a split-toned image. Next, rinse the print and immerse it in the tannic acid bath for as long as you want. The greater the concentration, and time of immersion, the deeper the color. I've had students leave a print in the tannic acid bath for 24 hours. The darks are beautiful but the highlights get hammered and will turn a sepia tone most of the time if the immersion is too lengthy. If you are seeking an image effect that feels like the Stone Age . . . this is your toner. Wash the print for 20 minutes when it's done with the chemistry.

Violet Tones #1

Prepare a weak borax solution and immerse the print in it until you see a color change that pleases you. The concentration of the borax to water is flexible and you should play around with it. This particular toner often looks good in the wet state but has a tendency to flatten out after drying. Water type will play a role in determining the degree of violet you might get. A caveat: often this lovely violet will revert back to the original cyanotype blue in a few days so don't be upset if that happens. If you really like the violet, do a violet gum over the cyanotype.

Violet/Gray Tones #2

You can occasionally get the violet/gray shift by making a solution of 5 g of lead acetate in 100 ml of distilled water. This works best if the lead acetate solution is not acidic, i.e., pure water is pH 7. Immerse the print in this solution until you see a color that you like. Then, wash the print well for 15 minutes. Be cautious of the lead acetate because it is not one of the harmless chemicals. Do not dispose of lead acetate down the drain and continue to reuse the toner formula until it doesn't do anything anymore. It is possible to continue this formula by immersing the print in a bath of citric acid following the wash. This bath will result in a very deep blue/violet.

Violet Tones #3

Age your cyanotype print for 24 hours and re-wet before beginning the toning sequence. Prepare a tray with a liter of water and to this add a splash of household ammonia. Stir the ammonia into solution and immerse the wet print. You should get an immediate violet image that is really quite lovely. Don't admire it for too long a time as it will begin to fade away. Remove the print before you

Figure 7–18
Emily Barton, *Self Portrait*, 1987—toned cyanotype
Emily made this 4-piece heavily toned cyanotype montage when she was a student of mine at Harvard. Emily is the author of two best-selling novels, *The Testament of Yves Gundron* and *Brookland*.
(Courtesy of the artist)

get to the point where you love it and place it in a tray of warm water. Wash for 20 minutes and hang to dry. Enjoy it for a short time . . . it will not be permanent.

Purple-Brown Toning

Mix up a *hot* solution of tannic acid at 70 g to 1000 ml water. To this solution add a drop or two of pyrogallic acid. Then, immerse the print until the blue turns to a lilac color and rinse the print for 5–10 minutes. If you like the color, simply complete the wash stage and don't do any additional toning. If you wish to go to the purple-brown, immerse the print in a caustic potash solution made with 15 grams of caustic potash to 1000 ml of water until the desired color is achieved. After toning, wash the print well for 15 minutes.

Figure 7–19

Willis Odundo Making His Cyanotype, 2006, Kageno Kids, Kenya

Jayne Hinds Bidaut is a volunteer artist/teacher for Kageno Kids in Kenya, an outreach program that transforms communities suffering from oppressive poverty into places of hope. Kageno Kids focuses on the children, primarily orphans, living within those communities. One of her students is Willis Odundo and she made this image of Willis showing his friends how to make a cyanotype. Willis lost both of his parents to HIV/AIDS and now lives with his grandmother and has recently been sponsored so that he can attend primary school. If you want to help this outstanding organization, go to www.kagenokids.org for information.

(Courtesy of Kageno Kids and Jayne Hinds Bidaut)

Gray to Reddish Tones

Mix up a solution of 48 g of copper nitrate dissolved in 100 ml of distilled water. Then, add 5 drops of household ammonia and mix it well into solution. Immerse the print until the desired color is achieved and wash the print well in running water for 15 to 20 minutes.

Eggplant Black Toning with Dark Cyan

Begin with a dense and over-exposed cyanotype. Age your cyanotype print for 24 hours and re-wet before beginning the toning sequence. Immerse the print in a very weak sodium carbonate dilution (a pinch of sodium carbonate to 2000 ml of water) until the lightest highlights open up. Immediately move it to a wash tray for 10 minutes.

Then, immerse the bleached print in a strong tannic solution, 50 grams to a half liter of water) for another 5 minutes and wash the print again for 10 minutes. Return the print to the weak sodium carbonate bath and a lovely rose color will appear. You may stop here if you want and rinse for 20 minutes.

However, if you want the eggplant black with deep cyan then take your print, after it has rinsed for 10 minutes following the last sodium carbonate bath, and immerse it in a tray with a small amount of ammonia to a liter of water. Observe the changes and stop it when the color you want is reached. Finally, wash the print well for 20–30 minutes.

Figure 7–20
Willis Odundo, *Cyanotype*, 2006, Kageno Kids, Kenya
This is Willis Odundo's finished cyanotype.
(Courtesy of Kageno Kids and Jayne Hinds Bidaut)

Figure 7–21
Michele Robins, *Tokyo Harbor*, 2006
Michele, a Ph.D. Clinical Associate at the University of Pennsylvania
Medical School, made this outstanding cyanotype using a map of Tokyo
as her substrate.
(Courtesy of the artist)

Violet-Black Toning

Age your cyanotype print for 24 hours and re-wet it before beginning the toning sequence. Mix up a weak solution of sodium carbonate as in previous formulas, and immerse the print until it has turned a pale yellow. Wash the print for 10 minutes. Then, mix a solution of 8 g of gallic acid, 0.5 g of pyrogallic acid, and 1000 ml of water and immerse the print until the desired color is reached. Wash the print for 15 to 20 minutes and hang to dry.

Red-Brown Toning

Age your cyanotype print for 24 hours and then immerse it in a solution of non-detergent (also known as non-sudsy) household ammonia and water, mixed in solution at approximately 32 ml to 1000 ml of water until the print turns a violet color. Wash the print for 15 minutes and then immerse it in a strong solution of tannic acid and water (50 g to 500 ml water) for 5 to 10 minutes.

After the tannic acid bath, wash the print for 5 minutes. If you like the brown color, stop the process at this point and wash for 20 minutes. If you feel like going on, immerse the print in a strong solution of sodium carbonate until a deep red—brown appears and then wash the print well for 20 minutes.

Dark Blue/Blue Violet/Rose Split

Follow the directions for the rich red-brown toner. After washing, quickly immerse the print in the strong tannic acid again and then wash the print for 5 minutes. Then, immerse the print in the gold—borax toner formula used for salted paper toning (400 ml distilled water, 3 g borax, 6 ml 1% gold chloride) until you see the split. Finally, wash the print for 20 minutes.

Figure 7–22

Catherine Jansen, *The Blue Room*, 1981—cyanotype installation

Catherine Jansen has been inspiring students and artists for decades and her *Blue Room* is a work that I have been showing in lectures for many years. I have seen this image instantly transform a student's approach to alternative process image making.
(Courtesy of the artist)

Figure 7–23
Lisa Elmaleh, *Self*, Santa Fe, 2006
SVA graduate Lisa Elmaleh produced this piece in my alt pro workshop in Santa Fe in 2006. This image is a relatively accurate interpretation of her quiet and introspective personality.
(Courtesy of the artist)

Cyanotype: Variations & Adaptations

OVERVIEW & EXPECTATIONS

In this chapter, I'll explore the possibilities of creating large cyanotype murals with sensitized fabrics. In addition, I'll discuss other variations, and possible adaptations, of this very flexible process. We will describe Dr. Mike Ware's New Cyanotype process, cyanotypes on alternative materials, cyanotypes combined with other alternative processes, and ways in which the process is incorporated into artist's books, sculpture, and ceramics. I'll also introduce you to a number of ways in which you can prepare non-traditional substrates, such as glass and ceramics, for cyanotype printing.

Cyanotype on fabric printing is a wonderful and engaging way to make photogram murals, unique clothing, installations, bed linens, quilts, costumes, or anything else that you feel might be improved if it had one or more of your images on it. It is also a terrific way to make giant photograms with a group, especially brand-new students in a first project, in that it allows them to play with translucent, transparent, and opaque elements, such as their own bodies, in order to make a collaborative piece of art. A cyanotype mural activity also teaches them, in the best way possible, what photography is really all about.

You are also going to be introduced to the great concept of bringing photography to places where the medium could not normally be taught or learned. In this chapter you are going to see examples of work done by children in Kenya with Jayne Hinds Bidaut and in Nicaragua with Ronnie Maher. If you are inclined to make a difference in this world with your photographic work, you will find this idea compelling and just about perfect.

Figure 8–1

Cyanotype Mural, *Maine*, 1999

I begin every alternative process class and workshop, weather permitting, with a cyanotype mural. This exercise gets everyone involved and together immediately and provides me with a captive audience for 20–25 minutes where I can talk about the history, cultural influences, and chemistry of alternative processes.

(Courtesy of the author)

THE CYANOTYPE MURAL EXPERIENCE

Materials You Will Need

Fabric: The Simple and Perfect Solution

I'm going to begin by making your life really simple. Instead of hand dunking and hanging a huge piece of fabric in the dark, and being blue for the next week, the easiest way to do the cyanotype mural is to buy the fabric already coated, guaranteed and ready to go . . . you will be extremely happy you did this.

Go on line and order a pre-coated cyanotype fabric, in sizes ranging from 12" squares, for quilting, to 9' × 18' for wall hangings and clothing. The site address: www.blueprintsonfabric.com. Linda Stemer runs the show and pre-coats and sells high quality prepared fabrics, i.e., 100% cotton, raw silk, Chinese silk, etc. Linda is a terrific human being, so don't be afraid to call her.

Fabric: The Less Simple Solution

If you insist on coating your own fabrics, a good idea if you intend to make a cyanotype on your own pajamas, you will need 100% cotton, silk, or linen fabric. . . anything from clothes to bed sheets to canvas. It is imperative that you use the best fabric you can afford. Be sure to wash new material several times in complete hot water cycles to remove the manufacturer's sizing. It is also a known truth that 100% cotton labels do not always mean that the fabric is 100% cotton. Just ask printmakers about how difficult it is to get true 100% cotton print-making papers.

During recent summer alternative process workshops in Maine, Colorado, and Oklahoma, we have used several different types of king-size sheets from discount stores and catalogues. In each case, the thread count was between 230 and 300 and the material was labeled as being 100% cotton. The best results came from Martha Stewart sheets purchased at a mall discount store that had a label declaring they were manufactured in Pakistan. The identical sheet, labeled "*Made in the USA*," felt "*crispier*" when wet but was indistinguishable from the Pakistani-made sheet after an identical exposure and development. However, when both sheets had "*dried down*," the Pakistani sheet remained rich and saturated with a wonderful blue color, whereas the USA-made sheet had faded by nearly 50%. We repeated the test with a longer exposure and more chemistry on the USA sheet and achieved only a slight change in color density.

Synthapol: Sizing Remover

To remove sizing from new fabric, there is a product that fiber artists use called Synthapol. It can be purchased from the Dharma Trading Company. Synthapol is normally used to remove any loose dye particles at the end of the fabric dyeing process. Synthapol prevents the migration of dyes that may wash out. Synthapol may be found wherever fabric-dyeing chemicals are sold. Follow label directions.

If You Don't Have Any Synthapol

The first thing you should do when you bring home fabric is to run it through several complete hot water wash cycles in the laundry. The purpose of this washing is to remove the sizing put into the sheets during manufacturing. The hot wash with a little soap loosens the sizing and a hot rinse clears it away. *If you rinse with cold water, you simply reset the sizing that remains in the fibers.*

My last recommendation, if you are not going to be purchasing pre-sensitized fabric, is to try to buy used sheets and linens from hotels, as they have been washed hundreds of times and are probably perfect for your needs. You can also go online to a site like Craig's List and ask for old, used sheets. I know it sounds a little kinky but you can get anything there pretty quickly.

Development Equipment: Trash Can & Hose

A large plastic trashcan that is either very clean or lined with a 39 gallon/contractor's grade plastic trash bag. You'll need the garden hose to fill up the trashcan.

Or Better Yet . . . The Ocean!

You may not always be making your mural near an outside spigot that a hose can be attached to. In these situations, you always have nature. Keep in mind that one of

Figure 8–2
Bayside Cyanotype Mural, *Maine #1 & #2,*
2004—**cyanotype mural**
As part of my Teacher's Workshops, with
Craig Stevens, at The Maine Photographic
Workshops, we take the participants to an
old seaside vacation community called
Bayside. Then we tell the teachers to inspire
the vacationing children there and teach
them how to produce a cyanotype mural
using the ocean for the wash-development.
(Courtesy of the author)

the beauties of this process is that you can safely use the ocean, or a river, for your washing out the unexposed iron salts in your cyanotype mural. When asked by concerned passers-by about how we might be fouling the environment I simply point out that we are adding a little additional salt to the ocean. The idea of processing in a trash bucket with a garden hose, or in a surf line at the ocean, is so seductively low tech that even if you have no interest in doing a cyanotype mural you owe it to yourself to have the experience.

Instant Oxidation & Gratification

A quart of drug store grade (3%) hydrogen peroxide for instant oxidation and gratification. The rapid deep blue that is achieved in a hydrogen peroxide bath is exciting but don't worry if you don't have any; the cyanotype will get deep blue on its own as normal oxidation occurs.

Push Pins & Clothesline

You will need push pins or a clothesline, strung high between trees, for drying. Don't forget the clothespins.

Figure 8–3
Bayside Cyanotype Mural, *Maine #3*—**2004**
Here's the finished mural and the kids who made it. As soon as the documentation is done we have a raffle and one of the kids gets to take it home.
(Courtesy of the author)

Dry Ground

A dry ground area to lay out the fabric and the students. If the ground area is damp the cyanotype mural will begin to develop during the exposure. . . eliminating your highlight areas. If your location is a problem then lay down a plastic tarp, or an inexpensive plastic drop cloth, sold in every hardware store in the world.

CHEMISTRY: A & B

Chemistry—Home Made Coating

If you are not purchasing a pre-sensitized fabric and have chosen to coat at home, good luck. Here are a few things to consider. The easiest and least expensive way to deal with the hand coating task is to buy the chemistry in bulk form. Mixing the cyanotype chemistry is quite simple and very inexpensive when purchased through a chemical supply. If you are pressed for time, and don't object to paying more money than you need to, you can buy your solutions in wet or dry pre-measured kits from the Photographer's Formulary or Bostick & Sullivan. You'll need a small digital gram scale for gram weight measuring and these can be found on eBay for very little cost. Type in "jeweler's gram scale" and the bargains will appear.

On average, it will take 3000 ml to 4000 ml of sensitizer to coat a king-size sheet with a dunk-style coating technique in a plastic tub. If you decide to be frugal and purchase the raw chemicals from a chemical supply, all you will need at home is an inexpensive gram scale. One pound (453 g) of both ferric ammonium citrate and potassium ferricyanide will cost less than $40 and will make more solution than you will likely use in a year. By comparison, an average prepared kit, yielding 1000 to 2000 ml of prepared solution, cost about $20. The following formula will yield 2000 ml of working solution.*

---

* Neither of the chemicals in this formula poses a serious health risk unless you are one of the very few people who may have an allergic reaction to them. Ferric ammonium citrate is often found in iron and vitamin supplements and potassium ferricyanide is a stable compound that only becomes a risk if it is heated above 300°F or if it is combined with a strong acid. Wear latex, or nitrile, gloves when mixing and coating to simply avoid becoming blue for a few days.

Figure 8–4
Detail from an Oklahoma O.S.A.I. Mural, 1999
This is a detail of a mural from my 1999
workshop made at The Oklahoma Summer Arts
Institute (OSAI).
(Courtesy of the author)

Cyanotype Stock A

200 g   ferric ammonium citrate
1000 ml   distilled water
Stir these 2 components into a uniform solution.
Pour the solution into an opaque storage container
and label it.

Cyanotype Stock B

80 g   potassium ferricyanide
1000 ml   distilled water

Stir these 2 components into a uniform solution.
Pour the solution into a different opaque storage
container and label it.

You now have two separate 1000 ml opaque bottles:
1000 ml of Stock A and 1000 ml of Stock B. Let the two
solutions "ripen" for 24 hours. If you experience fading
after your first test try doubling the amount of chemistry
in the same volume of water, double coat, or change
material. If the problem doesn't go away then you are
probably dealing with something simple like not enough
exposure. Very little can go wrong with this process.

Coating: The Spray Method

In a room with a very low light level, mix equal parts of the Stock A and B solutions together (*your working sensitizer*) and pour them into a garden supply, heavy duty, spray bottle. Put on some old clothes you don't care about any more, latex gloves, so you don't turn blue, and a respirator. If you are planning to make a mural using the spray technique, hang the material on the line that you will dry on first . . . that way it can dry right where you sprayed it. The room you use must be able to become almost dark for the lengthy drying period.

Coating: The Dunk Method

For large mural pieces, using sheets or sizeable pieces of fabric, I advise you to use the dunking method. With this coating technique the entire sheet goes into the solution at once, which nearly guarantees an even coating. *Whether you are spraying, painting or dunking a fabric area, lay down newspaper and plastic sheeting to protect the floor from blue staining.*

Mix your prepared stock A & B solution so that you have an adequate amount of liquid sensitizer to totally saturate the piece(s) of fabric. Remember that a king-size cotton sheet will absorb about 4000 ml of sensitizer. A flannel sheet will take twice as much. Again, don't forget to put on a pair of latex gloves and wear old clothes that you don't care about. I once gave a 40" × 60" paper coating demo where I thought everything had gone really well. I walked home in a light mist and upon arriving discovered that my clothing and skin had turned a curious and semi-permanent speckled blue. The daylight had exposed the splattering and the mist had "developed" it during my walk. The speckling on my skin eventually wore off. Don't be alarmed if your clothes or skin get stained a little.

Next, take a large plastic tub and pour the A and B cyanotype solution into it. Turn down the room lights and immerse and knead your material into the solution until you are sure it has been completely coated. One immersion coating is sufficient as long as it is a saturating one. If you do *not* elect to use the dunking immersion method, I strongly advise applying a double coating to the material by either a brush or spray technique. Honestly, the dunking method is easier, cleaner, and much less of a hassle.

Your life will also be easier if you are in the same room where you will be hanging the coated material to dry. The ceiling should be higher than the sheet is long and you will need to have installed a taut clothesline to hang the soaking sheet on for drying. This hanging part is much easier with helper friends, a ladder, and good quality clothespins. Hang the sheet and make the room as dark as possible for the dry time. If you are in a hurry, you can go into the room and begin to blow-dry the material. Be forewarned that that is quite a tedious and annoying way to spend an hour or two. Be sure to wear a respirator if you decide to blow-dry. Once the material is dry, it is UV light-sensitive. Bag it and hope that the humidity in the air doesn't begin to develop the material. In this homemade coating situation it is best to use the material within 12 to 24 hours. If you have coated and hung the fabric in a damp environment such as a cellar, 12 hours may be stretching the limits.

THE BEST SOLUTION:

www.blueprintsonfabric.com

THE PROCESS

Almost 100% of the time I do cyanotype murals with large groups of people. Students, family gatherings, strangers I run into on the beach, it is simply more fun to have the mural experience with lots of people. It goes without saying that sunlight is your best and only UV source for murals of this size. It is possible to make an exposure under fluorescent lights but it's going to take a very long time and will eliminate the possibility of using human beings as subjects.

I usually begin by taking a group of people outdoors and explaining to them how we are going to create, together, a cyanotype mural. If these people are my students then they have already seen examples of the cyanotype murals in presentations and in real life on the floor, or walls, of my classroom or lab. I show them the black plastic bag that contains the pre-coated fabric and explain to them that the cotton material inside is coated with two simple iron salts . . . ferric ammonium citrate and potassium ferricyanide. I explain that these two chemicals are relatively safe, that they are salts that they

Figure 8–5
Kageno Kids, Kenya, *(preschool) Cyan Mural*, 2006
Jayne Hinds Bidaut is a volunteer for Kageno Kids, in Kenya, and this is a document of one of the murals she made with the pre-school kids.
(Courtesy of the artist and Kageno Kids)

will reduce from a ferric to a ferrous state during exposure. I then explain the chemistry and its role in the process . . . the ferric ammonium citrate is the "light trigger" and the potassium ferricyanide is responsible for making the piece cyan blue. I quickly explain what they will do and then tell them that I will continue the conversation once we begin the exposure.

It is important to do this exposure on a large surface that is free of moisture, as the process is a water development one and if there is moisture underneath the fabric it

Figure 8–6
Nicaragua Project, 2006 (NicaPhoto)
In 2005, Ronnie Maher volunteered to visit Nagarote, Nicaragua and conduct a photo workshop for the Jerónimo López Youth Project. Ronnie now makes several trips a year and is a N/NSCP board member. NicaPhoto stands for The Norwalk/Nagarote Sister City Project (N/NSCP), a partnership for sustainable community development between Norwalk, Connecticut, and Nagarote, Nicaragua. These young people are part of the López Youth Project where most of the 200 plus families struggle to get by on less than $2 a day. The Youth Project, which now has over 150 teens, provides year-round activities designed to offer young people an alternative to gangs, drugs, and crime prevalent in their neighborhoods. To learn more about the project, visit www.NicaPhoto.com
(Courtesy of the Ronnie Maher and NicaPhoto)

is likely that the highlights will be less than sparkling . . . they will have been developing during the exposure. I then ask everyone to go and gather objects to use with him or herself when we make our giant photogram.

When everyone returns from collecting . . . gather the people and props together and make decisions as to who and what will go where and for what period of time. You can move objects around during the exposure which will provide ghost images, double exposures, and illusions of movement. In a recent Maine Photographic Workshops Alternative class, we used an old bicycle as the central element in a mural. With an early morning light low on the horizon, the shadows of the bike, with one student appearing to ride it while another sat in the bike's basket, provided a wonderful illusion of depth and movement.

Various tie-dye techniques, such as small tufts of fabric tightly bunched with small rubber bands, will yield interesting star-like results, i.e. tie-dye. Misted water spray and water droplets thrown from your fingers will also create interesting abstract drawing elements, while long hair, grasses, and plant life always look great.

When everything is ready, assign one person to each corner of the fabric and whip the material out of the plastic bag or container that has been holding it. Lay it out and immediately cover it with your objects and the people who will be *exposed*. I then tell them to leap onto the fabric and to find a comfortable position to remain still in. The exposure will be taking about 18–23 minutes, depending on the time of year. A standard time will be 18 to 21 minutes, between 10:00 A.M. and 2:00 P.M., in the summer months and 23-25 minutes in the fall. I don't bother trying to make murals in the northeast in the winter.

Everyone on the sensitized fabric is now my captive audience and I use this opportunity to entertain and educate them. I begin to tell them the history of the process and to put what they are doing in context with the history of photography and the time it was created by Sir John Herschel. (*Please refer to A Little History in the Chapter 7, Cyanotype.*) I'll ask if anyone remembers the chemicals in the sensitizer and re-state the oxidation state conversion from ferric to ferrous that is taking place. Ask this question every few minutes during the exposure and by the end of the exposure everyone will be able to impress their friends with their new-found knowledge.

Figure 8–7
Christopher James, *Rachel with Wings,* **Maine, 1995**
Rachel with Wings *was made during a workshop cyanotype on fabric mural project. I made the image with a pinhole camera and Polaroid Type 55, P/N Film.*
(Courtesy of the author)

Figure 8–8
Kageno Kids, Kenya, With Their Cyanotypes, 2006
(Courtesy of the artist and Kageno Kids—photograph by Jayne Hinds Bidaut)

I ask the people on the mural to look at the color of the fabric. I want them to make the connection between the original bright chartreuse when we laid it out and the color as it changes during exposure. As the exposure goes along, the chartreuse yellow-green turns to a blue and eventually to a slate gray. This slate gray is the color we are seeking. I tell them that the only serious error they can make is to under-expose the mural. Please be patient and go the distance on the exposure . . . no matter how much your subjects complain.

With a minute to go, I quickly outline everything that is about to happen. I warn them that the exposure is about to end and that when I count to 10 they must leap off the fabric, grab any objects they have, and we'll race with the exposed fabric to the trash can filled with water, or to the river, lake, or ocean.

DEVELOPMENT

Develop your image in an appropriate body of water. Developing container options might include medium-sized trays for moderate-sized pieces, lawn & leaf bag lined trash cans (39 gallon size) for larger ones, and kiddy pools for very large ones. Wash the fabric in refreshed, moving water until the highlights are pure white or the original color of the fabric. Clearing the unexposed (still chartreuse-colored) sensitizer will take between 10 and 15 minutes.

If you are using a hose and a trash bucket, 4 to 5 complete water changes with a lot of sloshing around should do the job. On a hot and humid day, you might see an interesting sight. Some of the people who were props in the mural may have blue hands, faces, arms, and other body parts that were in contact with the sensitizer during the exposure. Small children who jump onto the fabric with wet bathing suits will always pre-develop the fabric directly underneath them and usually a segment or two of their skin.

If anyone is concerned about getting a chance to have blue skin then you can place a clear acetate, plastic, or food wrap between their skin and the sensitized fabric during the exposure. If someone does get stained, the blue can be scrubbed off easily with a phosphate based soap. If some of the blue stays on the skin it should be gone in a day or two. In decades of doing this I have never seen, or heard of, a problem.

You will notice that the shapes in the mural where people perspired have very interesting edges—scalloped and similar to tone-line drawings. In almost all hot humid day mural exposures you will be able to tell what kind of underwear your subjects are wearing . . . because the extra layer of fabric blocks their perspiration from reaching the fabric . . . this is always funny when everyone is examining the finished mural. Continue the water rinses until the highlights are clean and there is no more yellow salt run-off visible in the water.

Figure 8–9

Mike Ware, *Mandorla 1987–1999*—New Cyanotype

Although Herschel's was the first of the iron salt/non-silver processes, it has weathered the medium's transitions essentially unchanged since the year he combined the chemicals he received from Dr. Smee. Mike Ware decided to address the shortcomings of Herschel's original cyanotype process in order to make it even better and produced a new cyanotype process that is both user friendly and a fine addition to the alternative process menu. *(Courtesy of the artist)*

Instant Oxidation & Gratification

Now it is time for the "wow" factor. I make the last dump of the wastewater and re-fill the trashcan. Once there is sufficient water in it, I take the 3% hydrogen peroxide and casually dump a quarter to half a bottle into the can, explaining how precise measuring is critical to the success of this step. I do this to make them understand that this is play and that it is ok to change the rules.

The blue in the cyanotype will darken immediately and make everyone who participated in the mural feel very positive about the entire experience. Save the hydrogen peroxide solution if you are making a bunch of images. After 20 to 40 seconds, remove the material from the hydrogen peroxide bath and place it in clean, refreshed water for 4 to 6 complete fresh water exchanges. If you are at the beach, or some other natural body of water, fill your trash bag half way with water (don't try to pick it up) and pour in a little hydrogen peroxide. Add the yet-to-be intensified fabric and swirl it around for 20-40 seconds. When the time is up, just drop the sides of the plastic bag and continue with the washing cycle. *Note: if you are at the ocean you will want to eventually rinse the fabric in fresh water. The rush is not immediate but you will want to do it when you're back in civilization.*

Following the final wash, you can dry the mural by stringing it up on a clothesline, laying it out on the lawn, taking it to the side of the house, you decide. This sets you up to begin toning, dying, combining techniques, sewing quilts, or whatever else you had in mind. Think about it, this is just the beginning of the possibilities.

Post Exposure Washing Care

If you decide to make cyanotype clothing it may be socially appropriate to wash it on occasion. Cyanotypes will change to yellow if washed with phosphates. Try to avoid using detergents or laundry soaps containing phosphates. If you need to wash the fabric use a product like Seventh Generation laundry detergent, Dr. Bonner's Peppermint Soap, or a dish detergent such as Ivory or Dove. Dry cleaning is not recommended.

WARE'S NEW CYANOTYPE
A Little History

As you may recall, Sir John Herschel discovered the cyanotype process in 1842, three years after the "official" proclamations of the discovery of photography by Daguerre, Bayard, and Talbot. Although Herschel's was the first of the iron salt/non-silver processes, it has weathered the medium's transitions essentially unchanged since the year he dreamed it up. Mike Ware, in England, decided to address what he considered the shortcomings of Herschel's original cyanotype process in order to make it better. Mike is predisposed to these kinds of improvements and has done an incredible amount of work in the field of photographic science, including the modification of other iron-based processes, such as the Argentotype and the Chrysotype.

Mike is exceedingly generous and forthcoming about what he knows, and because I am under the illusion that he is Herschel's good-natured doppelgänger, I thought it would be a good idea to include his New Cyanotype Process in this book. With Mike's permission, the following represents an abridged version of his adaptation and its application. For a complete rendering of the entire New Cyanotype Process I suggest that you see Mike's book; *Cyanotype: The History, Science & Art of Photographic Printing in Prussian Blue* (London, The Science Museum and National Museum of Photography, Film and Television, 1999). This excellent text is obtainable from www.siderotype.com.

The Six Shortcomings of the Traditional Cyanotype Process According to Dr. Ware

1. The exposure times are often very long and tiresome.

2. Part A (ferric ammonium citrate) and Part B (potassium ferricyanide) must be stored in separate bottles, because Part A becomes an excellent environment for mold growth within a short period of time. This problem can be reduced with thymol crystals that sit on the surface of the solution.

3. The sensitizer, A and B mixed in equal proportions, is not absorbed completely or very well by the paper or fabric it is coated upon.

4. The traditional salt, ferric ammonium citrate, is notoriously variable in its composition, and stability, and performance and suppliers samples vary enormously.

5. Due to the colloidal nature of Prussian blue, much of the image, if not overexposed to the point of solarization, usually washes away in development.

6. The staining of highlights by transfer of colloidal Prussian blue in the wet processing

Chemical Solutions for the Six Problems

If ammonium iron(III) oxalate (aka ammonium ferric oxalate) replaces the ferric ammonium citrate in the solution these 3 things happen:

1. The cyanotype sensitizer becomes more light sensitive, resulting in shorter exposure times.

2. The sensitizer doesn't get moldy.

3. The sensitizer penetrates and is absorbed by cloth and paper fibers more easily than the conventional sensitizer.

4. What's more, ammonium iron(III) oxalate is obtainable universally as a highly pure, consistent chemical, unlike ferric ammonium citrate. It is however a bit more expensive.

5. The form of Prussian blue made with ammonium salts, rather than potassium, does not disperse so easily on wet processing, but binds to the paper better.

6. There is less likelihood of stained highlights.

However, ammonium iron(III) oxalate, when mixed with potassium ferricyanide, tends to crystallize out potassium iron(III) oxalate, which is not very soluble, and form a "gritty" solution that may cause unwanted textures on the print surface.

Realizing this, Mike decided to substitute *ammonium ferricyanide* for the *potassium ferricyanide*. This, however, was a problem because the ammonium ferricyanide was unobtainable commercially and quite complicated to make. His solution was to eliminate the potassium ions from the formula altogether and replace them with ammonium ions so making the ammonium ferricyanide "in situ."

Voila! All of the shortcomings could be addressed simply by eliminating the majority of the potassium ions in the formula. To do this, Mike added a hot, concentrated solution of potassium ferricyanide to a concentrated solution of ammonium iron(III) oxalate, allowing it to cool and create crystals. He then filtered off the solid potassium iron(III) oxalate that was the result of the process. A simple and single-part sensitizer was created. Best of all, Mike had successfully eliminated all the little things that he perceived as shortcomings with the original Herschel process.

THE SENSITIZER

The Simple Solution: The New Cyanotype Kit

Photographer's Formulary, in beautiful Missoula, Montana, makes Mike's New Cyanotype Printing Kit, in pre-measured and ready to use amounts. Each kit has a single sensitizer (the beauty of the process) and comes in a 100 ml amount . . . and makes about fifty 8" × 10" prints when applied with a glass coating rod. The formula was first published in the January/February 1997 issue of Photo Techniques. Now, buying a pre-made kit may not be as romantic as following the directions below, but it is a whole lot easier.

The Less Simple Solution: Make Your Own

Note: **This sensitizer solution is toxic if ingested and it will stain skin, and any other absorbent surface it encounters . . . be very careful, wear latex gloves, and don't splash.**

  30 g ammonium iron(III) oxalate

  10 g potassium ferricyanide

0.5 ml of 20% ammonium dichromate solution, or 0.1 g of solid ammonium dichromate—if you can weigh it. You can use potassium dichromate here instead.

Distilled water to make 100 ml of solution

Preparation of the Sensitizer

So there is no misunderstanding here, considering the fact that this formula is not the easiest to make the first time you try it, I am going to use Mike's specific words:

Figure 8–10

Vincent Carney, *#51*, 2005—Ware Cyan w/ 10% citric development

Vincent made this print using Ware's new cyanotype formula, developed in a 10% citric acid solution, and printed on handmade paper.

(Courtesy of the artist)

"The preparation of this sensitizer solution calls for a bit more experience in chemical manipulation than is required to make a traditional cyanotype sensitizer, so don't undertake it unless you are fairly confident. This work should be carried out under tungsten light, not fluorescent or daylight. Please note that all of the chemicals in the formula are poisonous!"

One more thing before the formula: If you are the least bit unsure about undertaking this chemical task but still want to try the formula, remember, it is available in kit form.

Preparation of Sensitizer: One Step at a Time

Step 1 Heat 20 ml of distilled water to about 110°F in a small Pyrex glass beaker. Add 10 g of potassium ferricyanide, *stirring constantly*, until it completely dissolves.

Step 2 Heat 30 ml distilled water to 110°F and dissolve in it 30 g of ammonium iron(III) oxalate.

Step 3 Add 0.5 ml of a 20% ammonium dichromate solution (*previously prepared by dissolving 4 g of the solid in distilled water and making up to a final volume of 20 ml*). Mix thoroughly.

Step 4 Now add the hot potassium ferricyanide solution to the ammonium iron(lll) oxalate solution. Stir this well and set the mixture aside in a dark place to cool to room temperature and crystallize. The solution should take about 60 to 90 minutes to cool.

Step 5 Separate most of the liquid from the green crystals by decanting or filtration. The green solid potassium iron(III) oxalate is then disposed of safely (*it is poisonous*). The volume of solution extracted should be about 60 ml.

Step 6 Make up this olive-yellow colored solution with distilled water to a final volume of 100 ml. The sensitizer can be made more dilute (e.g., up to 200 ml): it will be faster to print but yield a less intense blue.

Step 7 Filter the sensitizer solution and store it in a brown bottle kept in the dark. Its shelf life should be at least a year.

The contrast of the sensitizer can be *decreased* by adding citric acid, so that it can even accommodate a negative density range of 2.6 or so. Conversely, the contrast can be *increased* by the addition of more ammonium dichromate solution.

Sensitizer Color Warning: The Cure for the Blues

The ammonium or potassium dichromate can be omitted from the formula, but with the consequence that your sensitizer may change color, going from the light greenish yellow to a deep blue, be aware that the chromatic strength of the sensitizer can be a staining agent. This deep blue is the result of impurities in your chemistry. The easiest solution to a deep change of color is to let the solution sit unmolested in the dark for a few days and to let the dark blue precipitate settle to the bottom of your bottle. Then, very

gently, filter your rested sensitizer through a coffee filter into fresh, amber colored, glass bottle.

The solution for preventing the formation of dark Prussian blue precipitate is to incorporate a dichromate. The impurities in the chemistry can be counterbalanced with the addition of the tiny amount of either ammonium or potassium dichromate to the sensitizer as in step 3. The dichromate will increase the contrast sensitivity of your sensitizer, so be aware that this will be the outcome of your cure for the blues.

To Tween or Not to Tween: Use of Wetting Agent

Unlike the traditional cyanotype formula, in which a wetting agent (*a surfactant that facilitates the absorption of chemistry into paper*), Ware's New Cyanotype sensitizer solution is more readily absorbed making the use of a wetting agent almost unnecessary. There are a few hard-sized papers, such as Ruscombe Mills' Buxton, where the wetting agent, Tween 20, can greatly improve the process of coating and the ability of the paper to retain the deep blue during the entire processing sequence. I usually add 1-2 drops of 20% Tween solution for every 30 drops of sensitizer when I'm preparing my sensitizer in a shot glass.

Coating Techniques: Puddle Pusher or Hake Brush

For coating the sensitizer, I would recommend either using a Puddle Pusher or a traditional hake brush. If you decide on brush coating, I suggest that the brush be employed exclusively for this process and no other. I am a firm believer in the idea that each process should have its own brush. Be sure to place the brush in a holding beaker filled with distilled water after each coating and to blot it dry before the next.

Your other coating tool option is to use a glass rod or Puddle Pusher. A Puddle Pusher is essentially a small diameter glass rod with a fused handle so that you can get a good grip on it. Here's how you use it.

Go out and purchase a nice heavy piece of 1/4" plate glass that will be larger than your paper. Lay down several sheets of newsprint from a drawing pad on the glass and tape them down to prevent them from moving during the coating procedure. Take your glass rod, or Puddle Pusher, press it to the paper just outside of the area that you will be coating. Then, pour the sensitizer, which you have deposited into a good shot glass, along the top edge of the area you will be coating. Consult the Pt/Pd, or Ziatype, drop charts for an idea of how much sensitizer you'll need.

Keeping the glass rod pressed against the paper, quickly slide the glass rod lengthwise from side to side in the solution until it is evenly distributed along the Puddle Pusher's surface edge. Now, slightly raise the rod and place it along the back edge of the solution. Then drag the solution, with significant pressure, across the paper until your coating area is covered.

Repeat this single stroke in the opposite direction if there is an obvious abundance of solution left after the first pass. Using the glass rod, or Puddle Pusher, is the best way to avoid roughing up and disturbing the smoothness of your paper's fibers. This technique also presses the sensitizer deep into the paper, which enhances the quality of your final print. The down side is that you don't get to have the romantic brush strokes.

Stainless Steel Coating Rods

One additional type of coating tool that I've been fooling around with is a stainless steel coating rod made by R.D. Specialties in Webster, New York. Randy Nelson is the guy to get in touch with. The coating rods are 3/8" stainless steel, wire wound, coating rods #44 in 8", 10", 12", 14" lengths with 2" unwound on either end for holding. They are beautifully made and come with a tube protector. Check out their info in the Resources section of this book.

Drying the Sensitizer

It doesn't really matter if you let the sensitized coating dry at its own pace or if you heat dry it with a hairdryer. If you do use a hairdryer, dry from the back of the paper rather than the front. Print the sensitized paper within a few hours but, again, don't bother wasting your time if the coating has turned from its light greenish yellow (that chartreuse color again) to a deeper bluish green.

This deeper blue green color would mean your sensitizer has been compromised by either chemical contamination or a poor choice of paper. Start over and consider using a higher quality of paper as the first step in making corrections. Adding some 5% citric acid to the sensitizer will also help suppress this problem. Try to use a paper with as little additive as possible, i.e., Buxton or Silversafe.

Negatives

The best negative is one with a long density range of at least 1.8, similar, but a bit more dense than one you would use for Pt/Pd. Mike advises extending from base + fog (0.2) to a D-max of 2.0 or more. This is achieved by "overdeveloping" the negative as much as 70% to 80%.

Exposure and Development

No matter what light source you are using, sun or UV lamp, exposure is *significantly shorter* than is required for a traditional cyanotype exposure. A 4- to 5-minute exposure in a standard UV printer, or a 1- to 2-minute exposure under average sunlight will be normal. Nonetheless, it wouldn't hurt to do a step test before trying larger pieces. Expose the print using a hinged back contact printer so that you can monitor the exposure during the printing-out stages. Continue your exposure until your shadows and non-negative covered sensitizer areas are a pale silver-gray, as in the traditional cyanotype exposure. Look at the shadow areas and if they appear a bit "solarized" then you are likely done.

Development is the same as the traditional cyanotype process. However, you can realize a significant intensification by developing in a citric acid solution. Following the development, wash with running water until the yellow is cleared from the print borders and highlights. In almost all circumstances the wash cycle will be complete after 20 minutes. If you are processing your exposed image in "hard" water, the kind that makes it difficult to get a lather going with soap, you should be aware that the alkalinity of this water type is destructive to the blue in your cyanotype.

Figure 8–11

Galina Manikova, *Xiamen*, China, rm. 16, 2006

This is a general view of Galina's exhibition in Xiamen, China, made during her artist in residency. See more on her web site, www.wailingwall.no. The exhibition included about 50 silk panels cyanotype images on, exposed in the sun in a big contact frame from digital negatives.

(Courtesy of the artist)

Wet Development with Citric, Nitric or Hydrochloric Acid

Stronger shadow values can be obtained by immersing the print first in a 1% to 2% diluted bath of citric acid. Immersion time in the acid bath should be limited to about 30 to 45 seconds. This is immediately followed by a 20-minute wash/rinse in running water. Remember, as in the traditional cyanotype your goal is to eliminate the yellow from your print's highlights.

In his book on the New Cyanotype process, Mike notes that the citric acid may make the print more susceptible to light fading if it is not fully washed out. Therefore, he recommends using 1% nitric or hydrochloric acid in place of citric. For group use, in a classroom or workshop, stick with the citric acid solution, due to the liability of exposure to nitric and hydrochloric acids.

Change the citric acid bath every 5 to 10 prints. The yellowing in the print will go away during the bath and should be followed by a 20- to 30-minute water wash. If you still have stains, try a second immersion in the citric acid bath. Unlike prints made in the traditional cyanotype process, very little of the image will be lost and whatever does thin out, such as reversed shadow values, will return to a desired tonal saturation during the drying process. You might also consider an immersion in a 1%–5% oxalic acid bath to help with any highlight dullness.

Sensitizers on Glass, Ceramics, & Alternative Surfaces:
Dow-Corning Z-6040 Hardening for Glass, Ceramics, etc.

To have a good coating of a colloid-based (gelatin) emulsion, you need to have a hydrophilic (meaning it likes water) base surface, to lower the surface tension difference between the liquid emulsion and that surface . . . in this case, gelatin and non-absorbing glass or ceramic.

One solution to the problem can be found by adding a "surfactant" like Tween. Surfactants have a multiple personality, both hydrophobic (meaning it does not like water) and hydrophilic, at each molecule end. This essentially means that the surfactant can make an interface between opposite materials like glass and emulsion.

Once you have coated your glass or ceramic you do not have a guarantee that your dried emulsion/sensitizer will stay on the surface you've applied it to. To get things to stick you have two options. The first is subbing the glass plate with a very diluted hydro-alcoholic solution of gelatin + hardener as described in different ways above. The second solution is adding a surfactant (a surface active substance like a detergent) to the process. This addition will make a very strong adhesion both to the glass surface and to the gelatin. Try a silicium-based surfactant like Z-6040 from Dow Corning. A part of it binds chemically to the gelatin while another part of it sticks to the glass surface. If you add 1% to the emulsion you should realize a strong adhesion to any difficult surface.

Gelatin/Glyoxal Hardening for Glass & Ceramics

Make no mistake about this . . . putting any alternative sensitizer/emulsion on glass is not for the timid or insecure, but it can be done well if you follow some simple rules. Basically, it is the cleaning of the glass, cleaning it very well, that is predominately important. The glass should be scrubbed with a coarse kitchen sponge (like the yellow and green Brillo variety) that has sponge material on one side and an abrasive material on the other. You do not want to scratch the glass. Begin cleaning with vinegar, or stop bath, and then continue with soap and water until the water no longer beads up on the surface of the glass. You want to see it run smoothly. Now you can be sure that the gelatin will adhere to the surface.

Once the glass is perfect, and dry, you need to pour a warm gelatin, with the Glyoxal added to it, over its warmed surface. (*See the section on single-step gelatin—Glyoxal paper sizing, Chapter 15*) You may need to apply the warmed gelatin a few times so that you have several layers of thin coats rather than a single thick coat. Be very careful; move slowly, you don't want bubbles in the gelatin. Dry between coats.

Next, add several drops of concentrated gelatin to a few ml of your warmed cyanotype sensitizer before coating it on glass. Try to keep everything you're using warm: that includes the glass, the gelatin, the sensitizer, the brush water, the brush, everything. Now pour the cyanotype sensitizer, with gelatin, over the hardened gelatin on glass. Tip the glass and let the excess run off. When the sensitizer begins to set up, lay the glass plate on a totally flat surface in the dark for drying. You will want to keep the sensitizer from making puddles. If you do see bubbles, you can try misting the surface of the gelatin with alcohol. You can get misters at garden supply stores.

You may want to go directly to an etched, or sandblasted, glass. Sand-blasting puts a nice "tooth" on the glass and this certainly makes it easier to coat. However, sandblasting will severely compromise the transparency of the glass. If this doesn't matter to you, find a headstone memorial company and ask them to sandblast your glass for you.

Beer, Sodium Silicate*, and Corn Starch Hardener

Here's one more idea from an old recipe that I had in some notes. I have no idea where the original came from,

---

* Sodium Silicate is also called waterglass or liquid glass. It is available in aqueous solution and in solid form, and is a compound used in cements, passive fire protection, textile and lumber processing.

Figure 8–12

**Malin Fabbri, *The Big Eighteen Wheel Bus*, 2007—photo illus-
tration, cyanotype, and hand-applied color**

The Big Eighteen Wheel Bus *is an illustration for a children's
song and book called* Mamma rushes in *written by Gary Fabbri.
The book is about the dangers that can happen to a child when
growing up and how the child's mum is always there to save
him. Malin used several different photographs of buildings, the
street, and the boy and integrated them with scanned illustrations of the bus, the dog and the driver. The image was then
turned into a digital negative and printed as a cyanotype. The
bus was finally hand colored to achieve a bright red color.
Malin Fabbri is the editor of www.alternativephotography.com—
a great source of information and research for alternative photographic processes on the web.
(Courtesy of the artist)*

but it's a fun technique. Begin by taking about 500 ml of
beer and let it get flat and non-bubbly over the course of
a few hours. When the beer is ready, add a tablespoon
(for soup) of baking soda and 40 ml of sodium silicate.
Stir it into a solution and wait a while for it to age. When
the stars align, warm this solution up and pour it on a
warm piece of glass and dry it flat. After it is dry, then
coat with cyanotype or any other sensitizer.

Chrome Alum Hardening

Chrome Alum is a hardener that is used in fixing baths
for silver photography. It is very effective in hardening
gelatin but has a short life in fixing baths and can leave
a green stain. As a result, it is used mainly for high
temperature processing and in the manufacture of
emulsions.

The following is a paper sizing process that Sandy
King employs in his excellent carbon process technique.
This formula works for gum bichromate printing and
there is an even-money chance that it will be another
option for you to use as a sizing for glass (remember to
clean it first), Plexiglas, or ceramics. It's fairly simple, so
give it a shot.

Ingredients:

30 g of gelatin dissolved in a liter of water
Add 3 g of chrome alum which is first dissolved in
50 ml of warm water. You may also substitute 2-3 ml
of glyoxal or formalin in place of the chrome alum,
but be sure that you have superior ventilation in
your coating area. If you use chrome alum, let it
age for a week or so before use. If you're in a hurry,
use glyoxal or formalin.
Add 2-3 g of cornstarch to this combined solution if
you want a matte finish to your printing surface

Coating Sequence:

This is normally a paper application where the paper is
first soaked in warm water for about 10-15 minutes.
Then the paper is squeegeed on a flat surface and wiped
gently with a paper towel. If you are using glass then you
already have a flat surface, so simply warm the glass with
a hair dryer. The rest of this sequence will be the same
with paper or any other substrate. Simply apply the
warmed gelatin, with a hardener, to the surface by pouring or brush. Sandy figures it takes 100 ml of solution to
coat a 22 x 30 piece of paper. Obviously, glass isn't going
to absorb much solution, so plan accordingly.

CERAMICS, BOOKS, MAPS, TREE STUMPS, GUMS, & B-V-D'S

I'll close this chapter with a few quick ideas that you might want to try out. Some, like gum bichromate over cyanotype, I'll go over more thoroughly other chapters.

A Few Words Regarding Ceramics

All completed ceramic entities go through four basic stages: wet, dry, bisque and finally burned. One can apply sensitizer on clay at each of these points in the process although some of the stages will require a bit more play and experimentation than others. Here are a few, very brief and non-specific, ideas for you to consider.

Dry clay, unfired and essentially raw, can accept a good deal of sensitizer and gelatin-based emulsion. You might want to try impregnating cyanotype, Van Dyke, kallitype into the very absorbent dry-state clay. It's a good idea to add a little prepared gelatin to any of these sensitizers before applying them to the clay. Dry clay is also an ideal surface for experiments with dichromated gelatin, gum bichromate, and gumoil.

Bisque-Fired Clay is an excellent substrate for experimentation. This is the stage in ceramics that comes prior to glazing and a final kiln firing. A bisque fire is performed in order to drive off the water that is left in the clay. If you fail to remove the moisture from the clay before final firing, or if you bisque fire at too high a temperature, your ceramic object will explode and destroy everything else in the kiln (*you will not be popular*). Proper bisque firing is essential because even if the clay is very dry there is still moisture inside the clay molecules. It is important to fire bisque slowly. Cyanotype, kallitype, gum bichromate, collodion, and salt process can be used directly on bisque-fired ware by contact printing from a full format negative, using UV light. As well, if you like working with hand-applied emulsions and direct projection, this is fine surface to work with.

Lastly, cyanotype, kallitype, and salt print emulsions give brown and black colors when fired onto clay in the final kiln firing. You're going to have to know a good deal

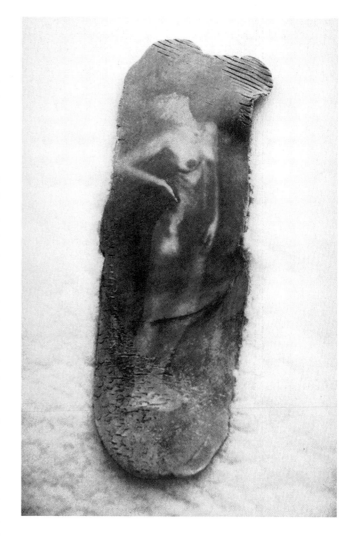

Figure 8–13

Galina Manikova, *Ceramics 01*, **1987-89- stoneware and cyanotype**
This is a stoneware ceramic panel about 70 x 180 cm with an unfired cyanotype image. It was made in 1987-89 period prior to Galina's exhibition at Henie Onstad Centre for Contemporary Art at Hovikodden nearby Oslo. *(Courtesy of the artist)*

about ceramics before you engage in this hybrid adventure . . . or you're going to have to collaborate with a ceramicist. Glazing chemistry and kilns are not to be taken lightly. If you are interested in having an inspiration in this area I would strongly recommend using Galina Manikova as your inspiration. Check out her web site.

If you want to have a lot more information about ceramics and photo-sensitive applications, please check out Chapter 17 . . . The Dusting-On Process.

Figure 8–14
Phoebe McCormick, *Shinto Views*
This is a lovely small artist's book made with cyanotype contact prints and bound with decorative paper.
(Courtesy of the artist)

One of the real benefits of using nice paper and making your own sensitizers to apply on them is that you can easily adopt the concept of artist's books into your creative process. It isn't difficult to begin seeing your individual pieces as pages and then it's just a matter of learning a few simple bindings and techniques for covering, containing, and display. Text can be added with your ink jet printer and in no time at all you have become a publisher.

Another variation on the alternative cyanotype, or almost any other process, theme is to combine processes. One of the most consistently positive combinations is the cyanotype gum bichromate where the cyanotype functions as the base blue value.

Consider making a cyanotype as your first color impression. It provides a strong and finely detailed blue (*or some other color if you tone your cyanotype first*) and gives an easily visualized "map" to register and work upon. You may also consider making a gum "pass" on top of a platinum/palladium print if you want to raise some eyebrows. Actually, this combination was quite popular with many Pictorialists in the early part of the 20th century. The additional gum bichromate step helps bring out and define complex shadow details and often provides additional depth to the image. If you intend to try this, begin with a brief green or blue gum exposure as Steiglitz did. If you want to experiment a bit . . . try running a cyanotype process on top of a high quality paper

Figure 8–15

Sarah Van Keuren, *Audrey, 1999*

Sarah's pinhole-cyanotype-gum bichromate is a terrific example of employing an assortment of alternative process options within a single image.

(Courtesy of the artist)

Figure 8–16

Christina Z. Anderson, *Holiday Cheer*, 2006

Six months after the 2006 hurricanes devastated the southern United States, Christina traveled there to document the aftermath. She wrote, "*To say I was unprepared for the extent of the devastation is an understatement.*" She translated this image into a combination of cyanotype and gum bichromate with a background layer of starry fabric to counterpoint the spray painted Merry Christmas message on the wrecked car. The print has multiple layers of gum printed on top of the starry cyanotype layer. The gum layers are printed in tricolor gum, but with one negative, to achieve a complementary warm tone effect to contrast with the blue of the background.

(Courtesy of the artist)

Figure 8–17

Grace Huang, *Norman in Blue*, 1989

Grace made this stuffed cyanotype pillow of Norman on a set of, reportedly, his flannel pajamas.

Figure 8–18

Elmar Stolk, Cyanotype on Tree

Elmar Stolk was a student of Phillipe Moreaux's at the St Joost Art School in the Netherlands. Passionate about his very specific natural materials, Elmar carried out extensive research into the supports for his images. Large sculpted tree trunks, for example, received a delicate cyanotype layer. He would impregnate watercolor paper with a mixture of chromate salts and cucumber juice pigmented with some mushroom spores. Phillipe wrote to me recently and related how Elmar had photographed a Magpie and had then printed the image in a photo egg-tempera (the eggs acting as the colloid) made from the eggs of the same bird he had taken a picture of.

(Courtesy of the artist)

ink-jet print or ink jet-ready rice paper. In the kallitype chapter I'll tell you how to combine it with Van Dyke.

For the cyan-gum combination you need to think of the piece in stages. The simple way to conceive of the process is to produce a nice cyanotype and take it all the way through the process. Use a paper that will be able to hold up to a lot of gum abuse, such as Fabriano Artistico or Lana Aquarelle. Do a single step gelatin sizing on top of the completed cyanotype and then move on to your gum bichromate process. If you intend to only use a single pass of gum, or several very light passes, you might be able to avoid the sizing step. As you will see in the paper sizing and preparation section of the book, the primary purpose of sizing is to keep your highlights from being blocked up.

Sarah Van Keuren and Christina Z. Anderson are two of the best artist-teachers working the hallowed halls of academia today and they are exceptional practitioners of this particular technique combining cyanotype and gum.

Some additional and interesting options for your cyanotype menu would be to use alternative substrates for your prints with the intention of providing context to your syntax. Excuse me, that's academic speak meaning the materials you work with, and the way you choose to work with them, are visually compatible with your ideas. Here are a few examples.

Elmar Stolk was a student of Philippe Moreaux's at the St Joost Art School in the Netherlands. Passionate about his very specific natural materials, Elmar carried out extensive research into the supports for his images. Large sculpted tree trunks, for example, received a delicate cyanotype layer. He would impregnate watercolor paper with a mixture of chromate salts and cucumber juice pigmented with some mushroom spores. Phillipe wrote to me recently and related how Elmar had photographed a Magpie and had then printed the image in a photo egg-tempera (the eggs acting as the colloid) made from the eggs of the same bird he had taken a picture of.

Another variation that you might find very interesting is a combination of cyanotype and Van Dyke processes.

The B-V-D (blue-van- dyke) process is an odd and charming hybrid. When everything goes well, you will get a wonderful split-toned image incorporating deep ultramarine blues that split with a variety of mid-tone earth colors that range from greens, grays, and blacks to golden yellows. At times, when the negative is not too high in contrast, the result is often a bas-relief-like effect. Rather than duplicate information, I'll direct you to the Van Dyke chapter where the instructions will be found.

The reason I got into alternative process image making, when I was in graduate school at R.I.S.D. decades ago, was because it was more fun than almost anything I had ever done, it made my work unique, and it was extremely flexible. No matter what direction I decided to wander in there was a way to facilitate what I wanted to do, in whole or in part, with an alternative process. The reason that the cyanotype process has its own chapter on variations and adaptations is because it is more flexible than any of the others. It has two salts, is water-processed, is unfailingly loyal in its ability to give you something nice if you follow a few simple directions, and it can be married to almost any other process or artistic discipline. All in all, the perfect blue process.

Figure 8–19

Sarah Lydon, *Horse Portrait in Blue Van Dyke*

Sarah Lydon made this very successful B-V-D image in my alternative process class at Harvard University in the late 1980s. It accurately describes the effects that are possible when all the pieces in the B-V-D puzzle fit. *(Courtesy of the artist)*

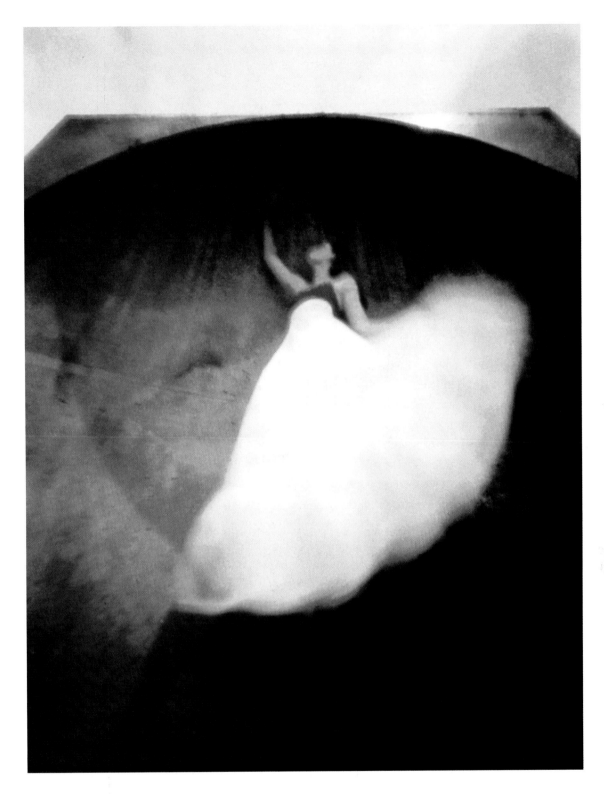

Figure 8–20

Diana Hooper Bloomfield, *Dancer, 2006 – cyanotype on Pt/Pd*

Diana's image of her daughter, Annalee, is part of a longer project which began in 2002. The image was made with a 4x5 pinhole camera and B&W film and then scanned and enlarged, to an 10x8 digital negative, using an Epson 2200 printer, and Pictorico OHP digital inkjet film. She then printed in Pt / Pd on Ruscombe Mills Buxton paper, and when dry, she re-coated the paper with cyanotype, re-registered the negative on the Pt / Pd image, and exposed to UV light again.

(Courtesy of the artist.)

The Argyrotype Process

OVERVIEW & EXPECTATIONS

In this chapter, I will begin with "a little history" regarding the argyrotype process to illustrate the technique's chemical DNA connection to Sir John Herschel's Argentotype, one of that distinguished gentleman's extensive menu of *Siderotype* processes. (*For more, please go to* http://www.siderotype.com/ Siderotype, a word first employed by Herschel to define an iron-based photographic print . . . but more on that in a moment. I will also describe to you how Dr. Michael Ware (*Herschel's contemporary good vibe doppelgänger*) addressed the short-comings of this antique process and modified its chemical recipe and workflow so that it might be equal to the investment of time, and materials, an artist would dedicate to producing a first rate argyrotype print.

I'll give you an overview of the Argentotype process, and then move into the argyrotype, discussing its chemistry, paper considerations, how to coat the sensitizer, toning options, the importance of humidity to color, how to construct a simple humidity box, trouble-shooting, and how to achieve different color tonalities by controlling the spontaneous marriages of toners and humidity. I'll also briefly describe how to combine the argyrotype process with an ink jet print for a different image variation.

The argyrotype is a process that is practiced by few people at the moment, but I predict this is going to change quickly. The process is a fairly new addition to the genre of alternative options and now that Bostick & Sullivan is making the sensitizer the major excuse for avoiding an attempt . . . the making of silver sulphamate . . . is no longer an excuse. If you are seeking a relatively simple, but endlessly variable, technique in the Siderotype arena this is one that is well worth your time to explore. Its ability to render values as perfectly as can a Kallitype have been well documented and to me, it is one of the best techniques available on the alt pro menu.

Figure 9–1

Christopher James, *Gellért Baths*, Budapest, 1983/2006—argyrotype printed in heavy fog

The argyrotype is another of Mike Ware's Herschel adaptations (Argentoype, 1842) and is rapidly gaining fans for its primary attributes . . . range of tonalities, controllable variations color, and user friendliness. This print is one I made from an ink-jet negative on a perfect day for an argyrotype . . . glowing dense fog and high heat and humidity.

(Courtesy of the author)

A LITTLE HISTORY

Sir John Herschel had a very productive year in 1842, creating three separate, iron-based, photographic processes . . . the Cyanotype, the Chrysotype, and the Argentotype. The Argentotype is just one on his menu of Siderotype processes (Siderotype, from the Greek *sideros*, a word first employed by Herschel to define an iron-based photographic print) a list of which would be quite lengthy if it were complete. Among the ones that are best known under this banner are: Argentotype, Aurotype, Chrysotype, cyanotype, ferrogallic process, Kallitype, Kelaenotype, Nakahara's Process, Palladiotype, Platinotype, Satista, and Van Dyke. The Kallitype, Van Dyke, and argyrotype processes are essentially direct adaptations of Herschel's Argentotype.

Herschel's Argentotype Process (1842)

Argentotype Sensitizer:

   20 g Ferric Ammonium Citrate

    5 g Potassium Oxalate

100 ml Distilled Water

Exposure in direct UV light: 2–5 min.

Developer:

Blue-Black Tone:

  20 g Potassium Oxalate

 1.5 g Silver Nitrate

100 ml Distilled Water

Black Tone:

  10 g Potassium Oxalate

 1.5 g Silver Nitrate

100 ml Distilled Water

Fix:

10 % Sodium Hyposulfite 5 minutes

       (*Sodium Thiosulfate*)

Wash: 10–30 min.

Figure 9–2

Sir John Herschel, *The Honourable Mrs. Leicester Stanhope*, 1842— Argentotype from engraving

One of 43 prints sent to The Royal Society for exhibition in 1842, the year that Herschel discovered the cyanotype, Argentotype, and chrysotype iron based processes. The image is from an engraving that must have pleased Herschel greatly as he used it often when testing new ideas.

(Courtesy of The Gernsheim Collection, Ransom Center, University of Texas-Austin, TX)

In Herschel's original Argentotype recipe, he coated his paper with an iron salt of ferric oxalate (*as in platinum/ palladium and Kallitype*) or ferric citrate. This iron salt was combined with silver nitrate, and dextrin (starch) as a sizing, (if the paper required that step) and coated upon a piece of rag paper. The contact image was printed-out (POP) in the sunlight whereupon the *ferric* salts were reduced to a *ferrous* (metallic) state due to the influence of UV light. The exposed printed out (POP) image was then wash-developed in a distilled water and silver nitrate solution that freed a precipitate of metallic silver from the silver nitrate to form the image. In some cases, the developer included 10–20 grams of potassium oxalate (*historically used in a platinum/palladium*

Figure 9–3
Mike Ware, Glade, *Stanton Moor*, 1983–1991—argyrotype on Silversafe paper
(Courtesy of the artist)

developer) in order to influence the color in the blue-black to a more black hue.

The Argentotype was unique at the time due to the seductive richness of the darker tonalities that the process made possible. Don't forget, this is 1842 . . . a scant three years after the "official" announcement of photography and the photographic options were a tad limited. The technique's primary shortcoming was that it was perceived as being a process that could not generate a print that would withstand the passage of time. In other words, its archival stability was in question. This was partially due to the technique's post-print tendency to fall victim to the oxidization and sulphiding of silver when ferric iron remained in the paper after processing. This was very often the case during Herschel's time and the majority of the Argentotype prints were highly unstable and have, as a result, faded. The Argentotype process, with minor modifications became the prototype for Arndt & Troost's Brownprint (Van Dyke & Kallitype) process in 1889. An interesting bit . . . for a brief time, the term Argentotype was used to describe all bromide printing processes.

Mike Ware who has re-configured Herschel's original cyanotype process, so that many of its less than ideal character traits have been addressed, came up with another process adaptation when he tackled Herschel's 1842 Argentotype. Dr. Ware's intention was to adapt and simplify the original process so that it was a more accessible and predictable one. With Herschel's Argentotype process he accomplished this by altering, and substituting within, the historical chemical formula, thus making the process one that was more user friendly. He named the process the argyrotype . . . which my students immediately re-named *R-G-ROW*.

What follows are essentially notes adapted from Mike's writings and our e-mail correspondence over the past few years. These notes also incorporate observations I've written down during my classes, workshops, and in my lab. At the conclusion of the chapter there is a large section that detail's Amy Sue Greenleaf's argyrotype toner and humidity experiments and I'm pretty sure you will find these more than helpful in your own experimentation. As for chemistry . . . you have an option here, as you do with Mike's New

Cyanotype formula. You can order the required chemistry and play with the formula or you can go the efficient route and get a perfectly excellent, fully prepared, and ready to go, argyrotype solution in a bottle directly from Bostick & Sullivan.

WARE'S ARGYROTYPE PROCESS

The Chemistry

Iron-silver-based, brown, images are made up of metal particles that are significantly smaller than those bits that comprise a black valued silver gelatin print. As a result, these small specks are far more susceptible to re-agents (a re-agent is a substance that causes a reaction in another substance; it essentially means to *"re-act"*) that decompose (*oxidize*) and break down (*bleach out*) the silver. Such re-agents, employed to *"fix"* the image in an iron-silver process, are necessary to prevent these same prints from holding onto residual ferrous and ferric (iron) salts in the print. Left behind, they are, in great part, responsible for fading and loss of image integrity. On the other hand, if you let the re-agents do their usual efficient thing, the image will etch or bleach away before you have a chance to show it off and enjoy it. Mike Ware's argyrotype process addresses this persistent problem. Here's how he explained it.

Mike's solution was to trade the traditional silver nitrate for a chemical that possessed (unlike silver nitrate) a non-oxidizing and negatively charged ion (*anion*) that would not cause a degradation of the image during the wet stages of development and fixing. Mike's choice for this new chemical alternative was *silver sulphamate*. The change, however, presented a small problem, as it was necessary to make silver sulphamate in your lab since it wasn't for sale anywhere.

THE ARGYROTYPE SENSITIZER

Option #1: Buy It in Prepared Solution

To deal with this issue you have two options. Option #1 is by far the easiest and best idea . . . you simply purchase the argyrotype solution in prepared form from Bostick & Sullivan. You may or may not find it in their product index, but you can certainly ask for it and they will make it up for you.

Option #2: Make It Yourself Method

Option #2 allows you to remain a purist and spend your time making the sensitizer in your lab . . . not an entirely easy task. If you're interested in going on with this process, rather than purchase the prepared argyrotype sensitizer, here are the ingredients, and directions, for the preparation of the sensitizer.

The Argyrotype Ingredients & Formula

7 g   Sulphamic Acid (NH_2SO_3H)

7 g   Silver (I) Oxide (Ag_2O)

22 g   Ammonium Iron (III) Citrate (green

0.2 ml   Tween 20 (*assists absorption efficiency*)

Distilled water to make 100 ml of total solution

Step 1   Dissolve the 7 g of sulphamic acid in 70 ml of warm distilled water.*

Step 2   Add the 7 g of powdered silver (I) oxide (*in small portions*) to the warm sulphamic acid solution, stirring as you go until it is all dissolved.

Step 3   Next, add 22 g ammonium iron (III) citrate to your in-progress warm solution stirring constantly as you go. Allow the solution to cool at this stage.

Step 4   Then, add the 0.2–0.5 ml (a very few drops) of Tween 20 and mix it well into the solution.**

Step 5   Finally, add ambient temperature distilled water to make a total volume of 100 ml. The solution, if all is correct, will be a dark, and clear, olive

---

* Contrast can be increased by adding another gram of sulfamic acid to the 100 ml of sensitizer solution.

** There is a debate over the effectiveness of Tween as an additive and you may elect not to use it if you're not having any sensitizer absorption problems when coating your paper. You will know if you need it by the deterioration of the image in the sodium thiosulfate fixing bath. More on this later on.

Figure 9–4

Amy Sue Greenleaf, *Self Portrait & Paperhouse #2*, 2003—argyrotype

Amy Sue, a Pennsylvania chemistry teacher with an MFA from The Art Institute of Boston, was one of the first people I taught the argyrotype process to. She took the technique to a new level, doing an exhaustive study of the relationship of toners, humidity, and color. This is one of her best, I think.
(Courtesy of the artist)

green. If you see sediment you may strain the solution through a coffee filter. This will, of course, leave you with less solution.

Step 6   Store this olive-green sensitizer in a dark glass bottle. It has a shelf life of approximately 1 year and should be filtered if you see a dark precipitate. Be cautious when handling the sensitizer, as it may be irritating to the skin.

THE PROCESS

The argyrotype process is not terribly complicated once you have the sensitizer prepared (or delivered) and you'll find it similar to the simplicity of the Kallitype. The contact negative you use should have an average negative density, in the 1.5–2.2 range, and have the characteristics you would consider appropriate when using a 0 grade paper in conventional wet-lab printing. I have found that the process is a pretty flexible and forgiving one and that it is often possible to make a perfectly fine print from a variety of negatives. The argyrotype does not appear to be a process that will punish you for having a negative that is not ideal for a UV exposure. Along with conventional large format, cliché verre or calotype negatives I would strongly recommend using Pictorico OHP ink-jet film generated digital negatives with a color layer (*see The Negative chapter*) and trying many density and contrast variations to see what you like.

TABLE SET UP FOR ARGYROTYPE

- Prepared argyrotype sensitizer in a 25, or 100, ml bottle w/ dropper cap.

- A bottle of Tween 20*

- Fresh and un-scratched sheets of lightweight clear acetate: (*for humidity control*)

- Clean paper for the table surface

- Paper for coating**

- Shot glass (*use the same drop counts as in the Pt/Pd and Ziatype drop count charts*)

- A new hake brush (label for argyrotype only)

- A Puddle Pusher or Glass Rod if not using a brush

- Clean distilled water in a beaker for brush washing

- Custom cat carrier humidifying box or cool mist steamer

- Pencil

- Contact printing frame

- Negative for contact printing

- Paper towels

Coating Argyrotype

Set yourself up in your working space, in low tungsten or subdued daylight. When you are ready to begin you will need to decide your coating method. Brush coating and rod coating each have pros and cons. Brush coating provides the romantic hand applied edge but consumes more sensitizer than you need to use to make a print. Rod coating is economical and allows the sensitizer to be pressed deeply into the paper fibers . . . and in this particular process that may be important. In both hake brush and rod coating methods, it is a good idea to use Tween 20 in your formula. A drop or two, depending on the size of your coating area, is recommended.

I personally prefer brush coating and I make up my sensitizer formula using drop counts in a shot glass instead of dipping my brush into a beaker of sensitizer. The dip method is not only non-economical, but also it leaves open the possibility of sensitizer contamination. Drop count charts, for size referencing, can be found in the Pt/Pd and Ziatype chapters but to make this simple, a 4 × 5 negative will require approximately 20–24 drops of sensitizer in a low humidity environment. Always use a plastic eye-dropper, as the dropper hole is uniform from dropper to dropper. Glass eye-droppers aren't as reliable in that regard. When you have your drops of argyrotype sensitizer in the shot glass, and you have added a drop of Tween to the solution, you're set to go.

Coat your paper with the sensitizer using either a hake brush or coating rod. Once coated, allow the solution to "set-up" in the paper by leaving it alone for about 3–10 minutes depending upon the relative humidity in the working space. The paper needs to get adjusted to the sensitizer and if you force dry with a hairdryer, your tonalities will be uneven. I use an empty drawer in the lab and when I cannot see a damp sheen on the paper's surface, when it no longer reflects light, I consider the paper ready. Humidity plays a role in the color of the image but I'll deal with that aspect a little later in this dialogue.

---

* Tween 20 is a non-ionic surfactant that assists your sensitizer in finding a secure "home" in the fiber of the paper you have selected. It also helps to minimize the leaching of colloidal metal during the process. You'll know if you should use it as an additive (a drop or two to your sensitizer) if you see staining or if your image falls away in the fix.

** The right paper is very important. It must be sized to be able to withstand extended immersion and free of additives. Some papers that work well include: Bergger's COT 320, Ruscombe Mills Buxton, Atlantis Silversafe, Weston Parchment, Saunders Somerset Satin, and Whatman's Watercolor. Crane's Platinotype is not recommended for this process.

Figure 9–5

Madeleine Patton, *Self and Lisa*, Santa Fe, New Mexico, 2006—Toned argyrotype
Madeleine made this argyrotype print of herself and workshop buddy, and calotypist, Lisa Elmaleh in my Santa Fe Workshop in 2006.
(Courtesy of the artist)

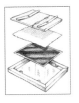

Once the coating and semi-drying is complete, place your contact negative in a contact-printing frame, with your sensitized paper, and clear acetate sheets, and exposed to UV light. I like to use two sheets of clean and un-scratched acetate in the frame set up. These two sheets are placed on both sides of the sensitized paper and this acts as an "envelope" of sorts, keeping the humidity in the paper and protecting your negative from the dampness of the sensitizer. If you dry your paper well you might consider eliminating the acetate altogether. So the set up in the contact frame goes like this: glass > negative > acetate sheet > sensitized paper > acetate sheet > hinged back of contact frame. Again, when I do this process in my workshops at The Anderson Ranch Arts Center, or The Santa Fe Photography Workshops, where altitude and very low humidity are a constant, it is the lack of humidity that is at issue. Ideally, your paper, and ambient humidity, should fall into the 40%–80% relative humidity range. Most of the time, in these environments, I don't worry about it and dispense with the acetate. If I need humidity, to influence color, I can always use the cat carrier humidity box.

Exposure

The image is "printed out," as in a POP process, and the tonalities you see following the exposure, and prior to toning and fixing, are moderately close to what you'll get when the process is complete. Toning, fixing, and drying will change the colors and densities so this is an approximation. Print characteristics are also dependent upon the time of day, season of the year and weather conditions.

Your argyrotype exposure should run between 2.5 to 6 minutes. At this stage in the process, the printed-out color will be an orange-sepia on an ochre background. I recommend that your UV exposure should continue until you over-expose your image, perhaps in the 15%–20% range. Although dry-down is significant, similar but not quite as severe as in Van Dyke, you will lose density in the sodium thiosulfate fixing stage. My recommendation for over-exposure should not be considered gospel. The first few times I demonstrated this process everything looked spectacular until the clearing stages . . . then a lot of the print washed away. Subsequent testing with different papers, adding Tween to the sensitizer, and acidifying the first bath with citric acid, did a lot to correct the problems. If you're doing everything correctly, you may find that a slight underexposure is best. Your decision will be based on the relative humidity, the paper choice, and your adaptations, if any, of the sensitizer and development chemistry.

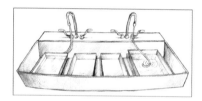

SINK SET UP FOR ARGYROTYPE

Tray 1 A very clean tray filled with *distilled* water. Agitate the print for a minimum of 10 minutes and change the water in the tray at least once during this stage.

Tray 2 A second tray with clean distilled water.

Tray 3 Gold Ammonium Thiocyanate Toner

(*Toning is optional and done prior to the fixing stage.*)

Tray 4 2% sodium thiosulfate fixer

Mix: 20 grams to a liter (1000 ml) of water.

Time: 2–3 minutes with agitation.

Tray 5 Final wash in fresh running for 20–30 minutes

Argyrotype Wash—Development

Following exposure, your exposed print is wash-developed in *distilled water* for 10 minutes. It is important to use distilled water during this stage, with a minimum of at least one change of fresh distilled water, as tap water will most often discolor the image due to chlorine content. The thing that must be avoided in the first wash is not chloride (Cl-) but chlorine (Cl2). Chlorine is a powerful oxidant and is used in bleaching and disinfectants. It is often added to public drinking water as a way to "purify" that water and protect the population from the perils of nature and the various little microorganisms that reside in it.

Water Dechlorination

Here's the problem . . . this same purifying chlorine simultaneously oxidizes the silver metal image to silver chloride (AgCl). The result is often a paper tonality that ends up with light, coffee & cream colored, tinting in the highlights. This, in turn, results in an image loss because that nice coffee colored tint will then dissolve in the sodium thiosulfate fix. If you still have this coffee & cream color after 10 minutes, then extend the wash time another 5–10 minutes and strongly consider a squeeze of lemon or a hefty pinch of citric acid to lightly acidify the water.

Here's the same issue with a twist. If your image disintegrates in the fixer, it may not be silver chloride that is the problem. In recent years, many municipalities have switched over from chlorine to chloramines. Chloramines are a combination of chlorine and ammonia (*both of which are toxic to fish life by the way*) and it's quite possible that silver chloramine compounds are even less soluble than silver chloride. This might explain why my argyrotypes behave very differently in urban and rural locals. If you are experiencing a persistent degradation of your image's integrity in the fixing stage, and you have acidified your distilled water, and extended the wash-development time, then you may have to resort to a dechlorinator . . . a chemical that home aquarium and aquaculture enthusiasts use to dechlorinate their fish tanks and ponds. You can find this product at your local pet store and each has a different dosage per amount of water to dechlorinate. A few drops to a tray of tap water will probably do the trick.

Figure 9–6
Cig Harvey, *Pears & Radiator*, 2004—argyrotype
Cig Harvey, on my faculty at The Art Institute of Boston, is easily one of the best alt pro artist/teachers inspiring students today. Known primarily for her artist's books, editorial illustration, and high-end fashion work, she continues to excite students to the possibilities of alternative process printmaking.
(Courtesy of the artist)

Again, if you do not use distilled water, de-humidified, or rainwater, in your first wash-development bath, you will notice an abundance of milky white turbidity, or cloudy liquid, leaving the print. This is a silver chloride (AgCl) precipitate due to chloride ions in the wash water reacting with the excess silver ions of the sensitizer; this is to be expected for the first wash, using tap water. You're going to see a little of this turbidity in distilled water but you will not see as much, nor will your print be as likely to turn the coffee & cream color in the highlights and disappear in the fix.

A public water supply tap water is more often than not totally unsuitable for the argyrotype's wash-development. Another warning sign . . . if you see your highlight, and mid-tone, colors turn to a red or buff brown in the tap water it probably means that the paper fibers may be failing to trap the tiny silver particles in the paper and you are going to lose your image. It is also likely that insufficient Tween has been used in the sensitizer preparation or that the paper is unsuitable for this process. If you don't have a choice, or any distilled water, re-humidifying the exposed

print for 10–30 minutes *before* the wash-development stage. Place the print face down in the distilled water and leave it alone. This may minimize the leaching effects. You might also consider using a gold toner prior to the fixing stage.

Toning and Final Wash

One of the most effective argyrotype toners is the traditional formula used for POP toning; the gold ammonium thiocyanate toner. This toner, and its use, is detailed shortly.

Following the toning stage, the print is immersed in a 2% (20 grams to 1000 ml of water) sodium thiosulfate fixer solution for 3 minutes. The fixer, as in the Van Dyke process, will often cool the color of the image. Consult the charts that follow for color shifts that take into consideration fixing before and after toning in this process.

The print is then washed in running water for 20–30 minutes and hung to dry. Be aware that the "*dry-down*" in argyrotype is significant and you should print accordingly. Air-drying will result in the color staying in the range that you ended with your wet stage. Drying with heat will result in darker and cooler values in the print.

Argyrotype Gold Ammonium Thiocyanate Toner

Toning is optional and traditionally done prior to the fixing stage. One of the gold toners used in argyrotype toning is the traditional POP gold ammonium thiocyanate toner. It is simple to make yourself or you can purchase it from Bostick & Sullivan. It arrives, in liquid form, in two A & B solutions.

Note: Gold toner gets better over time as long as you don't make it from scratch every time you need it. When it's time to replenish the toner, just add the 50 ml of the gold, and the 50 ml of ammonium thiocyanate, to the used toner. When you're done toning, save the toner and make the new toner for the next session with the old. Over time, as the gold toner filtrate is used to make the new toner solutions, the toner seems to get better and better, and the more difficult tones will be easier to achieve.

Solution A
0.2% gold chloride (*Notice that this is 0.2% and not 2%*)
Solution B
2% ammonium thiocyanate

These two solutions are mixed in a working solution using the same formula you would use in POP gold ammonium thiocyanate toning:

A: 50 ml of the .2 % gold chloride (Note . . . . 2 % not 2%)

B: 50 ml of the 2 % ammonium thiocyanate

C: 900 ml distilled water *

Note: Add additional gold chloride and ammonium thiocyanate to the working solution after every 5–6 toned prints.

Fixer: (2 % sodium thiosulfate solution)

Fixing the argyrotype is done following the toning. A 2% sodium thiosulfate fixing solution is prepared by dissolving 20 g of the sodium thiosulfate crystals in 1 liter (1000 ml) of water. This bath has an effective working capacity of about ten 8" × 10" prints. You should change the solution regularly during a lab session. The fixing solution removes insoluble silver salts. If you opt to fix the print, and not tone it first, you will notice that your image will often intensify, demonstrate an increased separation in its shadow areas, and change color slightly.

Again, the recommended fixing time is 3 minutes. Extended fixing times will often result in loss of image density especially in the highlights. This tendency may be used to reduce the density in an overexposed print. As an aside, the density of an over-exposed print can also be reduced by briefly immersing the print in a hot selenium bath. I have had some success with a 1-part selenium to 80 parts water bath. As always, be cautious whenever using selenium.

One other consideration regarding your fixing bath. If you are working with an image that has a very delicate degree of highlight detail, you may find it beneficial to make your fixing bath slightly alkaline by adding a small amount of ammonia to it. Although this technique will diminish the degree that the silver is reduced, the downside is that you may end up with the problem of too much residual iron in the print.

Your Image Fails in the Fixer: Part II

Here's the situation . . . besides the issue with the chlorine or chloramines, other threats loom. You have done everything perfectly and your image has survived and looks terrific. Feeling pretty good, you head to the fixer and within a minute, your image disintegrates and falls off the paper. What happened?

One of the causes could be a physical problem of the paper's fibers being unable to trap the nano-particle silver, when confronted with the fix. This has happened to me in a demonstration when I had done everything

---

* When you are finished with the gold ammonium thiocyanate toner, filter your prepared working solution through a coffee filter. Keep the liquid filtrate, and use it in place of the distilled water when making your new gold toner solution.

perfectly and it finally appeared to be a paper problem. The first thing I did was change to a higher quality paper, one that I knew did not require sizing. That solved half of the problem. Then I re-humidified in two ways; first with the cat carrier humidity box and second by dampening the paper's rear surface with a wet sponge before sensitizing the front. This assisted in getting the sensitizer more embedded in the paper's fibers . . . it also diluted, to a small degree, the concentration of the sensitizer. Still, there was a problem with the sensitizer's ability to penetrate the complexity of the paper's fiber structure.

If the sensitizer just sits in the pores (the microscopic indentions you can see in a sheet of paper if your eyes are still good), then it's bound to wash out. You need to get the sensitizer deep into the paper's fibers and this is where Tween 20 comes into play. By adding a drop of Tween 20 to your sensitizer, say 1 drop to a 24 -drop mix in your shot glass, you should solve your problem. By the way . . . 2 things to remember about Tween 20: only add Tween to a fresh coating solution as it loses its effectiveness as it ages. Do not add Tween to the entire bottle of sensitizer.

Controlling Image Color by Controlling Humidity

Along with that repair I would make doubly sure that my paper had some humidity in it before coating, exposure, and development. By humidifying your paper, 1 > before you coat it, 2 > after you coat it just prior to exposure, and 3 > just prior to wet processing (*assists in bringing out highlight details*), you greatly assist the sensitizer in penetrating the paper's fibers and you will give yourself a far better chance of success. Humidity is a real working tool in the argyrotype process.

By humidifying your paper before you expose it, and prior to the first stage development—wash, you can control (to a degree) changes in the color of the image. Colors can range from warm browns to violet browns, in an un-toned print, to a darker brown, peach, or black in a toned print. In the summer, when humidity is the norm,

extra humidification is often unnecessary. There are a number of ways in which you can humidify your paper in any of the humidifying stages. Here are a few.

The Cat Carrier Humidity Box

This is a paper humidifying technique I used in graduate school at R.I.S.D. when I was into printmaking. Since the argyrotype's color is so dependent upon the degree of humidity within the paper you may wish to add some control to the situation by constructing your very own personal cat carrier humidity box. Here's how to do it:

Go to a discount store, or eBay, and buy a medium-sized cat carrier . . . the kind made of plastic, with a carry handle, and perforations in the sides so the cat doesn't suffocate on the way to the vet. Build a shelf about halfway from the bottom of the carrier, supported by wood blocks, and tack a sheet of heavy-duty plastic screening to the blocks. You now have a shelf that will accept humidity from top and bottom.

Get a large plastic lawn and leaf size (39 gallon) trash bag and cover the carrier except for the front entry door. In the bottom of the carrier, place a glass baking dish or plastic tray that will hold a large car washing sized sponge. Soak the sponge in hot water, add a little bit more to the tray, place the sponge in the tray, and slide it in the carrier.

Finally, place the paper you are using on the plastic screening shelf and seal up the cat carrier by closing up the plastic bag. Your paper will humidify evenly in a few minutes and by controlling the humidity in this way you can control color, the evenness of the sensitizer, and prevent the splotches that sometimes occur when the paper is unevenly damp.

Cool Mist Humidifier

You may use a cool mist humidifier, which can be purchased in many drugstores for about $20. My own Sunbeam Safety-Glow Cool Mist humidifier actually has a built in green glow so you can observe the degree of reflective sheen on the paper while under low light levels.

Figure 9–7

Amy Sue Greenleaf, *Snow*, Pennsylvania, 2002—toned argyrotype

This is another print by Amy Sue that nicely illustrates the split toned color flexibility that can be achieved with the argyrotype process. *(Courtesy of the artist)*

The Where You Are Technique

This is easy . . . if you are in the South, working at low altitude in the summer, or anywhere in Malaysia, then you do not have to worry about humidity or building a humidity box. If you don't live in a humid climate try and keep the relative humidity in your working space in the 50%–60% range with either a de-humidifier, or a humidifier, and you'll be fine.

Remember, if you humidify your sensitized paper prior to exposure (*a good idea*), be sure to use 2 clear and thin acetate sheets on both sides of the sensitized paper. This is the same advice I'll give with another humid sensitive process, the Ziatype. Without the clear acetate sheets, there is a decent chance that you will forever bake the argyrotype sensitizer into your favorite negative during the exposure. I have learned this lesson the hard way . . . more than once.

Remember as well that you may also control the color of the print, and the degree of highlight separation in the final print, by humidifying the exposed print prior to development. After exposure, allow the exposed print to sit quietly in a low light environment for 5–20 minutes. Or, put the print into your cat carrier humidity box for a few minutes before going into the first of your distilled water baths. Experiment a little to see the level of control you can effect using this technique.

AMY SUE GREENLEAF'S ARGYROTYPE COLOR TESTS

Note: The humidity charts that follow are only provided as an approximation. Time of year, type of humidifying box, degree of dryness before humidification, and type of paper will all be variables. The color change during the exposure will be a good indicator of the degree of humidity in the paper. Pay attention to the color during the exposure and adjust your humidity to get the desired color change. Below is a chart to indicate the color change during the exposure for bone dry to very humid paper.

Color After Exposure Prior to Toning, Fix, & Final Wash

Humidity: Bone dry ←————————→ humid

Final color: orange rust   rusty/red   red/brown   dark brown   black

Retaining Humidity During Exposure

The process is very sensitive to humidity, so a visible line can easily show up on the print from the hinge back printer. I found that the paper was "dehumidified" even with tape over the hinge. It is best to put acetate on both sides of the paper when humidified to create an "acetate sandwich." The acetate keeps the paper at an even humidity and protects your negative. The "acetate sandwich" is even more critical for papers that are thin, as they tend to lose their humidity quickly.

TONERS & COLOR OPTION CHARTS

No Toner

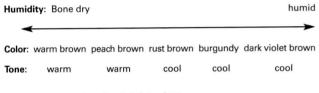

Humidity: Bone dry ←————————→ humid

Color: warm brown   peach brown   rust brown   burgundy   dark violet brown

Tone: warm   warm   cool   cool   cool

Dry Paper in Gold (Au) Toner

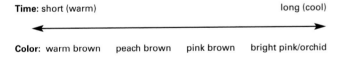

Time: short (warm) ←————————→ long (cool)

Color: warm brown   peach brown   pink brown   bright pink/orchid

More time in Au toner = more pink/purple tone. Darks go from warm brown to cool brown.

Humidified Paper in Gold (Au) Toner

Time in Au: short (warm) ←————————→ long (cool)

Color: warm dark brown   warm black   cool dark black

More Time in Gold Toner Equals a Cooler Set of Tonalities

Burgundy/violet tint > to dark brown > to black. As the darker tones become cooler and black, the whites cool and tend to the blue-whites. This gives the added impression of depth.

Color Tonality Suggestions

Warm Brown to Peach (no humidification): Coat your paper with the sensitizer and dry it with a hair dryer. Dry beyond the point at which it is bone dry. Expose your print and notice that during the exposure the color turns from a yellow-green to an orange/rust color. Following exposure, "develop-wash" the print in distilled water for 10 minutes and then fix the exposed print for 3 minutes. Tones will darken in the fix and turn a warm, milk chocolate, brown. The final wash is for 20–30 minutes in fresh water.

Brown Pink: Follow the steps for Warm Brown but tone in gold ammonium thiocyanate toner after the distilled water wash and prior to fixing. Immerse the print in the gold toner for 5–30 minutes. Visually monitor the change in tone. The color will go from peach to pink. If you want some of the peach to remain, remove the print from toner right before you see the pink color. The longer the print is in the gold toner the more pink it will become until it is almost an electric pink (pink/purple or orchid color). After toning, rinse in distilled water for 10 minutes and then fix the print for 3 minutes. Highlights will darken and the tone will cool down in the fix. The final wash is for 20–30 minutes in fresh water.

Dark Brown Peach (humidification): Coat and dry your paper. Humidify the paper for 5–15 minutes. During exposure, the color will turn from yellow green to a dark rust color. Following exposure, "develop-wash" the print in distilled water for 10 minutes. Immerse the washed print in fix for 3 minutes. The prints tones will darken in fix. The final wash is for 20–30 minutes in fresh water.

Cool Dark Brown: Follow steps for Dark Brown Peach except place in gold toner for 3–6 minutes. Rinse in distilled water for 10 minutes. Fix for 3 minutes and tone will darken and cool down. The final wash is for 20–30 minutes in fresh water.

Dark Brown Burgundy: Coat paper and humidify it for about 20 minutes. When exposed the print color will turn from a yellow green to red brown (if it turns black it is over-humidified). Following exposure, "develop-wash" the print in distilled water for 10 minutes and then go to the fix for 3 minutes. The fix will cool the tone down and the burgundy tint should still be evident. The final wash is for 20–30 minutes in fresh water.

Black Burgundy: Follow steps for Dark Brown Burgundy except place in gold toner for a short amount of time. The burgundy tone should disappear quickly. As soon as you see a burgundy black remove print and place the print in fix for 3 minutes. Many times the fix will cool the tone down and the burgundy will not be evident . . . if not, try again. The final wash is for 20–30 minutes in fresh water.

Warm Black: Coat your paper and humidify it for 20–35 minutes. When exposed it will turn from a yellow green to dark brown. (*If it turns black, it is over-humidified.*) Following exposure, "develop-wash" the print in distilled water for 10 minutes. Then, immerse the print in gold toner for 2–3 minutes. You will see hints of violet/ burgundy that disappear quickly and then will turn a warm black. Fix for 3 minutes and tone will cool down. If it doesn't work the first time, because this is a difficult color to get . . . try again. The final wash is for 20–30 minutes in fresh water.

Warm Black II: Coat your paper and humidify it for 20–35 minutes. Expose in UV light. Following exposure, "develop-wash" the print in distilled water for 10 minutes. Immerse the print in selenium at a 1:100 dilution for a short time. At this dilution, you will not get an extreme color shift but you will notice that your highlight may open up a little. Rinse after you are done for 5 minutes and then go to the fix for 3 minutes. The final wash is for 20–30 minutes in fresh water.

Cool Violet Black: Coat your paper and then humidify it for 40–60 minutes. When exposed, it will turn from a yellow green to black. Although extensive humidification is necessary it is possible to over-humidify, resulting in splotchy values during the exposure. "Develop-wash" your print for 10 minutes in distilled water and then go to the fix for the usual 3-minute. The fix will cool the tone down and the violet should remain evident. The final wash is for 20–30 minutes in fresh water.

Cool Black: Coat your paper and follow the steps for Cool Violet Black. After exposure, develop-wash the print in distilled water and then immerse the print in

gold toner for 3–5 minutes. The longer the print is immersed in the gold toner, the cooler, and more black, the tonalities. Fix the print for 3 minutes and notice that the cooling down of tones is not as evident this time. The final wash is for 20–30 minutes in fresh water.

Selenium Toner: Selenium is extremely aggressive even at the 1:30 dilution (*1 part selenium to 30 parts distilled water*). The shorter the amount of time in the selenium the better. The color tones in selenium will be different and can be combined with other toner types as long as you rinse adequately between toners. Experiment but be careful with selenium and wear gloves and work in a ventilated space. Remember that you can reduce density in an overexposed print with a selenium bath. 1:100 as a dilution would be a judicious starting point to experiment with this technique. The final wash is for 20–30 minutes in fresh water.

Black Yellow: Coat your paper and humidify it for 30 minutes. Expose in UV light and then "develop-wash" the print for 10 minutes in distilled water. Following the rinse, immerse the print in the gold toner for 3 minutes and then rinse again for 10 minutes. Next, immerse the print in a 1:30 selenium bath for 1–10 seconds. At this concentration, a lengthy selenium bath will eat the print. Rinse well again for 10 minutes and immerse again in the in gold toner until desired color. Fix for 3 minutes and then place the print in a fresh water final wash for 20–30 minutes.

ADDITIONAL IDEAS
Combo Printing

Consider printing an argyrotype on top of over-exposed cyanotypes for blue, sepia, and metallic green splits. Also, try gum bichromate prints on top of argyrotype for additional color rendition. You will likely have a few toning tests that did not work out as planned but that have an interesting coloration. Running a gum bichromate pass on top of an argyrotype is fun and thrifty. You may need to size your argyrotype paper if you intend to do many gum passes . . . (see paper preparation).

Figure 9–8

Matt Gehring *untitled* 2006—digital argyrotype

This print is a nice example of the effect that can be created when an argyrotype is printed on top of an ink-jet print.

(Courtesy of the artist)

Argyrotype on Ink-Jet Prints

This is a nice idea that was developed by a few of the guys in a recent advanced alternative process workshop of mine at the Maine Photographic Workshops.

Step 1 Begin with a digital image, either through a scanned negative or a digital file.

Step 2 Convert the image to CMYK in Photoshop and print everything (C-M-Y) except the black channel on a Cranes Platinotype or similar paper.

Step 3 Then make a digital negative using Pictorico OHP film by inverting and printing only the black channel at 100% opacity. (*see Chapter 5, Digital Options*)

Step 4 After the ink-jet print is dry, coat it with the argyrotype sensitizer and lightly dry it with a hairdryer from the backside of the paper.

Step 5 Once the print has been exposed (approximately 5 minutes), wash-develop the print in distilled water for 10 minutes, fix for 3 minutes, and final-wash for 20 minutes.

The Van Dyke, B-V-D, & Brownprint

OVERVIEW & EXPECTATIONS

In this chapter, I'll introduce you to the Van Dyke, B-V-D (*Blue-Van Dyke*), and Brownprint processes and you will see their relationships to one another and to others in the alternative process family. Iron based alternative processes fit into two separate, but often confused, categories. One group incorporates ferric ammonium citrate, like cyanotype, in its sensitizer. The other group incorporates ferric oxalate as in the kallitype process. The group with the ferric ammonium citrate in the sensitizer "prints out" (POP) during the exposure and is wash-developed in water. The group with the ferric oxalate in its sensitizer prints out as well but in a "stage whisper" of sorts and requires a developer (DOP) to be fully realized. Both groups yield prints that are sepia/brown, with exceptions, and are often referred to as a single category called the kallitypes.

In the first edition of this book, I incorporated the Van Dyke, B-V-D, Brownprinting, and kallitype processes into a single chapter. In this edition, I am splitting them up so that there is better distinction between the Van Dyke, its variations, and the kallitype. As in the calotype and salted paper chapters, the kallitypes share a common history and I will provide that in two parts with a little overlap . . . assuming that you will eventually get around to reading both chapters.

I will explain how to make the sensitizer, how to adapt it to contrast control, how to tone and process the Van Dyke, and how to avoid the pitfalls that have plagued the process from its inception. I'll also give you a quirky little process called B-V-D, or Blue-Van-Dyke, that is a combination of an over-exposed cyanotype and a half strength Van Dyke. It never comes out the same way twice and that is why most students seem to love doing it . . . it's like opening a present.

In the next chapter I will continue with the kallitype process . . . describing a more sophisticated technique that uses ferric oxalate instead of ferric ammonium citrate in its sensitizer and one that "develops-out" chemically. By experiencing the differences in the kallitypes, you will gain an understanding of how each unique process works, how the idiosyncrasies in each can be borrowed to achieve specific looks, the circumstances under which one process might be preferred over another, and how they might be combined to provide something new for your alternative process toolbox.

Figure 10–1

Christopher James, *Ferris Wheel & Corpse,* Delhi, India-1995

This image describes the way I think about India when I consider all of the images I've made within her borders. This is one of those "gift" moments when the reality and the metaphor merge. The plastic camera was the ideal tool for me to use as it captured the image moment the way I remembered it rather than the way a quality lens would.

(Courtesy of the author)

A LITTLE HISTORY

The standard Van Dyke formula that we most often use for the Van Dyke process is not that different from the original Brownprint *ferricitrate*–silver nitrate, water-developed process developed by Arndt & Troos in 1889. In that formula, the instructions called for mixing all of the ingredients and then adding the solution to warm gelatin just prior to use. The majority of contemporary papers have a gelatin, or other organic binder, in them already so the gelatin part of the formula is unnecessary.

Arndt and Troost Brown Print Formula — 1889

100 g	Ammonio-citrate of iron (*ferric ammonium citrate*)
20 g	Silver nitrate
20 g	Tartaric acid
15 g	Gelatin
1 liter	Water

For about 40–50 years, following its invention, the Arndt & Troost Brownprint, or Sepia Print, process was not called Van Dyke . . . a term that was, in that era, reserved for a photo-lithographic process used in map production (*remember Elizabeth Fulhame's idea that silver salted paper could be used for that purpose in the late 1700s*). At some point, in the early 1900s, someone, probably in the United Kingdom, looked at the color of his or her Brownprint and was impressed by the print's romantic sepia hue. The color characteristics, are reminiscent of the paintings of Sir Anthony (Anton) van Dyck (1599–1641) a Flemish artist, known for his subjects sharp pointy beards and lush sepia tonalities, and for being the premier court painter in England. Just speculating, but someone may have been sufficiently dazzled to change the name of the process. Aside from that, there isn't a significant amount of Van Dyke history. Kallitype, on the other hand, is rich in it, but that will come in the second half of this account in the following chapter.

Figure 10–2
Deborah Copaken, NYC, July 1987—Van Dyke
Deborah, a student of mine at Harvard, and author of the book *Shutter Babe*, began her career as a student by interpreting her powerful documentary images using alternative process techniques. This is a Van Dyke from a late 1980's series she called *Shooting Back*.
(Courtesy of the artist)

HOW VAN DYKE WORKS

The VDB (*Van Dyke Brown*) process, like the cyanotype, produces an image due to the reaction/reduction of ferric (iron) salt to a ferrous state during exposure to UV light (*a Sir John Herschel Argentotype technique from 1842*). The Van Dyke process employs a sensitizer formula consisting of ferric ammonium citrate, tartaric acid, and silver nitrate and is wash-developed in distilled and fresh water. The Van Dyke print is then either toned in one of several toning options, for color and archival reasons, or immediately fixed in a 3% sodium thiosulfate bath and washed for *permanence* . . . an often oxymoronic term when applied to Van Dyke because of its long history of dysfunctional processing directions passed along for decades in many alternative process texts and teaching. This problem, compounded with inadequate final washing, has led to a lasting perception of impermanence for this under-appreciated process.

The century long rap against this process, under any of its names, has been its lack of archival integrity. Most of this reputation is due to the major problem that plagues much of alternative process technical history . . . that one piece of bad information is like a line of bad genetic code that just keeps being passed along, from one generation to

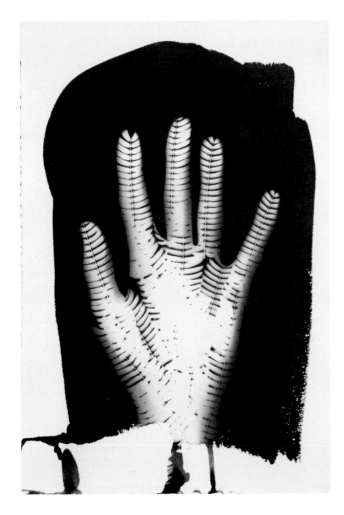

Figure 10–3
V. Elizabeth Turk, Fall 2006 #11—VDB
Atlanta alternative process artist and professor, V. Elizabeth Turk, made this compelling hand photogram using the Van Dyke process.
(Courtesy of the artist)

the next. That's just one of the problems. The others revolve around the failure to completely remove the residual iron compounds from the paper, fixing recommendations that employed concentrations that were far too strong, and that call for immersion times that were far too long. Still another issue involves dealing with the silver chloride or silver chloramine formed in the wash-development. Chlorine will react directly with image silver to form silver chloride. The thiosulfate fixer is then needed to remove the silver chloride trapped in the paper's fibers, and this step has to be done well in order to prevent problems down the road for the print. For such a simple process, and it really is almost as basic as the cyanotype, it has truly been an un-loved one. This is unfortunate because it is really a lovely technique with equally beautiful coloration.

The Brownprint's sensitizer is similar to the Van Dyke's, except that it incorporates oxalic acid in place of the tartaric acid (a chemical often employed to assist in keeping highlights from getting muddy). The Brownprint also requires development in a borax and water formula versus the water-only wash-development required in its Van Dyke cousin. The Brownprint's Borax developer is highly alkaline and that fact leads to the formation of iron hydroxide (*close to being rust but wet*) is quite difficult to remove. However, should you want to try it, just employ the salted paper technique of immersing your print in a bath of salted water that has been made slightly acidic, lowering its pH, with the addition of a healthy pinch of citric acid. This should fix the problem if your water is alkaline. The brownprint is the least commonly practiced among these three kallitype options. More on this idea later in the fixing instructional stages of the Van Dyke process.

You will notice that when a Van Dyke image is immersed in a fixer, the pleasant warm yellow brown colored image that emerged in the wash-development will change to a cool brown. Depending on the strength of the sodium thiosulfate fixer concentration, the print may also begin to show signs of "etching" and image deterioration. As fixing times approach traditional recommendations, more of the image slowly disappears and if the subsequent wash times are inadequate, then the un-removed residual fixer, trapped in the fibers of the paper compounds the problem. It is important that your prints are not over-fixed due to either concentration or immersion time and that you absolutely clear the paper of all trapped chemistry by the conclusion of the processing sequence.

THE VAN DYKE PROCESS

Table Set Up For Van Dyke

- Digital gram scale
- 1 dark glass brown bottle for 300 ml of sensitizer
- Stirring rod
- Dry chemistry for A, B, C (and Contrast A) formulas
- Plastic or glass beakers (3) for mixing the sensitizer

- Tape for labeling
- Sharpie/water proof marker for labeling
- Clean paper for the table surface coating area
- Distilled water

VAN DYKE SENSITIZER

There are three primary chemicals involved in creating the Van Dyke sensitizer: **Part A**: ferric ammonium citrate* (brown or green), **Part B**: tartaric acid, and **Part C**: silver nitrate.

You have a choice . . . you may make up the Van Dyke sensitizer from scratch, a relatively simple task and good for you to do, or you may purchase the sensitizer in a kit form and get right to making prints. If you mix the sensitizer yourself, you will need to let it age for a few days. We'll cover the homemade method now.

You will be mixing three separate solutions known as A B & C, in three separate beakers. Parts A, B, and C, will then be combined in a specific sequence into a single solution. Once combined, they are stored in a single opaque glass bottle that must hold at least 300 ml of liquid sensitizer.

When mixing, be sure to only use *distilled water* and non-metallic stirrers. You can work fairly easily under low ambient light when preparing the A, B, and C solutions but once they are combined you must be careful of exposing the sensitizer to strong UV light. The final mixing should be conducted in a moderately low light environment. This recommendation does not imply a darkroom-like environment but you should be cautious that no direct sunlight illuminating your working space and newly prepared chemistry.

There are several excellent businesses that market prepared dry and wet mixed Van Dyke and kallitype kits. (*See Appendix F*) Each of these kits essentially follows a variation of the traditional Van Dyke formula that is given in this chapter. Of course, it's always more economical to buy the raw chemistry and mix the formula yourself but the kits are terrific if you are into instant

gratification. Use a digital, or triple beam, gram scale to weigh out your chemicals. I started using a 200 g capacity digital jeweler's scale (*sometimes referred to as a street scale*) that I got on eBay for a few dollars a short time ago and much prefer it to the triple beam; it also fits in your pocket.

The Van Dyke Formula

Van Dyke Part A

   27 g ferric ammonium citrate (*brown or green variety*)
100 ml distilled water at room temperature

Place the distilled water in a plastic or glass beaker, slowly add the ferric ammonium citrate and stir the solution until it is uniform.

Van Dyke Part B

  4.5 g tartaric acid (*Note: this is 4 point 5, not 45*)
100 ml distilled water at room temperature

Place the distilled water in a plastic or glass beaker, slowly add the tartaric acid and stir the solution until it is uniform.

Van Dyke Part C

  12 g silver nitrate
100 ml distilled water at room temperature

Place the distilled water in a plastic or glass beaker, slowly add the silver nitrate and stir the solution until it is uniform.

Silver Nitrate Advisory

Be very careful not to get silver nitrate on your skin or clothing. It is both an oxidizer and caustic. Be extremely careful about accidentally putting silver nitrate in your eyes . . . Do not touch your face when mixing the chemistry or making Van Dyke prints. I advise reading about silver nitrate in the chemical section and then being sure to wear safety goggles during the mixing. If you happen to get raw silver nitrate on your skin, wash the exposed area with cold water and treat in the same manner as a burn. The silver nitrate will give you a brown henna like "tattoo" (the silver has simply bonded

---

* Ferric ammonium citrate is an "ill-defined" compound. There is no formula for it in the Merck Index and each batch of ferric ammonium citrate is slightly different from another. After a batch of sensitizer has been made and sits for a day or two, a white precipitate will often form. This formation can be addressed by adding a small amount of tartaric acid to the ferric ammonium citrate solution. Regarding the preference between brown or green ferric ammonium citrate . . . brown works equally well and it appears to hold onto the precipitate a bit better than the green version. Use either color with confidence.

with the proteins in your skin) and will be with you for a few days. It's possible to scrub off the stain with a pumice stone but that causes discomfort and your skin is in no immediate danger . . . eventually, a new layer of skin will grow and replace the stain.

Mixing Sequence for the Van Dyke Sensitizer

When the Van Dyke Parts A, B, and C have been successfully and separately mixed, you will be able to combine them into a single light-sensitive solution that you will then place in a dark glass bottle. All chemical resource suppliers carry these bottles. Follow the sequence carefully.

Step 1 In moderate ambient light, add Part B (*tartaric acid*) to Part A (*ferric ammonium citrate*). Gently stir the two parts together into a single solution.

Step 2 Then add Part C (*silver nitrate*) to the new solution that is composed of Parts A and B and pour the combined solution into the dark glass bottle that will hold the total volume of the liquid. Label the bottle, noting content and date and allow your new Van Dyke solution to age for a few days before use. Do not put it on the windowsill.

The mixed Van Dyke sensitizer will stay useful for about 12 months if stored in a refrigerator. However, *do not store this, or any other chemical solution, in your family refrigerator. It is not worth the risk that someone in your home will mistake the contents for a food product and do harm to her or himself. Instead, especially if you have children in the house, purchase a small, dorm-size, refrigerator for your darkroom and keep it locked.*

CONTRAST CONTROL FOR VAN DYKE

It's interesting to listen to the "*my-way-or-no-way,*" pontifications of many alt pro workers surrounding the control of contrast in the ferric-silver processes. For the most part, subtle adaptations to Van Dyke and kallitype are inconsequential, and major ones, such as adding a dichromate to the first water development bath, or the sensitizer itself, are

often too aggressive. Here are 3 recommendations for making a difference in your print's contrast with the best one, in my opinion, presented first. As an added thought, don't forget that if your negative isn't correct for the process you are performing you can always go and make another, more appropriate one, in Photoshop with Pictorico OHP ink jet film. *(Please see Chapter 4, The Negative)*

The Liam Lawless Contrast Control Sensitizer for Van Dyke

In this unique, and effective, contrast control formula, Parts B & C are identical to the traditional formula and mixed the same way. Part A is different, as you can tell by the addition of the ferric citrate to the Part A mix. Don't get strange when the ferric citrate doesn't completely dissolve in the solution immediately . . . it will eventually. What you are going to do is make this sensitizer in the same manner that you made the traditional one. The only difference is Part A's ingredients and how you mix the modified contrast control sensitizer.

Liam's Contrast Control Part A

18 g   ferric citrate
9 g   ferric ammonium citrate
100 ml   distilled water

Notice that this is different from the traditional Part A in that it now has ferric citrate and less ferric ammonium citrate. Place the distilled water in a plastic or glass beaker, slowly add the ferric citrate, and then the ferric ammonium citrate, and stir the solution until it is uniform.

Standard Van Dyke Part B

4.5 g   tartaric acid (*Note: this is 4 point 5, not 45*)
100 ml   distilled water at room temperature

Place the distilled water in a plastic or glass beaker, slowly add the tartaric acid and stir the solution until it is uniform.

Standard Van Dyke Part C

12 g   silver nitrate
100 ml   distilled water at room temperature

Place the distilled water in a plastic or glass beaker, slowly add the silver nitrate and stir the solution until it is uniform.

Mixing the Van Dyke Sensitizer

When the Van Dyke Parts A, B, and C have been successfully, and separately, mixed you will be able to combine them into a single light-sensitive solution that you will place in a dark glass bottle. All chemical resource suppliers carry these bottles. Follow the sequence carefully.

Step 1   In moderate ambient light, add Part B (*tartaric acid*) to Part A (*ferric ammonium citrate & ferric citrate*). Gently stir the two parts together into a single solution.

Step 2   Then add Part C (*silver nitrate*) to the completed Step #1 solution (Parts A and B) and pour the combined solution into the dark glass bottle that will hold the total volume of the liquid. Label the bottle, noting content and date and allow the your new Van Dyke solution to age for a few days before use. Do not put it on the windowsill. You now have a new Van Dyke sensitizer formula to play with.

Step 3   To make a 1:1 Van Dyke Contrast solution all you need to do is take a fresh dark brown glass bottle and fill half of it with the traditional Van Dyke sensitizer and the other half with your new Van Dyke Contrast Control sensitizer. Label the bottle as **Van Dyke Contrast Formula 1:1** and date it. Allow the your new Van Dyke solution to age for a few days before use.

You can make a different variation on this contrast control theme with any proportion that you wish but keep in mind that the more aggressive your sensitizer concentration, the more aggressive the results . . . this often means that your tonalities might be a bit ragged and un-smooth if your contrast concentration is too aggressive. That action does indeed increase contrast but too much of it has a distinctive downside. The traditional Van Dyke sensitizer is pretty fast and will give you 10–12 steps on a 21-step calibrated scale. If you use a 1:1 Van Dyke Liam's Contrast Controls sensitizer, you are going to lose a few steps overall and this relationship is what visually provides the sensation of higher contrast. Bottom line: if you need to increase the contrast in your Van Dyke then this is the best way to do it . . . just be conservative in how you apply the idea to your negative and it should work out fine for you.

Figure 10–4

Gwen Walstrand, *Becoming,* **2005—Van Dyke**

Gwen writes. *"The photograph—at once an object, an image, a memento, a reference to absence—is physically touched by reality and credibility, but shaped and skewed by the thoughts of the photographer. By using the specifics that photographs can render, I attempt to connect places and ideas through visual associations."*
(Courtesy of the artist)

10% Potassium Dichromate Contrast Option

A second way to effect contrast is to use a traditional dichromate additive. This particular contrast control technique irritates many people. . . but is a blessing for others. No matter, it is an aggressive solution to a low contrast problem and it does work . . . not well, but it works. To see if it works for you, mix up a 5% to 10% solution of potassium, or ammonium, dichromate and put it in a labeled bottle. Do not store it anywhere where a small child could get access to it and mistake it for refreshing lemonade like drink.

To make a 10% solution: Mix 10 g of potassium, or ammonium, dichromate with 100 ml of distilled water. If you see that additional contrast is required in your print, and you are not going to try Liam Lawless' Contrast Control

Formula above, then repeat your printing steps, go through your first 5 minutes distilled water bath, and then add 10 drops of the dichromate solution to every 500 ml of water in a second water tray. If you find that the contrast is a little too intense, simply add fewer drops to the bath next time.

Sun & Shade Contrast Control

When I'm printing in many alternative process techniques I often make small contrast alterations during the printing stage of the process by conducting a percentage of the exposure time in open shade and then hitting it at the end of the exposure with a good blast of direct sunlight in order to bring in the shadow areas. It is a low impact solution and it works for me. Don't expect to see major contrast changes . . . this technique is for fine-tuning.

TABLE SET UP FOR VAN DYKE WITH PRE-MIXED SENSITIZER

One of the nice things about the ever-growing popularity of alternative process photography is that many of the formulas and materials are available pre-mixed in kit form from such companies as Bostick & Sullivan and Photographer's Formulary. I have worked for years, in workshops and classes, with the ready to go Van Dyke from Bostick & Sullivan and recommend it highly. If you elect to buy the chemistry pre-mixed, here's your set up.

- ◆ Van Dyke sensitizer (*made up 24–48 hours in advance*)
- ◆ Plastic beaker or paper cup for sensitizer
- ◆ Shot glass and eyedropper if you want to prepare formula by drop counts
- ◆ Clean paper for the table surface coating area
- ◆ Paper for coating
- ◆ New hake brush (labeled Van Dyke)
- ◆ Clean distilled water in a beaker
- ◆ Pencil
- ◆ Hair dryer
- ◆ Contact printing frame
- ◆ Negative for contact printing

Figure 10–5

Karén Oganyan, *The Market*, 1997—Van Dyke on newsprint
Karén made this terrific piece when he was a student in my department at The Art Institute of Boston. Karén, from Eastern Europe, had a very unique perspective on life and made a series of Van Dyke prints on the pages of the worlds newspapers . . . while listening to Jimi Hendrix at full volume.
(Courtesy of the artist)

THE PAPER

Many papers will work well with this simple iron process but using the best that you can afford will yield a better image in any alternative process. When I say the word "best," I am referring to papers with manufacturing controls that eliminate most of the impurities that will affect your image. (*Please see the section on paper preparation in Chapter 15.*)

Among papers that I feel perform well the top choices of many Van Dyke printers is Cranes Platinotype and Stonehenge 90# white; both provide rich, deep brown-black darks and clean contrast in the whites. One of my personal favorites is Bergger's Cot 320 (it is necessary to use *Tween* in the sensitizer formula), as it has a luxurious finish and weight. It is a bit expensive but if you can afford to give yourself a treat it is a nice experience. Other papers that work well include; Ruscombe Mills Buxton, Weston Parchment, Lenox 100 and Arches HP 90#, Arches Aquarelle, Saunders Somerset, Whatman's Watercolor, and Fabriano Artistico. Each of these papers will exhibit a unique set of traits and colors. One of my former students at The Art Institute of Boston, Karén Oganyan (from Latvia), made a wonderful portfolio of Van Dyke images on newsprint. Although these prints will eventually decompose, due to the quality of newsprint in general, the effect was excellent.

A properly prepared, and exposed, Van Dyke can exhibit a significantly long tonal scale with fine resolution. In general, a smooth-surfaced, and heavyweight, hot press paper is a common choice than a lightweight paper with a lot of textural "tooth," as is found in cold press papers. Of course, the choice of paper is entirely dependent on your intentions for the image, so play around with several and see what works best for you.

SIZING

Sizing is not critical with either Van Dyke or kallitype. If you are using high-quality watercolor, stationary, or printmaking papers, they are likely to be adequately sized during manufacturing and will stay in decent shape even in processes that require long immersion times. There are some exceptions to this but you'll know them pretty quickly when the papers show spots or fall to pieces in the wet stages.

If you are using inexpensive, esoteric, or homemade papers, please refer to the sizing recommendations given in the Paper chapter, where I discuss preparation and sizing for gum bichromate. If you decide that sizing is part of your strategy, whether in an effort to produce an image with deeper tonalities or because you intend to incorporate a good deal of post-print manipulations, I recommend using the gelatin sizing. A good reason for sizing your paper is that these extra steps will often result in an increase in the print's D-max and crispness in the highlights.

THE NEGATIVE

The Van Dyke process is a contact printing process and again you will need a negative that is the same size as your final print. Van Dyke has a moderately extended tonal range and negatives that work well can be compared to those you would use with platinum/palladium, kallitype, and argyrotype. Equating it to silver gelatin printing, you can expect to achieve decent results with negatives that would print well on a normal grade #0 or #1 silver gelatin photographic paper. Some prefer a negative that has a negative density range of 1.5 to 1.8, similar to Pt/Pd. If you are planning on combining other processes with the Van Dyke, you will find that it is a quite forgiving and flexible process for such adventures.

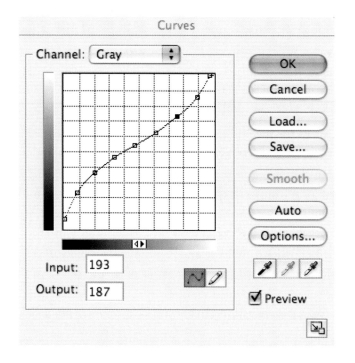

Figure 10–6

Van Dyke Custom Curve Profile Sample

This is one example of a custom curve profile for Van Dyke and how it would look after loading it following a curves adjustment.

My best recommendation to you is to begin learning the process of making enlarged duplicating negatives on Pictorico OHP ink-jet film. I would also strongly recommend adopting the habit of using customized curve profiles for the particular process you are engaged in and assigning a color layer to that curve profile to function as a UV filter.

COATING THE PAPER

Use a high-quality hake, or jaiban, brush or a glass rod (Puddle Pusher) for coating. You could use a foam brush but it isn't particularly economical as the brush absorbs too much sensitizer. In all cases, you must *not* use a brush with metal parts, for applying the sensitizer. Work in subdued ambient light on a clean surface and brush the sensitizer on your paper in delicate vertical, and then horizontal, strokes. Work quickly with a very light touch on the paper surface, but do not splash, because the silver nitrate component in the sensitizer is not good for your skin, or eyes, or for similar body parts belonging to people who may be standing near you. Be sure to complete an entire print area in the vertical strokes before changing direction and going horizontal. If you neglect to do this, your surface area will have an uneven application of sensitizer and in this process, almost more than any other (except for salted paper), you will see the mistakes.

Coating Van Dyke can be tricky. Once the sensitizer begins to "set up," or lose its sheen, during coating, additional brushing will often show up as streaking or exhibit a mottled appearance in your final image. You can determine when the sensitizer has begun to set up if you look at its surface reflection and observe that it is more matte than wet-glossy. As long as the surface appears wet and reflective you may continue to lightly coat your paper. Excessive brushing, or brush pressure, will adversely affect the fibers and the smoothness of your paper's surface.

If you have too much sensitizer on your brush you will probably end up with puddles of sensitizer on the surface of your paper. These puddles will dry thickly and often appear as dark metallic islands of solarization in an undeveloped and exposed print. These islands will then fall away from the image in the initial wash or during the fixing stage leaving you with big discolored and vacant areas within the coating.

If you are new to the coating experience, I strongly recommend practicing the coating technique with a yellow/green watercolor solution, working in the same level of light that you will be working in when you coat "for real." This practice will improve your coating skills and

will save you a great deal of aggravation and money. If you are "brush-impaired," consider purchasing a Puddle Pusher from Bostick & Sullivan and learn how to use it. (*Instructions are in The Platinum/Palladium Process, Chapter 13.*) One additional piece of information that you may find useful: I have found that excessive humidity sometimes leaves a less than pleasant speckling effect on the print. This is especially noticeable in the kallitype process and I recommend being sure that your emulsion is bone dry before exposure. If your working space, or environment, is fecund with excessive humidity, you might consider investing in a dehumidifier for your space.

Once the paper is coated, allow it to sit for a minute or two before accelerating the drying process with a hairdryer set on a cool setting. During this waiting period, wash your brush in distilled water and pat it dry with a paper towel. This may sound a bit compulsive but be careful not to let a wet brush rest on a paper towel . . . the reason they are so white is because of the bleach used in manufacturing and you do not want the bleach to become a part of your sensitizer for subsequent applications.

You can play around with the print color and hue of the Van Dyke by making very slight adjustments to your sensitizer coating solution. Experiment with a drop, or two, of 1%–5% gold chloride, or a 1% potassium chloroplatinite, for every 25–30 drops of solution.

PRINTING OUT

Van Dyke is an iron-silver printing-out process. This means that it does not need a developer to be realized following the exposure. It can, like other alternative processes, be examined during the exposure as long as you maintain the registration of paper and negative. A contact-printing frame is ideal for this purpose due to its hinged back as this construction will allow you to release the tension from one half of the contact frame and lift a portion of your paper to examine the exposure. The other half of the frame will continue to be closed, keeping registration of the negative to the coated sensitized paper. Examine and evaluate your exposure in low illumination to determine when your exposure is complete.

Unlike a kallitype exposure that is ready when there is a "*stage whisper*" of an image, the Van Dyke requires you to expose until you have a moderate over-exposure. Although the image will darken and cool, from warm/orange to brown, through the processing stages, the "bleach-back" effect on the Van Dyke process is a constant fact. Van Dyke also, as I've written already, has a significant dry-down factor.

I recommend that you do some test strips, or use a grayscale step strip film that you can print simultaneously with your negative, to provide you with an idea of where to go with your exposure times. Obviously, each negative, time of year, time of the day, and type of light source will require a different set of calibrations. Begin your exposure tests with 30-second intervals in the sun and write all of the pertinent information for your image in pencil on your print in order to evaluate your printing strategy. A Van Dyke, on a nice summer's day with bright sun and a decent negative, will be properly exposed in about 2 to 6 minutes. A UV Box exposure will be just slightly slower.

Figure 10–7

V. Elizabeth Turk, *Summer 2006 #2*—Van Dyke

This is another wonderful example of the Van Dyke process by Atlanta artist V. Elizabeth Turk.

(Courtesy of the artist)

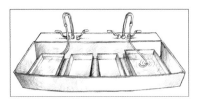

SINK SET UP FOR VAN DYKE

Processing the Van Dyke Print

Tray 1 Initial wash development in *distilled water* (5 minutes) if you have to use tap water, add a pinch of citric acid to the water to make it more effective. It will not hurt to add the pinch of citric acid even if you are using distilled.

Tray 2 Wash development /running water (1–2 minutes). Split this wash time up into two parts. The first part will be a tray of fresh water with a pinch of citric acid. The second part will be simply fresh running water.

Tray 3 3% sodium thiosulfate fixing bath (1–1.5 minutes) Mix: 30 g sodium thiosulfate, 2 g sodium carbonate, to 1000 ml water.

Tray 4 Optional sodium sulfite fixer clearing bath (1–2 minutes) Mix 10 g sodium sulfite to 1000 ml water. Or, Working Perma-Wash mix (3 oz to a gallon) diluted 50%/50% with water.

Tray 5 Final wash

After the exposure, go to a low light wet working space and remove the print from the contact-printing frame. You are going to wash-develop your newly exposed Van Dyke in 2 successive water baths, tone if you desire, or go directly to the fixer. In the wash-development you will see a pleasant warm sepia-yellow image that will make you feel good. Don't fall in love with this color because it is going to change soon.

Even if you coat and expose well, the success of your final print is only partially guaranteed. In Van Dyke, the complete success of your print is determined by how well you finish processing your image following the exposure. Van Dyke is a POP (Printing Out) process, versus a DOP (Developing Out) process and so the first, and second, wash-development baths are critical.

Tray 1 Use Distilled Water & a Pinch of Citric Acid

A great deal of the literature, and "expert" Internet newsgroup information, regarding Van Dyke processing has instructed the reader to use a single water wash-development bath followed by the sodium thiosulfate fixer. Most of the time this only results in Van Dyke prints that turn a dull coffee & cream brown in their highlights and that sadly leach out of the paper during and following the final wash. There is nothing so disconcerting as hanging a new Van Dyke on a line and watching the brown values slide off of the print like rain on a dirty window.

If the print manages to survive the wet stages, it still often fades away due to the inefficiency of the processing cycle. This, of course, is why the reputation of the potentially amazing Van Dyke has always been less than positive.

The first step in the wash-development part of this process is to immerse your print in a clean tray of distilled water with a pinch of citric acid added to it to slightly acidify the water. Do not use tap water for this first wash-development as there may be chlorine in the water supply, added as a disinfectant, and this is a powerful oxidant. If the silver oxidizes during this stage, highlights will often turn a light coffee tan.

Here's the same issue with a twist. If your image disintegrates in the fixer, it may not be silver chloride that is the problem. In recent years, many municipalities have switched over from chlorine to chloramines. Chloramines are a combination of chlorine and ammonia (*both of which are toxic to fish life by the way*) and it's quite possible that silver chloramines compounds are even less soluble than silver chloride. If you are experiencing a chronic degradation of your image's integrity in the fixing stage, and you have acidified your distilled water, and extended the wash-development time, then you may have to resort to a dechlorinator . . . a chemical that home aquarium and aquaculture enthusiasts use to dechlorinate their fish tanks and ponds. You can find this product at your local pet store and each has a different dosage per amount of water to dechlorinate. A few drops to a tray of tap water will probably do the trick. Uber-Chemist, Howard Effner, writes that this solution to the problem is "overkill":

"The little bit of free chlorine or chloramines in tap water will not survive long once the print goes into the wash water. The residual Fe+2, from the image, will quickly reduce elemental chlorine to chloride ion (Fe+2 goes to Fe+3). If there is silver ion present (from silver nitrate) it will quickly precipitate the chloride ion as insoluble silver chloride. This is the basis for the classical gravimetric chloride determination. The silver in an image will not be attacked by chlorine.* Thiosulfate will be needed to remove the silver chloride that is attracted to or trapped in the network of paper fibers. The anti-chlorine stuff is probably something like a solution of sodium thiosulfate—thiosulfate will take chlorine to chloride ion quantitatively. Just add a ml or two of 10 percent thiosulfate to the wash water and POOF it's gone."

Is that clear?

If you do not use distilled water, water from a dehumidifier, or rainwater, in your first develop—wash bath you will notice a milky white turbidity, or cloud, leaving the print. This is a silver chloride (AgCl) precipitate due to chloride ions in the wash water reacting with the excess silver ions of the sensitizer; this is to be expected for the first wash. . . if you are using tap water. You're going to see a little of this turbidity in distilled water but you will not see as much, nor will your print be as likely to turn the coffee color in the highlights and disappear in the fix.

Tray 2 Lightly Acidified Fresh Water

This second tray consists of a lightly acidified fresh water bath. Very simply, fill a tray with tap water, add a pinch of citric acid to it and agitate the tray for 2–3 minutes. Then

---

* One of my chemist friends disagrees and says that the silver will be attacked especially as it's colloidal (nano-particle). There will be a quiz in the morning.

simply let fresh water run into the tray for an additional 2–3 minutes and that should do it.

You may notice that you print is fading a little in these successive acidified baths but the image should return nicely in the fix. It will not be the romantic yellow brown, though, so get used to the idea that the print will cool off in color in the fixer.

What You Are Looking At after the Wash

Another thing you will have to get used to . . . the "dry-down" (*darkening and closing up of the print's values as it dries*) that comes after all of the processing is done. Van Dyke has a more significant "dry-down" than most any other alternative process.

If you are experiencing a significant loss of image density, or wish to see highlights that have a bit more pop to them, consider changing a few things, like the paper you are using, or the age of your sensitizer (*fresh sensitizer is less desirable than sensitizer that has aged for a few days*). Or try adding Tween to aid in the paper being able to absorb the sensitizer more deeply, or using Liam's Contrast Control Formula. You might also consider gelatin sizing the paper before coating. Again, if you are not using distilled, or demineralized, water for the first bath you might consider adding a pinch of citric acid or a squeeze of lemon to this first wash. Citric acid will reduce the alkalinity of the water.

The other side of this balanced sword is the addition of sodium carbonate to your sodium thiosulfate fixer formula. This is an option designed to increase the alkalinity of the fixer and will help prevent "bleach-back" (*hydrolysis and fading in the fix stage*). The pH of your water and the effects of the chemistry on your printing should determine your use of adding citric acid to reduce alkalinity or adding sodium carbonate to increase alkalinity. Get some pH Indicator paper to see what the pH of your water is.

FIXING VAN DYKE

A 3% Sodium Thiosulfate Fixer Solution

  30 g sodium thiosulfate
1000 ml of water
Optional: Add 2 g of sodium carbonate to minimize the "*bleach-back*" effect of fix.

"Bleach-back" is a term that describes what happens to your print when it is attacked by the fixer and experiences rapid image deterioration. The sodium carbonate makes the solution slightly alkaline but will make the simplicity of removing iron salts from the paper a bit more complicated. It is an option and not necessary if your water is alkaline to begin with. Store your sodium thiosulfate fixer in any clean plastic chemical container. *When you use a fixer this weak, it will be necessary for you to change the solution every 8 to 10 prints. I recommend having a multiple-tray set-up for the fixer and that you spread your fixing time between 2 baths.*

Processing Step #2: Fixing the Print

Pour a 3% sodium thiosulfate fixing solution into a clean tray and immerse the washed print in it for no more than 1 minute. Some of the artists working in Van Dyke prefer an extremely brief fixing time; one that I know uses a 2% fix solution made with 20 g of sodium thiosulfate to 1000 ml of water and fixes for as little as 20 seconds, at just that point when the print turns darker and cooler. I am not entirely convinced a penalty does not come into play for this short a fixing time and am content recommending a one-minute fixing time. Remember, half of the problems that plague the process are due to inadequate washing.

As mentioned before, the use of a double tray set-up with separate 3% sodium thiosulfate solutions will allow you to run 10 to 12 average size prints before a fresh change of chemistry is necessary. During the fixing stage, the warm sepia-brown color of the print will change. You may lament a little because that lovely romantic yellow-brown pre-fix color might have been perfect for you . . . you can always get some of it back through toning formulas, tea, coffee, watercolor, dyes, or combining it with another process such as gum bichromate. Instead, you will get a much stronger and dense brown black that will dry even darker than what you are looking at in the tray. As I've said before, the Van Dyke dry-down is not subtle.

Figure 10–8

Stefanie London, *Untitled*—1992—Van Dyke and gum bichromate

Stefanie, a student of mine at Harvard, and later on a member of my faculty, is one of the most productive and innovative artists I've known. This is one of her Van Dyke and gum gouache pieces. The text reads, *"I used to think the airport was the best place to die. All those people coming and going, as if the forces of passage swirling there would carry me too . . . to places faraway and exotic."*
(Courtesy of the artist)

Processing Step #3: Hypo-Clearing Option

If you wish to accelerate the removal of the residual sodium thiosulfate that has permeated the fibers of your paper you may use either a 50% dilution of a gelatin silver paper strength hypo-clearing agent or a 1% solution of sodium sulfite. In both cases, immerse your fixed print for one minute.

Processing Step #4: Final Wash

The purpose of the final wash is to remove the last remnants of the sodium thiosulfate fixer from the print. If you used the diluted hypo-clearing bath you will final-wash your print in fresh water for 20 minutes. If you are not using a hypo-clearing bath, wash the print in slowly running water for 30 to 40 minutes and then hang it on a clothesline to dry. You may acidify this final wash bath with a pinch of citric acid if you have highly alkaline water. I strongly recommend that all alternative process prints be line-dried versus rack-dried. It is far too easy, especially in a group lab situation, to encounter contaminated screens.

If you are unhappy with the image because the tonalities are too thin, save the image and try a Van Dyke/palladium or a Van Dyke/gum bichromate combination technique. If you feel that your contrast is too flat, try ironing the print with a hot iron or placing it in a dry mount press. This action will also change the color of the image. Your other options are: start over, re-coat using Liam's Contrast Control Formula and re-expose your image again on the same paper. Or, go with the standard formula and process it with a first bath containing a 10% potassium dichromate addition. If you feel that your darks are weak and your highlights are muddy, try a gelatin sizing prior to sensitizing the paper or change papers. If that doesn't work, scan your negative into Photoshop, increase the density and contrast, print it out on Pictorico OHP, and get back to work.

TONING THE VAN DYKE PRINT

A Pre-Fix Toning Process for Van Dyke

This is a toning process that can be used for both Van Dyke and kallitype and is employed *prior* to the fixing stage. This toner will help prevent "bleach-back" and will make it more permanent than a conventional Van Dyke print. *If you use this toner, it is not necessary to add sodium carbonate to your fixer.*

TONER OPTIONS: BEFORE FIXING

Gold Toner

5 g	citric acid
1000 ml	distilled water
5 ml	5% gold chloride

5 minutes or until you like it . . . *Faster when fresh*

Palladium Toner

2 g	sodium acetate
2 g	citric acid
400 ml	distilled water
30	drops of 20% palladium chloride

Gold or Palladium Toning Sequence

Coat and expose your Van Dyke print in the traditional manner. Go through the double-wash cycle beginning with distilled water. Mix the toner by combining the ingredients listed in the recipes above. Tone the print in either of the solutions until you like what you see and then immerse it in fresh running water for 5 minutes. When that rinse step is done, immerse the print in your 3% sodium thiosulfate fixer for 1 minute. Then, immerse the print in a hypo-clearing agent for 1 minute and final-wash the print.

Photographer's Formulary Gold 231 Toner (warm yellow-brown color)

Mix together Part A and Part B of the Photographer's Formulary Gold 231 in the same manner as you would for silver prints. The directions are in the kit and they are easy to follow. The Gold 231 formula will clean up your highlights as it alters the color. Be careful; sometimes it changes things too much and you may want to dilute the

Figure 10–9

V. Elizabeth Turk, *Espiritos del Jardin # 11—1997*

This is a representation of one of V. Elizabeth Turk's large Van Dyke photogram murals from her *Espiritos del Jardin* series. The work is 104" × 31" in size. *(Courtesy of the artist)*

Figure 10–10

Erin Kawamata, *Tea test #1, 2006*—VDB and tea Bags
This lovely, and innovative, Van Dyke was created by sewing together tea bags and sensitizing them with VDB. In this example of Erin's work, the context and subject are in perfect harmony.
(Courtesy of the artist)

solution with a little distilled water. The working life of this toner is very short. With conventional silver prints you can effectively tone six 16" × 20" images before it stops working well. Tone the print in either of the solutions until you like what you see and then immerse it in fresh running water for 5 minutes. When that rinse step is done, immerse the print in your 3% sodium thiosulfate fixer for 1 minute. Then, immerse the print in a hypo-clearing agent for 1 minute and final-wash the print.

Gold 231 to Lead Acetate (pencil lead/blue color)

The sequence of Gold 231 to lead acetate is an interesting toning process. The Gold 231 will slightly bleach the image and change its color to a warmer yellow/brown. After the gold toning, wash the print for 20 minutes in running water. Then, immerse the image in the lead acetate solution. This will restore a little of the image that was lost and change the color to a pencil lead/blue-black. Be careful with the lead acetate and wear gloves when you use it. Tone the print in either of the solutions until you like what you see and then immerse it in fresh running water for 5 minutes. When that rinse step is done, immerse the print in your 3% sodium thiosulfate fixer for 1 minute. Then, immerse the print in a hypo-clearing agent for 1 minute and final wash the print.

Selenium

Although I have heard other Van Dyke practitioners discuss this toner as an option, I personally found that it has a very strong bleaching effect even in radically dilutions. The reason for this is that Selenium Toner is 30% ammonium thiosulfate which is, as you know, a form of fixer. To use it, I recommend a significant dilution (100:1 maybe) and perhaps with a paper strength hypo-clearing (sodium sulfite) mix in place of the water to neutralize the sodium thiosulfate. I also suggest using a warm solution to intensify the reaction in a shorter period of time. Selenium must be handled carefully so please read the chemical section in Appendix A for more information first.

Blue Toner

Believe it or not, the standard cyanotype chemistry, along with a little acetic acid, makes a fine blue toner. It seems illogical to make a Van Dyke blue but a split toning might be possible if you experiment with diluted concentrations. Simply mix:

  20 ml of cyanotype Part A: (ferric ammonium citrate)
  24 ml of cyanotype Part B: (potassium ferricyanide)
1200 ml of water
 140 ml of 28% acetic acid

To use this formula, pre-soak your print as you would in any photographic toning process and then immerse it in

Figure 10–11

Dan Dakotas, Taos Guadalupe, Santa Fe, 2006-VDB
Dan made this terrific Blue-Van Dyke during my 2006
Santa Fe alternative process workshop. The technique
requires an over-exposed cyanotype followed by a
diluted Van Dyke sensitizer with the negative slight out
of registration.
(Courtesy of the artist)

the blue toning solution. Agitate the tray until you are pleased with the results. Then, wash the print for 30 to 40 minutes.

For split tones with this formula, or to partially eliminate a bit of color from a too-blue print, mix up a solution of 5 g borax with 1000 ml of water and immerse the print until you begin to see the change. This formula can also be employed as a toner for kallitype prints if for some reason, you want them to be blue. Try diluting the blue toning formula to see if a split can be negotiated with the Van Dyke print. Then again, if you want a semi-predictable split, try the B-V-D process.

THE BLUE-VAN-DYKE (B-V-D) PROCESS

In a workshop several years ago, after an afternoon of cyanotype frustration (*the result of contaminated storage bottles*), I "threw in the proverbial towel" and suggested to

the class that it was time to invent something new with the crap cyanotypes we had created. I can't remember if our cyanotypes were actually overexposed or simply too saturated with contaminated blue staining to be worth saving, but these were going to be our test prints.

Because the Van Dyke was the next process in the workshop's curriculum sequence, the sensitizer was already mixed and had aged the prerequisite 48 hours. I decided to take it and coat one of the very dark cyanotypes and see if anything would happen. Immediately, the visual cyanotype pigmentation broke down to a pale yellow-brown. Remembering the account of Fox Talbot's surprise when he tried to re-sensitize a badly executed salted paper, I dried the newly re-coated paper and placed the negative slightly out of registration on the re-sensitized and dried paper. This wasn't difficult to do, because the original cyanotype, having not been sized, didn't quite match in registration anyway. As it turned

Figure 10–12
Ashley Rose, *Between Autumn & Summer 2006 #1*—**BVD**
Ashley Rose was a student of V. Elizabeth Turk's in Atlanta and this is an example of her work using the BVD—Blue Van Dyke technique.
(Courtesy of the artist)

out, this slightly off-registration was one of the big reasons the experiment eventually worked.

The first test coating of Van Dyke was full strength and the changes to the prints were not very interesting except for the off-registration parts. Those parts showed tinges of goldenrod yellow splitting with the blue of the cyanotype.

We hashed it out for a while and moved on with the experiments; now the Van Dyke sensitizer was diluted by 50% with distilled water. This time, the split separation was truly pronounced and everyone in the workshop ran off to make horribly over-exposed cyanotypes so they could work with the new process for the rest of the day. This is what I've discovered about a workshop class . . . if you make a mistake,

and if it's an attractive mistake, the mistake will be incorporated into the way the process is done from that point on. For the last decade or so I have intentionally made mistakes in demos knowing that something good was going to happen that they could adopt . . . it instills the idea of play in the process. In any event, the students in the workshop quickly named the process *Cyan-O-Dyke*. This led to some class discussion regarding the political correctness of the inadvertent innuendo and the process was instantly renamed Blue-Van-Dyke . . . or B-V-D in order to keep it a little edgy.

The B-V-D process is a weird and charming hybrid. When everything goes well, you will get a wonderfully split-toned image incorporating deep ultramarine blues that split with a variety of mid-tone earth colors that range from greens, grays, and blacks to golden yellows. At times, when the negative is not too high in contrast, the result is often a bas-relief-like effect.

Several elements appear to have a lot of impact on the success of the image. The first is the length of the original cyanotype exposure; it must be over-exposed by a lot. Another is the dilution and freshness of the Van Dyke sensitizer. The process does not perform well with full strength or old Van Dyke chemistry. The sensitizer must be cut with distilled water to at least 1:1 and the sensitizer must be fresh. I would recommend using Liam's Contrast Control Sensitizer as the sensitizer for the B-V-D instead of the traditional formula to see what will happen. The negative also plays a large role because those whose subject matter demonstrates a great degree of linear delineation (versus mass), high contrast, texture, and energetic pattern always seem to make a better B-V-D than those negatives with a long continuous tonal scale.

A Few Final B-V-D Ideas

◆ Use a high-quality rag paper that can handle two separate processes, a lot of chemistry, and extended wash times. You may wish to pre-soak your paper in hot water, gelatin size, and perhaps harden the gelatin with formalin or Glyoxal. This is especially important if you intend to do a gum print on the B-V-D print. Keep in mind that the best B-V-D splits occur when the negative and the first cyanotype image are slightly out of register. You can make this happen easily whether you gelatin size or not.

- If you under-expose the cyanotype and use a strong Van Dyke solution, all you will get is a solid color print that resembles a Cyanotype after a strong tannic acid/sodium carbonate toning sequence.

- A different technique worth considering is to print the cyanotype step with a negative and then make the Van Dyke with a film positive of the same image. You will end up with a split-toned, tone-line separation. One more idea is to make a first cyanotype pass with one negative and then take a completely different negative and use it for the Van Dyke exposure. Play with this process, altering the chemical formulas of both sensitizers, knowing that you are going into uncharted process land. If you happen to refine the Blue-Van-Dyke, to a point where it will do exactly what you want it to do each and every time, please let me know. I will rename the process after you in the next edition of this book.

- Lastly, if you find that you went too far with your Van Dyke portion of the printing experience, simply immerse the print in a tray of water with a little hydrogen peroxide and a good deal of your blue will return.

THE BROWNPRINT PROCESS

Here is brief description of the Brownprint process in the event that you want to try your hand at it. It is a loyal member of the kallitype family and is similar in many ways to the Van Dyke, with the exception that it employs oxalic acid, in place of tartaric acid, in the sensitizer. Another minor difference is in the development bath, which is a mixture of water and borax (as in one of the kallitype developers), rather than straight water, (as in Van Dyke). The color of the brown in the print is similar to that of Van Dyke in that the golden brown turns to a darker neutral brown after development. Feel free to try the toning processes from the kallitype, salted paper, and POP chapters and be sure to adhere to the fixing and washing guidelines. **Follow the notes for the Van Dyke process, for everything but the sensitizer chemistry and the first development**.

Figure 10–13

Ryan Wing, *Bicycle On The Lawn*, Oklahoma, 1998

Ryan made this BVD print while a student of mine at the Oklahoma Summer Arts Institute in 1998. This technique works best when the negative has a good deal of graphic detail and texture.

(Courtesy of the artist)

The Brownprint Sensitizer

To 30 ml of distilled water add:

    2.5 g of ferric ammonium citrate

    0.4 g oxalic acid

      1 g silver nitrate

Dissolve the ferric ammonium citrate and oxalic acid solution completely, and in subdued light add 1 g of dissolved silver nitrate.

    Let this mixture stand in a dark glass bottle for 24–48 hours in subdued light. You may see a precipitate and if it is a problem you can filter it with a coffee filter. If you find that your contrast is consistently low in your prints you may wish to gelatin size your paper or to add a drop of a 10% potassium

Figure 10–14

Betty Hahn, *Dark Peony on Gold—1982*

This is an example from Betty Hahn's abundant portfolio dealing with the potential of inter-disciplinary alternative process techniques. Betty, who lives in New Mexico, has long been one of the leading influences in the resurgent alternative process movement.

(Courtesy of the artist)

dichromate solution to the sensitizer to boost contrast. Should you elect to add the potassium dichromate, you may make an additional precipitate that will also require filtration. If you find that this percentage is too aggressive, simply halve the solution to 5% and try it again.

Use a quality 100% rag paper like those recommended for the Van Dyke Process and apply the sensitizer in low light with a hake brush or a Puddle Pusher. Cool air–dry the coated paper and load it into a contact frame, being sure that the negative you are using will yield a "right reading" print in the finished version.

Exposure

Expose the sensitized paper in the sun or with a UV exposure unit and use a hinged contact printer to hold registration during visual inspections. Exposure times will approximate those of Van Dyke and kallitype and will be in the 2- to 6-minute range.

Development

During exposure, periodically check your print for exposure density. Expose as in a kallitype, looking for a *stage whisper* (like a kallitype) version of the image. Development will resolve the balance of the image. Following exposure, develop the image 5–7 minutes in a bath consisting of:

- 1 liter of distilled water
- 1 teaspoon of borax well mixed into solution

Fixing the Print

Fix the image in your Van Dyke Fix (3% sodium thiosulfate solution): 30 g of sodium thiosulfate dissolved in 1000 ml of distilled water. Fix the print for 1 minute. The image will darken in the fixer and the highlights will, if your karma is pure, clear out.

Final Wash

You may use a commercial hypo-clearing bath at half strength or a 1% solution of sodium sulfite to assist in the removal of the residual hypo. If you use the hypo-clearing bath, wash your finished print for 20 minutes in fresh water. If you go straight from the fixer into the final wash, it may be necessary, as in the case where your water may be too alkaline, for you to add a non-scientific pinch of citric acid or a squeeze of lemon to the wash water to acidify it . . . total wash time will be 40 minutes.

The Kallitype Process

OVERVIEW & EXPECTATIONS

In this chapter, I'll introduce you to the three separate versions of the 1889–1891 Dr. W.W.J. Nicol kallitype processes. You will see their relationship to one another, as well as to the Herschel Argentotype (1842), to the Arndt & Troost "Van Dyke"/Brownprint (1889) from the preceding chapter, to others in the iron-salt alternative process family, and to the contemporary kallitype practiced today.

As I wrote in the Overview part of the Van Dyke chapter, ferric-silver (iron salt & silver) based alternative processes fit into two separate groups. One category incorporates ferric ammonium citrate in its sensitizer, "*prints-out*" during the exposure and requires only a water development to complete the process. The other category uses ferric oxalate as its "*light-trigger*," prints-out as a "*stage-whisper*," and requires a chemical developer to be fully realized. Both types yield prints that are similar in hue, with exceptions having to do with specific toners and developer choices, and both fall into an overall family.

By experiencing the uniqueness of the various kallitypes you will gain an understanding of how the process differs from the Van Dyke, a process that it is often confused with, and how its evolution is remarkably similar to the platinum and palladium chapters that will come later on in this book. Kallitypes provide tonalities of sepia-brown, red, aubergine, and chocolate-black. In some developers the black color, and range of value, is equal to platinum/palladium prints and can often fool an expert.

I will explain how to make a variety of kallitype sensitizers, how to use them, how to process the print, and how to tone and fix the image so that it will be more flexible . . . and archival. One of the many new additions to this chapter will be a hybrid developer that I've been working with in my classes and workshops for the past few years that eliminates the chronic yellowing and coffee & cream highlights that are so common in the process.

In the kallitype processes, the ferric ammonium citrate that you have become accustomed to using will be replaced by ferric oxalate . . . which will become a familiar chemical to you when we get to platinum and palladium printing. The silver nitrate that you have been using consistently

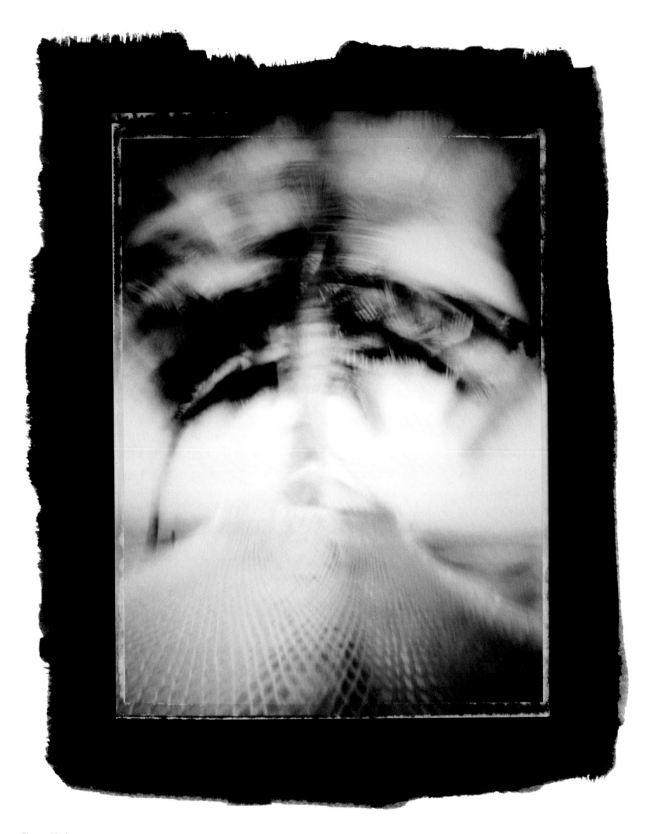

Figure 11–1

Christopher James, *Hammock & Palm*, Mexico 2006—kallitype

I made this image, using a Zero Image Zone Plate 4 × 5, at our friend Jeff's casita on a beach in San Pancho, Mexico. I was looking for a way of describing how I felt when swinging in a hammock, under his palm trees, listening to the heavy surf, with pelicans flying in formation overhead, and thinking about all the snow in Boston.

(Courtesy of the author)

until this point will remain in the formula. Instead of the water wash-development you have been using in the last few processes, we will be returning, as in the calotype, to a chemical development of the image. Considering what you have learned so far, I doubt that you will have much trouble assimilating the kallitype into the menu of things you can do in the alternative process genre.

A LITTLE HISTORY

The kallitype (from the Greek word *kalli* meaning beautiful) is a member of the iron-based Siderotype (*from the Greek root word "sideros" which means "iron"*), which was first named, and explained, by Herschel in 1842. Although the Van Dyke and the kallitype processes are quite similar, being iron based, each has its own unique characteristics and idiosyncrasies. In Van Dyke, ferric ammonium citrate is the active UV light-sensitive component in the sensitizer (*I like to explain it to my students as the "light-trigger"),* whereas in the kallitype, ferric oxalate performs that role . . . just as it does in platinum and palladium printing. The kallitype sensitizer of ferric oxalate and silver nitrate is coated onto a quality rag paper stock using a hake brush, or glass-rod, and exposed to UV light until a "stage-whisper" is seen. It is then developed in your choice of chemical developer options in order to allow for a variety of color renditions. The print is then distilled water washed, cleared in EDTA (*if you are using a borax/sodium borate developer*), toned in your choice of toner, fixed with a simple sodium thiosulfate bath, and washed. The kallitype is a close cousin to platinum/palladium in its reliance on ferric oxalate and a metallic salt (platinum chloroplatinite or palladium chloride) to make an image. Many artists consider the kallitype to be the equal of Pt/Pd and there are some knowledgeable folk who still have difficulty distinguishing between the two when the color and image tonality are made to look alike. This

was a major selling point of the process when it was first offered to the public. The problem . . . they were not even in the same parade when it came to permanence.

By 1842, the techniques that would evolve into the kallitype and Brownprint/Sepiaprint/Van Dyke processes, based on the work of Sir John Herschel's Argentotype, Chrysotype, and Cyanotype techniques, had chemically evolved into printmaking options for photographic image makers. Although Herschel had accurately described how the kallitype process would eventually work, it was not developed and patented until 1889 by Dr. W. W. J. Nicol.

Nicol's kallitype processes consisted of three variations on a theme and were named creatively as Kallitype I, II, & III. Nicol's Kallitype I process came in two versions and incorporated a ferric sodium citrate (*an iron salt*) and potassium oxalate sensitizer. It also required a developer made with silver nitrate and potassium oxalate to bring out the image. It's interesting to see the chemical relationships among Nicole's kallitypes, Herschel's argentotype, the Willis Platinotype that preceded it, and the Van Dyke/Brownprint that was developed at nearly the same time. For a historical/chemical perspective, here are Nicol's three kallitypes, in case you want to try them out.

Nicol's Kallitype I Process

Kallitype I Sensitizer
20% solution ferric sodium citrate
5% solution potassium oxalate

Kallitype I Developer for Blue Black
20% solution Potassium oxalate
1.5% solution silver nitrate
.880 ammonia*

The instructions for mixing called on the artist-scientist to mix together the silver nitrate and potassium oxalate solutions and then, a drop at a time, add the 1% saturated ammonia solution until a precipitate (*a physical solid that separates out of a solution*) formed on the surface of the sensitizer. Then, while stirring continuously, he or she would add additional drops of the .880 ammonia solution until the surface precipitate dissolved and the sensitizer showed clarity.

Nicol Kallitype I Clearing bath

  20% solution of potassium citrate

1-2 ml Ammonia .880 1% solution*

Fixing called for two successive clearing baths consisting of the potassium citrate and ammonia mix. Time in each tray was 5 minutes. If you intend to do this process, I would go a slightly different route and recommend a first wash of distilled water and citric acid followed by a light sodium thiosulfate fix and final wash.

Contemporary Clearing & Fix Alternative for Nicol I

Begin with 1 liter of distilled water to which you've added a healthy pinch of citric acid and clear the print for 5 minutes. Follow this clearing bath with a 5% sodium thiosulfate fixing bath (*50 g to a liter of distilled water*) for 1 minute and a final wash of 30–40 minutes.

The kallitype II formula was patented two years later (1891) and incorporated the ferric oxalate salt and the silver nitrate into the same sensitizing formula. This, you will see very soon, is pretty close to the kallitype process we practice today.

Nicol's Kallitype II Process

Nicol's Kallitype II Sensitizer

  20 g ferric oxalate

    8 g silver nitrate

120 ml distilled water

5–10 grains of oxalic acid

Add the ferric oxalate and the water together in a Pyrex measuring beaker (*kitchen measuring type will be fine*) and place it in a saucepan filled with water. Put the saucepan on the stove, or hot plate, and slowly bring up the heat until the ferric oxalate dissolves completely. Add the oxalic acid and then filter the solution through cheesecloth, the foot of a panty-hose, or a coffee filter. Then add the silver nitrate to the filtered solution and store the final volume in a dark glass bottle in a low light environment.

Kallitype II Developer for Black Tones

  113 g borax

   85 g Rochelle salt

   29 ml 1% potassium dichromate

1200 ml distilled water

Kallitype II Developer for Purple Black Tones

  113 g borax

   57 g Sodium Tungstate

1200 ml distilled water

In this kallitype II developer, you can see the first instance of the classic Rochelle salt and borax solution that is still used by many today. You can also see the addition of potassium dichromate in the developer. In many alternative processes, adding potassium dichromate is a choice you would make if you were trying to stimulate a chemically instigated boost in the contrast. At low percentage dilutions, however, potassium dichromate in the developer is added as a way of opening up shadows. One other bit of info . . . if you have trouble with crystallization in your developer you can modify the formula with 3 g of tartaric acid.

Kallitype II Clearing & Fixer

Since the Kallitype II process is so similar to the contemporary kallitype we do today, I am going to recommend that you follow the clearing and fixing baths for the contemporary version. Just go to the clearing and fixing instructions for Development Method #1 (Contemporary Clearing & Fix Alternative for Nicol I) instructions.

Nicol never got around to putting a patent on his kallitype III. In this process, all of the chemistry was combined into a single solution and once it was applied, and the paper was exposed, it printed out (POP) completely . . . as long as the sensitized paper remained uniformly damp throughout the process. This was a difficult trick to pull off, although the concept is a very nice one . . . kind of like the Argyrotype that does work well. Doing this process well is quite difficult but I am sure that some of you are going to enjoy trying to do it a great deal. Here it is if you want to give it a shot.

---

* Note: The aqueous solution of ammonia is basic. The maximum concentration of ammonia in water (a saturated solution) has a density of 0.880 g/cm³ (grams per centimeter) and hence is known as ". 880 Ammonia." Be very, very careful if you ever work with this concentration, as it is very nasty stuff. Be sure that you are working in a real chemistry lab with superior venting before attempting this Nicole formula.

Nicol's Kallitype III Process

Nicol's Kallitype III Sensitizer

17 g	ferric oxalate
4.7 g	potassium oxalate
4.7 g	silver nitrate
120 ml	distilled water

Kallitype III Clearing Bath: The Alka-Seltzer Formula

30 g	soda citrate*
5 g	citric acid
1 liter	distilled water

If you read the ingredients in Alka-Seltzer, you'll see that it is made of citric acid and sodium bicarbonate of soda. If clearing your highlights is causing indigestion you may want to consider giving yourself and your print an Alka-Seltzer.

Back to the history . . . In Nicol's kallitype I process, the paper was coated with an iron salt and potassium oxalate sensitizer and then exposed and developed in a solution of silver nitrate and potassium oxalate. This is quite different from the modern kallitype, in which the silver nitrate and ferric oxalate are combined in the sensitizer. By keeping the chemistry separate, Nicol's method overly complicated the procedure, as the increasingly exhausted silver nitrate developer could not be accurately replenished or counted on for consistent results.

As noted above, in 1891, Nichol secured additional patents for his iron salt and silver nitrate sensitizer modification and for a developer using Rochelle salts (*sodium potassium tartrate*) that mirrors the contemporary kallitype process. Although these changes were positive, the widely attempted technique was considered complicated and exceedingly temperamental. As editor John Tenant wrote in the February 1903 edition of *The Photo-Miniature #47*, "... the Kallitype process appeals, with peculiar force, to those with a lot of leisure time on their hands." In that very same issue of *The Photo-Miniature*, Henry Hall countered Tenant's lack of enthusiasm for the kallitype process and attempted to stimulate a public confidence in the practice of the technique with his article entitled *The Kallitype Process*.

For the next 15 years, the kallitype struggled to achieve even a modicum of popularity. To the dismay of the kallitype's champions, the advent of commercially coated papers, generated from such processes as Willis' ferric oxalate & chloroplatinite Platinotype (1873) and Pizzighelli's sodium ferrioxalate & sodium chloroplatinite POP Platinum (1887), proved to be more seductive as an alternative to hand coating. Given the Byzantine complexity of the written directions, and its reputation for impermanence, the process did not appear to have a bright future.

A few separate issues contributed to the permanence problem. One of the most significant had to do with the early procedure's high alkaline content developers, i.e., those with a great concentration of borax/sodium borate. This difficulty was coupled with not quite accurate fixing and wash recommendations, in which a bleach-like ammonia fixer devastated the image while it was supposed to be fixing it. In time, a mild sodium thiosulfate fixer (*sometimes with a tiny amount of ammonia added*) was substituted for the ammonia but this change only partially corrected part of the problem . . . and did little to dispel the public's perception, or the reality, of kallitype image fading.

During this same difficult time for the kallitype, the process was also being touted as being "*almost like platinum*" in its use of ferric oxalate and metal and was, for a short while, commercially produced and sold as an inexpensive alternative to the much pricier Platinotype paper. Unfortunately, the stability of the kallitype, with its silver, was no match for the Platinum; in addition, because of its flawed directions, the public saw the kallitype paper as an inferior alternative instead of a less expensive one. Coinciding with all of its other marketing problems, the kallitype had to contend with the beginning of the gelatin silver chloride paper revolution . . . it never had a chance.

Over the years, the kallitypes have been adopted by photographic artists for short periods of time and have gone by several different commercial names, including, Polychrome, Satista, Sensitol, Platinograph, and Soline. Dick Stevens's 1993 *Making Kallitypes: A Definitive*

---

* To prepare the citrate of soda dissolve 112 g of citric acid in 20 oz. of water, and add 133 g of the dried bicarbonate of soda.

Figure 11–2

Christopher James, *Rockets*, Mexico, 1992—kallitype

This image was made with a plastic Diana camera outside Pátzcuaro, Mexico, during the annual Dia de los Muertos rituals.

(Courtesy of the artist)

Guide is a pretty good resource if you want a grand tour of the process. As well, today there are many artists doing wonderful work with all of the kallitype processes, including Atlanta's Elizabeth Turk; Latvia's Karén Oganyan; and Philippe Moroux of the Netherlands, who creates mythical panoramic kallitypes with his hand-made pinhole cameras.

THE CONTEMPORARY KALLITYPE PROCESS

In the kallitype process a 100% rag paper is coated with a mixture of ferric oxalate and silver nitrate. After the sensitizer has dried, it is coupled with a negative that will be the same size as the final print, and exposed to sunlight, or mechanical UV light source. When the ferric oxalate and the silver nitrate sensitizer are exposed to the UV light, the ferric oxalate in the sensitizer reduces to a ferrous state (*ferrous oxalate*), which then reacts with the silver nitrate, changing the silver metal salt into a partially realized metallic silver. This exposed kallitype is

then processed in one of a selection of developers that is determined primarily by the individual artist's preference for specific colors and tonal renditions. These developers can be traditional kallitype variations or those that you would use in other processes such as traditional platinum or palladium printing, i.e., sodium acetate or ammonium citrate. I will also give you information about an alternative developer to work with that I've had great success with in workshops, and classes . . . a hybrid developer consisting of equal parts sodium acetate (*a traditional black kallitype developer*) and ammonium citrate (*a low impact palladium developer*). This new developer has been remarkable in yielding clear white highlights in situations where those highlights used to be a light buff. I'll also toss in suggestions for a few others to test out . . . among them an excellent sodium citrate developer.

It would be very easy to make this chapter complicated. One of the primary reasons that this beautiful process had such a short popular life was that the technique was explained in a far more complicated manner than was necessary. I've decided to provide a simple set of instructions and a few alternatives to get you started. If you really become enamored with the kallitype process you will find out how kallitype really complex it can be. The following silver nitrate and ferric oxalate formula is considered to be a standard and can be found in many historical and contemporary alternative process documents.

TABLE SET UP FOR KALLITYPE

- ◆ Kallitype A & B sensitizer (10% silver nitrate and 20% ferric oxalate)
- ◆ 2 screw cap droppers for A & B
- ◆ Clean paper for the table surface
- ◆ Paper for coating
- ◆ Shot glass
- ◆ New hake brush
- ◆ Clean distilled water in a beaker
- ◆ Pencil

Figure 11–3
Philippe Moroux—*Le jour de l'éclipse*
This is another beautiful pinhole generated kallitype, taken on the coast of Normandy during a solar eclipse.
(Courtesy of the artist)

- ◆ Hair dryer
- ◆ Contact printing frame
- ◆ Negative for contact printing
- ◆ Paper towels

The Kallitype Sensitizer: A & B

Kallitype Part A

10 %   silver nitrate solution

Add 10 g of silver nitrate to 100 ml of distilled water and mix it into a uniform solution. Be very careful with silver nitrate, especially in relation to your eyes. This chemical can cause blindness if you are careless about splashing or touching your eyes.

Kallitype Part B

20 %   ferric oxalate solution

Add 20 grams of powdered ferric oxalate to 100 ml of distilled water and stir into a uniform solution. Quality silver nitrate and ferric oxalate can be purchased through Bostick & Sullivan. Please refer to the chemical section before using these chemicals.

Keep both solutions in separate, labeled, dark glass bottles, with separate dropper tops, and never mix Parts A and Part B together in amounts greater than you intend to use immediately because it does not keep well in a combined solution. Once silver nitrate is mixed with any organic "stuff" it has a short life.

Silver nitrate, in a pure state, is quite stable but not when combined with other chemistry. As for the ferric oxalate, it has a mixed solution shelf life of about six months. I recommend buying it in a dry-pack powdered state versus the prepared liquid mix and then preparing it 24 hours before use. The dry ferric oxalate powder will last for years.

In the event that you find your old ferric oxalate responsible for fogging of your image, there is a remedy. Go to the drugstore and purchase a 3% solution of hydrogen peroxide, the same solution you use for first aid and for accelerating the oxidation of a cyanotype. Add several drops of the hydrogen peroxide to the ferric oxalate and swirl it around to mix it into solution. *Do not put the cap back on the bottle right away because the new solution creates a gas*, which like any other gas, will expand and exert a great deal of pressure in an enclosed container. If you are pretty sure that your ferric oxalate is past due, just call up Bostick & Sullivan and buy some new ferric oxalate in the mixed 20% solution or dry pack powder . . . and no, I don't own shares of the Bostick & Sullivan family business.

Figure 11–4
Rachel Woodburn, *Secrets*, 2006—kallitype
Arizona photographer, and AIB MFA candidate, Rachel Woodburn, has been making kallitypes for years and was one of my "lab-rats" when we were re-working the kallitype chemistry and process in 2006. Rachel's work centers primarily upon the women in her family . . . with the children as the principal storytellers and interpreters of the adult interactions.
(Courtesy of the artist)

Working with the Sensitizer

You will be mixing your sensitizer with a plastic eyedropper and a decent quality shot glass. Always use machine made plastic eyedroppers, because they will give you a consistent drop size. Hand-made glass droppers are unique per dropper.

Use a shot glass made for drinking in a bar rather than one with a picture of Niagara Falls on it made for a display shelf. The reason is simple . . . a drinking shot glass is heavy, has a thick glass bottom and a short barrel. The heavy weight at the bottom prevents it from falling over in a light wind or due to a clumsy gesture.

The short barrel reduces the amount of sensitizer left in the shot glass after you pour the sensitizer on the paper you are coating. This is economical and smart.

Using separate Part A (*silver nitrate*) and Part B (*ferric oxalate*) bottles and droppers, add equal drops (1:1) of Part A and Part B into your very clean, heavy-duty, shot glass. You will then swirl the solution together as you would do when mixing a platinum/palladium formula. The hand and wrist gesture is similar to the way someone swirls wine when they are pretending that they know something about the expensive wine they are evaluating. If you notice a precipitate of ferric oxalate on the surface of the solution you will have to filter it into a new glass bottle, using a coffee filter placed in a funnel, before applying it to your paper.

Generally speaking, a 4×5 negative, on a good quality paper, will require 8–10 drops of Part A and an equal number of drops of Part B to cover the printing area and allow the signature hand-painted border area that is common to many hand-applied sensitizers and emulsions. Adjust the number of drops proportionally to the size of your negative. You can easily refer to the Platinum/Palladium and Ziatype Drop Charts for a good idea of the total number of drops you will need for a specific size contact negative.

Later on, if your kallitypes show signs of "bleach-back" (*hydrolysis and fading of the image*), you may try eliminating that particular problem with a modest sensitizer modification. Simply add a bit more Part A silver nitrate to your A & B formula and you should see a difference . . . providing your developer and paper choices are compatible, you are clearing properly, you are not over-fixing, and your chemistry is fresh. Silver nitrate reacts to UV light once it is in a marriage with any organic matter, even dust, so always be attentive to the luminosity in your lab. Air-dry your sensitizer application in the dark or blow-dry it, from the back of the paper, using the cool setting and working in low ambient light.

Tween 20

Tween 20 is a non-ionic surfactant that assists your sensitizer in finding a secure "home" in the fibers of the paper you have selected. It also helps to minimize the leaching of colloidal metal during the process. You'll know if you should use it as an additive (*a drop or two to your sensitizer mix*) if you see staining or if your image leaches away in the sodium thiosulfate fixing solution.

Tween 20 is optional and can be added to your shot glass sensitizer formula to facilitate the absorption of the sensitizer into the paper substrate. Some say that it works great, enhances the D-max of their images, and yields a smoother-looking print. Others claim it ruins their work. As an example, when I print on Cranes Platinotype, I don't use Tween 20 as there is no apparent need for it. However, when I switch to Cot 320, depending on the process, the paper requires the addition of Tween to help emulsify the sensitizer. Tween 20 gets your sensitizer into the paper's fibers in a way that simple brush applications cannot.

To Make: a 5% solution, add 5 ml Tween to 100 ml of distilled water.

To Use: add one drop to every 20–40 drops of kallitype sensitizer.

Gold and Mercuric Chloride Additives

If you really know what you are doing with chemistry you can experiment with tonal and color modifications to the kallitype formula by adding drops of an additional metal solution to your sensitizer. The two most common, and traditional, additives are gold chloride and mercuric chloride. Both yield a warm olive-black and of the two options I recommend the gold chloride because it is less dangerous to use and far easier to obtain in a prepared 1% solution. The normal working formula is 1 drop of 1% cold chloride to every 20 drops of A and B sensitizer mix.

Mercuric chloride is prepared by mixing 1 g to 30 ml of distilled water. This working solution is used like the gold chloride solution; 1 drop to each 20 drops of A and B sensitizer mix. Please do not be alarmed when your A and B sensitizer clouds up when the mercuric chloride is added because this is normal. Be sure to dedicate a coating brush for this mercuric chloride enhanced formula and prepare yourself for possible clearing and staining problems, especially if you gelatin-size your paper for this process.

Note: Mercuric chloride is seriously toxic and is very hazardous to your health. It is listed as a Schedule I poison and all safety precautions should be attended to when using it.

COATING THE PAPER

The humidity in your coating area is going to play a role in the success of your kallitypes. Excess humidity may result in speckling and linear streaking in your image. Do your very best to work in a low humidity environment and get a dehumidifier for your working space if you get into the process. Remember to turn it off when you're done working. If you can't get rid of your humidity, (if, say you are living in Singapore), then you might want to think about using Nicol's kallitype III process or Mike Ware's Argyrotype instead.

Kallitype coating should be done under subdued light. Personally, I have always enjoyed working under multiple strands of miniature non-blinking Christmas lights because they provide enough illumination to see everything that is going on and they impart a festive atmosphere to the coating area. In truth, as long as direct sunlight, or fluorescent light, is not significantly illuminating your lab area, you are pretty safe until the final drying stage of your sensitizer, when you will want to be in a slightly darker environment.

When your brush is ready to use, *gently* coat the paper using long strokes, alternating between vertical and horizontal coverage, until the coating is even. As with Van Dyke, once the sensitizer begins to set up (*ceases to be reflective*) it is time to stop brushing.

Coating with a Glass Rod Puddle Pusher

With the glass rod method, place the rod flat on the paper at the top of the marked-out negative area. Then pour your prepared sensitizer solution along the back edge of the rod. Without lifting the rod from the solution, move it side to side in the sensitizer until the solution is spread evenly across the rod. Next, pick the rod up slightly, and lift it over, and behind, the elongated line of sensitizer. You are going to be pulling/pushing the sensitizer so that it covers the negative/print area. At this point, the rod is flat on the paper, behind the sensitizer, at the top of the paper. Now, with pressure, evenly drag the rod across the paper. If you have a puddle after the first "push," then repeat the step in the opposite direction. This is the same technique you would use when

Figure 11–5

Marissa Molinaro, *Self—Boston*, 2006—kallitype

Floridian, and recent graduate of The Art Institute of Boston, Marissa Molinaro, made this self-portrait with her pinhole camera and Type 55 P/N film. She then translated the image as a kallitype.

(Courtesy of the artist)

performing a platinum/palladium or a Ziatype coating. Again, either way you coat your paper it is a good idea to practice, on some scrap paper, ideally with some yellow watercolor in the same lighting conditions in order to get the feel of the coating technique.

If you are planning on using a hairdryer to speed up the drying process then it is important not to blow hot air on the freshly coated kallitype sensitized paper. Excessive heat will result in fogging and muddy highlight areas. Set the hairdryer on a cool setting and blow-dry the rear of the paper . . . pulling the sensitizer into the paper fibers. The print must be "bone" dry before printing or you'll get unpleasant texture surprises.

PAPER

The papers that I like for kallitypes are similar to those that I recommend for the Van Dyke and Argyrotype. My top choices will include Bergger's Cot 320 (*using Tween in the* formula) as it has a luxurious finish and weight. It is a bit expensive but if you can afford to give yourself a treat it is a nice experience. Other papers that work well include

Stonehenge 90# white, Crane's Platinotype, Ruscombe Mills Buxton, Weston Parchment, Lenox 100 and Arches HP 90#, Arches Aquarelle, Saunders Somerset, Whatman's Watercolor, and Fabriano Artistico. Each of these papers exhibits a unique set of traits and colors.

EXPOSURE

The kallitype-sensitized paper must be exposed in contact with the negative in sunlight or in a mechanical UV printing unit. Typical exposures will vary between 1–3 minutes in bright summer sun to 4–6 minutes in bright shade . . . which helps boost contrast slightly and opens up the shadows. Of course this is totally dependent on the time of day and your negative density (*which should be in the 1.5 to 1.8 range*). You'll need to do exposure tests but the best way to evaluate your progress during the exposure is to open your contact-printing frame and examine the paper in subdued light.

Unlike with the Van Dyke, you are not looking for a resolved POP version of your image during the exposure stage. Instead, as in a platinum/palladium print you will be waiting to see a pale positive image. In platinum/palladium I refer to this look as a "*whisper*." In the kallitype process I describe the value I am seeking as more of a "*stage whisper*," meaning that there is a bit more density to the whisper. Test strips will give the most accurate results but will change meaning at different times of the day and season of the year. After your paper has been exposed, develop it immediately.

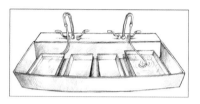

SINK SET UP FOR KALLITYPE

Tray Sequence

Tray 1 A very clean and dry development tray & a bottle of prepared combo developer. Development time will be 8–10 minutes.

> *Primary Developer: Combine prepared sodium acetate and prepared ammonium citrate developers in equal proportions. Or, see the text for developer alternatives, i.e., 20% Sodium Citrate developer, Henry Hall's Developer, Ammonium Citrate Develop, etc.*

Tray 2 A distilled water and citric acid clearing bath. For every liter of distilled water add a very healthy pinch of citric acid . . . perhaps a tablespoon. I once recommended just a running water bath but too often I experienced a rust-like colored fade on the print. Distilled water with a little citric acid appears to cancel out that problem. Rinse for 4–5 minutes.

Tray 3 **Optional** **EDTA** clearing bath depending on the choice of developer. Please refer to the text for specifics. Mix: 1 tablespoon to a liter of water. EDTA time . . . 5 minutes.

Tray 4 **Optional** **Toning Baths**: Toning must be done *before* fixing the print. Toning baths will alter the image color and often aid in the archival properties of the print. Please refer to the text for specific formulas and times. My favorite for this process is the .2% gold chloride/2% ammonium thiocyanate toner generally used for POP (printing out paper) toning. Average toning time for a cool valued rendition: about 8–9 minutes to as long as 30 minutes.

Another Toning Option—Platinum Toner: Mix up a formula of 5 g of sodium citrate plus 5 ml of platinum solution #3 (a 20% Potassium Chloroplatinite solution) per liter of water. Tone your print for not less than one minute. Your image will lose about 1/2 step of density during toning . . . this is normal.

Tray 5 **5% Sodium Thiosulfate fixing bath:** (2 minutes)

Mix: 50 g sodium thiosulfate to 1 liter water
5 ml household strength ammonia

Tray 6 Final wash for 20–30 minutes

Figure 11–6
Brandon James, *k1*, 2002—kallitype
Brandon's work deals with measuring, collecting, calculating, keeping records, and somehow, quantifying our natural surroundings. The images are made for the viewer to discover and are of past experiments that have been abandoned. The intent is to leave more questions than answers, with only the photograph to explain.
(Courtesy of the artist)

DEVELOPMENT

The kallitype is developed according to the color one wishes to see in the finished print. Each developer formula results in varying tonalities of black, blue, sepia, reddish brown, aubergine. I'll provide you with a few variations of development and clearing. *Developer #1* relies on traditional formulas and is much like Nicol's kallitype II recipe. With #1 you must run the print through a clearing bath of EDTA prior to toning and fixing the print. The developers that follow are standard kallitype formulas and have been around for a long time. In general, I am recommending that you read these formulas for informational value, and for further experimentation. I'll also recommend that you make your life simple by using the Developer #2 or sodium citrate versions as they generally yield very clean highlights. Notice that most classic kallitype developers contain tartaric acid, often used as an additive to assist in preventing ferric staining (yellowing) in the highlights . . . a significant, and long-term, issue with this process. I have a cure for the problem in Developer #2 below.

Developer Method #1: Classic Black/Brown Developer

1000 ml   of distilled water
  100 g   borax (*anhydrous*)
   75 g   Rochelle salts
    3 g   tartaric acid

Step 1 Warm 750 ml of distilled water to about 80°F to 85°F and pour it into a plastic beaker.

Step 2 To the warm water, add and dissolve 100 g of borax (sodium borate), stirring constantly.

Step 3 Dissolve 75 g of Rochelle salts (*sodium potassium tartrate*) into solution. Rochelle salts are very difficult to saturate and you will likely have to filter the leftover sediment from the solution before adding it to the borax.

Step 4 Add 3 g of tartaric acid to the water-borax-Rochelle salt solution and stir until it is dissolved . . . good luck.

Step 5 Finally, add distilled warm water to make a 1 liter working solution.

Kallitype Developer Warming & Cooling Control

Modify the formula to suit your taste. Use less borax and add more Rochelle salts and you will warm the print's coloration. If you use less Rochelle salts and add more borax to the formula you will cool the hues. It is advisable to work with a warm developer because borax (*anhydrous rather than hydrated*) will not stay in solution under 78°F. An electric Crock Pot is an ideal warming tool that will keep your solution at a constant warm temperature. This Crock Pot is not to be used for stews and soups after you are finished with it . . . it is now a lab instrument.

Crystallization Problem Solution

Feel free to modify the proportions of the borax and Rochelle salts in these and the formulas that follow. If you find that you have a lot of crystallization going on in the developer, remember to add some extra tartaric acid to the solution.

An example would be a formula consisting of 75 g of borax to 40 g of Rochelle salts in 1000 ml of distilled water. If this solution is left to age for 8 hours, and a print is developed in it, it is likely that there will be a coating of fine crystals on the print when you remove it from the developer. If you add 15 g to 20 g of tartaric acid to the developer, the crystals will dissolve. Factors that will change your coloration will be the paper that you are using and the developer's proportions; here are a few suggestions for beginning experiments.

Sepia Tones

◆ Use the black–brown formula #1 but use 50 to 75 g of Rochelle salts in 1000 ml of distilled water and eliminate the borax.

Cool-Brown Tones

◆ Use the black–brown formula #1 but use 75 to 100 grams of borax in 1000 ml of distilled water and eliminate the Rochelle salts.

Gray-Blue Tones

Step 1 Begin with 750 ml of warm (+ 80°F) distilled water in a clean plastic beaker.

Step 2 To the warm water, add 40 g of borax (*sodium borate*) and stir it into solution so that the chemical is dissolved entirely.

Step 3 Dissolve 40 to 50 g of Rochelle salts in the borax and distilled water beaker.

Step 4 Add 3 g of tartaric acid to this mix and stir it into the solution.

Step 5 Finally, add warm distilled water to make 1000 ml. Stir this solution well and allow it to age for 6 to 8 hours.

Figure 11–7

Peg Fredi, *Thou Shalt Not From This Grove*, 2005—kallitype

Part of photography's magic is the ability to compose scenes, (as opposed to taking a photo of things that present themselves) and Peg Fredi is a fine storyteller in both her words and images. The relationship of the child, the vulture and clean dress on the laundry line is reminiscent of a page from a Faulkner novel visually narrated.

(Courtesy of the artist)

ALTERNATIVE KALLITYPE DEVELOPERS

Developer #2: Ammonium Citrate & Sodium Acetate

About a year ago, in the midst of a workshop, I was getting a bit frustrated with the fact that my students were unable to clear the highlights in their kallitypes. The prints looked great going into the first wash but soon lost their white integrity. Because of the brown leaching, I recommended that we begin to add Tween to the sensitizer. That helped but didn't completely deal with the problem. I then made a change in the first wash, going from a running water rinse to a distilled water bath. This helped a little bit more. The problem was the iron and chlorine/chloramine in the public water supply.

I then went a step further and added a pinch of citric acid to the distilled water and this action continued to improve the quality of the highlights but not enough to inspire the chorus of oohs & aahs that usually accompany a new demonstration. Then I decided to try something new; I made up a new developer to go with the new wash cycles.

Two of the #2 developers, ammonium citrate and sodium acetate, are often used as platinum/palladium developers (*processes that also use ferric oxalate in their sensitizers and require a developer to realize the image*) and they are fine options. What is really quite nice about these two developers is that when they are combined in equal volumes, and used as a single developer, the kallitype avoids the vexing, and quite long term, problem of buff colored highlights. Here are several developers to play with.

Sodium Acetate & Ammonium Citrate Combo Developer

This is a really easy solution to a long-term problem. Mix together 500 ml of the sodium acetate developer and 500 ml of the ammonium citrate developer and blend them into a single solution. Use them in exactly the same manner that you would the other developers. This developer is wonderful to work with because it appears to solve the problem of buff colored highlights. Average time in developer is 8–10 minutes in order to convert all of the residual ferric salts that are in the paper fibers.

Replenish with fresh developer every 12 prints or as needed, and like a Pt/Pd developer, don't throw it out when your printing session is done.

Sodium Citrate—20% Solution (*Sepia brown*)

I like this developer a great deal as it is simple and efficient and really clears in the highlights nicely. I'm not sure if it is any better than the combo sodium acetate/ammonium citrate developer but at the very least it is another very good alternative. Development is at least 8–10 minutes in order to convert all of the residual ferric salts that are in the papers' fibers. Replenish the developer at a rate of 400 ml for every 1000 square inches of paper surface. If you don't replenish you will not be able to clear the paper well and staining will occur. This is also the developer that has been tested and used for adjusting contrast by adding potassium dichromate to it. Please refer to the test information to follow.

20% Sodium Citrate Kallitype Developer
200 g   sodium citrate
1 liter   distilled water

Ammonium Citrate (*Warm reddish-maroon*)

There are two options for adding this developer to your chemical toolbox. The simplest option is to purchase a prepared bottle of ammonium citrate developer from Bostick and Sullivan. This is their kit developer for platinum/palladium and is a good option because it is pre-mixed in liquid form, reusable until it runs out, and relatively safe. The other excellent advantages of this developer are that it is very consistent, and provides fine grain. Ammonium citrate yields a bright brown to warm reddish-maroon color depending on the paper you are using. It tends to be a contrasty developer. Or if you want to make it yourself, here is the recipe.

- Make up a 20 % solution of ammonium citrate by mixing 200 g of ammonium citrate to 1000 ml of distilled water.

Develop by inspection and don't worry about over-development. The standard development time will be 8–10 minutes. Replenish the developer at a rate of 400 ml for every 1000 square inches of paper surface.

Sodium Acetate (*Neutral black-maroon*)

- Mix 75 g of sodium acetate to 750 ml of warm distilled water.
- Add 3 g of tartaric acid to the sodium acetate and distilled water mix and stir into the solution.
- Finally, add warm distilled water to make a working solution of 1 liter.

This developer tends toward softer contrast than does the ammonium citrate. Develop by inspection and don't worry about over-development. Development is at least 8–10 minutes in order to convert all of the residual ferric salts that are in the paper fibers. Replenish the developer as needed.

Henry Hall's Sodium Acetate Option (1903)

This is a nice neutral black version of the earlier sodium acetate developer. It is Henry Hall's version from his article in *Photo-Miniature #47*, 1903. In Hall's formula the sodium acetate is doubled to 150 g and the tartaric acid is halved to 1.5 g. The total volume remains the same at 1000 ml. Those who use this variation describe the coloration of their prints, as being blacker than it would be with the sodium acetate version above.

150 g   sodium acetate
1.5 g   tartaric acid
1000 ml   warm distilled water

Kallitype Contrast Control: 5% Potassium Dichromate & Sodium Citrate Developer

Here is another way to control contrast; this time, you will be manipulating your developers rather than your sensitizers. Make a 5% potassium dichromate solution and add it to the developer in various proportions depending on how contrasty you want your image to be. The basic rule with this technique is that the more potassium dichromate you use the more contrast, and less tonal separation, you'll get. Begin by making up a few liter bottles of a 20% sodium citrate kallitype developer. Then add anywhere from 1 ml to 10 ml of the 5% potassium dichromate to that liter of sodium citrate developer. Here are the results of a few tests that Sandy King made with Stouffer 21-step wedges.

Figure 11–8

Sandy King, *Interior of Museum*, 2005—kallitype

Sandy King is a photo historian and landscape photographer, the author of *The Book of Carbon and Carbro: Contemporary Procedures for Monochrome Pigment Printmaking,* 2002. Recently retired from Clemson University, Sandy's current thinking about photography harkens back to the earliest days of the medium. Defined as the *neutral vision* . . . the idea that the lens is an artificial retina capable of revealing to us things independent of our senses. This is a relatively objective way of seeing, defended in the 1920s and 1930s by the members of the school of straight photography, who held that photography has certain basic qualities which, derived from its technical parameters, endow it with a specific mission and impose on it certain mechanical principles.

(Courtesy of the artist)

Potassium Dichromate and Sodium Citrate Test #1

Sensitizer: 1 part ferric oxalate + 1 part silver nitrate

Expose 100 seconds in UV ULF 28

Develop in 20 % sodium citrate solution

Add 1 ml of 5% potassium dichromate per liter in developer

Result: 14 stops .15 dMax to paper white = 2.10

Potassium Dichromate and Sodium Citrate Test #2

Sensitizer: 1 part ferric oxalate + 1 part silver nitrate

Expose 100 seconds in UV ULF 28

Develop in 20 % sodium citrate solution

Add 4 ml of 5% potassium dichromate per liter in developer

Result: 12 stops .15 from dMax to paper white = 1.80

Potassium Dichromate and Sodium Citrate Test #3

Sensitizer: 1 part ferric oxalate + 1 part silver nitrate

Expose 100 seconds in UV ULF 28

Develop in 20 % sodium citrate solution

Add 10 ml of 5% potassium dichromate per liter in developer

Result: 10 stops .15 from dMax to paper white = 1.50

EXPOSURE

Looking for the Stage Whisper and Development

Once the exposed print has reached the "stage whisper" it is time to develop it in one of the developer formulas above. The processing technique is a pouring action rather than an immersion . . . exactly like a platinum/palladium development.

Begin with a totally immaculate and dry tray . . . for every single print. Place the exposed print in the bottom of the dry tray and quickly pour the developer over the image. Be sure that you don't stop to admire your image halfway through the pour. This is not as critical as it is in platinum/palladium, but get into the habit of covering the paper all at once with this development method.

You will see the resolved image in an instant but it is not done developing yet. It is quite important to let the print develop out for the correct amount of time. The developer needs time to reduce the ferric salt to a ferrous state and this process will take a little bit of time. Be patient and give it 8–10 minutes for the full effect.

Don't be alarmed by the density of the image. You might notice that the image gets a bit "orangey" looking. On occasion, the image will appear to be fading . . . don't panic. It will come back nicely and you actually want the print to be too dark at this stage. The density will diminish in the clearing and fixing stages as the print makes its way through the process. The dry-down is pretty hefty

and you will get all of the densities back—in fact, you'll probably get more than you want. After the development stage, immerse the print in a distilled water bath with a pinch of citric acid added to it. Most important . . . once your print is out of the developer, pour the remaining developer back into the developer bottle (*you will not be throwing it away*) and then clean, wash, and dry your development tray for the next print.

I realize that a skilled practitioner can usually immerse a print in the developer without problems but I am recommending that you get into the habit of processing this way for a few reasons. First, it is good practice for the very fussy development process you will experience in platinum and palladium printing. Second, it reduces contamination problems that are a big part of the kallitype's difficulties. Third, it allows you to keep better track of your developer usage so that you can replenish with more accuracy.

WASHING & CLEARING

For the developers used in Developer #1 (with the borax and Rochelle salts), it is important to run the print

Figure 11–9
Galina Manikova, Kallitype on Ceramic, 1999
(Courtesy of the artist)

through an EDTA clearing bath prior to fixing or toning. With the sodium acetate, ammonium citrate, combo, or the Henry Hall Method #2 developers, it is possible that the EDTA clearing steps required in Method #1 will be unnecessary. That said, it is a good idea to do them anyway. Rinse your print in an acidified distilled wash bath and then follow it up with an EDTA bath. It is essential that you remove all of the ferric salts that remain in the paper or your print will fail.

Your first tray rinse should be a liter of distilled water and a hefty pinch of citric acid. Rinse for about 4–5 minutes.

EDTA

The second clearing bath is going to be made up of EDTA and water. EDTA (*ethylenediaminetetra acetic acid tetrasodium salt*) crystals are very effective in clearing the highlights in kallitype and platinum and palladium prints. EDTA is safe; it is not flammable, or reactive. It is a low impact chemical used as a food preservative in yogurt. In the EDTA clearing bath, unexposed ferric salts are removed from the print, which, if left in the paper, would cause unsightly brown staining relatively soon after you hang your print up to dry.

Preparing the clearing bath is simple, pour in a Tablespoon or two of EDTA crystals and drop and stir it into a liter of distilled water. You will notice that it is pretty alkaline (*slick feeling on the fingers*). If you feel better about measuring, make a 4% solution. Immerse your print for 5 minutes. You should see the color of the water becoming slightly yellow as the un-converted ferric iron salt is washed out. When you do, change the bath. EDTA crystals can be purchased from the same source as your developer chemistry. In a clearing bath emergency, say you are out of EDTA or citric acid, go to the store and buy some 7-Up® soda. This solution will work pretty well and is fun to use in a demo.

TONING THE KALLITYPE

Following the clearing stages, *and prior to fixing*, you are able to tone the image. These toning steps in the process permit change to the print's colors and values as well as help to preserve the print from long- and short-term deterioration. Toning is an option and is not necessary if you

Figure 11–10
Christopher James, *Pilar*, Mexico, 2005—kallitype
This is a simple portrait of my friend Pilar, who makes the best soupa de pablano in Mexico.
(Courtesy of the artist)

like the color of your print after the development, fixing, and dry down. The first toning recommendation is the same gold toner found in the Van Dyke chapter. It will help prevent the print from suffering the ill effects of "*bleach-back*" in the fix and will make it more permanent than a conventional kallitype print. Think of it as gold plating the print. One additional benefit of toning is that toners will often correct an over-exposed shadow area in your print by converting it from a solarized looking density to simply a dark one. In most cases, the toners that you would use for salted paper, POP, or platinum/palladium will work with the kallitype. Please refer to those chapters for the formulas. The following represent a few recipe options to add to your "toolbox." Split tones, where two or more colors are visible within the image, are possible if you play with the toning dilutions, toning sequence combinations, toner temperature, and/or type of developer used to process the print.

A Basic Gold Toner for Kallitype: Before Fixing

  5 g   citric acid
1000 ml   distilled water
  5 ml   5% gold chloride
5 minutes or until you like it . . . *Faster when fresh*

Palladium Toner

  2 g   sodium acetate
  2 g   citric acid
 400 ml   distilled water
30 drops of 20% palladium chloride

Gold or Palladium Toning Sequence

Coat and expose your kallitype print in the traditional manner and then go through the double wash cycle beginning with the acidified distilled water. Then, mix the toner by combining the ingredients listed in the recipes above. Tone the print in either of the solutions until you like what you see and then immerse it in fresh running water for 5 minutes. When that rinse step is done, immerse the print in your 5% sodium thiosulfate fixer for 1 minute. Then, immerse the print in a hypo-clearing agent for 1 minute and final wash the print for 30–40 minutes and hang the print on a line to dry. Presto! A beautiful print gold-toned kallitype.

Figure 11–11
Lisa Elmaleh, *Individual*, 2006—kallitype
Lisa made this montage from a series of photo booth generated picture strips and translated them into a composite kallitype.
(Courtesy of the artist)

Black Toning Formula

To 100 ml of distilled water add:

   0.5 g   of sodium acetate

   0.5 g   of citric acid or sodium chloride

7 drops   of palladium chloride (20%)

Immerse the print in this solution for 5 minutes with constant agitation. Then, rinse the print for one minute. Go to the fixing stage, and fix the print for 1 minute in the 5% sodium thiosulfate fixer. Finally, remove the print from the fix and place it in a clean water bath. If you wish, you may immerse the print in a hypo-clearing agent for 1 minute to shorten the final wash time. Wash the print for 20 minutes and hang on a line to dry.

Selenium Toner

Make up a very dilute solution of this toner, say 1%, to begin testing, i.e., 10 ml of Kodak Rapid Selenium Toner to every 1000 ml of distilled water. As always, avoid touching the selenium toner with bare skin as the body absorbs this liquid and keeps it. When you are ready, tone the immersed print until you see what you like. There is a chance you will not be immediately pleased . . . be patient. If it's too aggressive, tone the print in gold first, rinse for 20 minutes, and then go to selenium. Next, using tongs, remove the print and place it in a water bath for one to two minutes. Next, go to the fixing stage and fix the print for 1 minute in the 5% sodium thiosulfate fixing bath. Remove the print from the fix and place it in a clean water bath. Immerse the print in a hypo-clearing agent for 1 minute and then wash the print for 20 minutes and hang on a line to dry.

FIXING THE PRINT

This is the part of the process that contributes to the kallitype's poor reputation for fading. The majority of literature, old and new, on the technique recommend concentrations of sodium thiosulfate fixer that are too strong and immersion times that are too long. The bottom line here is that you need to rid the print of any unexposed silver salts. And the difficulty with that job, and the kallitype process, is that if your fixer is too strong and/or your immersion time too long your print is going to be etched away. Take your pick . . . now, or later. If you do it right, the print will be fine for a very long time.

Chances are if you have followed the procedure to this point your print is looking pretty good, so it makes sense to do the final steps perfectly. This includes a sodium thiosulfate fix that will adequately remove any traces of the ferric salts, or the effects of chlorine in your tap water (silver chloride), from your print.

The 5% Sodium Thiosulfate Fixing Bath (with an added alkali)

Step 1   Dissolve 50 g of sodium thiosulfate into 1000 ml of distilled water.

Step 2   When the sodium thiosulfate has dissolved, add 5 ml of *non-detergent* household ammonia, *or* 3 g of sodium carbonate, and stir it into solution. This makes the fixer slightly alkaline and greatly helps prevent *bleach-back* or the loss of your image in the fixer. *Bleach-back* is just a nice compound word for a terrible moment in the process when your print disappears in the fix. Just for your info . . . another way of reducing the problem is to increase the amount of silver nitrate in the sensitizer.

Step 3   Fix your print for 1 minute with constant agitation.

A one-minute fixing time should not cause your print to fade. My own 10-plus-year-old kallitypes, gold-toned, with an alkali fixer, and a short 1-minute fixing time, haven't faded or died.

HYPO CLEARING OPTION

If you wish to accelerate the removal of the residual sodium thiosulfate that has permeated the fibers of your paper you may use either a 50% dilution of a gelatin silver paper strength hypo-clearing agent or a 1% solution of sodium sulfite . . . these are the same thing only one costs more than the other. In both cases, immerse your fixed print for one minute.

FINAL WASH

If you have used the half strength hypo clearing, or sodium sulfite bath, then your final wash time will be 20 minutes long. If you have not used these baths then wash your prints for about 30 to 40 minutes, depending on how well you like your print.

Again, the most chronic problems in kallitype are those of over fixing, under washing, and that of leaving iron salts and silver chloride residue behind in the paper's fibers after the washing stage. The reason iron remains in the image is that insoluble compounds of iron (*ferric salts*) have formed in a wash that is too alkaline . . . this is why we throw in the pinch of citric acid and use distilled water in the first rinse after exposure. Don't be discouraged if the first few kallitype attempts are not what you had in mind when you decided to try this process. Play around with the technique, make a few free associations with the alternative cousins, cyanotype, Van Dyke, and platinum/palladium, and see how your own experiments and adaptations change the final image.

Figure 11–12

Yvette Dubinsky, *Here and Gone*, 1998

This is the work of St. Louis artist, Yvette Dubinsky. The cyanotype, kallitype, gum bichromate, and mixed media piece measure 45.5" × 23.5" and is good example of the interdisciplinary options in alternative processes.
(Courtesy of the artist)

The New Chrysotype Process

OVERVIEW & EXPECTATIONS

My intention for the new chrysotype chapter is to offer you enough information and knowledge to make chrysotypes and to inspire you to further your investigations in the process. My friend, the brilliant Dr. Mike Ware, who resurrected Sir John Herschel's original chrysotype process (1842), has written two books relating to the process and it would be absurd for me to try and replicate the depth of the information you can excavate by consulting them.

Mike Ware, *Gold in Photography: The History and Art of Chrysotype,* Abergavenny: ffotoffilm publishing, 2006

Mike Ware, *The Chrysotype Manual: The Science and Practice of Photographic Printing in Gold,* Abergavenny: ffotoffilm publishing 2006

There is also a web site that Mike, and his editor-publisher Paul Daskarolis have created that is dedicated to the *siderotype* (from the Greek *sideros*—iron), a method of printing images utilizing light sensitive iron salts in combination with salts of gold, platinum, palladium, silver and others. The site address: www.siderotype.com

So, you may ask, why another iron process . . . and won't this one be hellaciously prohibitive due to the cost of gold? The answers to those questions are precisely the reasons you should learn it.

- ◆ Gold has a higher covering power than other noble metals such as platinum and palladium. As a result, you will use less of it making a print and will find that it is actually less expensive.

- ◆ The new chrysotype can be thought of visually in the same way that you think about platinum and palladium. The new chrysotype print is matte and the tonal scale is equally delicate and extensive as its Pt/Pd siblings.

- ◆ The other great attribute of the new chrysotype is the vast menu of tonalities that are possible. Whereas you are somewhat limited in hues of neutral gray and brown with platinum and palladium, the new chrysotype offers split-color options involving grays, pinks, magentas, browns, violets, blues, and greens. This range of color, as you will see, is predicated upon the chemistry of the sensitizer and the conditions of the processing.

- ◆ Lastly, among the primary reasons for making this a process to embrace is the elegance and permanence of the new chrysotype print.

Figure 12–1

Mike Ware, *Noto Antica*, Sicily, 1987/2002—new chrysotype

This image is an example of Mike Ware's improved adaptation of Herschel's original chrysotype process from 1842. In 1987, after several years of painstaking testing, seeking possible compounds that could bind to and stabilize the gold (ligands), Mike came up with a method of printing images utilizing light sensitive iron salts in combination with salts of gold. This was probably the first new printing process, utilizing noble metal, to be created in over a century.

(Courtesy of the artist)

A LITTLE HISTORY

A fair distance on the historical siderotype trail has been traveled in previous chapters involving the iron-based processes, so I'll simply refer you back to the Cyanotype, Anthotype, and argyrotype chapters for the bulk of information. In this brief section I'll offer a brief description of Herschel's original chrysotype process and workflow and a few reasons why the process disappeared for so long . . . until Mike Ware, with his knowledge of modern chemistry, resurrected it under the banner of new chrysotype.

Most normal individuals would be content to invent, or discover in their lifetime, a single new process to make photographic images and history. In 1842, Sir John Herschel created three of them—the cyanotype, the Argentotype, and the chrysotype. Each of these

techniques has a place in the *siderotype* family, a word first used by Herschel to describe an iron-based photographic print. A number of authors have pointed to the fact that the English summer of 1842 was meteorologically "brilliant" and this fact may have had a great influence on how much work Herschel was able to accomplish. Herschel had also recently moved from London to the crisp and clean air of Kent, and was greatly inspired by his new environment.

Herschel was well aware of the work his friend, and scientific colleague, William Henry Fox Talbot, had accomplished with calotype and salted paper and was enthusiastically capable of making images in various shades of brown. As described in the Cyanotype chapter, Herschel's fortuitous correspondence with young Dr. Alfred Smee, and Smee's ability to provide Herschel with (new to him) the deeply colored salts of ferric ammonium citrate and potassium ferricyanide, and the amazing weather in the summer of 1842, all led to a extraordinary period in which Herschel changed the very foundations of the new photographic medium.

Figure 12–2

Sir John Herschel, *JFWH #23*, 1842— chrysotype

In his set of 43 specimens exhibited at the Royal Society in 1842, (now held by the HRHRC) this image was printed by Herschel as both an anthotype (#1) and as a chrysotype (#23). This print is a chrysotype because it is a negative and because of the density of the purple colour. The anthotype is a positive image and pale lilac in color. The image was originally published in Friendship's Offering 1839, vol. 8 p. 289; it's called A Scene in Italy, engraved by H. Cook from a painting by J.W. Wright. (See p. 82 of Mike Ware's book *'Gold in Photography'* for additional details) *Courtesy of The Gernsheim Collection, Ransom Center, University of Texas-Austin, TX*

One of the things that Herschel understood was that when sunlight fell upon his ferric ammonium citrate sensitized papers, the resulting ferrous iron could also be used to reduce* precious metals from their respective salts. This meant that he could make images in silver (*Argentotype*), gold (*chrysotype*), and mercury (*celaenotype*). It was Herschel's groundbreaking work in this area that eventually led to Willis's platinotype process. There were problems however.

In 2004, Mike Ware wrote an excellent piece for Double Exposure, *A Golden Legend: Chrysotype Re-invented*.

> "Owing to the powerful chemical reactivity of gold chloride, which is incompatible with the iron salt that he used, Herschel had to place this gold salt in a development bath, which rapidly accumulated impurities and decomposed—a highly uneconomic procedure. The expense of gold compared with silver, and chemical problems of image fogging, prevented the embryonic chrysotype process from gaining admission to the repertoire of photographic printing media."

Besides the expense, another problem, one that continues to have ramifications, was the fact that Herschel's chrysotype process announcement to the Royal Society, was misreported in the August 1842 issue of *The Athenaeum*, a popular and important periodical of the time for scientific and literary news. The transcriber confused Herschel's chrysotype with his cyanotype process by indicating the inclusion of ferro-sesquicyanuret of potassium (potassium ferricyanide) in the chrysotype technique. Herschel corrected the record two weeks later in a response to The Athenaeum (below) where he provided details for his chrysotype technique. Unfortunately, the misinformation had a life of its own . . . like a bad review.

In 1849, Henry Snelling's, *The History and Practice of Photography*, got it wrong and this source is still being referenced as historical fact.

"A modification of Mr. Talbot's process, to which the name of Chrysotype was given by its discoverer, Sir John Herschel, was communicated in June 1843 to the Royal Society, by that distinguished philosopher. This modification would appear to unite the simplicity of photography with all the distinctness and clearness of [Talbot's] calotype. This preparation is as follows. The paper is to be washed in a solution of ammonio-citrate of iron; it must then be dried, and subsequently brushed over with a solution of the ferro-sesquicyanuret of potassium (potassium ferricyanide). This paper, when dried in a perfectly dark room, is ready for use in the same manner as if otherwise prepared, the image being subsequently brought out by any neutral solution of gold. Such was the first declaration of his discovery, but he has since found that a neutral solution of silver is equally useful in bringing out the picture. Photographic pictures taken on this paper are distinguished by a clearness of outline foreign to all other methods."

Herschel's Chrysotype—From The Athenaeum August 20, 1842

"The preparation of the chrysotype paper is as follows: dissolve 100 grains of crystallized ammonio citrate of iron (ferric ammonium citrate) into 900 grains of water (approximately 2 fl. oz.),** and wash over with a soft brush, with this solution, any thin, smooth, evenly-textured paper. Dry it, and it is ready for use. On this paper a photographic image is very readily impressed: but it is extremely faint, and in many cases quite invisible. To bring out the dormant picture, it must be washed over with a solution of gold in nitro-muriatic acid,*** exactly neutralized with soda (bicarbonate of

---

* Reduce: the word describes reduction/oxidation and all chemical reactions in which atoms have their oxidation state changed.

**Note: Herschel's formula for the chrysotype states that 100 grains ferric ammonium citrate is dissolved in 900 grains of water. The best I can figure is that this weight is based on a system of liquid measure conversion established in 1618 in the London Pharmacopoeia, adopting the Roman gallon as a basic liquid measure converting units of liquid capacity into apothecary weights. This would mean that 900 grains is 58.32 grams of water, which has a volume of 58.22 ml at 20 C, which is 2.05 fluid ounces.

***Note: nitro-muriatic acid is another term for *aqua regia*, meaning "*King's Water*" in Latin. It is formed by freshly mixing concentrated nitric acid and concentrated hydrochloric acid, usually in a volumetric ratio of 1:3 respectively. It is one of the few reagents that dissolve gold and platinum, i.e., noble metals.)

soda), and so dilute as to be not darker in colour than sherry wine. Immediately, the picture appears, but not at first of its full intensity, which requires about a minute and a half to attain (though, indeed, it continues to darken for a much longer time, but with a loss of distinctness). When satisfied with the effect, it must be rinsed well two or three times in water (renewing the water), and dried. In this state, it is half fixed. To fix it completely, pass over it a weak solution of hydriodate of potash (potassium iodide), let it rest a minute or two (especially if the lights are much discloured by this wash), then throw it into pure water until all such disclouration is removed. Dry it, and it is thenceforward unchangeable in the strongest lights, and (apparently) by all other agents that do not destroy paper."

In 1984, Mike Ware was awarded a Kodak Photographic Bursary to support an investigation of the iron-based methods of precious metal printing. This interest sprang out of his professional research as an inorganic chemist at Manchester University. In collaboration with Professor Pradip Malde, they developed an improved method of printing-out in platinum and palladium. This research led to Mike's interest in gold and his belief that there was a means of stabilizing gold prints within an iron-based sensitizer . . . rather than in the economically unfeasible developer that Herschel had originally used.

In 1987, after several years of painstaking testing, seeking possible compounds that could bind to and stabilize the gold (ligands), Mike came up with a solution using an inexpensive compound to reduce the gold. This was probably the first new printing process, utilizing noble metal, to be created in over a century.

Figure 12–3

Tom Hawkins, *Coast, Bonaire*—new chrysotype

Tom's chrysotype image of the historical slave huts on the coast of Bonaire (a great hore entry dive site by the way) illustrates an example of the range of the color range one can achieve in the process.

(Courtesy of the artist)

MIKE WARE'S NEW CHRYSOTYPE PROCESS NEW CHRYSOTYPE SENSITIZER

There are three separate ways of creating a new chrysotype sensitizer, each with it's own unique degree of complexity. For our purposes I will detail the least complicated of the three forms, what Mike Ware calls the "S-version" (sodium method) and recommend that you investigate his book, *The Chrysotype Manual*, if you are interested in trying your hand at the other versions. Just for your information, the other two versions are called the "M-version" (Methyl sulphoxide) and the "P-version" (for pH parameter).

Chemicals Required for the Chrysotype Sensitizer

A—3,3'-Thiodipropanoic acid
   (aka: *3,3'-Thiodipropionic acid*)
B—Either/Or
   B1—Sodium tetrachloroaurate (III) dihydrate
   (aka: *sodium gold chloride or sodium chloroaurate*)
   B2—Hydrogen tetrachloroaurate (III) trihydrate
   (aka: *chloroauric acid or gold(III) chloride hydrate*)
C—Ammonium Iron(III) oxalate trihydrate
   (aka: *ferric ammonium oxalate or iron ammonium oxalate*)
D—Either/Or
   D1—Sodium carbonate
   D2—Sodium hydrogen carbonate (baking soda)
E—Tween 20
F—Distilled water

TABLE SET UP— MAKING CHRYSOTYPE SENSITIZER STOCK A-B-C

- One 50-100 ml graduated glass measuring cylinder
- One 100-200 ml Pyrex glass beaker

- One large plastic beaker (500 ml)
- One small filter funnel
- Filter papers (#1)
- Two glass stirring rods
- Plastic eye droppers/pipettes
- Gram scale
- Electric hotplate
- Plastic spoon
- Three brown glass bottles with screw caps (50 ml)
- Labels and marking pen

The new chrysotype sensitizer is made up of three separate solutions.

- **Solution A: ligand***
- **Solution B: gold**
- **Solution C: iron**

PREPARING STOCK SOLUTION S-VERSION CHRYSOTYPE

Stock A: Ligand

Step 1   Weigh out 12.5 g of 3,3'-Thiodipropanoic acid and transfer it into your 500 ml beaker, or measuring cylinder

Step 2   Weigh out 7.4 g of sodium carbonate (anhydrous) or 11.8 g of sodium hydrogen carbonate

Step 3   Add 30 ml of distilled water to the Thiodipropanoic acid and stir it into suspension with your glass rod

Step 4   Slowly add the sodium carbonate powder, in small portions, to the Thiodipropanoic acid in suspension. Carbon dioxide gas will form, the solution will foam and effervesce—it is harmless. Stir this well and allow the foam to subside between additions of the sodium carbonate. Continue this until the sodium carbonate is in

---

*A *ligand* is an ion, a molecule, or a molecular group that binds to another chemical entity, especially a metal ion, to form a larger complex.

Figure 12–4

Roger Vail, *Easter Rainforest Sunrise*, Easter, 1983–2000—new chrysotype
Roger was one of the first people to "road-test" the new chrysotype in a Monterey, CA, workshop he organized for his students and Mike Ware in 2000. *(Courtesy of the artist)*

clear solution. Small residual bits and particles do not matter.

Step 5   Pour this solution into a small 50–100 ml measuring cylinder and make it a final total volume of 50 ml with your pure water. Stir this into solution.

Step 6   Filter the solution through a #1 filter paper directly into the stock bottle. The solution will be like syrup so be patient. The bottle should be labeled:

Solution A: Ligand—New Chrysotype "S" (Disodium thiodipropanoate 1.4 molar)

Stock B: Gold (B-1)

Step 1   Carefully weigh out, or transfer, 5.0 g Sodium tetrachloroaurate(III) into a Pyrex glass beaker with a 100 ml capacity. Use plastic to measure and transfer.

Step 2   Add 25 ml of distilled water, at ambient temperature, to the gold salt in the beaker. Use a little water, squirted from an eyedropper, to wash out and transfer any residual gold left behind on your plastic spoon.

Step 3   Filter the gold solution carefully into a measuring cylinder (50–100 ml) using the funnel and a #1 filter paper.

Step 4   Add distilled water, a little at a time, to the filter paper, allowing it to pass through to wash out most of the residual yellow solution, and to make up the final volume to exactly 36 ml in the measuring cylinder. Mix this solution thoroughly.

Step 5   Transfer the solution carefully from the measuring cylinder to the stock bottle. This solution is stable indefinitely Label the bottle with the date of the mix and the following:

New Chrysotype: S-Version, Solution B: Gold (Sodium tetrachloroaurate 0.35 molar)

Stock B: Gold (B-2)

This B-2 option may be less expensive and more readily available than B-1. If hydrogen tetrachloroaurate(III) is cheaper or more readily available than the sodium salt, then you can make your gold solution from it. The following is the procedure for neutralizing this acid with anhydrous sodium carbonate or sodium hydrogen carbonate:

Step 1 Carefully weigh out, or transfer, 5.0 g Hydrogen tetrachloroaurate(III) into a Pyrex glass beaker with a 100 ml capacity. Use plastic to measure and transfer.

Step 2 Add 30 ml of distilled water, at ambient temperature, to the gold salt in the beaker. Use a little water, squirted from an eyedropper, to wash out and transfer any residual gold left behind on your plastic spoon. With gentle agitation the solid will easily dissolve into a yellow solution at room temperature.

Step 3 Weigh out 0.673 g of sodium carbonate (anhydrous powder) using a chemical gram scale. If you have trouble measuring such a precise amount, you may round the weight off to 0.7 g . . . OR use 1.07 g sodium hydrogen carbonate.

Step 4 # Slowly add the sodium (or hydrogen) carbonate, in very small portions, to the solution of chloroauric acid. There will be a good deal of effervescence as carbon dioxide gas is created. Swirl the solution, and continue adding the solid to completion and no further effervescence.

Step 5 Add pure water from the washbottle to make up to a final volume of exactly 36 cc in the measuring cylinder with thorough mixing.

Step 6 Filter the solution carefully from the measuring cylinder to the stock bottle using a #1 filter. Label the storage bottle with the date of the mix and the following:

New Chrysotype: S-Version, Solution B: Gold (Sodium tetrachloroaurate 0.35 molar)

Stock C: Iron Solution

Note: The following steps must be carried out under subdued indoor lighting . . . avoid daylight.

Step 1 Weigh out 30 g of ammonium iron(III) oxalate into a small 100 ml Pyrex beaker

Step 2 Add exactly 33 ml of distilled water from a measuring cylinder at ambient temperature. If the solution becomes to cold, gently warm it in a bath of hot water to assist the dissolving.

Step 3 Within 5 minutes, the solid will have dissolved to form an emerald-green solution. The total volume should be 50 ml.

Step 4 Filter the solution through a #1 filter in a funnel directly into a dark brown storage bottle (50 ml).

Step 5 Store the bottle at room temperature. If after several days, you see needle like crystals, re-filter the solution. This solution is very close to saturated and if it cools to below 68°F some crystals may form at the bottom of the storage bottle. Gently warm the solution to dissolve them. The solution will keep indefinitely. Date it and label:

New Chrysotype: All Versions, Solution C: Iron (Ammonium iron(III) oxalate 1.4 molar)

TABLE SET UP FOR MIXING SENSITIZER— VERSION S

- Several (6) graduated syringes capable of measuring 1 & 2 ml
- Three to four 50–100 ml brown glass bottles for sensitizer
- Clean trays (5)
- Clean table surface or glass plate for coating
- Paper for coating*
- Shot glass: heavyweight and stout
- A Puddle Pusher or glass rod
- Custom cat carrier humidifying box or hydration chamber
- Pencil & ruler
- Contact printing frame
- Negative for contact printing
- Paper towels
- Tape

---

* The right paper is very important. It must be sized and able to withstand extended immersion and free of additives. The best papers for this process include Ruscombe Mills Buxton, Atlantis Silversafe, Weston Parchment, and Bergger's COT 320.

Mixing the Chrysotype Sensitizer

Contrast is controlled by the molar ratio of the ligand : gold (A : B) which can be varied between 2 and 6. A "standard" value is 4 and is recommended for first trials with the sensitizer. The molar ratio of gold to iron (B : C) is always 1. OK, this may be a bit complicated but I'll try to make it clear.

The ligand (A) and iron (C) solutions have the same molar concentration of 1.4 molar. This is 4 times the molar concentration of the gold (B) which is 0.35 molar. The volume ratios for your standard sensitizer mix are determined by this information. This means that a standard volume ratio for the sensitizer would be set up like this: **Ligand : Gold : Iron = A : B : C = 4 : 4 : 1**.

Volume ratios can be varied between the following parameters: **A : B : C = 2 : 4 : 1** to **A : B : C = 6 : 4 : 1**.

The lower, than the "standard" value of 4, ligand (A) to gold (B) ratios, the faster the printing speed but the less stable the sensitizer. The tonal range will be longer and the maximum density will be higher. Highlights have tendency to fog.

Higher ligand (A) to gold (B) ratios, than the "standard" value of 4 provide more a more stable sensitizer, a slower printing speed, higher contrast, and slightly lower maximum densities with clean highlights. Increasing the value of iron (C) has no obvious benefit.

Mixing the solution must be done in the following sequence of steps.

Step 1 Deliver the volume **A** (ligand) solution into a shot glass using a graduated syringe.

Step 2 Add the volume **B** (gold) solution, drop by drop, from a separate syringe, swirling the shot glass. Allow time between drops for the gold solution to become clear and colorless.

Figure 12–5

Mike Ware, *Gull, Orkney*—new chrysotype

A great deal of Mike's inspiration and imagery come from his sojourns to the Orkney Islands where abundant evidence remains from the ancient Orcadians to the Vikings. The islands lie off the northern tip of Scotland. . . where the North Sea and the Atlantic come together.

(Courtesy of the artist)

Step 3 When Step 2 is complete, add the volume **C** (Iron) from a third syringe. The sensitizer will now turn a pale yellow-green.

Step 4 Mix the solution of **A : B : C** thoroughly using a fourth syringe.

An 8" × 10" piece of paper, using a "standard" volume ratio of 4 : 4 : 1, will require about 1.25 ml of solution per sheet if you are rod coating. Considering the expense of the sensitizer, I would strongly advise using a glass rod or puddle pusher. Please consult the platinum/palladium chapter for instructions on how to use the rod.

COMPONENT VOLUMES TO MAKE 10 ML SENSITIZER—VERSION S

Ligand: Gold Molar Ratio	Volume A Ligand 1.4M	Volume B Gold 0.35M	Volume C Iron 1.4M
2	2.86 ml	5.71 ml	1.43 ml
2.5	3.33	5.33	1.34
3	3.75	5.00	1.25
4 standard	4.44	4.44	1.12
5	5.00	4.00	1.00
6	5.45	3.64	0.91

 Note: Once the components are in solution the sensitizer will be stable for about 30 minutes. Version S will be useable for about 2 hours.

Coating

Coat using a Puddle Pusher or glass rod rather than the traditional hake brush. This is far more economical considering the cost of the gold. Your coating technique should be smooth and accomplished and I would strongly advise practicing with yellow-green watercolors before committing to gold.

Humidity

Predictable results for image color can be controlled by the relative humidity of the paper. Different degrees of humidity can be used as a tool and you should consider building the cat carrier humidity box described in the argyrotype chapter or investing in a humidity chamber that is controlled. A high relative humidity (RH) will yield neutral grays. Very Low RH will give almost no image printout with faint values in the darkest shadows. In this case, the image is entirely generated via development.

The colors will show pink to dull-red shadows and grey-blue high values. The mid-tonalities will show purple and magenta shadows evolving into blue highlights. Experimentation, your method of hydration, the season

of the year, and where you live will all be relevant factors. Water hydration, where the print is humidified over distilled water for up to 30 minutes is one method. (*See, Chapter 9, the argyrotype chapter for information about the cat carrier humidity box.*) Salt hydration chambers, where the RH is controlled by saturated solutions of specific salts is a second hydration option and details for building one can be found in Mike Ware's *Chrysotype Manual*.

Exposure

Exposure times are equivalent with, or even shorter than, platinum/palladium and are somewhat dependent upon the ligand : gold molar ratio. Most exposures in UV light sources will run about 2–3 minutes. Higher RH in the paper means that the developer will have little to do and is equivalent to a step. Lower RH means that developer will have a 4- to 6-step influence on the final image. It would be wise to do test strips before committing to full sheets of paper.

CHEMISTRY REQUIRED FOR CHRYSOTYPE PROCESSING

Developing Agents (1 or more of the following)

◆ 1% Disodium EDTA

   At low RH neutral brown tones in 5–10 minutes. High RH yields greens.

◆ 1%–2% Citric Acid

   At, low RH pinks, red shadows, blue highlights in 1-6 minutes—longer immersions intensify reds—may block up. High RH produces blues.

◆ 1%–2% Tartaric Acid

   Neutral to red tonalities depending on RH.

◆ 1%–2% Oxalic Acid

   Longest tonal range and dramatic red—blue splits depending on RH.

Clearing Agents

- Tetrasodium EDTA
- Sodium sulfite or sodium metabisulfite

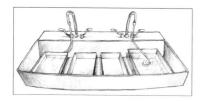

SINK SET UP FOR CHRYSOTYPE

Tray 1 **Disodium EDTA—OR—alternative developer** options listed above. Mix 1% solution: 10 g to a liter of tap water. Each liter of developer is good for 2–3 prints. Do not use tetrasodium EDTA which is less expensive and used later as a clearing bath.

Tray 2 **Rinse:** 30 seconds in running water

Tray 3 **Tetrasodium EDTA—Clearing Bath #1**

Mix 5% solution: 50 g in 1 liter of tap water—10 minutes.

Tray 4 **Rinse:** 30 seconds in running water

Tray 5 **Sodium Sulfite—Clearing Bath #2**

Mix: 2.5 % solution: 25 g in 1 liter of tap water—10 minutes

Tray 6 **Rinse:** 30 seconds in running water

Tray 7 **Tetrasodium EDTA—Clearing Bath #3**

Mix 5% solution: 50 g in 1 liter of tap water—10 minutes.

Tray 8 **Final Wash**

PROCESSING THE CHRYSOTYPE

Post-Exposure Hydration (Optional)

If you are seeking a lower contrast, with the longest possible tonal scale, then post-exposure hydration is strongly recommended. This procedure, conducted in a warm water hydration chamber (such as the cat carrier humidity box) will allow the print to develop almost to completion before the paper is immersed in the developer. Hydration can be from 2 to 15 minutes and this step will shorten tray development to about 1 to 2 minutes. Tonalities will also be smoother.

Figure 12–6

Pradip Malde, *Irkutsk*, Siberia, 1995—new chrysotype
Long a collaborator with Mike Ware, and once a resident of the Orkney Islands, Tanzanian born Pradip Malde has been at the forefront of alternative process adaptations.
(Courtesy of the artist)

Although this step gives a very long tonal scale, it does diminish the opportunities for dramatic split tones because of the lack of developer influence. Spot development can be accomplished by breathing your own warm breath in localized areas of the exposed paper.

Normal Chrysotype Processing

Step 1 Select one of the developers (Disodium EDTA, Tartaric Acid, Citric Acid, or Oxalic Acid) and mix a liter of it in Tray #1. Remember, the developer is good for only 1–2 prints before you will need to re-mix. The primary role of the developer is to clear the print. Develop, with vigorous agitation for up to 10 minutes.

Step 2 Rinse the print for 30 seconds.

Figure 12–7
Mike Ware, *Poppies*, 1990–2002—new chrysotype
Mike Ware has successfully adapted each of the three Herschel iron based processes from 1842; the Cyanotype, the Argentotype, and the Chrysotype. This example of his New Chrysotype process illustrates the wonderful split-tone potential of the process.
(Courtesy of the artist)

Step 3 **Clearing Bath #1**—Immerse the print in 5% Tetrasodium EDTA for 10 minutes and you will see the red tones emerge and intensify in this bath. This bath can be used many times.

Step 4 Rinse.

Step 5 **Clearing Bath #2**—Immerse the print in a 2.5% sodium sulfite or sodium metabisulfite for 10 minutes. This bath should be made fresh for a single printing session only. Do not store it or re-use.

Step 6 Rinse

Step 7 **Clearing Bath #3**—Immerse the print in a second bath of 5% Tetrasodium EDTA for 10 minutes. This bath can be re-used many times, and can replace Bath #1 when #1 is exhausted.

Step 8 **Final Wash**—30–60 minutes

Drying the Print

Lay the washed print on a near vertical piece of glass or clean Plexiglas and let the print drain. After it has shed most of its water then lay it out on a flawlessly clean plastic screen or hang on a line to dry.

Last Comments

This process is not for those who desire instant gratification. Even if you know what you are doing, have everything in place, and can manage a working session in the lab without distraction, an average print will take about 2.5 hours from beginning to end. Be patient and enjoy performing the newest original alternative process.

The Platinum/Palladium Process

OVERVIEW & EXPECTATIONS

Over the years, platinum—palladium (Pt/Pd) is the process that surfaces first when I ask students, "What process do you want to learn more than any other?" Perhaps it's the beauty of this nearly perfect alternative printmaking technique. Possibly it's the meticulous way a Pt/Pd print is analyzed, constructed, de-constructed, and realized. Maybe it's simply the romantic cachet of using precious metals, sunlight, and water to make an image . . . that alone does it for me . . . Whatever "it" is there is no contesting that the process is beautiful to work with and that it resides on a very high perch in the alternative processes pantheon.

In this chapter, I'll begin with the usual "A Little History" section. Then I'm going to make a conscious effort to demystify the process. You will learn the chemistry and sequence of the various stages to a finished Pt/Pd print. I will suggest alternatives to traditional platinum/palladium chemistry and provide you with an easy to comprehend sensitizer "drop chart" that is based on the type of negative you have in hand, rather than the print you would like to make . . . just like real life. I'll also offer a trouble-shooting list to assist in hunting down problems that may show up in your work. Finally, you'll get some brief suggestions for combining platinum/palladium with such techniques such as Van Dyke, cyanotype, and gum bichromate.

Figure 13–1

Christopher James, *Dying Man*, Mukti Bhavan, Benares, India, 1985—Pt

There isn't enough room in this space to tell you the whole story of this image. If my home were on fire, and I had time to grab one negative, after family and dogs, this would be the one.

(Courtesy of the author)

A LITTLE HISTORY

As is the case with nearly every refined alternative process, the art of Pt/Pd evolved over a lengthy period of time and through the efforts, and serendipitous accidents, of many artists, scientists, physicists, and entrepreneurs.

In 1804, Adolph Ferdinand Gehlen (1775–1815) was the first to observe and record the reaction, and effects, of light on platinic chloride salts. He noted that UV light would alter the color of the platinum salts to a tint of yellow and cause the ferric salts to precipitate out into the ferrous metallic state.

In Captain W. de Abney's books, *Platinotype* (Sampson Low, Marston & Co., London, 1895) and in its U.S. version, *Platinotype* (Scovill & Adams of New York, 1898), Abney gave credit to Adolph Ferdinand Gehlen for first documenting the photochemical property of platinic chloride. He wrote, "*Gehlen found that an ethereal solution of platinic chloride, when exposed to light, first turned a yellow colour, and eventually threw down metallic platinum in the form of a thin film on the sides of the vessel.*" So far, so good, except the actual color was more of a dark brownish-red that eventually went to a straw-yellow color as it was exposed to UV light. In a subsequent paragraph, Abney writes, "*Gehlen, as far back as 1834, showed that an ethereal solution of platinum, after a short exposure to light, was reduced by ferrous sulphate.*"

Two problems need to be pointed out because this inaccurate information is continually repeated in photo history texts. The first problem with the attribution by Abney is that Gehlen had been dead for 19 years when he made his observations . . . that may explain why he is able to see an ethereal solution. The second problem is that the ferrous sulphate would have reduced the platinum salts even if they hadn't been exposed to light.

My friend, Dr. Mike Ware, in a correspondence with me during the writing of this chapter, sent along the following reference, which I would not have been able to comprehend even if I had stumbled on it . . . and for that I am grateful. Mike wrote, "Gehlen's publication of these observations is well-documented. The full reference is: A. F. Gehlen, "Über die Farbenveränderung der in Äther aufgelösten salzsauren Metallsalze durch das Sonnenlicht." *Neues allgemeines Journal der Chemie, III, 566 (1804).* Gehlen was editor of this journal at the time. He showed that the chlorides of iron, uranium, copper, and platinum, dissolved in ether, were all photo-sensitive.

That is a nice reference and does much to explain the various paths that led from Gehlen's investigations. Then Mike wrote, "*You owe me—for all of those umlauts*" . . . I believe an "umlaut" has something to do with the way vowels are pronounced in German language. But, how does one repay an umlaut? I digress.

The first known preparation of platinum(II) chloride is credited to Heinrich Gustav Magnus (1802–1870), a German chemist and physicist who, in 1828, discovered the first of the metal complex platino-ammonia compounds . . . (*Magnus' Green Salt* or, if you're showing off, *tetre-ammineplatinum(II) tetrachloroplatinite(II)*). These compounds were relatively unknown until the 1870s when a simple method of preparation, utilizing a menu of reducing agents, was finally devised. It is this modern compound, potassium chloroplatinite, or potassium tetrachloroplatinite, that is essential to the success of the process as its reduction to a metallic state is a simple one of Platinum(II) chloride and ferrous oxalate leading to black platinum tonalities.

At approximately the same time, in 1831, Johann Wolfgang Döbereiner (1780–1849) observed the decomposition of ferric oxalate upon exposure to UV light and scientifically calibrated its sensitivity. He found that a solution of ferric oxalate was decomposed into carbonic acid (carbon dioxide) and ferrous oxalate by the action of the blue-violet ends of the spectrum, but not by the rays of red or yellow . . . a finding quite compatible with the experiments of Sir John Herschel with tincture of rose leaves that same year. Döbereiner also recorded the light sensitivity of platinum salts, manganic oxalates (*containing manganese*) and tincture of iodine. His scientific observations are relevant because they form the foundation on which many non-silver processes, especially those that incorporate iodine, have been built.

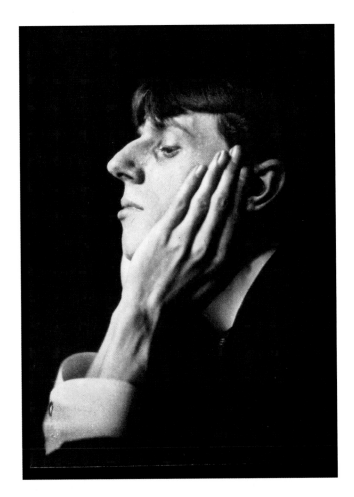

Figure 13–2

Frederick Evans, *Portrait of Aubrey Beardsley*, 1895—Pt

Evans was a photographic purist; some would say a *zealot*, who scorned any artist who strayed from the truth and essence of the medium. His subject, Aubrey Beardsley (1872–1898), was a self-taught illustrator influenced by Japanese woodcuts, the silhouette simplicity of Greek vase painting, and the flamboyance of French Rococo. Beardsley enjoyed a brief career with his erotically decorative, monochromatic, illustrations and died of Tuberculosis at the age of 27. The confluence of personalities between Beardsley and Evans is why this image has always been one of my favorites.
(Courtesy of George Eastman House/International Museum of Photography)

Aqua regia (*Royal Water*) is a mixture of concentrated hydrochloric and nitric acids and is one the few re-agents (*a substance used to begin a chemical reaction*) that is able to dissolve metallic gold and platinum. In 1831, Sir John Herschel noticed that when he neutralized a platinum solution in aqua regia with calcium hydroxide (lime), and then placed it in a dark environment . . . nothing happened. However, when he exposed it to sunlight, a precipitate was formed. In a report to the British Association at Oxford in 1832, Herschel reported that when this solution was subjected to light it clouded and then "*threw down a white, or, with excess of platinum, a yellow precipitate.*"

Robert Hunt (1807–1887), a Herschel contemporary, conducted experiments in the early 1840s using platinum chloride on silver iodide coated papers. Later, when he mixed platinum chloride with a solution of potassium cyanate it yielded a faint *whisper-like* latent image upon exposure to sunlight. Hunt then placed the paper in a solution of mercury salts (*mercurous nitrate*) that allegedly gave him a lovely image, which, like most everyone else's lovely images, faded away over time . . . even if kept in the dark. It is, according to Mike Ware, unlikely that this image contained platinum—more likely silver and/or mercury. As an aside, Hunt is recognized for his discovery of ferrous sulphate as a developing agent (1844), for his work on the influence of the spectrum on light-sensitive materials, and for being one the founders of The Royal Photographic Society.

In 1858, C. J. Burnett was the first to demonstrate a semi-controlled adaptation of these previous experiments using sodium chloroplatinate. His platinum-based experiments were not, according to Burnett himself, entirely successful. However, his uranium prints, developed with a solution of silver nitrate, and toned with gold, platinum, and palladium, delighted Burnett and he happily exhibited what could be called the first Palladiotype prints.

According to Abney, "*In the Liverpool and Manchester Journal of May 15, 1858, Burnett proposed to prepare paper, either plain or collodionized or gelatinized, with ammonio-ferric oxalate, and develop it with gold or palladium, or develop with silver and tone with platinum, gold, or palladium, fixing with ammonia or oxalate of ammonia.*" Abney then added this somewhat snide remark, "*It is difficult to know exactly what merit is to be assigned to Burnett; his papers are very numerous, and it is not easy to distinguish actual experiment from mere suggestions.*"

Abney's snideness aside, it is significant that Burnett came so close to actually discovering a truly accessible and practical platinum/palladium process . . . one that was essentially a mirror of the Willis method that is our contemporary version. Burnett was using ammonio-ferric oxalate, and he already knew that platinum salts, could be employed as developers. Had Burnett not been so inquisitive, experimenting with every type of salt in existence, he would undoubtedly have arrived at the solution to the platinum/palladium process nearly two decades before Willis.

In 1872, William Willis (1841–1923), seeking a way to make a photographic print that was both stable and user friendly, conducted an involved series of experiments, using potassium chloroplatinite and ferric oxalate. He was successful in reducing the ferric oxalate to ferrous oxalate by exposure to UV-containing light. Then, by using a heated potassium oxalate developer, he was able to make soluble the ferrous oxalate, which consequently reduced the platinum salt to platinum metal.

Willis was granted several patents between 1873 and 1887 for his discoveries and successfully launched the first commercial platinum paper enterprise, The Platinotype Company. Several years later, in 1892, he introduced a cold development process that resulted in his work gaining immediate acceptance as an accessible photographic printmaking technique that lived up to his claims that it was both permanent and not difficult to do. One additional important element relating to Willis's investigations can be read in Mike Ware's excellent article, *The Eighth Metal*, in which he details evidence from indicating that as early as 1880 indicating that Willis was aware that his platinotype chemistry was inhibited by the gelatin sizing in paper and that to achieve success it was necessary to avoid paper sized with that additive. Ware speculates that the eventual success of manufacturing platinum papers, in 1892, indicates that Willis had solved the problem with the possible use of alum-rosin sizing.

Beginning in the early 1900s, commercially produced platinum and palladium papers were available in Europe and the United States (*even Kodak made them*) and were very popular due to the beauty of their tonalities and permanence. The palladium process, which is essentially the same as platinum, with the principal exceptions of cost and color, was introduced during World War I. This was fortuitous as platinum was virtually impossible to get after the beginning of The Great War's hostilities, as it

Figure 13–3

Gertrude Käsebier, *Blessed Art Thou Among Women*—1900 (platinum print)

Gertrude Käsebier was a prominent member of England's The Linked Ring (*its first American woman*), and one of the primary influences in the Pictorialist movement. Stieglitz was a fan of hers, publishing her in *Camera Work* (1903–1917) and exhibiting her work in his 291 Gallery. Like the majority of the *pictorialists*, she was devoted to ideal, romantic and nostalgic visions of life.

(Courtesy of George Eastman House/International Museum of Photography)

was a strategic metal in weapons manufacturing. With the advent of the commercially perfect, and readily available, papers, hand-coating techniques became a non-issue and the process became *the* way for both photographic artists and amateurs to make prints. This was encouraged, in great part, into the 1920s by the popularity of the "*Pictorialist*" aesthetic.

Figure 13–4

Peter Henry Emerson, *Gathering Water Lilies, 1886—Pt*
(Plate #9 from Life and Landscape on the Norfolk Broads)

Peter Henry Emerson (1856–1936) said, " . . . *only a vandal would print a landscape in red or in cyanotype.*"

(Courtesy of The Getty Museum)

Pictorialism

Beginning with Hill and Adamson's calotypes (1843–1847) of the member's of the newly formed Free Church of Scotland, there have been photographers who approached image making with more expressive and personal intentions than those founded on practical science or serendipitous discovery. The first scientist to officially adopt the subjective side of image making was the outspoken, and quite curmudgeonly, English physician Peter Henry Emerson (1856–1936) who, by virtue of his revisionistic views of art history, and demonstrative ego, was able to spawn a movement in photography that led away from the evidentiary virtues of science to the less-defined and subjective virtues of fine art. It is a movement that continues to this day and is, in some romantic photographic circles, the driving force of contemporary photography.

Emerson spent much of his self-important photographic life tormented by the debate between those who believed photography could be distilled into a set of hard and fast rules and those who believed it was a flexible form of expression and impression. In 1886, Emerson began a series of lectures defining the correct, naturalistic, approach to the new medium. Trashing such image-makers as Henry Peach Robinson, he defined a position in which a photograph always aspired to represent an artist's true aesthetic vision, as painting did in the Impressionist movement.

Emerson made up a lot of *camera-club* like rules for photography; including centralized subject matter, differentiated focus, natural settings, and candid posing; and once said, in reference to a cyanotype print, "no one but a vandal would print a landscape in red or in

Figure 13–5

Henry Peach Robinson, *Fading Away*, 1858—albumen

One of the leaders of the Pictorialist movement, Robinson was torn between the passive relationship of the camera to the subject and his deep compulsion to influence the compositions . . . as would a painter. *Fading Away* is his most well-known piece and a composite image of 5 separate negatives. The interesting thing about this piece is how angry it made people. It seems that the theme was fair emotion for a painter to interpret but far too sensitive for the accuracy of a camera. When viewers were told that their emotions had been manipulated by photographic shenanigans, they were livid.

(Courtesy of George Eastman House/International Museum of Photography)

cyanotype." In 1889 he published his grand theory of artistic photography in a book entitled, *Naturalistic Photography*. The following year, Emerson changed his mind.

Emerson's idealism came to an abrupt, and ironic, halt in 1890 when Ferdinand Hurter (1844–1898) and Vero Driffield (1848–1915) divulged their findings on the direct quantitative linkage between the amount of exposure given a film and the resulting corresponding densities on that film following chemical development . . . the characteristic curve of film. In addition, they devised a theory of controlling the development of the latent image. Emerson was aghast; convinced that this "scientific proof" cast his own beliefs in doubt, he withdrew his claim that photography was pure art and promptly released a new book titled *The Death of Naturalistic Photography*. But it was too late; many

photographers had already become disciples of the Pictorialist vision he had championed.

Shortly after Emerson's first book, more than a few photographers began to see themselves projecting artistic reflections as their respective efforts often mirrored the styles and ideas of the Impressionist painters. Groups of photographers bonded together to ensure that their voices would be respected and their work shown. They established "clubs" such as the legendary The Linked Ring Brotherhood (London, 1892) and the Photo-Secession (New York, 1902) that achieved its singular strength through the peculiar and dominant personality of Alfred Stieglitz and the reach and reputation of his magazine, *Camera Work* (1903–1917). These two groups were the strongest advocates for alternative process image making and the concept that it was appropriate for photographers to have hands and heart . . . as well as eyes.

Figure 13–6
Alvin Langdon Coburn, *Flatiron Building, NYC, Evening*, 1912—platinum
One of the founders of the Photo-Secession, and member of The Linked Ring, Coburn was an articulate warrior against conventions and restrictions that restricted the new medium of photography. Attracted to Cubism, he was one of the first to apply that genre's style to photography in his Vortographs, created by attaching a kaleidoscope mirror to his camera. This image of the Flatiron Building is one of his more romantic images and was also made as a Pt and gum bichromate print.
(Courtesy of George Eastman House/International Museum of Photography)

Ironically, the rebellious nature of the pictorialists became bloated with its own pedagogy and a pedantic assortment of inflexible rules as to what a proper image *must* be. At this point, the photo-secessionist movement underwent a transformation toward a far more conservative and visual theology. This visual "*religion*" made a home for itself in obsequious camera clubs and lock-step generic salon competitions. In modern nomenclature, the word *pictorial* most often describes, positively or negatively (depending on who is speaking) a work of art that is "*painterly*," hand-made, romantic, trite, a cliché, and personal.

With the advent of smaller format cameras and rolled film, and of George Eastman's "you press the button and we do the rest" enterprise in Rochester, photography became a democratic reality. Social documentation, photojournalism, and work with commercial intentions began to replace the classical pictorialism that was perceived by many as a privileged and elitist kingdom within the medium . . . sort of what's happening because of Post-modernist photography today. In addition, significant changes in conceptual and perceptual thinking in the arts, i.e., The Bauhaus, put an aesthetic dagger into the once unchallenged Pictorialist heart. At this point in history, the use of platinum and palladium as the primary vehicle for image making ebbed. Within the last decade, though, the process has experienced an unprecedented re-birth in response to the mushy democracy of digital photography, the work of contemporary artists, alternative process courses in the world's colleges and universities, and the always sold out workshops in alternative process disciplines.

Figure 13–7

Marie Leon, *Portrait of Henry & William James*, London, c. 1905—Pt

A rare portrait of Henry & William James taken in Marie Leon's Regent Street studio in London.

(Courtesy of the author)

Figure 13–8

Michael Kenna, Mont St. Michel, 048, 2000—Pt

Ever since seeing one of Michael's images in Chuck Rynd's Equivalents Gallery in Seattle, many years ago, I have been a fan of his work. He is, in my opinion, a consummate artist and craftsman with very few peers. This image is one of a portfolio in platinum documenting his work at Mont St. Michel in France.

(Courtesy of the artist)

HOW PLATINUM/PALLADIUM WORKS

Here is a quick overview of the process. Pt/Pd is based upon the foundation that specific ferric salts will be reduced to the ferrous state when exposed to the ultraviolet (UV) range in the spectrum. Once that happens, these reduced ferrous salts can be solubilized by development utilizing any of a wide menu of developer options that are selected for color and rendition personality. This development stage results in a reduction of the platinum or palladium salt to a metallic platinum or palladium image, depending upon the salt chosen in the sensitizer, which is then cleared by dissolving any residual ferric salts in consecutive clearing baths composed of either hydrochloric acid, citric acid, or EDTA. The paper is then washed in fresh water, and if contaminant and ferric salt free, will last as long as its paper support.

There are three primary ingredients that go into a platinum or palladium sensitizer. Each is kept in its own separate dark glass bottle and the sensitizer is created on a print-by-print basis using an eyedropper and a shot glass.

Platinum Sensitizer

Solution # 1   Part A: ferric oxalate

Solution # 2   Part B: ferric oxalate with potassium chlorate

Solution # 3   Part C: potassium chloroplatinite/sodium tetrachloroplatinite (II)

Palladium Sensitizer

(*Note: a different Part C*)

Solution # 1   Part A: ferric oxalate

Solution # 2   Part B: ferric oxalate with potassium chlorate

Solution # 3   Part C: sodium chloropalladite

These solutions are mixed together in a shot glass, in precise droplet-based formulas, to form a light-sensitive solution. (*Please refer to the drop chart.*) The droplet mixture is then gently swirled together and deposited in the center of the paper (*if you are coating with a hake brush*) or along the edge of a Puddle Pusher (*if you are coating with a glass rod*).

Once the sensitizer is on the paper, it is necessary to execute your coating quickly and efficiently. You will be working with a very small amount of liquid and it is imperative that you quickly cover your entire printing area with the solution in the shot glass. Any unevenness in your coating will make itself evident in your final print. Once the paper is coated, it is allowed to sit for a minute, or two, and is then cool air-dried. The coated paper is then placed along with a negative in your hinged back contact printer and exposed to UV light.

During the Exposure

Once you begin to expose your negative and sensitized paper to UV light, a chemical reaction occurs that reduces the ferric salts in the formula to a ferrous state. The image at this point would be visible even if no platinum or palladium salt was present in the solution. This image, unlike many other iron-based processes, cannot be evaluated in a printing-out (POP) manner. Whereas you were seeking a "*stage whisper*" in the kallitype process you will now be looking for a very faint "*whisper*" of your intended final print. This means that the image is simply undistinguished, a little more than latent, and a hint of what you are hoping for following the development stage. If you can see the image clearly prior to development, you have badly over-exposed your print and it will be necessary to think about an alternative way of developing it using distilled water or glycerin.

Following exposure, the paper is developed in one of several developer options where it is instantly reduced to a metallic platinum, or palladium, to the degree that the negative density has permitted exposure. At first, the image you will see is ferrous iron based but will convert to platinum or palladium metal in the developer. The developed print is then cleared in an EDTA bath sequence to remove any leftover iron salts, leaving an image made entirely of platinum or palladium. The print is then washed for permanence.

Figure 13–9

Nancy Marshall, Deer Offering – 1995 - *platinum / palladium print*

To make this image, Nancy used an 8 x 10 Deardorff and a Taylor Hobson Variable softness portrait lens. For her work with the Deardorff, Nancy has also used a zone plate pinhole lens, a Conley portrait lens that will cover 5 x 7 and thus vignettes, a Turner -Reich convertible lens, and a Schneider lens for a 4 x 5 in order to create circles.

(Courtesy of the artist)

The Pt/Pd process has a potentially extreme tonal range, which many practitioners feel is significantly able to render values well beyond that of a traditional silver gelatin paper. It is also able to provide incredible depth and detail in the shadows. These very long tonal ranges, regardless of lengthy exposure times, are partially the result of an odd exposure characteristic called *"self-masking"*—a term that describes what happens during long exposures when light continues to expose highlights after the shadows have reached a degree of exposure that essentially transforms them into a filter, slowing down additional exposure in the thinner (shadow) portions of the negative.

Similar in many ways to the kallitype, the Pt/Pd process is far more consistent and easier to work with. While not as simple as the Ziatype, it's very close. Platinum/palladium print color ranges from cool to warm and is controlled by a number of factors, including developer selection, developer temperature, chemical additions to the sensitizer formulas (*such as gold chloride*), and mixing the two different Part 3 Pt/Pd (or Ziatype's LiPd) sensitizers together. Palladium is warmer than platinum but their tonal ranges are essentially identical. Both *"noble"* metal variations are as permanent as your attention to good technique, fresh chemistry, and the paper they are printed on permit.

Figure 13–10

Suzanne Solis, *Susquehanna*, Harrisburg—1998

Suzanne provides yet another example of the beauty that can be created when combining a pinhole negative with the platinum/palladium process.

(Courtesy of the artist)

Figure 13–11

George Tice, *Men's Room, Hotel Shelburne, Atlantic City, NJ—1975*

George made this platinum print as part of his extensive portfolio documenting his home state of New Jersey. One of the acknowledged masters of the platinum medium, George has demonstrated a life long commitment to photography and to teaching others the beauty of the platinum/palladium process and fine print making.

A FEW OTHER THINGS YOU WILL NEED

UV Light

The summer sun is, even though it is inconsistent, my favorite light to print in. However, a UV light printer is very consistent and necessary for printing during the winter, on overcast days, and in the colder climates. The sun is the better option because it is free and has a nice ambience. When used with open shade during exposure it also can be used as a natural contrast control tool.

Chemistry

It is critical that you purchase fresh platinum or palladium chemistry from a reputable supplier. Freshness is essential for the Part A (ferric oxalate) and Part B (ferric oxalate/potassium chlorate). Without question, it makes a great deal of sense to purchase your A & B ferric oxalates from a chemical supplier who makes it for a living rather than making it at home. Buy it in a dry powdered state (*called a dry-pack*), or pre-mixed in a liquid state that comes in a dark glass bottle. Dry-pack chemicals will be good for years. In a liquid solution, ferric oxalate Parts A and B will be past their prime in 6 months, even if refrigerated. The Part C solution, the precious noble metal salts, will last for years in liquid form.

I recommend the purchase of the pre-mixed wet pack or dry pack kit where all you have to do is add distilled water and wait 24 hours before using it. A kit from Bostick & Sullivan will come with the developer (*ammonium citrate*), a clearing bath (*EDTA*), and the three A B & C solutions in amber bottles. Sometimes they come with droppers, but I suggest purchasing a good plastic set from your local pharmacy. Remember that plastic eyedroppers are preferable to glass, because their drop size is more consistent. In most cases, you can also order your paper from the same suppliers.

Figure 13–12

Dick Arentz, *Grand Canal*, Venice, 1996, Palladium

Dick literally wrote the book on platinum & palladium printing and is one of the world's leading authorities on the technique.

(Courtesy of the artist)

The Negative

A contact negative is essential for printing due to the slow speed of the sensitized paper . . . a constant characteristic of all alternative processes. Negatives can be made in camera in the traditional large format way, through an inter-negative process using an interpositive to negative multistage duplicating film, or using Pictorico OHP ceramic dust coated ink-jet film.

Ideally, the finest quality negatives will be produced in camera. Generally speaking, if you can make a good silver gelatin print from your negative the chances are good that it will be inappropriate for Pt/Pd. Your negative should have an average negative density range between 1.5 and 2.0 and would be best suited for grade 1 or 0 conventional wet lab silver gelatin paper.

Note: Please go to Chapters 4 and 5, the Negative and Digital Options chapters for details on negative production.

Papers and Sizing

The bottom line is that inexpensive, poorly made papers will frustrate you when working in almost any alternative process. The exceptions might be cyanotype and Van Dyke, but it is best to always purchase the best quality printmaking or watercolor paper that you can afford. The paper must be free of impurities and with a surface that is compatible with your intentions. Ideally, it is 100% rag with no brighteners or buffering and has a pH between 5.5 and 7.5.

Often you will find a lovely handmade paper that simply will not hold up under the lengthy wet stages of the process, or will have ingredients accidentally blended in to it (for instance, metallic bits) that are incompatible with the Pt/Pd process. Occasionally, when you use a metal utility knife or paper cutter to trim the paper to size, metal shavings from the cutting process may get on the paper. So for this process it is best to tear the paper using a heavy ruler. This will give you a deckled edge. If you object to that look, you may trim the paper after the process is complete.

Figure 13–13

Dan Burkholder, *Pigs Frozen in Paradise*, 1994—Pt

This is a print that makes me laugh every time I look at it. Recently, Dan and his wife Jill moved from Texas to the beautiful countryside of upstate New York. About this image he wrote, "*The church and pigs were photographed separately in Mexico. These were my early digital days and I was experimenting; the "frozen" icicles effect. Many people adore it; few have the courage to purchase it.*"

(Courtesy of the artist)

🐷 **Note: Please go to Chapter 15, the Paper chapter for all of the details.**

THE CHEMISTRY

As mentioned before, there are three basic ingredients in the platinum/palladium sensitizer. In this chapter, we'll be using an ammonium citrate developer and EDTA for our clearing bath.

The A-B-C Sensitizer

◆ Part A: ferric oxalate

◆ Part B: ferric oxalate & potassium chlorate (*contrast control*)

◆ Part C: 20% potassium chloroplatinite (Pt) or palladium chloride (Pd)

◆ *Optional*: a few drops of 1% gold chloride solution

The primary differences between the platinum and palladium chemistry are the price of the *noble* metal and the color of the finished print. Palladium yields a print warmer in tone while the platinum yields a cooler black and white image. The combination of the ferric oxalate solutions will be slightly different depending on which Part C (platinum or palladium) you select. The best thing about the prepared kits is that the proportions have been worked out for you and the ferric oxalates are fresh. You can also purchase the optional 1% gold chloride in solution, paper, bottles, and droppers at the same time.

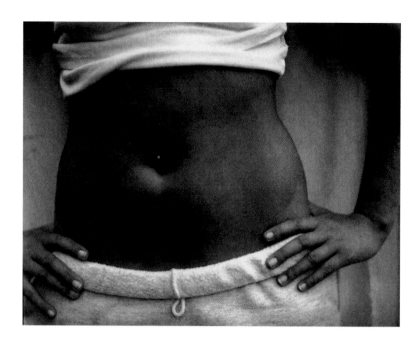

Figure 13–14

Laura Bennett, *Jivan At Nineteen*, 2005—Pd

Laura made this 8 × 10 palladium image of her oldest daughter, immediately after Jivan had her belly button pierced. *(Courtesy of the artist)*

The Developer

During exposure, the ferric oxalate is converted to a ferrous oxalate state. In the development stage, which is always an instantaneous and exciting event, the ferrous oxalate functions as a reducer, removing platinum or palladium from the salted sensitizer compound and precipitating those metals into the paper as pure platinum or palladium. This conversion begins during the exposure but requires the developer to complete the process.

One of the traditional developers for this technique has been potassium oxalate, a rather toxic chemical soup that is not particularly user-friendly. Other developer options have included sodium acetate and ammonium citrate. I recommend using ammonium citrate, (*ammonium carbonate neutralized with citric acid*), which is a lot more amiable than potassium oxalate. Each of these developers provides a slightly different print color and the one that you select should match the intentions that you have for the image. Ammonium citrate yields a slightly cooler color than potassium oxalate. I also find that potassium oxalate appears to be richer in the darks than ammonium citrate or sodium acetate. You may also cool the color of a print by working with a cooler developer. Conversely, heating the developer will warm the print color.

Almost all Pt/Pd printers keep the same base developer stock forever and refresh it with new developer when the volume drops due to paper absorption and evaporation. You may wish to remove the sludge that collects on the bottom of the developer container. If you find it necessary to decant the developer, simply pour it into a new non-metallic container, using a plastic funnel lined with a coffee filter.

Never throw out your developer: it gets better with age. Although this is conventional wisdom, there is evidence that developers, like everything else, deteriorate with advanced age. You will know when your developer is not behaving well. Until then, keep recycling, decanting, and adding fresh developer to your stock bottle.

SEVERAL PLATINUM/PALLADIUM DEVELOPER FORMULAS

Ammonium Citrate Developer

This is a common, and relatively safe, developer and one that I use in classes and workshops. Ammonium citrate yields a cool brown to ochre brown tonality. You can make it warmer by heating it to about 100°F prior to developing. It is an excellent solution and can be purchased pre-mixed from Bostick & Sullivan. You can also buy the ammonium citrate powder and easily make it yourself. Here's the mix:

250 g   ammonium citrate
1 liter   distilled water

Potassium Oxalate Developer

Potassium Oxalate is used as a 35% solution and, as mentioned earlier, its toxicity is not to be ignored. If you do decide to use potassium oxalate, due to its reddish-brown warmth and richness in the darker values of your prints, I am recommending that you work in a well-ventilated space, that you wear Nitrile gloves, and that you keep splashing to a minimum. Heating this developer will result in warmer values in the dark areas of your image. Here's the formula for making a full liter plus of the developer.

450 g potassium oxalate powder
1350 ml distilled water

Sullivan's Cold Bath Developer

150 g Potassium Oxalate
75 mg Potassium monobasic phosphate
Distilled water to make 1 liter

THE CLEARING BATHS

The traditional Pt/Pd clearing bath was a dilute solution of hydrochloric acid. A gentler alternative is citric acid. The most common clearing bath is tetrasodium EDTA (*ethylenediaminetetra acetic acid tetrasodium salt*), a preservative often found in commercially processed foods such as yogurt. Tetrasodium EDTA is significantly less hazardous than hydrochloric acid, whose fumes are unpleasant. Hydrochloric acid also makes the fibers in the paper too brittle. This clearing stage is critical, because it is absolutely vital to remove the unconverted ferric salts from the finished print. The EDTA clearing formula is not compulsively exact and should be set up in 3 separate and consecutive 5-minute baths.

A Two-Stage EDTA Clearing Set Up

There are two types of EDTA. The one that is now most common is *tetrasodium* EDTA that has an alkaline pH of 9. This high pH can lead to the retention of iron(III) and yellow staining in the highlights. As a remedy for this problem, prepare a first tray with *disodium* EDTA that is acidic and has a pH of 4- 5. It is also more expensive.

Tray 1 30 g disodium EDTA into 1 liter of water

Tray 2 30 g tetrasodium EDTA into 1 liter of water

Tray 3 30 g tetrasodium EDTA into 1 liter of water

Figure 13–15
Sandy Rosenberg, *British Museum*—1996 (platinum/palladium contact print)
(Courtesy of the artist)

Formula for EDTA Clearing Bath: Kitchen Blend

1 heaping tablespoon of tetrasodium EDTA (30 g)
Water to make 1 liter
Sodium sulfite (25 g) (*for a post-EDTA bath if highlights are yellow*)

Emergency Clearing Bath

In an out-of-clearing-bath emergency, you can go to the supermarket and buy 7-Up® soda or make a very dilute solution of Lime-Away® tile cleaner (*which is used to remove calcium*) and see if either works for you.

Another Clearing Option

Another emergency option is Kodak Hypo Clearing Agent. I know of one platinum/palladium printer who clears his prints by giving them a short fresh water rinse and then immersing them in a standard hypo-clearing bath (*sodium sulfite and water*) for 5 minutes. I suppose this works well enough, but I continue to recommend EDTA as your first option.

THE SENSITIZER FORMULA

Again, I recommend that you purchase the pre-measured and fresh chemical kits that are on the market. This would allow you to spend more time making prints rather than rambling around in your lab weighing and compulsively mixing chemicals with gloves on your hands and a respirator on your face. However, if that kind of thing makes you happy, here is the traditional formula for platinum and palladium.

Platinum/Palladium Part A (*ferric oxalate*)

  55 ml distilled water at 120°F
  16 g ferric oxalate
    1 g oxalic acid (optional)

Platinum/Palladium Part B (*ferric oxalate and potassium chlorate, this is your contrast control*)

  55 ml distilled water at 120°F
  16 g ferric oxalate
  0.3 g potassium chlorate (*for platinum*)
      or . . . 0.6 g potassium chlorate (*for palladium*)*
    1 g oxalic acid (*Optional but helpful for the blacks*)

A short time ago, I was having a conversation with someone who was recommending the use of ferric ammonium oxalate (*as found in the Ziatype Process*) in place of the traditional ferric oxalate. This, he said, results in a warmer image with a bit more contrast and requires a longer than normal exposure time. Mike Ware, responding to this idea, expressing the thought that there was a risk of ferric potassium oxalate crystallizing out of the sensitizer if you simply substituted the ammonium salt. This was the primary reason for the "all ammonium" formula in the Ware-Malde version of the Platinotype. Keep this idea in mind if you feel like experimenting someday.

Another formula modification that you might wish to explore is Willis's addition of lead oxalate to the formula. Willis's mix: 0.44 g of lead oxalate to each 60 ml of A

and B sensitizer. Platinum images with this formula are cooler, show more contrast, have crisper edge definition and are richer in tonality. Be careful with lead oxalate if you decide to experiment; it's toxic.

Platinum Part C

  50 ml distilled water at 100°F
  10 g potassium chloroplatinite

Palladium Part C:

(The following are two different recipes for palladium prints.)
Palladium Part C—Option # 1
  51 ml distilled water at 100°F
    9 g sodium chloropalladite

Palladium Part C—Option # 2
  50 ml distilled water at 100°F
    5 g palladium chloride
  3.5 g table salt (*sodium chloride*)

Mix all of the individual solutions, put them in dark brown glass bottles with dropper tops, label their contents with contents, and date them so that you know how old they are. Label them with the letters A, B, and C, and let them sit for at least 12 hours. The platinum solution is supersaturated at room temperature so will deposit crystals on cooling. A & B have a shelf life of 4–6 months. Part C is good forever. Store your A-B-C mixed chemistry in a dark and cool place to extend the shelf life.

Note: Some texts have recommended the refrigerator as a fine place for the storage but I advise against it especially if there are children in your home. Aside from the obvious lethal danger of an accident of ferric oxalate, this chemical may also form into insoluble chunks in the refrigerator. If you are going to refrigerate your chemistry, go buy a small dorm room–size unit and keep it in your lab.

---

* Please note that the amount of potassium chlorate changes in the Part B mix depending on whether you are making a platinum or palladium image.

Figure 13–16

David Michael Kennedy, *Rain Luna County*, 1989—Pd

David Michael Kennedy is well known for his extraordinary platinum/palladium work and documentation of the landscape and culture in the southwest. Anyone who has spent time in this amazing landscape will recognize this moment. This is my favorite landscape photograph. *(Courtesy of the artist)*

PLATINUM/PALLADIUM DROP CHART

The emulsion formulas in the following Pt/Pd Drop Chart, are dependent on the density and contrast of your negative. This is an important distinction because the majority of previously published drop charts were formatted to achieve the contrast of the print you desire and hope to finish with. They assumed that your negative was always appropriate for the process, which is seldom the case unless you are using custom curve profiles and producing digital negatives for contact printing. It has been my experience that the reading of the negative is more relevant than wishful thinking about what kind of print you would like. By setting up the drop chart for the negative in-hand I am allowing for flexibility in the learning process. I assume that not everyone who wants to print platinum or palladium has the ability to fine-tune each negative so that it is perfect. In addition, most people do not have a densitometer sitting around the house.

In the drop chart, notice how the proportions of Part A and Part B change to deal with the contrast of the resulting print. Also note the total number of drops of A & B to C and how the ratio is constant in all formulas. Be cautious that the greater the concentration of Part B (*ferric*

	4 × 5	5 × 7	8 × 10
Extremely Soft Negatives:			
A	0 drops	0 drops	0 drops
B	5 drops	11 drops	22 drops
C	6 drops	12 drops	24 drops
Soft Negatives:			
A	1 drop	4 drops	8 drops
B	4 drops	7 drops	14 drops
C	6 drops	12 drops	24 drops
Average Negatives:			
A	3 drops	7 drops	14 drops
B	2 drops	4 drops	8 drops
C	6 drops	12 drops	24 drops
Contrasty Negatives:			
A	4 drops	9 drops	18 drops
B	1 drop	2 drops	4 drops
C	6 drops	12 drops	24 drops
Very Contrasty Negatives:			
A	5 drops	11 drops	22 drops
B	0 drops	0 drops	0 drops
C	6 drops	12 drops	24 drops

oxalate—potassium chlorate) in the formula the more "grainy" your print will be. Part B is the primary control of the contrast in your final print; *the more B in the formula, the more contrast in the print . . . and grain.*

You can elect to add 1 or 2 drops of 1%—5% gold chloride to your formulas. This change will slightly elevate the contrast and will have a modest effect on the color of the final print. As well, after you fall in love with this process, you may wish to experiment with sensitizing formulas that incorporate both Pt/Pd salts. This decision will change both the color and the contrast of your images. A good way to begin thinking about this is to learn the Ziatype Process that comes later in the book, where these changes are a normal part of the process.

Nearly every text I've read uses a drop chart formula based on the print desired. I suspect that the proportional recommendations in the chart below originated with Paul Anderson, who was the accepted authority on non-silver and special processes in the early part of the 20th century. The concept goes back to Pizzighelli & Hübl. To my knowledge, only Nancy Rexroth, in her great pamphlet, *The Platinotype 1977,* constructed her chart as the following one does . . . based upon the type of negative that the artist will be working with.

Figure 13–17
Tracy Longley-Cook, *Boxed Wing*, 2002—Pt/Pd
Currently a graduate student at Arizona State University,
Tracy is one of the best new alternative process artists.
(Courtesy of the artist)

TABLE SET UP FOR PLATINUM/ PALLADIUM

Three dark, glass bottles w/ prepared platinum or palladium A, B, & C sensitizer. Label and date each bottle.

- A—ferric oxalate
- B—ferric oxalate and potassium chlorate
- C—palladium or platinum solution
- Three screw cap eye droppers for A, B, & C
- Pt/Pd drop chart (*see text*)
- Clean paper for the table surface

- Paper for coating
- Shot glass . . . *(drinking type rather than a tourist keepsake)*
- A new hake brush (*label for Pt/Pd only*)
- Clean distilled water in a beaker for brush washing
- Pencil
- Hair dryer
- Contact printing frame
- Negative for contact printing
- Paper towels

PREPARING & COATING SENSITIZER

Prepare an area in your lab with subdued light and be sure that it is absolutely clean and dry, and prepare yourself for some moderately compulsive behavior.

Set up a coating area and have a good quality shot glass (*for swirling the drops together*) with a short and heavy barrel. This type of shot glass is important so that you don't leave too much solution behind when you dump it on the paper for coating. Also, you will need a pencil for marking the area of the paper that these drops will have to cover and for writing your formula, and printing information. For coating you will need a hake brush *without* a metal ferrule. This brush, once it is used for coating platinum/palladium, should be labeled accordingly and not be used for any other process. An alternative to the brush, especially if you feel brush impaired, is a glass rod coater, i.e., Puddle Pusher. You also need paper towels and two glasses of distilled water—one for wetting your brush prior to coating and the other for cleaning it afterwards. You may also want a hairdryer set on a cool setting.

Finally, you will need your labeled A, B and C formulas in their individual brown bottles with droppers and a decent quality paper to coat upon. When you are making up your sensitizer, always remember to replace the top on the bottle before it spills. It is a time-honored laboratory fact that little bottles filled with precious, or dangerous, chemistry will always fall over if you forget to put the top back on.

Figure 13–18

Christopher James, *Vatican Bride*, Rome, 1987—Pt-Pd

Vatican Bride is a Diana plastic camera generated image. The negative was translated, via direct duplication film (*SO-132—no longer available*) and printed in platinum.

(Courtesy of the author)

Write Down the Information You Need

The first thing you will do with your paper is take your pencil and write everything you will need to know when you evaluate the print at the end of the process. I set up my information in a line at the bottom front of the sheet of paper I'm going to coat like this:

> Process > Weather, Sun, & Time > Drop Count of ABC > Exposure > Place > Date

Mark the Negative Area

The next thing I will do is lay my negative on the sheet of paper and place it where I want the image to be. I then go to just outside the edges of the negative and place a small L-shaped bracket at each corner. This shows me the area that I will be coating and where I will be depositing my sensitizer from the shot glass. It also assures me that I won't be wasting any sensitizing formula.

Drop Count the Sensitizer

Under low light, add the appropriate number of drops of Part A (*ferric oxalate*) to your shot glass and put back the top on the bottle. Then, take Part B's bottle, and dropper, and add the drops of B (*ferric oxalate and potassium chlorate*) to the shot glass. This is the component in the sensitizer formula that will function as your primary contrast control. Replace this top as well. To complete the sensitizer formula, take Part C's dropper and add drops from C to the shot glass. Part C is your precious noble metal salt . . . either platinum or palladium. You will notice that it may appear that you do not have enough solution to coat the negative area of your paper. Don't worry, with a little practice, you will discover that the amount is quite adequate. In the beginning, if you find that this is not the case, and this is especially true at high altitude and in low humidity environments, simply work with a drop count that is proportionately greater. I tell my students to use the 5×7 formula drop count for 4×5 negatives when they are first learning how to coat.

Wet your hake brush in the distilled water and blot it dry with a paper towel. Avoid using a white paper towel because of the bleach used in manufacturing to make the towels white. Do not shake out your brush with a sassy snap of your wrist, as that action will almost always result in random spray on someone's print or paper. This wetting in distilled water, and blotting, steps are done to prevent the brush from completely absorbing the emulsion, to add a little moisture to the paper, and to give you a decent chance of applying a smooth coating with your very small quantity of sensitizer solution. Be careful that your brush is not too damp because that is an even bigger problem. You will know if the brush was too wet because you will see dull streaks in the print where the water diluted the sensitizer and the tonal values will be pasty and flat. A little practice with watercolor paint and your hake brush will show you the way.

Coating the Paper

Swirl the A-B-C solution around in the shot glass and do one of two things. Your first option is to pour the shot glass solution into the center of the marked out print area and begin by lightly brushing over the entire area with complete horizontal coverage, followed immediately with complete vertical coverage of your negative area. Quickly repeat this sequence until your coating is smooth and free of obvious brush strokes. Keep your strokes light and airy and avoid pressure, as that friction will simply disrupt the fibrous paper surface once it is damp. Do not be concerned if your brush strokes exceed the dimensions of your negative area. Those roughly painted edges are the "signature" look of the hand-coated print. However don't go to far outside your negative area as this will result in blacks that are not reaching their potential. In addition, do not fuss over any hairs from the hake brush that might fall out of your brush during the coating. These hairs can be easily removed during or after the drying stage with a flick of your fingernail. Again, be sure to be light, fast, and delicate with your brushing technique.

Coating With a Puddle Pusher

Your other coating option is to use a glass rod or Puddle Pusher. You can buy a Puddle Pusher with a handle from Bostick & Sullivan or you can go out and purchase a lab grade glass rod and a nice heavy piece of ¼" plate glass that will be larger than your paper. Tape your paper to the ¼" glass sheet and place your Puddle Pusher firmly on top of the paper just above your coating area. Pour the contents of your shot glass along the back edge of the Puddle Pusher and then quickly slide the glass rod lengthwise from side to side in the solution until it is evenly distributed along the surface of the Puddle Pusher's back edge. Slightly raise the rod and lift it over the line of sensitizer so that it sits along the back edge of the solution. Then drag, or push, the sensitizer solution, with pressure, through your coating area. Repeat this single pressurized stroke in the opposite direction if there is an obvious abundance of solution left after the first pass. This is the best way to avoid roughing up and disturbing the smoothness of your paper. Unfortunately, you don't get romantic brush strokes in the final print.

Once your sensitizer is on the paper, let it sit quietly in the paper for 2 to 5 minutes in subdued light. After this waiting period, while you are cleaning the shot glass, take your hairdryer, put it on a cool setting, and gently blow-dry the backside of the paper. If you are working in a space without excellent ventilation, wearing a dust mask is a sane idea since some ferric oxalate in the formula will become airborne during the blow-drying. The best thing for the paper, and you, is to allow the paper to dry naturally. It will not take very long, as there is very little sensitizer in the paper.

Stainless Steel Coating Rods

One additional type of coating tool that I've been fooling around with is a stainless steel coating rod made by R.D. Specialties in Webster, New York. Randy Nelson is the guy to get in touch with. The coating rods are ⅜" stainless steel, wire wound, coating rods #44 in 8", 10", 12", and 14" lengths with 2" unwound on either end for holding. They are beautifully made and come with a tube protector. Check out their info in Appendix F of this book.

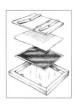

EXPOSURE

When your paper is "bone" dry and has a snap to it when you flex it . . . you will hear the sound clearly once you know what to listen for . . . take your negative and place it on the dry sensitized paper so that the final print will be "*right-reading.*" Put the negative and the coated paper into a hinged back contact printing frame *so that you can monitor the exposure* and get ready to go sit in the sun . . . or, less romantically, beside your UV exposure unit. If you are using a UV unit, do not look at the light source during the exposure (*it is like a tanning booth*) and turn the unit off before checking on the exposure. Printing times will be dependent on the negative's contrast, density, and the formula you are using. A high-contrast sensitizer mix may require as much as a 50% increase in exposure. A higher contrast formula will result in more grain in your final print. Try your best to control your contrast via your negative and sun/shade printing times rather than A-B-C formula and exposure time.

Looking For The Whisper

Expose your paper until you see a "*whisper*" of detail in the print. This process does not have the same personality in its printing-out stage as many other iron-based processes. This is why keeping track of your progress with notations on the paper is so important. With an average negative, in summer sun, your exposure will run in the 3-to 7-minute range if you are working between 10:00 AM and 3:00 PM. At high altitudes, in places like Santa Fe or Aspen, the exposure will be shorter than it will be at sea level. If you use a UV exposure unit figure on an exposure time that will be a bit longer than summer sun. This is all relative, of course, and it has a great deal to do with your negative, formula, and many other small considerations. You might want to print a Stouffer film gradation value scale to see what levels of tonalities you will be getting with the formula and exposure time you've selected. Write all of your information down and take the print through to completion . . . then make adjustments and do it again. Within a print or two you will be pretty close and you will not have driven yourself crazy with formulas, charts, and graphs. There are several excellent books to read if you wish to know absolutely everything about this process . . . and how to use all of those graphs and charts. My favorite of these is Dick Arentz's *Platinum and Palladium Printing*: 2nd Edition from Focal Press.

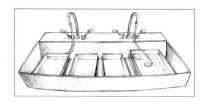

SINK SET-UP FOR PT/PD:

Tray 1 **Labeled For Pt/Pd Only.** A very clean, and dry, development tray and a bottle of prepared developer nearby. Developer is selected based upon color choice, i.e., ammonium citrate, potassium oxalate, etc.

Tray 2 Distilled water tray (*agitate for 1 minute*)

Tray 3 **disodium** EDTA clearing bath

Tray 4 **tetrasodium** EDTA clearing bath

Tray 5 **tetrasodium** EDTA clearing bath

(*Mix: 1 Tablespoon EDTA to liter of water. Five minutes in each tray with agitation.*)

Tray 6 **Optional** if highlights are yellow even after the third EDTA bath. *Mix: 4% solution of sodium sulfite. (4 g of sodium sulfite to each 100 ml of water)* **To Use**: *Rinse print following last EDTA bath for 2 minutes in running water and then into the sodium sulfite solution for 5 minutes.*)

Tray 7 Final wash in clean running water for 20–30 minutes.

Figure 13–19

Vaughn Hutchins, *Oak Pine Rock*, 2005-06—Pt /Pd

This image is a fine example of why Vaughn is well respected and known for his elegant craftsmanship in both Pt/Pd and carbon.

(Courtesy of the artist)

DEVELOPING THE IMAGE

After the exposure, take your closed contact frame into the sink area. Have a very clean and very dry tray waiting for you that is **only** used for developing platinum and palladium prints. I want to emphasize the importance of an exclusive tray for development, because chemicals from other photographic procedures may be present no matter how well you wash your trays, especially in a communal lab.

Take the exposed paper from the contact frame, place it face up in the bottom of the very dry Pt/Pd Only tray. Notice the very pale whisper of the image. If you can see the image clearly, then you may want to forget about the chemical development and use distilled water as a developer instead. If your pre-developed image looks correct, quickly, with complete coverage, pour the developer on the surface of the entire print. Any hesitation, as you pour your developer, will result in uneven development. This unevenness will show itself as a distinct flaw in the image. I prefer using either a wide mouth plastic bottle or a Pyrex measuring cup for the pouring, and to hold my developer between prints. Development is nearly instantaneous. You may leave the paper in the developer for up to 2 minutes if you want but it really isn't necessary. Examine the print and you will notice that its highlights are yellow. This is normal and this yellow will clear after the 3 stages of clearing baths.

Figure 13–20

Catherine Harris, *Fresno*, 1986—Pt /Pd

This Pt/Pd image was made by Catherine when she was a student of mine at Harvard University. Catherine, if you see this, please get in touch with your address so that I can send you a copy of the new edition.

(Courtesy of the artist)

FIRST WASH AND CLEARING

I like to put the developed paper into a bath of distilled water for a minute before going into the clearing bath sequence. This provides me with an opportunity to evaluate whether I want to bother going through the 15 minutes of clearing. It also gives me an idea of what I will change with a subsequent formula, that I'll be making while my print clears. Also, the water bath gets some of the developer and residual ferrous salts out of my print and keeps my clearing baths fresher.

Preparing Three Trays with the EDTA Clearing Bath

Tray 1 30 g disodium EDTA into 1 liter of water

Tray 2 30 g tetrasodium EDTA into 1 liter of water

Tray 3 30 g tetrasodium EDTA into 1 liter of water

In the past, this clearing step was done with a 0.5% to 1% hydrochloric acid dilution. This is a little strong for our needs and so we will be using EDTA. This is a kitchen-casual clearing bath formula and is quickly made and near goof-proof. As I wrote several paragraphs back, the common method of using EDTA is to prepare 3 separate baths of tetrasodium EDTA by mixing 1 heaping tablespoon—about 30 grams—of EDTA to a liter of water. Occasionally, if yellowing is showing up in the highlights, you can toss in a tablespoon of sodium sulfite.

In this EDTA set up, prepare 3 trays of the EDTA but make the first tray a disodium EDTA that is more acidic than tetrasodium EDTA and will be a cure for the yellow that sometimes presents itself when the print has completed the process. I provide this formula in non-metric measure because most of my students forget about the gram scale at this point in the procedure and just guess at the amounts. If you want the gram weights check the Sink Set Up section to follow. Fortunately, the EDTA clearing bath formula is very flexible and anything close to this mixing suggestion will be satisfactory.

Place the print into clearing bath #1 (disodium EDTA) for 5 minutes and periodically rock it gently. During this first bath clearing time, pour your developer back into its bottle or holding beaker. NEVER THROW YOUR DEVELOPER AWAY! Also, because you have the time, wash and thoroughly dry your development tray so that it is ready for the next print or person who uses it.

Refreshing the Clearing Baths

After 5 minutes, place the print in clearing bath #2 (tetrasodium EDTA) for another 5 minutes. You should begin to see highlight and shadow definition clearly at this stage and the yellow tint in the highlights should be nearly gone. After another 5 minutes, place the print in the final clearing bath #3 for an additional 5 minutes. Change your clearing baths often . . . about every 8–10 prints.

Sodium Sulfite Bath: If You Don't Use Disodium EDTA

If you haven't been adding the sodium sulfite, and find that you are still having problems with yellowing in your highlights following the third EDTA bath, you might want to try this recommendation. Make up a fourth tray with a 4% solution of sodium sulfite (*4 g to 100 ml of water*) and set it in your sink. Following the third EDTA bath, rinse your print for 2 minutes in distilled water and then put it in the sodium sulfite solution for 5 minutes. Then follow the final wash instructions.

FINAL WASH

After the clearing bath sequence, wash the print for 20 to 30 minutes in fresh running water and hang it on a line to dry. As with any alternative process, screen drying is just asking for trouble because other people in the lab may not have the same compulsive lab habits regarding cleanliness that you do. If you intend to make another print from the same negative it would be a good idea to force dry the first one so that you can adequately evaluate what you did. Dry down on Pt/Pd is significant and trying to evaluate the formula you used, without this dry down step, will be difficult without experience.

NA2: CONTRAST CONTROL

Another modification worth looking into, and one considered worthwhile by several artist/chemists who have taken the time to investigate it, is the *magic bullet* of contrast control—sodium hexachloroplatinate(IV).

Note: It has been pointed out that controlling the contrast of a palladium print with a platinum salt (to prevent the precipitation of palladium) is a very expensive solution to the contrast problem. Keep this in mind when making your negatives.

Na2 is indeed an interesting tool to have in your toolbox. It works by substituting drops of one of the several different pre-mixed percentage solutions of sodium chloroplatinate in place of Part B ferric oxalate—potassium chlorate . . . the traditional contrast control. I had to make a decision at the onset of this chapter as to how deeply I wanted to go into this rather complex and formula heavy technique and decided to provide a definition of the technique and then to send you to Dick Arentz's excellent book where you will find an abundance of charts, graphs, equations, formulas, citations and drop counts . . . all focused on this method of increasing contrast in your platinum palladium print. I think there are less detailed ways of improving contrast in your platinum/palladium prints and I recommend beginning at your negatives before going to more chemicals.

Figure 13–21
David Strasburger, *Ferrara,* **2004—Pt/Pd**
David writes, " *This image of my friend Chiara was made in Ferrara, Italy. She is the city's archeologist and anybody who does any serious digging has to ask her for permission. Once the city was tearing up a downtown intersection to put up new traffic signals when the backhoes unearthed a practically intact wooden ship. When she told this story the part that got to me was the location—what's ship doing there? Chiara was totally matter-of-fact: in the Middle Ages, the river Po ran through Ferrara, not around it. We took Chiara and her husband to Fenway Park to see the Red Sox, and Chiara fell in love with Johnny Damon. She wouldn't let anyone else use the binoculars for the whole game."*
(Courtesy of the artist)

That said, I am overwhelmingly impressed with the scope of Dick's investigation of Na2 and doubt that I can improve upon it in any way. Therefore, I am going to give you his brief summary, below, of how it works and recommend that you look into his book for the details.

"Sodium Chloroplatinate (Na_2PtCl_6), when used with the palladium salt (Na_2PtCl_4, has the effect of consuming the ferrous oxalate, which normally would reduce the palladium salt to metallic palladium. The net result is a disproportional slowing of the process of reduction, more at the highlights than the shadow areas of an image. This decreases the exposure scale of the paper, increasing its contrast."

TROUBLE–SHOOTING & OTHER THINGS TO CONSIDER

Only Change One Thing at a Time

If you are running into problems, it is prudent to alter only one factor at a time. If you change both the exposure and the sensitizer formula simultaneously you will be hard-pressed to figure out which change made the difference. Later, when you are more proficient at this process, you can make multiple corrections with more confidence.

Coating & Humidity

It's a good idea to print coated paper very soon after it is dry. The hygroscopic nature of paper means that it will always collect moisture from the air and this may result in foggy tonal values in your print. A little humidity is fine so don't get too compulsive about it. Cold and dry weather can also have a less-than-pleasing effect on your printing. In the winter, humidify your working space to about 55% to 60% humidity. Light Impressions sells an inexpensive hygrometer to measure the relative humidity level in your work space (*see Appendix F*). In addition, if your image looks great in the developer but looks weak following the washing and clearing baths, there may have been too much humidity in the lab. Try to coat and dry within a 10-minute time period . . . including the 2 minutes you let your print meditate after the coating step.

Tween 20

Tween 20 is a non-ionic surfactant that assists your sensitizer in finding a secure "home" in the fibers of your paper. Some papers don't require it while others benefit greatly. Tween 20 also helps to minimize the leaching of colloidal metal during processing. You'll know if you should use it as an additive (*a drop or two 20% concentrate to a 5" × 7" sensitizer mix*) if you see staining or if the image fades quickly in the clearing baths.

Open Shade Exposure for Contrast

A longer printing time, in open shade, out of direct sunlight, will increase your contrast in a non-chemical way. This is my favorite method of printing most alt pro work. One of the best demonstrations I ever gave was at The Maine Photographic Workshops where my exposure time, in a dense fog, was nearly 45 minutes.

Warm & Cold Developers

Cold developer is appropriate whenever you have overexposed your print. Cold developer will give more contrast to your image than a warm developer as well as rendering a slightly cooler tonality. Warm developer is appropriate whenever you have under-exposed your image. It was not unusual, according to Pizzighelli and Hübl, to place an under-exposed print into boiling developer to make up for an inadequate exposure time. A warm developer will give a slightly warmer image. A warm developer may also help with any staining problems you may be having. Heat to about 100°F.

Too Much Exposure

If you radically overexpose your print, you can develop it in distilled water. You may also add a little developer to this water at the end of the wash-development to "punch" it up at the end. There is a technique, covered in several texts on this subject, concerning localized brush development with glycerin. If you're interested in glycerin development, some of the historical texts describe it well and there is also a good description of the technique in Nancy Rexroth's *The Platinotype, 1977*. I don't practice this technique and so will pass on incorporating it into this text.

Bronzing

You may, from time to time, see an effect that is referred to as "*bronzing*"—especially with palladium. This is an almost solarized metallic look in the darker values of your print and is often the result either dampness in the paper or of an inappropriate negative density for the process resulting in your exposure being far too lengthy. The biggest reason for bronzing is that you have not coated your sensitizer well and it is puddling up on the paper and drying too thickly. During the exposure, this puddle area bronzes and if it is in an area of the negative that is thin, and the exposure is too long, then the problem leaps out at you. This bronzing occurs in many alt pro techniques and can be rectified, to a degree, by toning and/or changing the sensitizer formula. In Kallitype, toning will often take care of the problem. In palladium, a few drops of platinum Part C often fixes the problem. One last fix you might want to try is cutting back on Part B (*ferric oxalate & potassium chlorate*) contrast control.

Fluorescent Light and UV

Try not to let your sensitized coated paper to sit out under fluorescent light because this type of light does indeed emit a degree of UV and may contribute to fogging.

Fogging Fix with Hydrogen Peroxide

If you are experiencing a fogging in your image and have tried everything you can think of, including exchanging all of your ferric oxalate for fresh, and changing papers, you might want to give 3% hydrogen peroxide a try. When mixing up your sensitizer, add a single drop of 3% hydrogen peroxide to every ml of sensitizer in your shot glass. This action slightly narrows the exposure scale and makes the image a bit brighter.

Fogging & Drying Temperature

Another cause of "fogging" is that you may have dried your sensitized paper at too hot a temperature. Try to print in a manner that permits you to let your paper dry on its own or, at the very least, to sit quietly for at least 2 minutes in subdued light after you coat it. I like to lay a freshly sensitized paper down in a clean drawer in the lab and let it dry peacefully. When it's time to finish the drying stage, be sure that the hairdryer is set on a cool setting and be sure to dry from the back of the print first.

Fogging & Muddy Highlights

If you have foggy or muddy highlights in your print, here are some of the reasons; the paper was fogged by strong light before exposure; the ferric oxalate is old and it's time to replace it (*use wet mix within 6 months*); your negative was too thin; your exposure was too long; the sensitizer formula you selected was an incorrect analysis of what your negative required; there was moisture in the paper; your hairdryer setting was too hot; cold and dry weather dominated your lab space . . . or, bad karma.

Paper Sizing & Print Color

If you decide to size your paper with gelatin expect the coloration to cool and blacks to take on a bluish black hue. If you use starch, instead of gelatin, you will see an increase in the warmth of the hues. (*See Chapter 15, the Paper chapter.*)

Testing Ferric Oxalate

Ferric oxalate doesn't last forever . . . especially when it's in solution. In a dry state, it is good for 25–30 years. Once mixed with distilled water, however, it has a shelf life of less than 6 months. Here's a simple test to see if it has turned on you. Make up a normal sensitizer formula and coat your paper. Once the paper is dry, develop and clear it in the normal fashion and hang it up to dry. If you see any coloration in the paper you can attribute this tone to one, or all, of the following; your coating area is too bright with UV; your clearing bath is not working well; or your ferric oxalate is too old. To see if it is the ferric oxalate, add 1 to 2 drops of 3% hydrogen peroxide to either ferric oxalate Part A or Part B and run the test again. **DO NOT PUT THE CAP BACK ON THE BOTTLE** that you added the hydrogen peroxide to as a gas will be building with the addition and you don't want the bottle to explode. If, at the end of the second test, you see a yellow tint, then it is either the ferric oxalate or ineffective clearing baths. If the tint is more grayish, then your coating area is too bright. If it is a chemistry problem I advise buying fresh ferric oxalate.

Saving & Decanting Developer

Never throw your developer away. You can filter it with a coffee filter when it gets too "sludgy," and you can add fresh developer to it at anytime to keep the container full and prevent evaporation. It is good lab practice to re-fresh your developer at the conclusion of each lab session. Think of this in the same manner that you would sourdough starter for sourdough bread. Some developers last for decades and simply get better with time.

Emergency Part C Replacement

If you are all of a sudden out of Part C . . . you can always replace it with some lithium chloropalladite from a Ziatype kit. It isn't ideal but it works well enough and will increase your contrast without adding to the B drop count.

Alternative Clearing Baths

In most cases, a clearing bath must be acidic in order to remove residual iron salts. EDTA possesses unique chelating properties (*chelate comes from the Greek word chele, meaning great claw of a crustacean*) in which the residual iron salts are bound to the EDTA's atoms. EDTA is made more effective, even though it is alkaline, when sodium sulfite is added to it.

Be very cautious about the concentrations of your clearing baths and about keeping track of the time that your print is immersed in each of them. Besides EDTA there are other choices for clearing . . . in case you run out of EDTA.

- **Citric Acid:** 1% solution
- **Oxalic Acid:** 1% solution
- **Phosphoric Acid:** 2%

  (*Be careful . . . this comes in a 75% solution and you must remember to always add the acid to water and not water to acid*)

- **Hypo Clearing Agent (Perma Wash):** This clearing bath is used at regular strength but you should add 30 g of EDTA to it before use. The hypo-clearing solution itself has citric acid and either sodium sulfite or sodium metabisulfite in it (this is also used to clear gum prints) and is effective at clearing papers that seem to resistant to clearing. Be extra vigilant when clearing palladium, as it is more susceptible to bleaching out than platinum.

Metal Bits and Old Hair Dryers

As hairdryers get older they begin to break down. Often you can see the sparks. Sparks mean metal and you do not want little metal shards shooting onto your newly sensitized paper. This causes little black spots. If you are going to use a hairdryer, blow only on the back of the paper and only on a cool setting.

If Your Image is Too Weak

If your image is too weak and thin it might be because; your coating brush had too much moisture in it; the paper was too damp when you made your exposure; your chemistry was not fresh; you made an incorrect evaluation for your Part B concentration and added too much; you used an exposure time that was too short; you used a negative that was either too flat or too dense . . . or . . . bad karma.

Black Spots, Streaks, & Blemishes

If you have black spots, streaks, and blemishes, some of the causes may be that: there were alkaline and oily fingerprints on the paper before or after, coating; your print experienced metal contamination from a metal ferrule on the brush, mat knife, an old hairdryer, or paper cutter; moisture or chemistry contaminated your working area; your developing tray was not completely washed or dried; you used contaminated brushes; your brush wash water was contaminated (*change it every time you make a print*); there were impurities in Part C of your formula; you were working next to others who think an extravagant impressionistic brush gesture is required for coating; your developer technique was too slow or hesitant . . . or . . . bad karma.

Yellow Stains

Yellow stains are most often chemistry related. If you have a yellow-stained print it is the result of an active pH flux (the pH is too high) due to the formation of insoluble iron oxide complex. The stains might be there because: your ferric oxalate is no longer good (*see the test for ferric oxalate in this section*); you forgot the clearing bath; your clearing bath is exhausted; your clearing bath is not the right one for the paper you are using; your developer has become too alkaline . . . possibly due to the paper you are using, and a small amount of citric acid

Figure 13–22

Laura Dietz, Cambridge, Massachusetts, 1987—palladium

Laura made this elegant palladium image while a student of mine at Harvard. She made the original with infrared film and then translated that image to ortho film processed with a continuous tone developer for her contact negative. *(Courtesy of the artist)*

can slightly adjust the developer back to an acidic state. Another reason would be that you are using EDTA that is used up or that you didn't use a first EDTA bath with disodium EDTA. There are a lot of other reasons . . . but karma has very little to do with yellow stains in platinum/palladium printing.

5% Gold Chloride to Sensitizer

The most elementary way to alter your print color is to add gold to your sensitizer. Adding 1–2 drops of 5% gold chloride to every ml of sensitizer will cool the values of your print.

Figure 13–23

Craig Barber, *Paul's Place*—Pd

Craig wrote, "*This was one of those end of the day, light looks great, but not much of it, shots. This is a 60-minute exposure. It was dead calm with darkening skies; no sooner did I finish my exposure, and put my gear away, when the skies opened up and it began to rain in torrents.*" Craig, works with a 25% Pt/75% Pd mix and develops in ammonium citrate at 100°F.

(Courtesy of the artist)

Gold Toning

Gold toning, following clearing and washing can create some interesting changes of color in your prints. Palladium becomes somewhat reddish-purple while platinum becomes more bluish-purple. Here's a simple gold-toning formula.

Part A:

    4 g sodium formate
1000 ml   distilled water

Part B:

  10 ml 5% gold chloride (*you can get this pre-mixed*)

Mix A & B together and pour the solution into a clean tray. Immerse your recently cleared, washed, and damp print in the toner and observe. You will notice that the darker values are change color and that the highlights are cooler. The toning time is subjective but the print will normally be done in 10 minutes with fresh toner. Subsequent prints will take longer as the gold solution weakens.

When you are satisfied with the print, put it into a bath of film or paper developer (*called a clearing bath in many texts*) for 1 minute and then do a final wash for 30–40 minutes.

- HC-110 mix: 50 ml HC-110 film developer to 1000 ml water

- Or Dektol: 250 ml stock solution to 1000 ml water

Art Wax

One last thing; I have found that a finger-rubbed application of Dorland's Art Wax to your alternative process prints, after they have dried, will always enrich the blacks and soften highlights that may be a bit hot. This is very simple and a nice way to finish off a print. All you need to do is lay down your dried print on a hard and flat surface and then, with gentle swirling action, rub a very even and thin layer of Dorland's Art wax over the entire print area. Once that is done, take a hairdryer and begin to gently blow hot air onto the wax-coated area. You will see the wax melt and then dry down into the paper texture. What is different is that you now have a protected image where the darks have been intensified by the wax application. You'll like this a lot and the organic wax is entirely beneficial to your print.

HAVING A BAD DAY? TRY THESE OPTIONS

There are explanations for almost every problem one might encounter with the platinum/palladium process but sometimes even the best Pt/Pd printers have bad days and can't explain what it is that is going wrong. That's life and sometimes you just have bad karma . . . so relax, go watch a movie, change processes (cyanotype always works) and live to print another day.

Some days, everything you print seems just a bit off. On these special occasions you might want to take your less-than-successful prints and experiment with them after they have been washed, dried, and flattened. Try other alternative processes in combination with your recently not so successful platinum/palladium. Many alternative processes can easily be applied on top of Pt/Pd prints and it has been quite common, throughout the technique's history, to combine delicate gum bichromate or light cyanotype prints on top of a Pt/Pd print for additional coloration and depth. For the last few years I have made a habit of applying short, dark pigment, gum exposures to any print that seems weak in the shadows and have actually salvaged quite a few that I would otherwise have normally trashed. This particular technique, by the way, was a favorite of such historical luminaries as Edward Steichen, George Seeley, and Alfred Stieglitz.

Cyan & Platinum/Palladium

Cyanotype is often effective in adding density to weak shadow areas. Make up a standard A and B cyanotype formula, dilute it, and coat your dried and flattened Pt/Pd print. Briefly expose your negative, in registration,

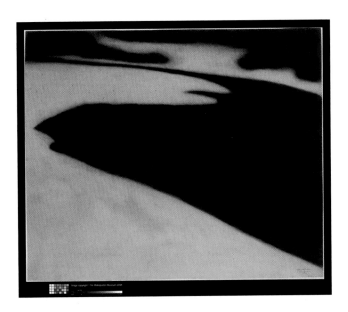

Figure 13–24

George Seeley, *Winter Landscape*, 1909—Gum & Pt
One of my favorite photographers from the Photo-Secession was George Seeley. His influences were strongly rooted in painting and this Pt/gum bichromate image is a perfect example of how he married his two passions. *(Courtesy The Metropolitan Museum of Art, Gilman Collection, Gift of the Howard Gilman Foundation, 2005, Image © The Metropolitan Museum of Art)*

and follow the traditional cyanotype process. I would recommend a specific dilution but the degree of blue you want in your shadows will dictate that choice for your print.

Gum & Platinum/Palladium

Pt/Pd and gum bichromate is a really wonderful combination technique and I recommend it highly as a way of intensifying your shadows and adding color to an essentially monochromatic process. Gum and palladium are made for one another since the warm values of the palladium make a nice bed for almost any hue. If you simply intend simply to intensify your shadows, then there is no need to size your paper as your gum exposure will be a very short one and will only harden the dichromate, gum, and color sensitizer in the most open portions of your negative. If you're going to do a number of gum impressions, I would recommend hardening and sizing your finished Pt/Pd print and using a relatively sturdy weight of paper for the initial Pt/Pd print. For complete instructions on paper preparation and gum printing, please see those chapters.

Figure 13–25
Edward Steichen—*The Pond—Moonrise*, 1904—Pt & gum bichromate
On February 15, 2006, an astonishing price of $2,928,000.00 was paid for this print, by an unidentified collector at a Sotheby's auction. The Met had acquired the print as part of the great collection from the Gilman Paper Company (*The Waking Dream*). The museum already possessed another version of the print, hence the decision to deacquisition. A third print from this negative, but in Pt and cyanotype (Figure 7–5) is in the collection of MOMA.
(The Metropolitan Museum of Art, Gilman Collection, Gift of the Howard Gilman Foundation, 2005, Image © The Metropolitan Museum of Art)

Intensification in Palladium & Gum

If you really want to see a beautiful intensification in your palladium prints try doing a gum bichromate coating with just a mixture of thalo green and lamp black watercolor, gum Arabic, and potassium dichromate. Make the exposure a quick one but long enough to hold the gum to the paper.

Van Dyke & Platinum/Palladium

I began experimenting with the Van Dyke/Palladium process around 1990 after making an aesthetically impaired Van Dyke during a demo for my alternative process class at Harvard. Although it still provides surprises from time to time, like any experience with a second process in combination with Pt/Pd, it is a technique that can produce absolutely beautiful tonalities and color variations. The primary elements to look for in a successful VDB & Pt/Pd print are warm and deep shadows and luminous highlights . . . provided you clear your print well. When wet, the highlights seem to glow from the inside of the paper. The technique works best when you begin with a Van Dyke and over-expose the image. The over-printing with Pt/Pd will often open up the shadows and give life to the highlights. You have a better chance at success when Parts B and C of the Pt/Pd sensitizer formula make up the primary drop load.

Don't be surprised to see the image bleach to yellow and fade when you first coat the palladium on top of the over-exposed Van Dyke. Don't worry. Once the paper is dry, register your negative to the original Van Dyke and expose the recoated paper to UV light. You will have to test to see what your exposure time will be but look for the whisper before taking development action. Process the palladium image normally, paying close attention to the recommended EDTA clearing bath times. After the clearing, wash your print in cool running water for 30 to 40 minutes and hang it up to dry. In most cases, if the print looked great when it was wet, then it will likely dry-down too flat. Print for an image that is a little weak in the wash and you should end up happy when all is said and done.

Figure 13–26

Peter Liepke, *Manhattan Bridge At Sunset*,
3-color gum over Pt

Peter's Manhattan Bridge at Sunset image
was first printed it in platinum only. He then
tried it as a gumoil print, but eventually felt
that a 3-coat gum bichromate over platinum
would be the best combination to produce
what he had envisioned when I originally took
the photograph.
(Courtesy of the artist)

Figure 13–27

Margaret Mateskon, *Maggie Pool*, 2006—
Pt/Pd & on digital ink-jet

Maggie, a student of Christina Z. Anderson's at
Montana State University, began her redheaded
woman series a year ago . . . because she has
red hair. That instigated her interest in the iconic
pin-up and its projected strength, sexual aware-
ness and independence . . . qualities she found in
the World War II–era pin-ups when women were
raising families, running every industry, and building airplanes and tanks for the war effort. This
piece is a marriage of a 20th-century pin-up,
printed on a 19th-century platinum, on top of
21st-century ink-jet print.
(Courtesy of the artist)

The Ziatype Process

OVERVIEW & EXPECTATIONS

In this chapter, I'll offer a little history about how the Ziatype came into being and show, as in nearly every process that is covered in this book, how connections from the past were instrumental to the way we practice a specific process today. I'll describe how the Ziatype works, its chemistry and where to get it, detail the technique, and provide you with a "drop chart" that works like the platinum/palladium chart you used in the previous chapter. From these Ziatype formulas, you will clearly see how slight variations in the drop counts and chemistry will impact the colors and contrast of your finished prints. You will then learn the process and how to mix and apply the sensitizing formulas to your paper. I'll describe exposure considerations and what to look for in a Ziatype printing-out process (POP) and will conclude the chapter with additional considerations and suggestions as they apply to the technique.

The Ziatype process is one of the most accessible and "user-friendly" processes I've worked with in the past decade. It is also one of the most flexible and open to individual invention and inspiration. Nearly every time I teach this process to a class or workshop, I end up seeing an interesting adaptation and a new way for me to think about working with the technique. Have fun!

Figure 14–1
Christopher James, *Painters*, Rangoon, Burma, 1982— Ziatype
This is a Ziatype print I made from a 1982 Burma Project negative translated to a Pictorico OHP contact size ink-jet film.
(Courtesy of the author)

A LITTLE HISTORY

The Ziatype process can be seen, from most every angle, sitting upon a foundation of platinum and palladium history. As these two processes have so much in common, it would be a good idea to go back to the Pt/Pd chapter and read the A Little History section and then come back and begin here. There is a brief overlap for continuity.

In the late 1880s, Captain Giuseppe Pizzighelli (1849–1912) and Baron Arthur Von Hübl (1852–1932) expanded upon, and modified, Willis's work. Among their achievements, they created a sensitizer that incorporated sodium, or ammonium, ferric oxalate into the sensitizer as a substitute for the ferric oxalate in the Willis formula. Pizzighelli humidified the paper prior to exposure, and because the humidification created a printing-out effect, he was able to eliminate the need for the potassium oxalate liquid development in the Willis technique. The process was a POP—printing-out process that required only humidity to assure the resolution of the image.

During this adaptive process, the platinum salt in the sensitizer was reduced, and converted, into metallic platinum *during* the exposure rather than as a result of development. Following a brief clearing bath with distilled water, the image was immersed in an acidic solution (*a 0.5%–1% hydrochloric acid bath*) for clearing, then washed.

Pizzighelli continued to experiment with other "*double salt*" formulas and discovered that with the addition of sodium ferric oxalate, potassium ferric oxalate, or ammonium ferric oxalate, he could alter the sensitivity and color of his prints. At the completion of the exposure, Pizzighelli's image would appear, with the exception of the clearing and wash stages, exactly as it would in the finished print stage of the process. Pizzighelli commercially manufactured his *Pizzitype* printing papers, using sodium ferric oxalate, and enjoyed a short and modestly successful run as an entrepreneur. Also marketed was Dr. Jacoby's

Platinum Printing-Out-Paper. . . a reported favorite of Alfred Stieglitz. Eventually, due to several insurmountable technical problems encountered in the manufacturing process and a relatively brief shelf life, due to its super absorptivity, the printing-out platinum papers disappeared from the marketplace.

In 1986, Pizzighelli's research was expanded and refined through the efforts of Dr. Michael Ware and Prof. Pradip Malde, who successfully developed an ammonium-based method of Pt/Pd printing by substituting Pizzighelli's potassium chloroplatinite with ammonium chloroplatinite/ammonium chloropalladite, which is more soluble in water. These are referred to as "*ammonium salts of platinum and palladium*" and were integrated into the process in order to realize a greater degree of chemical solubility and a more hygroscopic paper surface. In the Ware-Malde variation, the color of the print, and that print's contrast variables, are dependent on a balanced formula and by paying close attention to, and controlling, the degree of *humidity* in the paper prior to exposure.

In the early 1980s, when Bostick & Sullivan was a fledgling enterprise, founder Dick Sullivan also began to investigate the work of Willis, Pizzighelli, and Hübl. He happened upon a reprint of Ernst Lietze's *Modern Heliographic Processes* (Visual Studies Workshop, 1974) in which there was a full description of Pizzighelli's formulas and workflow. Sullivan tried some of the formulas and found them unforgiving and quite temperamental. He did confirm that if one were to coat a paper with a palladium salt, and ammonium ferric oxalate, and then humidify and expose the sensitized paper, the image would print out and appear as it might following a standard wet development. This was something that most likely happened during Pizzighelli's own investigations and may explain how he ended up with an alternative system following his partnership with Hübl.

In 1995, Sullivan renewed his research by investigating double-palladium salts and took on the challenge of making a process that was easily accessible to those who were interested in exploring the simplicity, and advantages, of a POP method over the traditional Pt/Pd development (*DOP. . . develop-out*) process. Sullivan's (*as he refers to it*) "big gestalt" came about when he was trying out various double salts of palladium and happened to see a brilliant POP/printed-out image when he tested with the lithium salt. He wasn't looking for a POP but was primarily seeking out variables in coloration and was actually expecting to see a dramatic red or blue. It was at this point that he happened on the powerful POP effect of lithium. Realizing that lithium was hygroscopic, he then tested with ammonium ferric oxalate, which is also hygroscopic, and that led to his big A-ha moment when he remembered that Pizzighelli once had a commercially viable paper with problems that couldn't be remedied at the time. At this point, he began to build a system. Sullivan's intention was to distill the information that had been learned, from Pizzighelli-Hübl to Ware-Malde, and then create a fluid printing system that was uncomplicated and where all of the variables, except humidity, could be controlled through flexible drop-count chemical recipes.

In the Pizzighelli, and Ware-Malde, processes the color and the contrast of the final print are realized by controlling chemistry and humidity. Ware & Malde differ from Pizzighelli by using ammonium salts versus Pizzighelli's sodium salts. In the Sullivan process, the color and contrast are controlled in great part by chemistry. . . specifically the drop-count sensitizer mix. Humidity plays a role but less so than Ware-Malde. I suspect these brilliant gentlemen would respond that there is a great deal more to this than I'm relating in this brief summation. . . and I would not argue. However, it's time to move on to the process.

Figure 14–2

Dick Sullivan, *Feed Store*, Las Vegas, NM, 2000—Ziatype

Dick Sullivan is the irrepressible co-founder and proprietor, along with his wife Melody Bostick, of Bostick & Sullivan—my favorite source for alternative process materials and chemistry. As well, Dick is the creator of the Ziatype process and this image is an example of his work.

(Courtesy of the artist)

A LITTLE CHEMISTRY

After extensive testing of complex palladium double salt formulas, using nearly all of the alkali metals that were affordable and safe,* Sullivan found that a combination of lithium chloropalladite and ammonium ferric oxalate would make a simple and flexible formula that resulted in prints that were neutral-black in color.

Sullivan also discovered that by modifying the formula with cesium chloropalladite (*see the lower end of Group 1 in the periodic table*) either in a mix, or by completely replacing the lithium chloropalladite, he could achieve the same tonal range but produce a print with reddish to brown-black coloration. At this stage, Dick secured the assistance of Carl Weese, who participated in the testing of the process from his studio in Connecticut. They discovered that some of the technical issues that worked in Dick's Santa Fe, New Mexico, studio (*high altitude and very dry*) did not work the same way in Carl's Connecticut studio (*low altitude and humid in 3 out of 4 seasons*). They continued to sort out the kinks and eventually came up with a system that was both rational and predictable. Dick named this new process *Ziatype* after the circular Anasazi Pueblo icon for the sun.

It has been suggested by some that cesium chloropalladite is not truly an ideal option because it is low in solubility. This causes the crystals to precipitate out in the sensitizer. Personally, and I've been working with Ziatype since Dick Sullivan put it on the market, I don't experience this particular problem as long as I keep the solution hot. The principle and primary differences between the Ziatype and the Ware-Malde processes are:

◆ Sullivan's Ziatype utilizes the unique color polarity of lithium and cesium to control color range at a relatively constant humidity and the color differences are more pronounced than when using the ammonium salts of the Ware-Malde method. Granted, there are also a lot more solutions to play with in Ziatype.

◆ The Ziatype differs from Ware-Malde by using palladium alone instead of palladium and/or platinum, and then by using the more unusual lithium and cesium double salts of the palladium. In the early testing stages of the Ziatype, platinum salts were tried but Sullivan and Weese found that they could not make a pure platinum Ziatype. There was, as well, according to Sullivan, a 3-fold difference in cost difference between palladium and platinum at that time and their focus was directed to palladium.

◆ In the Ziatype, color and contrast are independent of one another and determined by the recipe that the user selects. Humidity is, as it is in the Ware-Malde method, an important element but not to the same degree. In the Mike Ware—Pradip Malde method, using the ammonium salts of Pt/Pd, color and contrast are controlled with the balance of humidity and the ratio of the platinum and palladium salts.

◆ Just for the record, both methods are first-rate adaptations and well worth the time to learn how to do them well.

HOW ZIATYPE WORKS

The Ziatype, and Ware-Malde, methods are different from traditional platinum/palladium working methods in that it is a printing-out process. This means that the values within the image are nearly fully realized at the conclusion of the UV exposure and that you can define the finished density, and look, of your image by inspection during the printing-out stage of the process. I use the word "*nearly*" as there is, as in every alt pro process, a significant dry down to consider when evaluating your POP image. Chemical development is not required in Ziatype or Ware-Malde and the odds for a successful print are generally quite good within the first few attempts by a new Ziatype or Ware Malde printer.

After you determine that the print has met your intentions during the exposure, all you need to do is rinse the print in distilled water, clear the highlights in a simple EDTA bath, and complete a final wash. Beyond this simplicity, the Ziatype is more flexible than the traditional platinum/palladium process, has a greater range of color options, demonstrates less grain in the image, is easier to manage in regard to control of contrast, and equals the quality of platinum/palladium.

*Potassium, sodium, ammonium, barium, zinc, tin, tungsten, magnesium, lithium, and cesium (See the references to cesium on this and following pages.)

Figure 14–3
Jonathan Bakos, *Lowell, MA. Facade*, 2006—Ziatype
Jonathan is one of my current students at The Art Institute of Boston and he apparently heard the Ziatype sirens calling his name, as he is now one of the best practitioners of the technique that I know.
(Courtesy of the artist)

As in some other alternative processes, the Ziatype retains the traditional "*self-masking*" characteristic of platinum/palladium. Self-masking is the term that describes what happens during lengthy Pt/Pd exposures when UV light will continue to expose highlights after the shadows have reached a degree of exposure that basically functions as a filter, slowing down additional exposure in the thinner sections (*the shadows*) of the negative. All in all, the Ziatype is a terrific technique to begin learning about quality complex alternative process image making as well as being the most complex user-friendly process I have encountered.

TABLE SET UP FOR ZIATYPE

Make your life very simple by purchasing all of the Ziatype chemistry at once in kit form from Bostick & Sullivan. A standard kit will contain bottles of afo, LiPd, gold, Tn, ad (these non-standard abbreviations are defined below) and Tween. The prepared Ziatype sensitizer components: 25 ml bottles w/dropper caps

- ◆ **afo**—(ammonium ferric oxalate)
- ◆ **LiPd**—(lithium palladium chloride. . . aka lithium chloropalladite)
- ◆ **Gold**—(5% gold chloride)
- ◆ **Tn**—(sodium tungstate)

- ◆ **ad**—(ammonium dichromate: 1%, 2%, 5% concentrations) *(Be careful with this chemical, as it is very aggressive in the sensitizer. A 1% solution is preferred.)*
- ◆ **CsPd**—(cesium chloropalladate—palladium)
- ◆ **sfo**—(sodium ferric oxalate)
- ◆ **Tween 20:** (dilute 1:3)
- ◆ **Photoflo 200**—*(Mix 1 drop to every 10 ml of distilled water for working solution.)*
- ◆ Ziatype drop chart (see text)
- ◆ Clean sheets of lightweight clear acetate (*humidity control*)—or Krystal Klear acetate envelopes for both storage and printing
- ◆ Clean paper for the table surface
- ◆ Paper for coating: COT 320, Crane's Platinotype, Buxton, Arches Platine, and gelatin salted paper using salted paper sizing #1
- ◆ Shot glass
- ◆ A new hake brush (Label for Ziatype only)
- ◆ Clean distilled water in a beaker for brush washing
- ◆ Optional: steamer/humidifier
- ◆ Pencil
- ◆ Contact printing frame
- ◆ Negative for contact printing
- ◆ Paper towels
- ◆ Photo paper box, or drawer, for drying. *(Allow 15-30 minutes of drying time in the box or drawer after coating.)*

ZIATYPE CHEMISTRY

Abbreviation Symbols for Ziatype

afo

ammonium ferric oxalate

sfo

sodium ferric oxalate

lfo

lithium ferric oxalate

LiPd

lithium palladium chloride*

CsPd

cesium chloropalladate-palladium

ad

(1 drop at %)

ammonium dichromate

Tn

(warmer tones, reduces contrast)

sodium tungstate

gold

(cooler tones, boosts contrast)

gold chloride (5%)

*lithium chloropalladite

5% Gold: Color & Contrast Control

Gold provides cooler values and hues in the purple, blue, gray range. Exposure times *increase* with the addition of more gold in the sensitizer, as does the contrast of the print. When gold is 20%–25% of the drop count the mid-tones cool considerably and the Dmax and contrast rise. When gold is 40%–50% of the drop count you will see more blue in the print. At 80% you will get lavender.

In order to do this, you are able to substitute the 5% gold chloride for lithium palladium chloride (LiPd) on a drop-by-drop exchange. Don't exceed an 80% LiPd to 20% gold ratio or you'll have to use a double strength ferric ammonium oxalate and a 10% gold chloride mix with the LiPd and gold and contrast will go up significantly.

5% Gold: Color Control Swap w/ LiPd

If you want to slowly adjust the color of your print, consider this gold for lithium palladium swap. A single drop of gold in exchange of a single drop of LiPd will provide a reddish burgundy shift. As you make the drop count exchange greater, say 6 drops of gold out of 8 LiPd, your color will shift radically to purple lavender.

Part C Palladium(II) Chloride Swap for LiPd for Contrast

If you find it necessary to boost your contrast in the midtones of your print, you may consider up to a 20%–25% swap of the lithium palladium chloride (LiPd) with an equal number of drops of Part C, palladium chloride from your platinum/palladium process chemistry.

Split Tones & Humidity

If you steam your sensitized paper completely prior to exposure, and you have successfully sandwiched the paper with acetate sheets on the front and back of the paper (*to hold in the humidity*), you will get a neutral black print using a standard 12 afo + 12 LiPd formula.

If the print is dried before exposure, the print will have a brown tonality and will be less deep in the darker values. If you dry your print, expose it, and then steam it, the print will develop out completely and will yield a rich sepia color. Variations of the process, using this knowledge and formula alterations will produce splits.

Ziatype Drop Count Formulas

afo	lfo	sfo	LiPd	CsPd	gold	ad	Tn	color	contrast
12			12					neutral slate grey black	low
12				12* warm				warm brown	low
12			12			2%		neutral	low/med
12			12			5%		warm	medium
12			12			20%		warmer	high
12			10		2			cool	medium
12			8		4			very cool	high
12			4		8			purple lavender	very high
12			9		3		2	green blue	low medium
12			11		6			blue black	medium high
12			12				2	slightly warm sepia	medium
12			12				3	very warm sepia	low
	12		12					red warm	medium
6	6		12					warm	low

(Tables courtesy of Sullivan & Weese, *The New Platinum Print*)

Red Shadow Tones with Cesium Chloropalladite (CsPd)

There is only a single formula in the Bostick & Sullivan Drop Chart that incorporates Cesium Chloropalladite (CsPd) but that doesn't mean this formula is the only one that works. Cesium chloropalladite can also generate prints in a non-humid state. . . steaming actually produces a cooler image while a dry print yields warmth. Using CsPd in **exchange** of LiPd will give you deep red tones in your shadows when the exchange is a total substitution. You **must** be sure that the CsPd remains warm, perhaps even hot, throughout the process. It must be heated in a non-metallic beaker before use and it will precipitate out at ambient room temperature if it cools.

Figure 14–4
David Stinchcomb, _Food Lion_, 1994—Ziatype
Oklahoma artist David Stinchcomb took a workshop with me many years ago and has stayed in touch with new work. David's Ziatype was the first print I had seen executed in Sullivan's new process and I was immediately impressed with the simplicity and quality of the technique.
(Courtesy of the artist)

Sodium Tungstate: Warmth and Lowering Contrast

Using sodium tungstate (Tn) in your sensitizer formula will both lower the contrast and add warmth to your print. The 40% solution that comes in a Bostick & Sullivan Ziatype kit can be used as an additive directly into a standard afo and LiPd mix. The more sodium Tungstate in the formula, the warmer and softer the final print will be.

Ammonium Dichromate: Big Contrast Change

The Ziatype kit comes with an ammonium dichromate (ad) solution that is used principally as a contrast control agent. As is, I personally find it really aggressive and not appropriate for my negatives. As a result, I seldom use it in my sensitizer formulas.

When I teach the process, I generally have my students prepare percentage dilutions of the ammonium dichromate and urge them to use a drop at a time if at all. Printing times also slow down with the addition of ammonium dichromate and since this process is humidity dependent that fact is important . . . the

longer the exposure, the more likely the paper will dry out. If you need to control contrast, I recommend beginning with drops of 5% gold chloride. You can also try the Part C swap with LiPd or do the sun/shade exposure technique where the bulk of the exposure is done in open shade with a last minute hit with direct sun for the shadows.

It is really important to remember that the "self-masking" trait of this process will be _lessened_ by the inclusion of ammonium dichromate in the formula

Tween 20—
(_polyoxyethylenesorbitanmonolaurate_ . . . there will be a spelling test in the morning . . .)

Tween 20 is sold as 10% solution. It is a non-ionic, polysorbate, surfactant that promotes the ability of the sensitizer to penetrate deeply into the paper's fibers in your sensitizer formula. I recommend using it for this process at a 1:3 dilution. You can add 1 drop of Tween per sensitizer mix or combine Tween with a Photoflo wetting agent (_diluted to 10%_) and use 1 drop of each. The point of this addition to the formula is to assist the sensitizer in finding a secure home in the paper fibers.

Figure 14–5
Manikarnika Cremation Grounds, Benares, India, 1985—Ziatype
This Ziatype image is from my Benares Project series documenting death rituals in Benares, India. The original negative was a Tri-X 6 × 9 translated into a digital ink-jet contact negative for the Ziatype printing.
(Courtesy of the author)

THE WORKING PROCESS

You will need most of the same supplies and the same environment necessary for Pt/Pd and your coating area and set-up will be identical . . . as will your need for a hinged back contact-printing frame. The Ziatype can handle a greater range of negative densities with ease (*negative densities of .8 to 2.0 due to the ammonium dichromate and gold contrast control*) but a long tonal scale in your contact negative is still preferable to one that is limited. Consider creating a digital negative on Pictorico OHP.

Because the sensitized paper will be slightly humidified when the exposure begins, you may need a package of clear, and thin, acetate sheets to place between the negative and the sensitizer to protect the negative. Only use a high-quality acetate sheet without imperfections as those flaws will degrade your final print. If you don't use acetate, there is a good possibility of baking your sensitizer to the negative in humid conditions . . . I have done this on several occasions.

Set yourself up in a clean, dry, and low-light work area that is the same as you would work in for Pt/Pd. Then arrange the small bottles of Ziatype chemistry in the order that you intend to use them; each of these bottles will have its personal dropper. I generally mark the butcher's paper that covers my coating area with a labeled location site for each of the bottles. This is really necessary with Ziatype as there are so many bottles on the table, especially when you have a selection of ammonium dichromate percentages and are working in a group situation such as a workshop.

Figure 14–6
David Stinchcomb, Bandelier, NM—Ziatype
Here is another Ziatype image from David's excellent portfolio of alternative techniques.
(Courtesy of the artist)

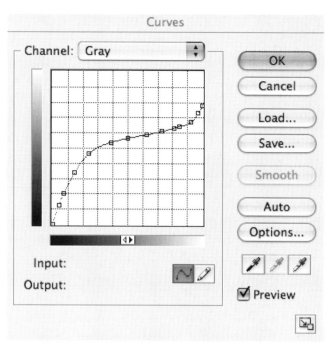

Figure 14–7
Ziatype Curve Profile
This is an example of a Ziatype curve profile that you can load during a curve adjustment sequence in Photoshop.

Acetate Sheets and Static Electricity

You will also want to have your clear sheets of acetate near by and if it is winter, or you are at high altitude, and the air is dry, it is important not to create a lot of static electricity (meaning the sheet becomes a dust-magnet) when you remove them from the package. I like to turn on an electric teakettle and remove the acetate near the steam.

The Ziatype Negative

The Ziatype process is very flexible and you can make a very successful print with a negative that has a base plus fog of 0.2 and a Dmax of 2.0 or greater. In other words, your negatives can have a very long density range that can exceed the range you would want for platinum and palladium printing. The Ziatype is also 2–3 stops faster than traditional developing out Pt/Pd.

Pyro-processed negatives that would print on a grade II silver gelatin paper work extremely well with the Ziatype process. My friend David Stinchcomb has done a bit of work with the concept of the Pyro tint benefits for a Ziatype and has worked that idea into the production of his digital negatives on Pictorico OHP. Please return to Chapter 5, Digital Options to get a full Color Layer workflow for making digital negatives for Ziatype.

Moisturizing Your Brush

Before you begin to work, immerse your Ziatype-dedicated hake brush in a glass of distilled water. The reason for this is that your volume of sensitizer solution will be rather spare and if your brush is bone dry then it will absorb all of the liquid, leaving you very little to coat the paper.

Also have an additional beaker of distilled water for washing your brush between coatings. This wash water should be changed quite often. To one side, have your recently cleaned contact frame, a package of fresh and clear acetate sheets for the negative/sensitized paper separation, your negative, and a clean piece of paper that you have torn with a straight edge so that it fits within the dimensions of your contact printing frame.

Making a Ziatype

The first part of this process involves determining what kind of print you want and what contrast and color you want it to be. The next step involves counting

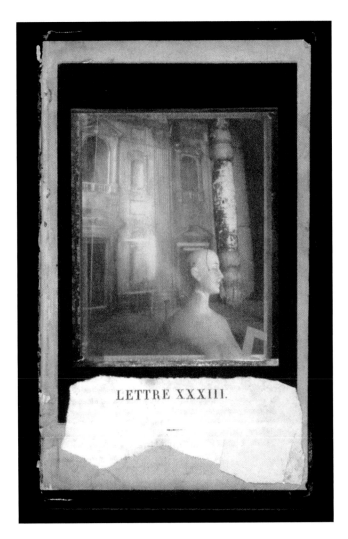

Figure 14–8

Jesseca Ferguson, *Letter XXXIII*, 1998—pinhole Ziatype

This is a fine example of Jesseca Ferguson's work incorporating Ziatype and collage.

(Courtesy of the artist)

exposure, and weather notations on the lower margin of the paper to assist in the evaluation of the print during the lab session.

The next step is to pour the mixed sensitizer formula into the center of the marked-out area on the paper where your negative will go for the exposure. Then, with a quick and very gentle touch, brush the solution into that area. As with other brush applications, alternate your vertical and horizontal strokes over the full negative area to guarantee a smooth and complete coverage. As an alternative coating method, see the platinum/palladium chapter for Puddle Pusher directions.

After the coating step, I allow the emulsion to "*set up*" in the paper for 1 to 2 minutes. If you are experiencing very high humidity in your working space you may want to consider using your hairdryer, on a cool setting, by blowing gently on the backside of the paper. Humidity is essential to the print quality of your Ziatype and it may take you a little while to evaluate the ideal state of humidity in the paper. This is not difficult and simply takes a little practice to figure out. When working during the more humid summer months in New England this aspect of the process is not a great problem. However, when I teach in Santa Fe, or at Anderson Ranch in Aspen, there is no humidity and the process gets a bit trickier. In these situations I am sure to add Tween to my sensitizer and do my best to humidify my working space . . . if only with an electric teakettle boiling water.

My personal method of evaluating when it is time to expose the negative is when I can no longer see a reflective sheen on the paper's surface. I also know that the paper is ready for printing when it appears dry but doesn't have the "*snap*" of perfectly dry paper when I flex it. Also, I know the time is right when the back of the print is "cool" to the touch using the pulse-taking side of your wrist, like checking the temperature of milk in a baby's bottle. Try not to touch the paper surface with your fingertips, as they are sources of alkalinity and oil.

Your working space would be considered ideal if the relative humidity in it were between 50% and 65%. This may mean, especially in arid climates, and during the winter months, that you should consider purchasing a humidifier for your lab or working space. You can calculate your lab's humidity with an inexpensive hygrometer, available from Light Impressions.

the drops of each solution in the sensitizing formula into your shot glass and swirling them together so that the solution is uniform. Consult the drop count chart and do exactly what you did when mixing sensitizer formulas for both the Kallitype and Pt/Pd. So far, this is identical to the procedure you use in preparing a sensitizing solution in platinum/palladium printing.

The next step is to place your negative on the paper you are going to sensitize, in the location where you want it to be in the final print, and mark the paper on the outside corners of the negative with an "L"-shaped pencil line. This tells you where to coat the paper and allows for a little over-run for the brushstrokes. While you have the pencil in hand, make all of the necessary formula,

For more information See Michael Ware's article, "Platinum Reprinted" (British Journal of Photography, October 1996) or Pradip Malde's, "New Solutions for Platinum Printers," (View Camera Magazine, October 1994).

I like to build the Ziatype sandwich on a clean piece of paper before loading the contact printer. The layers are arranged on a clean surface in the following order:

1. A sheet of new acetate that is larger than the negative but smaller than the inside dimensions of the contact printer.

2. Next is your newly sensitized and not quite dry paper. By the way, the paper recommendations for Ziatype are the same as for Pt/Pd.

3. Next, place a second sheet of acetate on the sensitized paper so that now you have acetate on both the front and back of the sensitized paper. This will be a pseudo humidifying envelope and will prevent the paper from drying too quickly during the exposure. Also, because your exposure will generate heat, the humidity will actually build during the exposure. This is the part of the process experience where I discovered that I could ruin my favorite negatives if I didn't use acetate between my negative on the sheet of acetate.

4. Now, lay your negative on the sheet of acetate, within the coating area of sensitizer, so it will be "right-reading" on the paper in the final print.

5. Take hold of all of these pieces on the corners, lift them up, and flip them over into the contact printing frame so that when you close up the frame you will be looking through the glass at your right-reading negative > the first acetate > the sensitized paper > the other acetate sheet > the back of the frame. Now it is time to expose the paper to the sun or by placing it in a mechanical UV light source.

Again, Ziatype is a printing-out process and you must be able to inspect your print during the exposure sequence in order to determine when the print is ready for washing and clearing. Ziatype exposures happen pretty quickly so be aware of the outside border's color shift and think of it as your D-max or maximum density.

Figure 14-9
Dick Sullivan, Tucumcari, NM, 2000—Ziatype
(Courtesy of the author)

The average Ziatype exposure will probably not be longer than 6–8 minutes, so it is a good idea to begin checking on your printing out progress after 3–4 minutes of UV exposure. When you do this, be in subdued light. Also, remember that the orange color that you are looking at is only the sensitizer and that you are looking for tonal gradations that will make you happy after the exposure, washing, and clearing are complete.

If you find that your exposure is happening too rapidly and that you are blocking up in the shadows and getting very little contrast (*no self-masking is taking place*), then try placing the contact frame in an open shade location. This will lengthen your exposure time and boost the contrast of the final print. If you opt for a shade exposure, it is a good idea to give the print a minute or two of straight sun at the conclusion of the shade exposure to intensify your shadows. This practice will give you a little more control over your tonal scale. If you are using a UV mechanical printer, try placing a sheet of Pictorico OHP film over the contact-printing frame during the exposure. If that isn't enough, try 2 sheets or put an 18% color layer, printed out on Pictorico, using the instructions given previously. Again, don't be alarmed by the orange color of your sensitizer during inspection because it will wash out. It is important that you learn how to read your highlights through this orange filter.

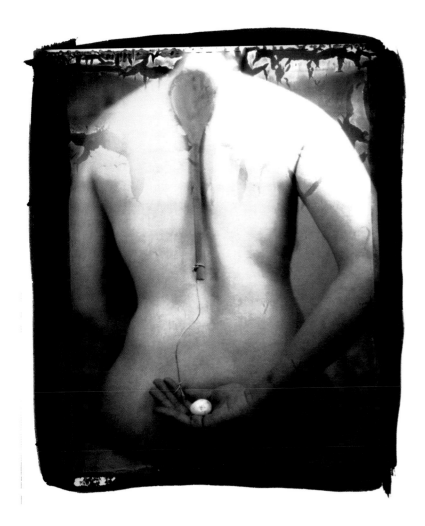

Figure 14–10

Jessica Somers, *Motherhood*, 2007—Ziatype on salted gelatin paper

Jessica was in an advanced alternative process workshop of mine in 2007 and worked with me in experimenting with a variety of papers and paper preparations, with Ziatype sensitizers . . . this one a Ziatype on salted gelatin paper. Jessica writes, "My photographs explore the struggle and balance between the choices one makes and the uncontrollable circumstances that intervene with these choices." *(Courtesy of the artist)*

ZIATYPE ON SALTED GELATIN PAPER

During a recent Advanced Alternative Process workshop, at The Maine Photographic Workshops, I was giving a Ziatype demonstration using the super tough Kozo paper but was unhappy with the way it was translating the negative. I decided to extend the demonstration by printing on a piece of paper that had been gelatin sized and salted for salted paper printing (see Gelatin Salting #1). Still less than thrilled after printing several versions, I decided make a Ziatype on a piece of Arches Platine that had also been salted and gelatin sized.

The first print resulted in beautiful, and deeply rich, shadows . . . but highlights that were too pink for my taste. I removed the gold chloride from the Ziatype formula and replaced it with a drop of 5% ammonium dichromate in order to keep the contrast in the final print. That strategy was successful at eliminating the pink highlights (because gold was out of the formula) but

the delicate highlight details were completely blown out by the vigorous percentage of ammonium dichromate. At that point I had a choice of using a less aggressive potassium dichromate solution or changing the printing strategy. I decided to make a sensitizer consisting of a simple AFO (ammonium ferric oxalate) & LiPd (lithium palladium chloride) neutral black mix (about 1:1) and expose the print almost entirely in the shade with 2 minutes of straight sun at the end of the exposure sequence to enhance shadow integrity.

I was really surprised. The values in the final image were simply amazing . . . far richer and more satisfying than any Ziatype I had ever printed. I asked my workshop students to give the Ziatypes on salted gelatin paper a try and within a few attempts they had all produced beautiful images. If you are looking for a new technique, you may find this variation very satisfying.

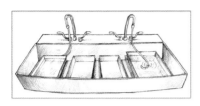

SINK SET UP FOR ZIATYPE

Tray 1 A very clean tray filled with running water for 4–5 minutes

Tray 2 1.5% Citric acid bath

Mix: 1 tablespoon (approximately 15 grams) of citric acid to a liter of warm water for 5 minutes. This is a 1.5% solution.

Tray 3 Clean water rinse for 1 minute.

Tray 4 1.5% Sodium Sulfite or EDTA bath

Mix: 1 tablespoon (approximately 15 grams) of sodium sulfite to a liter of warm water for 5 minutes. This is a 1.5% solution.

Tray 5 Final wash for 20 minutes

Fresh Water First bath

When you are satisfied with the way your print looks, immerse your paper in fresh running water for 4–5 minutes. Unlike many of the previous processes, a distilled water first bath doesn't seem necessary. If you can't seem to clear the yellow from your highlights, this might be one step you should consider doing. Right away, you will notice the orange clearing from the paper and also that the print is beginning to lighten a little while exhibiting a bit more contrast than you had planned for. Relax; the density and contrast of the image will return to the way you wanted it after the final washing and dry-down of the print.

Citric Acid Second Bath

After 4–5 minutes in clear running water, take your print and place it in a bath of 1.5% citric acid (15 g/1 heaping TBS to a liter of water) for 5 minutes. Agitate the print gently during this clearing stage.

Sodium Sulfite or EDTA Third Bath

Next, make up a 1.5% tray of either sodium sulfite or EDTA, (15 g/1 heaping TBS to a liter of water) and agitate gently for 5 minutes.

Figure 14–11

Tricia Hoffman, *Figure Study #26*, 2004 (2007)—Ziatype

Tricia took my alternative process workshop in Maine in 2007 and produced this evocative, and dramatic, Ziatype. The unique graphic across the top of the image is the result of a fault in the peel apart process of Polaroid's Type 665 film. Tricia is not sure how it happened and hasn't been able to recreate the effect since. The negative was contact printed with a Ziatype sensitizer on Cot 320 paper. The deep blue tonality comes from a high drop count of gold chloride in the sensitizing formula.

(Courtesy of the artist)

Final Wash

Your final wash should last for at least 20 minutes and at this stage in the process your print should appear slightly soft and incomplete in the highlights and mid tones. If it looks perfect, then you are going to be unhappy after the dry-down, as all of the values will likely be about 15% darker.

After washing, do not, under any circumstances, use a screen rack for drying if you are working in a public or workshop darkroom. There is no possible way these screens are uncontaminated. Hang the print on a wire with clothespins and wait until it dries to determine the next step. If you are in a hurry, just blow-dry the print. Following this dry stage, check your notations against

Figure 14–12
Christopher James, *Drivers—Giza, Egypt,* 1992—Ziatype
Drivers, Giza was made with my Diana plastic camera that had been adapted with a Graflex shutter (*the single element plastic lens was glued onto the shutter*) in order to allow me to shoot in low light level situations. The weather was very unusual for Giza: freezing cold and light snow.
(Courtesy of the author)

the prints that have come before, and decide if you have made the right choices. If not, begin the process again knowing that you can alter contrast, color and temperature of the print with a simple change of the proportional drops in the sensitizer.

END THOUGHTS

Art Wax

As with many other alternative processes, except albumen, carbon, and gum bichromate, consider a final application of Dorland's Art Wax to enhance the shadows and to protect the print. Again, all you need to do is lay down your dried print on a hard and flat surface and then, with gentle swirling action, rub a very even and thin layer of Dorland's Art wax over the entire print area. Once that is done, take a hairdryer and begin to gently blow hot air onto the wax-coated area. You will see the wax melt and then dry down to the paper texture.

Too New for Rules

Every POP process is a little different and will change, depending on heat, time of year and day, relative humidity of both your workspace and printing area, and UV source. Like other POP processes, the Ziatype is "self-masking," and its final resolution is linked to exposure and sensitizer formula. The variables are infinite and a creative person can use this chemical flexibility to completely manage the process to suit individual intentions. As its inventor, Dick Sullivan, will readily admit, the work on this process to date may be only the tip of the iceberg. It is, despite its chemical bloodline, a relatively new technique and there may be some wonderful and quirky adaptations waiting in the wings that can be added to the tech notes. Of all the alternative processes I have worked with over the last 30 years, the Ziatype is the most "user-friendly." If you are a newcomer to the alternative process genre, or a teacher of alternative processes, you may want to consider it as one of your first processes.

Paper and Alternative Substrates: History, Considerations, Preparation, & Sizing

OVERVIEW & EXPECTATIONS

This chapter will provide a brief overview of paper including a compressed version of its very interesting history, considerations for its use, and information about a few of its unique attributes that will connect with your future work in alternative processes. I'll begin, as always, with a little history. Then I will continue with a few things that you should know about papers. I'll also deal with specific types of paper that, in my experience, are excellent for making alternative process prints.

The reason that this chapter arrives at this point in the book is that it precedes gum bichromate . . . a process that absolutely requires you to be well versed in the preparation of paper for that process to achieve any degree of success. I'll deal with a menu of considerations for each step and offer you formulas for the most common procedures, including the sizing and hardening variations employing the use of gelatin, formalin, glyoxal, gesso, polyurethane, arrowroot starch, liquid emulsion hardener, and gum arabic–bichromate sizing. I'll also touch upon some considerations for the preparation of single and multi-stage alternative processes in this book.

By the end of this section, you will know when it will be necessary to use these techniques and when it might simply be a redundant step or a waste of time . . . such as in single pass gum in combination with processes like cyanotype, Ziatype, or platinum/palladium. The paper you are using rather than the process you are working in often informs this decision.

Figure 15–1

W. H. Schilling, *Paper*, 1994—gum bichromate

(Courtesy of the artist)

A LITTLE HISTORY

The concept of a flexible and transportable surface (i.e., unlike the Rosetta Stone) upon which to enter harvests, tomb inventory, warships on the horizon, drawings, writing, and other marks has a history that precedes that of the accepted origin of paper in ancient Egypt in the neighborhood of 3000–4000 B.C.E . . . a thousand years after the great Pyramid at Giza was erected. Ironically, there are no examples of this earlier material with writing on it, so the Egyptians get the glory.

The plant first used to make a flexible writing surface is called papyrus, a 10- to 13-foot reed indigenous to the marshes and riverbanks of the Nile River. The transformation of the papyrus reed, into a writing surface, was described by the eminent Roman naturalist Gaius Plinius Secundus (23 A.D.–79 A.D.), affectionately known as Pliny the Elder. In his 37-volume text, *The Natural History (Naturalis Historia),* the first encyclopedia by the way, in Volume XIII (*the section that dealt with aquatic plant life*), Pliny the Elder explained papyrus as a material that was made from the peeled core pith (*approximately 68% cellulose*) of the papyrus reed's stem. This white pulp was soaked in hot water, layered in perpendicular strips, pounded flat, re-layered at right angles to the first layer, re-pounded, and finally dried under a heavy weight.

The theory is that the sugar and natural cell sap (*the arabans and the galactans*) in the plant are the bonding agents that hold the pulverized pulp together. Intentionally adding starch to the pulp mixture, as a step in the making of paper, was not practiced until 300 B.C.E. When the weight was removed, the papyrus was made suitable for writing by polishing it with a smooth stone or by vigorously rubbing it with the heel of one's hand. This rubbing was also how papyrus was erased in times of draught when there was no fresh papyrus to write on. This led to the origin of the word "*palimpsest,*" where the ghosts of previous marks could be seen behind the fresh inscriptions.

The credit for the actual invention of paper is given to Ts'ai Lun, a eunuch and very highly ranked official in the Imperial Court of Emperor Han Ho Ti (*Han Dynasty*) in 105 A.D. According to legend, Ts'ai Lun stripped bark from Mulberry trees, pounded the bark fibers into pulp and formed the pulp into sheets. Later, he greatly improved the quality of his paper by adding sesame fibers and old cloth rags to his mulberry bark pulp mixture. Tsai Lun achieved great wealth and status in the Emperor's court for his paper but unfortunately managed to get himself embroiled in a little palace intrigue that ultimately led to his being ostracized and eventually committing suicide.

The Chinese went on to improve the papermaking process, advancing the technique by using plants such as bamboo (*which they cooked in lye to eliminate the bamboo fibers*) and incorporating sizing and dyes into the pulp in order to make the paper less susceptible to the ravages of time, insects, and weather. China managed to keep Ts'ai Lun's papermaking process a secret for five centuries . . . that is, until several Chinese papermakers were taken hostage (c. 750 A.D.) by the Ottoman Turks. The Chinese papermakers, being quite pragmatic and practical, taught their captors how to make paper in exchange for their heads. Immediately, the Turks adopted the process and established a thriving papermaking industry. In very short time, the practice of papermaking swept through central Asia and the Himalayan regions of Tibet and India. Paper mills were also launched in Baghdad and Damascus.

The exact path of how paper eventually arrived in Europe is a little fuzzy. One of the accepted theories is that the knowledge entered Europe in the 10th century during the Crusades via Spain, on the heels of the Moorish conquests of North Africa and Spain . . . think Alhambra. By 1180, a papermaking mill was operating near Valencia, Italy, and in 1283 the still very operational, and famous, mill in Fabriano, Italy, was established. It was here that major adjustments were made to the manufacturing process and this revolutionized what was to become the "art" of papermaking. The mill workers of Fabriano replaced the traditional mortar and pestle with a water-powered hydraulic hammer for pulverizing linen rags. They also introduced gelatin-glue sizing (*instead of*

Figure 15–2
Pinky Bass, *Cuerpos Santos III (Ivy Brain)*, 1986–2006

Cuerpos Santos III (Ivy Brain) is part of a series using hand-made paper, Van Dyke brown for printing, iconic stamps from Mexico, and embroidery thread. The pieces in this series are 8 × 15 and were made 1986–2006.
(Courtesy of the artist)

starch), which made the paper better able to withstand the rigors of wet immersions and aging. Fabriano also introduced the *watermark* as a sign of the paper's authenticity, and their papers were so highly regarded that they soon became the only choice of drawing paper for artists such as Michelangelo, Brunelleschi, Raphael, and Bodini.

By the late Middle Ages, and into the 15th and 16th centuries, paper was being manufactured and sold throughout Europe. The Reformation, jump started by Martin Luther's *95 Theses on the Power of Indulgences*, in 1517, required an unfathomable amount of paper to write about the new theology. With the spread of

moveable type throughout Europe (*it had actually been available in Asia since 700 CE and in Gutenberg's print shop since 1455*) to publish all of these new ideas, the papermaking industry boomed. Paper merchants became mill owners, and made their presence felt in the evolving publishing industry, as the hard reality of paying for the paper "up front" became the norm.

Technology continued to improve, and by the end of the 16th century, a small mill could turn out 4000 sheets of paper a day. This amazing growth led, of course, to serious supply problems with raw materials such as rags. This, of course, led to government regulations that, true to form, made the problems worse. An effort to find a replacement papermaking material did not succeed until the mid-1800s. Prior to 1853, there was no process for producing pulp, via washing and bleaching in a single operation . . . although the British government had granted a patent to Charles Watt and Hugh Burgess for their improvements in the wood to paper process. Then, in 1854, Marie Amed and Charles Mellier received a patent for the first chemically treated wood pulp . . . the advent of very cheap paper that you do not want to use for your alternative process printmaking.

PAPER TYPES & CONSIDERATIONS

Papers are made using three specific techniques: handmade, cylinder mould-made, and Fourdrinier machine-made. Handmade papers, in the style of Ts'ai Lun, are lovely and esoteric but are generally inadequate substrates for alternative process work due to the inevitable abuses of long water and chemical immersion times. There are exceptions, of course, like Buxton paper from Ruscombe Mill and Fabriano Esportazione, a paper that requires four separate craftsmen to make a single sheet.

Cylinder mould-made paper provided an efficient industrial speed to papermaking with the look, feel, surface, and composition of a handmade paper. Cylinder mould-made paper is drum rolled rather than mould and deckle made, as in the handmade process, and will likely be the type of paper you will use for most of your alternative process work. Mills that produce high-quality cylinder mould-made papers include Fabriano, Arches, Saunders, Somerset, Rives, Whatman, and Cranes. If you are unsure about the paper you are buying, simply ask the proprietor of the art supply or go online and research the paper.

Most machine-made papers are not likely to be of particular interest to you. Wood pulp, whether chemically treated, or unadulterated, lacks the archival quality of mould-made papers made from cotton rag. There are a few machine-made papers that are perfectly adequate for many alternative process endeavors and these are manufactured as acid-free or *"high alpha cellulose"* papers. They are chemically treated to be neutral and contain less of the "lignin" found in most wood pulp papers. This gives the paper a similar integrity to a cotton-based paper. The distinctive difference is the paper's performance when subjected to long immersion times in water. In this situation, cotton-based stock is superior. Mills that make quality machine-made papers, that you can use for drawing and transfer processes, would include some brands of Fabriano, Cotman, Canson, and Strathmore. Again, it is a good idea to ask about the paper's manufacturing process if you do not know it.

When buying paper, you want to know who made it, what manufacturing process was used, the manufacturer's stated purpose or function of the paper, its ream or gram weight, its watermark, its color, its sizing, and its surface texture. There is often a lot of talk about the concept of *"acid-free"* paper. According to accepted standards, this means a paper has a neutral pH of 6.5 to 7.5. Keep in mind that paper that is made acid-free may not be able to stay that way over time. When buying a paper, look for the words "neutral pH" rather than acid-free. Neutral pH implies that the paper is neither too acidic nor too alkaline . . . it is in the middle.

Acid-free paper occasionally has alkaline buffers, like calcium carbonate, to make the paper less acidic. Avoid trying to perform iron-based processes on buffered papers as the buffering sometimes makes the paper too alkaline and reacts with the chemistry, i.e., *taking the pH from a neutral 7 to a pH of 8.5.* My feeling is that the paper will remain in neutral pH state as long as it is well cared for but that extended exposure to lab chemistry, careless handling, or polluted air, will likely affect its status. Then again, perhaps considering all of the chemistry you're about to introduce to your paper, it may not matter if you are overly fussy.

Be aware that paper is also often manufactured with optical brightening agents. These are incorporated into the paper with the explicit purpose of making the paper appear whiter and brighter when it is for sale on the shelf. These optical brighteners wear out and eventually the paper goes back to being what it was in the first place. There is evidence that optical brighteners actually make the paper a bit dull looking once the brighteners lose their effectiveness. You'll know if there are optical brighteners in your paper because it will glow like a shimmering blue-white Hollywood-like alien when placed under a UV light source.

By and large, your choice of paper will depend on
your intentions and the process that you are using it
for. Surface is an important consideration. Platinum/
palladium, Ziatype, and the Kallitypes, for instance,
look best to me when the technique is performed on a
hot-press paper in which the surface has been made
smooth with a hot rollers during manufacturing. If you
were doing gum prints, you might look for a paper that
had more *ream* weight (*the weight of 500 sheets*),
meaning that it might be a 300 lb. paper versus a 90 lb.
paper that you would use for salted paper printing. If
you were going to really abuse your paper with many
hand techniques, you might even consider one of my
favorites, a super-heavy paper such as Arches 1200 lb.
CP that comes in 40" × 60" sheets. Again, all of your
decisions should be based on what would be best for the
translation of your intentions and your individual taste.

With few exceptions, those being alternative substrates such as glass, tin, steel, plastic, toast . . . the one
basic fact of alternative process life is that to make a
print it is necessary to lay down a sensitizer, or sensitized
colloid emulsion, on a piece of paper. This is nice
because it is romantic and a pleasant exercise to prepare
and hand coat your own paper. The downside of this
experience is that it is absolutely necessary to remove
any unused residual chemistry from the paper's fibers at
the conclusion of the process or your efforts will have
been in vain as the print will fade and yellow. The other
problem is that the sensitizer might not get deep enough
into the paper's fibers. In this scenario, the print will disappear right before your eyes as you process it.

Most of the time, alternative processes involve the
sensitizer being applied directly to the paper. The exceptions are those processes, such as carbon that employs a

Figure 15–4

Susan Arena, *Midnight at Giza*, 1988—emulsion and oil paint

World adventurer, artist and, mom, Susan Arena made this piece as part of a portfolio while a student of mine at Harvard. It was the beginning of her dedication to painting, an art form she has taught at Yale and practiced since.

(Courtesy of the artist)

tissue transfer to a paper support, or gum bichromate, where it is necessary to prepare your paper with a hardened or sized gelatin emulsion in order to keep the dichromate sensitized pigment from penetrating your paper's fibers. In this situation, the sensitizer rests on the hardened gelatin layer that has been bonded to the paper substrate. We'll be getting to this shortly.

The paper you select should be compatible with the process you are performing. In other words, if you are making a gum bichromate print, you will not likely be selecting a delicate rice paper to perform it on as the process will require repeated long soaking and wash-out times and your paper will simply not be up to the task of staying in one piece even with sizing. You will also want a paper that is acid-neutral (6.5–7.5) and can be categorized as archival. You will hope for a paper without additives, except for a bit of internal sizing to enhance wet strength, and to allow for a smoother application of sensitizer when not using a surfacant, such as Tween 20, in your sensitizer. All other consideration, such as surface, texture, and color, are subjective choices.

Iron-based processes, such as cyanotype and Van Dyke (*they employ ammonium iron(III) citrate*) generally have a problem penetrating the fibers of paper they are coated on, and often sit on the paper's surface in the form of crystals. When this happens, the image always looks great prior to processing and then, because the sensitizer has not been able to penetrate the paper, the image drops out of the paper and goes down the drain. These processes would benefit from Tween in their sensitizers and you would benefit by making a different choice of paper.

Processes that use ammonium iron(III) oxalate, such as new cyanotype, Chrysotype, Ware-Malde Pt/Pd, and Ziatype, have much less difficulty in penetrating paper fibers and this makes the use of an additive such as Tween unnecessary most of the time. The downside of this is that often the sensitizer may go too deeply into the paper's fibers and the resulting print ends up looking washed out.

The happy medium is a paper that allows the ammonium iron(III) citrate processes to penetrate and the ammonium iron(III) oxalate to sit up and not penetrate too deeply . . . that has the other features essential to alternative process printing. Not many papers are able to do all of these tasks equally well. Here are a few papers that I personally like to use and that satisfy many who work in the alternative process genre.

RECOMMENDED PAPERS

Bergger's Cot 320

Bergger's Cot 320 is my personal favorite paper. There isn't a single quality that I do not like about this paper. It does require a drop of Tween in the sensitizer for several processes but this hasn't caused any problems for me. Cot 320 is 100% cotton rag and has a luxurious finish, and weight. It survives well in a tray of water, dries reasonably flat and doesn't "pill" easily if your coating technique is a little rough. It is expensive (like Buxton) but if you can afford to give yourself an art-treat, the experience working with it is well worth the expense.

I order Cot 320 for all of my classes and workshops and use it for personal work the majority of the time. I especially like Cot 320 for albumen, salted paper, Ziatype and Ziatype on salted gelatin paper. I will be doing extensive testing with it this year as a carbon transfer support following multiple coatings of gelatin and glyoxal sizing and hardening . . . go to my web site for details and updates.

Buxton/Ruscombe Mills

This paper is the most frequently mentioned as a favorite by my alt pro friends and deserves all of its praise and following. The Ruscombe Mill paper makers, originally in Gloucestershire, England, but now relocated to Margaux, France, are renowned for their excellent attention to detail and for producing a paper called Buxton that is perfect for a variety of alternative process printing. In 1992 Mike Ware, and Ruscombe Mills' Chris Bingham, collaborated on an idea to produce a handmade paper that would be ideal for the iron based process research that Mike was so heavily involved in. After a great deal of testing they arrived at the type that is now called Buxton whose primary attributes included: 100% cotton alpha cellulose, wove laid (*no watermark*), internally sized with *Aquapel* for superb wet strength, no chalk alkaline buffer, natural white and no brighteners, no additives of any kind, and a neutral pH of 7.5 . . . essentially the perfect paper. There is also a gelatin-sized version of this paper called Talbot that is particularly well suited for gold processes such as Chrysotype and the very fussy calotype process. Buxton also performs well with single coat gum bichromate applications which would make it an ideal paper to use if you were performing a platinum/palladium print and wanted to do a single pass gum on top, *without* having to size the paper, to intensify shadow details or add a tint.

Arches Platine

This paper was designed specifically for platinum printing. I personally like the smooth finish and color of this 100% rag, neutral pH, paper, and the fact that it has no buffers (*alkaline reserves*) or optical brightening agents and it coats very easily. It is, indeed, quite an excellent paper for platinum/palladium and Ziatype, fair for cyanotype and Van Dyke but not, interestingly, a particularly a good choice for Argyrotype. This paper looks great with albumen but will dry a bit yellow in high heat or humidity. Basically, I wouldn't recommend it for albumen. Arches Platine has decent wet strength, but I have found it not the best choice in a group situation as its surface is often compromised by a lot of movement and handling in the washing trays. Arches Platine paper is made by the Arjomari-Prioux Mill (*they also make*

Rives) in France. If you want to see a really nice effect, gelatin size this paper with salted paper gelatin sizing #1 and do Ziatypes on it.

Crane's Platinotype

I've been using Crane's Platinotype for years in workshop and class situations as it is durable, compatible with most processes, has terrific wet strength, doesn't require Tween (except for Argyrotype or Ziatype at altitude), has a great finish, and a nice overall color. It clears well and is manufactured with a neutral pH. It is also affordable, and for a student this is extremely important. It has always been a great paper at a reasonable price.

In the past year (2007), though, Platinotype has been very inconsistent in quality and more than a few of the paper sellers that I trust have stopped ordering this paper until Crane can correct their inconsistencies. These problems show up as small black spots in the paper during processing and unevenness in the sizing. I have also noticed that the paper does not work as well for iron-based processes as it once did. Hopefully, this is a temporary problem and this excellent paper will be back in the marketplace by the time that this book comes out. In the meantime, I would recommend an alternative such as Cot 320 or Buxton . . . if you can afford it.

Lanaquarelle

Since 1590, the Lana mill has producing fine art papers for artists in all disciplines. Lanaquarelle is made on a cylinder mould machine, giving it the look and feel of a handmade paper. This 100% cotton paper is perfect for gum bichromate printing at 140 lb & 300 lb hot or cold press and in workshops and class situations, this is the paper I always demo gum bichromate with. It is a mould-made, neutral pH, 100% rag; calcium carbonate buffered (*to make it slightly alkaline*) paper and is colored natural white or buff. Lanaquarelle is a great paper for long soaking processes such as gum but I avoid it for cyanotype due to the calcium carbonate buffering which tends to have a slight bleaching effect in the manner of sodium carbonate.

Arches Aquarelle

This is a nice paper for an iron print—gum bichromate combination printing. Try a gelatin-glyoxal single step sizing process after the cyanotype is completed. Sized properly, Arches Aquarelle is an excellent choice for gum bichromate printing.

Arches 88 Silk Screen Paper

Mould-made in France, this clear, white paper is recommended for screen-printing and intaglio presswork. Arches 88 is a heavyweight (140 lb) 100% cotton fiber paper, it's acid-free, neutral pH, buffered, and is un-sized for high absorption. This paper, like Somerset Satin, has been reported to be quite excellent as a substrate for albumen printing.

Somerset Satin

Somerset Satin is a 100% cotton, pH neutral, mould-made paper that is a favorite of albumen printers. It is made in England by St. Cuthberts Mill, is both internal and surface sized, and has 2 natural deckles. Somerset is known for its excellent quality for printmaking. The paper is ideal for drawing, charcoal, pastel as well as digital applications.

Lana Royal White/Lana Royal Crown

Lana Royal Crown is made by the Lana Mill in France and is a mould-made, 100% cotton, neutral pH, alkaline-buffered paper with 2 deckle edges and a smooth surface. Many like it for the Kallitype process.

Weston Diploma Parchment

Weston Diploma Parchment is produced by the Byron Weston Paper Co. (a division of Crane Paper) in Boylston, MA. The paper is warm-white 100% rag denim, 177 gsm,* no brighteners, no buffering, is rosin alum sized, and has a pH in the good neighborhood of 5.5 to 7.5. It has also been manufactured for more than 50 years so the track record is strong. As well, it appears that this paper is excellent for several processes such as Pt/Pd, cyanotype, and Kallitype. It does not perform well on the notoriously fussy Argyrotype.

---

* The weight of metric paper is given in grams per square meter (gsm). One square meter is one A0 (34" × 44") size sheet or 16 A4 (8.5" × 11") size sheets. In the United States, paper is given in pounds per 500-sheet ream of uncut C (17" × 22") size paper. Note that each type of paper has a different "base size," so 200 gsm of one paper will give a different Lbs/ream equivalent than another.

Diploma Parchment clears very quickly and the incidence of black spotting with salt and albumen is reportedly almost non-existent. It has a very smooth surface on the "felt" side, which is retained even after extensive wet processing—unlike some heavily calendered commercial papers. The processed sheet dries satisfyingly flat without cockling or curling, and there is no need for pressing. Weston Diploma Parchment paper coats easily and economically with all my sensitizer solutions using either the rod-coating or hake brush methods. The specific coating volume needed is about 22 ml. per square meter. The paper is well sized, has a nice hand and is sufficiently absorptive to not require the addition of any surfactant (e.g. Tween 20) or wetting agent to the sensitizer solutions. One caveat: It is very fragile after extended soaking but will hold up well if you're gentle with it. If you're interested in a sample, at no charge, the contact is John Zokowski, jzokowski@butlerdearden.com, who you will find most helpful.

Rives BFK

This is a pretty nice paper but, in my experience, it has not held up well in long soaking situations. Like the Arches papers, Rives is also made in the Arjomari-Prioux Mill in France. It is a mould-made, 85% cotton, 15% linen, internally sized, acid-free and buffered paper without optical brightening agents. This is a traditional intaglio printmaking paper and is unbeatable on a flatbed press. I would not recommend it for long wet time processes, but it humidifies evenly and well.

Cranes AS 8111

This is an expensive, lightweight, kid finish, stationary and I like it as a base for calotypes. Be careful when it is wet . . . although the wet strength is good, it is not great.

Fabriano Artistico

From the famous, and ancient, Fabriano Mills (1283), this 100% rag, neutral pH, and gelatin sized, paper is one of the most beautiful made. It comes in both hot and cold process but is rather thick and requires a lot of sensitizer for a good coating. I like this paper sized as a gum bichromate printing stock and also for any combination process where I intend to do a lot of post-print work and montage-collage work. You might also want to try gum printing on the less expensive, but also acid free, **Fabriano 5,** which is 50% pulp and 50% rag. Also, **Fabriano Perusia** is a paper that is traditionally recommended for gum bichromate printing.

Hahnemühle Photo rag ink-jet paper

This is the paper that I use personally for almost all of my carbon-based ink-jet printing. It is, in my opinion, the best ink-jet paper made in the world. It is also a great paper to use for salted paper printing, gum on ink-jet, and Pt/Pd on ink-jet.

Kozo

This rice paper is made from mulberries and is a delicate and translucent paper with extraordinary wet strength . . . you can literally wring the water out of it and lay it flat. This paper has no added buffers or brighteners. Kozo is fairly white to begin with and the papers are not bleached . . . except sometimes with sunlight, so it isn't acidic from the processing. The main reason for buffers is that the bleaching process to whiten cotton or wood pulp generates a lot of acids and they destroy the paper later on. Kozo and Gampi are also very low in lignin content and the fibers they use are far stronger and longer than western papers. There are Kozo scrolls in Japan which are 800+ years old, and the scrolls still roll/unroll without cracking or falling apart. The thicker paper even mixes in that abaca/Manila hemp fiber which is generally considered the strongest natural fiber in common usage. Use it for processes that can perform well on thin papers with short immersion times such as Pt/Pd, Ziatype, and salted paper.

Stonehenge HP 90 lb

Stonehenge 90 lb has received rave reviews for its ability to work well with Van Dyke . . . specifically due to the deeply rich sepia tonalities and the extra contrast it seems to bring to the technique without use of a ferric citrate contrast control. Many papers are not suitable for VDB but both Stonehenge and **Arches 90 lb** hot press watercolor, which is heavily sized during manufacturing, keep the sensitizer on the surface, preventing it from sinking too deeply into the paper's fibers.

Figure 15–5

Stephen Livick, *Kali Mural #530*, 1991—gum bichromate

This is a great example of the scale and quality of Stephen Livick's gum bichromate murals. This is Mural No. 530, 1991, Edition of 3, Full Color Gum, 240cm × 300cm (95" × 115").

(Courtesy of the artist)

Strathmore Bristol

Very smooth surface—tends to break down in long wet immersions due to the layering that is standard in Bristol manufacturing.

Bienfang 360

Bienfang 360 is a specially formulated graphic arts paper made to accept felt nib markers with heavy coverage without bleeding through to the next sheet. Colors flow smoothly yet hold sharp edges. Bienfang #360 has the attributes of vellum and is a beautiful paper to work with

if you can deal with the wrinkles at the conclusion of the process. It is a paper with excellent translucency and you can purchase it in blocks.

Atlantis Silversafe

Atlantis Silversafe is highly recommended for Platinum/Palladium and Argyrotype. It is 100% cotton, free of calcium carbonate buffering, and weighs in at a healthy 200 grams. Originally developed as archiving separation sheets in museums, the paper has a lot of fans.

SIZING PAPER

The majority of cylinder mould-made papers can be purchased with internal sizing—where alum-rosin, or Aquapel, is integrated into the pulp. External sizing—usually gelatin is where the sizing is applied to the paper's surface, or combinations of the two. Paper is sized in order to provide it with a little more integrity and wet strength in long water baths and in order to bond the fibers of the paper. As well, it is intended to prevent inks and paints from penetrating too deeply. Papers that are not sized are referred to as "water-leaf" papers and are mostly unsuitable for alternative process work unless you decide to size the paper yourself. Papers can be sized with a variety of pH neutral sizing agents and some of these are gelatin and starch. Just for your information, be cautious about using papers that are heavily sized in manufacturing when you are doing platinum printing as the platinum(II) binds to the gelatin, and this makes the reduction to metallic platinum more difficult than it needs to be.

A paper that does not deal well with extended immersion times should be sized and hardened to prevent a loss of the paper's integrity and/or to avoid highlight staining. Some customized handmade papers and rice papers are examples of fragile paper that will probably not hold up well with repeated immersions in water. If you are working with a process in which the sensitizer becomes one with the paper, as it does in cyanotype, Van Dyke, and Kallitype, you may wish to add an initial gelatin sizing and hardening step for the purpose of improving the highlight and shadow clarity. If you are using a colloid/chromate process, such as gum bichromate or Dusting-On, then you will most certainly want to size and harden so the chemistry and pigment remain on a layer above the actual paper. Basically, if you plan to do any of the following things you should consider preparing your paper with one of the sizing and hardening recommendations that follow.

- If you intend to employ mix media techniques, or work in two or more alternative processes on the same paper and extended or multiple washing stages are going to be involved.

- If you intend to register negative(s) for multiple applications of color or impressions, as you would in a straight gum bichromate process, or when using the gum technique to enhance shadow density in a different process with more than a single, or short time, pass.

- If you intend to work with customized or handmade papers that are fragile. When working with an unknown paper, it is a good idea to purchase a sheet and immerse it in water to see how it will hold up. There is little point in investing time, chemistry, and money in a paper that cannot survive the coating and washing adventures.

- If you intend to use liquid, hand-applied, photo-sensitive, emulsions on paper, you have an option to gelatin size, or produce a gum/dichromate hardened layer, in order to keep your highlights clean. Another option is to use a product like Maco's Black Magic VC Liquid Hardener. Adding this hardener to your paper developer will greatly improve the paper's ability to deal with the exposed and developed liquid emulsion.

Following these guidelines will help you develop a technique that can satisfy your intentions without the aesthetic confusion of stained and muddy highlights, blocked-up shadow details, and out-of-registered images. Please note that the purpose of this chapter is not to lay down dogma. There are artists who have defined a personal working system in which these steps are omitted, ignored, or modified. Examples of their work often prove their point but, for the most part, following these sizing steps will make the gum bichromate process, in particular, far less frustrating for the beginning alternative process artist.

SHRINKING

Quality, 100% rag, printmaking and watercolor papers will change dimensionally after being wet. These papers are made of cotton rag fiber; so like a pair of jeans, they shrink after washing. If you intend to make two separate impressions on a single piece of paper, as in gum bichromate printing, or if you are combining gum with another process, or combining two or more processes, it is necessary to shrink you paper first. If you don't, then registration will be difficult.

Figure 15–6

Judy Seigel, _Lunchtime Nap_, NYC—gum, paint & varnish

Without a doubt, Judy Seigel is one of the leaders of the alternative process renaissance that is taking place in schools and artists' studios around the world. Judy is a teacher and the founder/editor of _The World Journal of Post-Factory Photography_ a warrior in the alt process newsgroup circuit, and the best line editor in the business. _(Courtesy of the artist)_

Shrinking your paper is a simple process of hot water immersion and drying in order to tighten up the cotton fibers. Fill a tray with hot water, 120°F to 140°F, and soak your paper for 20–30 minutes. Be sure that each sheet is completely saturated by gently shuffling through the sheets. Pull the sheets from the tray one at a time and hang them with clothespins on a secure line until they are dry. Be careful when handling the paper because the fibers will be fragile.

PAPER PREPARATION FOR GUM BICHROMATE

There are a few ways to go here. The simplest and most effective way to size and harden your paper is to use a mono-bath method in which gelatin and glyoxal (_sizing and hardening_) are combined and used simultaneously. This method works well and I have found it quite satisfactory and easy to do. The technique makes it an excellent single-stage option in a class or workshop situation where space and time are considerations. The only other consideration that you will want to keep in mind is whether you single or double coat your paper. This will be decided based on how thick and absorbent your paper is and whether or not it has a manufacturer-integrated sizing such as Aquapel in it already.

You can also consider the traditional two-stage sizing and hardening technique, which has been used by gummists for ages. Hardening a gelatin emulsion, with formalin or glyoxal, after the gelatin has been applied to the paper, will help in some single-pass alternative processes where you might be experiencing dull, or flat, imagery due to the paper absorbing too much of the sensitizer. The process we will be focusing on here is gum bichromate. There are several traditional sizing and hardening methods in this section for you to try. Some are, in my experience, more effective than others, and I'll be clarifying those techniques in a minute. Although I have included the formalin (*formaldehyde*) hardening instructions, I am recommending that you consider glyoxal as an alternative due to the toxicity of formalin.

The caveat on the glyoxal MSDS data sheet indicates that insufficient testing has been done with glyoxal, making it difficult to determine if it is actually less toxic than formalin. (It is less volatile, however, so you will absorb less of it.) The possibility that glyoxal is less dangerous does not excuse you from wearing gloves and a dual-filter respirator when working with it. I make this point because the fumes from the glyoxal are less acute than those of formalin and that fact may cause you to let your guard down . . . don't. Glyoxal is, however, easier to buy in this age of *Homeland Insecurity*. In that regard, I have included two variations, a single and a multiple-step version of the glyoxal hardening formula.

I strongly recommend that you do not work indoors with formalin or glyoxal unless you have a lab designed with an excellent in-flow to out-flow ratio of air probably on the order of 5:1. A casual attitude about liquids that can mummify dead things is unwise. *See Appendix F, the Appendix for vendors of formalin and glyoxal.*

GELATIN SIZING & HARDENING PROCESSES

Table Set Up for Glyoxal—Gelatin Single Coat Sizing Process

- 28 g Knox gelatin (4 seven-gram packets per box)
- Baking Soda (1/2 teaspoon)
- 1-liter cold distilled water
- Electric kettle to heat water to 140°F
- 1 large and very clean tray (for hot water)
- 1 smaller tray—paper size (for sizing solution)
- Pencil for marking paper
- 2"–3" foam brushes
- Beaker with water for brush cleaning
- Paper towels
- Clothesline and clothespins
- Paper (Lana Aquarelle is excellent)
- Zipper-top bag (freezer type) for storage after drying
- 40% glyoxal

Gelatin Sizing

The first stage of a sizing and hardening process involves coating your paper with a plain unflavored gelatin. This step will prepare the paper for the glyoxal, formalin, or chrome alum hardening step. In a single stage, monobath, variation, both the sizing and hardening stages are done at the same time.

In my watercolor painting, I always pre-coat my watercolor paper with a gum Arabic and water wash solution. The gum Arabic creates a barrier between paper and paint that can only be compromised with excess water. This technique protects the paper's whites from one or two invasions of painting with a wet brush and allows me to re-enter the dry painting and open up highlight details. In alternative processes, gelatin sizing performs this same task . . . protecting the paper from pigment and multiple water exposures; this makes it easier to keep the highlights clean and the shadows detail-defined.

Gelatin: Photo or Food Grade

You need a good quality gelatin with a "bloom" value between 200 and 250. Bloom value is the measure of the gelatin's strength or firmness. The best grade of gelatin is referred to as a photographic grade and that can be purchased at any decent photographic or chemical supply. Bostick & Sullivan sells a photographic grade gelatin with a bloom value of 250.

A simpler option is to go to the market and buy a box of Knox (or some other version) unflavored gelatin (28 grams) that generally is sold in a pack of four or more envelopes containing 7 g each. Do not buy Jell-O®, even though it might work. Knox gelatin tends to be a little soft, bloom value wise, but is perfectly suitable for learning the process.

While you're at the market, buy a few gallons of distilled water. You will also need a pot and a hotplate to heat up the water-gelatin mix, a tray for the paper and solution, and a clothesline to hang the paper to dry. You may find it necessary to have a glass rod or a squeegee to pass over the gelatinized paper after it comes out of the tray to eliminate air bubbles. If this is so, you will also need a clean and flat surface to squeegee on.

THE GELATIN SIZING: STAGE # 1

Step #1—The Bloom

Begin by adding four 7 g envelopes of gelatin (28 g) to about 300 ml of *cold* distilled water. The total volume, when mixed, will be 1 liter (1000 ml). Stir the solution gently to avoid creating bubbles and then let it "*bloom*" (*swell up*) for about 20 minutes. For smaller batches of sizing simply proportion the gelatin and water to make the amount that you need, i.e., 7 g of gelatin to 250 ml of distilled water.

Step #2—Heating the Gelatin

Add the rest of your water and slowly heat the water and gelatin solution, stirring gently, until the temperature reaches approximately 100°F. Then, pour your heated gelatin solution into a warmed tray that is large enough to accommodate

Figure 15–7

Christopher James, *Irezumi #2*, 1986—watercolor, gum, chine-collé, & carbon
This painting is an example of my work in which I begin the piece by laying down multiple layers of gum Arabic in order to change the way paint sets up on the surface of the paper.
(Courtesy of the author)

your paper. If you can't afford, or find, a large enough tray, then try using a Pyrex lasagna tray or a wallpaper paste trough and hand rolling your paper through the sizing. These troughs are available at a local hardware or paint store and are also excellent for processing RC mural paper. While the solution is still hot, immerse your paper in the warmed gelatin solution be sure that it is completely covered.

Note: If it is cold in your workspace, take a tray that is larger than the one your gelatin and paper will be using and fill it half way with very hot water. Then float your gelatin paper tray in it and this will keep your gelatin warm and liquid during the coating.

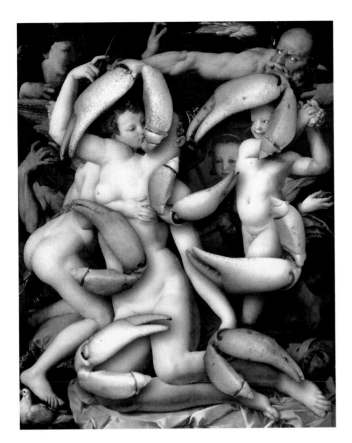

Figure 15–8

Doug Prince, *Construction-014—2003*

The process of creating images is quite similar in both Doug's photo-sculptures and digital constructions. The most obvious difference is that one is black & white and 3-D on film while the other is 2-D digital in color. In Doug's recent work, the worldwide web offers a limitless resource of imagery generated from all of the world's peoples. As an appropriator of this trove, Doug uses the monitor of his computer in much the same way he used to use the viewfinder in his camera.

(Courtesy of the artist)

Step #3/Hang to Dry

After the paper is saturated, drag it slowly over the edge of the tray, being sure to eliminate any air bubbles that have formed. One technique I have used is to lay the paper on a clean sheet of Plexiglas® (*larger than the paper*) and drag a glass rod, or rubber squeegee over the surface. This drives the sizing into the paper's fibers and also leaves a drip-free piece of paper. You can use a windshield wiper blade for this purpose in a pinch. Size as quickly as you can, because the gelatin becomes increasingly difficult to work with as it cools. Gelatin will also go bad and has a dis gusting smell after a few days, so coat as many paper sheets as you intend to use.

Hang the sheets to dry on a clothesline. After the gelatin-sized sheets have dried, it will be time to work with the chemicals that harden the gelatin that you have just applied. Remember, if you are only going to make a single pass on this paper, the hardening stage may be unnecessary. Be aware though that in the gum process, un-hardened gelatin sizing will often stain more easily than hardened gelatin.

Brush Coating Gelatin Sizing: An Alternative Technique

I generally encourage immersion in gelatin simply because of the importance of keeping the gelatin in a warm state during the process. However, this does have a downside, as over-saturated gelatin areas occasionally makes it difficult for the gum emulsion to adhere to the prepared paper. A more economical technique is to keep your gelatin in a warm condition and quickly brush coat, with a foam brush, your solution on the side of the paper you intend to make your print on. You may have to coat twice when using thick and porous papers but it is not complicated and the paper dries quickly. If you are going to make multiple passes, be sure to shrink and dry your paper before brush sizing.

GELATIN HARDENING WITH GLYOXAL: STAGE #2

The Glyoxal Option

To ensure that you have the best surface to work on, it is necessary to harden your gelatin, and there are a few options for you to consider. Glyoxal and formalin produce similar results and play the same role. Most importantly, they must be treated with equal respect. Glyoxal is the hardener that I use personally and the one that I teach with. If you prefer, you may follow the coating instructions for the formalin Stage #2 variation that follows. Here are a few important things for you to know about using this chemical.

Working Glyoxal Solution

To make a working glyoxal hardening solution: add 15 ml of a prepared 40% glyoxal solution to every 1000 ml of distilled water. You may make smaller total volumes by proportioning the amounts of glyoxal and distilled water to suit your working needs. A 40% glyoxal solution can be purchased through Bostick & Sullivan, Photographers Formulary, Artcraft, and several of the other chemical suppliers that are listed in Appendix F.

Glyoxal and Bicarbonate of Soda

Mix the glyoxal and water solution in an extremely well ventilated space . . . preferably outdoors. To this prepared glyoxal solution, add 1/2 teaspoon of baking soda (*bicarbonate of soda/sodium bicarbonate*) per liter of solution. This sodium bicarbonate addition makes the bath more alkaline, which helps to strengthen the bond between the sizing and hardener. This additive can also be added to the formalin solution to perform the same function. If you intend to save the glyoxal beyond a single day you should add 10 ml of methyl alcohol to it. This will keep it viable for a few extra days. Formalin, on the other hand, will keep indefinitely.

Again, be aware that there has not been enough testing of this chemistry to know whether glyoxal is actually safer or more toxic than formalin. One thing for sure: formalin or glyoxal hardened paper, even after drying outdoors, will continue to *outgas*. This will cause unpleasant things to happen to your eyes, nose, and throat and you should be aware of this when storing the paper. Try your best to dry the recently sized and hardened paper in a well-ventilated space or outdoors.

Immersion Technique in Glyoxal

Immerse your gelatinized paper in a tray of glyoxal hardening solution for 5 minutes. A sufficient time for you to be able to give it a nice rinse afterwards without undoing the act of hardening. At the same time, the rinse will reduce the possibility of your paper yellowing later on. If you choose the brush coat hardening option your hardening time will obviously be shorter than 5 minutes. This shorter time will not require a rinse following the hardener but you will not be able to store the hardened paper for a long time without yellowing.

Rinsing After Glyoxal Hardening To Prevent Yellow Staining

If you harden your paper in an immersion bath of glyoxal for 5 minutes the next step is a good rinse. After the glyoxal is allowed to permeate the sized paper completely, it should be rinsed for a few minutes in a fresh, cool, water bath before it is hung to dry on a line. This removes excess glyoxal from the surface of the paper. If you forego this step, the paper may turn a little butterscotch-beige in the highlights down the road . . . sometimes even before you use the paper. Rinsing permits you to store the paper for future use.

GELATIN HARDENING OPTION: STAGE #2
The Formalin Option

Formalin sizing works well as a sizing-hardening agent and was once the only sizing choice for serious gum bichromate printers. Formalin and formaldehyde are interchangeable in this context. Formaldehyde (HCHO) is a colorless, flammable, poisonous gas with a stifling odor. Although formaldehyde is a term applied to many hardening instructions in alternative texts, pure gaseous formaldehyde is uncommon because it readily polymerizes into solid para-formaldehyde.

Formalin, a 37%, by weight, solution of formaldehyde in water (*with 15% methyl alcohol*) is commonly used as an antiseptic, disinfectant, preservative for biological specimens, and as one of the hardening agents for gelatin in this section.

Working Formalin Solution

To make the formalin hardening solution, you will need to add 25 ml of formalin to 1000 ml of distilled water. You may make proportionately smaller total volumes if your needs do not call for 1000 ml of solution.

Set up your trays outdoors, where it will be a sane idea to stand with the wind at your back, and prepare the formalin solution. Wear Nitrile or latex gloves and a good dual-filtered respirator. Then set up a clothesline for

Figure 15–9
Judy Seigel, *Probably Viollet-le-Duc*, 2003
He was the 19th c. French architect of gorgeous chateaux, which the NY Times Building on 43rd Street features in NYC. Here is one version of each inside a scribble turned into a negative as "frame." Three gum coats, plus solvent transfer (flower).
(Courtesy of the artist)

hanging the hardened paper and take your dry gelatin-coated paper and immerse the sheets, one at a time, in the formalin solution. Add other dry gelatin-coated sheets to the tray and shuffle them gently, from bottom to top, until they are completely coated. Carefully remove the sheets and hang each on the clothesline to dry.

There are no safety shortcuts here. Do not take chances with formalin. There is a reason it was the primary chemical used by morticians to embalm bodies and why every frog you ever dissected in high school was in a bottle filled with it. Don't even begin to think about the fact that your nose was inches away from that formalin-preserved frog, indoors, during all of those biology labs. Remember please, chemistry that can preserve dead frogs is probably not healthy for the living tissue. Of course, you can argue that food preservatives perform a similar task, but that is a different book.

Clean up by pouring any leftover formalin hardening solution into a labeled glass jar and tape it shut. Be sure to store the jar in a place that cannot be reached by small children. This working solution will, obviously, keep indefinitely. The alternative to formaldehyde is glyoxal. Following are instructions for using glyoxal following the gelatin sizing.

GLYOXAL—GELATIN SINGLE COATING OPTION

For quite a long time, I have been using a single-stage gelatin and glyoxal-sizing technique. It works reasonably well and is a fine alternative to multi-stage sizing if you are only going to be doing a gum bichromate pass, or two, or adding a gum pass to an existing print done in another process. In this sizing and hardening procedure, the glyoxal is added to the prepared warm gelatin and the paper is immersed and hung to dry. If you wish, and are in a particular hurry, you can simply coat the solution on the paper with a foam brush in a single step and hang it up to dry. In both of these scenarios you should rotate the solution laden papers every minute or so until the gelatin begins to set up. This prevents the gelatin from building up too heavily in the lower end of the paper. Here's the technique.

Step 1 Weigh out and mix 6.5 g of gelatin into 250 ml of distilled water and let the solution sit and bloom quietly for about 15–20 minutes. It is easier to make a larger volume of solution if you intend to coat a lot of paper. Keep your proportions the same, i.e., 250 ml water, 6.5 g gelatin, 15 ml glyoxal.

Step 2 After this "blooming" period, slowly bring the solution to a temperature of 140°F, but *do not let it get hot enough to boil*. I prefer to prepare the solution in a plastic beaker, which is placed in a pot of hot water. In this manner, I can better control the temperature and a beaker's shape allows me to stir the solution with more efficiency.

Step 3 When the solution has warmed, add 15 ml of the prepared 40% glyoxal to it and stir easily until it is in solution. This all-in-one solution can then be employed via an immersion technique or by coating with a foam brush. When brush coating this solution, be quite careful to go lightly with the brush so as not to disturb the surface of the paper. A single coating will be sufficient. Personally, I prefer the immersion technique.

Step 4 This step is quite important. Be sure to rinse the paper in a bath of cool fresh water after an immersion technique. If you're brush coating, the rinse is unnecessary. Hang the paper to dry and flip it over after 1 minute to prevent buildup of the gelatin on one edge.

ALTERNATIVE STAGE #1 SIZING OPTIONS

Going backwards for a minute, there are a few Stage #1 sizing options and methods that you can use in place of gelatin. These include Arrowroot, Chrome Alum, Acrylic-Gesso, and others.

Old Dickie's Instant Sizing

This procedure is courtesy of Dick Sullivan. Take a sheet of 1/4" plate glass that is larger than your paper to be sized and place it on a flat surface in a horizontal format. Gather your materials: the prepared gelatin sizing, your paper, a glass rod or a Puddle-Pusher, a turkey baster, tape, and a car window wiper or squeegee. Be careful when using the wiper or squeegee to avoid roughing up the surface of the paper. Then, take the paper that you intend to size and tape it securely to the glass along the edges.

Now, partially fill your turkey baster with the gelatin. Take your glass rod and place it flat on the paper. Squirt the gelatin solution along the bottom edge of the rod and drag, as in a rod coating technique, the gelatin across the paper's surface. Quickly take the car window wiper and gently squeegee-dry the paper. Drying is instantaneous and coated papers can be stacked immediately, allowing your workflow to be more efficient.

Arrowroot Sizing

Arrowroot starch is a sizing option that is generally recommended by manufacturers of alternative process materials. Using arrowroot prevents liability problems and is really safe to use. Arrowroot sizing is smoderately effective and is best used in a lower grade level teaching situation where liability, health concerns, or student maturity might be an issue. Think about it: What type of cookie is the first one that an infant gets to gnaw on with its gums? That's right—arrowroot cookies.

To make a solution, place 20 g of arrowroot starch in a cooking pot and add a small amount of hot distilled water. Stir this concoction until you have a paste. Then add 1000 ml of distilled water and stir it into the

Figure 15–10
Christopher James, *Ocean #13*, 1997
(Courtesy of the author)

solution. Put the pot on low to medium heat. Stirring constantly, bring the solution to a low boil for 5 minutes. Allow it to cool to room temperature and store it in a Tupperware -type container. This solution will spoil in a fairly short time, so use it within 24 hours of making it. It is applied to the paper by dunking, brushing, or squeegee, and the papers are line dried.

Gesso-Gelatin Sizing: RG-4A Gesso— Gelatin Sizing

This sizing option comes from Judy Siegel's *The World Journal of Post Factory Photography*, which is sadly no longer in publication. The sizing is called Bernie's Gesso-Gelatin Size and is the invention of Bernie

Boudreau, *"gum printer to the stars."* There are several variations of this sizing and I'll pass along the one that seems to be most universal.

To make this size, add 1 part thick Gesso (Gesso gets thicker with age) to 3 parts 3% Knox gelatin. If your Gesso is fairly new and too fluid, increase the gelatin to 3.5%—4% concentration.

Judy wrote that her best results came with this RG-4A Gesso-Gelatin formula sizing, a gum emulsion of equal parts gum Arabic and ammonium dichromate, and carmine red, viridian green, and Phthalo blue colors.

Gesso—Acrylic Medium Sizing

This is a pretty good formula for preparing more porous materials, such as artist's canvas or linens. In a plastic container, combine equal parts of white gesso, acrylic gloss medium, and water. Stir these ingredients into a smooth solution and coat your papers with a brush. Some artists who employ this sizing technique often apply a new coat between each gum bichromate color application and I have had good results with this sizing technique when making black gum bichromate images on canvas. This particular sizing technique does not seem to be totally compatible with liquid emulsions and it does have a tendency to flake off in odd places.

Acrylic Matte Medium & Water:

Make up a solution of acrylic matte medium and water in a proportion of 50%—50% and brush it on your paper of choice with a foam brush. After it dries, which doesn't take very long at all, coat the paper with your gum bichromate sensitized emulsion. My students who have used this method like it for the speed and not having to use glyoxal.

Gum Arabic—Dichromate Sizing

As mentioned earlier, I have long used gum arabic and acrylic sizing paper surface preparation for my paintings. Gum provides a simple layer for the paints to lie on and this allows me to go into the painting with a wet brush in order to pull out highlights and detail that may have been compromised by the ebb and flow of painting. A gum arabic-dichromate sizing works in much the same way, but remains effective long after a single immersion in water. The reason for this is the gum is mixed with a light-sensitive ammonium dichromate, which will harden the gum on exposure to UV light. The process is a quick and efficient sizing/hardening technique that was fashionable many years ago. Here are two variations of the technique.

Gum Arabic—Dichromate Sizing Version 1

Mix up a gum bichromate solution consisting of 5 ml of potassium, or ammonium, dichromate, 10 ml of gum Arabic, and 10 ml of water. Do not add any watercolor pigment unless you want to make a colored background. Coat this solution on your paper and expose it to sunlight or in a UV light exposure unit, for 5 minutes. After the exposure, wash the print for 15 to 20 minutes in clean running water and hang it up to dry on a line. What you have made is a hardened, and tan-colored, bichromate surface that will protect the paper sufficiently during liquid immersions. This tan undercoating is particularly nice when combined with a cyanotype blue print.

Gum Arabic—Dichromate Sizing Version 2

A variation of this sizing technique is to mix up equal proportions of a *saturated* solution of ammonium, or potassium, dichromate and an equal amount of liquid gum Arabic. (Ammonium dichromate is in a saturated solution at 25% to 30%. Potassium dichromate is in a saturated solution at 10% to 13%.) This solution is coated on a paper, which is hung to dry in the dark, and then exposed to UV light for 1–3 minutes. The paper is then washed well until it exhibits its natural paper coloration. If the white of the paper doesn't wash clean, then the following sodium metabisulfite bath comes into play.

Sodium Metabisulfite Clearing Bath

This clearing bath, one that is commonly employed in the gum bichromate process, is made by mixing 5 to 10 g of sodium metabisulfite into 1000 ml of water. The exposed paper is either immersed in the solution or sprayed on the paper for not more than a minute. You should see the staining go away. After the sodium metabisulfite, wash the paper well for 10 minutes and hang it on a line to dry.

Double Coating Gelatin – Glyoxal Sizing for Rives BFK

If you are working with a paper that has decent wet strength, like a good printmaking paper such as Rives BFK, but you know that it may have trouble holding up after 2 or 3 passes, then consider double coating and sizing. I know that Tony Gonzalez uses this technique and it works perfectly for his usual 12-pass gum process on BFK. Pre-shrink your paper in a bath of hot water and then size the paper in the gelatin-sizing bath followed by the glyoxal. Dry the paper and then repeat the sequence. This double sizing may seem over zealous, and choosing a more gum-friendly paper, like a Lana Aquarelle, will make this two-step process unnecessary. However, this labor-intensive sizing process will allow you to go through a dozen gum bichromate passes without staining your highlights.

Note: For information regarding gelatin and chrome-alum hardening on difficult substrates, such as glass and ceramics, please refer to Chapter 8, Cyanotype Variations chapter.

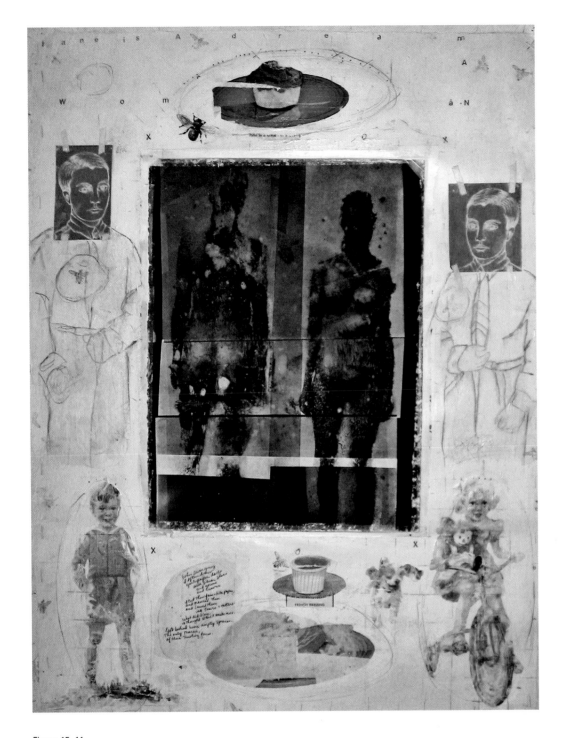

Figure 15–11

Maryjean Viano Crowe, *Fun With Dick & Jane*, 2003—mixed media

Maryjean is one of my favorite artists and people . . . often a difficult combination to find. This is an example of MJ's eclectic imagination . . . a mixed media piece made of cyanotypes, platinum prints, drawing, paint, and collage.

(Courtesy of the artist)

The Gum Bichromate Process

OVERVIEW & EXPECTATIONS

Here's the truth . . . In gum bichromate printing, there are very few *absolutely correct* ways to do anything. Here's another bit of reality . . . In my experience, gum bichromate printers are the most passionate, and hard-headed, of all alternative process artists when it comes to their particular way of doing the process. I can just imagine many of my friends reading that last sentence and saying, "He's talking about me!"

When the gum bichromate process is broken down into its three components, and explained in the simplest of ways, it appears to be amazingly uncomplicated. However, to nearly every one of my students who has been seduced by the process, and for those artists who are dedicated to it, gum bichromate reveals itself to be one of the most complex in the alternative process genre.

Gum printing is ridiculously seductive, due to its limited chemistry, simple water development, unlimited color potential with watercolors of the artist's choice, and its flexible ability to be coupled with a wide range of other alternative and graphic arts techniques. I think of gum as the photographic ambassador to the graphic and fine arts. Because of its pigment and substrate options and brush application, gum bichromate printing is one of the few photographic processes capable of achieving that wonderful element of *gesture*—gesture being the evidence of painterly expression, of the *artist's hand*, in the creation of a mark. Sadly, in conventional photography, the element of gesture is rare (and often mistaken for camera movement).

In this chapter I will, as always, offer you "a little history" and describe how the process works. I will then discuss the negative, how to generate a set of CMYK negative separations with ink-jet printer output, and relaxed registration techniques . . . this will allow you to place multiple applications of color on the same piece of paper without losing the original details of the image. You will also learn how to make a gum print from a single contact negative.

Figure 16–1
Christopher James, *John Q. W/His Own Negative*, 2005,
cyanotype & gum
This portrait of John Q. began its life as a relatively high-contrast cyanotype. Once dried, the print was sized with gelatin and hardened with glyoxal so that I could do multiple gum bichromate passes. The reptilian texture in the face is made by splashing water on a fresh gum application and blotting with paper towels prior to exposure.
(Courtesy of the author)

Figure 16–2

Christina Z Anderson, _Crack a Girl's Ribs_, 2005—gum

One of the true believers in the alt pro renaissance, Christina Z. inspires and turns her students into zealots . . . I know because I have had them in my work-shops and they are very well-schooled and enthusiastic. This piece is from her series, The Love Comic Project. From the late 1940s to the 1970s, Love Comics taught romance rules to women: girl falls in love at first sight, some conflict arises, but she finally gets the guy, and after a single kiss they marry and have babies. All stories end happily with a "completed woman," in 3 to 6 pages. They are perfect illustrations of culturally distilled encoding that, unfortunately, still influences. Christina prints her gum from tri-color separation negatives with a cyanotype first layer

(Courtesy of the artist)

You'll learn about mixing the chemistry for the sensitizer and the relationship among the three primary ingredients in the technique: gum Arabic, a dichromate (potassium or ammonium) sensitizer, and pigment . . . generally watercolor. This will be coupled with instructions for applying the sensitized emulsion, processing the print, and re-applying sensitized coatings for subsequent layers and depth. I'll discuss development-clearing gum prints, and conclude the chapter with a comprehensive trouble-shooting section.

Considering the basic simplicity of the process you'll notice that there seems to be an unexpected abundance of information. Part of the reason is that I want you to see the infinite menu of variables within gum printing. If you investigate the process beyond this book, you will find published evidence that will occasionally seem

contrary to some of the information in this chapter. You need to be aware that gum bichromate printing suffers from the same problem as do many other alternative processes . . . untested and erroneous instructions that are endlessly repeated as gospel.

You'll find that you will not have trouble making good gum bichromate prints if you follow the instructions in this chapter, and the Chapter 15, the Paper chapter (dealing with paper preparation) that precedes it. Of course you're going to have issues to deal with, everyone does with gum, but the path I'm laying out for you is a well-tested one and you'll be fine. Just relax, take your time, keep notes of what you are doing, and realize that the gum bichromate process will reward you individually as you modify the myriad elements of the process to suit your own personal working style, imagery, and intentions.

A LITTLE HISTORY

An interesting hypothesis from a book by Picknett & Prince entitled *Turin Shroud—In Whose Image? The Truth Behind the Centuries-Long Conspiracy of Silence* (Acacia Press, 1994) suggests that Leonardo da Vinci (1452–1519) may have been the creator of the Shroud of Turin by using a mixture of dichromated egg with human or animal urine. Guess whose image is on the Turin shroud? . . . None other than Leonardo da Vinci's, of course. The book's authors, if correct, would give Leonardo da Vinci credit for the first photographic image, several hundred years before the medium's "official" beginning. To put this curious factoid in context, the publisher's catalogue is rife with books dealing with conspiracy theories dating back to the fourteenth century. Who knows? Considering everything else da Vinci has accomplished, it might very well be true.

The earliest attributable considerations regarding the effect of light on bichromates seems to be the intellectual property of the French chemist, Louis-Nicolas Vauquelin (1763–1829), at the tail end of the 1700s. Although Vauquelin published over 378 separate papers on chemistry, the bulk of his writing did little more than provide analytical observations and data. Interestingly, he was one of the first academics to consider instructing his students by means of actual, hands-on practice in the laboratory and for that he gets a big round of applause.

Mungo Ponton (1801–1880), the Scottish inventor (*with the all-time best name in the history of photography*), expanded on Vauquelin's analytical wisdom in 1839 when he discovered that paper impregnated with potassium bichromate (*bichromate and dichromate are the same thing, by the way*) was sensitive to light. In Ponton's process, paper was coated with a potassium dichromate solution and exposed to sunlight using objects to create a photogram negative image. The exposed print was then washed, to remove any unexposed dichromate, and dried; leaving a light buff-colored sepia print that consisted of chromium dioxide. The print was rather handsome at first, but tended to fade to a delicate gossamer-like green after several months. Ponton's single-solution Pontontype is directly related to the idea behind Poitevin's Dusting-On process (1858) and a sizing technique for liquid emulsions on paper . . . both of which are covered later in this text.

A year later, in 1840, Edmund Becquerel (1820–1891) added to the rapidly expanding base of photographic knowledge by producing images using iodine in combination with starch. Specifically, he showed that he could produce electric currents by exposing certain liquids and metals to UV light and had invented a machine called an *Actinometer* that could calibrate and measure the response of those materials to light. This discovery eventually led to the development of the photoelectric cell. It was Becquerel, by the way, who first figured out that continuing the Daguerreotype's exposure through a red glass filter could intensify the final plate.

In 1854, William Henry Fox Talbot began working on the concept by observing the ability of potassium dichromate to have a hardening effect upon a colloidal gelatin directly proportional to the degree of UV light that the gelatin received. Fox Talbot's modest success in this area was followed by the work of Alphonse Louis Poitevin (1819–1882), who continued the investigation of how bichromates were able to render gelatin insoluble upon exposure to light. In 1856, Honoré d'Albert Duc de Luynes, an exceedingly wealthy arts patron, put up a prize of 10,000 francs to anyone who could describe a photographic printing process that was permanent. Poitevin won the prize for two processes: the Carbon Print and the Collotype. Additional history will be forthcoming in Chapter 17, the Dichromate Options chapter but, in the meantime, here are a few other related techniques to consider.

Figure 16–3

Felix Nadar (a.k.a. Gaspard Félix Tournachon) 1820–1920, *Portrait of George Sand*, **1877 (from Galerie Contemporaine, littéraire, artistique)**

Nadar had a brief, but stunning, career as a photographer in the mid-1800s primarily due to his extraordinary social connections within the French artistic and literary circles. His list of occupations and interests included poacher, freedom fighter, smuggler, cartoonist, and proponent of heavier-than-air-flying machines. His photographic studio became the main office for *The Society of the Encouragement of Ariel Locomotion by Means of Heavier than Air Machines*. Nadar was the President and Jules Verne was the secretary. This is a Nadar Woodburytype of his friend, and novelist, George Sand, who is remembered for her notorious affair with Chopin, her wardrobe of men's clothing, her feminist politics, and for writing 80 novels about love, nature, and morality. *(Courtesy of The George Eastman House, Rochester, NY)*

Woodburytype

Walter Bentley Woodbury (1834–1885) is credited with the creation of the Woodburytype (aka *Photoglyptie—Stannotype—Photomezzotint*) in 1864–1866—a process that was widely practiced for nearly 25 years and known for its amazing tonal range and ability to render values without any grain whatsoever. In fact, as is true of most people who invent new processes, the genius of Walter Bentley Woodbury was assisted by several decades of experimentation by a host of other artist/scientists/entrepreneurs such as Mongo Ponton, Becquerel, Fox Talbot, Poitevin, Beuregard, Paul Pretsch, and John Pouncy.

To produce a Woodburytype, the artist would make a thick gelatin relief on a piece of carbon paper by exposing it to a continuous-tone negative. The relief image was dried and then compressed into a lead intaglio plate under enormous pressure from a hydraulic press. The lead, having taken the detail of the hardened gelatin impression, would now become the printing plate for the

next step. The lead intaglio plate was encased in a mold and pressed against a fine-quality paper. Pigmented gelatin ink was then poured into the mold, where it deposited the gelatinized ink in proportion to the depth of the plate. Interestingly, the Woodburytype is generally a dark reddish brown and seldom printed in black, even though any color could have been used.

Corot's Cliché Verre Etchings on Glass

A fascinating bit from the same time period . . . the French painter, Jean-Baptiste-Camille Corot (1796–1875), tried his hand at processes utilizing bichromates and colloids and made cliché-verre prints on glass using pure albumen as his sizing agent. He also made colloidal etchings by coating glass plates with wet sensitized collodion emulsion. The plate was then exposed to light, which darkened it entirely. Corot then etched into the darkened emulsion, and when finished, contact printed the plate to a piece of sensitized paper for a paper print. Corot and others also utilized a technique in which they would burn a tallow candle close to a glass plate, leaving a soot-blackened sheet of glass. The soot was then drawn into with a variety of mark-making tools to create a negative plate of lines and textures. The etched soot on the glass was then used as a contact negative in conjunction with a sensitized sheet of paper.

The Fish-Glue Process

As an aside, there is another really interesting technique known as the Fish-Glue Process that applies these same principles, but does so for use on a metal plate substrate. Alphonse Louis Poitevin is credited with the invention of this process. In the Fish-Glue Process, ammonium dichromate and water-soluble fish glue were mixed and coated on a metal plate. Following exposure, the un-exposed and un-hardened glue (*acting like gum Arabic does in a traditional gum process*) washed off the plate, which was then dried, and heat hardened. The heat hardening produced an enamel-like surface that was subsequently acid etched (*likely with dilute nitric acid or a Dutch Mordant*) and used in an intaglio press, un-inked, to make a bas-relief image. Fish glue is still being manufactured and can be purchased, should you get an urge to try this seldom-used technique. You might also want to test it with household white glue. (*See Resource section F in the Appendices for a supplier of fish glue.*)

Gum and Pictorialism

In the late nineteenth, and early twentieth, centuries, photographic image makers viewed themselves as dedicated artists rather than as the gentleman scientists, as had photographers of a half-century earlier. Some even began referring to themselves as *Pictorialists*. They worked extensively with the gum process, due to its ability to mimic the painterly image and to express the artist's intentions and feelings. For critics of the movement, this categorized the imagery as warm, romantic, and fuzzy.

Indeed, gum bichromate was championed in America by the *Photo-Secessionists* (*first cousins of the U.K.'s The Brotherhood of the Linked Ring*), a coalition

Figure 16–4

Robert Demachy (1859–1937), *Cigarette Girl, (gum bichromate print reproduced as a photogravure in Camera Notes, Vol. 6, No. 1, July 1902)*
Robert Demachy was an artistic force in the 1880s and began to interpret his work in gum in 1894 as it allowed him to use considerable handwork and was similar to the feelings he had when looking at Impressionist painting. Demachy founded the Photo-Club de Paris and was a stalwart member of The Linked Ring as well as an honorary member of The Royal Photographic Society. In spite of his success, Demachy divorced himself from photography in 1914. *(Courtesy George Eastman House)*

of photographers such as Edward Steichen, Gertrude Käsebier, and Clarence White, and, in due time, Alfred Stieglitz, who were dedicated to Pictorialist expression in the medium. Their inspiration came from the aesthetic integrity of multiple European organizations, such as the Wiener Kamera Club in Berlin, that struggled to have their photographic art appreciated within its own unique context rather than as an imitative reflection of "reality." This is, of course, the principle argument born of the aesthetic ruckus started by Peter Henry Emerson in 1889.

Figure 16–5

Stephen Livick, *Kali Mural #528*, 1991—gum

This image is another example of Stephen Livick's artistic and technical dexterity. This Canadian artist is one of the most fearless gum bichromate artists that I know of. Each of his mural size works takes a minimum of three months to execute.

(Courtesy of the artist)

HOW GUM BICHROMATE WORKS

John Pouncy had come to a conclusion, the underlying principle being: a mixture of a potassium, or ammonium, bichromate salt (*dichromate and bichromate describe the same thing*) in a saturated solution is mixed with a colloid, such as gum arabic, gelatin, glue, or starch. This UV light-sensitive liquid mixture is then applied to a substrate, such as paper, and dried. A contact negative, the same size as the finished print, is placed in direct contact with the dried sensitized coating in a contact-printing frame and exposed to sunlight. The portions of the sensitized paper affected by UV light through the negative will then become insoluble in direct proportion to the amount of light received.

By itself, the dichromated salt and the gum Arabic (*sap from an Acacia tree*) will produce a buff or tan-colored image. This particular sensitizer is often employed as a preliminary sizing layer for hand-applied liquid emulsions and unique substrates. If a coloring agent, most often watercolor pigment, but occasionally a gauche or a metallic powder, is added to the dichromate and gum Arabic sensitized mixture, the color of that pigment will remain in the UV light-hardened emulsion.

Again, because the dichromate/pigment/gum arabic mixture will harden in direct proportion to the degree of UV exposure received. In a first exposure, the thinnest parts of the negative (*the shadows*) will allow the most exposure, and will cause the image upon the coated paper to become the most insoluble and hardened in those areas. The densest parts of the negative (*the highlights*), will require more exposure and will as a result, harden less during the same exposure time. This means that during the wash-development stage the un-hardened pigment simply falls away from the paper leaving the highlights color-free. This is exactly why sizing is so important. It is also why, if you didn't yet read the previous chapter on paper preparation, you probably don't understand what you just read. The other factors that will influence the outcome of your gum print are many, but the most relevant include the dichromate sensitizer-to-pigment ratio, and the amount of pigment in the sensitizer mix, the paper you choose, water type and temperature, paint type and color, and how all of these work with the chemistry and your individual technique.

A FEW WORDS BEFORE WE BEGIN

Any change in the principal components of the gum process (gum type, sensitizer type and strength, ratios of one to the other, water type, temperature, paper, time of year, etc.), on any given day, may change the final results in a gum print. This is exactly what makes the process so interesting and so much fun to do. As long as you avoid investing your self-worth and abilities as an artist, in the success of every print, you will be fine. Be patient and don't try to become the "best" at this process. My friend Judy Seigel has probably spent more time and energy exploring the variables of this gum process than anyone I know and she is still coming face-to-face with the unexpected tricks or treats of the process. It would be a "fool's errand" to try to conquer gum bichromate printing in a short time. Judy offers decent advice when she suggests that one can come to a working truce with gum simply by paying attention. The gum bichromate process is amazingly fluid and flexible and should be approached with a spirit of play, adventure, and discovery.

THE GUM BICHROMATE NEGATIVE

Because gum bichromate, like other alternative processes, is a contact printing process, it is necessary to work with negatives that are the same size as your final printed image. The vast majority of gum printing experiences require more than a single exposure and multiple "passes" (*applications of sensitizer and subsequent exposure*) of sensitized color are the norm. For this reason, it is common to have a set of *registered* negatives, fine registration, with which to successfully print a selection of highlights, mid-tones, and shadow details on the same paper. Of course, if you wish to be more free form than that, and not have anything match up, that's perfectly fine as well. Registration is important if you really want to control how the print will evolve.

If your intention is to have a single color gum, with many applications of the same color, one negative may be all that you will require. If your intention is to deepen the shadows of a previously made print, such as a cyanotype or platinum/palladium, then a single negative may be adequate. With a single negative, it's only necessary to adjust the concentration of pigment, exposure, and/or amount of sensitizer in order to make a resolved image.

Figure 16–6

Judy Seigel, *Two Men & Tree*, 1983–2000—gum

Judy writes, "This piece has 3 coats of sensitizer exposed through the negative on Strathmore Bristol. It also has a coat of green, made with a positive 'negative' but not on the figures."

(Courtesy of the artist)

It is advisable to have negatives that would be appropriate for a normal grade of silver gelatin paper. This means that the negative will have an average negative density of 1.0 to 1.8. This is a general suggestion, unless you intend to make gums with inter-disciplinary intentions, where the tonal values are secondary to the concept. If you are looking for a full tonal range, and gum is more than capable of giving this, it is best to avoid negatives that are too high in contrast . . . unless, of course, that is what you're looking for.

There are a host of film varieties and developers available for nearly any type of negative interpretation you could wish for. For the last few years, I have been separating transparencies into separate CMYK (*C= cyan, M= magenta, Y= yellow, K= black*) files in Photoshop and printing them out digitally on Pictorico OHP ink-jet films. I have also been taking original color or black &

white images and converting them to CMY and CMYK negative sets for gum printing. One of the workflows that you can read about in this, and in the Digital Options chapter is how to apply custom curves to your digital files that are designed for the process. You can make your own or you can go to the Internet and find many free versions to test out. ***Note:*** *Please refer to Digital Options, Chapter 5, for a complete workflow regarding making a color layers on a digital negatives.*

In almost every situation, digital negatives are perfectly satisfactory for gum bichromate printing and they provide a flexibility and speed in negative reproduction that only Polaroid matches. You may also wish to consider using negatives made from laser copy machines or making your own with a cliché verre technique. Refer to Chapter 4, (The Negative), for more information.

MAKING DIGITAL SEPARATIONS FOR GUM PRINTING

Simple Workflow In Photoshop

Note: There is relevant information here that can be applied to many processes and it especially important to see this B&W to CMYK workflow in context with the process and related illustrations.

Gum bichromate artists have always had to accomplish a few tedious tasks before getting to the fun parts of the process with all the colors and splashing around in the sink. Along with paper sizing, making CMYK (Cyan, Magenta, Yellow, & Black) negative separations was one of my least favorite things to do for a day in the studio. In the beginning you could shoot the separations in camera or move to the darkroom with an existing negative, and do your separations there with various film types, filters, and projection. Then along came digital imaging, Adobe Photoshop, and Pictorico OHP.

In the first edition of this book, I was all impressed with Photoshop v.5 and by the fact that I could make CMYK (*cyan-magenta-yellow-black*) separations from a black and white source with only 26 easy steps . . . I called it the "speedy, non-fussy version." Now I'm using

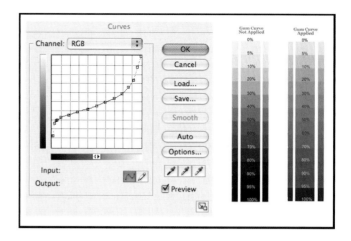

Figure 16–7

Applied Gum Bichromate Curve and Comparative Step Wedges
As an example of the tonal increase possible with custom curve profiles, I went to Malin Fabri's alternative process web site and took advantage of a free custom curve download made by David Hatton. This illustration shows what the adjusted curve looks like and how a step wedge indicates the increase in steps due to the curve adjustment.
(Courtesy of www.alternativephotography.com)

Photoshop CS2. Next month I'll probably be using Photoshop CS3. No matter; the fact is that with CS 2 or 3 I can now tell you how to go from a black and white (grayscale) source to CMYK, or from a RGB (*red-green-blue*) source to CMY (*cyan-magenta-yellow*) or grayscale in a flash. Best of all, it really is speedy and simple . . . even for the technical neophyte.

These sequences are a good start. They are not the last word in making digital separations on Pictorico OHP film, going from grayscale to CMYK, or RGB to CMY, nor is it inflexible. For instance . . . if you flip and exchange Step E with Step C, your separation negatives will look different.

These particular workflows are ones that I worked out via e-mail exchanges with several friends—David Stinchcomb, in Oklahoma, Tony Gonzalez in New York, and xtine Burrough in California. Their brains don't melt when they think about things digital and they have been a great help in getting this information into a simple and easy to follow workflow. Tony's 3-color CMY workflow will come later in this chapter.

As with any alternative syntax in any medium, individuals will adjust the steps in any process to suit their individual needs. Again, these are only workflow recommendations, but they work and will certainly get you started.

One other thing to consider: The separations that I am offering here are simple workflows designed for those who just want to have an easy and more than adequate way to generate their digital negatives quickly. If you are really serious about perfection and knowing everything there is to know about this subject, then you will want to consider graduating to advanced level considerations such as those developed by Dan Burkholder or Mark Nelson. Dan's web site (www.danburkholder.com) and book are amazingly complete and he has custom profiles and instructions for just about everything you will need. You can find Mark Nelson's advice in Dick Arentz's *Platinum and Palladium Printing: 2nd Edition.*

C-M-Y-K GUM SEPARATION NEGATIVES

On Pictorico OHP in Photoshop

Note: In this example, you are starting with an RGB color file and your intention is to convert it into a set of B & W, C-M-Y-K negatives that you can use in gum bichromate printing.

R-G-B TO GRAYSCALE C-M-Y-K SEPARATIONS

On Pictorico OHP In Photoshop

Step 1 Open up your image file and work on it in Photoshop until it meets your expectations and intentions. Save it with a label that will indicate that it is specifically for the particular set of CMYK negatives you are making.

Step 2 Go to > Menu Bar, then to > Image, then to > Mode, then click > CMYK

Step 3 Go to > Image, then to > Adjustments, to > Curves and click >Load

Note: You have an option at this point in the process. Some gum printers want a set of negatives that are really "punchy" and have a good deal of contrast. If you are one of these gummists then this is where you will go to > Image, then to > adjustment and click > Auto Levels. If you are

Figure 16–8

John Quackenbos, 35mm Transparency, 1999

This is the 35 mm color transparency of one of my workshop classes executing a cyanotype mural.

(Courtesy of the artist)

seeking a more true-to-life CMYK interpretation of an actual color set, then you might want to skip this step. Try it both ways and see what you like. At some point in the process you will be adjusting levels, and by doing so, the contrast levels of your negatives. Depending on the type of negative separation set you want, contrasty, or sort of true to life, you can adjust now or after you make your separation set.

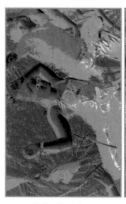   

C - Cyan Separation   M - Magenta Separation   Y - Yellow Separation   K - Black Separation

Figure 16–9

C-M-Y-K Gum Separation
Grayscale Sequence
This is a C-M-Y-K set of separa-
tions, in grayscale, made to print
a 4-color gum bichromate.
(Courtesy of the author)

Step 4 Find your > Gum Curve (the. sacv file) and > click Load.*

Step 5 Go to > Image, then to > Adjustments, and click > Invert

Step 6 Next, go to the palette that is probably on your screen, indicating Layers, Channels, and Paths. Click > Channels and, using the tiny arrow on the top right corner of the palette, click > Split Channels. Presto! . . . Photoshop will automatically create 4 separate, and distinct, B & W negatives for you. These are your CMYK separations.

Step 7 For each of these negatives . . . Go to > File and to > Save As. Title your negative to as whatever you need to name the file in order to remember it. I name my sets by the title of the image and what color negative I will be applying when gum printing. i.e., Cyan, Magenta, Yellow, or Black.

Step 8 Go to > Image, then to > Adjustments, and > click Levels and adjust them manually . . . bringing the left and right adjustment markers to the extreme ends of the Levels histogram. Do this step for each of your separations. Keep in mind that you are making a unique set of negatives here and that you can adjust the contrast of these negatives using Levels or Curves to suit your needs or the type of color you are using.

Figure 16–10

John Quackenbos, *Cyan Mural*, Maine-4 color gum, 1999
This is the gum bichromate print made from the C-M-Y-K set of separations.
(Courtesy of the artist)

This will make sense once you begin doing the actual gum printing.

---

* Free Curve Profiles

The most immediate, and simple, solution for getting a free Curve Profile for gum bichromate printing is to go to Malin Fabbri's excellent alternative process web site, www.alternativephotography.com. In their negatives and curves section, you will find a number of free profiles that you can download and use to make negatives. I personally like David Hatton's Gum Curve but you can easily begin with that and adjust it to fit your intentions. Then simply save it as a curve to use another day.

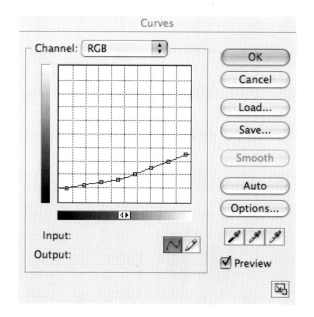

Figure 16–11
Gonzalez CMY Gum Curve Profile
This is the C-M-Y (no K = black) custom curve profile that Queens College—CUNY professor and artist, Tony Gonzalez, applies to his gum bichromate negative set. Notice that it is quite different from the Hatton curve in Figure 16–8 but that it adequately represents Tony's palette and working style.
(Courtesy of the artist)

Step 9 Go to > Image, to > Canvas Size, and give yourself a little white, black, or gray border to use for registration marks, pin holes, or other miscellaneous marks that will be your guide for gum registration. You can apply registration marks automatically with your printer in > Print With Preview. . . See Below.*

Step 10 Print out the CMYK negative separations using Pictorico OHP ink jet film.

R-G-B TO C-M-Y/GRAYSCALE GUM SEPARATION NEGATIVE

Note: In this example you are starting with a color file, perhaps R-G-B, and your intention is to convert it into a

set of C-M-Y grayscale negatives that you can use in your gum bichromate printing.

Step 1 Open up your image file and work on it in Photoshop until it meets your expectations and intentions. Save it with a label that will indicate that it is specifically for the particular set of C-M-Y negatives that you are making.

Step 2 Go to > Image on the Menu Bar, then to > Mode . . . then click > Multichannel

Step 3 Next, go to the palette, that is likely on your screen, indicating, "Layers," "Channels," and "Paths." Click >Channels and using the tiny arrow on the top right corner of the palette, in this box, click > Split Channels. You will automatically create 3 separate, and distinct, B & W positives for your C-M-Y separations. Execute the following steps for each of the C-M-Y files.

Step 4 Go to > Image, to > Adjustments, and click > Auto Levels. Or click > Levels instead and adjust your negative manually to your own taste. At some point in the process you will be adjusting levels, and by doing so, the contrast levels of your negatives. Depending on the type of negative separation set you want, contrasty, or sort of true to life, you can adjust now . . . or after you make your separation set.

Step 5 Go to > Image, to > Adjustments, and click > Invert

Step 6 Go to > Image, to > Adjustments, to Curves, and click > Load

Step 7 Find your Gum Curve and click > Load.

Step 8 Go to > Image, to > Canvas Size, and give yourself a white, or black, border to use for registration marks, pinholes, or other miscellaneous notes.

---

* Adding Registration Marks

If you want to add registration marks to your film, make sure that you have enough room outside of the image to do so. I will add here that this is how my Epson printer software allows me to create registration marks. Most printer software packages come with a method of adding registration marks to the printed works, but you may have to dig around in your own print dialog box to find something like "output," "crop marks," "printer marks," or "registration" . . . isn't that annoying? Anyway, after you check to see if you have enough room on the outside of your image . . . Go to File > to Print With Preview. There is a blue box under the Preview image, and if you click on it you will get a choice of Color Management or Output. Choose Output and you will get a rather large menu of things you can set up before printing . . . one of these items is registrations marks. Check that box and if you have enough white space around your negative the marks will appear. If they don't appear, check the box that says scale to fit media and they will pop up because the program automatically resizes the image to include everything necessary.

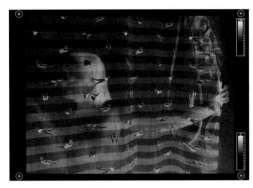

CYAN NEGATIVE

MAGENTA NEGATIVE

YELLOW NEGATIVE

CMY GUM PRINT

Figure 16–12
Tony Gonzalez, Jaclyn Curtain, CMY Separation Set
This is the negative separation pack that was generated with the negative and custom curve profile above. *(Courtesy of the artist)*

Step 9 Go to > File and to > Save As and title your negative to whatever you need to name the file in order to remember it. I label mine by the title of the image and what color negative I will be applying when gum printing.

Step 10 Check your levels one last time and continue to print out the negative separations using Pictorico OHP ink-jet film.

REGISTRATION

Registration is done after sizing/hardening. If you intend to make multiple passes, or if you are working on a more complex gum, such as trying to duplicate a color transparency from 4 CMYK separations (*see the workflow above*), it will be necessary to register your negatives. If you don't register them, you will often get curious and unexpected results where none of the C-M-Y-K separations line up. This accident may well be a *good* technique if you use it intentionally.

There are many ways to register negatives and paper. Some of the methods include Photoshop registration marks (*see above*), paper punches, pushpin holes, stick-on transparent registration targets applied during negative

production, or an old dye transfer punch-board that can easily be found on eBay. You can also register simply by laying your coated paper on a light table and quickly registering your negatives to the sensitized paper and locking it in with pieces of transparent tape. This is harder to do with darker color layers of course. Don't stress about the light from the light table. Even though your dried emulsion is sensitive to light, you still have plenty of forgiveness in the emulsion speed and will have time to secure the registration without fogging the image . . . as long as you're really quick about it. The point of registration is to give yourself a repeatable and mechanical way of accurately aligning your negative, or a different one, on the same piece of paper. This is especially true when a different color is assigned to each negative and where it is difficult to see the base image after recoating.

A Simple Registration Technique

On a light table, register all of the negatives to be used in your print. With a mat knife or sliding blade paper cutter, trim the margins at different lengths of all but one negative so that when they are in registration each piece of film will have a different height but will still be in registration with

Figure 16–13

Tony Gonzalez, Jaclyn Curtain, 2005—CMY gum bichromate

Here's Tony's finished C-M-Y gum bichromate print from the negative set in Figure 6–12. I really like the delicate tonal nature of Tony's custom curve profile for gum printing. It permits delicacy and allows the process to express subtle tonal shifts, something that gum has not been given a lot of credit for being able to do well.

(Courtesy of the artist)

the others. Run a strip of tape across the packet of trimmed edges so they can be picked up as a set.

When this is done, place the packet of taped negatives on the area of your *sized* paper that you will be printing on. Move the sized paper and the taped negative pack to a clean and porous surface (such as Foam Core) that will accept a pushpin and poke a pinhole through at least three margins of the negative set and paper. These holes will serve as your registration reference guides later on. Of course, if you wish to have a lot more control, then your registration techniques will have to be a lot more sophisticated than what I've described. If you have a strong urge to make this process more complicated, please feel free to do so.

THE GUM BICHROMATE RECIPE

The sensitizer emulsion for gum bichromate printing is prepared in simple and separate steps. You begin by mixing your dichromate solution. Most gummists use either potassium or ammonium dichromate but it is also acceptable to use sodium dichromate . . . although I don't know anyone who does. Potassium dichromate is a bit softer than ammonium dichromate but clears out in the highlights better than does ammonium dichromate. Potassium dichromate

yields a bit more contrast, takes a little bit longer to make a complete exposure, which is good, and usually avoids yellow dichromate staining. Most serious gummists that I know use potassium dichromate. Just for the record, the difference in saturation between ammonium dichromate (25%) and potassium dichromate (13%) may be the reason for the way they behave differently. If you were to add water to the ammonium dichromate, taking it to a 13% solution like the potassium, it is probable that you will avoid some of the less aggressive traits of ammonium dichromate, i.e., less concentration softer print.

Whichever dichromate you elect to use for your sensitizer is added to a mixture of gum arabic and watercolor paint to make the complete sensitizer solution for coating. Additional water can also be added and will help make your emulsion smoother. The proportions of gum arabic to sensitizer can be adapted to suit your contrast and exposure time requirements as well. Some gum practitioners also substitute a liquid rabbit skin glue or albumen for the gum arabic. Immediately you can begin to see that the process is not one where hard and fast rules apply.

Potassium & Ammonium Dichromate

Potassium, or ammonium, dichromate is your UV sensitive component and is added to your mix of liquid gum Arabic and watercolor pigment to create the sensitizer emulsion that will be coated upon your paper. It is a typical alternative emulsion, suitable only for contact printing under UV light. You don't have to worry very much about working with it under normal low light conditions because your sensitizer isn't that sensitive until it is dry. I once gave a gum printing demonstration in a motel lobby where the motel's yellow sheets were hung over sun filled windows. I performed another gum demonstration in the back of a van in a parking lot on a rainy day—and had no problems with fogging there either. Avoid long periods of time under excessive fluorescent light as you would with other alternative processes.

An Interesting Fact Regarding Dichromates:

The speed of the emulsion will be slower in proportion to the pH of the water used in creating the coating solution. The more alkaline the water is, the higher its pH (*above 7*) and the less the dichromate's sensitivity to UV

Figure 16–14

Sarah Van Keuren, *Geometric Seascape,* **2001 digital gum**

Sarah is a professor at the University of the Arts in Philadelphia and another hero in the resurgent alt pro movement. Her print, "Geometric Seascape," made in 2001, is a transitional piece for her, derived from an 8" x 10" b/w pinhole negative that she scanned and used to create a set of color separations in Photoshop. She then enlarged the negatives using a Scitex imagesetter and printed out a C-M-Y-K negative set. Sarah then printed from the 4 negatives in cyanotype, and gum, using layers that did not correspond closely to magenta, yellow and black, i.e., the "magenta" was Perylene maroon.

(Courtesy of the artist)

light. Conversely, the more acidic the water, the lower the pH (*less than 7*) and the greater the dichromate's sensitivity to UV light.

Making a Stock Saturated Dichromate Solution

Dichromates are used in gum sensitizers in a saturated solution. A saturated solution is defined as one in which no more of the dry chemical can be dissolved in water without creating insoluble sediment.

As mentioned earlier, ammonium dichromate is *saturated* at around 25% to 30% while potassium dichromate is saturated at 10% to 13%. Ammonium dichromate is more sensitive than potassium dichromate (*due to more dichromate ions in the solution*), but the only differences that you might notice will be shorter exposure times and a slight increase in contrast. Potassium dichromate is a little softer and you will experience an easier time clearing the print with potassium in your sensitizer. Again, one factor will impact another, such as the pH of the water you saturate with, and you'll need to work out your own system to accurately predict outcome.

Let's say that you are going to use potassium dichromate in your sensitizer and you need to make a saturated solution. Knowing that potassium dichromate become saturated between 10% and 13%. Take digital gram scale

and weigh out 10 g of potassium dichromate and stir it into solution in 100 ml of water. This makes a 10% working dichromate solution . . . simple, huh?

There is a range here and if you opted to make a saturated solution of 13% then you would be using 13 g to the 100 ml of water and this would be making a slightly faster sensitizer. In truth, you don't need a scale at all. Just keep adding the dichromate to the water until the dry chemical ceases to dissolve any more.

You can experiment and decide what strength is best for your own work. In any case, this saturated dichromate solution, whether it is potassium or ammonium, will last for a very long time when stored in a dark airtight bottle. Be sure to label the bottle with information regarding its contents, its percentage, and the date it was mixed. Be sure that the bottle has a plastic cap . . . no metal ever! Lastly, be sure to store it in a safe place where children cannot reach it; when mixed, dichromate solutions look a lot like a sugared drink!

Note: Be cautious in how you handle ammonium or potassium dichromate: It is dangerous and poisonous and highly allergenic. Never put bare skin in contact with any dichromate solution. This chemical can cause lesions on your tender flesh through contact and

Figure 16–15

Christopher James, *Grace in Gum,* **1977**

This is from a series of gum bichromate portraits that I made from damaged inter-negatives that had been thrown in the trash in the Harvard photography labs. The final negative was enlarged on SO-132 direct duplicating film (sadly no longer made) and then used for several days worth of gum bichromate exposures with paint, ink, dyes, bleaches and etching tool abrasions in wet gelatin emulsion.

(Courtesy of the author)

can damage your lungs by breathing it in its dry state. Be very careful with storage and never leave the chemistry unlabeled or where children can get their hands on it. Please reference the chemical section in Appendix A before using dichromates.

WATERCOLOR PIGMENTS

The watercolors you use must always be "professional" artist quality, *not* student or "*academy*" grade paint.

Inferior paint often does not clear well in the highlights, or the shadows, and can be one of the reasons, besides poor paper preparation, bad gum Arabic, and too much sensitizer in the formula, for paper staining. There are almost no exceptions to this warning about academy grade paint. The best paints that I've used are made by Schmincke Horadam Aquarell, Winsor & Newton (professional grade only), Linel (Lefrance & Bourgeois), and Sennelier. Stephen Livick recommends adding twice the amount of pigment to gum ratio if using Sennelier (*12 g pigment for every 12 ml of potassium dichromate*). Each of these manufacturers has types of paint that are better than others and you will spend a little money testing them.

Watercolor paint is composed of finely ground pigments mixed with gum Arabic for body and glycerin or honey for viscosity and to assist in bonding the color to the substrate. The only other ingredient you're likely to encounter will be clove oil, which is added to prevent mold growth.

It would be a simple task to begin writing about watercolor paint but a much larger one to finish telling you everything there is to know about it. I'm going to explain a few basics and then leave the rest up to you. I would like to recommend that you try to locate a book called *The Wilcox Guide to the Finest Watercolour Paints*, by Michael Wilcox. You may also try to access the related web site which is mind-boggling . . . just Google it. This site should satisfy even the most demanding scholar, which is lucky for you because copies of the book are quite rare. Just to give you an idea how precious the book is . . . as I write this, there were two used copies on Amazon and they are over $165 each.

For beginning work, it is a good idea to have "primary colors" from a single maker on hand. Schmincke or Winsor & Newton are good choices. The primary colors include red (*alizarin crimson, Permanent Carmine*), blue (*Phthalo or cobalt*), and yellow (Lemon Yellow, *New Gamboge or Cadmium Yellow Medium*). Winsor & Newton's Naples yellow is also a really nice color and is creamier than the other yellows, as is Transparent Yellow. You may also wish to have a black (*Lamp Black*) and a gray such as Davy's Gray, which is a very pale creamy greenish slate color. If you need a stronger green I would recommend Oxide of Chromium over a straight green, as it will clear better. You can also mix your own green from the blue and yellow you have in your primary set. Of course, you may use any color you wish from the manufacturer's stock as long as the quality is good. Be aware that some colors are suspect in regard to permanence and ability to clear in the wash development stage. Those of you who are color blind, or color-impaired, might be considered creative, so don't avoid the gum bichromate process for those reasons.

It would be numbing to provide a complete list of recommended paints because there are so many different brands of watercolor and gouache (*watercolor with white pigment added*), and a color from one manufacturer will behave quite differently than the identically "named" color from another. You will have to discover those that are best for you within the parameters you work in. Keep careful notes and you'll work it all out eventually. I would recommend going to the firestorm that is the alt process newsgroup and checking out their archives that discuss gum bichromate color. Note: Daniel Smith, one of the best art supplies to be found anywhere, gives information re: such things as "light-fastness" in their catalog. Daniel Smith also makes and sells their signature line of high quality watercolors and these can be found on their site . . . www.danielsmith.com.

Testing Pigments For Gum Printing

One of the best methods of testing a particular pigment for gum bichromate printing is to mix together a gum formula consisting of 12 ml gum Arabic, 12 ml saturated potassium dichromate, and 1 g of the pigment being tested. Coat and dry your sized and hardened gum paper, place an opaque object, like a coin, in the sensitized area, expose it to UV light for 15–20 minutes, and then process it normally in a soaking wash-development bath for 30 minutes. The paper under the opaque object should clear completely in the wash development bath. If it does not, the paint is not a suitable one for gum bichromate printing. Or, you need to work on your sizing technique.

The Most Often Recommended Paints/Pigments Based on Gum Performance

OK, OK . . . I know that I said I wasn't going to list all of the paints but this short list will be enough to get you started on your experimentation with color and paint.

Lefrance & Bourgeois/Linel: (Founded in 1720)—Natural Earth (Lightfast Raw Umber) Helios Yellow, Ruby Red, Hortensia Blue, Ivory Black, Peach Black, Cobalt Blue, Warm Green, Warm Sepia, Bayeux Violet, Naples Yellow, Viridian, Venetian Red

Winsor & Newton: Cobalt Blue, Permanent Rose, Terre Verte, Oxide of Chromium, Naples Yellow, Rose Madder, Alizarin Crimson (hue), Lamp Black, Permanent Magenta

Sennelier: Cobalt Blue, Phthalo Blue, Lamp Black, Phthalo Green Deep, Sennelier Red, Veridian, Warm Sepia, Permanent Magenta, Cerulean Blue (*very heavy paint!*), Yellow Ochre

Schmincke Horadam Permanent Carmine (magenta), Cadmium Yellow Middle (yellow), Phthalo Blue (cyan)

PAPER FOR GUM BICHROMATE

It is important to use a paper that is well made and able to stand up to all sorts of abuse and have superior wet strength. No wimpy papers are suitable for gum bichromate printing. They must be able to withstand repeated washing times of extended duration as the process requires a complete wash after every pass and there is no limit to the number of passes you might perform in a single print. For minimal passes, a paper with a weight of 140 lb might be adequate.

For gum projects with several applications, exposures, and development experiences, a 300 lb paper will work well. I have used 1160 lb Arches when I have intended to make gums where I could use power tools and sanders as part of the working process. In all cases, even with high quality watercolor papers, you must gelatin size and harden the sizing if more than a single pass is planned for. Please refer to the previous chapter for specific information and recommendations for paper.

My personal paper favorites are 300 lb Lana Aquarelle, well-sized 300 lb Fabriano Artistico (a luxury experience), and 300 lb Arches Aquarelle.

GUM ARABIC

Gum Arabic, or gum acacia, can be traced back in time to 2650 B.C.E. where it was harvested from the sap of various species of Acacia trees in Nigeria, Cameroon, Chad, Mali, and the Sudan. The Acacia trees grow primarily in the sub-Saharan (Sahel) areas of Africa and the Sudanese variety is considered the premium grade. In gum printing, the dichromate is added to the gum to create the liquid foundation of the gum sensitizer.

Grades of Gum Arabic

Gum Arabic can come in a variety of purities. Superior Selected Sudanese/Nigerian gum Arabic is considered the premium grade and has a very pale color and clarity. This gum Arabic is hand selected, cleaned, and sifted free of any impurities and alien organic matter. This is the grade of gum Arabic that you would want to use with delicate colors such as yellow. It's also very expensive. Winsor & Newton sells this expensive Sudanese grade.

Kordofan No. 1, is a good grade of gum Arabic and quite excellent for gum printing. This grade has a slight haze and is pale to dark yellow. I believe that Bostick & Sullivan sells the slightly hazy, pale yellow, Kordofan#1. This brand is good for just about everything. After #1 comes the "Siftings" grade, which, can be recognized by a cloudy and yellow amber color. This is pretty common and a step up from the lowest grade, "Dust #3," which is opaque and dark amber-brown. You'll find this grade in printmaking studios in art departments with small budgets. To be considered saleable, the gum Arabic must have minimum moisture content of 12%–14%.

New vs. Old Gum Arabic

One thing that seems to make a difference is the age of the gum Arabic. I've heard from more than one gum bichromate worker that the way ammonium dichromate mixes with pigment, and the way it hardens during UV exposure, is better when the gum has aged a bit rather than when the gum is fresh and new. Older gum Arabic tends to adhere to the paper more effectively and is somewhat responsible for more predictable and cleaner looking prints. Tony Gonzalez told me that he has four gallons of the stuff aging in his darkroom.

A few gum bichromate artists claim that different types of gum arabic have different printing speeds. They are probably correct, but I'm not sure you should lose sleep over this possibility. Gum arabic is also handy for masking.

Essentially, you are buying the sap from an acacia tree and the color of it does not always determine the quality. Most art supply outlets sell it by the quart or gallon to meet the requirements of printmakers and lithographers.

Preparing Gum Arabic Solution from Dry Gum

Mixing gum Arabic from a dry state is relatively simple . . . it just takes a little longer to get to the stage where you can use the gum. The mix is essentially a 1:6, i.e., 30 g of photo quality gum Arabic to 180 ml distilled water. Put the two ingredients together in a glass or plastic beaker and let them stand for several days until the gum dissolves. Any residue can be filtered or strained off leaving you with a clear gum Arabic to work with. Some of my friends add 0.50 g of mercuric chloride to the solution as a way of preventing bacterial and fungal growth in the solution. I'm not an advocate of this practice if you are not extremely familiar with chemistry and related safety precautions . . . this amount of mercuric chloride is lethal.

Using Glue as a Substitute for Gum Arabic

There is a nice idea for using liquid glue as a substitute for gum arabic. This formula is from the Randall Webb and Martin Reed book, *Spirits of Salts*. First, make up a 5% potassium dichromate sensitizer (5 g to 100 ml of distilled water). Next, place a small amount of watercolor pigment, about the size of a #2 pencil eraser, in a ceramic cup. Then add 5 ml liquid glue to the cup and stir it into the paint. The Webb-Reed book indicates that you shouldn't be concerned if the mixture is a "rubbery mess" but that could be their sense of humor. Add 5 ml of the 5% potassium dichromate mix to the "rubbery mess," mix the ingredients together, quickly coat your paper with a thin coating of the solution, dry it thoroughly, put the coated paper and negative in a printing frame, and expose in UV light. Presto!

TABLE SET UP FOR GUM BICHROMATE PROCESS

Glyoxal—Gelatin—sized paper

A small measuring beaker able to measure in single ml increments

Clean paper for the table surface

A selection of hake or foam brushes for coating paper

Clean water in a beaker for brush washing

Pencil for marking paper with procedure notes

Contact printing frame

A selection of professional quality watercolor paints in tubes.

(*Basic colors will include red, yellow, blue, and black. If separating CMYK, cyan, magenta, yellow, and black.*)

Gum Arabic

A saturated solution of potassium or ammonium dichromate

Negative/CMYK negatives for contact printing

Paper towels

GUM BICHROMATE SENSITIZER EMULSION

The Best Gum Sensitizing Emulsion

I imagine that that headline got your attention. The truth of the matter is that nearly everyone I know who is good at this process has their unique way of performing it and this includes their recipe for the sensitizer emulsion. There are also so many variables to take into consideration that it is a small wonder that anyone agrees on anything connected to the process.

The general consensus among contemporary gum bichromate printers is to use a sensitizer that will expose easily and clear quickly. The gum to sensitizer ratios run from 3:1 to 1:1 with variations in the proportions depending upon when the "pass" occurs in the printing sequence. We'll get to this later but essentially what this means is that if you are making a yellow pass, your first sensitizer might be a gum to dichromate sensitizer ratio of 1:2. A second pass might then change to a gum to dichromate ratio of 1:1 and by doing this you will experience an increase in printing speed, and a reduction in contrast.

If you take all of the variables out of the equation; the paper is fine, the sizing is perfect, the paint and gum is of excellent quality, and the dichromate is mixed to a perfect saturated state, then the ideal base sensitizer emulsion would be . . . 1 part gum to 1 part dichromate sensitizer and some paint . . . usually 1/2" to 1" out of the tube.

A 1:1 Sensitizer Using Potassium Dichromate

All variables in place and in good order, this formula is generally very successful and the proportions of potassium dichromate to gum are similar to the mix used by many of the most technically successful gum artists. Use the following ingredients and mix them according to the directions for ammonium dichromate. Pigments have different densities and different manufacturers make similar colors in different concentrations. Therefore, the amounts used in an 8" x 10" formula such as this one will fluctuate, depending upon the color and make of the paint. Figure a half-gram weight to be in the ballpark.

◆ 6 ml of gum Arabic

◆ 1/2" to 1" watercolor pigment

◆ 6 ml of saturated potassium dichromate solution

Begin by taking a clean paper cup and adding 6 ml of gum Arabic to it. Then add your watercolor paint and stir it into the gum. You can add a little water if you want a less dense solution. Now it's time to sensitize it. Add 6 ml of your saturated potassium dichromate and stir it into solution. Your sensitizer is ready to go.

Figure 16–16

Carmen Lizardo, *American Flag Blue House*, **2006 —gum**

This great 22" × 30" gum is from Carmen's American Flag series. Carmen talks about this piece better than I can. . . *"How do I belong to America when I belong no place else? This is one of the questions that birthed my American Flag series. I was born and raised Dominican yet have come alive, as an artist, as a woman, in America. Come alive in a culture, and English tongue, that is as alien and ambivalent to me as it is welcoming and inspiring. This series is a narrative of the journey of discovering the American in me. The source images were taken in the Dominican Republic, my home country, and in New York, my home."* (Courtesy of the artist)

Gum bichromate artist, Carmen Lizardo, uses a thinner sensitizer and mixes her formula using simple "kitchen" measures: 1 tsp gum, 1 tsp ammonium dichromate, 1 tsp, pigment, and 1 tsp distilled water. There isn't much chance of this formula being misunderstood. Carmen says that she does alter the pigment to gum—sensitizer ratio depending on the intensity of the pigment, i.e., cadmium red vs. a Davy's Gray.

Stephen Livick, who is one of the very best gum printers around, has a very basic initial sensitizing emulsion formula that is similar to many other great gum printers. The sensitizer is based on a 1:1 ratio of gum to potassium dichromate sensitizer with varying degree of paint

Figure 16–17

Tony Gonzalez, *Rachel, Nail Polish*, 2004—gum

Here's another example of Tony Gonzalez's gum bichromate work from his Bather Series. These images are generated from CMY digital negative sets printed out on Pictorico OHP ink-jet film. *(Courtesy of the artist)*

depending upon color. He mixes 12 ml of gum and 12 ml saturated potassium dichromate. To this, he adds:

- First Coat: 2.5 grams Linel's Helios Yellow
- Second Coat: 2.5 grams Linel's Ruby Red
- Third Coat: 4 grams Linel's Hortensia Blue

Notice that Stephen doesn't have a black (K) pass as he feels the 3-color sequence makes quite enough black for his imagery. Tony Gonzalez is another gum printer who also foregoes the black pass in favor of a cyan.

3-COLOR C-M-Y GUM BICHROMATE

It isn't always critical to have a set of CMYK separations to make a beautiful gum bichromate exposure. Tony Gonzalez, who teaches at Queens College in New York, has a terrific workflow that utilizes cyan, magenta, and yellow negatives that are made on Pictorico OHP ink jet film and an Epson 1280 printer. (*See Figure 16-12.*)

In detailing the way he works with making his CMY negatives, Tony explained that he did extensive testing using his Epson 1280, Pictorico OHP film, and Media Street inks. After about a year, he determined the percentage of black ink that would be equivalent to the density of silver in the Stouffer 21 Step Tablet. Knowing that a

65% black density is equivalent to step #2, 70% black is equivalent to step #3 and so forth. Tony then based his curve profile on an 8 step (*including Dmin and Dmax*) tonal scale that is more or less the tonal range he concluded that he could achieve in his gum prints.

As you can see in the following description of an 11-layer set of exposures, Tony is printing two very short black passes but is using his Cyan negative for the exposure. (If you forgot how to make a cyan negative, you can refer back in this chapter for instructions or go to Chapter 5, Digital Options). In the following gum workflow set, Tony uses the following Schmincke Horadam watercolor pigments. These are not the most expensive watercolor paints, but they work extraordinarily well for him and for the way he has worked out his system.

Gonzalez's C-M-Y-K Gum Color Equivalents

- Magenta: Schmincke Horadam Permanent Carmine
- Yellow: Schmincke Horadam Cadmium Yellow Middle
- Cyan: Schmincke Horadam Phthalo Blue
- Black (*using the Cyan negative*): Winsor & Newton Lamp Black

Gonzalez's Gum Recipe

For the sensitizer, the gum to dichromate ratio is 1:1. For his negatives, Tony uses 12 full eyedroppers of gum and 12 full eyedroppers of ammonium dichromate. He uses a 1 ¼ inchworm squeeze of pigment for Cyan, Magenta, & Yellow paints. For the black equivalent, use a 1" worm squeeze of W & N black paint but use the cyan negative for the 2 exposures.

Gonzalez's Exposure Unit

Note: Exposures are made using an exposure unit with an outside dimension of 18" × 32". Inside the unit are three 24" double fluorescent fixtures with 6 Phillips, F20T12/BL, 20-watt fluorescent UV Black Lite bulbs, with approximately 1" between each bulb. There is 4" between the bulbs and the negatives. All bulbs are controlled by an on/off toggle switch. You can purchase these bulbs inexpensively. See Appendix F.

Gonzalez's Gum Bichromate Workflow:

Layer 1 Magenta Negative—at 1:2 gum to sensitizer ratio

Exposed for approximately 4 minutes and develop for 1 hour.

Layer 2 Yellow Negative—at 1:2 gum to sensitizer ratio

Exposed for approximately 4 minutes and developed for 1 hour.

Layer 3 Cyan Negative—at 1:2 gum to sensitizer ratio

Exposed for approximately 4 minutes and developed for 1 hour.

Layer 4 Magenta Negative—at 1:1 gum to sensitizer ratio

Exposed for approximately 4 minutes 45 seconds and developed for 1 hour.

Layer 5 Yellow Negative—at 1:1 gum to sensitizer ratio

Exposed for approximately 4 minutes 45 seconds and developed for 1 hour.

Layer 6 Cyan Negative—at 1:1 gum to sensitizer ratio

Exposed for approximately 4 minutes 45 seconds and developed for 1 hour.

Layer 7 Magenta Negative—M at 2:1 gum to sensitizer ratio

Exposed for approximately 2 minutes 30 seconds and developed for 1 hour.

Layer 8 Yellow Negative—at 2:1 gum to sensitizer ratio

Exposed for approximately 2 minutes 30 seconds and developed for 1 hour.

Layer 9 Cyan Negative—at 2:1 gum to sensitizer ratio

Exposed for approximately 2 minutes 30 seconds and developed for 1 hour.

Layer 10 Cyan Negative—at 2:1 gum to sensitizer ratio

Exposed for approximately 2 minutes and developed for 1 hour.

Layer 11 Cyan Negative—at 2:1 gum to sensitizer ratio

Exposed for approximately 2 minutes and developed for 1 hour.

A TRADITIONAL GUM SENSITIZER EMULSION FORMULA

- 9 ml of gum Arabic
- 1/2" to 1" of artist's grade watercolor pigment
- 3 ml of saturated ammonium or potassium dichromate

This is a time-honored formula that you'll find in a lot of literature and one that tends to clear very well due to the abundance of gum in the sensitizer. It does, however, provide a rather soft impression in each pass. Begin by adding the 9 ml of gum Arabic to a small plastic, paper, or glass container. Next add the watercolor paint and stir the paint into the gum until it's smooth. To sensitize this paste, add 3 ml of a saturated ammonium, or potassium, dichromate solution and stir it into solution. Please be aware that this formula is one of those old "horses" that has made its way from one source to another since the beginning of time (*more or less*). It works perfectly well but it isn't, by any means, the last word in gum formulas. I like it for workshops because not many things go wrong with it. Each individual will adopt his or her own personal working styles, techniques, and mixes to suit their intentions and their imagery. In addition, each person's coating technique, washing style, or purist to non-purist approach, will be different according to who they are and what it is they need from the ratios and combinations of gum, paint, and dichromate. As they say in the gum labs, "It's not how impeccable your formula is, it's how you use it."

An Alternative Sensitizing Formula: "The 5-10-10"

Here's another formula that I like for large pieces because the sensitizer doesn't dry as quickly and the details are pretty nice after each pass. This sensitizer formula makes a coating that is texturally smooth and a bit pale. As I said, it's a good choice for print details that are delicate and built up patiently over subsequent exposures. This is also great formula for darker colors used to increase shadow depth in gum and combination processes such as gum and cyanotype.

- ◆ 10 ml of gum arabic
- ◆ 10 ml of warm distilled water
- ◆ 1" or more of quality watercolor paint
- ◆ 5 ml of ammonium or potassium dichromate

Cyanotype or Sensitizer Without Pigment First Pass

When your paper has been correctly sized and hardened, and you have registered your negatives with the paper so that multiple applications of exposure are possible, it is time to coat the paper. If this is your first experience with gum, or if you have not had any success with the process before, choose one of the dichromate formulas above and prepare for success.

Select the color(s) you wish to mix for the first coating. Generally, a lighter value is used first so that you can get a sense of where you will be going with the print. This lighter color is often used to print for the highlights in your negative. Measure a small amount of watercolor pigment into the gum and stir it well until it is thoroughly in solution. Now add the dichromate sensitizer under low light and stir slowly until all of the ingredients are melded together as one.

It is not uncommon to make a first exposure using only the gum arabic and the sensitizer. This exposure, providing it is not too long, will give you a light tan-colored image of your negative. You may also elect to begin your first gum exposure on top of another non-silver process such as cyanotype. In this case, your initial base color will be blue and will take the place of the Cyan in your C-M-Y-K sequence.

It is quite permissible to work under normal room light conditions, but I generally prefer to *mix* my colors under a brighter light so I can better evaluate them. It is also a good idea to paint a piece of the scrap paper with your intended emulsion and blow-dry it to quickly see what the color will look like when it's not wet. Keep in mind that when you add the dichromate to the watercolor/gum arabic solution the color will change due to the orange color of the dichromate sensitizer. Don't worry about this change, because the orange color will wash out during processing.

COATING

Coating a gum bichromate emulsion on paper is not difficult but requires practice. There are several ways to coat well. The standard technique is to work on dry, gelatin-sized and hardened, watercolor paper using a hake or foam brush. Mark the printing area with light pencil registration marks, and quickly brush-coat in even vertical, and then horizontal, strokes. Work fast, lightly, and smoothly until the emulsion just begins to become tacky. Select the width of your hake brush by the size of the area that you are coating. Obviously, a 1" brush is a more difficult tool to work with if your coating area is large. It is much less expensive to use a hardware store type of foam brush and this type of brush comes in wide assortment of sizes. I personally prefer working with the hake brush. This is because the hake brush absorbs less of the sensitizer emulsion and can be easily washed for additional use. Judy Siegel makes a case for using a foam brush saying that all

Figure 16–18

Ernestine Ruben, *Big Bird*, **China, 2007—gum**

Ernestine has been making powerful visual statements for most of her long and productive artistic life. This piece is from her brand new China portfolio. Big bird is a gum print utilizing two negatives with the second negative (as in some of the other images) created from digital captures of reflections of metallic materials. She described the reflection as being made in freezing cold weather so that she could introduce the feeling of fresh air, breezes and birds in a rather dead, used up, and dormant landscape. She combined the images digitally and Big Bird was given Cobalt blue as a color instead of white, which makes it appear that it is a gum over a cyanotype.

(Courtesy of the artist)

you need to do is gently moisten the brush with a dropper of distilled water and gently blot it with a paper towel. She's probably correct, but I'll stick with the hake because it simply feels better in my hand. Again, be careful to paint lightly, to cover the entire area that will be printed, and to be graceful with the coating.

When the emulsion begins to "set up" (*looks and feels more gummy than liquid*), take a clean, and dry, 4" hake brush and very gently whisk it back and forth until all of your application streaks have blended into a smooth coating. Barely touch the paper when doing this and you will appreciate the results. Of course, if your intention is to have a coating that is not smooth but more "*painterly,*" just go with your instincts and coat gesturally to your heart's content. When you are satisfied with the look of the coated surface, allow the sensitized paper to dry in a low light level environment; don't force-dry it with a hairdryer unless you have it set on a cool. Write down all of the technical information, such as the coating formula, paint amounts, and type, date, time of exposure, and stage of the print. Write this information also on the back of the paper for reference. Gum printing is about strategy and acquired knowledge more than intuition and impulse.

Figure 16–19

Melissa Good, *Occupancy/Vacancy*—**1998**—**gum**

Melissa, a former student of Sarah Van Keuren's in Philadelphia, created this strong gum bichromate print as part of a portfolio of portraits.

(Courtesy of the artist)

An Alternative Wet Coating Technique

An alternative method of coating is to initially soak the prepared paper in room temperature water. After removing your paper from the water bath, gently blot it until it is slightly damp with no visible water reflection on the surface. Be careful not to abuse the paper's fibers when blotting. Coat the paper in exactly same manner as you would with dry paper. You should notice a smoother coating, and will probably find it unnecessary to use the 4" hake brush for evening the emulsion coating. Dry the coated paper in a low-light environment, or force-dry the print with a hairdryer set on a cool setting. It is a good idea to contact print immediately after the paper's fresh emulsion has dried. The wet coating method will give you a somewhat lighter image, which is perfectly fine because you will be building your image over time with multiple applications.

An Alternative Spray Coating Method

For really large gum bichromate pieces, you might want to investigate the possibility of spray coating your sensitizer. The proportions are identical to the smaller print sensitizer formulas . . . you just use a lot more of the stuff and it gets increasingly expensive. Don't even think about this unless you are willing to build a ventilation spray booth with great ventilation, are willing to wear a full haz-mat body suit with goggles and dual-respirator, and are all alone. I wouldn't dream of spray coating in a group experience due to the danger of dichromate contamination.

EXPOSING THE NEGATIVES

It is pointless to attempt, or recommend, a uniform gum "*standard*" for exposure, as the variables are too numerous to define such a paradigm. These variables include density, quality, and type of pigment, humidity, time of day, negative density, strength of sensitizer, type of gum arabic, type of paper, and/or anything else that is a part of the process. There is no such thing as a "*correct*" exposure. As with most elements of this process, each part of the process is a variable that will change when another variable enters the equation. To compound the problem, you need to know what the exposure time will be as checking on the print during the exposure will tell you next to nothing about how things are going.

The exposure must be made, as in every alternative processes, with a UV light source such as the sun, a 1000 watt quart lamp, or a hellaciously expensive graphic arts, vacuum frame, exposure unit with a 3000 watt ultra violet light source. I really like these units but they are really only practical for an institution or the idle rich.

The advantage of a mechanical UV printing unit is that it is consistent year round, 24 hours a day. Gum artists working with a UV exposure unit are able to calibrate their work with less guesswork and they can better evaluate exposure times in a deductive manner. Other gum artists like the more organic and casual ritual of

Figure 16–20

Cheryl Harmeling, *Brynmore*, 1998—gum

This is an image from a portrait series that Cheryl created while at The Art Institute of Boston. Cheryl used the plastic camera to generate negatives for her black gum bichromates because of the camera's facility with mass over detail.

(Courtesy of the artist)

printing in the light of the sun. In my experience, sunlight appears to provide a "*crispier*" image and a faster exposure time. As with all of the alternative processes, you will need a hinged-back contact-printing frame for printing. You can also use 2 sheets of plate glass . . . especially for larger works where a contact sheet is impractical.

It might be a good idea when beginning a new print to make a test strip of exposures using a Stouffers 21-step-wedge. If you don't have one of these, lay opaque strips over the contact frame holding the negative and sensitized paper. Remove a strip every 20 to 40 seconds during the exposure. When using dark colors it is not a bad idea to increase the number of test strips. Don't forget to keep notes of what you are doing, including formula, time of day, and test strip times. After making the test exposures, develop the test print and you will have a pretty good idea what exposure times you should use that day. Remember that the gum process is an evolving one and is more like printmaking than like traditional silver gelatin printing. Make a plan for your printing strategies and be patient. Here are a some basic starting

exposure times to work with . . . mind you, I have no idea what your variables will be so don't be upset if my suggestion isn't dead-on for you.

◆ Sun—In the middle of the day, in the summer, with a light color and a perfect coating, on a beautifully sized and hardened paper, that is perfect for gum printing, with a negative that is not too dark, and not too light, in a geographical location that is temperate and bright, with a 1:1 gum to sensitizer ratio . . . I have no idea. You're going to have to test.

◆ 1000-watt quartz lamp—Figure about 15 to 20 minutes

◆ Tony Gonzalez's exposure unit—If you're using his unit, figure 2–5 minutes of exposure.

◆ 3000 watt Graphic Arts Exposure Unit—Figure 4 to 8 minutes—I've made Naples yellow exposures with this unit in a minute and a half so it is always best to run a few tests before you get too involved in thinking you have the exposures wired in. Don't forget: every single variable is going to change things.

Printing a Single Color Gum with a Single Negative

Quite often, especially in a workshop environment that compresses many alternative processes into a very short time, it is common to demonstrate the techniques of gum with a single negative. This is a cost-effective, and time-efficient, method of illustrating how the gum bichromate process works without taking the time to produce multiple densities with a complete set of C-M-Y-K negative separations.

By this point, you should be getting a good idea of how to think about gum printing so I'll not take a great amount of time discussing single coat strategies. Essentially, you're going to be using a single negative throughout the process. To get any kind of exposure diversity you'll have to switch up the following variables; gum to sensitizer ratio, choice of colors going from lightest to darkest, length of exposure times, and amount of water in the sensitizer.

In order to penetrate the highlight densities of your negative, make your first exposure a fairly lengthy one so that the highlight details will show. You may also refer to an earlier mention of printing with only a 1:1 ratio of gum Arabic and dichromate (no pigment) in order to lay down a tan-colored base to show highlight detail.

In a single negative/single color gum it is advisable to make the coatings thinner and less sensitive rather than use a normal sensitizer mix, playing with the ratio theories mentioned above. On subsequent exposures you can increase the ratio of gum to dichromate, back to the standard, adjusting your elements as you see the need. One thing to keep in mind when making a gum print from a single negative is that you do not want to print for the finished image on a single pass. The reason for this is that your shadows will block up. It's better to parcel out exposure time over several exposures, each taking a percentage of the total time necessary to complete the finished density. Again, keep notes on everything you do.

A Simple Single Negative Strategy

This is really basic but it does the job of letting you teach yourself the process. I'm going to keep this vague purposely because I want you to delve into the chapter and look for the answers. If you are brand new to this technique and have one contact negative to play with, here is a possible strategy for you. First, make sure that you have performed the gelatin sizing and hardening process perfectly. Now, try printing a single negative with a longish exposure and a small amount of paint. Then, for a second pass, after washing and drying the first pass, use a lot of pigment and a short exposure. For a third color pass, try using the right amount of paint, with the right amount of exposure. You should end up with your first good-looking gum print.

A Dichromate First-Step Strategy From the Past

A caveat: Although I haven't done this gum variation it sounds like it might be fun and a good solution for going on a gum printing vacation in the wilderness with pre-dichromated sensitized paper, a bottle of gum Arabic and a few tubes of paint . . . and making gum prints.

A while ago, I heard about a technique that Robert Demachy and some old time Gummists used to do. It's a different approach to gum bichromate printing and it works in an odd kind of way. Begin by gelatin sizing and hardening your paper as you would normally. Then make up a saturated solution of potassium dichromate (10%–13%) and coat it directly on your dry paper. The light level should be pretty low but the paper, once dry, will keep for a long time.

When you are ready to print, make up your gum and pigment formula and, if you think the solution is too thick, add distilled water in place of the dichromate . . . since it is already on the paper. Then all you do is expose and wash-develop in the normal manner.

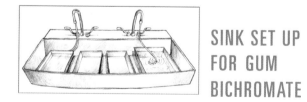

SINK SET UP FOR GUM BICHROMATE

Tray 1 A very clean tray filled with clean water

A soft hake brush for gently feathering the print during washing

Tray 2 A 1% solution of potassium metabisulfite for clearing highlights and intensifying color values if needed

Figure 16–21

Lisa Elmaleh, *The Long Goodbye*, 2006—gum

Lisa made this very large (30 × 90) gum bichromate print in my advanced alternative process workshop at The Maine Photographic Workshops in the summer of 2006. It was generated from a small series of boxed photographs of herself, her mother, and her grandmother. Those were translated into large contact films and printed sequentially . . . each image with 10 passes of color.

(Courtesy of the artist)

Tray 2 If you use potassium metabisulfite you will need to have a Tray #3 for a 30-minute final wash in cool running water. If you opt to spray the potassium metabisulfite on the freshly washed print, you will need the tray #3 as well.

WASHING & CLEARING

Development of the exposed gum print is very simple. You only need fresh water to complete the process . . . however, there are a few things you need to pay attention to.

Following exposure, immerse your paper in a tray, of ambient temperature water, that is larger than your paper. If the water is too hot you will unwittingly erase subtle details. If the water is too cold, the clearing will take forever. Gently agitate the paper, face down, for about 30 seconds and then very carefully change your water . . . holding on to the edge of your paper so that it stays still during the change. Place the print face down in the new fresh water bath and *leave it alone*.

The unexposed areas of the image will soften and drop gently to the bottom of the tray. If you agitate aggressively or run water on the surface of the emulsion you will wreak havoc on wet and fragile details in the image. Look across the paper's surface after your highlights have cleared and you will see a distinct bas-relief of the image. This relief exists because the exposed (*hardened*) areas of the image are still on the paper and swollen with water. The unexposed portions of the image will be lying peacefully on the bottom of your wash tray . . . providing your exposure was correct. If you exposed for too short a time, everything will fall off the paper. If you exposed for too long a time, nothing will.

In my experience, light colors will yield a perfectly developed print within 10 to 15 minutes. Black pigment prints will take much longer to clear than will prints with lighter colors. Single exposures with very thin colors such as Naples Yellow or Davy's Gray may take only minutes to clear. *Clear* means that the highlights are paper-base clean and the well-exposed shadow values have tonal delineation and detail.

Often you will initially see nice separation within your shadow details only to have them float away or drip off your print's surface. This indicates that you are close to having a correct exposure time but those particular areas simply haven't had enough exposure yet. Don't throw away the print. Wash it well, dry it and recoat with the same or a different color, and expose the negative again for a slightly longer time.

Prints that have been overexposed will show less contrast, flat highlights, or blocking in the shadows. Making a bath of 15 ml of ammonia, or household bleach, to a liter of water, can often repair these flaws. Be careful because this bath is very efficient at removing a lot of detail in a hurry, especially if the solution is hot. This particular remedy often becomes a technique, like spraying your cyanotypes with a mist of Tilex® toilet bowl cleaner for an unusual reticulated effect. If you are not into really aggressive gum printing (*and some people live for that effect*), I would simply re-do the print.

Another method for clearing heavily stained or overexposed prints is simply to let them soak overnight. Again, if you underexpose the print you only have to dry it, recoat it, register, and reprint the same color and negative. Your exposure on your second "pass" will likely require less time to achieve the effect you were going for in the original exposure because you will be building upon a layer of detail that already exists. Personally, I prefer a series of small exposures to one big exposure, but this is just a matter of personal taste and workflow.

Stopping Development and Re-Exposing

There will be times when you may not want to develop the print to completion or, conversely, when you wish to produce an image that is significantly different from one where you left the print to gently soak for a total clearing of the highlights. Incomplete development, where you leave a good deal of original color behind (*especially in the highlights*), can be achieved by stopping the development about halfway through and laying the paper flat, face up, on a blotting surface. If you hang it to dry, the colors will run. If you decide to abruptly stop development in progress, because you like the way it looks, you can harden the image by re-exposing the paper to UV light after it has dried.

Forced Wash-Development

On the other hand, forced development of the print, where you wish to eliminate or transform detail, can be achieved by running water directly on specific areas of the print. You may also change the way a print will look by using a brush, gloved finger or etching tool to mark in the soft and swollen pigment. Remember, in the wet state the emulsion is very sensitive to abrasion and abrasion is not always something to avoid. I have used a commercial handheld garden sprayer, the type that allows you to adjust water stream pressure and flow size, to "draw" into the soft emulsion. Use your imagination and have a good time with the options. If the end result is a mess, then chalk it up to experience and see if you can use the knowledge in a positive way. The fundamental wisdom of this is that the relationship of exposure and development depends upon a good marriage between the gum and the dichromate. The paint is the "unrequited suitor" and only stays in the relationship if the gum hardens and refuses to wash away.

A FEW WORDS: CONVENTIONAL WISDOM & STAINING

One of the "*old rules*" stipulates that a greater concentration of paint than "normal" (*whatever that means*) will result in the staining in your print's highlights. I have generally found that a greater concentration of paint in the emulsion will actually have the opposite effect and will result in *less* staining. Judy Seigel confirms this point in Issue #2 of her excellent, but sadly no longer published, *Post-Factory Photography Journal*. Judy is still doing reprints however and if you want to have a complete set they are available.

For many years, I have been laying multiple gum arabic washes, with batik resists, on watercolor papers prior to making my watercolor paintings. By doing this, I was able to paint and then return to specific sections with a wet brush to pull away painted pigment and expose highlights. This was possible because the paint was sitting on the gum Arabic rather than in paper's fibers. It made sense, the extra paint would not be a significant factor in staining when sitting in a gum arabic solution. In fact, I have always considered extra pigment (more than an 1", but not so much that flaking occurrs) as a quasi-filter, resulting in cleaner values and less stain potential. Be aware that a greater concentration of paint may also result in a shorter tonal scale, higher print contrast, and possible flaking.

Figure 16–22

Christopher James, _Sisters_, Takaragawa Baths, Japan, 1986—watercolor, resist, and gum Arabic

This 80 × 120 watercolor is an example of how I can work with highlight areas within my paintings by first laying down washes of gum Arabic and batik resist.

(Courtesy of the author)

Figure 16–23

Stefanie London, _Tulips_, 1989—gum and mixed media
Stefanie works with many materials in the translation of her intentions. This piece, made while a student of mine at Harvard, uses cyanotype, acrylic, gum bichromate and watercolor.
(Courtesy of the artist)

The Relationship of Sizing—Color—Staining

There is a relationship between the sizing formula you select and the final colors and highlight tonalities in the print. A hardened gelatin sizing, which allows for the successful clearing of highlights, will occasionally hold fast to the potassium, or ammonium, dichromate and stain your image. This result, in some cases, is a yellow tinting of lighter values within the print. These yellowish flaws can generally be cleared with a potassium or sodium metabisulfite bath following the wash-development. . . but there is a better solution to this problem; a fresh water rinse directly after the 5 minute Glyoxal hardening of your gelatin sizing. (_See Chapter 15, the Paper chapter._)

Rinsing After Glyoxal Hardening To Prevent Staining

After the (_5-minute_) Glyoxal (_Stage #2 in the Sizing and Hardening paper preparation for gum bichromate_) is allowed to permeate the gelatin sized paper completely,

it should be rinsed for 5 minutes in a fresh, cool, water bath before it is hung to dry on a line. This removes excess Glyoxal from the surface of the paper. If you avoid doing this step, the paper may turn a little yellow-beige in the highlights down the road . . . sometimes even before you use the paper for an exposure.

Clearing Stains with 1% Potassium Metabisulfite

In the event that you have dichromate stains in your highlights or borders (_the tan color_), you may clear them out with a simple 1% solution of potassium metabisulfite. Simply mix together 10 grams of potassium metabisulfite into 1000 ml of distilled water. Prints can be immersed or you may elect to spray the solution on the surface of a damp print. You might even consider selectively painting the potassium metabisulfite on problem areas. You can try sodium metabisulfite if you are low on potassium metabisulfite. You can also try potassium alum but this

Figure 16–24

Cig Harvey, *In You I Taste God*, from the Icon Series, 2006—white gum bichromate with encaustic

Cig Harvey, who teaches alternative processes in my program at The Art Institute of Boston, made this white on white gum bichromate of her husband Doug.
(Courtesy of the artist)

chemical may not help the archival intentions you have for your image. In any event, this clearing step, and subsequent wash, will be your final ones after all of your color impressions have been made.

Clear the print in the potassium metabisulfite bath until the stain goes away and then wash it for 30 minutes in clean running water. Be cautious of the percentage concentrations of the metabisulfite because they it may be more aggressive than you had anticipated. Also, don't use a sodium *bisulfite* bath as it softens the gum too much. Be sure to do a test piece before committing your print to a clearing bath and adjust the percentage strength as necessary. I suspect the 1% will work fine as long as your stains are not caused by overexposure . . . in which case you are out of luck.

You may also spot-clear with this solution using a small brush. If you notice that your emulsion has become fragile in the potassium metabisulfite clearing bath, you may want to consider drying the print and going to the final wash later on. If all attempts to clear your gum print have failed you can try a few things in the next printing session to avoid the same problem.

TROUBLE SHOOTING GUM BICHROMATE

Note: Any of these suggestions may be disregarded if they don't fit your working style.

First Rule of Fixing Gum Bichromate Problems

Many of the solutions for gum problems are mentioned in the earlier sections of this chapter. There are a lot of things to consider when tracking down gum vexations and this next section will deal with a lot of them. However, there is a rule . . . When hunting for remedies to problems . . . ONLY FIX ONE THING AT A TIME.

Sizing

If you are experiencing staining, the very first thing I look at is my gelatin sizing and hardening materials and technique. Did I take shortcuts? Did I make do with what I had rather than use the correct solutions? Fix this part of your gum technique and you are pretty much assured of eliminating the biggest staining problem. While you're at this thought, you might also consider using a different variety of paper. One more time . . . simply because it really does prevent the problem of yellow staining most of the time. After you glyoxal-harden your gelatin for 5 minutes, rinse the paper in cool running water for 5 minutes and line dry. Yes, I know, that was more than one change at a time.

Paint

Try duplicating your technique with a different brand of paint. Always use the highest-quality watercolors you can buy. Student-grade watercolors often have little quality to speak of and will often end up staining your print or washing out in splotches. Some colors are particularly tough to clear and personally I've had problems with greens. When I want a green I will generally mix a safe primary blue and a yellow rather than opt for the tube green. I will also lean toward greens that I trust and that always clear well, such as, Winsor & Newton's Oxide of Chromium.

Add Pigment

You might want to try adding more pigment to the sensitizer. This often is the first fix I'll attempt and it does work . . . in spite of the nasty things people on the alt pro discussion groups say about the idea.

Gum Arabic

Another fix is to try using a higher grade (*a more clear variety*) of gum Arabic, or add a little more of it to your sensitizer formula.

Dichromates

Try re-mixing a fresh dichromate in case of contamination, using less dichromate in the sensitizer mix. In my experience, potassium dichromate (which is slower than ammonium dichromate) demonstrates evidence of staining less than ammonium dichromate.

Changing Exposure Time

You might consider changing your specific color exposure times (*see Tony Gonzalez workflow in this chapter*) for multiple, and shorter, exposures.

Curve & Color Layer

Try using the custom curve and color layer described in this chapter. Simply having a negative that is less

difficult to print will often eliminate the subsequent staining of your image.

The Last Resort

There is a chance that everything you are doing process wise is correct and that you simply need a new negative. Then again, perhaps it's time to wave the white flag and give up on the one you're using for this process. This begs for the Pictorico OHP solution to the problem. Last, but not least, you can be upbeat about the entire experience, think about how much fun gum printing is, and start all over again. You might also consider using the print as a base for another process or a canvas for you to paint, paste, and play on.

First Impressions: Cyanotype First Pass

If you are having a hard time establishing a foundation for your gum print you might want to try one of my favorite techniques . . . consider making a cyanotype as your first color impression. It provides a strong and finely detailed blue (*or some other color if you tone it*) and gives a fine visual map to work upon. You may also consider making a gum "pass" on top of a platinum or palladium print if you want to raise some eyebrows. Actually, this combination was quite popular with many pictorialists in the early part of the century. The additional gum bichromate step helps bring out and define complex shadow details and often provides additional depth to the image. If you intend to try this, begin with a brief green or blue gum exposure as Steiglitz did.

To Darken an Image

Perhaps the solution is to simply repeat the negative, in registration, but with a less intensive exposure. You can expose for a shorter time, add a little water to your sensitizer, try a darker paint, a lighter version of the negative . . . especially if it's a digital negative, just adjust your curves. Also try a complementary color, or a *little* more dichromate in the formula. If you add more dichromate to the sensitizer mix you will experience a reduction of contrast and an increase in your exposure time. Adding more pigment to your sensitizer, which may initially seem like a good idea, may or may not work and the success of this choice will depend on a few other variables.

To Lighten an Image

The easiest solution to this problem is to use a lighter color or to dilute your sensitizer formula with a little water. You can expose your print for a shorter exposure but that really isn't the best approach to the problem because you want the exposure to be complete enough to harden everything in the print that needs hardening. Printing a lighter, or dilute, color is better than under-exposing. Short exposures will often yield more contrast because only the thinnest parts of the negative, your shadows, will react to the hardening effects of UV exposure, i.e., more of the pigment will remain unhardened during the exposure and will wash out during the wash-development.

Using less dichromate in the formula will result in a solution that is slower (*reduced sensitivity*) and has more contrast because only shadows will print-out. You may lighten the entire image by using less pigment in the formula and this will result in less contrast and possibly some unwanted tonalities in your highlights.

The cave person approach to the problem would be to wash the image in very hot water or try using a 5% solution of potassium metabisulfite, or ammonia.

To Increase Shadow Density Without Changing Highlights

The first thing I would do in this situation would be to make sure my negative set would accomplish this task for me. If you're impatient, try decreasing the exposure times of subsequent coatings. You may also try using less dichromate in the formula. Also try adding proportionately less pigment, by half, to each subsequent formula and exposure. This allows shadows to build slowly and may help minimize staining in the highlights. Many alternative gum artists will add more pigment to subsequent coatings to increase contrast. If you have the time, try both methods and determine which works best for you.

To Enhance Highlights Without Blocking the Shadows

Is your gelatin sizing and hardening technique imperfect? This could be a reason your shadows are blocking. Is your negative set right for your formula and exposure time? Those are the first questions I would ask and then I would make a quick print and see if I could fix the problem by adding additional gum to the sensitizer formula. Next, try a decrease in the amount of watercolor pigment you add to your sensitizer and modestly increase the exposure time. Both of these options will result in less contrast in the print. You can also achieve a full tonal range by altering the amount of pigment added to each additional coating but the success of this tactic will be dependent on several other factors.

To Reduce Contrast

Use lighter colors, use potassium dichromate instead of ammonium dichromate in the sensitizer, dilute the ammonium dichromate, use a higher concentration of dichromate sensitizer and decrease the amount of pigment, expose longer, and/or develop for less time. Dilute the sensitizer with gum or water. To tone down colors, try using their complements, instead of immediately reaching for a tube of black watercolor paint.

If the Highlights Will Not Print at All

This isn't unusual, especially if you are using a pinhole camera or making your negative set with ortho film. The first thing I would recommend would be "flashing" your entire image area without a negative in the contact printing frame . . . with only a 1:1 sensitizer coating of gum arabic and dichromate. Expose quickly, and you should be able to inspect the exposure (as there is not paint in the formula) looking for a "whisper" in the highlights. Eliminating the color will make your highlights a tan color. And will, if you get the exposure right, give you some highlight definition.

A Full Color Inventory

Some gum artists like to make up their color and gum emulsions in larger batches and store them in Tupperware® or urine sample containers from the local HMO health provider. This allows you to establish a color inventory and save time. Urine sample containers are great since most have an embossed graduate scale on the side and a very secure screw cap. Next time you go in for a physical check-up, pick up a few for free. *Do not add the dichromate yet.* The dichromate is added just before you intend to use the color. Keep the proportions of gum to color the same as when mixing small batches, i.e., 50 ml of gum to a 15 ml tube of watercolor paint.

Figure 16–25

Carmen Lizardo, *Santo niño de antoche*, 2006—gum

Here is another nice example of Carmen's mastery of the gum bichromate process.

(Courtesy of the artist)

This is not a recipe set in stone. Your gum, and the type of paint that you select, will dictate the proportions, and that will take a little testing. You are seeking a solution, so that when the sensitizer is added, and the exposure is correct, your print will clear quickly and easily with no staining.

Make Color Charts

Each new paper, paint type, sensitizer, sizing, hardener, and emulsion will show you a different look. Write this information on swatches, cut them into slide size shapes, and keep them in a slide sheet to use as a reference chart.

Try Painting on Gum Emulsions

Try painting on gum emulsions in selected areas of the print, i.e., eyes, clothing, lips, and so forth, instead of total paper coverage in the traditional manner. This allows you to add specific areas of color without affecting the entire print. To avoid a hard edge on the selective color, wet a fan-shaped watercolor brush in clean water and lightly drag it along the edge of the recently applied selected color before it dries. This "feathering" creates a softer edge line.

Create Area "Masks" Using Gum

Painting an extra coating of gum Arabic in the areas you do not want completely colored after exposure works quite well. You can also use other masking devices in conjunction with the negative, such as rubylith film or Mylar®. I like gum because it washes out well and can be blended unlike rubylith. The image in the emulsion achieves its tonalities based on the degree of its hardening. The harder it is after exposure, the less of it washes off. The less it is hardened, the more of it washes off. Pay attention to your exposure times.

Exposure

Exposure is controlled by several factors that you can keep in mind when creating print strategy. What is your source of UV light, the color of the pigment in the emulsion, the expected exposure time, the proportion of dichromate to gum, the thickness of the sensitizer, and the humidity?

Some practitioners find that the higher the humidity, the shorter the exposure. Others report the opposite is true in their work . . . go figure. Best bet in my experience is to keep the humidity above 45% and below 65%. Long exposures will result in less contrast because more of the sensitizer becomes insoluble and refuses to clear in the wash-development. Shorter exposures work in the opposite manner. Use your exposure control as a minor player in this drama.

Your Print Does Not Clear

There are a few things that could have caused this problem. The first, and most common reason, is that the idea of spending time gelatin sizing and hardening didn't appeal to you and so you thought that maybe, just this once, you could make a nice gum print without doing that step. Sorry, if your pigment goes into the paper's fibers, rather than sit on the surface of the hardened gelatin sizing, it will grab on and stain the paper exactly as paint is supposed to do. Other things that could have caused the print not to clear include; over-exposure or you may have used too much hair dryer heat.

Your Print Washes Down the Drain

This is really simple . . . Only a few things could have gone wrong for the print to completely leave the paper during the wash-development. Nearly 85 % of the time the reason is that your exposure wasn't long enough to harden the dichromate—gum—pigment sensitizer. The other three 5% reasons; you forgot to add the dichromate to the gum and pigment, the emulsion was still wet when you made your exposure, the gum Arabic that you used is impure or rotten . . . don't forget, it is vegetable matter.

Your Print's Surface Texture . . .

If your surface looks uneven, you can take a piece of fine sandpaper or steel wool and gently give it a nice matte-luster finish by softly sanding the surface in small circular swirls.

Emulsion Flaking Off

This problem generally happens when you have used too much paint or your sensitized emulsion was too thick when you painted it on. Add a little water to the sensitizing formula to thin it out. This will soften your image for that pass and give you a chance for some fine details.

Streaks in the Print

This generally means that your coating technique needs some work. It isn't fatal. Simply get some scrap paper, say the backs of prints that you don't like, and practice coating them with a non-sensitized mix of gum and paint. You'll be good at it soon. Another reason you might see streaking is that you didn't attend to your print in the wash stage . . . in other words, it stayed in the water but not necessarily evenly and/or completely.

Random Last Thoughts

Take your time learning gum printing and enjoy the simplicity of the process as well as its often-maddening complexity. Unless you wish to show evidence of working stress on the surface of your print, sometimes you just have to put the print face down in the water and do something else for a while (*this will make sense later on*). Gum bichromate is different from others in the alternative process genre and it is unhealthy for your creative self to think that there is a perfect way to do it. I write this even though I know of at least six gum printers who claim that their technique is sublime perfection and the "only way" the process can ever be performed. They are wrong. Being dogmatic about how to make a gum bichromate print is like telling a child that only blue crayons are acceptable for coloring a sky. The variables in gum printing are *infinite* and each individual's intentions will never be exactly like another's. Play and practice are the secrets to becoming a good gummist. Play with the myriad elements of gum and practice to make your personal technique compatible with your intentions . . . so that it works for you.

Dichromate Options: The Chromatype, the Dusting-On Process, Alternative Surfaces for Gum, 3-D Gum Bichromate

OVERVIEW & EXPECTATIONS

In this chapter, you will be introduced to a few esoteric chromium/dichromate-based processes that are interesting to do, are contemporary adaptations of older procedures, or are ones that enjoyed a limited degree of popularity at the time they were conceived.

I'll begin, as always, with a little history, but this time it will be in the context of an exchange of letters between Henry James (from the Ordnance Survey Office) and William Henry Fox Talbot. This correspondence is very interesting in that Henry James is writing to Talbot about his experiments with a process he calls *Photo-zincography*. He relates how the technique incorporates collodion negatives on glass, potassium bichromate, and gum Arabic, and that the process, when incorporated photo-mechanically, with a printing press, can be used to duplicate maps and manuscripts at the cost of a half-penny a page. Talbot replies suggesting that the idea of making a mixture of gum and potassium bichromate (*bichromate of potash*), the process James is describing, is protected by his exclusive patents . . . (Does this sound familiar?) What follows is pretty interesting.

The first process that I'll describe in this chapter is Robert Hunt's Chromatype process from 1843. From there, I'll give you a good deal of information about working with the ever-charming, and head-banging, Dusting-On process and how to incorporate the Dusting-On ingredients, and workflow, in the process with ceramics and coating on glass.

Then we'll jump ahead to a discussion of how to perform 3-D gum bichromate images and how to make the images, and 3-D glasses that you'll need to complete the illusion. There is more, but essentially the primary intention of this chapter is to stimulate your interest in inventing something new for yourself by using your knowledge of light-sensitive dichromate solutions. In its most basic form, that UV light causes a dichromate salt (*potassium, ammonium, or sodium dichromate*) to make a colloid, such as gum Arabic, gelatin, or honey, insoluble in water in proportion to the degree of exposure.

Figure 17–1

Naomi Savage, *Ozymandias*, c. 1965—acid etched plate

Naomi Savage has always been one of my favorite artists and she was always breaking the boundaries with her work. Really, Naomi was making alternative images before there were alternative images. She began her career in photography in the early 1940s, studying with Bernice Abbott at The New School. A few years later she assisted her uncle, Man Ray, and then set out on her own. *Ozymandias* is a prime example of Naomi's work. What you see here was a created with a bichromated emulsion on a silver plated copper sheet. Following exposure, the plate was deeply acid etched, inked and selectively wiped. Naomi saw her inked plate as the finished piece itself rather than escorting it through the traditional intaglio translation to paper. I have lived with this plate on my wall for years and never tire of its power and beauty.

(Courtesy of the author and artist)

A LITTLE HISTORY

In 1849, considering that photography had only been in existence for 10 years, Henry Hunt Snelling (1816–1897) published a very interesting book . . . *The History and Practice of Photography* (G.P. Putnam, New York*)*. In the book, he discussed the efforts of several enterprising individuals who sought to utilize chromic acid as an active agent in the making of photographic images. He documented how, in 1839, Mungo Ponton (*remember him from Chapter 16, the Gum Bichromate chapter?*) discovered that paper impregnated with bichromate of potash (*potassium dichromate*) was sensitive to UV light. In his *Pontontype* process, paper was coated with the bichromate of potash solution and exposed to sunlight using objects to create a negative photogram image. The exposed print was then washed, to remove any unexposed dichromate, and dried; what remained was a light buff colored orange-sepia print that consisted of chromium dioxide. It is not known if Ponton was aware of the 1832 observations of Gustav Suckow regarding the sensitivity of chromates.

Snelling went on to describe how Edmund Becquerel advanced the work of Ponton a year later, in 1840, by sizing the substrate with starch prior to sensitizing it with bichromate of potash (potassium dichromate) and how that enabled the conversion of a negative image to a positive "*by use of a solution of iodine, which combined with that portion of the starch on which light had not acted.*" He then went on to say, in a non-judgmental way, that clear and distinct pictures failed to be realized in either Ponton's or Becquerel's process.

A few years later, in 1843, Robert Hunt had an inspiration that incorporated the use of copper sulfate and potassium bichromate with direct positive images, of orange and lilac, in the camera obscura. In his book, Snelling related his impressions about Hunt's *Chromatype* process as being exceedingly simple to perform, resulting in images with a pleasing character, and ideally suited to

Figure 17–2

William Henry Fox Talbot At Home, 1839

(Courtesy of The George Eastman House/International Museum of Photography)

making images of botanical specimens, engravings, and the like . . . if only it were a bit more light sensitive.

Eight years later, in 1854, William Henry Fox Talbot added to this history by observing the ability of potassium dichromate to have a hardening effect upon a colloidal gelatin that was directly proportional to the degree of UV light that the gelatin received.

With that as your background, and more history to come with the Dusting On process, here is the exchange of letters between Fox Talbot and Henry James . . . no, not that Henry James. These letters were documented through the efforts of Dr. Larry Schaaf and The Correspondence of William Henry Fox Talbot Project. If you are interested in this fascinating collection, of over 10,000 letters to and from Talbot, 1800–1877, please go and visit: www.foxtalbot.dmu.ac.uk/contact/contact.html. By the way, all of the grammatical quirks and odd spellings are from the original letters.

William Henry Fox Talbot — Henry James Letters — 1860

Henry James to William Henry Fox Talbot

Date: 14 May 1860

Collection: Fox Talbot Museum/Lacock Abbey Collection Lacock

Collection number historic: LA60-019

Ordnance Survey Office

Southampton 14th May 1860

My dear Sir,

I have great pleasure in sending you some specimens of Photo-zincography. This. art promises to be of great importance to the public for the purpose of making fac-similes of ancient M.S.S. or rare works either in type, or engraved in outline. We have not attempted to copy any thing in which there is a gradation of shade, and the process is not suited for it. The process consists in this, a highly intensified negative is first taken on glass by the collodion method, a print is then taken on a sheet of very thin paper which has been washed over with a saturated solution of the bichromate of potash and gum, and dried. After exposure for one or two minutes, the Bichromate positive is laid on a sheet of zinc which has been previously coated with lithographic ink, and passed through the press. The paper is then submerged in a shallow vessel of hot water with a little gum in it, and the water is agitated and the paper gently brushed over the paper to remove the soluble bichromate, and the ink attached to it, this leaves the insoluble portion with the ink on it, or in other words a positive picture charged with ink, and ready for being transferred either to zinc, stone, or to the waxed surface of a copper plate—I prefer zinc for many reasons, and an examination of the specimens sent will enable you to judge of the degree of perfection to which we have already brought this art. We could copy any M.S. or rare book at a cost of half-penny a page—I have been anxious to give the fullest publicity to what we have done in this way, and I have therefore given an account of it, with a specimen, in my Annual Report to Parliament, and you will see an account of it, both in the Photographic News, *and the* Photographic Journal, *I believe a full account will appear in the next number of the latter which will come out this week–*

I am much obliged for the specimens of photoglyphic engraving, and it appears clear to me, that if you confine yourself to the copying of lines, you can produce very perfect copies, and they will be sharper and clearer than by photo-zincography –

But I cannot think that your Camera is exactly suited for this class of work—we have an 8 inch lens for ours, and you will see that we produce photographs of folio sized drawings, of the exact same dimensions as the original.

The engraving of Furness Abbey proves beyond doubt that you will also succeed with the half tints –

Has any account of your process been yet published? if so I wish to have a reference to it. I hope you may be able to pay this Estbt a visit, we have many things which will interest you here.

Yours very truly

Henry James.

William Henry Fox Talbot to Henry James

Date: 17 May 1860

Collection: Fox Talbot Museum/Lacock Abbey Collection Lacock

Collection number historic: LA60-020

May 17, 1860

I am much obliged to you for by your very friendly letter of the fourteenth and for the specimens which accompanied it—I have no doubt there is much in the Ordnance establishment at Southampton which would interest me greatly to see and I hope that some day or other I may have the opportunity. But the question which you have asked me in your letter, viz., Has Whether any account of your my process has been yet published? proves to me beyond a doubt that at present you are unacquainted with the fact that in 1852 I gave full publicity to an invention [illegible deletion] in photography, for which I took out a patent which process depends mainly on the fact (of which I was the first discoverer) that a mixture of bichromate of potash with gum when spread on any surface and exposed to light, becomes by the action of light insoluble in water so that if it were is immersed in water subsequently, the water washed removes only those parts of the Gum on which the light [has] not acted.

I subsequently in 1858 took out another Patent [for] improvements on the process, but these although considerable in themselves are not material to be here mentioned considered. I was strongly of opinion that this invention would prove of great utility whenever it came to be adopted in a large scale either by the Government or by some enterprising Capitalist or Company. But in 1856 or 1857 a Company was formed in London with the title of the Photogalvanographic Company who began operations on an extensive scale [1] Their process consisted in this: they spread upon Glass a mixture of bichromate of potash and gum : when dry they placed upon it a photograph or engraving and placed it in the light to obtain a photographic image on the gum—They then placed the sheet of glass in water which removed the insoluble [2] portion leaving a picture on the glass in very low bas relief. They then electrotyped the picture on the glass and thus obtained a copperplate impressed with a similar picture from which they printed in the usual manner in which engravings are printed numerous impressions by means of a Copperplate printing press.

This process being carried on in disregard of my patent right a correspondence ensued between my Solicitor and theirs, which proved unsatisfactory and I commenced an action against them in the Court of Queen's Bench. In consequence of this the Company, which I have no doubt thoroughly explored the matter question finding they had no case gave the matter up and dissolved the Company, discontinuing entirely their process of manufacture when of course the legal proceedings (against them) were dropped as I had not the least wish to give unnecessary trouble. One advantage however accrued, viz. that the patent was on this occasion very thoroughly explored by the lawyers and other persons employed by the Company who found no flaw in it ? if they had found any flaw in it, would have advised the Company to persevere.

With respect to your own very ingenious and successful process you will excuse me if I feel a certain degree of embarrassment [illegible deletion] in speaking to you, the inventor, on this subject. The fact is that I have spent a large sum of money upon the Science of my Photographic inventions (amounting to many thousands of pounds eight or nine-thousand pounds at the least) and it does appear to me a hard thing that when these inventions are, as many of them in succession have been, adopted by the Government for the Public Service that no portion of the advantage which thus accrues to the Public, is ever reaped by the original inventors—It is true that our Statesmen and public men at the head of departments Cabinet Ministers and the like have not the slightest wish to perpetrate an injustice but the facts of Science and the claims of Scientific men ???? too often remain unknown to them their thoughts being absorbed by other and higher matters–

I believe and I think it is capable of proof that considerable sums of money have been saved by the Public by the use of my inventions, yet never has the slightest acknowledgement been made by Her Majesty's Government. Now here is another beautiful and useful invention which you have brought nearly to perfection and which I assure you I admire very much : but it treads upon my rights as a patentee, and therefore if it is intended to employ it for the public service (which and I am confident sure might be done it would prove useful in many ways) I think the Government ought in the first instance to take a license from me for the use of that part of the process which was invented by me my invention. This license need not be calculated on such a scale as to place any impediment in the way of the full development free use of the Photozincography because another mode exists (of insuring a just remuneration) which I am sure would prove most satisfactory to everyone and this with your leave I will proceed to explain.

There are at the Admiralty and I have no doubt at the Office of the Ordnance Survey, and at other Government offices a very large number of maps plans drawings, etc., which it would be very useful impossible to publish but the thing cannot be of full size, because they would fill folio volumes; but which if reduced to a small octavo size by photography and then published would be make handy and useful books. But when maps and plans are so much reduced in a Camera the lines and names become so minute close and crowded that your they could not be rendered printed distinctly by your process of zincography whereas on the contrary by my photoglyphic process is capable of copying very the closest and finest engravings, sometimes without blurring a single line on the other hand your process has a great the advantage when the plate is large and lines or letters are bold—There being then this broad distinction between them it follows that both inventions might be largely employed in the public service without injuring interfering with each other and therefore if I have made myself intelligible explained the matter clearly it only remains it is for me to say that if you think fit to recommend to the head of the Ordnance department (is it not Sidney Herbert?) [3] to take a license for the Government use of my patent on behalf of the Government that license would of course include both your invention and mine and place the matter on a just and equitable basis—If in your opinion Mr Herbert would refer the question to the Government Solicitor for his opinion I should be happy to show that gentleman the paper legal proceedings which took place with the Photogalvanographic Company, as I have no doubt they too all the Gentlemen the discussion which then took place exhausted pretty nearly all that could be said on the subject.

I will say no more on matters of business at present but just advert to a perfectly true and just fair criticism which you have made on my photoglyphs 'from Nature'—These are certainly much too small, and do not do justice to the art by any means but the fact is, that as I have no assistant, I select small plates as giving me less trouble—and being well aware that The principle is exactly the same whatever the size of the plate But of course—the public taste will require larger views whenever the process which is now mainly experimental is judged to have come to that a sufficient degree of perfection which to use for the certain of for which a volume of specimens a volume of specimens is published–

Notes:

1. *The Photogalvanographic Company, involving Roger Fenton (1819–1869), photographer & lawyer, and Paul Pretsch (1808–1873), Austrian photographer & inventor; founder of the Photogalvanographic Company, produced heavily retouched photomechanical reproductions of photographs in direct violation of WHFT's patent for photoglyphic engraving, see Glossary.*

2. *WHFT obviously meant to say that it removed the soluble portion, leaving the insoluble portion on the glass.*

3. *Sydney Herbert (1810–1861), War Secretary, and hence James' superior, in 1860.*

Henry James to William Henry Fox Talbot

Date: 23 May 1860
Collection: Fox Talbot Museum/Lacock Abbey Collection Lacock
Collection number historic: LA60-022
Ordnance Survey Office,
Southampton
23rd May 1860
My dear Sir,

Before publishing my Annual Report to Parliament on the progress of the Ordnance survey in 1859, in which I have given an account of the process which I have called Photo-zincography and also a specimen, I obtained the written opinion of Mr Carpmael of the Patent office, through the Solicitor of the War office, and he says we can publish any thing by that process without "being subject to any patent".

Mr Mungo Ponton in a communication to the Edinburgh New Phil. Journal of May 1839, says "In the case of the bichromate of potash, again, the salt is exceedingly soluble, and paper can be easily saturated with it. The agency of light not only changes its colour, but deprives it of solubility thus rendering it fixed to the paper."

*Again I find that Mr Hunt discovered and published at the meeting of the British Association at [Cork?] in 1843, the process which he named **Chromatype** which is founded on the process of Mr Ponton—Mr Becquerel has also (in 1845–6) described the peculiar effect of light on the bichromate of potash, and therefore I am surprized now to learn that you could in 1852 claim to be the first discoverer of this property of the bichromate of potash upon which all these processes depend. I shall therefore feel obliged if you would state clearly what part of the process we employ in Photo-zincography you claim as your invention.*

I do not as yet see any purpose to which your photoglyphic process would be advantageously employed on the Ordnance Survey, we have to reduce 16 sheets, each 3ft × 2ft to the scale of 9in × 4in, and then engrave them on copper on one sheet—if you can show us how that can be accurately and economically done it may be of use to us –

> *Believe me very truly yours*
> *Henry James*

William Henry Fox Talbot to Henry James

Date: 13 June 1860

Collection: Preus Fotomuseum/Norsk Museum for Fotografi

Collection number: 001-HNX-16-C

Collection 2: draft in NMPFT/RPS Collection

Lacock Abbey, Chippenham

June 13th 1860

Dr Sir

Your letter though dated the 8th inst. [1] only reached here Yesterday. With your permission I will defer further consideration of the question of the zincography with reference to my patent, [2] for a couple of months, for the reason that I am going to the Continent next week, or very soon afterwards, being one of the devoted band of astronomers and men of science who intend health permitting—to observe the eclipse of the 18th July in the North of Spain –

From the particulars You mention in your letter of the present mode of engraving the Ordnance maps it results that the actual engraving is wholly done by hand—All that photography does for you is to trace out an outline which the engraver is to follow with his tool as closely as he can. But in a map 3 × 2 feet I think there must be some thousands of names and I do not see how these can be engraved by one man with less than several days labour. Consequently though I cannot estimate exactly the saving wch wd be effected by the photoglyphic process, I perceive that it must be considerable.

> *I remain*
> *Yours very Truly*
> *H. F. Talbot*
> *Col Sir H James &c Southampton*

Notes:

1. See Doc. No: 08113.

2. WHFT and James were in negotiation over the process of zincography employed by the Ordnance Survey Office, and whether it infringed either of WHFT's patents for photographic or photoglyphic engraving.

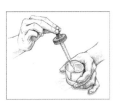

THE CHROMATYPE PROCESS

How to Make a Robert Hunt Chromatype (1843)

Step 1   **Immerse in Copper Sulfate**

Immerse the paper in a solution of copper sulfate made by mixing 3.70 g of copper sulfate to 30 ml of distilled water. After the paper is sufficiently saturated, hang it until it is partially dry.

Step 2   **Immerse in Potassium Bichromate**

The partially dried paper is then immersed in a *"moderately strong"* solution of bichromate of potash (*potassium dichromate*). I am assuming that since we generally use potassium dichromate in a saturated solution between 10% and 13% that Hunt means that this solution is pretty close to saturated. Begin testing at 11.5%. Other chromates can be used however; Snelling indicated that none were as successful as Hunt's chromate of copper.

Step 3   **Dry at a Little Distance From the Fire**

Now, according to Hunt and Snelling, you're supposed to dry your paper *"at a little distance from the fire"*; and the paper, once ready, would be fine for use for quite a while. Since the majority of you probably don't have a hearth fire burning at all times, I think that hanging the paper on a line in a low-level ambient light (not fluorescent) will be fine.

Step 4 Exposure

When the sun is out, try using a negative in a contact frame, or making a photogram of some sort directly on the paper's surface. Expose your chromate of copper paper directly in the sun for 15–20 minutes. The image that you will see after the exposure will be in the form of a negative.

Step 5 Silver Nitrate Wash

Now it is necessary to wash over the negative print with a solution of silver nitrate. This will provide, according to Snelling, an immediate and beautiful deep orange image on a tan (*and sometimes white*) background. I would recommend beginning with a 6% to 10% silver nitrate solution and adjust up or down from there for the best results. It shouldn't take more than a few attempts before you will know which percentage will work best.

Step 6 Fix with Distilled Water

The image must be fixed immediately by washing the exposed paper in distilled water (*try 2 baths at 5 minutes each*) and then line dry.

Option: Talbot's Potassium Bromide Fix

Although that is the only fixing requirement indicated in Hunt's process, you might want to try an experiment if you find that your image is yellowing. Perhaps, just for fun, try Talbot's potassium bromide Calotype/salt fix: 6.4 g of potassium bromide mixed into 300 ml distilled water.

Lilac Positives after a Salting Bath

If you elect to use this potassium bromide salt bath, you may see your image slowly fade, and if all goes well, be left with a delicate negative outline of the original. If you then dry the paper and re-expose it to bright sunshine, a positive, lilac colored, image will emerge in a few minutes.

Snelling relates, regarding the relative strength of the solutions, that if they are saturated (*such as the potassium bichromate at 10%–13%*) that a negative is produced. However, if the solutions are "*three or four times their bulk of water,*" that the picture darkens initially and then a bleaching effect takes place resulting in a faint positive which is then brought out with great delicacy by the silver nitrate bath.

Figure 17–3

Galina Manikova, ID—04, 1993—Dusting-On/Ceramic

Galina Manikova is one of the most productive artists I have ever known. Much of her work is motivated by the memories of her childhood and the images found in her family albums. This is Galina at age 5, or 6, sitting on a bench.

(Courtesy of the artist)

THE DUSTING-ON PROCESS: A LITTLE (MORE) HISTORY

The Dusting-On process is a curious alternative process technique that a many creative people had a role in developing. It began to evolve in 1832 with Suckow's observation of chromate sensitivity. Mungo Ponton's revelation, in 1939, regarding the light sensitivity of potassium dichromate, was immediately followed in 1840 by Edmund Becquerel's realization that the dichromate's unique properties and reactions were, in part, due to the starch used in papermaking and that the same results could be recreated with any organic substance, i.e., albumen, gelatin, gum acacia, and glue. In 1855, Alphonse Poitevin considered, and attempted, the application of the dichromate process to the photomechanical production of permanent prints and filed for his first carbon process patent.

In 1858, Henri Garnier and Alphonse Salmon recorded an odd photochemical reaction when they observed that ferric citrate showed less solubility in water, when combined with glycerin or alcohol, in those areas that had been exposed to sunlight. Based on this observation, they proceeded to make the first Dusting-On process experiments. Using paper or glass, the exposed chemical coating was then dusted with pine soot, or colored powder, whereupon it adhered to the more soluble, less exposed, portions of the substrate. The paper or glass was then "fixed" in a water bath where the un-hardened, more soluble, less exposed, iron salt dissolved and dropped away from the substrate.

Dusting-On has a complicated family tree its roots intersect with the work of Vauquelin, Ponton, Becquerel, Talbot, Archer, Garnier, Salmon, and Poitevin and many more. In 1858, Alphonse Louis Poitevin worked on a process that utilized a dichromate sensitized colloidal solution of bees honey and gum Arabic is often credited with being the first to then add pigment, as in the gum bichromate process, into the equation. Poitevin also conducted variations on the dichromate theme . . . among them, a perchloride of iron (*aka, ferric chloride and iron trichloride—this is a highly toxic chemical used to engrave metal plates*) and tartaric acid solution exposed under a negative that had been covered with collodion and transferred to a gelatinized paper. When mixed with gelatin, perchloride of iron/tartaric acid, it was exposed under a positive and could then be "developed" by dusting on directly. The best guide for this process is Poitevin's own book from 1863 in which he describes using both gelatin and gum base options.

How It Works

In the Dusting-On process, a transparent or translucent *positive* film, or image, is used rather than a negative. The reason for this is so that a powdered colored pigment can be dusted on the exposed print and the areas of the exposure that have not received a lot of UV light (*the darker shadows*) will still be tacky (*un-hardened colloid/dichromate*) and able to receive the powdered pigment following the exposure. Printed without any post exposure colored pigment application, exposures with this sensitizer will result in chromium dioxide, sepia colored images. This type of print is essentially Mongo Ponton's *Pontontype* technique that employs potassium dichromate as a solo sensitizer; left alone, unwashed, the image will eventually turn a pale green similar in color to oxide of chromium watercolor paint.

Dusting-On for the Deceased

The most bizarre variation of these concepts is attributed to one of the several books by Fraprie and Woodbury . . . each titled *Photographic Amusements: Including Tricks and Unusual or Novel Effects Obtainable with the Camera*. After a great treasure hunt, I located, and purchased, a 1931 version of one of their books hoping to find the exact description of the following Dusting-On technique. Alas, it wasn't the right edition but this is the basic idea.

In the Fraprie and Woodbury book I couldn't find, there is a Dusting-On technique that calls for the use of a dead person's cremated ashes for the pigment! The general idea is that you take a picture of the recently deceased. This practice was very common in the past when people died at home instead of hospitals. It is also why many older homes have double front doors so that the coffin and pallbearers could comfortably exit the house. I digress . . . in any event they made a transparent positive and then placed the positive in contact with a gelatin-sized paper coated with a potassium dichromated sensitizer and honey.

Following a UV exposure of the film positive, in contact with the gelatin sized and sensitized paper, all that you needed to do was humidify the paper and gently sprinkle the ashes of the recently cremated person over the humidified, and sticky, dichromate parts that had

Figure 17–4

Galina Manikova, *Blue & Fireproof*, 1989—Dusting-On ceramic

In this work, the images are transferred to both ceramic and metal using the dusting on method and very finely ground iron powder for dusting on metal plates that give the impression of shadows. The finished plates are covered with an overcoat of special hard glue to protect them.

(Courtesy of the artist)

not been hardened by light. The excess ashes were then brushed away, leaving an image of the departed in his, or her, very own ashes! Since reading about this process I have this vision . . . I see the bereaved family sitting in a circle, each holding an edge of the exposed bichromated image of the deceased, straws between the lips, all gently blowing on the paper, humidifying the portrait so that it will accept the ashes.

The Dusting-On process can be used on a variety of surfaces, including paper, glass, prepared metal (*see liquid emulsions on metal*) and canvas. The best rule for this technique is to have a good time with it

and not expect too much until you modify it to suit your working style.

Dusting-On Process with Ceramic Pigment

If we return to the basic premise of the gum bichromate/Dusting-On process, both processes are solidly based upon the concept that a colloid (*collodion, gelatin, gum, honey, bitumen, etc.*) can be made sensitive to UV light by the addition of a UV light-sensitive dichromate. When this sensitized colloid is exposed to UV light, the portions of the colloid that are exposed to the light will harden in direct proportion to the amount of the exposure. In other words, the colloid hardens, becomes less sticky, and will not dissolve in a wash-development bath.

However, in the Dusting-On process, unlike a gum bichromate process, the contact film is not a negative but a positive. If you were to work on a metallic plate, the final image would be realized by brushing over the exposed surface of the prepared colloidal metallic plate with ceramic pigment, or metallic enamels that would adhere to the exposed image in direct proportion to the amount of exposure the plate had received. After drying the plate, the image is covered with coat of gelatin or gum Arabic, and after drying, it can be spray glazed and kiln fired. Metal enameling does not require spray glazing. If you are performing this process, don't forget to add special flux compounds to the pigments.

Imagine a box with a black circle in the middle of it. If this is a positive image, and you lay this positive transparency in contact with the plate for exposure, the black circle in the positive film will prevent exposure (*hardening of the bichromated colloid*) on the plate and that circle will remain sticky after exposure. The outside area, around the black circle, will permit exposure to UV light and will harden. When a ceramic pigment is dusted over the exposed plate with a soft brush, the still tacky black circle will accept the ceramic pigment while the hardened outside area will not.

A Contemporary Dusting-On Process

In Norway, Russian artist Galina Manikova has been working since the 1980s with her contemporized Dusting-On process with ceramics. Galina's technique is a variation of a classic ceramist (*one who makes ceramic things*) procedure and is so mercurial that she describes her recipes and process as being one that is performed with a mixture of intuition, experience, and science. This way of working is quite like a chef in a kitchen, where a trip to the garden and the basic recipe are only the first steps in the cooking adventure.

Galina begins by spraying a layer of gum Arabic on either a bisque-fired piece of ceramic or a metal plate. Bisque firing is the first kiln firing of a ceramic work and is done to prepare the piece for glazing. The sprayer is a standard ceramic spraying gun used to apply glazes, and the gum Arabic can either be a standard gum bichromate formula or one that has been diluted somewhat. *If you were going to mix a powdered gum Arabic with water you would make this mix with 70 g of gum Arabic in 400–500 ml of distilled water.* In effect, the purpose of this step is to create a smooth surface so that the pigments do not hang themselves on the printing surface during the pigment dusting stage. Once this step has been performed, a solution of dichromated gelatin and sugar is applied and allowed to dry overnight.

Dichromated Gum Formula:

30 ml	dichromated gum Arabic (*1:1 potassium dichromate & gum*)
70 g	sugar
15 g	bee's honey
150 ml	vodka (40%)

Note: Spraying a dichromate is considered a dangerous activity! Do not perform this technique without using a ceramic spraying box, working in a room with excellent ventilation, and wearing a dual-filter mask, safety goggles, and Nitrile gloves only.

In our correspondence over the years, Galina and I discussed using alternatives to sugar, due to its tendency to crystallize, principally substituting the sugar with a thin dilution of non-crystallizing bee's honey or a syrup of any kind. The purpose of the syrup, honey or sugar solution is to keep the surface emulsion slightly sticky and tacky. To sensitize the plate, a solution of saturated potassium dichromate (10% to 13%) is mixed with the gelatin and honey/syrup solution in a ratio of approximately 1:1.

An alternative to this coating method is one that Galina uses where she coats the surface with the gelatin/honey/syrup as a base coat and when the surface is tacky, a saturated solution of potassium, or ammonium, dichromate is sprayed, brushed, or poured over the surface 3 times.

Note: if the emulsion is too tacky then the entire surface, even after the exposure, will accept the pigment. If the surface is too dry, the pigment will not attach to any part of it.

In total darkness (*very important for long exposures*), the image is exposed using a slide projector and its 250-watt quartz light source at a distance of 4' to 6' from anywhere between 30 minutes and 3 hours depending on the density of the *positive* transparency . . . slides/diapositives. The positive is most successful if it is high in contrast. After the exposure, brush fine ceramic or enamel powders over the surface to reveal the image. The powders will stick to the unexposed areas, while the areas that have been hardened by the UV light during the exposure will remain non-sticky and clear. Galina likes to use very finely ground pigment powders. The idea of using finely ground oxides, as opposed to stains or pigments, is that one can pre-fire it before eventually glazing in order to get rid of all organic matter. Organic matter will sometimes lift the glaze. If there is no need to glaze, one can use any fine powder and fire directly to the final temperature. That is what Galina did for her "Blue and Fireproof" installation, working at a brick factory and firing in a tunnel kiln along with the fireproof bricks to *1500°C*. One of her techniques was to use saturated oxide mixtures that gave a luster shiny golden color at that high temperature. When the application of the pigments is done, the ceramic pieces are fired at a high *stoneware* temperature (*1200°C–1500°C*) in a kiln. Metal surfaces are fired at a lower temperature than stoneware (*800°C—enamel/1000°C—bisque*) to get the iron powders to stick and are then re-fired at a stoneware temperature. In Galina's "Blue & Fireproof" (Fig. 17-4), she did not fire the stainless steel plates but dusted on using finely ground iron powder and then over-coating the plate with a hard glue to protect it.

Dusting On With a Glass Substrate

Another substrate that has all sorts of creative possibilities is glass . . . and in recent years, many artists have turned to this material as a surface for their work. Students often take the liquid emulsion route when thinking about working on glass while artists such as Mark Osterman, France Scully-Osterman, Mark Kessell, and Sally Mann are exploring wet collodion emulsions. (See the Wet Collodion/Gelatin Dry Plate chapter) Galina Manikova uses a process that incorporates a hardened/gelatin coating to prepare a surface for any number of applications including cyanotype, gum, and Van Dyke. To use glass as the substrate requires a slightly different strategy than ceramic, metal, or other non-porous surface.

If you want to work on glass you are going to have to prepare it first. The first thing that you need to do is clean it well with muriatic (hydrochloric) acid or a superior solvent. Don't even begin to think that a simple spray with a commercial glass spray cleaner, or soap, will do the job properly. You can purchase muriatic acid in a good hardware store or pool supply in a non-lethal dilution. Wash the glass with water following the muriatic acid and then dry it thoroughly.*

*Note: Vinegar is also a good option, followed by a concentrated sodium hydroxide and acetone of a re-agent grade (without oil), distilled water at the end.

At this stage, you might want to consider wearing a pair of those silly white gloves that curators, and your compulsive friends, make you put on when they allow you to look at their pictures. In other words, be careful not to leave oily fingerprints on the glass. Once the glass plate is dry, lay it on top of a, smaller than the glass, tray filled with hot water in order to warm the glass from below with a constant temperature. This prevents the gelatin from setting up too quickly after you pour it on. You can also use a portable hot air heater to warm the glass. Galina pointed out that this was an excellent option during the cold winter months in Norway (*where it is winter most of the year*) because it heats her studio at the same time.

Note: This gelatin coating is only a base . . . an under layer that is going to carry the emulsion.

Now, begin to think about layering on successive coatings of *warm* gelatin and glyoxal. (*See Chapter 15, the Paper chapter, please, for preparation instructions for gelatin sizing and hardening.*) This is the difficult part of preparing your plate. Please don't try to gelatin size your plate all at once with a single coat unless you are extremely good at coating, are a professor giving a demonstration, or very short on time. Instead, warm the glass, and the gelatin and glyoxal solution, and apply 3 very thin and delicate coatings . . . drying between each one. Pour the warm solution into the middle of the warmed glass surface and gracefully moving the glass plate around until the coating is smooth. Do not mix up more solution than is necessary to coat the glass plate a single time and a new mix should be made for each of the three separate coatings. This way you are eliminating the problem of disposal. One good trick is to angle the glass so that the small amount of excess gelatin and glyoxal runs offs into a separate tray. Once that step is done, lay the glass on a level surface and allow it to dry. Then repeat the process two more times.

A Coating Option

A coating option would be to apply a standard gelatin solution of 28 g gelatin to 1000 ml of water. Then, pour or spray the gelatin on the glass and allow it to dry. Then immerse (*do not spray*) the glass in a separate bath of prepared glyoxal that you have set up out of doors. After drying, repeat the process two more times. When using this method you would have to coat and dry your plate 6 times (*3 gelatin coats and 3 hardener coats*) before applying the dichromate/gelatin sensitizer. The good part of this idea is that your glyoxal stays relatively pure and you won't be confronted with having to dispose of the excess.

What you are seeking is a smooth surface without bubbles unless that is the effect you are looking for. The purpose of the gelatin is to allow the glass surface to accept a liquid sensitizer without running off or beading . . . like water on wax. When you are ready to sensitize the gelatin/glyoxal prepared plate, you will be adding a bit of prepared gelatin to your sensitizer as this will assist in the sensitizer adhering to the gelatin/glyoxal surface.

The Process on Glass

Once the gelatin or gum, base-coated, glass plate is ready for the Dusting On process, it is coated with a saturated solution potassium, or ammonium, dichromate mixed with albumen and honey. You may want to apply up to 3 separate coatings of the sensitizer with drying between each coat if you're looking for a very smooth coating. I'm not trying to be vague but there are a lot of variables at play here and you'll need to determine the number of sensitizer coatings you need as you go through several experiences with the technique.

When the sensitizer coating is dry on the glass substrate, it is exposed in contact with a *positive* film or projected positive transparency. The image is then revealed, after the exposure, by dusting on colored ceramic glazing powders, with a soft brush, which will adhere only to the unhardened parts of the exposure, that have not been exposed to UV light, and that have remained sticky.

For plates with a gelatin coating, the picture is then covered (*fixed*) with an alcohol solution containing a little acetic acid.* The alcohol is a 96% solution but in some countries "technical" alcohol is considered dangerous due to young people drinking it and being poisoned. It is now harder to find so as a replacement . . . please use Vodka. After the fix, the plate is washed in fresh water until everything but the colored image on the glass has washed off. Galina points out that it is absolutely necessary to harden the gelatin before washing and it may be necessary to wait a few days before the washing step as the hardening process of gelatin takes some time. When everything has been done, the glass plate is then fired in the kiln at about 580°C.

🦉 *Note: If you add acetic acid to gelatin, it will not solidify so quickly. If gelatin is dissolved in acetic acid, you can mix it with alcohol without precipitation, and this may be a way to prepare gelatin emulsions for spraying and airbrushing, etc.**

You might be tempted to go to a monument company, the businesses that sandblast granite grave markers, to have a sandblasted tooth etched into your glass. This is really effective as long as you don't object to losing your glass transparency. If this is important to you, use the gelatin and glyoxal method.

You need to prepare a "Goldilocks" working space for Dusting-On. Galina relates that it is important that the temperature, and humidity, of the working space be just right. By this she means that it is not too dry, not too hot, not too humid, and not too cold . . . just right. You will get the feel of what's right once you begin working with the process. The exception to the Goldilocks environment is if you are intending to put a dichromated gelatin on the glass for a Dusting-On process using glass enamels and a firing temperature that is suitable for the type of glass (*ceramic or metal* as well) that you are using. In this case, you should be trying to keep everything hot and humid. The key is that everything must be hot and humid for this to work properly. Galina advises a Finnish sauna as a Dusting-On studio.

🦉 **Note: If you want to work in ceramics, or glass for firing, then I strongly advise that you take a course or workshops in the discipline. As much fun as wet clay is, ceramicists have to deal with an abundance of less than safe issues, i.e., chemical glazes, kiln firings, etc., and you will need to know of these things before you work in a ceramic studio on your own.**

After all of the preparation it is absolutely necessary to expose the sensitized glass plate to UV light to harden the emulsion and allow it to air dry. It is important to be very careful when handling glass plates. In the wet stage it is quite easy to lose the entire image even after you have worked so hard to make a surface for it. One last bit . . . if you just want to put an alternative process on glass, even if you have no intention of firing it in a kiln, you need to add a gelatin solution to the new sensitizer. By the way, firing a new sensitizer, like cyanotype, can be pretty interesting.

The proportion is 1/3 gelatin to 2/3 new sensitizer, i.e., cyanotype or Van Dyke, by volume. Prepare the gelatin in the "kitchen style" 1 tablespoon of gelatin dissolved in as little water as possible. Begin with a little cold water, let the gelatin sit for a few minutes and then add

Figure 17–5
Galina Manikova, *Trees Series*, **1999—Van Dyke On/glass**
(Courtesy of the artist)

boiling water to dissolve. When you're ready to use it, mix it in the 1/3 gelatin to 2/3 sensitizer proportions before applying it to the glass. This will greatly assist in the bonding of the sensitizer and the emulsion.

Table Set up for The Traditional Dusting-On Formula

Part A *(The Sizing)*

Mix together 28 ml honey and 30 ml gum Arabic (*albumen, fish-glue, or gelatin may also be used*) in a beaker sitting in a tray of 130°F water. You can make a thinner solution

if you need to by adding 10 ml to 15 ml of distilled water to the solution. This is a good idea in the event that you are spraying multiple coatings.

Part B *(The Sensitizer)*

Part B is a simple saturated solution of either potassium (13%) or ammonium (25%) dichromate. Don't forget that you're going to add a few drops of prepared gelatin solution to this sensitizer in order to help it flow more smoothly on the substrate.

Materials Needed For Dusting-On

◆ A good quality paper or prepared sheet of glass, metal, or other substrate.

◆ A high contrast **positive** film image. The best way to get a great positive is to do it digitally using Pictorico OHP film. This way you can easily go for contrast (very important) and if your positive is ruined while printing then it is simple to make a new one. You can also use a single step ortho film positive, an acrylic lift positive, an RC print, a Calotype negative, etc.

◆ A hinged back contact printing frame.

◆ A few flexible plastic drinking straws or a piece of surgical tubing.

◆ Hot moist air from your body. You can also try using a travel-size clothes steamer.

◆ Feet from a pair of pantyhose for holding the powdered pigment or for making a sieve-like cover for a jar holding the pigment.

◆ Powdered color pigments (*see Appendix F for art supply resources and don't inhale*) or powdered graphite. A 400-to 600-mesh pigment is best.

◆ A shaving brush for sweeping away excess pigment.

◆ Many small bottles to hold your powdered pigments.

◆ Tape, or a rubber band, to secure the pantyhose feet on the jars.

The Process On Paper

Size and harden your paper using the traditional honey gum Arabic method. (*You might want to experiment with the normal gum bichromate paper at some point as well.*) Mix 2 Parts A—sizing with 1 Part B—sensitizer under subdued light and coat your paper evenly using the same technique that you would when coating a traditional gum bichromate. Dry the coating quickly with a hairdryer on a *cool* setting. A second coat is optional and may be necessary if you elected to thin the solution for a smoother first coating. Feel free to modify the proportion of Parts A and B as you delve into the mysteries of this technique. Remember, the higher the concentration of sensitizer in your formula, the faster the speed, but the lower the contrast of the resulting image.

Next, place a high contrast **positive** film in contact with the emulsion that will have a *slightly* tacky surface. A high contrast positive is the best way to learn the process because the technique is not one that is designed for subtlety or perfection and detail. Because of the tackiness, you may require a sheet of acetate between the sensitized emulsion and the positive film, as in the Ziatype, to prevent the dichromate sensitizer from becoming a permanent addition to your negative. When the dichromated paper and film positive are set in the contact frame expose the image under UV lamps or sunlight . . . *try 5 to 8 minutes in sun for a start.*

Hot and Humid Image Development

After the paper has been exposed you have a choice of how to humidify it. You can place the paper in a humid environment for 10 to 15 minutes, steam it with a handheld travel steamer, or begin to add the pigment immediately while blowing your warm breath through a straw or flexible hose. If you are working with the technique during the humid part of the summer it may not be necessary to do anything extra.

Put some powdered pigment in a bottle (*spice bottles work quite well*), and cover the opening with the toes of the pantyhose. Using a wide rubber band, or a snap tie, secure the pantyhose part to the bottle opening so that the two won't easily separate. You can also put the powdered pigment in the toe of a pantyhose foot and tie up the open part. Be very cautious about using powdered pigments. Some of them, particularly a few of the cadmium powders, are really quite harmful if ingested or inhaled.

The traditional method of development of your image, and the one that will amaze your friends and relatives, is realized by blowing your very own warm, and humid,

breath on small areas of the exposed image. You must be delicate here in order to make this process work. You also must work rather quickly. Humidify a small area on the image with your breath through a short piece of flexible rubber tubing. If the tubing is too long then your breath will cool too much on the way tot the paper. Then, gently tap the pigment in the toe of the pantyhose over that area. Wait a few seconds and delicately brush the excess pigment away with a soft brush. Quickly move on to another section, or re-humidify the same area, and repeat your previous actions. Areas that have not received a lot of exposure will not have hardened, and as a result, the gum in those areas will still be soft and tacky. Conversely, areas that have received a lot of exposure will have hardened and the added humidity should not affect them. A short piece of 1/2" rubber surgical tubing or a shortened drinking straw will work the best for isolated humidifying. You can get this tubing at a medical supply or a good SCUBA shop, as this tubing is excellent for customizing your gear set up if you dive wrecks or caves.

Remember that you used a film positive for the exposure. What that means to the dichromate, gum Arabic, and bee's honey emulsion is that the highlight areas of the positive film allowed light to pass through the film and harden the dichromated bee's honey and gum in proportion to the degree of exposure. This is a little different than gum bichromate exposure thinking. In gum printing, the shadows are the clear portions of the *negative* and permit complete exposure and subsequently dark areas on the final gum print. In Dusting-On, the shadows of the *positive* film are dark, preventing exposure and keeping the emulsion tacky so that it can take the colored pigment when the emulsion swells due to the application of humidity. When you dust a colored pigment onto the soft gum parts (*shadows*), those areas will accept and embrace the color. Conversely, the hardened parts of the exposure (*highlights*) will not swell enough to accept the color. Make sense?

If your pigmented image is too dark, it is likely that you have underexposed it. Conversely, if it appears to light, it is likely overexposed. Once you are happy with your print, re-expose it to bight sunlight until the tackiness is gone. It is entirely possible that you will not be enthralled with the first application of pigment. Repeat

Galina Manikova, _Metal_, 1997–2005, "ID" Series—photo on aluminium

Galina writes, "*This is one of the series of family album pictures on metal, produced in the period 1997 to 2002. I started this series while working at an aluminum plant in Hoyanger on the west coast of Norway. I was one in a group of artists who were invited to work in an industrial environment for a period of a month or so. The frame is made by casting aluminum into a sand form made by pressing different small toys into special oiled sand that is used for casting metals. The picture is made by projecting images on handmade photo emulsion and etching the plate after the image is developed. The emulsion functions as a resist. These are also based on my family album, this one is showing me at the age of 3, dragging a toy track.*"

(Courtesy of the artist)

the humidifying, dusting, and brushing sequence until you have created an image. You may mix, switch, and change colors as you go. After the pigmentation is satisfactory, you may fix the image with a delicate spray of artist's fixative, the variety used by artists working in charcoal.

Some Dusting-On Suggestions

Try the technique on paper and after you have washed the exposed print in water, to clear away the unexposed dichromate, you will be left with a tan-colored image that is swollen with water. Allow the paper to dry until the image is tacky and proceed with the pigment application part of the process. If you re-expose the pigmented image in UV light it will help harden the image. Again, if you opt to leave the dichromated image alone without washing or pigment application, you will have a light

sepia image that will eventually turn a pale oxide of chromium like green over time.

I recommend using a high-contrast film positive and single-colored pigment to begin learning how to do the process. It will be far easier to control the density of one color (*black or sepia perhaps*). Remember, another way to control contrast is to modify the concentration of the dichromate sensitizer in your formula. The more concentrated the sensitizer solution, the lower your contrast. Conversely, if you lower your dichromate concentration, your contrast will be stronger. This can be easily tested by using ammonium dichromate for one image and then re-doing the print with potassium dichromate . . . that will be a higher contrast by comparison. Try a Dusting-On technique on top of a traditional gum print. If you are using the same image at the same size, you may end up with a very interesting effect. Use your imagination and experiment.

CHAPTER 17 DICHROMATE OPTIONS: THE CHROMATYPE, THE DUSTING-ON PROCESS, ALTERNATIVE SURFACES FOR GUM, 3-D GUM BICHROMATE

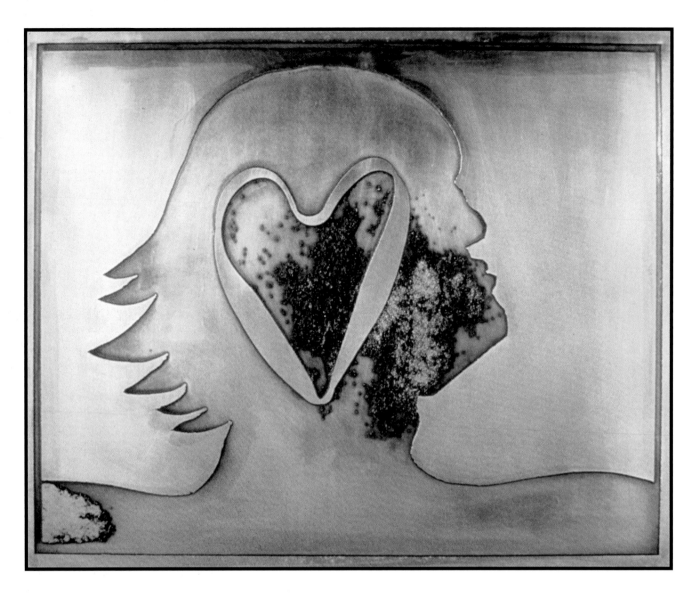

Figure 17–7

Naomi Savage, *Contradiction*

In Naomi Savage's powerful steel plate images, she has used the process of plate making and photo-engraving out of context; allowing the plate to be the work of art rather than the traditional intaglio end stage of a print on paper. In this piece, she has endowed the plate with oxidized plating techniques, acrylic paint, ink, and lacquer.

(Courtesy of the artist)

THE FERRO-TANNIC PROCESSES

This is an odd little hybrid technique that incorporates potassium dichromate in its material list and even though it's actually considered an iron-based process I'm going to drop it into this chapter for your amusement. The Ferro Tannic Process makes an ink black image because of the nature of ferrous sulfate iron salts that turn black when exposed to tannic acid. The Ferro-Tannic roots are quite similar to several other processes, such as the Ferro-Gallic,

Colas, Blackline (1860s), Heliographic or Makahara's Processes (late 1890s), which also used ferric salts (*ferric tartrate, chloride, and sulphate*) that are developed with either tannic or gallic acids. These other formulas can be found in *Nadeau's Encyclopedia of Printing, Photographic and Photomechanical Processes,* Atelier Luis Nadeau, 1989, and Cassell's *Cyclopaedia of Photography,* London, 1911.

The following formula is a modified one that will produce a gray/black image, but there is no guarantee that you'll like it or that you will find it superior to toning your cyanotypes black. As an aside, the propyl gallate found in some of these older formulas is a white, odorless, anti-oxidant powder that has been used since 1948 primarily as an ingredient to stabilize cosmetics. It has also been used as an additive preservative for meat, oils, and edible fats. Its importance and relationship to us is that it turns *black* in the presence of *iron or iron salts*.

The Chemistry: The Ferro-Tannic Sensitizing Solution

Step 1 **Mixing the Sensitizer**

Begin by making a sensitizing solution consisting of 50 g of potassium dichromate (*this bonds with the iron salts on paper*) dissolved in 150 ml of distilled water.

Step 2 **Dry and Expose**

Next, coat the paper with this solution in subdued light and let it dry slowly on its own. Then, put your negative, and the sensitized paper, in a contact frame and expose it in sunlight from 3 to 15 minutes depending on the density of the negative you're using.

Step 3 **Wash**

Wash the print for 30 minutes and then move directly into the intensification stage.

Step 4 **Mixing the Intensifier, Intensification, & Wash**

Make up an intensifying solution consisting of 1.6 g of ferrous sulfate (*green vitriol*) dissolved in 150 ml of distilled water. Immerse the print in the intensifier for 2 to 5 minutes and then wash the print for 30 minutes before moving on to the toning stage.

Step 5 **Toning & Final Wash**

The toning solution is made by dissolving 10 g of tannic acid into 150 ml of distilled water. Some find this dilution a little too anemic so feel free to make it stronger if you need to. Immerse the print in the toning solution for as long as you want to. The tannic acid creates *tannate of iron* that will result in gray-black tonalities. This is similar to the reaction you'll get when subjecting a cyanotype to a very strong tannic acid bath for a lengthy period. Fixing the print is optional. Should you elect to fix the print, make a fixing bath of 1:10 standard paper fix to water for less than a minute. After the toning, or optional fixing stage, wash the print in clear running water for 20 minutes and hang it up to dry.

A Simple Photo-Resist Formula for Intaglio

The following is a simple formula, for creating a resist, for an etching plate, using fish-glue, albumen, ammonium dichromate, and water. You will need:

30 ml	fresh albumen (egg white)
45	prepared fish glue
6 g	ammonium dichromate
	Distilled water

Step 1 Put 30 ml of fresh egg white (albumen) in a mixing bowl, add 30 ml of distilled water, and beat it well. You may use powdered albumen but because this formula requires only a single egg's albumen (approximately 30 ml) it really isn't worth the trouble to go get the powdered variety.

Step 2 In another bowl, mix 45 ml of prepared fish-glue (*LePage's or photo engraving glue*) thoroughly with 30 ml of distilled water. Slowly pour the egg mixture from Step #1 into the glue mixture, stirring slowly.

Step 3 Mix 6 g of ammonium dichromate with 30 ml of distilled water. Under normal room light, add the ammonium dichromate solution to the glue-egg colloid so that it becomes light sensitive.

Step 4 Then add 30 ml of distilled water, more or less, to the solution to determine the thin or thick quality of the emulsion you want to work with. You can also increase the sensitivity of the emulsion by adding more of the ammonium dichromate. Before the plate is exposed it is a good idea to "bake it" with a hairdryer set on a hot setting. This step ensures the best chance of the resist adhering to the plate through the development stage. Just blow-dry for a few minutes but don't put the plate in the oven because excessive time and heat will fog the emulsion.

Step 5 In low-level light, pour the colloid resist on your plate and rotate the plate in the air, emulsion side up, to ensure an even coating. You may want to use a brush for the coating but the pour and rotate method seems to provide a smoother surface.

Step 6 Once the plate's surface has dried, you may take a transparency (*a positive or negative*) and place it in contact with the sensitized emulsion. Remember, your decision as to whether you will use a positive or negative transparency is dependent on the stages that the plate will go through and where you want to end the process. Lay a thick piece of glass on the transparency and sensitized plate to ensure a firm pressure between the film and the plate and expose this "sandwich" to UV light. You may use either an exposure unit or the sun and you should definitely make exposure tests before committing your prepared plate to the UV light.

Step 7 Once the exposure is done, move to the lab for development. This stage is done easily in a bath of slightly warm water and continues, with gentle movement of the water, until the unexposed portions of the plate begin to fall away from the plate. The look here is quite similar to the way a gum bichromate print clears. Once you are content with the development, gently remove the plate from the water, blow-dry it, and place it on a hotplate to re-harden the resist that is left. This step is done until the resist that remains turns a deep brown. Once that happens, take the plate from the hotplate and let it cool before etching it with acid.

HERSCHEL'S BREATH PRINTING PROCESS

Although this little-known process doesn't truly fit in this chapter, it's a nice concept and conceptually it's works as well here as any other place I've tried it. I could have left it

out but then you wouldn't be able to read about it. In this process, you use your own warm breath to make an image visible. Herschel's Breath Printing Process is like writing secret messages in lemon juice as a child and holding the paper over heat to bring the message out. In it, Herschel coated his paper with a dissolved precipitate (*a solid separated from a solution by the action of a re-agent*) formed by combining silver nitrate with ferro-tartaric acid. He then exposed the paper with a contact negative in sunlight and subsequently discovered that the latent image could be brought forth by breathing on the exposed paper, or holding the paper over a streaming teakettle. Once humidified, the image was reported to have an extraordinary intensity. And that's all there is to this.

3-D GUM BICHROMATE PROCESS

In 1990, when Dan Estabrook was a student of mine at Harvard University, he decided to produce a 3-D Gum Bichromate thesis that was a great deal of fun due to the images themselves but also required a lot of often compulsively humorless faculty to walk around together as a group . . . wearing the custom-made, Buddy Holly-like, 3-D glasses that Dan had made for them to view his work . . . I still laugh when I think about it. In any event, I thought Dan's 3-D gum technique was really a great idea . . . a perfect balance of something complex, and amusing, and a process that I needed to include in this book for you to try.

Because the gum bichromate process is able to create colorful prints, in multiple layered exposures, it is possible to create 3-D photographs. This red-green "anaglyph" type of 3-D is simple once the theory behind it is understood, though it can be confusing to explain.

How 3-D Works

Extend your arms and hands in front of your face and using your thumbs and pointing fingers from both hands, make a diamond shape that you can see through. Look through the diamond-shaped hole, with both eyes open, and focus on something at a distance through the diamond. Now close your left eye. If you are right-handed and did not fall on your head when you were young, the object should have stayed exactly where it was when you looked at it through the little diamond shape with both eyes open.

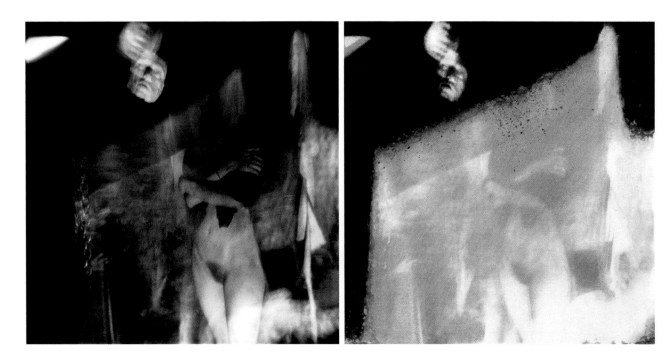

Figure 17–8

Dan Estabrook, 1990 *(B & W /3 –D gum bichromate)*

Here you see the transition of Dan's plastic camera image from black and white to 3-D color gum. The monochromatic version is a silver print from one of the duplicate negatives made for the gum print. The colored image is the result of assigning a single color to each of the negatives. The creamy orange and cyan blue, with a pass of black for shadow enrichment, will provide a 3-D viewing experience when the viewer wears red and green glasses. *(Courtesy of the artist)*

Now open both eyes and line up the object again within the small diamond shape. Close your right eye. The object should be gone from the hole and will have given you the impression that the object jumped to the left . . . or that your hands jumped to the right.

If this test didn't work for you, and you experienced it in a completely opposite way than I described, then you were probably born left-handed and society forced you to become a right-handed person. If this information explains a lot . . .you're welcome.

When the eyes look at an actual 3-D object, each eye sees the object at a slightly different angle. When your brain puts these two different views together, it perceives depth and space. Likewise, when wearing 3-D glasses, and looking at a 3-D "anaglyph" (*a composite picture printed in two colors that produces a 3-D image when viewed through glasses fitted with colored corresponding lenses*), each eye sees a slightly different view of the image. One eye sees through a red lens—blocking any image in red; the other eye sees through a blue (*occasionally green*) lens—blocking out blue. The brain puts these two different views together to perceive a three dimensional space.

The Negatives

It is not enough to have to have slightly different views of the same subject printed on top of each other. For the 3-D effect to work properly, you must have two separate views of the same subject. These are photographed side-by-side with a distance equal to the space between the eyes . . . approximately 2.5". One way to do this is to move the camera 2.5" to the left or right after one exposure and take another picture of the same non-mobile subject.

Of course, this way of working is a little annoying and only allows you to take images of things that will not be moving. The best way to make your parallel negatives is to get an old 3-D camera like the ones that were popular in the 1950s. A homemade solution is to take two plastic cameras, like Holgas, and reconstruct them so that when they are cut and reunited they will make a single, elongated, two-lens camera. Using a fine blade saw (*a straight ridge-back Japanese woodworker's saw*), cut off the left side of one of the cameras and then cut off the right side of the other. If you place the two cameras together you should have a long rectangular camera with the lenses 2.5" apart. In the event that you are tool-impaired I recommend going to a machine shop and having them make the cuts with equipment that is superior to what you have at home.

Once the cuts have been made, super glue the two cameras together and add a stiff brace, or two, to hold the unit rigid. Place the braces along the bottom and another, shorter one, in the front. Do not brace the back, because you will be unable to load film. When you load 120 mm film, you will insert the roll on the far left side and have your take-up spool on the far right side. I suggest practice loading in the dark to prevent fogging. The new Holga models have foam behind the take up spools so you will be able to avoid the dreaded "fat-rolls." Making the new camera light tight is also an important consideration.

Creating a "shutter-release" is also important, because you will want both exposures have to be made at the same instant. One solution is to take a lightweight metal rod and shape it like a big staple. Using super glue or a metal/plastic compatible epoxy, fuse the ends of your big staple to each of the shutter-releases. When shooting, depress both shutters at once by pressing down on the middle of the metal staple. If you have made your camera well, it will give you two negatives shot at the same time. Do a test roll and begin to modify the camera until it works perfectly.

Negatives: Digital or Film

In order to make the 3-D gums you will need to make enlarged duplicating negatives of both the left and right frames. Considering the process, I recommend doing this step digitally in Photoshop and printing your fine-tuned negatives on Pictorico OHP. (*Please go to Chapter 5 for instructions.*) The other option is to shoot traditional film in camera and work out a system for either moving your camera, or the subject, the required 2.5" so that you'll have 2 negatives to work with.

Once the two negatives are made, it is very important to register them in order to get the proper separation for 3-D. Be sure to label the negatives "left side"/"right side." This is an easy task to undertake digitally, and while

you're at it, you can make separate color layers of your two negatives, assign them the correct 3-D colors, put on your 3-D glasses, and actually see it's going to work.

The Process

Now that you have your 3-D negatives, the rest of the procedure is the gum bichromate process from Chapter 16 with a few minor adjustments. Begin by preparing your paper for gum bichromate following the gelatin/sizing instructions from Chapter 15. You may use any of the formulas but I will recommend the single stage sizing/glyoxal formula because you have enough to deal with already. If you recall, this technique calls for you to mix 6.5 g of gelatin in 250 ml of distilled water and let it bloom for 20 minutes. Then all you need to do is warm the gelatin to about 100°F. Then, slowly add 10 ml of 40% glyoxal to the solution and brush coat it on the paper, rinse it, and hang it up to dry outdoors. Again, when using glyoxal it is critical to be aware of all safety recommendations; work with the stuff outside with the wind at your back.

3-D Glasses

Traditional 3-D glasses are made so that the red lens is for the left eye and blue lens is for the right. Quite often a 3-D comic book comes with red and green lenses instead of red and blue. You'll get somewhat the same illusion, but the red and green glasses will function differently with the instructions provided in this chapter . . . I would recommend that you make your own. If you make the glasses yourself, try using an old pair of eyeglass frames without the lenses or construct a new design using a double-ply mat board. Theatrical acetates, the kind that are used to tint actors and theater sets, work exceptionally well. As an aside, if you shoot with infrared film that requires a 25 A red filter, it is far more economical to use this same color theater gel. One sheet will make about 30 25 A filters and the cost will be under $2.

The next stage, a most important one, is to create the right colors to make the best 3-D illusion for the red/blue glasses. Use a 1:1 sensitizer to gum formula from Chapter 16 that uses the potassium dichromate sensitizer. You may remember that 3-D comics are generally composed of very light tonalities and a successful 3-D image is often perceived as being out of registration and quite "pasty" to

Figure 17–9

Sandra C. Davis, *Mother*, 2006—gum bichromate on glass & light box
Sandra is currently a grad student at University of the Arts in Philadelphia. Each B & W Holga negative is scanned into Photoshop and negatives are made on Pictorico OHP as a set of CMYK color separations with custom curve profiles. The film is outputted on a Scitex image setter. Sandra uses double strength window glass and sandblasts on both sides with medium grade sand. The doll side of the glass uses the CMYK separations and is rendered in gum bichromate. She prints the negatives on one side in reverse order—black, yellow, magenta, and cyan. On the other side of the glass, she prints a layer of Antwerp Blue and a layer of Holbein Shadow Green. The glass is then installed in a darkroom safelight so that it can be viewed as backlit.
(Courtesy of the artist)

the naked eye. For thinner coatings, and a smoother image, you may want to add some water to your sensitizer formula and think about building density over a period of several thin exposures. For a pair of red/blue glasses, your primary gum bichromate colors will be a *Creamsicle*®–like sherbet-orange and a powdery cyan blue. You will have to make a number of color tests with different mixes and densities before you hit the perfect match while wearing the glasses, so be patient. Just remember to always use the same color, orange or blue, for the left and right negatives to correspond with the red lens or the blue lens. If you do not, your tests will not make any sense. I recommend buying a few 3-D comics and using them for color matching.

At the conclusion of your orange and blue gum experience, you can make several passes with a thinned-out (*with a few drops of water*) Lamp Black gum formula for the last stages. This additional black pass will enhance your shadow details and add an illusion of depth to the print. Another added bonus of the black pass is that it will also make your prints a little more dynamic to both the naked eye and to eyes wearing 3-D glasses. When you are done printing, you can touch up and enhance portions of your gum print with colored pencils. A quality

colored pencil set should provide you with the same density, and hue, as the watercolors you've been using in the gums. When everything is done, you can bask on your laurels and spend some time making and decorating a selection of 3–D glasses to give to your friends and neighbors so they can see your new work.

GUM BICHROMATE ON ALTERNATIVE SURFACES

The Basic Premise

Once you have worked out a way to be comfortable using the traditional gum bichromate on paper process, there are new worlds to conquer . . . including placing a gum image on an alternative surface. Paper is simple in that it is flexible and has a given "*tooth*" texture for the gum to "*hook*" into. Alternative surfaces, such as metal plates, stone, chalkboard slate, glass, mica, vinyl, or plastic, do not have this same tooth unless you make a conscious effort to create it.

Another huge difference in working on an alternative/non-paper surface is that the issue of pigment staining becomes irrelevant. Literally any portion of the image can be dislodged with water, sanding, abrasion, or

Figure 17–10

Christopher James, *Vatican Bride on Steel*, **acid etched steel plate with colloidal emulsion**

This piece is part of large series utilizing steel plates that I destroy with acids, and when satisfied with the surface, coat with a liquid emulsion for projection printing. The plate is then subjected to more torture with power sanders, etching tools, oil paint, and toners. *(Courtesy of the author)*

etching. The key task is to create a surface that will hold onto one or more coatings of a colloid-dichromate sensitizer. Eventually you will discover that multiple coatings are significantly more complicated due to the tenuous hold the initial application has on the substrate. In this situation, you may need to re-harden between coats or to seal each coat after it dries.

Tooth

Tooth is the surface texture of the substrate and is what's needed to hold onto an emulsion, or image, once it is printed. To create tooth, take your pick of a number of techniques. Acid etching of metal, or glass, sandblasting (*check the business directories for a sandblaster or tombstone etcher*), steel wool abrading, power sanding, multiple coatings of gloss polyurethane/spray paint, or

any other way you can think of putting a texture on whatever you are using for a printing surface. When I am working on metal, for instance, I buy large metal plates from an industrial roofing business as they have the huge pressure cutting machines as well. I then degrease the plate with a solvent, because metal plates almost always come with an oil coating to prevent rust before the sale. When the plate is degreased, clean, and dry, I smooth the surface with steel wool and proceed to give the plate multiple light coatings of spray gloss polyurethane. It is important to use gloss polyurethane because both the matte, and semi-gloss, polyurethane finishes contain wax in their formulas to create their non-glossy appearance. Wax, as you know, is not conducive to holding onto a liquid emulsion.

Figure 17–11

Bea Nettles, *Rachel in the Pines*, 1978—gum on vinyl

Bea Nettles has been an influence to so many young artists over years because of her fearless examination of personal family and friendship documents, her willingness to use any medium to express what she needs to say, and for her many self published artist's books. This piece is from her well-known book, *Flamingo in the Dark,* and measures 20" x 24".
(Courtesy of the artist)

One other preparation technique that I have used for metal plates is the application of a metal degrading acid before, or after, an aquatint (*a melted resin texture*). The most aggressive acid to use in this instance is nitric acid to water mixed in a 1:8 to 1:12 acid to water dilution. You may brush on the acid or immerse the plate (*as in a printmaking lab set-up*) but be sure to pay attention to all safety recommendations. *Nitric acid produces a dangerous nitrogen oxide gas when it is in contact with metal and you MUST use a ventilating hood when working with it.* If you have no experience with printmaking, or no access to a printmaking lab, you might consider using a copper plate and try the less dangerous ferric chloride to etch your plate with a texture. After etching and washing, seal the plate with several very thin coatings of gloss polyurethane spray. A good book on printmaking such as *The Complete Printmaker,* by Ross, Romano, and Ross provides many ideas and suggestions for altering your metal surfaces.

Note: I want you to be very conscious of your safety while attempting these processes. Working with acids, dust, chemicals, and such demands that you pay close attention to your health. Be sure that if you work with acids that you wear acid resistant, nitrile, gloves, and eyewear. Also, if there are airborne fumes and dust it is imperative that you wear a dual filtered respirator. A painter's paper mask is worthless for protecting you.

Coating, Exposure, Development, & Re-Exposure

Once the plate is prepared, it is time to put an image on it. The first thing that I do is to warm the surface of the alternative substrate that I'm using. This prevents the gum Arabic from "setting up" too quickly on a cold surface. For a metal plate, I fill a tray, one that is smaller than the plate, with hot water and then lay the plate on the top edges. The heat from the water in the tray, below the plate, keeps the plate at a constant warm temperature until I am satisfied with the look of the coating. Then I remove the plate and lay it on a flat surface to dry.

Coat the surface in the same manner as you would coat paper but with extra attention to getting the emulsion evenly spread, bubble free, and completely covering the entire printing area. Allow the emulsion to dry on its own. If you use a hairdryer you will only harden the emulsion . . . so don't. You may find it necessary to add water to your gum sensitizer due to the thickness of the emulsion and the lack of friction between the emulsion and the surface. You'll have to make this decision once your surface has been prepared.

For photo-ceramics, the gum coating was traditionally hardened in a solution of 10% boric acid in warm water and 500 ml of alcohol or a solution of aluminum chloride. For clearing the dichromates one used a 5% solution of sodium or potassium bisulfite. It is my experience that potassium dichromate works best. If one does not clear out the dichromate, it will give a greenish tone at firing, as it is a ceramic colorant in itself.

To make an exposure, place your enlarged negative in contact with the dry emulsion and put small pieces of tape on the edges of the negative to hold it on the surface of the plate. This allows you to monitor the exposure without losing your registration. If your plate is thin enough, you may continue to use a contact-printing frame. Be sure that your image will be "right-reading" when done and then place the plate in the sun for your exposure. It is better to overexpose, due to the fact that the "*hooking*" abilities of the emulsion are not as significant as when you are using paper. I use the term "hooking" in teaching when I am trying to paint a word-picture of what happens during a gum exposure. As exposure increases, the dichromated emulsion hardens in relationship to that exposure. In effect, it is hooking more tenaciously into the substrate. With metal or glass this can't happen and that is why the surface preparation is so critical.

Development is the complicated part. Lay your exposed image in a tray of ambient temperature water for 10 to 15 minutes and very gently move the water within the tray. Do not run water directly onto the surface of the image and *keep the image facing up during the wash* (unlike what you did with paper). Highlights can be assisted in clearing by means of gentle whisking with a watercolor fan brush but keep in mind that the surface image is extremely fragile. When you reach a point where the image pleases you, gently remove the plate from the tray, keeping it face up, and delicately begin to blow-dry the image. When it's dry, take the plate back into the sunlight for re-exposure of 5 to 10 minutes because this is an action that will help harden the image and make it less fragile. *Note: If you are in a hurry, and like a more organic look to your work, you can force develop with brushes, fingers, jets of water, etching tools, etc.*

Once the plate has been through those stages you may now go on to another coating, following the same sensitizing and exposure sequence. Your other option is to finish the plate with a spray coating of acrylic gloss polyurethane or clear acrylic spray. If you find that you are having difficulty retaining the first impression in subsequent coatings, you might want to give each coating a gloss polyurethane spray followed by a light steel wool sanding. If you detest your image you can plug in the power sander and eliminate it and begin again or retain the base image as a "canvas" for painting. Use your imagination and enjoy the possibilities.

Figure 17–12
Lois Johnson, *Transplants*, 1980—gum and drawing
(Courtesy of the artist)

The Carbon Print Process

OVERVIEW & EXPECTATIONS

In this chapter you will learn about the carbon process . . . in which a print is made with pigment and a bichromated colloid. The technique has several similarities to the gum bichromate process (primarily the phenomena of a bichromated gelatin hardening under the influence of UV light) but is infinitely more refined in its rendition of tonal values, in the subtlety of its highlights in combination with the depth and richness of its shadow details, and in having a true straight-line response to exposure. The carbon process is also revered for it amazing archival quality . . . and renowned for being labor intensive.

Curiously, in spite of its elegance and permanence, the carbon process is one of the least practiced of the alternative photographic processes. Part of the problem is that making your own carbon tissue is a bit difficult and finding a commercially made carbon tissue, until now, was equally so. Many years ago, a gentleman in Indiana, by the name of Dr. Green, conducted workshops and sold Hanfstaengl carbon tissue to a small group of carbon process aficionados who were working with the technique.

Within the last year, Dick Sullivan, of Bostick & Sullivan, with the assistance of Gordon Mark and Howard Efner, has been dedicating the majority of his time developing a reliable carbon tissue that you sensitize with potassium dichromate, use to expose your negative in reverse (flopped), and then transfer to a final support paper of your choice. Dick has recently written a manual to go with his new tissue and I have relied on his expertise to a great extent in the production of this chapter. I have also worked with his research team, in his Santa Fe carbon facility, in order to be sure that these instructions, his tissue, and your experience making carbon prints, are in harmony. For more information, go to www.carbonprinting.com.

Figure 18–1

Dick Sullivan, *Spahn Ranch*, 2007—carbon

Dick Sullivan made this image at the Spahn Ranch, a 500-acre wilderness area in the Santa Susana Mountains. If you remember black and white TV, the Lone Ranger (Clayton Moore) and his sidekick Tonto (Jay Silverheels) galloped past giant boulders on their way to "save the day" . . . then you have seen the ranch. Unfortunately, the Spahn Ranch is also known as the one-time residence of Charles Manson and his disciples, known as "The Family," who lived there in the spring of 1968 . . . the year of their very evil deeds.

(Courtesy of the artist)

A LITTLE HISTORY

A few decades following the celebration of the invention of photography, it became quite obvious there was a problem with permanence. Many of the treasured first examples of the new medium were rapidly disappearing as time and ineffective fixing or washing methods were causing the images to fade away.

In previous chapters, I've discussed the experiments, and process innovations, with dichromated salts conducted by Mungo Ponton, Edmund Becquerel, and Fox Talbot between the years 1839 and 1852. Ponton was the first to use these salts to make low contrast images on paper. Describing his discovery, he wrote, *"Paper immersed in bichromate of potash [potassium bichromate] is powerfully and rapidly acted upon by the sun's rays. When an object is laid in the usual way on this paper, the portion exposed to the light speedily becomes tawny, passing more or less into deep orange, according to the strength of the solution and the intensity of the light. In this state, of course, the drawing, though very beautiful, is evanescent. To Fix it, all that is required is careful immersion in water, when it will be found that those portions of the salt which have not been acted on by the light are readily dissolved out, while those that have been exposed to the light are completely fixed on the paper. By this second process the object is obtained white upon an orange ground, and quite permanent."* This last sentence, considering the concerns regarding permanence, was quite relevant.

In 1840, Edmund Becquerel deduced that Ponton's process was made better by the adaptation of starch, or other organic binders such as glue, albumen, gelatin and sugar. This recognition led to the pigment and chromate investigations, in 1855, by Alphonse Louis Poitevin, who is generally given credit for inventing the carbon process.

In Poitevin's technique, powdered carbon soot (usually lampblack) was combined with a bichromated gelatin and applied to a paper support. The sensitized paper was then coupled with a negative and exposed to sunlight where the bichromated gelatin hardened (became insoluble) in proportional relationship to the degrees of exposure received. As in the gum bichromate process, the least exposed areas of the print were most vulnerable to being washed away during the wash-development. Conversely, the areas receiving the most exposure were the darkest and the most permanent. Poitevin's process was similar to Ponton's, but in Poitevin's case, an actual pigment came into play and this was the first instance when a choice of color could be incorporated with a dichromated colloid. The process's sole weakness was the absence of half tones . . . the print was entirely black and white.

This problem was partially rectified through the work of L'Abbé Laborde, in 1858. He determined that the excessive contrast was because only the most deeply exposed portions of the print remained on the paper in the warm water wash-development following exposure. This happened because the upper-most surface of the dichromated colloid hardened first during the exposure, thus preventing additional exposure to the mid-tones beneath the hardened top layer. In the wash-development, the lower layers (those closest to the paper support) of the print were insufficiently exposed to anchor them to the paper substrate. Consequently, when the unattached lower layers released from the paper support, the well-exposed upper layers of the print tagged along for the ride down the drain. This discovery meant that the solution to the problem was at hand.

In 1858, C. J. Burnett partially solved the problem by exposing his negative to the backside of the pigment and dichromated gelatin paper. The paper, oiled for translucency, was contact printed with the negative and this strategy permitted mid-scale tonalities to be resolved properly . . . as the bichromated gelatin was hardening at the support layer first. To achieve the deep shadows, the exposure had to be quite lengthy and the texture of the paper obscured the clarity of the final image. Then, in 1860, a Frenchman by the name of Fargier patented a complex and difficult solution to the problem by incorporating the idea of image transfer with wet collodion. A description of Fargier's process can be found in Josef Maria Eder's book, *History of Photography.*

In 1864, Sir Joseph Wilson Swan (1828–1914) patented a practical, and easily accessible, solution to the confounding and vexing problems of carbon printing. Swan is primarily remembered for receiving a British patent for an electric light bulb in 1878, a year before Thomas Edison.

Edison, by the way, worked on improving Swan's invention and eventually obtained a U.S. patent for the bulb. Edison then initiated litigation against Swan for patent infringement and simultaneously commenced an advertising campaign claiming to be the true inventor of the electric light bulb.

Note: Eventually, in 1883, Edison and Swan went into business together forming the Edison & Swan United Electric Light Company.

According to W. Jerome Harrison's, *The Chemistry of Photography* (1892), Swan mixed a little sugar into gelatin to make it less brittle when it dried. This was combined with a dichromate and pigment (Swan also used red chalk as well as carbon for his pigments but it wasn't as archival) and applied to a glass plate. After making his exposure through a negative, the exposed glass plate was transferred under contact pressure to a pore-less waxed or gelatined paper support. Swan then used a rubberized latex glue to hold the gelatin image to the support.

In 1865 Swan received a patent for his carbon process innovations and introduced a ready-made carbon tissue and transfer sheet that was manufactured by his new company Mawson & Swan. In the Dublin International Exhibition of Arts and Manufactures of 1865, in Dublin, Ireland, three landscapes were exhibited using Swan's patented carbon process and these images were printed on tissue made by the firm of Mawson & Swan. Curiously, the company was also credited as the artists.

The Mawson & Swan carbon tissue consisted of a film of gelatin, in which finely powdered carbon was incorporated, and spread on paper. The tissue was sensitized by the photographer with a solution of potassium dichromate, and when dry, exposed under a negative. The face of the carbon tissue was then attached to a paper support and soaked in hot water until the original backing paper of the carbon tissue could be detached. Then the unexposed soluble gelatin was dissolved. As the picture was laterally reversed it had to be transferred a second time to its final support.

In 1868, Swan sold the patent rights to Autotype Company of England and one of the vice presidents of that new firm was J. Robert Johnson (not the legendary blues guitarist) who improved upon The Mawson & Swan carbon tissue. In 1869, he demonstrated that it was only necessary to first soak the carbon tissue in water for a short time in order to make it adhere to a waterproof support. The Autotype Company of England continued

to make the carbon process a better product and in their prime, they supplied carbon printers with 50 varieties of tissue in over 30 different colors.

A great many improvements followed and between 1870 and 1910 the carbon process enjoyed its greatest popularity and was employed as one of the primary processes for "fine art" photographic printing. Variations on the carbon and gum bichromate theme included Victor Artigue's artigueotype, in 1892, Thomas Manly's ozotype, in 1899, and the ozobrome, in 1905. The ozobrome was an improved adaptation of the autotype and was eventually given the name carbro process.

Of late, there is a renewed interest in these processes, in no small part, to Dick Sullivan's new, and easy to use, carbon tissue. Using Dick's tissue, one can easily make carbon prints on a great variety of surfaces including paper, glass, plastic, and canvas . . . and they will be as permanent as the substrate they are transferred to.

HOW CARBON WORKS

The carbon printing process is one that has a great many more steps than you will encounter in other alternative techniques. Each of these major steps has a plethora of simple little steps so be prepared to spend some time making a print. There are four phases to making a carbon print

Phase 1 **Sensitizing the carbon tissue**

Phase 2 **Exposing the carbon tissue**

Phase 3 **Mating the carbon tissue to the final support**

Phase 4 **Developing and drying the final image**

Here's a quick overview. A piece of very thin and flexible paper is meticulously coated with gelatin and a pigment. I strongly advise buying prepared tissue from Bostick & Sullivan rather than making your own. This prepared tissue is then sensitized in a dichromate solution. The sensitized sheet, which is called *carbon tissue*, is then dried, mated with a negative, and exposed with UV light in a manner similar to most of the other alternative processes.

The UV light causes the long chains of atoms making up the gelatin to become "cross-linked." This entanglement hardens the gelatin, and the degree of hardening is relative to the amount of light received through the negative, i.e. like in the gum bichromate process. The exposed tissue is

Figure 18–2

Christopher James, *Tea Boy*, Jaipur, India, 1994—carbon
This image was made in the back alleys of Jaipur where precious stones are traded, bartered, and sold. As is the custom, a sweet tea magically appears as soon as you are seated. Here's the recipe: **India Street Masala Chai**: 1" stick of cinnamon, 8 cardamom pods, 8 cloves, 2/3 cup milk, lots of sugar, 3 teaspoons of black tea . . . bring to boil and let it sit for a spell. Serve in clay cups for 2.
(Courtesy of the author)

then immersed in a cool water bath and mated to a sheet of microporous gelatinized or resin-coated paper and put under pressure for a period of time.

The mated pair is then immersed in a warm water bath until there is visual evidence that the tissue is ready to be separated from the support. This is often recognized as a delicate black cloud on the edges of the mated pair. The tissue is then peeled away from the support and washed until the unexposed gelatin is washed away—leaving a permanent carbon image. If additional clearing of the highlights is needed, the print is immersed in a bath of dilute potassium metabisulfite.

PHASE 1: SENSITIZING THE TISSUE

The Table Setup

- A 10% Potassium dichromate solution—100 g per liter of water
- Rubbing or isopropyl alcohol. Anywhere from 70% to 100% is fine.

- A clean tray for tissue sensitizing
- A larger tray to hold iced water and the tissue-sensitizing tray
- Bostick & Sullivan Carbon tissue cut to size.
- A window squeegee
- A large piece of plate glass or solid Plexiglas—larger than the tissue
- A bag of ice
- A pair of nitrile gloves

About Sensitizing

In this step, we will be making the carbon tissue sensitive to light. For convenience, we'll make the working solution from a saturated stock solution of potassium dichromate. This is exactly the same saturated solution you used in gum bichromate so you can use the same solution for carbon. You may recall that potassium dichromate is saturated anywhere between 10% and 13% depending on temperature.

Changing the percentage of dichromate in the working solution can control contrast. You can work with 0.5% to 6% but the outer extremes can be difficult to work with and will often present problems. A 0.5% concentration will yield a contrasty print, will result in longer exposure times, and is used for lower contrast negatives.

The higher percentages of potassium dichromate are for very contrasty negatives and will make softer prints. Solutions over 4% will often dissolve the gelatin. To counter this possibility, you will need to lower the temperature of the working solution. Higher concentrations of potassium dichromate will mean shorter exposure times.

The alcohol is not mandatory. Its purpose is to speed the drying of the tissue. Do not use ethyl or denatured alcohol as this type forms chemicals that harden the gelatin and will result in fog on the exposure.

For a platinum style negative that would print on a No. 0 enlarging paper, try a 2% solution. For a negative that prints on a No. 3 silver enlarging paper, try a 1% working solution.

Sensitized tissue may last for a day or so if left in a dry cool dark place and may last for weeks if frozen.

The Process: 10% Dichromate Stock Sensitizer Solution

Example: 1 liter of 2% working solution from stock

Step 1 Put 200 ml of the 10% stock solution in the beaker

Step 2 Add 400 ml of 55°- 65° F cool water to the stock solution

Step 3 Add the rubbing alcohol to bring the total to 1000 ml

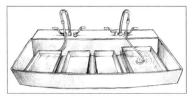

Sensitizing the Tissue: Cold Sensitizer Set Up

First, please put on a pair of Nitrile gloves before working with a dichromate, as it is carcinogenic. Second, if you have any dry chemistry left over, save it. Do not throw it out as a powder, as it may be combustible under the right circumstances. Only dispose of dichromates by flushing with large amounts of water.

The following can be done in a dimly light room. There should be no fluorescent light in the sink area while this step is being done. I've found that a very cool to cold sensitizer is better than sensitizer at an ambient temperature. The reason for this is that a colder sensitizer is far less likely to disturb the fragile state of newly immersed carbon tissue.

Take your large tray and half fill it with some ice and water. Then place your smaller sensitizing tray in the larger one and pour in the sensitizer. Let it chill. You will find it practical to wear a respirator mask as the alcohol/potassium dichromate solution is rather intense. Ventilation is important. It is also very important to wear protective gloves, as the dichromate is unfriendly to your person.

Place the tissue in a clean tray and pour enough dichromate solution to cover and flood the tissue. Gently rock the tray making sure the solution covers the tissue. If it becomes difficult to continue flooding the tissue with the solution, simply add more. With the iced tray system you shouldn't have any problems with the pigment. However, if you have not chosen to use the double tray set up you may see changes in your tissue during the sensitizing. *If pigment starts to flow off the tissue, stop immediately.* If this happens you will need to lower the temperature of your working solution. Higher percentages tend to melt the tissue and bleed pigment. Flood the paper for 2–3 minutes in the sensitizer.

The tissue goes from being insensitive to UV light when it is very wet, to highly sensitive when it is nearly dry, to a little sensitive when it is dry and ready for exposure. In a dry climate, the tissue may curl tightly and may have to be humidified before exposure. In a humid climate, it is necessary to see a slight curl to the tissue before exposure. This indicates that the tissue has dried and can be used. You may employ a fan for drying.

Squeegee & Drying Steps

Set up your sheet of glass, or solid Plexiglas, in the sink. Be absolutely positive that the glass is clean or you will see streaks in your final print.

After 3 minutes, remove the tissue and drain it briefly by holding it from a single corner. Then, place the tissue face up on your plate glass in the sink. Very gently, squeegee the face of the carbon tissue to remove the remaining solution. Do not turn the tissue over to squeegee the backside as this may damage the front.

Hang the tissue in a clean dark area to dry, as it is now light sensitive. Low ambient light will not expose the tissue so please don't get compulsive about the luminosity in your working area. In dry climates, like Santa Fe or Aspen, the tissue will be dry in less than one hour. In more humid climates, like summertime in Maine, the drying time will be a good deal longer.

 **Note: Dry tissue should curl a bit when it is completely dry. If there is moisture in the tissue then the mating steps will not work as well as the tissue will be too damp to create a vacuum with the mating paper. Be sure that the tissue is completely dry before exposure and mating.**

Note: I've found that unexpected changes in temperature and humidity, in our labs at The Art Institute of Boston, occasionally make the tissue curl tightly. One way to avoid this is to wait until your tissue is dry and is showing a slight curl. At this point, bag your dried tissue in a zip lock freezer bag. Store the bag in a freezer between printing sessions and the tissue should remain flat.

Spontaneous Exposure

As tissue ages it becomes more sensitive and at a certain point it spontaneously fogs. The time for this to happen is unpredictable. Sensitized tissue will usually last for a day or two but in some cases it spontaneously exposes in 24 hours. If your tissue has "blown" (which is what this spontaneous exposure is called . . . it is also called a "dark reaction"), it will fail to stick during development and will peel right off the support. It will also be leather-like while sticking to the tissue backing.

PHASE 2: EXPOSING THE TISSUE

Comments

Carbon tissue is UV light-sensitive (also slightly visible light sensitive) and can be exposed in mechanical light units that work for other alternative processes. The printing speed of the tissue will vary according to the

Figure 18–3

Brian Palm, *American Can*, **2005—carbon**
Chicago artist, Brian Palm, found the can while on a walk in the woods in Wisconsin. When I asked him what he wanted to say about the can, he replied that he could probably write a few paragraphs re: the ironic relationship of the object and the text. Sufficient, perhaps, to say that it's a great carbon print of an interesting object found in interesting times.
(Courtesy of the artist)

percentage of potassium dichromate it was sensitized with. Higher percentages are faster, and lower are slower.

Carbon tissue that is not dried sufficiently will melt and stick to your negative . . . this is obviously very bad for your negative. Carbon tissue that is too dry will coil up and be difficult to manage. The tissue is best exposed when it has some moisture in it but not so much that it melts onto your negative. A slight amount of moisture will make it easier to handle getting it into the print frame. Local humidity conditions will affect this. Dick Sullivan lives in Santa Fe and the humidity there can be measured in single digits in the winter. As a result, he needs to humidify his drying cabinet to keep the tissue from curling too much. An artist living in New Orleans may have the opposite problem, with the tissue being too moist, and will likely need to de-humidify their drying space. When I work with this tissue in New England, in the summertime, the tissue takes several hours to dry properly and it should exhibit a slight curl when it is ready.

You can use either a 1-or 2-mil (a mil is one thousandth of an inch or 25 microns / micrometers) piece of clear Mylar to separate the negative from the tissue. Mylar tends to cling and is difficult to handle so a better option is to use Krystal Seal envelopes. These are thin very clear envelopes that you can put your negative in. They are available from Bostick & Sullivan and many art supply stores or sources on the Internet. They range in size from 6" × 8" up to very large 23" × 31" inches.

The Safe Edge

One of the unique things you will do in carbon printing is to put a safe edge on your negative. The purpose of the safe edge is to prevent the over-exposed area outside the image from flagging during development and tearing part of the image off the support during the separation stage. *If carbon is exposed past the point of its Dmax it will not stick to the support.* This is due to it having hardened past the point of being able too absorb water during the mating phase. It is this absorption that creates the vacuum to make it stick.

If you make digital negatives put a mid-tone gray border around your print. If they are in-camera negatives, put a piece of masking tape around the edge of the negative. You can also put the negative in a paper or rubylith matt. You can also make an instant safe edge with the metallic slide masking tape. This will leave a white or gray edge around the negative that will not flag. If you are transferring to an RC digital paper, a safe edge isn't necessary.

The Setup

◆ A UV light source

◆ A piece of sensitized tissue

◆ A negative

◆ A contact printing frame or vacuum exposure unit

◆ Krystal Seal envelopes—or equivalent

◆ Black tape for safe edge

Exposing the Tissue

Expose the negative in a UV light source in much the same manner as you do in any other alternative photography process. There will be no stage whisper or print out of the image as there is in almost all other alternative processes. Sunlight will work but it is a second choice compared to using a controllable mechanical UV exposure unit with a vacuum frame or a hydroponics metal halide grow light. That said, sunlight exposure in summer, using a contact-printing frame, generally takes an average of 5 to 6 minutes at peak exposure hours in the middle of the day. If you are using a high intensity

Like gum bichromate, carbon will continue to "expose" after it has been removed from the exposure unit. You should go immediately to the mating step following exposure.

Figure 18–4

Vaughn Hutchins, *Oak Roots Merced River*, 1994–1995—carbon
Vaughn Hutchins's name was constantly mentioned every time I asked someone who was doing really strong carbon printing. He works at Humboldt State University and has been making carbon prints for 15 years . . . after reading about the process in View Camera Magazine . . . and then it took him a few years before he was happy with the quality of his print. Vaughn works with an 8" x 10" camera and contact prints directly from the negative. *(Courtesy of the artist)*

PHASE 3: THE MATING THE TISSUE TO THE SUPPORT

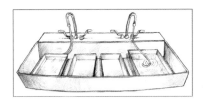

Sink & Table Set Up—What You Will Need

- An exposed piece of carbon tissue (from Phase 2)
- A piece of support paper cut to size (see below)
- A tray of iced or very cool water
- A piece of plate glass to squeegee on
- A heavy duty photo squeegee
- 2 sheets of Plexiglas larger than the tissue and the support paper
- Paper towels

Mating the Tissue to the Support

In the mating step, you will fill a large tray with iced or very cold water and immerse the support paper and the exposed tissue in the water bath with the image side of the tissue facing down, towards the transfer support. The tissue will begin to sink a little and you will then be able to guide it into position with the support material after 30 to 45 seconds. In certain conditions, a lengthy soak, prior to mating the tissue and support, will prevent achieving a tight bond during the mating stage. Mate the tissue and its support together while they are in the water, remove the mated pair from the water in a flat position, lay them on a sheet of Plexiglas and with a good deal of pressure, squeegee the pair together with an aggressive squeegee in several directions . . . then seal them with a second piece of Plexiglas.

Depending upon the support you choose, the mated pair will need to sit for as little as 5 minutes, or more than 30. If you are using a support, such as Photo Warehouse's Photo Quality Luster, your contact time will be between 5 and 7 minutes. During this time, the water will migrate into the gelatin creating a vacuum like suction that pulls the tissue and the support together. The gelatin surface of the support and gelatin of the tissue will lock together. This happens at the molecular level where the long stringy strands of gelatin mesh together in the manner of a hook and loop fastener.

Support Options

Carbon has been put on a variety of surfaces; paper is the most common, but canvas and glass were often used in the past. Traditionally the surface to which carbon is transferred is called a "support." This probably evolved since carbon tissue was also originally on paper, so it lessened any confusion as to precisely what was being referred to. Here are some options for supports.

Ink-Jet Photo Papers

This is undoubtedly the best choice for a beginner. The variety of surfaces and weights are endless. However, you will want a photo quality ink-jet paper and one that is microporous. Microporous is not a term that describes papers that are blasted with tiny holes during manufacturing. In ink-jet printing, the term indicates that the papers are covered with a coating of extremely fine silicon particles. There are millions of these silicon particles on the paper and they are designed to bond with pigmented inks. During the mating phase, between the tissue and the paper support, these particles grab hold of the gelatin surface of the tissue and hold on like a vise. Shedding and blistering, the most common problems with carbon are thus almost nonexistent. Some of these ink-jet papers wrinkle on their surface when they are wet so you will need to test the paper before investing in a large batch. Digital papers come and go so I'm not going to list a lot of them.

As of July 2007, the best of these would be Professional Grade Photo Quality Luster from www.ultrafineonline.com. This is the very best paper to use when you are first learning the process. You may, or may not, like the surface after the drying. It looks a lot like ink-jet paper. For a more artful surface you may want to consider glyoxal hardened gelatin sizing on fine art paper although I haven't had much success with this idea to date. Other ink-jet papers that work well are Canon Photo Paper Pro, Ilford Galerie Smooth Gloss, and Moab Lasal Photo Gloss.

There are some very high-end ink-jet papers that are similar to fine art papers that are not microporous and they do not work. You will know because the image will slide right off of the surface as soon as you separate the tissue from the support in the hot water development bath. You might also notice that the tissue won't bond with the paper and when you separate it all you will be left with is a yellow dichromate ghost of your image.

Yupo

Yupo is a synthetic paper used for a wide range of printed applications such as maps, catalogues, manuals and labels. It is very durable category 5 polypropylene plastic film, is completely recyclable, and is available in most art stores. It has become quite popular with watercolorists. Yupo also works without any additional sizing and is a good support for the beginning carbon printer. It is, however, a bit trickier than ink-jet photo paper. Yupo has the added benefit of being reusable. If you don't like the print, wash it in some household bleach and rinse it in hot water and reuse it. Yupo should also be washed with some detergent and hot water before first use to remove any release agents left during its manufacturing process. If your art store does not carry Yupo, it is available from Bostick & Sullivan and from many sources on the Internet.

Fixed Out Photo Enlarging Paper

This is a choice of many contemporary workers. If you happen to find a load of out-of-date paper, consider yourself lucky. If it is foggy because it is old, fix it in Farmer's Reducer instead. It should be soaked for 5 minutes in warm water before mating it to the exposed tissue.

Art Paper

To date, no one has found an off the shelf art paper that works without extra sizing. Art papers, such as Rives BFK, need to be sized twice with a 4% warm gelatin mixture combined with 3 grams of potassium alum (a hardening agent) per liter. Please consult the Paper preparation chapter for full details on paper sizing. Caveat: In most cases, the paper will need to be sized far more heavily than you normally would for gum bichromate.

Another idea, and one that my students and I are just beginning to work with, is taking a paper such as Cot 320 and performing a glyoxal/gelatin hardening preparation on it and then using that paper as the transfer support. I suspect that you may have to do this sizing process twice before the paper is completely perfect for the transfer.

Preparing Fine Art Papers For Carbon Supports

I'm still working on this idea and most of the solutions that I've run across don't work very well. Honestly, if the surface of the microporous Professional Grade Photo Quality Luster support were just a little bit more attractive I wouldn't keep trying to find a way to get printmaking paper to accept a carbon transfer. I know that I could muddle through a double transfer sequence, like carbon on canvas, but the fact is the Luster works beautifully and even the novice can make a carbon print in a short order. Not so with exotic supports.

In any event, I had this idea the other day about taking a sheet of Lanaquarelle and glyoxal sizing it with several light coatings using the single bath immersion technique. I tried a piece of paper prepared with a single gelatin glyoxal hardened surface but it simply wasn't microporous enough and the tissue couldn't bond properly. I thought, what if I did these three, or four, times with a thicker gelatin? Well, I haven't yet and since this manuscript is due in a few days it doesn't look like I'll know the answer in time. However, this evening, Dick Sullivan sent me an e-mail and told me that Andrea Zalme in Canada had a process of gelatin sizing her support and this is what she does. Again, I haven't tried this either so I can't say if it is great or not . . . all I know is that it apparently works for her and it is relatively close to my idea so you might as well give it a shot.

Step 1 Brush size 2 coatings of 6% gelatin on warmed paper . . . drying between the first and second coatings.

Step 2 Andrea then sprays on a third coating of gelatin in a spray booth with a professional spraying apparatus.

Note: I'm not sure why you couldn't immerse your paper in a solution of warmed gelatin and get just as good a finish.

Step 3 After the paper is completely dry, apply a cold glyoxal directly to the gelatined surface with a foam brush. Dry the paper and then wash it in cold water for 30 minutes.

Note: I'm not sure why Andrea is recommending the drying before the rinse but if it works for her then it wouldn't be a bad idea to try it this way.

Step 4 When mating the tissue and the support in the water tray, immerse both for one minute and then (and this will be tricky) squeegee the tissue and the support together underwater. Remove the paired tissue and support and place them on a sheet of glass or Plexi and squeegee once again.

Step 5 Keep them mated for 1 hour.

Note: To me this seems like a long time to mate and I would see about going to the hot water separating bath at different times to see if a shorting mating might be possible.

Standard Procedure for Mating the Tissue to the Support

Step 1 Place the chosen paper support in the tray of iced or very cold water with the side you will mate to facing up.

Step 2 Place the exposed tissue in the tray of ice-cold water, with the exposed side facing down towards the support paper, and allow it to soak for 1 minute. Agitate and wipe the surface of the tissue with a latex gloved hand to remove any microscopic or larger air bubbles trapped on the surface during this time.

Step 3 With the gelatin of the tissue directed downwards, facing the support, put the two sheets together and pull them from the tray. Keep the pair horizontal and moving quickly to the Plexiglas surface where you will squeegee, carrying as much water as possible.

Step 4 Firmly squeegee the two together. The first stroke should be firm followed by increasingly firm strokes. Four to five strokes should be sufficient. The reason for carrying the water between the pair to the squeegee glass is to have a flood of water on the first stroke. This flood will carry away any air trapped between the mated pair.

Step 5 Allow the mated pair to sit for at least 30 minutes, pressed between 2 sheets of glass or thick Lucite, if you are using a support like Yupo. If you are using an RC digital printing paper such as the Photo Quality Luster mentioned earlier, the mating time is 5 to 7 minutes. Longer mating times will not hurt; in fact, they will actually help reduce the chances of blistering and shedding. In the early days of carbon printing, it was common to expose and mate tissue in the morning and develop them in the afternoon.

Figure 18–5

Margret Hall, *Emmaline*, 4 o'clock Sun, 2007—carbon
Maggie made this carbon print during my advanced alternative process workshop in Santa Fe. She wrote, "Going home to Kansas from Boston, my sanity returning slightly as I finally got to photograph those I love." *(Courtesy of the artist)*

PHASE 4: DEVELOPING THE PRINT

Table Set Up

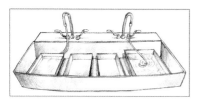

- A mated pair of tissue and its support
- A large and clean tray for processing
- A very good supply of hot water
- A thermometer that will read 105°F/40°C

The Procedure

Step 1 Fill the tray with 105°F to 110°F water.

Step 2 Slip the mated pair into the tray, submerge them and don't fuss with tray or the water.

Step 3 Wait 3 to 5 minutes. Watch the edges where the tissue meets the support. When the pigment begins oozing from the edges and it looks like a grey silt-like cloud leaking from the pair's edges, you are ready to separate the pair. This oozing indicates the gelatin is melting and that the tissue can be removed.

Step 4 Peel the tissue from the gelatin support diagonally, from one corner to it's opposite corner. There should be some resistance so don't be afraid that you will rip the tissue or the support. If, in doubt, let it sit a little longer. Start from one corner and hold the paper support steady while removing the tissue.

Step 5 Once the tissue backing has been removed, dispose of it, as it is no longer needed in the process.

Step 6 At this point you should see a sheet of black and shiny, how do I put this? . . . goo, gunk, crud, gloop . . . you get the picture. If the support, like Yupo for instance, floats, you can turn the support over by holding two sides and letting it bow. This will prevent any air bubbles from forming. Most ink-jet papers will sink so just let them sit on the bottom. Ink-jet papers should be agitated rapidly to speed development. There is little danger of shedding the image.

Step 7 Continue to monitor the temperature in the tray. If it drops below 95°F, add more hot water to bring up the temperature.

Step 8 Every so often, turn the print over and observe the development. There will usually be a fringe of tissue sticking to the print outside the image area. This can be removed during development by rubbing it off with a gloved finger. However, this task is a bit more difficult when using ink jet papers. The fringe can also be removed after the cold-water step (next) by laying it flat on the glass and wiping it off with a paper towel.

Step 9 When you hold the print out of the water, and do not see the carbon leeching off of the support, the development is complete. Look at the white border color . . . if it's not completely white when the water runs off, then it's not ready to be transferred. Place the print in a tray of cold water to set the gelatin.

Step 10 Clear the print in a solution of potassium metabisulfite that is made by dissolving 5 g per liter of water. Clear until there is no yellow from the dichromate in the print. This may take up to 10 minutes or longer. If the clearing is difficult, the rule is warmer, stronger, or longer.

Step 11 Hang the print to dry.

Toning

If you feel like toning, there is a chocolate brown toner that is quite excellent. Simply immerse the carbon print in a 1.5% solution of ammonium dichromate for a few minutes, wash in running water for 5 minutes, fix in standard silver gelatin print fixer for 3 minutes and wash for 20 to 30.

Comments

Every carbon printer will have her or his own technique for developing prints. The variations are endless. Typical of alternative process artists, no two carbon process printers agree on the details and exact steps. Depending whom you talk to, development time varies from 5 minutes to 15 or more minutes. Some printers develop face up and agitate the print in the water. This speeds development but risks edge frilling . . . just as in gum bichromate wash-development.

CARBON ON CANVAS

You can make some very interesting carbon images on canvas that serve as a final image or the first stages of a painting that will follow the creation of the carbon image. The initial set up is time consuming but it is not particularly difficult to do. A. M. Marton's, *The Modern Methods of Carbon Printing*, 1905, has enough information to begin to describe the working process.

Step 1 Scrub the canvas well with a brush and soap and dry it completely.

Step 2 Make a gelatin solution consisting of 80g gelatin and 1 liter of cool water. Allow the gelatin to bloom for 30 minutes and then add 2 g of chrome alum that has been dissolved in a small amount of hot water. Stir the dissolved chrome alum into the gelatin solution in small increments.

Step 3 Apply the gelatin alum solution to the canvas with a brush. Dry the canvas and repeat this step with a second application.

Step 4 Go through the carbon steps and have your carbon image on a temporary support and ready to transfer. This is a technique referred to as a double transfer because you are transferring your carbon image to a support that will then be used to transfer to a second, more stable, support. A temporary support will be glass, a nice thick sheet of white Lucite, or vinyl (like the material grandparents often use to cover their furniture

Figure 18–6
Molly Geiger, *My Bees*, Vermont, 2007—carbon
Molly, grew up on a farm in Vermont and has a passion for honeybees whose hives she tends with her father . . . who knows everything about them. Like Winnie the Pooh, she is fascinated with how they work, live, and produce her favorite food in the world: honey. This image was taken during a day of bee-keeping and honey collecting.
(Courtesy of the artist)

Figure 18–7
Brian Palm, *Long Lake Ladder*, 2005—carbon
(Courtesy of the artist)

between holiday gatherings). Each of these materials needs to be cleaned with bleach and hot water and then coated and buffed with Johnson's Floor Wax. This leaves a super thin molecular film that will release the carbon image to the second support/canvas. Car wax, like Turtle Wax, does not work.

Step 5 The next step is to put a third coat of the gelatin-chrome alum solution on the canvas. The carbon print is then transferred from the temporary support, of glass, Lucite, or vinyl, by pressing it into direct contact with the wet third coat. The mating is allowed to dry and the print is then separated from the temporary substrate and the canvas.

If you want the glossy new transfer to dull down a bit simply soak it in cool water and hang it up to dry. If you want a matte surface mix a little cornstarch with your gelatin solution and brush on a thin coating. At this point

you have a carbon print on a piece of canvas or the beginning of a very interesting adventure into painting on carbon-based photographic imagery on canvas.

MAKING YOUR OWN CARBON TISSUE

If you decide not to purchase the prepared and perfect tissue from Bostick & Sullivan then you will be interested in the following information. Some carbon printers will want to make their own tissue. This is a messy process so it should be done where sooty gelatin and drips on the floor will not matter to anyone. It is nearly impossible to make tissue without also making a mess; and generally you will be limited to a maximum size of 20" × 24".

The Set Up

◆ A flat piece of plate glass at least 2 inches larger in all directions from the size of the tissue to be made. Level the glass on 4 pieces of modeling clay using a spirit level. Have the edges of the glass sanded by your glass shop or tape them to prevent cuts.

- A baine marie, double boiler or crock-pot.
- A 1 liter beaker or suitable glass vessel.
- 90 g 250 Bloom hard gelatin. Knox gelatin from the supermarket can be used in a pinch but it tends to wash out in the highlights.
- 30 g table sugar
- 10 g glycerin—available in most drug stores
- 12 g paint store lampblack pigment. Benjamin Moore stores usually sell pigment in 1 quart cans. This is far more economical than art store pigments.
- Strong paper or wallpaper liner. Wall liner is best. One can use non-woven interfacing material from a fabric store. This can be washed and re-used after printing the tissue.
- A modular picture frame the size of your tissue. This can be one of the many brands of metal frames commonly used for photographs and other art.
- A rubber kitchen–type spatula. A spoon will do in a pinch.
- A large comb with coarse teeth.

The Process: Making the Glop

Step 1 Fill the beaker with 750 ml of cold water, the colder the better. Gelatin swells better in cold water.

Step 2 Let it sit for 20 to 30 minutes to swell.

Step 3 Fill beaker with water to the 1 liter mark.

Step 4 Place in the crock-pot with enough water to reach the midpoint of the beaker and bring up the temperature. You can set the crock on high.

Step 5 The gelatin will melt in about a 30 to 45 minutes.

Step 6 Add the sugar and stir until dissolved. Adding the sugar adds air to the mix so you will want to do this before it sits to de-bubble.

Step 7 Add the glycerin.

Step 8 Add the pigment and stir . . . mixing it well. You do not want any pigment sitting on the bottom as it will clump and get grainy if it cooks there.

Step 9 Turn the heat to low. You will want to keep the gelatin in a liquid, fairly fluid state to allow the bubbles to escape. The bubbles will take some time to rise to the surface and escape. Even the tiniest, almost invisible bubbles will expand considerably in the warm developing water and leave pits in your image.

Step 10 Let the gelatin mixture sit in its hot state for at least 1.5 hours to let the bubbles rise and disappear. They are hard to see; they look like a fog in the mix. Any bubbles in the gelatin mix will end up in the tissue, and then will end up in your prints.

Laying Out the Support

Step 1 Clean the leveled plate glass.

Step 2 Wet the wallpaper liner and gently squeegee down on to the leveled glass.

Step 3 Place the picture frame face down on the wall liner. The frame keeps the glop on the glass.

The Pour & Spread

Step 1 Transfer the gelatin to a small pitcher or large measuring cup with a pour spout. The beaker may be hot and awkward to hold.

Step 2 With the pitcher in one hand and the comb in the other, pour the hot mixture and spread evenly about with the comb. Work quickly and quit when you have a good coating, evenly spread, on the wallpaper liner. If your mix gets cool, and starts to set, the comb will leave rake marks in the gelatin. You will need to throw that attempt out and start over.

Step 3 Let the tissue set for about ½ hour.

Step 4 You can then cut with a knife or a razor blade around the inside edge of the frame to free it from the gelatin.

Step 5 Lift up the tissue and hang it up on a line to dry. It will be surprisingly heavy.

Step 6 When dry it can be used like any other tissue.

Figure 18–8

Rachel Woodburn, *Quiet*, 2007—carbon

Rachel made this carbon print during my advanced alternative process class at The Maine Photographic Workshops in 2007. Her ability to make carbon prints in high heat and humidity is, in part, due to having learned the process in Dick Sullivan's carbon facility in Santa Fe a few weeks earlier . . . where the conditions were ideal.

(Courtesy of the artist)

POP: Printing-Out Paper

OVERVIEWS & EXPECTATIONS

In this chapter, I'll introduce you to the POP (*Printing-Out Paper*) process. POP is a generic name, first used by Ilford Ltd. in 1891. It was used to describe a number of products, and techniques, that shared similar chemical and working characteristics with albumen and salted paper: simplicity, flexibility, versatility, and the fact that the paper "prints-out" without requiring a developer to be fully realized.

Although POP commercially, and chronologically, succeeded salt and albumen in the alternative process timeline, it is significant in that it further democratised the medium of photography . . . allowing anyone, anywhere, the ability to make photographs easily with commercially prepared gelatin sensitized papers and simple chemistry.

This chapter will provide you with the information you need to replicate the POP process as it was conceived by Peter Mawdsley (1874), William de W. Abney (1882), Johann Baptist Obernetter (Munich, 1884), and Raphael Eduard Julius Liesegang (Düsseldorf, 1886). Fortunately for you, there is a lovely POP paper still being produced commercially by the Chicago Albumen Works. With a box of this excellent Centennial paper, you can easily, and successfully, accomplish a POP print in combination with gold and platinum toners. As always, you will learn a little history, how to work with Printing-Out Paper, and the chemistry involved in the fixing and toning of a POP image. At the conclusion of this section, you will have a new, elegant, and richly colored option in your alternative process toolbox.

Figure 19–1
Christopher James, *Driver*, Delhi, India, 1994—POP
(Courtesy of the author)

Figure 19–2

Paul Géniaux, *Confetti Fight in Paris***,** c. 1900—POP

I love this image of a confetti fight in Paris during the Feast of la Boeuf Gras. Paul Géniaux, like Atget, was considered a fine photographic craftsman whose subjects celebrated the men and women of the "small trades" and the street life of Paris. This print can be seen in the collection of the Musee d'Orsay, my favorite museum in the world.

(Courtesy of the Musee d'Orsay, Paris)

A LITTLE HISTORY

In earlier chapters, we have been moving around within the early history of these processes and have seen how the scientific, and creative, explorations of Schulze, Scheele, Hellot, and Fox Talbot had taken the processes to this point. We'll pick it up in 1873 with Peter Mawdsley's first develop-out (DOP) gelatin silver paper . . . which were not commercially available until 1885.

The first silver gelatin-based, printing-out (POP) papers were first manufactured and made available to the German public by Johann Baptist Obernetter (1840–1887) in 1884. That same year, although some sources cite the year as 1886, Raphael Eduard Julius Liesegang began to manufacture a sophisticated collodion printing emulsion that he called Aristotype, named by utilizing the Greek words *aristos* (best) and *typos* (type). The following year, 1885, Joseph Barker, of London, set up a production plant that he called Britannia Works which eventually was re-named Ilford Limited. It was in Ilford's packaging and advertising, in 1891, that the term POP was first used.

POP papers were far less difficult for the amateur to work with than any commercially prepared products,

Figure 19–3
E. J. Bellocq, a Storyville Portrait, 1911—1913
E.J. Bellocq, was an eccentric and curmudgeonly, commercial photographer, in the early part of the 20th century. His private life was infinitely more interesting than his professional life and when he died in 1949 he left a collection of 8" x 10" glass plate negatives documenting the opium dens and prostitutes of the Storyville district of New Orleans. In the late 1960s, Lee Friedlander purchased the plates and began to contact print the work as Bellocq had originally done, with printing-out paper (POP) toned with gold chloride.
(Courtesy of The Minneapolis Institute of Arts, Accession Number :80.11.31—printed by Lee Friedlander—The Miscellaneous Works of Art Purchase Fund)

most specifically albumen. Much as albumen rose to popularity over less convenient imaging systems, POP papers gained acclaim because they were far easier to use. Ultimately, they replaced commercially produced albumen papers in the marketplace. This did not, however, happen overnight. The new POP paper was very similar to the albumen paper it was supplanting. It contained an excess of silver nitrate in a gelatin binder (*rather than an albumen binder*); the printing speed of the two papers were similar; both printed-out as it evolved through the exposure; their processing workflow were nearly the same, and its contrast, coloration, and surface were remarkably alike.

However, unlike albumen, POP paper did not suffer from silver sulphide yellowing and fading. As well, as just mentioned, POP papers used gelatin as a binder. This natural protein, isolated from animal skins and bones, didn't crack as easily as did albumen when it dried, and it also functioned as a protective colloid for silver halide crystals. In solution, gelatin will prevent crystals from growing too large. In a photographic context, the absence of gelatin as a binder for a silver halide/salt would result in crystals growing into a size far too large for a photographic emulsion to deal with for any degree of success.

By 1889, automated production, of continuous roll collodion POP paper was underway, when Dr. A. Kurtz began producing his Celloidin (*meaning pyroxylin or collodion*) POP paper in Germany. That same year, in the United States, there were several POP operations already in business. Among them, Jamestown, N.Y.'s New York Aristotype Company, Kuhn Crystallograph in Missouri, and Western Collodion Paper Co. of Cedar Rapids. Iowa. Shortly thereafter, in 1892, George Eastman (*the proverbial 900-pound gorilla in the living room*) began manufacturing a POP paper called *Solio*. Eastman Kodak continued to produce this paper as Studio Proof until 1987 when they determined that the market had expired.

They were wrong.

As the medium of photography entered the 20th century, there were several manufacturers that were supplying the POP demands of amateur and professional photographers and the paper could even be purchased in novelty party flavors of pink and mauve to go along with the traditional burnt sienna. Today, POP papers such as the excellent Centennial POP are made and distributed by Kentmere Ltd. and the Chicago Albumen Works (*curiously located in Massachusetts*) in sheets and 40" x 100' rolls. We will deal with these pre-coated POP papers in this chapter.

Figure 19–4

Linda Connor, *Benares*, 1979—POP

Having spent a significant time in my life in Benares, India, I have lived with a reproduction of Linda's photograph of the ghats on my office wall ever since removing it from a magazine. Linda's work has been dedicated to the visual exploration of sacred spaces for over 35 years in countries such as Africa, Vietnam, Nepal, India, and Turkey. *(Courtesy of the artist)*

HOW POP WORKS

POP papers are unique among commercially produced photographic papers in that they have a menu of characteristics that not only make them perfect for contact-printing large format negatives, due to their exceedingly long tonal range, but also they are quite elementary in terms of the technical demands they impose upon the maker. POP papers are UV-sensitive, contact-printed, and require you to have a negative the same size as your final image. They feature a very slow speed emulsion that *"prints-out,"* meaning that you can examine your print's progress at set intervals during the exposure. This concurrent evaluation of your image's progress is one of the factors that make the process so appealing to both serious photographic artists and students. Aside from the ease of evaluation, the POP print has a particular characteristic curve that results in a perfect combination of attributes . . . a delicate and smooth tonal structure with detailed shadows and soft highlights. The paper features a self-masking attribute in the shadows, so more exposure yields reduced contrast. These tonal values can be further enhanced with an extensive menu of archival, toning options incorporating gold, borax, platinum, and palladium.

In the POP process, UV light creates a printed-out image by decomposing an excess of silver chloride and liberating decomposed (*photolytic*) silver in the sensitizer. The common light sensitive silver chloride ingredient, in combination with the excess of soluble silver salts, is converted into metallic silver having a deep russet/chestnut brown color, as it prints-out. The silver salts in a POP emulsion are spread uniformly throughout the gelatin binder; in contrast, in the albumen print, the silver salts are coated upon the surface of the prepared albumen. The unique reddish coloration of the POP print comes from this uniform dispersal of the silver salts and from the absorption of short spectrum wavelengths by the smallest particles of silver in the gelatin binder.

As with salted paper exposures, I recommend that you avoid facing the sun directly during your entire exposure. As an alternative, I find that making my exposures, in an area of open shade produces a smoother range of tonalities and less blocking in the shadows. You will still enjoy a thoroughly exposed print; it just takes a bit longer. The benefit of this strategy is that you gain a bit more flexibility in the subtle interpretation of values and a slight increase in contrast, which is especially helpful in the event that your negative's density range is a little low. Should you find that a good deal

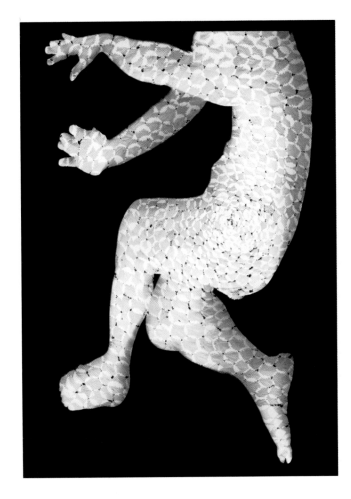

Figure 19–5

Martha Madigan, *Shiva, 1995-96 (72" × 53" gold-toned POP image)*
Martha Madigan created this double-exposure POP (*printing-out paper*)
image by initially creating the photogram of the body and then making a
second exposure with a pattern of natural elements overlaying the white
area created by the body during the first exposure. The POP print was then
gold-toned to create split coloration.
(Courtesy of the Artist and Jeffrey Fuller, Fine Art, Philadelphia)

of contrast is desired, you can actually expose your negative
under fluorescent light (*it emits a small degree of UV light*)
for a 12- to 24-hour exposure. By and large, POP negatives
should have a high-density range and be moderately high in
contrast. Do your best to avoid over-exposure, as that fault
compresses the density scale to a great degree.

At this point, you are aware that the key attribute of
the POP process is that the image is printed-out during
the exposure and that no post exposure development is
required in order to realize the image. The print's color,
following exposure, and prior to the toning and fixing
bath stages, is a characteristic rusty-plum in concert with
a bronzed olive solarization.

When the POP exposure has been completed to your
visual satisfaction, the print is washed in distilled water
where a good portion of the unexposed silver is removed
from the print. If you elect to use running water from the
tap during this pre-wash stage, you will see a milky white
residue form in the wash water that looks identical to
what you saw at the same stage in the salted paper and
Argyrotype processes that you learned earlier. This
milky residue is the excess silver nitrate reacting with
the tap water to form insoluble silver chloride.

Using distilled water eliminates a fair degree of this
white residue as it avoids the chlorine, or chloramine,
that is often added to public water supplies. You can also
begin with a distilled water bath and switch out to running water after 2 to 3 minutes. When the wash water
runs clear, it is a sign that the excess silver has been
washed from the print. At this point in the procedure,
the image is unstable, but tonally rich, and you have to
make a decision about where you are going next.

You have a choice between fixing the print, or toning
it first and fixing it later. If you elect to fix the image
immediately after the first wash you will notice that a
percentage of your image's total density will lessen. After
fixing, in a standard 15% sodium thiosulfate fixing bath
(*150 g to 1000 ml of distilled water*), the color of the
print will change from its familiar plum-red to a warmer
orange-brown. I recommend that you add 2 g of sodium
carbonate to every liter of the fixing bath to make the
bath slightly alkaline. The print that is exposed and fixed
without a toning stage is traditionally called a "*proof*."
This form of POP print lacks a great deal of what the POP
image can provide and will be a warm plum-orange-
brown color. Simply for the pleasure of experiencing the
diversity of colors available in the POP process I strongly
recommend a toning stage *prior* to fixing and final washing. Gold-ammonium thiocyanate and platinum toning
will produce lovely "*tonal splits*" and I have made very
complex splits incorporating selenium with them . . .
more on toning shortly.

There are several excellent POP toners on the market and a few of them are single-stage, monobath, variations on standard gold toners and sodium thiosulfate
fixer. One of the best is Photographer's Formulary POP
Combined Gold Toner-Fixer. This is a simple and reliable combination fixing toner and is good for about

Figure 19–6

Christopher James, *Mosque, Cairo*, Egypt, 1992—POP

I made this image of the two boys, outside a mosque in Cairo, with my plastic Diana camera with a mechanical shutter adaptation. The negative was translated digitally on Pictorico OHP ink-jet film and contact printed on Centennial POP paper. *(Courtesy of the author)*

30 8" x 10" prints. With the traditional toner to fixer processing sequence, fixing in a sodium thiosulfate bath follows toning of the print. This is followed by a final wash in clean water for 20 minutes.

A TRADITIONAL POP EMULSION

Considering the excellent quality of the Centennial POP paper, and the fact that it is not at all easy to make this product without the proper coating machinery, it is unlikely that you will want, or need, to make your own POP emulsion. If, however, you have an overwhelming urge to see if you can actually do it (*and I do know people like you*), or you want the POP process to perform on an alternative paper surface, here is a simple formula to follow in order to make 1000 ml of POP sensitized emulsion. Don't forget that silver nitrate, once it is in solution, has a brief life span.

POP Solution A

1.5 g	ammonium chloride
5 g	sodium potassium tartrate
80 g	plain gelatin
750 ml	distilled water

POP Solution B

25 g	silver nitrate
10 g	citric acid (*more of this will increase the contrast in the print*)
250 ml	distilled water

POP Additives to A & B Mix

50 ml	alcohol
30 ml	of 2% chrome alum

Begin by making Solution A and Solution B in separate *non-metallic* beakers. Placing the beakers in a tray of hot water, warm the temperature of each solution to around

100°F, and very slowly add Solution B to Solution A, while stirring at a steady and continuous rate. You will notice that the thoroughly mixed solution is cloudy. Let it sit for 10 to 15 minutes and then add 50 ml of alcohol followed by 30 ml of a 2% chrome alum solution. When done, you should filter the solution (*a cotton-wool blend sock works quite well*) and then coat your paper before the gelatin "sets up."

Coating is done in the same way as for other hand-applied sensitizers; you have your choice of brush coating or tray floating (*see albumen*). For either choice, be sure to keep the sensitized emulsion from attaching to both sides of the paper. Work efficiently and don't rush the coating process, because the imperfections will make themselves evident during the washing, toning and fixing stages. At the end of the process, you will have proven that you can make a POP emulsion and will also have likely decided that buying a box of Centennial POP paper is an easier way to go.

TABLE SET UP FOR POP

- A box of Centennial POP paper
- Maybe a pair of white cotton gloves if you're nervous
- Clean paper for the table surface coating area
- Pencil and paper for taking notes
- Contact printing frame
- Negative or photogram materials for contact printing

FORMULAS AND WORKING POP PROCESS

Centennial Pre-Coated Paper

The following represents the working process using a pre-coated Centennial POP paper. Be very careful when handling and storing POP paper because it does not appreciate high humidity or excessive handling. Be sure that your hands are entirely free of moisture and chemistry before touching the paper. The paper's surface is very similar to a 111 surface Agfa Portriga (some readers will recall the sad day that this beautiful silver gelatin

Figure 19–7

Leah Sobsey, *Lily,* **2006—POP**
Leah is an artist and educator and currently teaches at UNC Greensboro and the Center for Documentary Studies. This piece is a very nice example of the great color variations possible when making POP photograms. *(Courtesy of the artist)*

paper was discontinued) and it will show your fingerprints if you touch the surface excessively. If you cannot limit your touching to the edges (*which will also likely leave a blemish*) I recommend a pair of the compulsively fresh & white photo-gloves that graduate students are so fond of wearing when looking at prints. Keep the paper tightly sealed in a plastic zip-lock bag and, if possible, at a temperature lower than 70°F. When you are not printing, it is a good idea to store the paper in the refrigerator.

As mentioned earlier, POP papers share characteristics with albumen and salted paper printing techniques. You can work with the paper in low-ambient, non-fluorescent light for limited periods of time and this same light will be appropriate for inspection of the print-out during the exposure stage. Use a hinged back contact frame for inspection and lightly overexpose your image to just past the point where you were happy with it.

You're going to lose a bit of density in the fix and then get most of it back during dry-down. When your exposure is complete, you will have a plum-red/russet colored image. This coloration will fluctuate depending on the time of day, relative humidity and air temperature. Don't be concerned with these differences because the toning stages will change them. Exposure times will vary but begin testing with single minutes in mind and depend heavily on visual inspection during the exposure. You should have the exposure wired in after a few prints.

The negative that works best for this process is one that is quite contrasty, and that has a long negative density range with strong shadows and highlights. A negative density range of 1.6 to 2.0 will work very well. Also, glass plate negatives from the late 19th and early 20th centuries, print beautifully with POP. One more thing to know before the exposure, POP paper, under the right circumstances, will deposit silver nitrate on your negative. If you are anxious about your negative, and it is a particularly humid day, think about separating your negative from the POP paper with a thin, and clean, sheet of acetate. Also, because this is silver nitrate we're talking about, never touch your eyes while handling POP paper without taking some time to thoroughly wash your hands first.

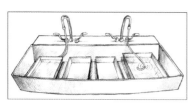

SINK SET UP FOR POP

Tray 1	*Distilled* water . . . 2–3 minutes.
Tray 2	Fresh water bath for 2 minutes
Tray 3	Toning baths
Tray 4-A & 4-B	Fixer—15% sodium thiosulfate (150 g sodium thiosulfate to 1000 ml of distilled water. Add 2 g of sodium carbonate to this fixer to increase the bath's alkalinity. Make up 2 separate trays and split the total fixing time between them.)
Tray 5	Final wash—running water

FIRST WASH

Salt Wash Bath

In the past, I simply washed my exposed POP prints in a distilled water bath for 2 minutes and then moved them to a fresh running water bath for 5 more. For the past few years, I've been incorporating the same slightly acidic salt wash that I use for salted paper printing and albumen, in an effort to eliminate stain goblins and to facilitate a smoother toning process.

The first bath in the processing sequence consists of a slightly acidic salt bath whose purpose is to precipitate the free (or excess) silver by producing silver chloride. If you have no salt in this bath, you will not be removing the free silver and this will create problems with toning, as the gold will not adhere to the silver unless the free silver is eliminated. Following your exposure, immerse your print in this bath of salted water that has been made slightly acidic (lowering its pH) by the addition of citric acid.

    10 g   citric acid—(*this is just a pinch*)
    30 g   kosher salt
1000 ml   distilled water

Immerse your print in this solution under low to moderate light, and agitate slowly for about 5 minutes. Following this step, move your print to a tray for a fresh running water bath for an additional 2–3 minutes. If the milky residue leaving the print in the first wash bath bothers you, there is a partial solution. You can experience less of it if you begin with a short distilled water bath.

POP TONERS

The traditional step at this point in the POP process is to tone the print with one of several toning options. The most commonly used is a POP gold chloride—ammonium thiocyanate toner. The ingredients can be purchased in a raw chemical state, in a partially prepared state (1% gold chloride and ammonium thiocyanate in separate solutions), or in monobath gold toner-fix combination. Again, these toners are used following your water wash to remove residual silver chloride and *before* the sodium thiosulfate fixer. Toners from both albumen and salted paper printing can be tried and the following ones are the most common for POP.

Figure 19–8
Linda Connor, *St. George Book II*, Ethiopia, 2006—POP
Linda writes, "My primary concern as an artist is that the work operate not only as fact, but also as metaphor. To a certain extent, I'm working as a poet would, coaxing out layers of meanings."
(Courtesy of the artist)

Gold — Ammonium Thiocyanate Toner

This toner is available from several suppliers and can be purchased in two separate prepared solutions. Should you wish to make it yourself, this is the traditional formula that has been around for a long time.

Stock Solution A

10 g   ammonium thiocyanate
500 ml   distilled water at 120°F

Stir the 10 g of ammonium thiocyanate stirred into 500 ml of distilled water. Once the solution is prepared, pour it into a glass bottle with a secure top and allow it to sit for 8 to 12 hours before use.

Stock Solution B

1 g   gold chloride
500 ml   distilled water at 70°F

Stir the single gram of gold chloride into 500 ml of distilled water at 70°F and pour the solution into a glass bottle with a top. This is the same percentage used as a supplement to platinum/palladium chemistry. If you buy the 1% gold chloride solution, simply mix 100 ml of it with 400 ml of distilled water to make a 500 ml volume of Stock B.

Note: A good idea for this part of the toner, as well as a simple way to prepare the gold-alkaline toners, is to purchase a prepared 1% gold chloride solution.

Note #2: An even easier solution is to buy the gold ammonium thiocyanate toner already mixed in two separate bottles from Bostick & Sullivan.

To Use: Mix A & B together in the following proportions.

50 ml   of A (*ammonium thiocyanate*)
50 ml   of B (*gold chloride solution*)
900 ml   of distilled water

Toning will take 2 to 30 minutes; a sepia-orange coloration will show after a minute. The time differential is due to the relative age of the toner. Fresh toner tones faster. Do not be alarmed when it appears that the image is initially being destroyed in the toner. It begins its journey by fading your print. As the toning continues, the image will return and darken.

With agitation, as the toning time increases, the color will begin to cool, the highlights will turn light gray, and the shadows will intensify. Color changes will continue to take place, but in general, shorter toning times result in warmer images while longer times provide cooler ones. If it appears that nothing is happening here is what you do . . . Add 50 ml of Part A and 50 ml of Part B to the toner you are working with. In other words, you're refreshing the toner without adding new distilled water.

When the toning is finished, you can quickly rinse the print and head to the fixing tray.

Gold–Alkaline Toners (*gray silver-sepia to pink*)

There is another option available with gold toning and it features the addition of one of several alkaline chemicals to the gold chloride, Part B, of the gold–thiocyanate toner formula. This alkaline formula provides a nice range of subtle color shifts from silver gray to sepia to pink. Again, the Stock B gold chloride for these alkaline toners is prepared by diluting 100 ml of the 1% gold chloride solution with 400 ml of distilled water.

Borax Toning

For sepia tones: Add 4 to 5 g of borax to 900 ml of distilled or tap water. In this situation, the water type doesn't matter a great deal. Next, add 30 ml of the Stock B gold chloride stock solution to the Borax and water mix and enough water to make a working strength 1000 ml toning solution. You'll notice that the solution is yellow but in a few minutes that tint should be gone and the formula will be ready to use. The toning time is completely subjective. Figure anywhere from 2 to 15 minutes and keep in mind that shorter toning times will result in warmer tonalities. Also, a dry print is tonally cooler than a wet print.

Gold–Borax Albumen Toner Option

There is an alternative gold-borax toner that has traditionally been used for *albumen*, which you might want to experiment with. Dissolve 3 g of borax in 400 ml of distilled water and add 6 ml of a 1% gold chloride to the solution to the mix. Percentages of prepared gold chloride solution (*1% to 5% are most common*) can be purchased in a prepared state from most chemical suppliers. Toning will take 5 to 15 minutes, at 70°F, depending on the tone you are seeking. Prepare this toning solution at least an hour before use and try to have it at room temperature. If you find the toning less than active, add, or replenish, with 6 to 10 ml of the 1% gold chloride solution.

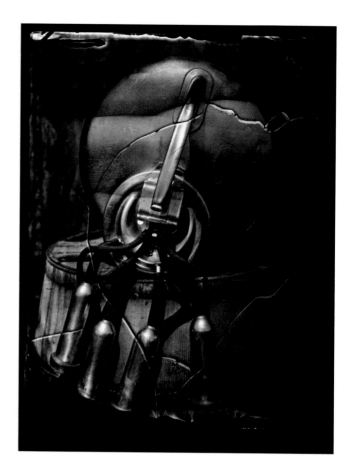

Figure 19–9

Margaret Adams, *Milking Machine,* **2006—POP**
Margaret is a former alternative process workshop participant of mine, and what will probably come as a bit of a surprise to her students at the Corcoran College of Art & Design, the former lead singer in a punk rock band. Margaret has been a "lab rat" tester for both of my books and I am ever grateful.
(Courtesy of the artist)

Sodium Bicarbonate—Gold Formula

This is another gold and alkali formula. For silvery gray tones, add 1 g of sodium bicarbonate to 900 ml of distilled or water from the tap. Then add 30 ml of the gold chloride stock solution to the sodium bicarbonate and water mix and enough water to make a working 1000 ml toning solution. Again, toning time is subjective.

Sodium Bicarbonate–Borax Formula Options

The range of coloration in the combination of sodium bicarbonate and borax with the gold chloride stock is as variable as the proportions you elect to use. In general, your prints will take on hues of pink to sepia. To make a working toning solution, add 1.5 g of borax and 3 g of

Figure 19–10
Christopher James, *Writing in Maine*, 1996—POP
This POP was generated from a pinhole camera with Type 55 Polaroid P/N film. *(Courtesy of the author)*

sodium bicarbonate to 900 ml of distilled or tap water.

Stir the chemicals into solution and then add 30 ml of the stock gold chloride and enough water to make 1000 ml. Toning time is again subjective. More borax, in proportion to the sodium bicarbonate, in your formula will result in a toned print that is less pink and more of a silvery gray-red. In most cases, shorter toning times result in warmer tonalities than do longer toning times. This is due to the gold in the formula.

Replenishment for Gold Toners

Gold is removed from the toning solution every time a print passes through it; the toner is essentially gold-plating the silver. As a result, it is necessary to replenish the toner with several milliliters of gold chloride after every 8" × 10" print or equivalent. For the *gold-ammonium thiocyanate* toner add 7 ml to 10 ml of both the Part A and Part B solutions to the toning solution.

For the *gold alkaline* toners, add 5 ml to 6 ml of the gold chloride stock after every 8" × 10" print or equivalent. If you are doing a lot of toning, as in a workshop or class situation, it is less tedious to simply replenish the toner as described above . . . 50 ml of A & B into the old solution.

Platinum Toner: Traditional Formula

You can realize warm sepia–neutral black tones using the Part C from your platinum process chemistry. The formula is made like this:

Part A: 7 g of sodium chloride combined with 3 g of alum in 500 ml of distilled or tap water

Part B: The 20%, Part C, platinum solution from the platinum process chemistry

Part C: The lithium palladium chloride from the Ziatype process

The working solution is variable. You may opt to use Parts A and B only or make a solution that combines all Parts A-B-C in a single toner. The number of drops of Part B, or Parts B and C with Part A, does determine print color, as will the time that the print is left in the toner.

Begin testing by adding anywhere from 2 to 10 drops of Part B to 500 ml of Part A. Immerse the print in the toner and time the toning until you like the color of the print.

For the second test, combine the same number of drops of Part B with the same amount of Part C and 500 ml of Part A. Tone your print for the same length of time and compare the results. This evaluation will give you a good platform for finding what works best for your intentions. Keep in mind that it is not a good idea to totally fall in love with your color or splits, as you still have both a fixing stage and dry down to go through. Both of these last two stages will alter your colors to a degree.

POP Platinum Toner (*neutral black-sepia*)

Bostick & Sullivan makes a prepared POP platinum toner using potassium chloroplatinite #3. The kit includes:

10 g citric acid
10 ml potassium chloroplatinite #3
1 empty 1000 ml plastic container for storage of the mixed solution

Figure 19–11

Martha Madigan, *Embodied #6*—1995–96—**POP**

This is a terrific example of Martha's amazing control with POP. This solar photogram print is gold-toned on printing-out-paper and is 24" × 20" in size.

(Courtesy of the Artist and Jeffrey Fuller, Fine Art, Philadelphia)

To make a POP platinum toning solution, measure out 10 g of the citric acid on a gram scale and dissolve it in 1000 ml of room temperature distilled water. This will result in a 1% solution of citric acid. To this solution, add 7 to 15 drops of the potassium chloroplatinite #3. The more drops added to the citric acid solution, the faster the toning. You may wish to add fewer drops to allow you to have time to adequately inspect your toning progress. *Note: Platinum toner does not have to be discarded after use.* If you feel that its effectiveness and speed are not what they used to be, add 5 to 10 more drops of the potassium chloroplatinite #3.

To use this toner, overexpose your POP print by 15% to 20% and follow that with a 5-minute wash in distilled water. Then, place the print in a clean tray, and immediately pour the platinum toner over its entire surface. Agitate the tray continuously during the toning process. The toner will make itself evident first in the deeper shadow areas of the print and then will work its way through the sequential tonal stages from dark to light. A short toning time results in a warmer print, while a longer toning period yields blacks and a cooler image. When you are content with the coloration, rinse the print for 5 minutes and proceed to the fixing stage.

Gold—Platinum POP Split Toner

You can achieve a nice gold-platinum split-toned POP print by partially gold toning the print (*a very short toning time in the gold-thiocyanate toner*), rinsing the print for 3–5 minutes, and then re-immersing the print in the platinum toner until you like what you see. The darker values will be purple-sepia in the shadows following the gold toner, while the highlights and lighter mid-tones will tone a cool-blue-black in the platinum. Always be sure to first tone with the gold because the citric acid in the platinum toner affects the gold toner in a negative way.

Figure 19–12
Christopher James, *Katie*, Oklahoma, 1999—POP
This is a pinhole image of Katie, one of my former workshop students at the amazing Oklahoma Summer Arts Institute . . . quite possibly the best high school age arts workshop program on the planet. The POP print was contact printed and subsequently toned in a sequence of toners including platinum, gold, and selenium.
(Courtesy of the author)

Gold–Platinum-Selenium POP Split Toner

This toning variation produces some intense results. My sequence begins with a very brief time, about 10 to 15 seconds, in a fresh gold–thiocyanate toner. Then, I remove the print before it has a chance to thoroughly change and place it in a rinse for 2 minutes. Then, go directly to the platinum toner for about 6 to 10 minutes. After the platinum toner, wash the print for 5 minutes and then immerse it in a 30:1 selenium bath at room temperature for about 10 seconds and proceed to the final washing and fixing stages. The print takes on an extremely rich plum-red tonality in the shadows with sepia to neutral black tones in the middle grays.

It's very easy to go too far with this toning process, as it gets away from you in a hurry. As always, when working with selenium it is prudent to wear gloves or use tongs.

FIXING THE POP PRINT

15% Sodium Thiosulfate Fixer Formula

150 g   sodium thiosulfate
1000 ml   distilled water

   * Make up 2 baths of 15% fixer and split the time between them.

Figure 19–13

Linda Connor, *Monastery Roof Spiti*, India, 1994—POP

Linda's technique is as distinctive as her images. She uses an admittedly cumbersome 8" × 10" large-format camera, which allows her to achieve a remarkable clarity in her images. She frequently resorts to long exposures that permit the representation of time and movement. Her prints are created via direct contact of the negative on POP printing out paper. In this process, the negative and paper are fitted carefully together and then the image is exposed through the sunlight in her garden. She then tones her images with gold chloride, which infuses the works with a rich patina reminiscent of the 19th-century photographic processes. *(Courtesy of the artist)*

To make a 15% sodium thiosulfate fixer, simply dissolve 150 g of sodium thiosulfate into 1000 ml of distilled water. If you wish to protect the gelatin with a hardener during the fixing and washing cycles, just add 60 ml to 70 ml of Kodak Liquid Hardener to the total volume. This addition is not necessary, so don't worry about it if you don't have any in the lab. Once you are finished with your toning, give the print a quick rinse in clean running water and then move it directly into a fixing tray containing the 15% solution of sodium thiosulfate. Fix your print for 3 to 5 minutes.

You are probably wondering why, after a slew of processes with very dilute sodium thiosulfate fixing times of a minute or two, we are now fixing with a

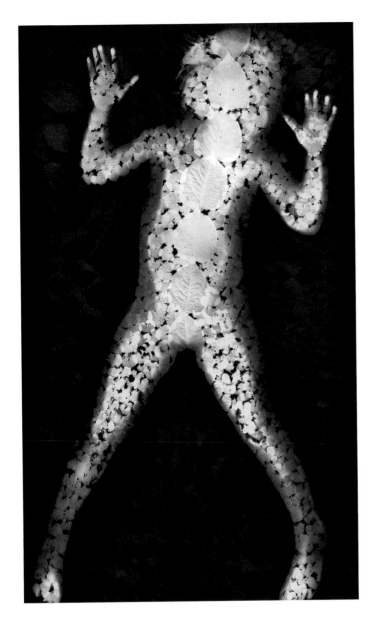

Figure 19–14

Martha Madigan, *Graciela-Growth-III,* **1993–2003—40" × 24" giclée**
Philadelphia artist Martha Madigan has been working in alternative processes for 30 years and since 1981 she has focused on the POP process. Many of her images are mural-size works in which she makes complex multiple exposures in sunlight on a single sheet of POP paper. *(Courtesy of the Artist and Jeffrey Fuller, Fine Art, Philadelphia)*

15% dilution for 3 to 5 minutes. It is due to the fact that silver is embedded in the gelatin rather than the easily accessible paper fibers found in a process like salted paper. I know of many POP artists who play it safe with a double fixing baths and I recommend this same idea to you. Simply split your fixing time between the two trays. This is important . . . After 5 prints, a new 15% sodium thiosulfate bath should be made and moved to the tray #1 position while the original tray #1 goes to the #2 position.

FINAL WASH

After the fixer, wash your prints well in clean, not too hot or cold, running water. If you are not intending to use a hypo-clearing bath then the recommended washing time is 40 minutes. If you do use a hypo-clearing bath, you may cut the wash time to 15 minutes. After the prints are fully washed, hang them on a line, back to back, with clothespins at the top and bottom. You may also elect to lay them on drying screens, but I would avoid doing so in any communal lab situation, as those screens are almost always contaminated with chemistry.

Tintypes & Hand-Applied Emulsions

OVERVIEW & EXPECTATIONS

In this chapter, I'll begin by discussing commercially made, hand-applied, liquid emulsions and will deal with their idiosyncrasies, and how they can be adapted for use on such alternative surfaces as glass, metal, and wood.

Please keep in mind that a great deal of related, and complete, information can be found in other chapters, such as Chapter 22, Wet Collodion & Gelatin Dry Plate Emulsion, Chapter 17, Dichromate Options, and Chapter 15, Paper. Be sure to check those chapters if you want to learn a lot more about wet and dry hand-made emulsions and how to prepare them for a variety of substrates.

I'll also be showing you how to make contemporary tintypes using commercial emulsions. But first, I'll give you a little history beginning with the Alabastrine process from 1864. I'll discuss the technique and various ways in which you can begin to think about using easily available commercial emulsions for tintypes . . . or how to go even deeper into the tintype process by returning to the technique of working with wet collodion (see Chapter 22).

Figure 20–1

Christopher James, _Steel Twins on Acid_, 1996—emulsion & paint on acid-etched steel

(Courtesy of the author)

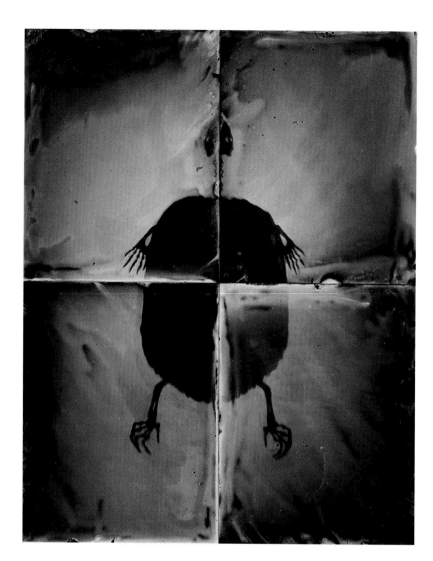

Figure 20–2

Jayne Hinds Bidaut—1999–2007—*Chrysemys Scripta Elegans—Turtle Skeleton*, 1999—Tintype

The power of organic simplicity is how I describe Bidaut's work to those who are unfamiliar with it. There is a grace to these small and precious memorials on metal. *(Courtesy of the artist)*

COMMERCIAL EMULSIONS

This section focuses on several different commercially made emulsion types, i.e., Rockland's Liquid Light, its superior companion emulsion, AG-Plus, Silverprint SE-1, and Maco's (*used to be Cachet*) Black Magic set of emulsion, hardener, and gelatin. The primary purpose of these commercially prepared emulsions is to provide photographers, and other visual artists, with a continuous tone, blue-sensitive, silver halide emulsion that can be applied easily to nearly any surface that will accommodate it.

Liquid hand-applied emulsions can be used alone, or in combination, with a great variety media, and have proven to be compatible with drawing, painting, sculpture, printmaking, alternative process techniques, and transfers. They can also be applied to a wide assortment of materials including plastic, paper, fabric, metal, and glass and assorted basic food groups such as Twinkies or toast. Personally, I feel that these materials are at their respective best when used in combination with other media.

Maco Black Magic Liquid Emulsion

Maco's Black Magic Liquid Emulsion, and its related products, is made in Germany and comes in several tonal varieties of normal, hard, and variable contrasts. It is, of all the commercially made emulsions, the one I personally use and highly recommend for work on alternative materials and surfaces. One of the primary reasons for my enthusiasm, other than its superior quality to all other options, is the Black Magic Liquid Hardener, added to the developer, which eliminates a lot of the soft emulsion damage that generally occurs during processing. Maco also sells a gelatin base sub-coating for problem surfaces such as glass, metal, and absorbent

Figure 20–3
Gary Emrich, *As in Titian Profane & Sacred,* **2004**
Gary builds his images in the computer, puts them on videotape, and re-photographs them off of a 1955 Zenith TV. The TV lets him control contrast and brightness, which is often a problem with these emulsions. He ages his emulsions for years and believes that the best emulsions are like wine and cheese . . . left to ripen they will get better. Slate tiles, paint, brushes, and flagstone have many layers of alkyd white paint underneath. There is a lot of oil retouching after the materials are dry and glass is the most stable of his substrates. Gary's artwork relies heavily on process, releasing him from traditional photographic perspective, scale, texture, materials, and preconceptions.
(Courtesy of the artist)

materials. Maco Black Magic Photo Gelatin comes in 250 ml bottles and is used in conjunction with Maco Black Magic Liquid Hardener, a formaldehyde-free hardening agent that assists the emulsion in adhering to difficult surfaces. A sub-coating that is made for the emulsion is a bonus and should be explored if your work generally calls for a primer. These products offer high speed and high silver content. Among its other salient features are a long shelf life, a product system, 3 different contrast emulsion grades, and consistent reliability.

Black Magic Liquid Hardener: A Solution for Fragile Emulsions

Adding Black Magic Liquid Hardener to the paper developer has proven to be a simple solution to the problem of a soft hand-applied emulsion breaking up or sliding off of the substrate it's printed on during the development and washing cycles. The hardener has an acidic pH of 3 and consists of 15% to 20% of a glutaraldehyde sodium

bisulfite compound, 1% to 2% of 5-nitrobenzimidazole nitrate, and 12% acetic acid. The manufacturer recommends that the working hardener/developer solution is made by mixing the hardener to the developer in a 1:20 ratio but I have found that an easier way to work with it is to simply add 2 capfuls of the hardener to a liter of Dektol developer mixed at 2:1. The hardener also works well with other liquid emulsion brands.

One additional benefit: the addition of the hardener to the developer appears to increase the contrast of the image. Two other options with Black Magic Hardener are adding the hardener to the liquid emulsion itself or adding it to the Maco Black Magic Gelatin used for preparing non-porous metallic or glass substrates.

To use the hardener within the emulsion itself, there are two steps to follow. The first is to make a stock hardening solution by mixing the hardener with distilled water in a 1:20 dilution. The second step is to then add the 1:20 hardening stock to the liquid emulsion using a ratio of 1:20. Make only the amount of emulsion with hardener that you intend to use immediately.

Kentmere Liquid Emulsions

Kentmere Fixed Grade Liquid emulsion is a light-sensitive silver bromide emulsion, which can be applied to various surfaces such as glass, ceramics, cardboard, fabrics, plastics, metal, etc. The fixed contrast is a standard grade #3, and is the same emulsion used to coat Kentmere Bromide #3 double-weight fiber-base paper. Kentmere VC (*Variable Contrast*) Liquid emulsion is a light-sensitive chloro-bromide silver emulsion, it can also be applied to various surfaces and is comparable to Silverprint's SE-1 Liquid Emulsion (sold in the United States as Luminos Silverprint). The emulsion can be purchased in fixed or variable contrast grades and can be used with variable contrast filters. As with other commercial liquid emulsions, this solid photographic emulsion is liquefied by heating it slowly in a double boiler like a bath of hot water. The cap to the bottle must remain on the emulsion bottle during this warming stage and only opened under safelight conditions.

Silverprint SE-1 Liquid Emulsion

The SE-1 emulsion gets a strong recommendation from those who use it in that it has the sensitivity of a grade 2 paper, can be easily diluted for different substrates, there is a "subbing" solution available for use on non-porous glass surfaces, it reacts well to toners, and has a warm black tonality. SE-1 also seems to be less prone to the fogging characteristics that are common in similar liquid emulsion formulas. For these reasons, Silverprint Emulsion SE-1 has recently become a student favorite. Be sure to look at the Black Magic Liquid Hardener information above for recommendations about using it with Silverprint SE-1. Adding the hardener to your print developer greatly assists in keeping the fragile emulsion on your paper from being compromised during the production process.

Figure 20–4

Deborah Luster, *Rosesucker Retablos III—1957 (liquid emulsion on aluminum with oil)*

This work is a wonderful example of the organic richness found in work. The piece was created with Silverprint liquid emulsion on aluminum panels and hand painted with oils. The image is from Deborah's *Rosesucker Retablos* portfolio that was initially published in *Conjunctions: 32* accompanying the poetry of C. D. Wright with translations by Gabriel Bernal Granados.

(Courtesy of the artist)

Rockland's Liquid Light & AG-Plus Emulsions

Liquid Light has become a generic term, like Kleenex, and is often used to describe any hand applied commercial emulsion and is the product most often experienced first by students and artists when working with this type of material. It is a basic black and white emulsion that is easy to use, quirky enough to teach you a lot about the foibles of liquid emulsions, and adequate for most applications. Liquid Light, like other emulsions, has a tendency to fog whenever safelight illumination is too close to the product.

Figure 20–5

Charlene Knowlton, *Triptych*, 1984—81" × 120"—emulsion and oil paint on wood

I first saw Charlene's work a few decades ago when she was making these huge tribal pieces out of a tiny garage space in Los Angeles . . . at least, that is how my memory recalls it. I wanted to put this piece in the first edition but couldn't find her to ask permission. With the Internet, it was easy, and here it is. This piece is an 81" × 120" triptych on plywood, hand-applied emulsion, and oil painting, and it's been a favorite of mine from the first time I saw it.

(Courtesy of the artist)

It often exhibits inconsistent behavior, although this might simply be the case of the diverse working styles of individuals. I've been using it for over 30 years and the product's idiosyncrasies have taught me a great deal about dealing with the eccentricities of hand-applied emulsions. It is also, due to its inconsistencies, likely the primary reason artists decide to learn wet collodion.

Ag-Plus is Rockland's premium gelatin-silver emulsion, with higher sensitivity (more silver), a major convenience if the emulsion is used in camera on metal or glass plates. It is also best to use when oversize prints are made at a considerable distance from an enlarger. Like Liquid Light, Ag-Plus photographic emulsion is completely free of phenol fumes, so is safe to use in any darkroom.

THE WORKING PROCESS

Paper Preparation

One of the primary complaints regarding commercial liquid emulsions is the inconsistent nature the product and final imagery. Most of these problems are easily dealt with by simply paying close attention to surface preparation, and the specific directions that accompany each type of emulsion. For instance, by sealing the pores in paper with a hardened gelatin or bichromate, the emulsion is able to "hook" into the sizing. This will result in a slightly glossier surface, more resolved blacks, less streaking in the brush coating, and it also helps in keeping the emulsion on the paper during the processing stages. Please refer to Chapters 15, Paper, and 17, Dichromate Options, for information regarding preparation of difficult substrates.

One example of a preparation technique is performing a traditional gum-bichromate exposure, on gelatin glyoxal hardened paper, without using pigment in the formula. This means mixing a solution of 1:1 gum arabic and a saturated potassium dichromate, or ammonium dichromate, and applying it in the area where you intend to place your image. Then, all you need to do is expose this coating to UV light for 10 minutes, and water process the paper. After the final wash, the paper is re-exposed to UV light for 5 to 10 minutes and line-dried. The paper can be flattened in a dry-mount press at a low temperature following the drying stage. The surface will have a light tan color and this color will take the place of white in your liquid emulsion image unless you decide to clear it in a 1% potassium metabisulfite bath to clear up the highlights. Now you have a gelatin-hardened surface that can be used as a substrate for liquid emulsions.

Working under Safelight & The Basic Process

First, it is important to know that these commercial emulsions have a strong tendency to fog while you are preparing to make images. It's easy to forget that in conventional darkroom printing (soon to be an alternative process?), you are simply opening your box of paper, slapping a sheet down on an easel, making a fast exposure, and moving right to the chemistry. With hand-applied emulsions, you are going to be applying your light-sensitive coatings to a substrate, drying it, generally aging it for 24 hours if you want a decent-looking image, and then making your exposure. Knowing this, it is very important that you reduce the amount of safelight illumination in your darkroom. Move yourself, or the lights, to a location that is light-safe. You can also put your safelight on a dimmer switch or simply drop a yellow or white towel over the safelight glass.

Begin by placing the *sealed* bottle of liquid emulsion into a large beaker of very hot water and wait for the emulsion to become warm and fluid. It gels and gets too thick to flow evenly as it cools and it's essential that the solution is warm for an even application of the emulsion. This warming step should take about 10 minutes.

If you intend to expose immediately after your coating is dry, begin to set up your chemistry in the darkroom sink. This set up is identical to paper chemistry but it is a good idea to omit the stop bath. In its place, fill a tray with water; this will act as your intermediate step between the developer and the fixer. To your developer, add 2 capfuls of the Maco Hardener. Use a non-rapid fix. Rapid fixers, made with *ammonium* thiosulfate, can often have a less than positive effect on the emulsion. Use regular *sodium* thiosulfate fixer like Kodak's Kodafix or prepare your own by making a weak solution as you have done with several of the processes in this book.

If you are working with paper, lay it down on a clean and dry surface, such as a sheet of 1/4" glass, and tape the corners to keep the paper flat. Surfaces that are not normally flat, like eggs or cupcakes, will have to be positioned to allow you to apply the emulsion. I will assume that you are using paper for these initial instructions. I like to put my paper through the dry mount press before coating. The best way to remove excess moisture from the paper is to place the paper in the press and then open and close it several times. You will see the steam escape at the back of the press.

When you are set up, pour a small quantity of the warmed emulsion on the paper's surface. Using a soft watercolor fan brush, a foam brush, a comb, a glass rod, or your fingers, quickly lay down a smooth coating in the area you intend to print in. If the emulsion begins to cool, it will gel and your coating will be dimensionally uneven—you may like this look. I have had students attempt to airbrush the emulsion but nozzle clogging is a definite problem on larger areas. After coating, allow the emulsion to air dry or blow-dry under very low safelight conditions.

Note: Commercial emulsions are best left alone to air dry in a paper safe, box, or light-tight drawer, for 24 hours.

Exposure time in an enlarger will range from 30 seconds to several minutes, depending on the negative and the size of the enlargement. If you project the negative in

Figure 20–6

Mari Gardner, *Ostrich Egg—1999 (ostrich egg with liquid emulsion image in sculptural motif)*

Mari Gardner created this piece while a student at AIB. Like most all of Mari's work over the last decade, it is created with the intention of showing both life and death in an organic and evolving state. Mari's work once used Plexiglas encased deceased life forms (her skunk made her a living legend at The Art Institute of Boston) as well as living vegetation such as the moss growing on top of her sculpture.

(Courtesy of the artist)

a slide mount from a slide projector, the exposure will be as short as a few seconds. This will, of course, depend on the distance between the projector and the coated paper. The slide projector is the best way to expose large mural pieces in a short time. An example of a large mural piece might be coated 4' × 8" sheets of plywood followed up with applications of paint as in the work of Charlene Knowlton (Fig. 20-5).

If you are looking for an image with a smoother surface, try dampening the exposed print with cool water

prior to development. Process this exposed paper normally in conventional silver gelatin paper chemistry, but remember to replace the stop bath with a plain water bath. Consider toning and split toning the image on any surface. Most toners have an effect and they are a bit different than what you might be used to with paper. With that in mind, try selectively painting the toners on the image. Stay loose and enjoy learning from the failures and occasional successes. The failures, meaning they were not what you were expecting, are potentially great substrates for applications of other materials and additional emulsion coatings.

WORKING ON GLASS, CERAMIC, & SIMILAR SURFACES

One of the great pleasures of working with liquid emulsions is seeing how many different surfaces you can get an image to print on. There is a separate section in this chapter on metals and tintype. *Note: For related information on the procedure for gelatin-glyoxal sizing on glass and other substrates, please consult the Chapter 8, Cyanotype Variations, Chapter 15, Paper, and Chapter 17, Dichromate Options.* You will also find other instructions for preparing glass and metal in the wet collodion and the gelatin dry plate emulsion chapter. Using multiple images, color, and texture, photographic artists are able to extend their working concepts in many alternative directions.

Gelatin/Glyoxal Hardening on Glass

Applying any alternative sensitizer/emulsion on glass is not a simple task, but it can be done well if you follow some simple rules. The glass should be scrubbed with a course kitchen sponge but avoid any abrasive material that may scratch it. Begin the cleaning process with vinegar, or stop bath, and continue it with soap and water until the water no longer beads up on the surface. When this stage is reached, you can feel confident the gelatin will adhere to the surface. Once the glass is dry, pour a warm gelatin-glyoxal mix over a piece of warmed glass. You may need to apply the warmed gelatin a several times so that you have multiple thin layers rather than a single thick coating. Be very careful and move slowly as you don't want bubbles in the gelatin. Dry the glass well between applications.

If glyoxal is unavailable, try spraying a series of thin coats of gloss polyurethane. It is important to use the gloss version of this canned aerosol polyurethane because it does not have a liquid repellent wax in its formula, as do the semi matte and matte versions of the product. Maco's Black Magic Photo Gelatin and Hardener, employed as a primer for difficult surfaces, is another product that can be used with its companion emulsion instead of polyurethane. It is especially effective on glass and similar hard surfaces. When this product is used on fabrics, it will save on emulsion use by limiting the absorption of the sensitizer in the material.

Simple Preparation & Coating

If you are going to be using spray gloss polyurethane, apply three to four very light applications and dry well between coatings. When it is time to apply the emulsion, you must first heat it so that it becomes more fluid. Heat in the same manner as described in the initial instructions. Several artists who work with liquid emulsion on glass are fond of additives in their sensitizer solutions. One of my students liked to add a small amount of exhausted fixer to his emulsion and his images seemed to benefit from this decision by being more brilliant in the highlights. Another student routinely added small amounts of D-72 developer to his emulsion. This addition worked well and resulted in more resolute blacks.

It is important to warm the surface that you intend to spread or apply your emulsion layer on. One method that I always use when working with sheet metal, or flat surfaces, is to fill a tray, that is smaller than the substrate you are coating, with very hot water and then lay the substrate (glass or metal for instance) on the edges of the lower tray. Wait a few minutes and the glass should be sufficiently warm to allow for a long and unhurried coating process. You can pick up the sheet of glass and rotate it, letting the emulsion flow evenly across the surface of the substrate. Once the emulsion has dried, store the coated substrate in a dark environment, such as a paper safe or cardboard box, for at least 24 hours. This aging process helps intensify the contrast of your image. Another option, especially when the surface is irregular, is to warm the object, that you'll be applying the emulsion to, with a hairdryer on a hot air setting immediately prior to coating. Spread on a thin application of emulsion and move the object around as the emulsion cools and gels. The heat ensures a smooth application, which is important because if it begins to set up too quickly the surface will gel in uneven clumps.

Sweet Cream Emulsion: Avoiding Bubbles in Coating

Bubbles are often a problem. Here is a way to avoid them.

Step 1 Warm the surface that you are intending to make an image on. You can use a dry-mount press, or hot water tray technique, for flat and thin objects or a hairdryer for three-dimensional ones.

Step 2 Make up a formula of:

- 60 ml of emulsion
- 7 ml of distilled water
- 1 ml of heavy sweet cream

Mix the ingredients together at 110°F, slowly and carefully pour the solution on the surface, and rotate the object using a technique similar to coating a wet collodion plate.

Printing on Glass

When printing, use small apertures to avoid fogging potential and when working with glass it is a good idea to place a sheet of non-reflective black velvet under the glass plate to avoid back-splash reflection of the projected light. When processing, use a slightly chilled chemistry and agitate very gently throughout the developing and washing process. If your chemistry is too warm, place a can of cold unopened soda, or ice, in a plastic storage bag and place it in the solution. This causes a quick chilling and does not dilute the solution.

Exposing in Developer

Another method of exposing, and processing a glass plate image at the same time, is to expose it while it is immersed in a tray of paper developer. This lessens the chance of damaging the emulsion during the working process. In the darkroom, under very low red safelight, take a dry tray and place a piece of paper, mat board, or

Figure 20–7

Jayne Hinds Bidaut, *Green Iguana, Held In Hand*, 1998–2007—tintype

Lizzie is an 11-year-old, 5-ft-long, male Iguana who was a casualty of the pet trade, and has lived with Jayne since he was 2, his age in the tintype. Lizzie is a sweet guy and he visits schools to help educate kids about the environment. He has had a big impact upon her work and has taught her many things. Jayne never had a desire to live with an iguana before she took him in, but now cannot imagine her life with out him. Lizzie does not live in a cage and travels with Jayne wherever she goes.

(Courtesy of the artist)

frosted glass, the same size and thickness of your coated glass, under the enlarger to focus the projected image. Remove the focusing material from the tray and replace it with your coated glass. Pour cool developer over the glass in the tray until it just covers the upper exposed surface. If you fill the tray too deeply with developer, the fluid will refract the light from the enlarger. Turn on your enlarger and make the exposure.

You will be able to observe your image developing during the exposure and I recommend allowing for extended development by occasionally turning off your enlarger and observing the changes that are taking place under safelight conditions. When you're satisfied, gently remove the exposed glass from the tray of developer and place it in a cool water bath. Try to keep the glass in a flat position during the transfer to lessen the chances of the image sliding around. Then fix and wash gently in the normal manner. If you find that your emulsion is having a difficult time remaining on the glass, especially if you haven't gelatin/glyoxal hardened it, then you will want to add 2 capfuls of Black Magic's Liquid Hardener to every 1000 ml of your paper developer.

EMULSIONS ON METAL

For years, I have been working with the application of liquid emulsions on metal plates such as stainless steel, aluminum, and copper. One of the best sources you will likely find for these plates is an industrial or commercial roofing company and most of the time they can cut the plates to your required size specifications with very impressive, room size, snipping machines. (*It's a good idea to smooth the sharp edges with a metal file.*) The plates are available in a variety of thicknesses and sizes including rolls and very heavy 4' x 8' sheets. Besides filing the edges, it is necessary to degrease the metal's surface because the majority of industrial metal sheeting comes with a thin oily coating to prevent corrosion prior to the sale. Steel roofing material, painted and ready to use in a variety of colors, costs about $40.00 for a 4' × 10' sheet. The cutting costs will be extra.

Note: In a few pages I'll be delving into tintypes and it would probably be a good idea to read that section along with this one as there is a lot of information that can be shared and mixed in the creation of images on metallic surfaces.

Materials You Will Need

- Liquid photographic emulsion (*Maco Black Magic Emulsion, Rockland AG Plus, Kentmere VC, Silverprint SE-1*)

- Maco Black Magic Hardener (helps adhesion and can be added to emulsion or developer)

- Maco Gelatin for odd and difficult surfaces such as glass

- Anodized aluminum or steel plates (prepared or un-prepared)

- A can of gloss, spray, polyurethane for surface preparation

- A darkroom

- Traditional paper chemistry in trays or spray bottles (*no stop bath*)

- Distilled water for developer mix

- Fixer—see recommendations

- Hot plate, double boiler, electric kettle (*for heating emulsion*)

- Plastic trays

- A tray for hot water that is smaller than the plate, for keeping the plate warm during coating. This prevents the emulsion, as in glass coating, from gelling too quickly.

- Glass cleaner/de-greaser and soft cloth for cleaning metal

- Hairdryer

- Film transparency for printing (*Pictorico OHP inkjet transparency, or negatives in slide mounts from projector*)

- Contact printing frame or enlarger

- Paper safe or light—proof storage box for drying sensitized plates

The Working Process

The working process is the same, in almost all respects, to the one described earlier in this chapter. The difference is in the substrate's metallic surface. Begin by preparing the

Figure 20–8

Deborah Luster, *Rosesucker Retablos, VI*, 1977—emulsion on aluminum w/oil
(Courtesy of the artist)

plate's surface by removing the oil that is generally sprayed on metal sheets to keep them shiny and corrosion-free. At this point, you may inflict almost any kind of distress, or mayhem, that comes to mind including my favorites . . . acid etches, power sanding, painting, hammers, and so on, until you get a surface that suits your intentions. If you want a pristine un-ruined surface, simply degrease and then lightly buff the surface with circular strokes using a fine grade steel wool. This technique leaves a lovely sandwashed like surface. You can also take your plate to a grave marker business and pay them to sandblast your plates . . . metal or glass.

Modern Options, or an art supply like Pearl Paint, has liquid enhancers like Copper Toner and Patina Green (*a nice antique verdigris*), which will distress the surface and add an aged color. You can also add color to the surface with gloss spray paints; especially if you do not wish to have your highlights look like the base metal surface.

You can substitute white, or any other color for that matter, in place of the clear polyurethane. Be sure that the surface is bone dry between applications. The polyurethane, metallic paint, and steel wool buffing will aid in keeping your emulsion on the metal during the processing stages. Liquid emulsions form a chemical bond with polyurethane and alkyd-based paints. I've had a lot of success prepping my plates with RustOleum spray cans. I recommend that you do a very light finish coat with gloss polyurethane over any colored spray paint.

OK . . . you are now in a darkroom environment and the light level is very low. When you're ready to coat, take your tray, which is smaller than the plate you are coating, and fill it with very hot water. Place the metal plate on top of the hot water tray and wait until it warms up. This action will allow you the time to smooth the emulsion at your own pace. Liquid emulsions tend to set and gel immediately if poured on a cold plate.

Heat up the liquid emulsion (*leaving it in the original bottle with the top on*) in a beaker of hot water. When it is warm, pour approximately what you will need to make a thin coating on the center of your metal plate. You can brush it on with a foam, watercolor, or hake type brush, move it around with your fingers, feathers work well, or simply pick up the plate and roll it around in the air to make your coverage smooth and even. If you decide to roll it around, and you notice that the emulsion is gelling in uneven layers, just put it back on the hot water tray until the emulsion warms up again. After your coating is done, it is important to age the plate in a totally dark environment for at least 24 hours. This step is taken to ensure a tonally rich image. In the meantime, prepare additional plates and metal test strips for the following day.

When you are set to print, expose your prepared test strips, determine the proper exposure and developing time, and make your finished print on the plate using traditional paper photochemistry. Be sure that the print chemistry is cool and remember to avoid using stop bath in the processing steps. Again, you may wish to substitute the traditional paper rapid fixer with Kodak's Kodafix or simple sodium thiosulfate. As well, if you are experiencing problems with your emulsion being too fragile, you should add 2 capfuls of Cachet's Liquid Hardener to every 1000 ml of your developer.

Liquid emulsions on metal are a challenge and doing them leaves the creative doors wide open to a vast array of post-image abuse and adornment such as paint, acid, cutting, welding, and the like. The good news . . . if you don't like the results, you can always go get a power sander and grind the image off the plate and start again. If you want to have a lot more control of the image making process on metallic surfaces then read on.

THE TINTYPE PROCESS: A LITTLE HISTORY

All photographers, at one time or another, have experienced the visual phenomenon of seeing their underexposed and/or underdeveloped negative film as a *positive* when viewed against a dark background. What you are seeing is "light scatter," where the visible light from the maximum density (highlights) is juxtaposed with the total lack of silver in the minimum density (shadows) areas of the negative. The tintype, Daguerreotype, Physautotype, and all direct positive collodion images made in camera rely on a super-fine silver particle size resulting in a lighter color of the metallic silver. Gelatin tintypes rely on either additional fine silver added to the image or bleaching.

The primary personality of the tintype was built upon this visual idiosyncrasy and the development of colloids as applied to photography. In 1847, a young medical student by the name of John Parker Maynard formulated an ingenious medical dressing, called *collodion*, a name taken from the Greek word *kollodes* meaning "glue-like," that could be used to treat wounds from explosives. Maynard made his collodion by adapting Christian Frederick Schönbein's nitrated cotton (*cotton fibers soaked in a mixture of sulfuric and nitric acids*) dissolved in a mixture of equal parts of sulfuric ether and alcohol. The result of Maynard's action was a clear and viscous fluid that dried to a durable and flexible *skin* that could be used by medical staff in a battlefield environment . . . in this case, the Crimean War. Collodion dried

Figure 20–9

Two Women Fencing, 1885—Tintype

This is one of my favorite art history photographs . . . I like it almost as much as the daguerreotype of the blind man holding the headless cat earlier in this book. What is so cool about tintypes is that they were so simple and inexpensive to make that people thought nothing of playing while they made pictures . . . a far cry from the serious nature of portrait painting and daguerreotypes.

(Courtesy of the artist)

quickly and could be applied directly to the bandages, covering a wound, to keep the injury clean and dry and to protect it from infection.

In 1850, Robert Bingham suggested the idea that Maynard's adaptation of Schonbein's collodion solution could be applied to photographic intentions as it appeared to be the perfect binder for holding a light-sensitive silver halide solution on glass . . . and later, to asphalted iron in the creation of ferrotypes or tintypes. Gustave le Gray followed soon after by publishing a formula, though it was theoretical at best. Subsequent refinement by Fredrick Scott Archer, and Peter Fry (1851), had an extraordinary and immediate impact on the medium.

In 1854, in the second edition of his manual, *The Collodion Process on Glass*, Fredrick Scott Archer described the Alabastrine process, that would eventually end up being called the Ambrotype, in a section detailing the whitening of collodion pictures as positives. Ambrotypes were made by underexposing a wet collodion/silver nitrate-sensitized glass plate with less exposure than would be required for making a printable negative. Archer described developing the plate with Pyrogallic acid developer that produced a dark-brown silver deposit. He then bleached the highlights in the image with mercuric chloride. Shadows were then established by dark-backing the plates in a variety of ways;

with a dark varnish medium made from asphalt dissolved in oil; lamp black added to an alcohol based varnish; dark cloth; or black paper.

Alabastrine Positive Process

Here is a really interesting description of Archer's Alabastrine Positive Process from John Towler's 1824 book, *The Silver Sunbeam*. In the first paragraph of the text, the sentence that truly gives a sense of how the public's democratic perception of photography was already beginning to take shape . . . Towler wrote, "*Naturally the operation must be very simple, and but a very small quantity of color must be used, otherwise the operation will become a work of art, and none but an artist could perform it.*"

Alabastrine from *The Silver Sunbeam* (1864)

I'm going to keep the text as written by Towler, as I think the archaic tone of the writing is rather charming and will set the right tone for your experimenting with the process. However, I will change the formula so that you can more easily attempt it in your own lab.

The coloring of collodion positives, as already remarked, may be effected on the whites of the picture, either before the varnish is flowed on, or upon the varnish itself: When well performed, it communicates life and roundness to a picture which before was flat and lifeless. The colors in use are in fine powder, and are laid on with a dry and very fine pencil of camel's, etc., hair. Naturally the operation must be very simple, and but a very small quantity of color must be used, otherwise the operation will become a work of art, and none but an artist could perform it. In all ordinary cases the color lies on the surface, and does not penetrate into the material of the film. In the; Alabastrine process, however, the film is so treated as to become permeable to varnish, and thus to exhibit the color, as it were, in the collodion; besides this the whites are still retained white, notwithstanding the impregnation of the film with the penetrating varnish. Positives treated in this manner are regarded through the glass and the collodion film; the pictures, therefore, are direct, as they ought to be. The mode by which the tones are preserved soft and white, and rendered at the same time permeable, is the following

Alabastrine Formula Solution

- 2.6 grams Sulphate of protoxide of iron (*iron(II) oxide/ferrous oxide*)
- 5.2 grams Bichloride of mercury (*mercuric chloride*)
- 2 grams Chloride of sodium (*kosher salt*)
- 120 ml rain or distilled water

Author's Note: Mercuric Chloride—Mercury(II) chloride (also known as mercuric chloride) was used as a photographic intensifier to produce positive pictures in the collodion process of the 1800s. When applied to a negative, the mercury(II) chloride whitens and thickens the image, thereby increasing the opacity of the shadows and creating the illusion of a positive image (*Towler, 1864*). Mercuric chloride is toxic, white, and a soluble salt of mercury (at 6%). It has been used in disinfectant, as a fungicide, and in photographic fixers. It's also odorless, colorless, and really dangerous which is why I'm letting you know about it here. Take all safety precautions when working with this chemical.

Regarding sulphate of protoxide of iron (iron(II) oxide/ferrous oxide) . . . this is a black powder, is very unstable, and can easily corrode into iron(III) oxide. This means that it may take a few tries before your Alabastrine process works. Ferrous oxide is often used in cosmetics and in tattoo inks.

Select for this operation a vigorous good positive; a faint and thin film does not answer well. One that has been rather under-exposed is most suitable. Then, whilst the collodion film is still moist from fixing, pour upon it a quantity of the above solution, and keep it in motion. At first the picture assumes a dead and gray appearance; but this soon chases, and becomes continually more and more brilliant.

It is sometimes necessary to add a little more of the fresh solution, and to retain this solution on the surface until the whites are perfectly clear. The time required for this operation varies according to the temperature and the thickness of the film. Heat promotes the effect; the plate is therefore frequently supported on the ring of a retort-stand, with the fluid on its surface, whilst a small flame is kept in motion beneath it. Unless this precaution be observed, there will be a liability to break the plate. It happens sometimes that a few minutes are sufficient; but generally more time is required. If no heat is applied, the operation may require in some cases as much as an hour. As soon as the whites have attained their utmost purity, the operation is complete. It is better to be quite certain that the whites have attained the purity required, than to shorten the time, and have the effect underdone. 'there is no danger in giving too much time; but it is a disadvantage to remove the fluid from the plate too soon; because in drying, the whites in such a case arc apt to grow darker again, and the picture assumes then the cold blue tone, which arises from treatment with corrosive sublimate alone.

As soon as the effect has been reached, the plate is thoroughly washed in several waters, and then dried over the spirit lamp. The plate is now ready for the first coating of varnish, which communicates transparency to the shadows, without at all impairing the whites.

The next operation is to lay on the colors carefully and artistically on those parts that require them. It is unnecessary to apply any to the Shades. Where much color is desired on a given surface, it is better to apply it by repetition, and not in one thick blotch. Colors thus tastefully laid on produce a very brilliant effect, by reason of the purity of the whites; and this effect is again increased by the softness communicated to the whole picture by the application of the penetrative varnish,

Figure 20–10

Jody Ake, *Untitled Self-Portrait—1999*
(*8"× 10" ambrotype***)**

Jody Ake is a contemporary artist who gives his audience something to consider when examining his self-portraits. A lot of Jody's work is created within a classical context and often he will use an alternative process to convey the image. This particular self-portrait is an ambrotype. Ambrotypes were traditionally made by producing an under-exposed, wet collodion, negative on glass and backing the glass with a dark background such as Japanned lacquer or black paper.
(Courtesy of the artist)

which causes the color to permeate into the pores of the film, or to be seen at least in full beauty from the opposite side. This varnish is nothing more than a very pure strong-bodied protective varnish. The picture so far finished is backed up with a piece of black velvet, but never with black Japan, which would injure the film.

The positive image was then placed in a decorative case that was often the same type that housed daguerreotypes. This ornate presentation method was also occasionally applied to ferrotype/tintype metal plates. The ambrotype, due to its relatively speedy exposure and clarity, quickly displaced the daguerreotype as the vehicle used for studio portraiture. With collodion you could make unlimited paper prints, particularly Carte d'visite

(*card of the visit*) prints, from a single negative and these prints could be given away or put into albums. The collodion positive process had its market . . .but it was only from the mid-1850s to the mid-1860s and the people making them were not called photographers, but Ambrotypists. The term "photographer" referred to those who made prints from negatives.

This is a good place to discuss a bit of the often re-cycled misinformation regarding photography and it's evolution . . . principally, that the wet plate collodion process is easier and less demanding than the daguerreotype. The idea of the daguerreotype being more difficult has passed down through the year by historians who have rarely done the either process. The daguerreotype is made almost exclusively with *pure elements* . . . silver, copper, iodine, bromine, mercury, and is essentially a hands off process; everything happens in the box. At the end you fix and tone with compounds.

The wet plate collodion process on the other hand is done with chemical compounds every step of the way resulting in hundreds of variant formulas, and shifting sensitivity, depending on the condition of the chemicals. Also, everything in the collodion process is applied with the hands and all decisions are made by inspection during the process. It's easy to make a mark on a wet collodion plate . . . not so easy to make a clean image with a full range of tones as made in the 19th century.

In 1853, French photographer Adolphe Alexander Martin described a collodion on metal process that introduced the concept of the ferrotype/tintype. No one ever saw an example of Martin's work, so it is more accurate to give credit to Daniel Jones and William Kloen who secured English patents for the process in 1856. In the United States, Hamilton Smith, who actually made images with the process, was also granted a patent and assigned his rights to his collaborators, William and Peter Neff, who commercialized the process and named it the Melainotype . . . *"melaino" means to blacken in Greek.*

The general public took an immediate liking to the images on metal and referred to them as *"tintypes"* even though the commercial manufacturers of the plates called them ferrotypes. The tintype was inexpensive for even the most meager wage earner, and required very little capital to investigate as a photographer. More importantly, any enterprising individual could easily afford to begin a business using the process. Peter Neff's booklet of instructions, *The Melainotype, Complete,* made it simple to adopt the process as a means of making a living and many took the chance and prospered ever after.

The technique of making a tintype was elementary. The chemical process and technique was nearly identical to the ambrotype (see Chapter 22, the Wet Collodion chapter for all details) but executed on a thin sheet of soft iron (*not tin*) that was pre-coated with a smooth, baked on, skin of asphaltum in a technique called japanning. The japanned iron sheet was then coated with collodion and sensitized immediately before exposure, as with all collodion plates, negative or positive. The plate was then exposed in-camera.

Figure 20–11
Little Gem Tintype of Lafayette Warwick—1850s
A Little Gem tintype measuring 1/2" x 3/4" and set into an embossed card.
(Courtesy of the author)

Following exposure, the plate was developed in the darkroom with acidified ferrous sulfate and washed. In some cameras there was a slotted bottom that led to receptacles holding the processing chemistry. The plate could then be taken from the darkroom, fixed in potassium cyanide and washed in a container of water. After washing the plate was air-dried and often varnished for protection and gloss. The metal tintype was more durable than a glass plate Ambrotype and eliminated the need for applying a dark backing since the image already existed upon a dark substrate . . . the japanned iron plate.

Although the image quality sometimes left something to be desired, in the right hands, a well-done tintype

Figure 20–12

Tintype Studio—c. 1850s

This image shows a simple scene of people waiting to have their pictures taken at a local tintype studio in the mid-to late 1850s.

(Courtesy of the author)

equaled a high-end ambrotype on glass. The tintype was extremely popular, especially during the period between 1860 and 1880, and used extensively by itinerant and holiday location photographers. Its ability to provide a sturdy image of the sitter, while that person waited for the results, made it the people's process of choice . . . much to the dismay of the fancy commercial studios.

Although the tintype image was reversed from actual life, it replicated the view of oneself that you would have by looking in a mirror . . . so no one seemed to mind. As well, because the tintype was faster than the daguerreotype, and less expensive than the ambrotype, the poses of the sitters were more personal, candid, and relaxed. No longer were the subjects forced into being steadied by braces. The tintype was the process that really democratized the medium and remained popular until the introduction of George Eastman's dry plate negative in the 1880s. (*The dry plate Tintype was introduced in 1891.*)

I have seen photographers using old tintype cameras in Central America, North Africa, and Southeast Asia and it is still commonplace to find itinerant street photographers making a living working with the process. Many of the younger street photographers have adopted Polaroid, introduced commercially by Edwin Land (1909–1991) in 1948, as a replacement for the more cumbersome process, but not the spirit of the tintype, nor the public's desire for simple, personal and inexpensive images. The tintype's primary attributes were its speed, economy, ability to record a candid pose, and durability. The tintype disappeared for a while but what it represented, a democratic visual history of all facets of society, merrily lives on. For the first time, wealth and education were not prerequisites for building a visual family history.

A CONTEMPORARY DRY PLATE TINTYPE PROCESS

First, if you are really interested in doing this process in the original collodion technique, I recommend that you head directly to the Wet Collodion & Gelatin Dry Plate

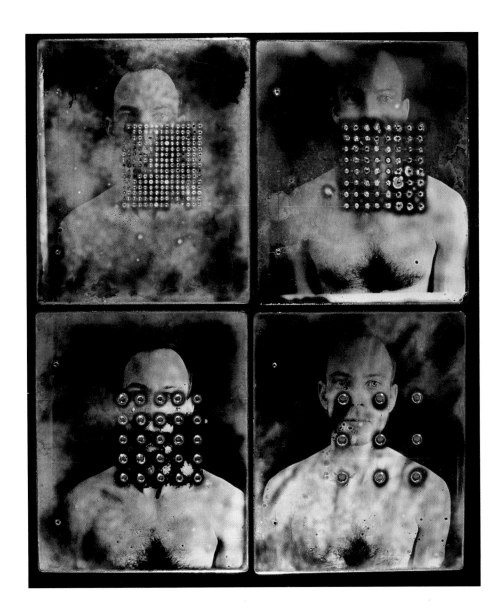

Figure 20–13

Scott McMahon, *Emulation of Self,* **2004—tintype**

Scott *Emulation of Self* tintype was printed on four separate black enameled, copper plates, each plate measuring around 6"x 5." For this work, Scott used a Luminos emulsion but that product is no longer made. A suitable alternative would be Silverprint or Maco's Black Magic. *(Courtesy of the artist)*

Emulsion chapter and consider producing your tintypes from scratch. The method that follows in this space is performed with a commercially made silver gelatin emulsion that varies quite a bit between brands.

The Rockland Colloid Company (www.rockaloid.com) makes a kit that claims to have everything you need to make tintypes. It comes with sufficient materials for creating five tintypes including your tests. However, my students have always experienced quite a few problems with this product, such as the pre-coated blackened sheets of metal being too large to fit a conventional 4" × 5" film holder, and frustration with the quality of the Liquid Light emulsion.

As an alternative to the kit, especially when your intention is to make more than a few tintypes, I am including the following technique using Maco (*it used to be called Cachet*) Black Magic Liquid Emulsion and Hardener. You can use a variety of commercial liquid emulsions, such as Rockland's AG-Plus or Silverprint SE-1, to prepare your own plates but in my experience, Maco's Black Magic Liquid Emulsion, in combination with their Liquid Hardener, works as well as any of the alternatives with the exception of making your own collodion emulsion.

THE METAL PLATE

What you need to do first is get your metal substrate. Thin sheets of metal can be obtained quickly, and inexpensively, at a building or roofing supply and spray-painted black with gloss black paint. Then all you need to do is follow the instructions that come with the Black Magic Emulsion or Gelatin. There are alternatives, however, and here are a few.

Anodized Aluminum Sheeting

Anodized glossy black aluminum is perfect for both this technique and for collodion tintypes. The company Lawrence & Frederick makes a terrific anodized aluminum sheeting on a roll in matte or glossy white and it is a superior product that quickly be painted black with a gloss black spray paint.

Metal Roofing Substrates

You may have noticed, especially in areas that get a lot of snow, that more and more buildings are sporting metal roof surfaces. This new metal solution is a far cry from the tin roofs of the past and they are extremely durable and come in a vast variety of finishes. Recently, I had to repair a section of my studio roof that was too flat for the slate that covered the majority of the building. I looked into metal roofing and after handling the samples, thought that they would make a terrific substrate for tintypes. If you want to give it a try (I haven't yet but I suspect it will work well) go to a local roofer and ask for some small samples to test on. Here are the types available at the present time.

Steel is the most common commercial grade metal roofing used today. It is heavier and sturdier than aluminum that is used primarily on residential property. Manufacturers offer a number of durable coatings and finishes that protect steel from corrosion. The roofing material is zinc-coated and then sealed with a coating of epoxy primer (this provides adhesion) and is then an acrylic top coating is baked on adding color and protection. These paint finishes are extremely durable. Ask for steel, as it's already painted with a baked-on color. My roofer says he'll cut it up for me and that I can buy 40 square feet for $40.

Aluminum is extremely lightweight, and is the material used in much residential metal roofing. It won't rust, but it must be painted or coated for appearance. Coatings are similar to those used on steel. There is also a pre-coated aluminum sheeting but I would stick with steel.

Copper metal shingles will last as long as the house. It will not rust, has no "finish" to scratch or peel, is soft enough to easily tool, and weathers naturally to a beautiful verdigris patina. It's very expensive.

Baked Copper Enamel Plates

If you know someone with a kiln, you should try your hand at preparing baked enameled glass on copper plates that are then fired in a kiln. In a way, this is exactly the way you might have made copper enameled pin jewelry in Hobby Hut at summer camp. The enameled copper plate is made up of powdered glass, sprinkled on a piece of copper, and fired to a glass surface in the kiln. The appearance can be different from that of a tintype made on an anodized, or painted plate, because enamels can be semi-transparent revealing the color of the metal underneath. They also have a luminosity and depth inherent in the glassy surface. Often the same effect can be achieved by spraying multiple thin coatings of gloss paint on anodized metal like the ones mentioned earlier.

An enameled plate often varies in thickness, forcing the emulsion to settle unevenly, creating variations in tone, and in some cases, abstracting the image entirely. Scott McMahon's wife, Christina Miller, is a ceramicist and makes his plates and her results are beautiful. Scott's plates seem to have luminosity that the spray-painted plates lack. In a way, they feel more like ambrotypes in that the photo emulsion rests upon the glass surface. Scott tells me that the baked enamel plates are also different from plate to plate. You might end up with thicker areas or dips in the surface and debris that might have been flying around in the kiln. It's hard to get real consistent results so each one is unique. This is good.

LAB SET UP FOR A CONTEMPORARY TINTYPE

◆ Liquid photographic emulsion (*Maco Black Magic Emulsion, Rockland AG Plus, Kentmere VC or Silverprint SE-1*)

◆ Maco Liquid Hardener additive

◆ Blackened plates—anodized aluminum, spray-painted black plates, japanned plates, enameled plates, steel or aluminum metal roofing material

◆ Tintype developer—commercial or homemade

- Distilled water for developer

- Fixer—Kodak powdered fixer

- Hot plate, double boiler, electric kettle, (*for heating emulsion*)

- Plastic or glass trays

- Glass cleaner and soft cloth for cleaning enameled or glass plates

- Hairdryer

- Positive transparency for printing tintypes (*film positive, Pictorico OHP ink-jet transparency, or slides*)

- Film or plate holder if shooting in-camera tintypes

- Contact printing frame if contact printing

- High quality varnish, i.e., sandarac varnish—see recipe in wet plate section

- Paper safe or light—proof storage box for drying sensitized plates

A Tintype Alternative

First, you will need a film **positive**. To produce a good tintype, especially during the learning stages, it is necessary to have a positive film image with good contrast and strong distinctive values. The positive film image can then be contact printed, projected from a slide projector, or exposed using an enlarger. You may also expose the sensitized tintype plates directly, as you would sheet film, in a view or pinhole camera. It is time-consuming but immensely gratifying . . . especially if you are making your own emulsion.

Liquid Emulsion

Set up your paper chemistry as you would for other hand-applied emulsion techniques. This means a developer with liquid hardener, a water bath in place of stop bath, and Kodafix or a weak sodium thiosulfate fixing solution.

To prepare the metal surface, thoroughly clean and degrease the metal plate and then, if necessary or desired, coat it with a several thin coats of polyurethane, RustOleum, dark varnish, or alkyd paint. Again, do not use matte or semi-matte spray paints, as there is wax in the formula.

Figure 20–14

Deborah Luster, St Gabriel, *Halloween,* **2000—***from the portfolio " One Big Self"*—tintype (*liquid emulsion on aluminum*)

Deborah Luster's work centers bringing forth the real person in her photographs. These images are rich and complex and often feature a great deal of hand-work and alternative techniques. The image, originally in tinted color, is Silverprint liquid emulsion on aluminum. The subject is Prisoner #298170, from New Orleans, born in 1968 and serving a 7-year sentence at the Louisiana Correctional Institute for Women. She works in the chair plant. *(Courtesy of the artist)*

Japanned Lacquered Plate

If you use a japanned lacquer (*called urushi and made from the sap of various natural sources such as sumac, poison oak, mango, cashew and poison ivy . . . so be careful, please*), you will have much better results. Unlike polyurethane spray paint, or shellac, a japanned lacquer contains no resins for hardening purposes and polymerizes in high humidity to form a hard, water-resistant film.

When preparing a sensitizing emulsion using AG-Plus, many of my students have had pretty good success adding Dektol paper developer, mixed with a little *really exhausted* fixer. The theory is that the high silver content of exhausted fixer becomes the *whitener* for the developer. This suggestion is not an exact science and you'll need to experiment quite a bit.

THE WORKING PROCESS

Clean Your Plate

Again, the working process is pretty similar to the one first described in this chapter and repeated in parts in the Metal section. Refer to those sections for specifics.

Coating the Plate with Warm Emulsion

Warm up the plate before pouring on the *warm* sensitized emulsion. Methods of keeping your plate warm include a hot plate at a very low setting (*around 115ºF*), a hairdryer, or placing the plate over a smaller tray of hot water and letting the resulting steam heat warm the underside of the plate. When the plate is sufficiently warm, pour a puddle of emulsion into the center of it and spread the emulsion around the plate's surface with your index finger. Make every effort to keep the coating even at this stage. Pick up the plate and rotate it around slowly, letting the emulsion spread evenly over the plate surface as it cools off. I like to keep the plate warm throughout the coating process and for this reason my preference is to use the hot water in a smaller tray beneath the larger metal plate.

Wait 24 Hours

Once your plate is nicely coated, the best thing to do is place it in a totally dark environment and leave it alone. Blow drying works for a demonstration but isn't very satisfying for honest work. If you must blow-dry the emulsion, use a cool setting. After the plate is dry, you may load it into a camera for an exposure or use it in a contact-printing frame with the film *positive*. For better results, after the plate has been coated, I like to let it age for at least 24 hours. This aging period will yield a bit more contrast in the final image.

Positive Film

Your best bet for learning this process is to make a strong, dense, and contrast-rich positive film on Pictorico OHP ink-jet film. Using Photoshop, work with your image until you see a great-looking image on your screen. If you can make your positive on a piece of Pictorico OHP Ultra Premium (rolls only at this writing), that would be best, as it accepts more ink and you can make a great negative using a single sheet of film. Do your best to make your positive film to look much like you would a traditional silver gelatin print with good overall densities and strong contrast.

Exposure

You're going to have to adjust to the way you think about the exposure. This is a reversal process and you are using a positive film. If the image on your plate is too light, then you need to be thinking about giving it less exposure time. If the image is too dark, increase the exposure time. You are going to have to make test strips to determine your exposure . . . either with an enlarger under low safelight, or in camera. Try exposing your plates in a pinhole camera . . . they work quite well. Pinhole camera exposures, in bright sun, with a 1.5 focal distance, run between 20 and 45 seconds.

As mentioned previously, several different light sources can be employed. Whatever type of light you elect to use, do a bit of testing first before committing your carefully prepared plates. If you use an enlarger, expose the plate, using a film positive like a test strip, at 5- to 10-second intervals. Remember, a tintype exposure is similar to direct negative-to-negative film like the no-longer-manufactured SO-132. The more exposure you give an area, the lighter the area will be in the final image. Slide transparencies are good sources for film positives, as are black and white reversal films and ortho-based dupe negatives. Begin your exposure times with a base time of 30 seconds.

If you opt for a view camera exposure, place your camera on a tripod and make an exposure using the sun as the light source. A sunny day starting time for tests might be f/5.6 for 1/2 second. The proper exposure should show a nice balance between highlights and shadows. If your plate is flat and lacks highlight detail then you should increase the exposure. If your plate is too light, with little contrast, you should decrease the exposure. Because this is a conventional emulsion, you may wish to use filters to enhance the contrast.

By the way, this is a perfect opportunity for you to try exposing your plates in a pinhole camera as the exposure will be a positive, just as it is when you load your pinhole with a piece of conventional photographic paper.

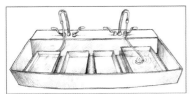

Tray 1 Tintype developer or commercial paper developer with hardener

Tray 2 Water bath

Tray 3 Paper strength fixer—Kodak powdered fixer works well, or sodium thiosulfate fixer. Fix plates several minutes or until milky white areas are clear.

Tray 3 Water or hypo-clearing bath

Tray 4 Final wash

Processing

You can use a manufacturer's developer or the developers mentioned below. Your darkroom needs to be very dark . . . much darker than it is for conventional silver gelatin printing. Don't be alarmed by the way the image looks during the developer stage. The plate, if you can see it well, may look a little flat. In fact, sometimes it doesn't appear that you have an image on the plate or that the image has been fogged. Let the plate sit in the developer as you agitate the tray very gently for 2–3 minutes. Then move it to a fresh water bath.

Two Developers

Developer #1

Mix up a tray of Dektol paper developer 1:10 at least 24 hours in advance of processing. To this developer, add a cap full of Maco Liquid Hardener to prevent your delicate emulsion from being damaged in the processing stages. The hardener is optional but I recommend it. Use at room temperature and develop your exposed plates in extremely low red safelight conditions, for 2 1/2–3 minutes . . . or longer if the developer is older.

Developer #2

Developer #2 works pretty well but has its difficult moments. It seems to be a particularly good developer to use on glass, so I am including it here in case you want to give it a shot. Begin by mixing up a Dektol developer solution of 1 part Dektol and 2 parts water. Then add a small amount of really exhausted fixer diluted with water 1:2. Age the solution for 24 hours before using. This developer is really inexact but fun to try.

After exposure, immerse the plate face up in the developer and watch for the first signs of density. You will notice that the image is a *negative*, which makes sense because you used a film positive to contact print it. Increasing your development time does not result in increased density and that is significant, because there is exhausted fixer in the developer. Negative quality at this stage is judged by how clean the white areas of the image are. Gently rock the tray during development. During development you may notice portions of the image are very dark—don't worry about it.

Rinse & Fixing Stages

After a minute or two, gently remove the plate from the developer and place it in a cool water bath. Then put the plate into a standard paper fix solution for 3–4 minutes or until the milky quality of the image has cleared away. At this point, the image will take on the appearance of a positive due to its underexposed nature and its dark negative space. Hypo-clear for 1 minute and wash the plate for 10 minutes and then let it sit flat to dry.

Closing Thoughts

You can prepare your plates with colors other than black spray paint. If you coat the plate white, the image whites will end up in pale sepia. If you use other color spray paints, the shadows and the highlights will take on variations of that color. The prepared kits have a developer that is ready to use as is. You might want to buy a kit in the event that the developer options presented here don't make you happy. After you have successfully negotiated a commercial liquid emulsion tintype, you may want to consider thinking about ways to make the results more personal. Finished plates can be painted, collaged, scratched, etched, or made into book covers . . . it's endless, so have fun with the opportunities.

The Albumen Process

OVERVIEW & EXPECTATIONS

This chapter is pretty direct in its intentions . . . to guide you into making albumen prints with as few problems as possible. I'll begin, as I do in every chapter, with "a little history" about the brief and luminous life of the albumen process . . . a beautiful and labor-intensive technique involving egg whites, salt, acetic acid, silver nitrate, and, occasionally, gold chloride. You will learn how the process works and how to prepare the chemistry with both the traditional, and contemporary, raw egg white albumen. I'll also be offering you Zoe Zimmerman's unique matte albumen method. This technique will be in print for the first time and is the one I use exclusively to introduce students to the process. It is also my favorite way to make an albumen print. I'll also describe the "instant gratification" and powdered albumen versions of the technique and will do my best to simplify the coating, printing, processing, toning, and fixing stages. I'll go over some trouble-shooting issues and discuss the importance of not taking too many short cuts. This technique is truly beautiful, and one of my personal favorites.

Figure 21–1

France Scully Osterman, *The Embrace*, 2002—gold-toned albumen print from 8" × 10" collodion negative [*Sleep* series]

As I will tell anyone who will listen, there are few who equal France when it comes to solving the complexities of an antique process. More importantly, is that her visual sense is as refined as her technical ability. This albumen print, for her *Sleep series*, is a good example.

(Courtesy of The Howard Greenberg Gallery)

A LITTLE HISTORY

The earliest photographic prints on paper were created using sodium chloride salted papers that had been sensitized in a bath of silver nitrate to create UV-sensitive silver chloride. The principle fault of the salted silver based processes of this particular technique was that the salted paper print was most often dull and lifeless due to a dilute 1:1 albumen and water surface coating, and to the absorption of the sensitizer by the paper's fibers.

You will recall—from the 1860 exchange of letters between Henry James and William Henry Fox Talbot (Chapter 17, Dichromate Options) that Fox Talbot had been thinking about gelatin and gum binders for silver nitrate since 1840 when he performed some experiments involving albumen on glass that he fumed with iodine and then sensitized with silver nitrate . . . creating a light sensitive silver iodide coating. In conjunction with that work, Talbot also conducted several experiments that included combining albumen with potassium iodide. According to his notebooks, none of these albumen binder processes met his expectations or were successful.

In 1844, in Boston (*home of the Red Sox*), John Adams Whipple (*see Fig. 1-6, his Daguerreotype of the Moon from 1852*) and his friend, William Jones, conducted a series of investigations using Fox Talbot's calotype chemistry on glass plates coated with milk. This proved to be less than successful so they switched to albumen as a binder and for the next several years worked on perfecting their new technique. Their work, like Talbot's early albumen experiments, was never officially recognized, nor formally presented or published.

In 1847, Claude Felix Abel Niépce de St. Victor (1805–1870), a career cavalry officer, and cousin of Nicéphore Niépce, published a detailed description, in the *Compte rendus des Séances de l'Académie des Sciences* (a prestigious French scientific journal that has been in existence since 1835), of his experiments incorporating starch, as a photographic binder, on glass. In his account, he described how a glass plate was coated with potassium

Figure 21–2

Nadar, *Self Portrait Carte d' Visite in hot air balloon*—1863—albumen
This is a terrific, and pretty silly, carte d'visite by Nadar, who was quite well known for his irrepressible personality, fascination with flying machines, and, one would think by looking at this image, his extremely short legs. His studio was a gathering place for the artistic and literate and he made his mark by photographing all of them. He was the first to use artificial light, to make pictures from a balloon, and for inventing the illustrated interview. *(Courtesy of the Getty Museum)*

iodide mixed in a starch binder solution of albumen. Once the solution had dried on the glass plate's surface, it was sensitized with a solution of aceto nitrate of silver (*silver nitrate with added acetic acid*) and exposed to sunlight in contact with a negative of some type. Following a rather fast exposure of approximately 20–25 seconds, the sensitized glass plate was developed with a solution of gallic acid (notice the direct relationship to Fox Talbot's initial calotype development technique), resulting in a finely detailed plate.

At the conclusion of his article, Niépce de St. Victor recommended replacing the starch with the superior albumen binder and briefly documented the preparation of the albumen and its use. Unfortunately, the process was unacceptable for portraits because an average exposure with his new technique took 15 to 20 minutes. Not only that, the development of the plate with hot gallic acid required hours of intensive labor and the rapid oxidizing nature of this acid, I will speculate, likely resulted in far more failures than successes. Even more unfortunately, Niépce de St. Victor's plates, notes, and journals were destroyed during the 1848 public riots of the second French Revolution,

In 1849, Louis-Désirée Blanquart-Evrard (1802–1872) devised an albumen paper process (a silver chloride sensitizer with an albumen binder) that was remarkably similar to Niépce de St. Victor's, and that featured the option of being exposed in either a wet or dry state. Coincidentally, Blanquart-Evrard's inspiration occurred at the same time when many photographers were adopting the practice of shooting very large glass plate negatives. This demanded a different and more explicit translation of detail than salted paper could ever provide.

Within a year of his discovery the entrepreneurial Blanquart-Evrard plunged into a very successful business of mass-producing albumen images utilizing his recently announced technique. In his establishment, Blanquart-Evrard worked with the top photographic artists of the day, i.e., Le Secq and Du Camp, and published the esteemed *Photographic Notes* with his partner, Thomas Sutton. Their enterprise, founded in Lille, France (1851), was the first commercial photographic printing and publishing firm in history.

At this point, the albumen concept was getting a lot of attention. Fox Talbot, as was his habit, quickly placed a patent on the concept of the iodide fuming sensitization of albumen. Niépce de St. Victor recovered from the riots and published a declarative manuscript on an improved albumen process (*including the addition of honey into the albumen binder to counteract the problem of cracking*), and John Whipple finally got around to publishing the work he did with Jones and placed a patent on his version of the albumen process . . . which also incorporated honey and bromide salts. In fact, it was Whipple who first incorporated honey into the albumen.

Blanquart-Evrard's albumen technique, when used in combination with Frederick Scott Archer's wet collodion glass plate negative process (1851), was considered the first true and repeatable paper-based imaging system capable of yielding values and details that were commercially viable and commensurate with the Daguerreotype image on silver-plated copper. In its formative stages, the

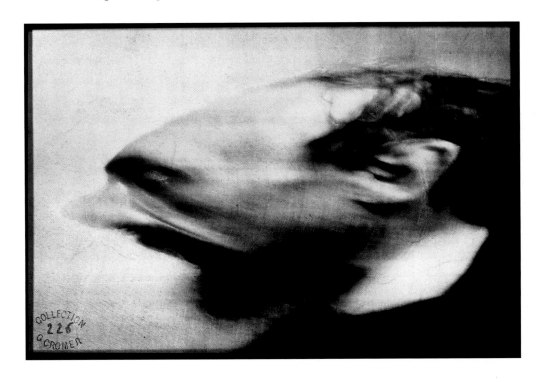

Figure 21–3
Louis Ducos Du Huron (1837–1920), *Self-Portrait made with a distorting camera,* **1888—albumen**
(Courtesy of The George Eastman House / IMP, Rochester, NY)

Figure 21–4

Robert Howlett (1831–1858), *Isambard Kingdom Brunel* **(Builder of the Great Eastern), 1857—albumen**

Robert Howlett and his partner, Joseph Cundall, were commissioned to document the construction of the mammoth coal driven steamship *The Great Eastern*. Howlett's supplement to the medium was his personal interest in exploring the meaning of documentary image making and the subjective view of the person, place, or thing being documented. Howlett manufactured, and sold, a portable darkroom tent but died at the age of 27, according to some speculators, from working with so much chemistry in his tent without adequate ventilation.

(Courtesy of The George Eastman House/IMP, Rochester, NY)

Figure 21–5

Lewis Carroll, (Charles Dodgson), *Irene McDonald***, 1863—albumen**
Lewis Carroll is remembered well for his brilliant fantasies of *Alice's Adventures In Wonderland* and *Through The Looking Glass*. He is also known for his photographs of children who he enjoyed dressing up and photographing according to his constructed tableaus. He was once quoted as saying, "*I am fond of all children, except boys.*"
(Courtesy of The Gernsheim Collection, Ransom Center, University of Texas-Austin)

results of the process were often flat and uninspiring. This problem was rectified by the adoption of a gold chloride toning process, which resulted in an intensification of print "color" and a variety of tonalities ranging from aubergine, purple, red, and brown to black. Aubergine was the color the early practitioners were aiming for and the intensification was needed due to the 1:1 albumen dilution.

For over 30 years, the albumen process was *The Process* in photography and its consistency—relative to other image making systems that were known at the time—rivaled silver gelatin papers in the modern day. Prepared albumen paper, *without the silver sensitizer*, was commercially produced for an exploding photographic marketplace

and the insatiable demand for the paper, by both professional and amateur photographers, was unprecedented. One of the most common, and oft repeated, anecdotes from that era is that the Dresden Albumizing Company, in Germany, used more than 70,000 egg whites per day to meet the albumen paper demands of the public. It is interesting to note that only women were hired to prepare the albumen paper because it was believed that their hands and touch were softer than a man's.

In the last few years, there has been a resurrection of the albumen process by contemporary artists whose work equals, and in some cases greatly exceeds, the qualities of the original albumen techniques. With the advantages of contemporary image making systems and concepts, photographic artists are once again being charmed by the absolute beauty of the process. Among the best are Zoe Zimmerman and France Scully Osterman.

Figure 21–6

Zoe Zimmerman, *Under Your Hat*, 2006—gold-toned matte albumen

This is a pretty recent image of Zoe's that illustrates her sense of humor and imagination as well as her personal albumen technique . . . one that requires zero days of refrigeration and skimming of foam. Her albumen method is, hands-down, my favorite way to make, and teach, albumen printing and a superior method for achieving matte albumen surfaces.

(Courtesy of the artist)

HOW THE TRADITIONAL ALBUMEN PROCESS WORKS

First, I am going to make a distinction between what I call the traditional albumen method and others . . . such as Zimmerman's matte albumen technique. In the traditional method, the preparation time is lengthy and quite fussy. In a more contemporary way, such as the matte albumen, the process is quite fast and less complicated.

A piece of fine-quality, lightweight drawing paper, stationery, vellum, or glass, is initially coated with a thin layer of albumen in a solution of either ammonium chloride or sodium chloride (*kosher salt*), in combination with acetic acid and distilled water. Don't simply go to the market and buy some table salt. If you are going to go the sodium chloride route, use kosher salt, rather than a conventional table salt, as it is pure sodium chloride and is not cluttered with additives.

Several days later, the prepared albumen paper is sensitized by floating it in a distilled water and silver nitrate solution in a tray for 3 minutes, or by brush coating. As soon as the paper is dry, it may be used. You will load your newly sensitized albumen paper into a contact printing frame with your negative (*negative density range is a high 2.0 to 2.2 with this process*) and exposed to UV light until the image prints-out and begins to show signs of dark metallic "bronzing" in the darkest shadows.

The exposed albumen paper is given an initial rinse in either tap water containing chlorine or distilled water with a pinch of sodium chloride (kosher salt) to remove a good portion of the excess silver nitrate by precipitation. It is vital to remove all of the excess silver before toning. At this point, think about either toning for color and permanence, or about going directly to a double-tray set up of 15% sodium thiosulfate (plus 2 g sodium carbonate to make the solution neutral). The prints will be immersed in the separate fixing baths for 2.5 minutes in each tray, washed for 20 to 30 minutes, and hung to dry.

The resulting print is quite often the perfect technique, even for the most discerning alt pro artist, due to its clarity, resolution, and surface elegance. The principal reason for this clarity is the albumen base support, which has an important function: it fills the pores in the paper, like a gelatin glyoxal sizing stage in gum bichromate, preventing the sensitizing solution from being swallowed up by the paper.

Another reason for the increased clarity is that albumen is an organic sensitizer that results in greater printing speed and contrast than can be obtained with plain salted paper. This results in the paper having a thin, and thoroughly saturated, sensitized "*skin*." It is this albumen skin, working as a colloidal binder, that holds the light-sensitive silver salt in suspension above the paper's surface, providing a finely detailed image that is essentially unaffected by the substrate's texture. Albumen is a beautiful thing.

Figure 21–7

Mike Robinson, *Flatiron Building, NYC—1996* (original albumen color)
Canadian photographer, Mike Robinson, made this albumen print of the famous Flatiron (*Fuller*) Building on 23rd Street in New York City. Designed by David Burnham, in 1902, it was one of the first buildings to utilize a steel sub-structure and heralded, at 287" tall, the age of the skyscraper. A curious fact: When the Flatiron building was erected, it generated a lot of wind speed at its base. That air turbulence attracted crowds of men hoping to get a peek at women's ankles as their long skirts were lifted by the wind. The crowds led to police patrolmen yelling the words, "*23-skidoo*" (in a reference to 23rd Street) at the gawkers to make them move along.
(Courtesy of the artist)

TABLE SET UP FOR TRADITIONAL ALBUMEN PAPER PREPARATION

- Pencil
- Electric hand blender wand (very inexpensive on eBay)

- Refrigerator (not required for the Zimmerman Matte Method)
- Cheesecloth or fine strainer
- A large funnel
- 2.5 dozen large eggs
- 28% acetic acid
- Distilled water
- Ammonium chloride
- Mixing bowl
- A new dark glass bottle for storing the albumen
- A marker and tape for your label
- Clothesline and clothespins

THE ALBUMEN

If you are into "process," you will have a lot of fun making the albumen solution from raw eggs . . . and you will end up with more yolks than you can safely consume. In the past I recommended considering the use of prepared powdered albumen . . . or developing serious cholesterol based passion for the leftover yolks, which can be used in making crème brûllée . . . see the great recipe below!

METHOD #1: TRADITIONAL RAW EGG ALBUMEN

Traditional Method

- 16 jumbo size eggs
- Good hands or a yolk separator
- 2 ml 28% acetic acid
- 15 ml distilled water
- 15 g ammonium chloride

If you double coat, you will need

- 500 ml of 70% isopropyl alcohol
- 15 g ammonium chloride

Separate the Yolks from the Albumen

To make 500 ml of albumen (*enough to double coat about 75 8" × 10" pieces of paper*) you will need about 16 large size eggs. (I recommended 2.5 dozen in case you decide to make the Zimmerman matte method or you get yolk in your whites and must begin separating again.) Carefully separate the whites from the yolks with a yolk separator, or with the shell halves like a professional chef, and add them into a non-metallic mixing bowl until you have 500 ml of egg whites (*albumen*). Avoid any shell bits, yolk parts, blood, or odd stringy stuff in the whites.

Note: If you make any mistakes at all, like a little bit of yolk in the albumen, start over. Some albumen printers separate their egg whites in small batches to avoid yolk contamination. When the albumen looks perfect, add it to the larger collection of egg whites. You should now have 500 ml of pure albumen in a non-metallic container.

Adding the Chemicals

To your 500 ml of albumen, add:

- 2 ml of 28% acetic acid
- 15 ml of distilled water
- 15 g of ammonium chloride

Whip It Good

Whip the egg whites into stiff peaks (*like the top of a Starbuck's latte*). If you are being true to this idea of tradition, you will be using a bundle of quills to whip the albumen. If you don't have time to pluck a goose, use an electric blender wand. Let the solution sit overnight, uncovered and un-refrigerated, just as they did in the 19th century. The foam will settle revealing to a clear yellow liquid with a thin crust of white dried albumen by the next morning. When you wake up, while the coffee is brewing, simply poke a hole in the crust and carefully pour out the clear albumen into a pristine and clean glass container. If you're careful, you won't even need a filter. Allow the solution to age another 24 hours at room temperature. Warmth breaks down the proteins but if you can't take the aroma, cover the container and put it in the refrigerator.

Strain and Refrigerate for a Week

On day #2, remove the now-liquid egg whites from the refrigerator and let them warm to room temperature.

Figure 21–8

Dan Estabrook, Interior, *Floating Cloth*, 1996— albumen

(Courtesy of the artist)

Remove the froth that has settled on top of the albumen mixture and strain the solution through cheesecloth. Return the solution to the refrigerator where it will do absolutely nothing for the next week.

Once your albumen has been removed from the refrigerator simply keep it at an ambient temperature out of direct sun. I store mine in a cardboard box with bubble wrap around the glass bottle. Your new albumen solution should be kept in a well-labeled container. If it gets too cold you will get dull images. If it gets too hot you will get a toxic omelet . . . trust me . . . this is not a pleasant situation. Clearly, you can see that this process takes some adjusting to. It is slow and methodical and totally antithetical to a 21st century instant gratification mentality. This is exactly why the people who make albumen images love the process.

METHOD #2: ZIMMERMAN'S MATTE ALBUMEN PROCESS

Method #2: Single Session Raw Egg Albumen Process

This is my favorite albumen method and one that I use in a class or workshop teaching situation for a single session demonstration. I really appreciate the simplicity of the technique and love the color and quality of the matte image on a perfect paper substrate. This albumen recipe was given to me by Zoe Zimmerman who is, in my humble opinion, one of the very best albumen printers working today. Zoe's signature matte albumen printing method varies from the traditional technique, both technically and visually, in several ways. You can print within an hour or two of your albumen preparation. It opens up the option of

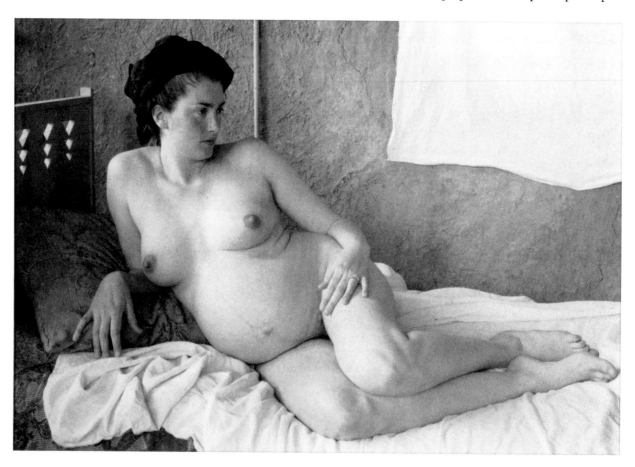

Figure 21–9

Zimmerman, *Renaissance*—matte albumen

New Mexico artist, Zoe Zimmerman is a master albumen printer whose subject matter is often classically compatible, as in the case of this figure study portrait, with her process.

(Courtesy of the artist)

making prints on a greater variety of papers, including thick printmaking papers, as no floating is required or necessary. As well, the highlights tend to be whiter than those in the traditional albumen print (*likely due to the citric acid in the formula*) and when toned with a thiocyanate toner, the prints mimic the tonality, surface and color (depending on time and mix) of a Pt/Pd print. Here's her process.

TABLE SET UP FOR ZIMMERMAN'S ALBUMEN PAPER PREPARATION

- A large 2-liter plastic beaker or mixing bowl
- Pencil
- Paper towels
- An electric plastic kettle—dedicated to heating salts and citric acid
- A large beaker of wash water (albumen gets sticky)
- Electric hand blender wand (very inexpensive on eBay)
- Cheesecloth or muslin for straining albumen foam
- A large funnel
- Distilled water
- 2.5 dozen large eggs
- Citric acid
- Sodium chloride
- Tapioca starch
- A new dark glass bottle for storing the albumen
- A marker and tape for your label
- A selection of fine paper for albumen coating (see below)
- A thick piece of Lucite or glass
- A good squeegee
- Clothesline and clothespins

ZZ Albumen Starch Solution

40g Sodium chloride
3g Citric acid
40g Tapioca starch
1 liter distilled water
2½ dozen eggs

Step 1 Mix the sodium chloride and citric acid into 950 ml of distilled water in a non-corrosive pot. Stir until the chemistry is dissolved and then bring it to a gentle boil. I like using an electric kettle with a hidden heating element. Look at Chef's Choice models.

Step 2 Meanwhile, mix the tapioca starch with the remaining water until it looks like paste and there are no lumps in it. Add this *roux* mixture to the boiling citric acid and sodium chloride salt solution from Step #1 while stirring constantly. Stir until the mixture appears translucent as opposed to white & starchy. This will take about 3 minutes.

Remove the mixture from the heat and allow it to cool to about 110°F. When the solution is sufficiently cool, remove the foam-skin from the liquid surface and strain the remaining solution through cheesecloth-lined strainer. You may have to do this a few times, but don't get compulsive about it.

Step 3 Next, separate the egg white from the yolks. Can you do this like a professional chef? Crack the egg cleanly and then shift the egg contents back and forth between eggshell halves as the white albumen slurps (I can't think of a better way to describe what the albumen is doing) into the holding container and the yolk stays in the shell. If not, use an egg separator.

Whip the egg whites in batches of 500 ml, with a hand-held blender wand, for one or two minutes. Allow the froth to settle, and strain the solution through a funnel lined with dampened muslin or cheese-cloth. This solution is mixed with an equal portion (500 ml) of the tapioca starch, sodium chloride and citric acid solution (1:1) and used as soon as it is ready.

You will notice that Zoe's method doesn't require a refrigerator period and this is bound to raise a few questions in the alt pro hen house, but I will ask all who doubt to remain calm and look at the quality of the prints for affirmation that the method works very well.

A Very Quick Word Regarding Paper

Hot press, and smooth paper works well for this process. Somerset Satin, or Arches 88 printmaking papers work flawlessly with the Zimmerman matte albumen method. Cot 320, Weston Parchment, and Buxton, are also recommended but Arches Platine has a tendency to yellow quite badly during the dry down. The albumen-starch solution can be applied to the paper with a hake brush, but a two to five minute immersion method works best. Weston tends to yield a more reddish color without toning while Cot 320 provides the richest shadows. Be very careful handling the albumenized Weston . . . it's quite fragile.

Step 4 The freshly mixed 1:1 albumen solution is now gently poured it into a very clean tray. Submerge sheets of paper completely in the solution, doing your best to be sure there are no air bubbles trapped on the paper's underside. Soak the paper for two to five minutes and then run it along the tray edge when removing it from the tray.

Step 5 Place the paper on a flat, smooth surface, i.e., glass, Lucite, or Plexiglas and with a single gentle but firm stroke, squeegee off the excess albumen solution from the paper on one side. A soft and flexible squeegee is necessary; Zoe uses a windshield wiper blade as they meet the requirements, are inexpensive, and come in a variety of sizes. Hang the paper on a line with clothespins to dry. After a minute, flip the paper 180 degrees . . . this will help prevent one side of the paper being more thick with albumen than another. Try to be sure that there is no excess albumen dripping down the paper's surface. This mistake will frustrate you if you overlook it. When the paper is bone dry, it is ready to be sensitized. It can also be stored indefinitely for later use. Be sure to mark your paper as "albumen" on the side that has been squeegeed. It is actually a good idea to mark your paper with paper type and process before you begin to do all of these steps.

ZZ Sensitizing Solution for Matte Albumen

60 g silver nitrate

7.5 g citric acid

500 ml distilled water

Step 6 In low ambient light, mix the silver nitrate and citric acid in the distilled water until fully dissolved. Pin the paper to a smooth, very clean surface, and using a hake brush, apply the sensitizer in smooth even strokes in one direction. Quickly dry with a blow drier until the paper is no longer glistening wet and then apply the silver nitrate in the other direction. Blow-dry again until the paper is bone dry. You are now ready to expose your print. You can coat for a third time but this may be overkill depending on the paper you are using. A thicker paper looks beautiful with a third coating.

You might also consider doing drop count formulas in a shot glass, per print, rather than risking contamination by re-dipping your brush in silver nitrate.

Step 7 Exposing, washing, toning, fixing, etc. can be done according to the instructions for traditional albumen printing in this chapter. I've found that a full range negative requires a 2-minute exposure in the low humidity environments of Santa Fe and Aspen. You can control contrast with sun and shade combination exposures using the shade exposure to determine the contrast and the sun to determine shadow densities.

WHAT TO DO WITH THE EGG YOLKS
A Great Recipe for Crème Brûlée

- 2000 ml heavy cream
- 20 large egg yolks
- 30 ml vanilla extract (*Xanath [Mexican] is best*)
- 400 g granulated sugar
- Serves a large class of 16–20

Step 1 Vigorously beat the egg yolks and granulated sugar in a large bowl, until the mixture becomes light in color and the sugar has dissolved.

Step 2 In a large saucepan, combine the heavy cream with the vanilla extract and bring the mixture to a simmer; when small bubbles have formed around the edges of the cream turn off the heat.

Step 2 Slowly pour the cream mixture into the egg and sugar mix, and with a wire whisk blend the two together gently. Then, strain the combined mix through a fine mesh strainer and cover the mixture with a sheet of plastic wrap, pierced several times to release any steam. Place the mix in the refrigerator overnight.

Step 4 Preheat oven to 350°F (180°C). Place 16 to 20 six-ounce ramekins (individual soufflé dishes) in a large baking pan that is deep enough that water can reach at least halfway up the sides of the dishes so that it can work as a double boiler (*bain-marie*).

Step 5 Fill ramekins ¾ full. Place the pan in preheated oven and pour hot water into baking pan so water level reaches halfway up the sides of the ramekins. Cover pan with a sheet of heavy-duty aluminum foil, sealing edges to retain steam. Cook 40 to 50 minutes or until the custard sets.

Note: To test for doneness, gently shake the individual ramekins; if the custard is a little wobbly return it to the oven and check again in 5 minutes. Look for a circular shape, about an inch wide, in the center of the custard that remains loose while the outside edges are firm.

Step 6 Remove ramekins from baking pan and chill custard in refrigerator several hours.

Step 7 To serve, put a thin layer of granulated sugar atop each custard; then, using a hand-held propane blowtorch, char the tops of the custards until the sugar caramelizes.

METHOD #3: POWDERED ALBUMEN

A few years ago, I became less enamored with the traditionally prepared albumen because of its "dead mouse" odorous rating factor. I tried the powdered albumen method for a while before switching to Zoe Zimmerman's matte albumen method and saw no distinctive difference between the real egg and powdered egg. The "dead mouse" factor was actually a bit worse with the powdered version but it could have simply been the brand that I was using. In case you don't like crème brûlée, here's the formula for the powdered albumen.

- 72 g powdered albumen
- 475 ml distilled water
- 2 ml 28% acetic acid
- 15 g ammonium chloride

Dissolve 72 g of the powdered albumen in 473 ml of distilled water. Add the 2 ml of glacial acetic acid and 15 g of ammonium chloride to the powdered albumen and distilled water solution and whip it into froth. Label the container really well and refrigerate the solution for 24 hours.

On day #2, remove the now-liquid egg whites from the refrigerator and let them warm to room temperature. Remove the froth that has settled on top of the albumen mixture and strain the solution through cheesecloth. Return this solution to the refrigerator for the next week. If this still takes too long for you, there is a modified instant gratification (*sort of*) version and that would be Method #4.

METHOD #4: INSTANT GRATIFICATION METHOD

- 72 g powdered albumen
- 10 g kosher salt (sodium chloride)
- 475 ml distilled water

I don't know if I should even tell you about this one. Sure, it's technically an albumen technique but it's a long way from the pristine beauty of really well done traditional albumen. However, always thinking about the positive application, I'll imagine that your particular image-making tastes may run to the more organic and free and this process may just be right for what you need to express.

First, dissolve 72 g of the powdered albumen in 475 ml of distilled water, and when it's in solution add 10 g of kosher salt (sodium chloride) and whip it into a nice froth. You will quickly notice that we're not adding any acetic acid and that we're using kosher salt in place of ammonium chloride.

Let it sit for a little bit and then skim off the frothy foam. Notice how we're eliminating the 24 hours in the refrigerator and the filtration step?

Now, take a hake brush and coat your paper with a smooth and even solution of the albumen. Notice that we've completely abandoned the concept of aging our albumen? Mark the front, or back, of the paper with a notation indicating which side has been coated and hang the paper up to dry for a day or two in a low light environment. This drying period will help harden the albumen so that it will accept the silver nitrate sensitizer.

After the two days, coat the paper with a 15% solution of silver nitrate sensitizer and get on with making your prints.

OLD ALBUMEN IS GOOD ALBUMEN

It should be noted at this point that old albumen is good albumen. Mike Robinson typically uses albumen that is over a year old because as it ages, the proteins break down, and this results in a drop in the pH level to around 6. This means that there will be less yellowing of the highlights in the final print. I have been using a bottle of albumen that is now 5 years old and really rather offensive . . . but it works beautifully. The problem is that it stinks so bad that I can only demo it outdoors in the summer and I notice, with each passing year, that my students stand further and further away from me while I'm showing them how to prepare the paper. This summer I threw it out and just used the Zimmerman albumen because it was ready in an hour and used up before it began to ripen.

THE CHLORIDE & NEGATIVE RELATIONSHIP

In the first stage of albumen coating, the amount of the ammonium, or sodium, chloride in the solution can be used to counterbalance the density of your working negative. Here's how . . .

Any normal density negative is considered "thin" for an albumen print. However, if that is the type of negative that you have to work with, you can still make a pretty decent print by cutting the amount of sodium, or ammonium, chloride in half and using a more diluted (*less than 15%*) silver nitrate-sensitizing solution.

Fox Talbot figured out that there must be an excess of silver to salt to make this work. Typically, a 4 or 5 to 1 ratio is used with long scale negatives with a density range of 2.0 to 2.25. If you increase this ratio, you will be able to print *flatter* negatives, but too much of an excess of silver to salt will cause problems such as bronzing and highlight yellowing.

AMMONIA FUMING FOR CONTRAST

If the silver-to-salt ratio is reduced, you run the risk of uneven or under-sensitizing and you'll see a malady referred to as "measles" (*the word says it all*) as well as flat and weak prints. One more thing to think about is that fuming the sensitized paper with ammonia will give you a significant increase in tonality and contrast when using flatter negatives. It also gives the silver halide a higher pH, which makes it more sensitive. The ammonia fuming technique is far easier than trying to fine-tune the silver to salt balance. Fuming is essentially subjecting the paper, or plate, to the fumes of a particular chemical in an enclosed environment. If you intend to try this method with any chemical that is particularly aggressive, like ammonia, please consider doing so in a space with decent ventilation. When France Scully Osterman and Mark Osterman fume (that's not the same as having a marital spat), they use a large plastic storage box for the task. The bottom of the box is covered with an even layer of wadded cotton and ammonia is drizzled evenly over this. The paper is taped, albumen side down, to the inside of the box lid and placed on the box. Usually about 4 minutes is enough. Be sure to let the paper out-gas for a few minutes before placing it in the printing frame.

TABLE SET UP FOR COATING TRADITIONAL ALBUMEN

♦ A thin, high-quality, writing or drawing paper (Somerset Satin & Arches 88 are very good for this process)

♦ A Pyrex lasagna-size glass dish or tray

- A pencil and notepaper
- Matt knife
- Clothesline and clothespins

Coating the Paper with Albumen

First, get a nice thin paper to work with. I recommend a 100% rag paper, such as Somerset Satin, Arches 88, Buxton, a high-quality stationary, vellum, or drawing paper. If you live in France, look for Mark and France Scully Osterman's favorite albumen paper, Canson Crobb 'Art. This is the only paper available that has the same weight and feel of the 19th century papers. I would also recommend, trying Weston Diploma Parchment, a paper produced by the Byron Weston Paper Co. (a division of Crane Paper) in Boylston, Massachusetts.

Next fill a lasagna size, Pyrex glass, baking dish, or a brand-new plastic tray (*that will always be for albumen coating*), with your prepared albumen solution. Take a piece of your paper and mark it with a pencil to indicate the side that is to be coated with the albumen.

Next, you need to float the paper on the surface of the albumen in the tray. A very good floating technique is to make a pseudo-origami "*serving tray*" out of your paper by folding up the 4 sides of the paper a quarter inch so that it looks like a tray. This fold can be trimmed off at a later time and it gives you something to hold on to during the floating steps while simultaneously preventing the solution from getting onto the backside of the paper, which will result in uneven densities in the finished print. When your tray is formed, set it carefully on the albumen, like putting a toy boat in a bathtub, and move it around a bit without making bubbles.

Float your serving-tray formed paper in the albumen solution for 3 minutes and then remove it by dragging it slowly and smoothly over the side of your tray. If your albumen solution has too many air bubbles in it then you might want to try slowly filtering it into another tray.

Check the paper again for any air bubbles. If you find some, pop them with a pin or toothpick. If it looks hopeless, and the albumen is still fluid on the paper, re-float the paper for an additional minute and then try removing it again, gracefully, by pulling it over the edge of the tray. Hang it on a line to dry and don't fuss with the paper by

trying to keep the albumen from collecting at the bottom of the recently hung paper. Just trim that edge off later along with the folded edges of the serving tray.

Glossy or Matte Surface

A dry albumen coated paper will have a nice semi gloss reflection. However, if you double coat, or steam the paper, it will become glossy. To make a true matte surface albumen coating all that you have to do is make an arrowroot starch solution and mix it into your prepared albumen before coating. Of course, you could also simply use the Zimmerman matte albumen method and save yourself a lot of trouble.

Arrowroot Starch For Matte Surface Albumen

    12 g Arrowroot Starch
    12 g kosher salt (*sodium chloride*)
    300 ml distilled water

To prepare a matte surface albumen coating, take 12 g of arrowroot starch and mix it into a paste with a little of your distilled water. Add 12 g of sodium chloride and the rest of the distilled water to the arrowroot paste and, in a clean pot, boil it for 1 minute. Once the solution has cooled off, remove the skim from the surface and mix the solution 1:1 with your prepared albumen coating solution.

TRADITIONAL ALBUMEN HARDENING OPTIONS: DOUBLE COATING

Single coating albumen generally *will not* require a hardening step. However, if you double coat, there are a few albumen hardening methods available to you before you sensitize the paper for printing. These methods will result in a glossier albumen print.

METHOD #1: THE HAY LOFT

According to James Reilly, 19th century albumenists simply stored their freshly albumenized paper in a warm loft for half a year. This was the amount of time it took to slow cure and harden the albumen.

Figure 21–10

Jesseca Ferguson, *Two Birds/Negative Island*, 1999—pinhole/albumen
This is a nice example of an albumen-based collage from the brilliant, and eclectic, Boston artist Jesseca Ferguson.
(Courtesy of the artist)

Method #2: Steam

In the 19ᵗʰ century, it was thought that steam would be an adequate vehicle for hardening albumen. The problem is that the level of steam that it's possible to generate at home isn't strong enough to do this task nearly as well as letting the albumen age in the hayloft for half a year. However, if you don't have a hayloft and wish to try the steam method, feel free. The worst it will do is remove the albumen. Steam was used however to make the paper more pliable prior to floating on the silver solution. To do so, steam the original albumen coated surface for one minute before the second albumen coating; obviously, this is like cooking an egg. A handheld clothes steamer or a piece of heavy-duty window screen, laid over a soup pot of boiling water will work as well. Another option is to use a steam iron and iron the albumen coated paper through a clean piece of thin paper; set the clothes iron on a silk setting. After steaming, hang the paper up to dry.

Method #3: Isopropyl Alcohol & Ammonium Chloride

Still another method, and really the most practical of the three, is to harden the first coating of albumen with a 500 ml bath of 70% isopropyl (rubbing) alcohol combined with whatever amount of ammonium chloride you used in the original coating, i.e., 15 g in our original formula, and immerse for 15–20 seconds. Be careful that you don't treat the paper in too strong an alcohol concentration, as it will dissolve the albumen, or for too long, as it may lead to cracking in the albumen surface.

Why are you doing the ammonium chloride again? Because it is possible that the isopropyl alcohol will cause the original ammonium chloride in the formula to leach out and abandon the albumen coating. Replacing this ammonium chloride with what you've included in your alcohol solution, makes up for the loss.

These techniques will prevent the first albumen coat from breaking down during the application of the second coating. Be careful of *blistering*, which is not an uncommon second coat experience. After hardening the coating, hang the paper using film clips on the top and bottom of the paper on a line in a dust-free place.

Silver Nitrate as a Hardening Agent

Just a quick bit of information that you are already accommodating in this process. A strong solution of silver nitrate will harden albumen whereas a less strong concentration will dissolve it. I am recommending a 15% silver nitrate concentration in this chapter, but you can easily, and effectively, increase that percentage up to 20% without a problem.

Flattening Albumen Paper

You will find that double-coated albumen paper is very difficult to keep flat. I like to use my old dry mount press (it's still good for something) for this purpose. When the albumen paper is dry, heat your press and when it gets to about 200°F, turn it off, and put your stack of coated paper in the press. Let the press cool, and in a few hours you'll have a stack of flat albumen sheets. Be careful not to burn the albumen.

TABLE SET UP FOR SENSITIZING TRADITIONAL ALBUMEN

- Flattened and sensitized albumen paper
- Pencil and paper for taking notes
- Scissors or matt knife for trimming paper
- Maybe a pair of white cotton gloves if you're nervous
- Clean paper for the table surface coating area
- Contact printing frame
- Negative or photogram materials for contact printing
- 15% silver nitrate sensitizer (30 g of silver nitrate & 200 ml distilled water)

15% SILVER NITRATE SENSITIZER

Sensitizing the Paper: 15% Silver Nitrate

- 30 g of silver nitrate
- 200 ml of distilled water

Under low tungsten, or ambient, room light, mix a 15% solution of silver nitrate being extremely careful not to get it on your skin or in your eyes. Silver nitrate is not light sensitive until it is combined, or comes into contact, with an organic material such as albumen, gelatin, or dust, or humans. Be cautious; avoid getting it on your skin, keep your hands away from your eyes, and be wary of fluorescent light as it emits low levels of UV light and may fog your paper.

Your albumen-coated paper can be sensitized by using either the "serving-tray" floating technique, rod - Puddle Pusher, or hake - foam brush application methods. Brush coating is less expensive but not as effective in my experience. Your newly sensitized paper will generally be acceptable for printing for up to a day after this step . . . but that is pushing it unless you make a formula with a preservative in it . . . see below.

The density of your print can be controlled, to a point, in this stage by adding or reducing the amount of distilled water used in making the silver nitrate solution. I have used 20% concentrations successfully. A more dilute solution, say 10%, results in a softer image and is generally less than satisfying. Whatever concentration you make, be sure to stir well, and when the silver nitrate is totally dissolved, pour it into a dark glass bottle and label it well. The solution is clear and can be mistaken for water so please don't be casual with it or with how you store it. Do not store it in the refrigerator where it can be opened by mistake.

15% Silver Nitrate Sensitizer with Citric Acid

There is a semi-popular theory that the addition of citric acid to the silver nitrate sensitizer will lengthen the time the silver nitrate solution will be suitable for coating. I believe this works as advertised. In other words, the citric acid works as a restrainer. This is the same formula that I use for salted paper. Add 5 g of citric acid to every 100 ml of sensitizer.

Acid Restrainers in the Silver Sensitizer in Humid Conditions

In exceptionally warm and humid conditions it is a good idea, some say imperative, to add a little citric or acetic acid to the silver nitrate sensitizer. This slows down the exposure time as the acidity acts as a restrainer, slowing down the interface between the silver and the halide salt. It will cause the print to become more red in color. This is a good formula and I advise using it for anyone printing in the summer at sea level or in relative humidity that is uncomfortable.

- 30 g of silver nitrate
- 200 ml of distilled water
- 4 g of citric acid (*will result in light-sensitive silver citrate*)

Silver Nitrate Replenishment during Sensitizing

If you are sensitizing your albumenized paper by floating it in the 15% silver nitrate solution, it will be necessary to replenish the silver nitrate as you progress. Make up a 25% solution of silver nitrate by mixing 25 g of silver nitrate with 100 ml of distilled water. After every 8" × 10" sheet of paper, add 15 drops of your 25% silver nitrate.

Precipitating Contaminates from a Discolored Silver Nitrate Solution with Kaolin

You can maintain a silver nitrate solution for years if you add 15 g of kaolin to every 1000 ml of your silver nitrate solution. Kaolin (*china clay*) is a clay mineral more correctly known as kaolinite. It is a mineral, soft, white in color, used as one of the primary ingredients in porcelain, and made up of individual crystals in its pure form. Kaolin's whiteness, opaqueness, large internal surface area, and non-abrasive quality make it an ideal filler material for chemical and paper production. Kaolin precipitates the organic matter that has combined with the silver nitrate and allows it to fall to the bottom of the container.

Be sure when pouring the silver nitrate into a tray or beaker for coating that you don't disturb the kaolin. The best technique is to use a small siphon to move the solution from the bottle to another location. (*An inexpensive siphon can generally be found at an auto supply store.*) After using the silver solution you must replenish it with your 25% silver replenisher or you'll soon have a weak solution that will give your prints the dreaded "measles."

The other 19th century method is to "sun the bath" by placing the silver solution in a large clear glass cookie jar. Stir in enough sodium bicarbonate to get the solution to reach neutral pH and set the jar on a sunny windowsill. The sunlight will cause the dark organic contaminates to precipitate and fall to the bottom of the jar. This technique was also used in the wet-plate process.

COATING SILVER NITRATE SENSITIZER

Set yourself up in a room with very low light. Put on a pair of fresh Nitrile gloves and remind yourself to be careful not to touch your face or eyes while you are doing this part of the process. You have coating options . . . float coating, rod coating, or brush coating.

Using the same technique that you employed in the albumen float coating, make your origami "serving tray" out of a sheet of albumenized paper, pour into a Pyrex casserole dish, or super clean tray, your silver nitrate solution and float the paper on the silver nitrate surface for 3 minutes. Gracefully peel the paper from the silver nitrate solution and be careful not to get any silver nitrate on the back of the paper. Hang it up to dry in a dust-free and dark environment and be sure to lay down a lot of newsprint underneath the drying line to catch the dripping silver nitrate.

If you elect to brush coat, you will be able to work more quickly and you'll have those romantic brush coating marks on the outside of your image area that show nothing existed on that paper until you put it there. The first thing to do is mark out where the coating will take place with 4 faint pencil "L" marks. I will recommend, as I do for salted paper coating, that you use a brand new foam brush for every paper you coat. These are very inexpensive brushes and by using a new one you avoid the problem of transferring organic (*albumen*) contamination from a previous coating to your silver nitrate. I will also use a hake brush for this coating stage but will thoroughly clean the brush in distilled water, and dry it, before going to the next piece of paper.

Tack down your paper on a very clean flat surface. Next, measure out your silver nitrate solution into a shot glass with an eyedropper. A 4" x 5" negative area can easily be covered with 25–30 drops of solution. When you're ready, pour the contents of the shot glass into the center of your coating area and brush the silver nitrate quickly, lightly, and evenly over the marked out dimensions of your coating area.

You can also pour a small amount of the silver nitrate into a plastic or glass beaker, or hot-liquid paper cup, and dip your brush into the solution. Brush-coat it in the same manner you have been using throughout—light, even strokes covering the full image area vertically and then horizontally. After the coating, allow the paper to air dry in the dark until it is "bone" dry. In environments where high altitude and lack of humidity are normal, you will find that the paper will dry very quickly . . . a very nice situation when working in albumen.

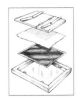

EXPOSING ALBUMEN
Exposure Control

Although you have about 24 hours to use the sensitized paper it is a good idea to expose the print as soon as the paper is bone dry. If you wait too long before exposing the paper, the contrast in the final image will decrease and you'll eventually get yellowing highlights due to *silver albumenate,* which begins to be created quite rapidly. (More on this in a few paragraphs.) If you know that you will not be printing the sensitized paper right away, consider using the silver nitrate with preservative citric acid formula. You can also use drops of acetic acid. With pH strips, monitor the bath as you gradually bring the pH down to about 3.

Place the paper and your negative into a hinged back contact printing frame, "right-reading" positioning, and go sit in the sun or shade with it. If you don't have sunlight, use a mechanical UV printing unit. As with POP and salted paper techniques, exposing in direct or indirect sunlight is a personal choice. Personally, I prefer to begin my albumen exposure in open shade and will take it practically to the end of the exposure in that light environment. At the end of the exposure sequence, I will give the exposure a 1- to 2-minute shot of direct sun to intensify the shadows. In the summer, an average negative will require 4–6 minutes in the shade and 1–2 minutes in the sunlight. Negatives with a lot of density will require longer exposure times while thinner negatives may demand that almost all of your printing is done in shade.

Albumen is a POP printing-out process and so you will be periodically examining your print during the exposure in order to determine when it is perfect. Exposure time is dependent upon the density of your negative, time of day, heat and humidity, etc., so it is important to write all of this information down when you're printing.

🐢 **Note: If the negative is an unvarnished gelatin emulsion film or plate, you should place a sheet of clear Mylar, or a Krystal Seal envelope between the negative and the albumen paper to prevent the excess silver from migrating to the film emulsion causing future damage.**

What to Look For

When you think it's time to check on the exposure, go into low light, release one side of your contact printer and check the image. Look for a purplish colored print with "*bronzed*" to solarized tonalities in the deepest shadows. Bronzing is a term used to describe having a metallic look to the darkest values. This will be the visual sign that tells you when the print is exposed well. Over-expose about 1 to 1.5 stops darker than you would like the finished print to be because it will lose a little density during the upcoming stages. This is similar to the recommendations I gave you for a salted paper print even though it requires less over-exposure than does salt.

Exposure & Silver Albumenate/Highlight Yellowing

You may recall that in the salt process I recommended facing the contact frame away from the sun and printing in open shade to achieve a modest contrast gain and a bit more control of your exposure. The albumen process, like all silver chloride printing out processes react in the same way. You may also place a sheet or two of tissue paper over the printing frame and print in direct sunlight to increase contrast. The best strategy with albumen paper is to process the print immediately. This action will reduce the amount of *silver albumenate* that is being formed during the albumen's extended contact with the excess silver nitrate in your sensitizer formula. The longer the silver nitrate excess in the sensitizer solution remains in contact with the albumen, the more likely it is that the highlights in that print will turn yellow over time. Silver albumenate does not "*fix-out.*" This results in white highlights turning yellow as in many historical albumen prints.

Yellowing of a finished albumen print is often the result of the wrong paper for the process. You may need to test papers to find out what works well for you but I would recommend beginning with Somerset Satin, Arches 88, or Cot 320, as they are all proven papers.

Figure 21–11

Christopher James, *Mary's Chair*, **Santa Fe, 2007**
—albumen

This print was made outside our lab building during my
2007 Santa Fe Workshops, Advanced Alternative Process
Workshop. I used Zoe Zimmerman's matte albumen
process and my demonstration, from cracking and preparing the 2 dozen eggs, making the pinhole, and completing
the finished print, took about 2 hours.
(Courtesy of the author)

Color & Exposure: Using the Right Negative

From a purely classical perspective, it is pointless to work
with a thin negative—because it will be near impossible to
get that lovely aubergine coloration in an albumen print if
your negative can't hold up to sufficient exposure. The
tone of the albumen print is dictated by how deeply you
can print. If you stop exposing too soon, you'll never get
the d-max strong enough to get rich tones.

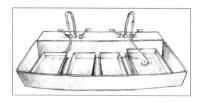

SINK SET UP FOR ALBUMEN

Tray 1   Salted tap water with citric acid

Tray 2   Fresh running water

Tray 3   Toner trays

Tray 4   Rinse tray

Tray 5 A   15% sodium thiosulfate fixing bath

Tray 5 B   Optional: Sel d'or Toner/fixer monobath

Tray 6   1% sodium sulfite hypo-clearing bath

Tray 7   Final wash in clear running water

PROCESSING ALBUMEN

Salt/Citric Wash First Bath

This first bath tray consists of a slightly acidic salt bath
whose purpose is to precipitate the free (or excess) silver by producing silver chloride. You will often see a
milky residue coming from the print's surface, as the
excess silver nitrate starts bonding with the chloride. If
you have no salt in this bath, you will not be removing
the free silver and this will create problems with your

toning, as the gold will not adhere to the silver unless the free silver is eliminated. Here's your first bath mix:

10 g citric acid
30 g kosher salt
1000 ml distilled water

Following your exposure, immerse your print in this bath of salted water that has been made slightly acidic with the addition of citric acid, lowering its pH. Under low to moderate light, agitate the print slowly for about 5 minutes or until no more milky precipitate is visible.

Following this step, move your print to a tray filled with fresh water and gently agitate. Repeat the fresh water exchange for 5 to 10 minutes. If you have a black plastic tray, this will help you to see when the water is completely clear.

ALBUMEN TONING

Optional Toning Prior to Fixing

Un-toned, an albumen print will be reddish-plum to warm brown in color. Toning the print, *prior to the fixing stage*, will provide you with options for the color of your finished work. It will also greatly assist in making the print archival and less susceptible to fading and yellowing as time goes on. Gold-toned prints will render a variety of colors depending on the length of the immersion, i.e., purple-brown, aubergine, slate gray, and blue-gray. The slate blue and gray tones are considered the least archival.

Albumen Gold Toner

2 liters warm distilled water
1 g gold chloride
8 g sodium borate

In a clean non-metallic beaker, carefully add 1 g of gold chloride to the distilled water and stir it into solution with a glass or plastic rod. Next, add the 8 g of sodium borate and stir until it is completely in solution. Filter the sediment that did not go into solution through a fine stocking or piece of cheesecloth and store it in a dark glass bottle. To tone the print, simply immerse the print in the toning solution and remove it when you are happy with the color. The print is then fixed and washed.

Salted Paper Toners for Albumen

Seeing as there are so many other similarities between the albumen and the salted paper processes, an option you might wish to consider is using salted paper toning formulas with your albumen. Please refer to Chapter 2, the Salted Paper chapter toning section for recipes and instructions for the following toners.

- Gold/borax toner (*warm/reddish color*)
- POP gold–ammonium thiocyanate toner (cooler whites and darks)
- Gold–sodium acetate toner
- Palladium toner
- POP platinum toners

FIXING THE ALBUMEN PRINT

15% Standard Sodium Thiosulfate Fixing Bath: 2-Tray Set Up

150 g sodium thiosulfate
2 g sodium carbonate (*to make the fix slightly alkaline*)
1000 ml distilled water

Your fixing bath will be a familiar one. Dissolve 150 g of sodium thiosulfate (*anhydrous/dry*), and 2 g of sodium carbonate, into 1 liter (1000 ml) of distilled water to make a 15% fix solution.

Make up 2 trays of this fixer. Immerse the print in the first fixing tray of this fixing bath for 2 minutes. Remove the print and immerse it in the second fixing tray for an additional 2 minutes.

On average, using a double tray fixing set up, you should be able to adequately fix up to 2 dozen prints before having to re-mix.

SEL D'OR TONER/FIXER MONOBATH FOR ALBUMEN

Sel d'or Toner/Fixer Monobath

Several years after the Daguerreotype process was announced, a French physicist, by the name of Hippolyte Fizeau, introduced an important process addition, called sel d'or (salt of gold), that gave Daguerreotypists a way to intensify and tone their work. Some time between 1847

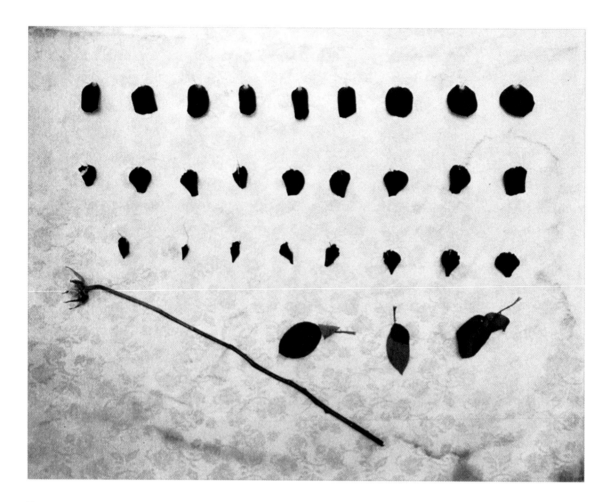

Figure 21–12

Dan Estabrook Rose, 1995—albumen with gold borax toner

Dan, who was a student of mine at Harvard, caught the alternative process bug early in his life and hasn't looked back since. He is one of the most innovative alt pro artists working today and has managed to marry the processes of the 19th century with the critical theory of the 21st.

(Courtesy of the artist)

and 1855, the process was supposedly incorporated into the calotype, salted paper, and albumen processes.

For many years, in the mid-19th century, sel d'or gold toning was commonly incorporated into the albumen and salted paper processes although it was quite difficult to predict whether the technique would improve, or fade, the print. When an albumen or salted paper print was immersed in the sel d'or toner/fixer monobath the image color would lighten (orange-brown) and then reconstitute itself to either a cool sienna, purple, or blue-black. The final image color is based upon the depth of the printing, the toning formula, and the length of time the print is in the toning solution. Print deeply if you intend to use this technique.

The sel d'or toner is actually a toning-fixing monobath and is constituted by mixing a solution of gold chloride into a solution of sodium thiosulfate and a little bicarbonate of soda, to make the solution lean a bit to alkaline. Using it allows the photographer to both tone and fix their print in a single action. Again, it is unpredictable and the following formula is more "kitchen-sink" than lab. Toning/fixing time is approximately 4 minutes following the wash stage.

Sel d'or Toner/Fixer Formula

500 ml water

75 g sodium thiosulfate

1 teaspoon bicarbonate of soda

3 grains of gold chloride (*use a 30 ml stock solution*)

Stock Gold Solution for Sel d'or Toner/Fixer

154 ml distilled water

1 g gold chloride in a glass ampule (*1 gram = 15.43 grains*)

Take your 1-gram ampule (*a sealed glass or plastic capsule*) of gold chloride and drop it into a bottle containing 154 ml distilled water. (Break the ampule and leave it there.) Because 1 gram equals 15.4 grains, and you mixed this amount with 154 ml distilled water, every time you need 1 grain of gold for a formula all you need do is add 10 ml of the gold stock solution.

1% SODIUM SULFITE HYPO CLEARING BATH

If you want to be absolutely sure that all of the residual fixer is gone from your print, you may mix up a solution of 1% sodium sulfite hypo clearing agent. Simply dissolve 10 g of sodium sulfite into 1000 ml of water and agitate your print for several minutes before going to the final wash.

FINAL WASH

Wash the toned and fixed image for 30 minutes and hang to dry.

Wet Collodion & Gelatin Dry Plate Emulsion

OVERVIEW & EXPECTATIONS

I'll begin by providing a little history about the discovery of collodion and its evolution into the wet plate collodion process that revolutionized photography. Wet collodion provided the detail prized in a daguerreotype, and the possibility to reproduce multiple prints from a single glass plate negative.

In the second part of this chapter, I'll be inviting Mark Osterman, of George Eastman House / International Museum of Photography, to contribute. Mark will be writing about gelatin dry plate emulsion. It might seem a little odd to hear a new voice this deep into the book, but in all honesty, Mark's knowledge of this topic is so thorough and complete that it doesn't make sense for me to tell you about gelatin dry plate emulsion when he can do it so well. I'm grateful to give the task to him and content that you can't get a better introduction to gelatin dry plate emulsion anywhere.

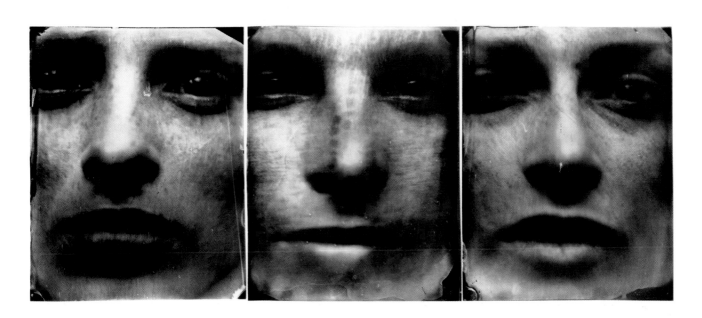

Figure 22–1

Sally Mann, Triptych, 2004 – wet collodion negatives

Left to right, an impressive set of 40" × 50" gelatin silver prints made from collodion negatives of Virginia, Emmett, and Jessie Mann . . . the same family line-up as the cover of Sally's book, *Immediate Family*. In some ways the expressions haven't changed, they're just 15 years apart.

(Courtesy of Gagosian Gallery, New York. © 2006 Sally Mann)

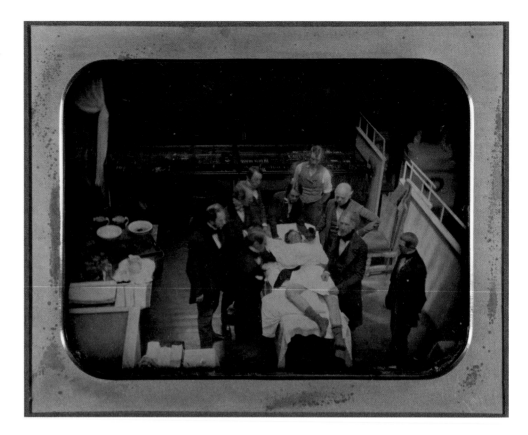

A LITTLE HISTORY

Prior to 1851, if you wanted to march in the fledgling photographic parade, the most relevant options avail- able, provided you didn't want your images to be botani- cal studies rendered in blue, were the daguerreotype, Talbot's calotype, or the albumen on glass negative.

The daguerreotype was known for its crystalline detail, preciousness of presentation, the time it con- sumed for its exposures, process, and the fact that it was a one-of-a-kind image. The calotype was a paper nega- tive suitable for making an unlimited number of positive salt prints.

Just a side note clarification; Talbot did make some developed-out positive prints, from his developed-out paper negatives, and these can be called calotypes. The calotype's resolution potential was inferior compared to

daguerreotype, due to the paper substrate, and it was also much less sensitive to light, making studio portrai- ture very difficult. Paper negatives were occasionally waxed or oiled in order to make them translucent enough for contact print printing.

The much-sought-after solution to their individual shortcomings would be a single process that could be both reproducible like the calotype, and finely detailed like the daguerreotype. Once the technique was discov- ered, glass would be the obvious substrate, because it was both clear and flat. The remaining big question, however, would be how to keep the light sensitive halides on the glass throughout the entire process. A clear, and flexible, binder was needed.

In 1845–1846, Christian Frederick Schönbein (1799–1868) discovered nitrated cotton, popularly known as *guncotton*, by soaking cotton fibers in a mix- ture of sulfuric and nitric acids. The cotton was placed in the acid solution for an extended period of time and was subsequently washed well until free of the acids. This ini- tial process yielded an unstable and flammable material that was initially used solely as an explosive.

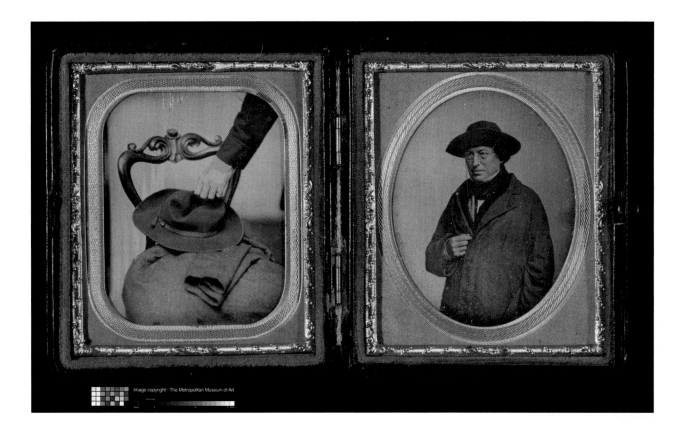

Figure 22–3

John Adams Whipple, Cornelius Conway Felton w/ His Hat & Coat, c. 1850—daguerreotype

John Adams Whipple, who, as Director of the Harvard College Observatory, also made extraordinary daguerreotypes of the moon, had a little postmodernism in him as well . . . which, fortunately, he was unaware of. This whimsical diptych of Cornelius Felton with his hat and coat is one of my favorite historical photographic illustrations.

(Courtesy The Metropolitan Museum of Art, Gilman Collection, Gift of the Howard Gilman Foundation, 2005, Image © The Metropolitan Museum of Art)

Ironically, in 1847, a young medical student by the name of John Parker Maynard formulated an ingenious medical dressing, called *collodion*, a name taken from the Greek word *kollodes* meaning "to adhere," that could be used to treat wounds from explosives. Maynard made his collodion by dissolving Schönbein's nitrated cotton in a mixture of equal parts of sulfuric ether and alcohol. The result of Maynard's action was a clear and viscous fluid that dried to a durable and flexible *skin* used by the medical staff during the Crimean War, in a battlefield environment.

Collodion dried quickly and could be applied directly to the bandages, as an adhesive, to keep the injury clean and dry and as protection from infection. In some accounts it is said that the collodion was applied directly to the wound but I am told, by those that know the sensation, that this ill-advised action is neither pleasant nor effective.

In January 1850, Robert Bingham proposed the idea that this solution could be applied to photographic use because it appeared to be the perfect vehicle for holding light-sensitive compounds on glass. Gustave le Gray followed soon after by publishing a formula, though it was theoretical at best.

In March 1851, Frederick Scott Archer published the technique and formula for the application of iodized collodion on sheets of glass for the purpose of making glass plate negatives. Archer described a process where potassium iodide was combined with a solution of dilute collodion. The plate was then immersed in a silver nitrate solution, resulting in light-sensitive layer of silver iodide. The sensitized glass plate was exposed immediately after being withdrawn from the silver nitrate, developed in a solution of pyrogallic acid, and fixed in sodium thiosulfate. The advantages were immediately evident. The process provided a sharp glass negative that was most

Figure 22–4
Jerry Spagnoli, Hands and Throat, 2001—daguerreotype
Jerry is one of the true antiquarian avant-garde and serves his passion well
as both an outstanding artist and teacher of the daguerreotype process.
This extraordinarily provocative piece is a fine example of his craft and
artistry.
(Courtesy of the artist)

Figure 22–5
**Frederick Scott Archer, Kennilworth Castle, 1851, Sel d'or toned Albumen
from collodion negative—S&O**
In March 1851, Frederick Scott Archer published the technique and formula
for the application of iodized collodion on sheets of glass for the purpose of
making glass plate negatives.
(Courtesy of Scully & Osterman Collection)

sensitive in the wet state, permitting exposures that were
dramatically faster than the calotype. Prints from wet-
plate negatives were also democratically priced, being a
fraction of the cost of the daguerreotype.

Soon after Archer published his technique, he realized
that an underexposed wet collodion negative, when laid on
a dark background and viewed in reflective light, would
appear as a dull positive. This phenomenon was enhanced
when he bleached the brown silver deposit to white with
mercuric chloride. Archer called these positive collodion
images "Alabastrines" playing on the white of alabaster.
Eventually, image-makers adopted ferrous sulfate developer and potassium cyanide fixer, a chemical combination
that eliminated the need for a bleaching step.

The early positive collodion plates were occasionally
referred to by the French as *daguerreotypes-on-glass*
and were common throughout the 1850s and 1860s.
However, most people called the plates ambrotypes, a
name introduced by Boston photographer Joseph
Ambrose Cutting after Marcus A. Root suggested the
name. The term ambrotype could be assumed to have
been taken from Joseph Ambrose Cutting's name but in
truth, it was actually derived from the Greek word
ambrotos, meaning *immortal* . . . referring to Cutting's
method of covering a completed image with a second
sheet of glass as in the fashion of preparing a slide for a
microscope. Interestingly, Cutting gave himself the
middle name of Ambrose to match the process. Today,
there are a fair number of artists using the wet collodion
process as their primary means of image translation and

Figure 22–6

Mark Osterman, Hesitation, 2006—tinted ruby glass ambrotype

Next to his wife France, Mark is one of the most knowledgeable people I have ever met when it comes to alternative/antique photographic processes. This terrific ambrotype is pretty close to accurately describing the feeling one gets just before pouring collodion on a glass plate. It is from his series, *Artifacts of the Process*.

(Courtesy of The Howard Greenberg Gallery)

expression. Their work is particularly meaningful because it incorporates the traditions and characteristics of the process while addressing the concerns and concepts of contemporary visual expression. Most prominent in this select group are France Scully Osterman, Mark Osterman, Sally Mann, and Jody Ake.

As an aside, it is quite common to see ambrotypes and daguerreotypes side-by-side and identically labeled in flea markets and antique shops. The daguerreotype appears as a metal mirror with a ghostly image residing in its interior. Due to its predominant reflective quality, observing the image is a bit like a looking at a "*little secret*" because only one person can see it well at one time. The ambrotype, on the other hand, is only as reflective as the glass itself and when made on clear glass it is often possible to see a slight separation between the image on the glass and the black backing behind it. This is especially evident if paper or fabric was used. This separation adds to a 3-D effect and is an instant clue as to the process.

There are many workable, published, and practiced formulas and the following descriptions represent a useful starting point should you wish to begin experimenting with wet collodion. The technique described herein is for the wet plate collodion ambrotype. To make a wet plate collodion *negative*, as in Archer's initial work, you would need to use a slightly different salted collodion solution (*increasing the iodide to bromide proportions at a rate of up to 4:1 in the formula to follow*), longer exposures, longer development, and a weaker and more acidic developer.

THE AMBROTYPE PROCESS

Although wet plate collodion work shares many of the same characteristics and sequences with traditional silver gelatin processes, it does require a few equipment adaptations. For one thing, the sensitized plate needs a special wet plate holder that replaces the view camera ground glass after focusing. A traditional wet plate holder is the best option but they are difficult to find and quite expensive.

Scully & Osterman Conversion Holder

The easiest way to create a wet plate holder is to adapt a conventional film holder by removing the dark slides and cutting a hole in the rigid septum that separates the two sides. This opening will be the size of the glass plates that you will be using. Drill two small holes on either side of the 4 inside corners of the opening and insert a clip made from a silver wire through each set of holes to hold the plate. Bend over the protruding ends of the wire and flatten them so that the dark slide can be removed without scraping. It is important that the collodion side of the glass plate is on the same plane as would be the film if it were being used normally. The sensitized plate is loaded collodion side down from behind and held in place by a spring made from a plastic yogurt container that is positioned between the back of the plate and the back dark slide as it's replaced. The front dark-slide is used as usual.

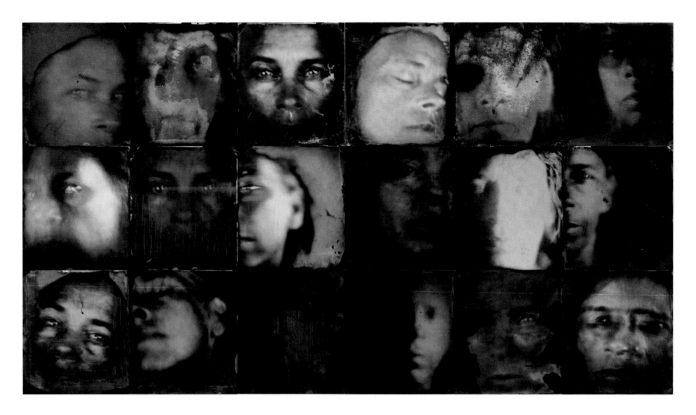

Figure 22–7

Sally Mann, Self Portraits, 2006—18 ambrotypes

Here's a piece of work you probably haven't seen yet. A while ago, Sally had a riding accident and her back was injured quite badly. During her rehabilitation, it was impossible for her to physically haul her camera around, so she simply stood in front of it and recorded this painful, and uncertain, period in her life. On the plus side, Sally's better and recently told me that she's in training for a 30-mile equestrian endurance race. Each ambrotype measures 13.5" × 15".

(Courtesy of the artist and the Gagosian Gallery, New York. © 2006 Sally Mann)

Figure 22–8

***Scully & Osterman* Conversion Holder**

This is an illustration of France & Mark's adaptation of 8" × 10" sheet film holders for 6½" × 8½" plates. The rear dark slide has been pulled to show the loose plastic spring that holds the sensitized plate against silver wire corners. Plates load from the back of the holder. This system is suitable for the collodion, calotype, and daguerreotype processes.

(Courtesy Scully & Osterman Studio)

Plate Dipper for Sensitizing and Fixing

While both sensitizing and fixing can be done in conventional trays, it is easier to use vertical glass or plastic tanks for these operations. The glass or plastic tanks should have an outer, light-tight box. Each tank should be equipped with a "dipper" or some mechanism for lowering and raising the plate in the solutions without touching the sensitized surface. In the 19th century, these plate dippers were made from glass, rubber, ceramic, or thick silver wire. One solution that works quite well is a 2" wide strip of Plexiglas® softened on one side over a stove burner and bent to have a 1/4" lip.

Glass Cleaning and Preparation

The glass plate is prepared by thoroughly cleaning a piece of clear or dark glass. Before cleaning the glass, remove the razor sharp burr on all the edges with a hand held sharpening stone. The glass must be totally free of any solvent, grease, and debris, or the collodion solution will not adhere to the glass effectively. One of the best cleaners is *rottenstone* which can be purchased at stores that sell furniture-finishing supplies. It is a fine gray powder and mixing it with equal parts of powder, water and alcohol produces a good glass cleaning solution. Apply this to the glass with one piece of cloth and vigorously buff the surface with another clean piece.

To verify if your plate is cleaned properly, breathe on the glass and check to see if there are streaks showing in the mist condensation from your breath.

MAKING PHOTOGRAPHIC COLLODION

I strongly advise not attempting to make your own collodion from scratch. Nitrating cotton is very dangerous. It is simply not worth the risk. Purchase the "plain" uniodized collodion from an alternative process supply or chemical lab and salt it at home in your well-ventilated lab or outdoors. **This part is important:** The fumes from the ether are very flammable and even a very small spark could ignite and cause an explosion. Mix the collodion solution outdoors when possible and do not smoke during the process. (*Imagine the non-smoking lecture here.*) If you are using a lab, be sure that the ventilation is excellent and that the fan motor is

Figure 22–9

Bev Conway, ambrotype of Sarazah, 2005
Bev Conway took a one-day ambrotype workshop with France Scully Osterman and her husband Mark Osterman, and produced this portrait of her friend Sarazah.
(Courtesy of the artist)

flameproof. If you use an in-line fan in your darkroom, be aware that it is likely to have an armature that generates a spark. Do not use that type of fan during this process.

A Scully & Osterman Collodion for Positives

♦ 236 ml plain collodion

♦ 155 ml ether

♦ 3 g cadmium bromide

♦ 155 ml of 190 proof alcohol

♦ 4 g ammonium iodide

Step 1 Add the collodion to a 550 ml glass bottle and then slowly add the ether. Cap the bottle, shake the solution, and place the bottle aside for a short time.

Figure 22–10

Mark Osterman, Solutions, 1999—tinted ruby glass ambrotype

(Courtesy Scully & Osterman Studio)

Step 2 Take a small glass beaker and pour 4 ml of distilled water into it. Then add 3 g of cadmium bromide to the beaker and proceed to break it down by crushing it with a glass rod. Hold the beaker over a flame and move the beaker around until the cadmium bromide dissolves completely. Once it is dissolved, slowly add it to the bottle containing the collodion and ether mix and shake the bottle.

You have now made *Part A.*

Step 3 Place the ammonium iodide in a glass beaker containing 155 ml of 190-proof alcohol and stir this with a glass rod until it dissolves.

You have now made *Part B.*

Step 4 To make the working solution, slowly combine Part B to Part A, shake the solution to mix it up. *Note: This will be the last time you will shake the bottle.*

Step 5 This formula has a relatively short shelf life of several weeks though it will keep longer if refrigerated. If you wish to make a collodion that does last longer, substitute the potassium iodide for

the ammonium iodide. This solution might be cloudy at first but it will clear given enough time.

Note: Some water is beneficial in collodion, however too much promotes the formation of lines in the surface of the film. If lines are a problem, the ammonium iodide and cadmium bromide may be dissolved in alcohol instead of water but do not use an alcohol lamp when mixing.

Coating the Plate

In daylight, hold the plate by the lower left corner and begin coating the plate by pouring a small amount of the collodion solution on the center of the plate, letting it flow to the corner being held but without letting it touch your fingers. Gracefully tilt it around to allow the coating to flow to successive corners. When 3 of the corners have been coated, tilt the plate at a 45-degree angle at the final corner and pour the excess solution back into the bottle. While draining, move the plate from side to side until the solution is even across the plate's surface. It is important that the coating is meticulous and that the excess is poured back into its storage bottle before the collodion begins to set.

Effect of Solvents in Collodion

Scully and Osterman often use an ether rich collodion formula for making ambrotypes where density is not only unimportant but detrimental. This helps establish a more delicate range of tones. A higher ratio of alcohol, though never more than 50%–50%, provides stronger deposits of silver when making negatives where density is desirable. Be warned, however, that alcohol also introduces water into the collodion, the main cause of ripple-like "crape" lines in the film.

Silver Nitrate Bath

Thoroughly dissolve 28 g of silver nitrate into 400 ml of distilled water. Pour this solution into your vertical silver nitrate tank. If you find that you're getting image fogging that is chemically generated, you may wish to test your silver nitrate bath with a piece of litmus paper to check its acidity. Ideally you want a pH between 3 and 4 to prevent fog. You may use either nitric or acetic acid but be aware that your film speed will drop as the solution becomes more acidic. Scully and Osterman also suggest leaving a plate coated with iodized collodion in your silver nitrate solution overnight to iodize the silver solution. Without excess iodides in the silver solution your images will be thin and of inconsistent density.

Before the ether evaporates from the collodion, the plate is immersed in a solution of silver nitrate for about 4 minutes. The environment for this stage is a darkroom with a red or deep orange-yellow filtered safelight or a room with deep red glass on the windows. During the immersion period, the silver nitrate bonds with the iodides and bromides in the salted collodion and creates a light-sensitive, silver halide deposit on, and just under, the surface of the collodion. Again, be sure that you are using a meticulously clean, glass or plastic, immersion "silver-bath" tank. Please read all relevant information concerning silver nitrate before beginning this step in the process.

When the plate is sensitized, and still wet, it is inserted into a light-tight plate holder and placed directly into the camera for the exposure. Be very careful during this stage, because the plate holder will be dripping silver nitrate. A technique that helps make less of a mess is to drain the silver nitrate sensitized plate over

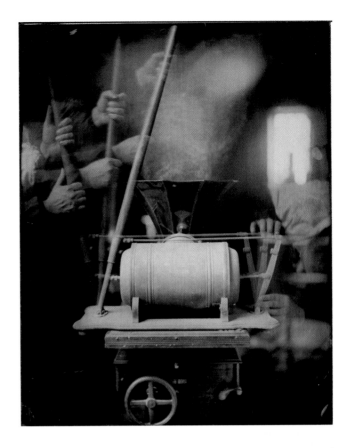

Figure 22–11

Mark Osterman, Blowing Smoke, 2001—tinted ruby glass and burnished ambrotype
This 8" × 10" ambrotype is from Mark's *Confidence* Series.
(Courtesy of The Ransom Center, U. of Texas–Austin)

the immersion tank, or a blotter, and to wipe off the rear of the plate before placing it in the plate holder. This technique prevents any excess silver nitrate from migrating to the front of the plate, a problem that will result in streaks called "oyster stains." Again, take all necessary safety precautions and under no circumstances touch anywhere near your eyes during the process because silver nitrate contact causes serious eye damage.

EXPOSURE

Once the plate holder is in the camera, remove the dark slide to expose the plate to the *inside* of the camera. When this step has been done you may then remove the lens cap from the lens and expose the plate to the subject outside receiving the light. Average exposure times can be as brief as a single second when working outdoors, in bright sunlight, and using period portrait type lenses.

Figure 22–12

Sally Mann, Jessie #34, 2004—ambrotype

A few years ago, Sally began photographing her children again. Although these new images were made with the mercurial inconsistencies of the ambrotype process, and so intimate that the portraits were absent of context, they were, for me, more starkly emotional, and real, than any she had done before. One reviewer wrote that they saw a fierce sense of presence in this work. Perhaps . . . but I feel this work speaks more of acceptance and knowledge . . . and of the importance of the moment.

(Courtesy of the artist and the Gagosian Gallery, New York. © 2006 Sally Mann)

Your personal working style will have to be worked out over time and will depend on several factors such as the lens that you are using, the age of your collodion, and the color of light in the scene. This process is most sensitive to blue, violet, and UV light but less so to shades of red, brown, amber, green, and yellow light. Remember, the success of an ambrotype, or a tintype, are dependent on keeping the deepest shadows from being exposed.

To make a negative, on the other hand, you would give the same scene twice the exposure and develop much longer with a weaker and more acidic developer to build up density. See the formulas to follow.

Note: A proper ambrotype (or ferrotype) needs *the correct* amount of exposure, as does a negative. It's just that a positive doesn't require as much exposure as a negative because you will be using a stronger developer and a shorter developer time. If you underexpose an ambrotype and push the development, you get an ambrotype with high contrast and no shadow detail.

Once the exposure has been made, replace the lens cap on the camera and then return the dark slide to the plate holder. Immediately return to the darkroom, or your antique, wet collodion darkroom wagon, and proceed with development. Development must be done before the collodion dries.

To process the plate, remove it from the plate holder, and then pour the developer across the surface of the collodion commencing from the edge of the plate. Do not pour the developer directly onto the plate, as this will wash away the silver droplets on the surface that are needed for full development.

Adding a drop or two of nitric acid to the developer will give the image a metallic silver tonality rather than the warmer tonalities one would get without the nitric acid. There are many variations of developer formulas and each wet collodion artist has a favorite one. This basic formula from Scully & Osterman is a good one for the characteristic 19th century ambrotype image tone.

THE PROCESS

Wet Collodion Developer: Positives

- 355 ml distilled water
- 15 g ferrous sulfate (or iron sulfate)
- 14 ml of glacial acetic acid
- 18 ml alcohol (190-proof [90%] grain variety) (*or just enough alcohol to allow the developer to flow onto the plate without beading up.*)

Wet Collodion Developer: Negatives

If you wish to develop wet collodion for negatives, just substitute the following wet collodion developing formulas from Scully & Osterman.

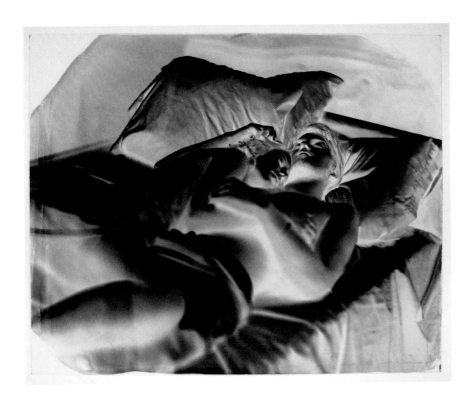

Figure 22–13
France Scully Osterman, The Embrace—
Collodion Negative
Here's the collodion negative that France made
for her albumen print . . . see Figure 21–1.
(Courtesy Scully & Osterman Studio)

Standard Wet Collodion Developer for Negatives

◆ 355 ml of distilled water

◆ 1 g pyrogallic acid

◆ 60 ml of glacial acetic acid

◆ 10 ml 190-proof "grain" alcohol

SOS Iron Negative Developer

This formula is particularly useful for use in hot weather when fogging can be a problem.

◆ 355 ml of distilled water

◆ 9 g ferrous sulfate

◆ 18 g of white sugar

◆ 10 ml of acetic acid

A properly exposed ambrotype will become visible within 3 to 5 seconds. You will see the exposed areas turn darker as they are reduced to metallic silver. Continue for 10 seconds. If the entire image is formed before 15 seconds, the plate was over-exposed. If you push the development longer than 20 seconds, the exposure was probably too short. *Development must be stopped before the details in the shadows are evident or the image will be fogged.* Extended development will result in gray images.

Stopping Development

At this point, the plate is washed with fresh tap water to remove the still active developer. Wash until the water ceases to bead up on the collodion surface. It is very important to wash the plate well before proceeding to the fixing stage that can be done in daylight. You will know that you have done this part incorrectly if you have blue stains on your plate. Again, continue washing until the water no longer beads on the surface of the plate.

Fixing the Plate

There are several fixing options. The simplest method is to use a rapid fixer such as Ilford or Kodafix and mix it up in a conventional film strength dilution. Another fixing option is to make a solution of sodium thiosulfate at a ratio of 150 g to 900 ml of distilled water. The two mentioned fixing agents however will never give as bright an image as those fixed with potassium cyanide . . . the traditional fixing agent for collodion positives. All fixers have a short effective life. You should use a new batch for every fixing session.

Figure 22–14

Chuck Close, Self-Portrait, 2000—daguerreotype

Another contemporary artist who has begun to create work in antiquarian processes is Chuck Close. Known internationally for his printmaking, painting, and photography, Close has pushed the boundaries of portraiture for well over three decades.

(© Chuck Close in collaboration with Jerry Spagnoli Studio, Courtesy the artist and Pace/MacGill Gallery, New York)

Potassium Cyanide Fixer

◆ 14 g potassium cyanide

◆ 950 ml distilled water

The cyanide fixer is made with 14 grams potassium cyanide dissolved in 950 ml water. Be very careful with potassium cyanide should you elect to use that fixer option. This is a very dangerous chemical. Take all prudent safety precautions when using it and keep the solution away from all acids lest you produce a cyanide gas.

It is important to remember that in traditional black and white silver printing the black parts of the image represent the developed silver. In the ambrotype and tintype process, it is the light-colored area that is the developed silver.

The purpose of these fixing baths is to remove the unexposed silver halides. The potassium cyanide version of the fixer is the preferred solution for collodion positives because it works quickly, produced a lighter and more reflective silver particle and leaves perfectly clean shadows in the final image. When using potassium cyanide, fix the plate until the unexposed (light-colored) silver halides are completely removed. Let the fixer continue its action for as much time as the original clearing, usually a several seconds, before moving the plate to a water wash bath. *It is essential that the plate be removed from the potassium cyanide fixer before the chemistry removes too much of the image silver.* If you have fogged the shadows of your image it is possible to clear these areas by extending the fixing stage. Wash the plate for at least a minute in clean water, though extended washing doesn't hurt the image.

Sodium Thiosulfate Fixer for Negatives

◆ 150 g sodium thiosulfate

◆ 950 ml distilled water

When making a collodion glass plate negative, sodium thiosulfate was used as the fixer because it left the collodion slightly darker when seen by reflected light. (See Fig. 22–15, Luis Gonzalez Palma.) It also eliminated the chance that the shadows would be dissolved in the fixing stage. When using sodium thiosulfate, fix the plate until it shows clearing and then extend the time by at least twice that time. Following the fixing bath, gently wash the plate in clean water for 5–10 minutes being very careful not to disturb the fragile collodion surface.

DRYING THE PLATE

Drying is done by using an alcohol lamp or you may air-dry the plate in an open rack. If you elect to use an open flame it is imperative that you move the plate continuously to ensure even drying and to prevent cracking the plate. Be aware that the water dries first and then the collodion coating. During this stage, the image is extremely fragile and all precautions must be taken to avoid harming the image. If you did not clean your plate well the collodion may begin to peel at this stage. Pyro-developed images are also prone to peeling if the plates are not previously subbed with dilute albumen.

Figure 22–15

Luis Gonzalez Palma, Yo #1, 2006—ambrotype

(Yo)—*por años sola me he gestado / poniéndome ese vestido que el tiempo diferia / mis manos disfrazaban sus caricias*

I first saw Luis's work at Houston FotoFest in the 1980s and even a hundred yards away I could tell it was special. In 2006, Luis began working with wet collodion (ammonium iodide). The pieces are tray-developed, fixed with sodium thiosulfate rather than cyanide, and traditionally varnished. They are back-coated with flat black spray enamel and the text is laser engraved into ¼" glass.

(Courtesy of the artist & The Schneider Gallery)

VARNISHING THE PLATE

Ambrotypes on glass and early tintypes (*on japanned iron plates*) were sold in either frames or decorative cases. Because these were protected from the air and abrasion they were often left unvarnished, a condition that also left the image silver a bright silver metallic color. When varnishing is employed, a protective coating of gum sandarac, alcohol, and oil of lavender is flowed over the plate. This varnishing step is, for many artists, the most complicated of all due to the difficulty of making a perfect coating. Unvarnished collodion images are prone to abrasions, peeling, and severe tarnishing over time. The varnishing step will impart a warmer tone to the image and slightly darken the image.

An ambrotype Varnishing Formula

- 414 ml of 190-proof grain alcohol
- 57 g gum sandarac
- 44 ml of oil of lavender

Mix the ingredients together until the gum sandarac has completely dissolved. Then, strain and filter the mix until you have a perfectly clear yellow varnish. You may have to filter the varnish several times before it is perfect. Before the varnish is poured on the dry plate it is a good idea to warm both the varnish and the plate. This is neatly done with a small spirit lamp, that burns alcohol with a controllable flame, and these can be easily found on the Internet. Then all that needs to be done is to pour a small amount in the center of the plate and move the plate around quickly until you have a complete and smooth coating. Pour off the excess back into its varnish bottle.

When the varnish appears to have set, hold the plate over your spirit lamp flame, moving it continuously, until the varnish is completely dry. Be careful not to proceed to this step until the alcohol from the varnish has evaporated or else the varnish will catch on fire and you'll drop your glass plate. This step is not difficult so please don't be too worried. One last note here: if the collodion that you were using is too old, the alcohol solvent in the varnish may destroy the image.

MOUNTING & PRESENTATION OF COLLODION POSITIVES

Single Glass Mount

The collodion image was made on a single glass plate and placed in a case with the collodion side down to prevent abrasion of the image. The plate was blackened to allow the shadows to appear black with a black asphalt varnish, dark fabric, paper, or japanned ferrotype plate. This allowed the viewer to see the image in a "right-reading" positive form.

Note: Applying black paint, black varnish or asphalt directly onto the collodion surface is not recommended. Historic examples are often found in very poor condition.

Double Glass Mount

This double glass method was more expensive and used when a collodion plate could not be turned over as in the case of ferrotypes, ruby glass ambrotypes, or on clear glass ambrotypes with delicate tinting on the collodion surface. Images were presented collodion side up and because of this they were laterally reversed. This allowed the subject to view their image as they saw themselves in the mirror . . . a very natural way of seeing ones portrait.

The Cutting Patent Method

A variant of the positive collodion on glass was invented by James Ambrose Cutting of Boston in 1854. A positive image on clear glass was sealed with a separate piece of glass applied to the collodion side of the plate. The cover glass was permanently cemented in place with small amounts of Canada balsam in the fashion of microscope slide preparation. Cutting used the term ambrotype in his English patent and although it refers specifically to collodion positives mounted in this fashion, all positive, in-camera, collodion images on glass were eventually called ambrotypes and the term became generic.

Relievo Variant

This last presentation method provided the viewer with a 3-D effect. The positive collodion image of a subject seated in front of a dark-colored background was made on clear glass. When the plate was processed, a black varnish was painted on the reverse of the plate but only in those areas where the subject of the image appeared on the plate. An optional method of the Relievo Variant is to expose a fully exposed and processed second plate and then lay the two plates of glass together, providing the impression that the subject was in relief against a light background. The most amazing 19th century relievos feature a complete second collodion image under the first with a scenic background (either real or painted) behind the subject.

TROUBLESHOOTING WET PLATE COLLODION

Failures and Imperfections of Wet Plate Collodion Glass Plates

Here is a very interesting list of some of the things that can go astray when making wet collodion imagery. This is a list from the Household Cyclopedia—1881.

Clouding—universal clouding from over exposure or diffused light in preparation or development of the plate, or alkalinity of the bath, or too much nitric acid in bath, or organic matter in the bath, or the use of colorless collodion; also vapors of ammonia or sulphuretted hydrogen. Such negatives may sometimes be recovered by the application of a weak solution of iodine, followed by hyposulphite of soda.

Spots Upon the Plate—from excess of bromide of potassium in the collodion, impure nitrate of silver in the bath, super-saturation of the bath with iodide of silver, dust upon the glass or coating, the concentration of nitrate of silver by drying before exposure.

Curtain-Like Marks Upon the Edge—from the plate being too dry before dipping, not long enough in the bath to remove the greasy appearance.

Wavy Lines—from the use of a glutinous, thick collodion from want of rocking when pouring off the collodion (common with cadmium sensitigus).

Rottenness of Film—from bad cotton or dipping too soon after proving before properly set.

Oily Lines—from the removal from the bath too soon.

Curved Lines—from the developer not covering the whole plate immediately.

Silver Stains—from reversing the plate between the bath and slide.

Figure 22–16

France Scully Osterman, The Assumption 1999—Relievo Variant triptych, three tinted double-plate relievo ambrotypes, tinted with gold leaf, 16" × 20"

The Relievo Variant provides the illusion of 3-D. In the most common example, the positive collodion image is made of a subject seated in front of a dark-colored background. This is made on clear glass. When the plate was processed, a black varnish was painted on the reverse of the plate but only in those areas where the subject of the image appeared on the plate.

(Private Collection)

Yellow Patches—imperfect removal of the iodide of silver in the fixing bath.

Scum upon the Surface—upon removal from the bath, over iodized collodion.

Image Black and White without Half Tones—from under-exposure in the camera.

Collodion Curls—from the glass upon drying from dirty glass, insufficient alcohol in the collodion, want of roughness of the edges of the glass.

Blueness of Film—want of iodizer in collodion.

Crystals on Film—when dried, hyposulphite not washed entirely out.

Developer Flows Greasily—from want of alcohol in developer.

Circular Transparent Spots—of large size, from pouring on the developer at one place.

Closing Thoughts

The wet collodion negative was used as the primary camera image for all of the major printing processes of the 19th century including; salted paper, cyanotype, albumen, carbon, Woodburytype, lantern slides, Orotones, milk glass positives, Ivorytypes, ceramic photographs, gum, platinum, gelatin and collodion printing-out papers. Dye sensitized collodion negatives were used for the first color processes. As well, as we've already discussed, the wet-plate collodion process was used for in-camera positive images such as the ambrotypes and tintypes and collodion emulsions were used for dry plate negatives, lanternslides and Collodio-chloride POP printing-out papers.

Learning the basics of wet collodion is generally much more difficult than other historic alternative printing processes. Actually, mastering a collodion variant requires a serious commitment. While you can teach yourself from reading this chapter, or other historic literature, the best way to shorten the learning curve is to attend a collodion demonstration, group workshop or arrange for a private tutorial. I've made several wet plate pieces with France Scully Osterman at my side and I can assure you that this is the best way to learn the information.

There are now many competent collodion specialists teaching the basics of the collodion process, though if you have the opportunity, seek out Mark Osterman and France Scully Osterman. Mark teaches the technical evolution of photography, from the earliest Niépce processes to making gelatin emulsions at the George Eastman House/International Museum of Photography. His wife France is equally well informed and I have her visit my alternative process class nearly every year at The Art Institute of Boston.

The Ostermans were the first to teach public workshops, publish serious primary research on the collodion process, and continue to be an influence on the photographic fine art community. They teach historic processes in their skylight studio in Rochester, New York, and at museums and schools internationally. This chapter, though not written by the Ostermans, made liberal use of their writings and formulas by permission and for that I am ever grateful. A more comprehensive manual on the collodion process can be purchased through their web site. For further information contact: Scully & Osterman, 186 Rockingham Street, Rochester, NY 14620. www.collodion.org

Figure 22–17
Mark Osterman, Turning The Tip, 2007—dry plate gelatin neg
This is silver gelatin print made from a hand-coated negative exposed in a skylight studio.
(Courtesy Scully & Osterman Studio)

MAKING, COATING, & PROCESSING A SIMPLE GELATIN DRY PLATE EMULSION*

A LITTLE HISTORY

By the 1870s, there were three major variants of the wet-plate collodion process: preserved (moist) collodion, dry collodion and collodion emulsion. Unlike the former two, collodion emulsion relied on actually adding silver nitrate to the halides in the collodion binder before it was applied to the plate. The basic concept that evolved from making collodion-based emulsions was the beginning of emulsion photographic technology for the next 150 years.

The use of gelatin as a photographic binder was suggested by several people but the first experiments with making silver halide emulsions with gelatin were conducted as early as 1853 by Marc Gaudin. His emulsion, which he called *Photogene*, was based on the combination of iodide and silver and was not successful. It was not until January 17, 1868 when W. H. Harrison published the first serious article on gelatin dry plates in the *British Journal of Photography*. Though imperfect,

---

* © 2007   Mark Osterman, Process Historian, Advanced Residency Program in Photograph Conservation. George Eastman House, International Museum of Photography, Rochester, NY.

Figure 22–18
Coated Gelatin Plates in Rack
Emulsion on the hot plate, coated plates
and an antique invalid cup used for pouring
the hot emulsion.
(Courtesy Scully & Osterman Studio)

Harrison's work helped to create new interest in the possibilities of the process, particularly in England.

In 1871 Dr. Richard Leach Maddox introduced the idea that gelatin emulsions should contain silver bromide, rather than silver iodide; the basis of modern gelatin emulsions for development. Improvements, such as washing the emulsion (J. Johnson, 1873) and ripening by heat to increase sensitivity (C. E. Bennett, 1874) were major contributions to the evolution of the medium. By 1877, gelatin technology was advanced enough to produce commercially manufactured plates though many professional photographers were not yet ready to make the transition from the wet plate collodion process. By 1880, gelatin emulsion plates were being manufactured on both sides of the Atlantic and being used by amateur and professional alike.

Like the daguerreotype, albumen on glass and collodion processes that preceded them, all gelatin emulsions begin as mostly sensitive only to blue, violet and ultra violet light. However, depending on the procedure, early gelatin emulsion plates could be from two to ten times more sensitive than the typical collodion negative. The sensitivity of early gelatin plates was even expressed numerically by how many times faster they were compared to a wet plate.

Making gelatin emulsions in the mid-1880s was not particularly difficult, once the basic concepts were

understood. Hand coating these early plates was also very easy since they could be applied to glass plates under red light. Today, an individual can, without expensive equipment, make a similar emulsion that is perfectly suited for hand coating plates for negatives, positive transparencies, opaltypes, orotones and gelatin tintypes.

The purest gelatin used in the earliest days of dry plates was probably not so different than good quality food grade gelatin available today. It was processed from the hides, bones and hooves of cattle. As the speed and spectral sensitivity of emulsions was increased, the purity of this bovine gelatin became more of an issue and photographic grade gelatin was improved. Photographic grade gelatin was, and still is, much more pure than the food grade variant. It is probably not a coincidence that the Genesee Pure Food Company (later to be known as the Jell-O Company) was established in Le Roy, New York, only a few miles from Rochester and the Eastman Kodak Company, the leading buyer of raw unprocessed gelatin.

BASIC THEORIES OF EMULSION MAKING

It's difficult to know just how much information to include in a basic set of instructions but the following will give the beginner a good start. Though it's really a suspension, the end product of this technique has become known as an emulsion. The goal is to produce a liquid that suspends the precipitated silver halide particles and keeps them from falling to the bottom of the beaker.

Types of Gelatin

There were three basic forms of processed bovine gelatin in the late 19th century; glue, food grade, and photographic grade. Glue is not suitable for photographic emulsions. It is possible to use some food grade gelatin provided that it is of reasonable purity, though photographic grade should always be a first choice.

Poor quality food grade gelatins may contain compounds that increase sensitivity of the emulsion causing non-image fogging. When using food grade gelatin, you will probably need to add more than the formula requires achieving the same jelling characteristics as the photographic grade. This is not a problem as additional gelatin can be added at any time as required to set into a firm jelly at room temperature.

Gelatins are occasionally assigned a bloom rating, important to the setting potential of your emulsion. In the nineteenth century, gelatins were offered as simply hard or soft. If you are able to purchase gelatin with a known bloom rating use the lower bloom (soft gelatin) for the first melt and the higher 250 bloom (hard gelatin) for the reserve gelatin added after ripening. A small percentage of softer gelatin in an emulsion allows the film to be penetrated by the chemicals more easily.

Relationship of Silver to Halides

The emulsion described herein is a silver bromo-iodide variety. The bromides are in excess to the iodides, and the total halides must be in excess to the silver. This is why the silver is always added to the bromide rather than the other way around. This excess of bromide to silver is important during the combining of the silver as it prevents potential fogging in the finished emulsion.

When looking at the formula, however, it appears that the weight of silver nitrate is actually larger than the total weight of the halides. This is because to accurately compare the ratio of silver to halides (bromide combined with iodide) one must convert the gram weights of the silver and halides to the molecular weight of those compounds being used.* This depth of understanding is only necessary if you are formulating your own emulsion formula or substituting one halide for another.

Sensitivity of Gelatin Emulsions

The speed in which you combine the silver solution with the gelatin halide solution (called **precipitation**) has much to do with the speed, density potential and resolution potential of the final emulsion. You have several ways to control this particular variable; the percent and purity of gelatin in the gelatin halide solution, speed of agitation when combining the silver with the halide, the opening of the orifice on your syringe and how quickly the silver streams from the orifice. *The slower the silver is introduced, the larger the silver halide grain size and the more sensitive the emulsion.*

When making your first emulsions, sensitivity is much less important than making a clean, fog free plate, with a good range of tones. A very slow, fine-grained emulsion is made by literally pouring the silver solution from a beaker, into the gelatin halide solution in a continuous stream while stirring.

Ripening and Digestion: Its Effect on Gelatin Emulsions

Once the silver solution has been added to the gelatin halide solution, the sensitivity of a simple bromo-iodide emulsion can also be increased by a process called **ripening**. The hot emulsion is kept at a constant temperature to promote the growth of larger silver halide particles that are more sensitive to light than smaller particles. The hotter the temperature of the emulsion and the longer the ripening period, the larger the silver halide crystal will become. After ripening, the emulsion is chilled, washed and subjected to another heat treatment called **digestion**. This is another opportunity for the silver halides to grow by heating the emulsion for a given period of time.

THE BOOK OF ALTERNATIVE PHOTOGRAPHIC PROCESSES SECOND EDITION

---

*A metaphor might be that the sweetening power of a sugar substitute might be stronger than plain sugar. Equal amounts of these two sweeteners will have a very different effect. Therefore, it will take less weight of the substitute to have the same effect as sugar because of its greater sweetness.

Eventually, heat digestion was replaced by chemical sensitization with ammonia, sulfides or other additives. It is digestion, however, that continues to increase the sensitivity *every time a gelatin emulsion is reheated.* If an emulsion is reheated too many times, or at too high a temperature, it will eventually become so sensitive that non-image fogging is the result. Reheating the emulsion also causes the gelatin to lose its setting characteristics which are absolutely crucial for successful coating and subsequent processing.

Washed Emulsion

When silver nitrate is mixed with a bromide and iodide, silver nitrate reacts with the halides creating a precipitate of light-sensitive silver bromo-iodide. In a process called double decomposition; a by-product of water soluble nitrates is also formed. When making developing-out emulsions with potassium bromide, the resulting water soluble potassium nitrate must be washed away. The first step in washing the emulsion is called **noodling**.

Chilling & Noodling

The potassium nitrate is washed out of the emulsion by first allowing the hot emulsion to chill in a refrigerator to a stiff jelly. Once chilled, the jelly like emulsion is cut into shreds with a silver or stainless steel fork or squeezed through the small openings of a die or mesh to produce emulsion noodles. These noodles give the emulsion a greater surface area which aids in releasing the water soluble potassium nitrate when they are washed in very cold water. Distilled Water is safer than tap water, though most tap water works fine. After washing the noodles they are drained of excess water and re-melted leaving behind only light sensitive silver bromo-iodide in a gelatin binder.

Noodle washing was eventually replaced by dialysis and later, the application of special washing gelatins that precipitated the emulsion so that the potassium nitrate could be siphoned off the top of the emulsion. For the amateur emulsion maker, old fashioned noodle washing is still the easiest approach.

THE EMULSION

The following instructions are based on a typical mid-1880s formula for making about 350 ml of a slow gelatin bromo-iodide emulsion for landscape work. You can make this emulsion more sensitive by adding the silver solution slower combined with ripening and digesting the emulsion longer; but it's better for the novice to start with slow, clean working emulsions.

EQUIPMENT & MATERIALS NEEDED

Equipment

Much of this equipment can be used for other historic photographic processes. The hot plate/stirrer, for example, is one of those pieces of equipment that is a great help for mixing all sorts of things. Pyrex glass beakers in assorted sizes are essential in every historic process darkroom. The crock-pot and potato ricer are however specific to gelatin emulsion making, an activity very similar to cooking.

◆ Safety goggles

◆ Latex gloves

◆ Pyrex "tempered glass" laboratory beakers; one 500 ml & two 300 ml size.

◆ 1½ quart Pyrex "tempered glass" loaf baking dish for chilling

◆ Heat source*

◆ Thermometer (digital thermometers are cheap and perfect for emulsion making particularly when they have a built-in alarm)

◆ 3 quart glazed ceramic or stainless steel mixing bowl

◆ Stainless steel wire mesh drainer big enough to rest in the opening of the aforesaid mixing bowl

◆ Small brown ceramic cheese crock with wire locking ceramic lid

---

* You can use a saucepan on a hot plate or the crock-pot (also listed), but a laboratory hot plate w/magnetic stirrer is perfect for emulsion making and well worth the expense. You can purchase them second hand on line.

- 1-gallon bag made of black plastic sheeting (must be opaque)
- Large plastic syringe (60ml/cc)*
- Heavy-duty stainless steel potato ricer
- Refrigerator (a small dormitory type is perfect or use your household refrigerator) and ice cube tray
- Electric crock-pot with at least 2 temperature settings
- 25" square piece of sheer white nylon or polyester cloth (for filtering)
- Stainless steel spoon
- Glass or stainless steel stirring rods
- Red or deep amber safe light
- Darkroom timer with sweep second hand

Materials Needed to Make 350 ml of Emulsion

The quantities listed below are for making one batch of approximately 350 ml emulsion. Naturally, it is a better plan to buy larger amounts any time you buy these materials, as they are generally less expensive when purchased in quantity.

- 1 liter distilled water
- 10.5 grams potassium bromide
- 0.4 grams potassium iodide
- 12 grams silver nitrate crystals
- 21 grams gelatin (photographic grade is best, but you can use food grade)
- 5 grams chrome alum (added as needed)
- 0.065 grams thymol
- 5 mls 95% grain alcohol

MAKING THE EMULSION
Step By Step

Take the time to read and visualize all of the following steps before you attempt to make the emulsion. You may want to practice Step 5 with plain water to feel comfortable with the technique. Preparing all the materials and equipment prior to working under safelight conditions will make the procedure much easier to perform.

Step 1 Put 3 grams photographic grade gelatin into a 500 ml Pyrex glass beaker with 85 ml distilled water. Allow at least 15 minutes for the gelatin to become fully swollen and easily flattened (or squished) between the fingers. This is called the "first melt" gelatin.

Step 2 Put 18 grams photographic grade gelatin into a 300 ml beaker with about 80 ml *cold* distilled water; or enough to just cover the gelatin. Allow this gelatin to absorb enough water to make it soft as tested between the fingers. This is called the "reserve" gelatin that will be drained of excess water and then added to the emulsion after the first melt.

Step 3 Dissolve the swollen first-melt gelatin by placing the beaker in a hot water bath such as a small sauce pan with water on a hot plate, or in a crock pot with just enough water to the level of the gelatin solution. You may also use a hot plate stirrer *as long as the solution is kept in motion with the magnetic stirrer* set on slow. Using a thermometer, try to keep the temperature around 120°F.

Step 4 Put 10.5 grams potassium bromide and .4 grams potassium iodide in the first melt gelatin and stir the solution until the halides are fully dissolved.

Note: Every operation after this should be done under red safe light. The darker the safe light and the less time you have the emulsion exposed to it, the better!

Step 5 **Precipitation:** Prepare the silver solution by dissolving 12 grams silver nitrate in a 300 ml Pyrex glass beaker with 85 ml distilled water. Heat this silver solution to around 120°F (50°C) and draw half of this solution into the syringe. Slowly squirt the heated silver solution at a rate

---

* The Terumo brand 60 cc Syringe with Catheter Tip is perfect except that the opening of the tip is too wide. Go to the hardware store and buy a tube of glue that comes with a separate tapered tip of the same size. Make a pinhole in the end of the tip with a hot needle and push this firmly over the catheter tip of the syringe.

of 40 ml per minute in a continuous stream *with the tip below the surface of the gelatin halide solution* while you stir it continuously (this is where a hot plate stirrer comes in handy). Refill the syringe and continue until all the silver solution has been added to the gelatin-halide solution. As you combine the silver with the gelatin-halide solution you will see the two clear liquids change into a milky white silver bromo-iodide emulsion.

Note: When making more sensitive emulsions you can be more accurate if you use a musician's metronome to keep you on track as you gently and continuously push the plunger of the syringe. Try to make the plunger pass a single ml marking on every click, or every other click, of the metronome.

Step 6 **Ripening:** After all the silver has been added, ripen the emulsion by maintaining the temperature at around 120°F for 15 minutes with constant gentle stirring.

Step 7 **Adding Reserve Gelatin & Digestion:** While the emulsion is ripening, begin draining all the excess water from the reserve gelatin. Too much water in the reserve gelatin can cause weak, thin images. When ripening is complete, add the reserve gelatin to the emulsion and stir until the new gelatin is completely dissolved. When you first add the reserve gelatin the temperature of the emulsion will fall. Bring the temperature of the emulsion back to 120°F and dissolve the reserve. Once the emulsion has reached 120°F maintain this temperature for about 5 minutes with gentle agitation to digest.

Step 8 **Chilling:** Pour the hot emulsion into the glass Pyrex loaf pan and carefully slide this into the black plastic bag. Secure the opening of the bag so that no light can fog the emulsion. Place the bagged emulsion in the refrigerator for several hours or until completely set to a stiff jelly. The reason that a shallow dish is used for chilling the emulsion is so that it will set the gelatin to a stiff jelly faster and more evenly than if left in the beaker.

Figure 22–19
Chilling Table Leveling
Placing the coated plate onto a leveled chilling table to set the emulsion to a firm condition before drying upright on a rack.
(Courtesy Scully & Osterman Studio)

Note: In the following steps, it is advisable to wear latex gloves; not because of potential silver stains to the hands, but to prevent contamination of the emulsion from your hands.

Step 9 Under red safe light remove the emulsion from the refrigerator and pull the dish from the bag. The emulsion will look white under the safe light (it is actually bright yellow). Scoop out the firm jelled emulsion with the stainless steel spoon and put it into the potato ricer.

Step 10 **Noodling & Washing:** Place the 25" sheer white nylon fabric in the stainless steel wire mesh drainer and lay the drainer in the mixing bowl. Squeeze the ricer to extrude emulsion noodles that will fall into the center of the fabric. When the emulsion is completely noodled into the fabric, gather the edges of the cloth and secure the bag of noodles with cotton string. Fill the mixing bowl with very cold distilled water (add a few ice cubes) and move the noodle filled fabric in the water with you're your hands for about five minutes. Let the noodles soak for five more without agitation. Change the water two more times and wash the noodles as before.

Step 11 **Re-Melt & Finals:** Drain the washed emulsion noodles thoroughly for at least 15 minutes. It is important to remove as much excess water as possible because too much water will dilute the emulsion causing cause weak, thin images. Place the drained noodles in a clean 500 ml Pyrex beaker. Re-melt the emulsion using the electric crock pot at around 120°F and add "finals." The finals listed below are chrome alum, added to make the emulsion set to a stronger film to withstand processing, alcohol to aid in coating and thymol, to prevent bacteria growth. Add the chrome alum solution drop by drop with agitation of the emulsion.

Chrome alum hardener:

The original 1887 formula does not include chrome alum. It is included here to help the novice emulsion

Figure 22–20
Noodling
A stainless steel potato ricer is used for noodling chilled emulsion. Make sure this is a heavy-duty model that will not bend when under pressure. [Note: These images of emulsion noodling were taken by white light for illustration purposes.]
(Courtesy Scully & Osterman Studio)

maker produce an emulsion that does not frill or melt during processing. You may choose to leave chrome alum out of the formula. It can always be added to the emulsion immediately before coating plates.

No chrome alum in the emulsion may result in a very fragile film that might melt off the plate if processed in solutions that are too warm. Too much chrome alum, on the other hand, will prevent the gelatin from absorbing the processing chemicals resulting in thin images and prolonged developing times.

The hardening effect of chrome alum continues long after the emulsion has dried on the surface of the plate, so it's best to use the plates within a week or so to keep

Figure 22–21
Mark Osterman, Eastman Kodak Headquarters, State Street, 2007—hand coated gelatin dry plate negative & positive
This is a test negative of Eastman Kodak Headquarters (I really appreciate the irony of this) and subsequent print made from that negative.
(Courtesy Scully & Osterman Studio)

development time short. There is no way to include the absolute correct amount because the characteristics of each source of gelatin are going to be different. The quantity of chrome alum may need to be decreased or increased as needed. Make only as much chrome alum solution as you will need as it goes bad quickly.

Finals

◆ 2 ml of a chrome alum solution (1.25 grams chrome alum into 25 ml distilled water) . . . Add the chrome alum drop by drop.

◆ 5 mls 95% grain alcohol

◆ 0.065 grams thymol

When the finals are added and fully incorporated into the emulsion pour the entire contents into a brown ceramic cheese crock, cover the opening with a piece of black opaque plastic and secure the ceramic lid with the wire spring. Place the emulsion filled crock in the refrigerator for future use. Remove only what's needed when coating a batch of plates by scooping out the chilled emulsion with a stainless steel spoon. The stock emulsion will last many months if kept cool and protected from white light.

This emulsion is fairly slow by modern standards and only sensitive to blue, violet and invisible ultra violet light. Assume an ISO rating of between 3 and 10.

COATING GLASS PLATES WITH GELATIN EMULSIONS

Coating glass plates with gelatin emulsions is a little different than working with a solvent based binder such as collodion, which relies on evaporation for the coating to set to a firm film. Gelatin emulsions must be heated to a liquid form, and once applied to the glass support, be able to set back into a firm jelly at an average room temperature. This so called "set time" or "setting time," is governed by the ambient temperature of the room, the bloom and percent of gelatin and the quantity of alum added as a "final" to the emulsion.

Shortening the setting time was almost always done by quickly lowering the temperature of the emulsion. The most common approach was to level a piece of marble or thick glass and place the coated plates upon the surface until the emulsion cooled and became firm. The setting of gelatin emulsions on paper supports was generally accomplished by chilled air.

The earliest commercially made gelatin dry plates were coated by pouring the emulsion by hand. An 1884 account of the coating operation at the Cramer Dry Plate Works in St. Louis was described as "eight busy men, with pitchers of emulsion on one side, a pile of glass on the other and in front of them, a peculiar leveling stand."*

The following instructions are based on the techniques of the early 1880s, before the invention of cascade or transfer coating and continuous belt chilling chambers. This system of hand coating with a chilling table is not difficult to master and enables one person to make dozens of plates in one sitting. The only real limitation is the capacity of the drying box.

EQUIPMENT & MATERIALS NEEDED

Equipment

- Glasscutter
- Cork backed straightedge
- Small sharpening (whet) stone
- 2" wide natural bristle paintbrush
- Soft natural hair make-up brush
- 2 wood plate racks (see Appendix F)
- Liquid dish detergent
- Rottenstone or calcium carbonate powder
- ½ yard fine cotton or linen cloth cut into 5" and 8" squares
- Small stainless steel container with lid (an old stainless steel film developing tank is perfect)
- Electric crock-pot with 2 temperature settings
- Small ceramic tea pot, antique invalid cup or glass gravy separator
- Electric laboratory hot plate
- Deep red safe light
- Paper towels
- 2 1' × 1' marble tiles or ¼ glass plates
- Small spirit level

- 2 wood leveling stands (see Appendix F)
- Drying box (see Appendix F)

Cutting & Cleaning Glass Plates

Window glass is good enough for hand coated photographic plates. Make sure you purchase these from a framing supply house in unopened boxes. The plates should be interleaved with paper to prevent surface scratches. If you have never cut glass before, pay a visit to a stained glass shop, purchase the best glasscutter you can afford and ask for a demonstration.

Cut the glass to the desired size and never lay the plate surface down on anything or it will become scratched. Place the plate upright against a wall or in a wood rack. It is extremely important to remove the razor sharp burr on all the edges on both sides with a small hand sharpening stone. Dust off the powdered glass dust with a stiff natural brush. This is also a good time to check if the plates fit your holders before you coat them.

Apply a drop of detergent to each side of the glass and wash the plate under warm running water rubbing the surface thoroughly with a small square of cotton cloth. If the plates are particularly dirty you may add a dusting of fine rottenstone or calcium carbonate to each side with the detergent. Keep washing in running warm water without the cloth until the water sheets off evenly. Handling by the edges only, place the plate upright in a rack on a piece of blotting paper to dry. Once dry, breath on the surface of the plate and rub the condensation with a clean piece of the larger cotton cloth squares until you see no streaks.

Heating and Pouring the Emulsion (*under red safe light*)

The whole coating procedure requires very little time; less than ten seconds for a 5" × 7" plate from the initial pour to placing the plate on the chilling table. It is similar to coating collodion plates, though not exactly. *Naturally all of the following is performed under deep red safe light conditions.* Before you turn off the white lights, level your chilling tables using the spirit level.

---

* *Philadelphia Photographer, Jan 1884, p. 11*

Figure 22–22

Coating the Plate triptych

In this triptych sequence you are seeing, from left to right: 1—the pouring of the hot emulsion onto the heated glass plate; 2—tilting the plate so that the emulsion flows to the far corners; 3—pouring excess emulsion back into the cup from the near corner.

(Courtesy Scully & Osterman Studio)

Step 1 Remove the emulsion from the refrigerator. Scoop out enough cold gelatin emulsion for several plates and place this in a stainless steel container (developing tank) with a lid. Put the tank containing the emulsion in a heated crock-pot and with enough water to keep the emulsion warm without having the container float or flip over. Heat the emulsion until it is very liquid. The actual temperature will depend on the pouring qualities of each batch of emulsion.

Step 2 When the emulsion is thoroughly liquefied, pour some through a large square piece of clean cotton fabric into the pouring cup (I prefer the antique invalid cup). Allow the emulsion to settle so that the bubbles rise to the top and pop. The pouring cup can be kept warm in the crock-pot between pouring plates.

Step 3 Slightly heat the plate of glass by placing it on the surface of a warm (not hot) laboratory hot plate covered with two layers of paper towels. While the plate is still warm hold it in the left hand with the fingertips supporting the back of the plate. Give the plate a quick dusting with the make-up brush.

Step 4 Holding the pouring cup in the right hand, pour a sufficient quantity onto the center on the plate (pouring too little is worse than pouring too much). Keep the plate level so that the creamy emulsion forms a perfect circle.

Step 5 Gently tilt the plate so that the emulsion flows progressively to all four corners without going over to the backside. Once the plate is completely covered, gently let some of the emulsion flow off one corner of the plate and back into the pouring cup and immediately afterwards pour some of the excess off from the opposite corner into the pouring cup.

Each corner from which you poured the excess will drip a small amount of emulsion that rolls to the back of the plate. Do not worry about this, it is typical of hand-coated gelatin plates and this artifact can be seen on historic examples. Any emulsion on the back of the plate can be removed with a razor blade after the emulsion is dry or after the negative is processed.

Step 6 Gently rock the plate for a couple of seconds so that the emulsion redistributes evenly on the surface. Immediately place the plate on the leveled chilling slab leaving a lip to hang over the edge of the slab for subsequent removal. The emulsion should still be warm and still fluid enough to level itself on the surface of the plate before it begins to set to a firm even coating.

Step 7 As the gelatin begins to set up you will probably see some dimples on the surface and possibly some dust. Move the plate to the next chilling table until the emulsion is firm enough to place upright on a rack in the drying box. You can test the firmness of the emulsion by touching one corner with your finger, though with experience you'll eventually have a sense when they're ready to be removed from the slab.

The slower gelatin plates are dried the better. Fast drying can cause ridges in the surface of the emulsion. Make sure the drying box is absolutely light tight but fitted with adequate ventilation. Collect the dry coated plates the next day and place them in a light proof box interleaved with clean paper until needed.

PROCESSING GELATIN EMULSION PLATES

The earliest developers used for gelatin emulsion plates were based on either **ferrous oxalate** or **pyrogallic acid**, known simply as **pyro**. Unlike the calotype, albumen negative or collodion processes that preceded gelatin technology, all of the developing agents for processing gelatin emulsions were used in an **alkaline** state. Ferrous oxalate was one of the first developers used for gelatin plates, though it fell from favor by the end of the century. Pyro was introduced in the 1850s to develop collodion negatives and has continued to attract devotees well into the 21st century for development of silver based film stock. Pyro development produces warm brown silver deposits with a slight yellow stain.

By the 1890s, **hydroquinone** and **metol** based developers were being offered by photographic suppliers. Metol developers produced cool, blue-black silver deposits and developed very quickly though with little density. Hydroquinone development resulted in warm black silver deposits that developed slowly with greater density potential than metol. By the late 19th century, most photographers chose either pyrogallic acid or a combination of metol and hydroquinone, simply called "MQ."

A typical developer formula for processing gelatin emulsions has the following elements; the **reduction agent** (pyro or metol/hydroquinone), an alkaline **accelerator** (ammonia or sodium carbonate), a **restrainer** (usually potassium bromide) and a **preservative** such as sodium sulfite. By knowing the function of these components, a photographer could tweak the formula to suit specific needs and correct exposure problems to some degree.

Development of emulsion plates is most easily done in a white tray so that the progress of development can be easily viewed by safe light. All other chemical operations can be done in any type of tray, though Pyrex glass is always the best choice as it is easily cleaned. Development is by a red safe light. The effect of over or under exposure can be seen during development and the knowledgeable photographer has the opportunity to adjust the developer as needed to produce the best possible results. It was typical in the 19th century for the photographer to have small dropper bottles of accelerator (ammonia or calcium carbonate) and restrainer (potassium bromide) solutions at the ready near the processing sink.

Processing the Negative [under red or deep amber safe light]

The exposed plate is placed, emulsion side up, into the white tray containing enough developer to cover the plate. The developer should be used at a temperature of around 65–68°F. It is necessary to rock the tray during the entire development so that fresh developer is always in contact with the emulsion.

When developing by inspection, the most common mistake is to stop development too soon. The maximum density areas of a negative always look much darker when working under safe light. It will be necessary to lift the plate from the tray and inspect the progress by looking through the plate, illuminated from behind by the safe light. No development time can be assigned, as there are too many variables with hand-made emulsions. An average, properly exposed landscape negative develops gradually with the sky visible first, followed by architecture and eventually well lighted foliage. Do not expect to see details in the deep shadows of foliage due the insensitivity of a blue-sensitive emulsion. Development can be carried out for 20 minutes if needed.

Once development is judged to be complete, the plate is washed under gentle running water for two minutes or in a tray with two changes of water and gentle agitation. Do not use an acid stop bath as this may shrink the emulsion causing frilling. Fix the negative in a tray of sodium thiosulfate for five minutes with occasional agitation. Wash the plate in several changes of fresh water or running water for at least 20 minutes and then place on a rack in a dust free place to dry.

FORMULAE

Kodak Dektol can be been used effectively for processing the emulsion described earlier in this section. Begin by using it undiluted and dilute with water if you feel the maximum highlight density is too strong. You may also make your own MQ (metol/hydroquinone) style developer. Kodak D-49 was originally formulated for processing bromide prints though it can be used undiluted for negatives made with ordinary blue-sensitive emulsions. When making alkaline developers, the ingredients should be added to the hot water in the order listed and each ingredient fully dissolved before the next is added.

D-49 Developer

500 mls   distilled water   (around 120°F)
3.1 grams   metol
45 grams   sodium sulfite
11 grams   hydroquinone
45 grams   sodium carbonate
2.1 grams   potassium bromide
Cold distilled water added to make a total 1000 ml

As with all MQ developers, metol and hydroquinone are the active developing (reduction) agents. Potassium bromide is the restrainer. Sodium carbonate is the accelerator and sodium sulfite, the preservative. If you want more density than extended development will provide, increase the hydroquinone. You may also raise the pH by adding ammonia or more sodium carbonate. This is most easily done by adding drops of household ammonia.

A good starting point is about 4–6 drops in 100 ml developer. Pour the developer from the developing tray into a glass beaker, add the ammonia to the developer solution and then pour the developer back into the tray. Raising the pH with ammonia or sodium carbonate will make the gelatin soften and more permeable so that the developer can be more effective, though too much will cause the emulsion to fog, lift from the glass and cause frilling.

Decreasing the potassium bromide restrainer in the formula will also cause the developer to work faster, though by doing this there is always a chance of causing fog. Tweaking the developer formula as needed eventually becomes intuitive.

Sodium Thiosulfate Fixer (working solution)

1000 ml   tap water
150 grams   sodium thiosulfate

TROUBLESHOOTING

Peeling Problems: On occasion, photographers had problems with the emulsion lifting from the edges of the plate; an effect called "frilling." Assuming the glass support was properly cleaned, this usually happened when the developer was either too alkaline or the temperature of the developer was too hot. A simple 2% alum hardening bath before or after development, or a little alum added to the fixing solution was usually enough to prevent frilling. If peeling is a persistent problem, pre-coat your glass plates with a 2% subbing solution of hard gelatin containing ½% chrome alum using the same method described for coating with the emulsion.

Image does not appear or takes too long to develop: The plate was either not exposed or the emulsion was too hard due to excessive chrome alum. A presoak in 70°F water for about 5 minutes will usually soften the emulsion for development. You may also add a drop or two of glycerin to the pre-soak. Adding a few drops of ammonia to the developer will also help, though excessive ammonia will soften the gelatin too much, causing frilling and fog.

Fog: There will always be some degree of fog present in gelatin emulsions. Too much fog is a problem. The most common causes of fogging are pre-exposure of the emulsion or the coated plate to white light or a faulty safe light. If the thin shadow cast on the negative by the plate holder is without fog; the problem is overexposure in the camera. Fog is also caused by using too warm or too alkaline a developer. Poor quality gelatin also causes fogging.

Thin, flat images: It is common for the beginner to produce thin images. This is usually due to overexposure combined with underdevelopment. Overexposure is responsible for detail in both the deep shadows and strongest highlights of the image. Using cold or dilute developer, not developing long enough or with enough agitation will also result in weak, thin images. Density is gained by proper exposure combined and prolonged processing with a strong developer and adequate agitation. Excess water in the emulsion from not draining the reserve gelatin or the washed noodles effectively is common cause of weak, thin images.

Too much contrast: High contrast is the result of underexposure and over development. If there is no shadow detail despite prolonged development, it is a clear sign of underexposure.

APPENDIX FOR GELATIN DRY PLATE EMULSION

There are three things you will need to construct before coating gelatin emulsion plates; 2 plate racks, 2 wood leveling stands for the chilling tables, and the plate drying box.

Wood Photographic Plate Racks

Vintage plate racks can be purchased at antique shops and on Internet auctions, though availability is uncertain. You can make a rack by drilling holes into the top of a wooden board and fitting a series of wood dowels. The size plate you wish to coat will dictate the size of the materials. A grooved plate rack can also be made, though this type is more requires the use of a table saw.

Leveling Stands for Chilling Tables

Materials
2 - 8" × 8" pieces of 3/4" birch plywood
6 - 1½" × 5/16" bolts
6 - 5/16" nuts
6 - ¼" flat washers
6 - 5/16" coupler nuts

A leveling stand is essentially a short adjustable tripod, with wide, flat top. Drill three 5/16" holes through the plywood. Countersink the holes so that the heads of the bolts sit below the surface of the plywood when installed. Install the bolts and attach the washers and nuts to the bolts on the underside of the plywood. Thread the coupler nuts on the end of each bolt. The coupler

Figure 22–23
Leveling Chilling Table
A leveling table is made of plywood featuring three adjustable leveling legs. The marble-chilling slab rests upon the leveling table in use. You can use plywood or you can try constructing a leveling table, using threaded nuts for the fine tuning, out of white plastic pipe that is abundant at Home Depot. The pipe can be configured as a tripod allowing for a very portable, and expandable, system. *(Courtesy Scully & Osterman Studio)*

nuts allow adjustment of the leveling stand from below. The marble (or glass) chilling plate rests upon the leveling stand to complete the chilling table.

Plate Drying Box

In time, you may want to make a sturdy wood box with filtered ventilation, but for your first experiments a cardboard drying box is easy to make and will do the job. You will need one, good quality, corrugated cardboard box and a couple extra sheets of single weight cardboard for constructing the ventilated light trap. The size of the box is dictated by the size and quantity of the plates you wish to coat in one session. While any tape will work, water-soluble gummed paper backed tape (available at art supply stores) never fails over time.

Simply put, the box must allow adequate ventilation without exposure to white light. Holes must be cut into either end of the box and then fitted with a light trap as illustrated. Tape the lid closed with black tape after you fill the box with plates and for extra protection pace a piece of dark cloth over the top.

Further Reading

The 19th century photographic journals are a great wealth of gelatin emulsion technology, particularly for the individual making and coating their own emulsions on paper and glass. English language publications include the *Photographic News, British Journal of Photography, British Journal Almanac, Philadelphia Photographer, American Annual of Photography and Photographic Times Almanac,* and *Anthony's Photographic Bulletin.*

The following out-of-print texts should be sought by every emulsion enthusiast. The more common titles are often quoted like scripture by a growing subculture of emulsion makers.

The Practical Working of the Gelatin Emulsion Process Captain W. De W. Abney, Piper & Carter, 5 Castle Street, Holborn, E.C. London, 1880

Modern Dry Plates or Emulsion Photography Dr. J.M. Eder, E. & H. T. Anthony & Co. No. 591, Broadway, NY 1881 (English edition)

Wilson's Photographics E.L. Wilson, No. 853 Broadway, New York, 1881

The Photographic Negative W.H. Burbank, Scovill Manf. Co., New York, 1888

Photographic Emulsions, Their Preparation and Coating on Glass, Celluloid and Paper, Experimentally and on the Large Scale E.J. Wall, American Photographic Publishing Co., Baker, 1929

Photographic Emulsion Technique T.Thorne Baker, American Photographic Publishing Co., Boston, 1948

Photographic Emulsion Chemistry G.F. Duffin, Focal Press, London & New York, 1966

Silver Gelatin; A User's Guide to Liquid Photographic Emulsion Martin Reed & Sarah Jones, Argentum/Aurum Press, 25 Bedford Ave., London, 1995

Finally, there is the Internet, where you will find a huge amount of information posted by individuals with a wide range of experience. In most cases, however, you will be better served to read the original texts and evolve though your own personal experience.

Figure 22–24
19th c. Gentleman Coating the Plate
(Courtesy Scully & Osterman Studio)

Light Marking: Photographic Alternatives

OVERVIEW & EXPECTATIONS

This chapter is a little different from the ones that preceded it. As in the others, there will be quite a few examples of specific techniques to learn and try but that is not the primary intention. This chapter is about alternative ways of making and thinking about photography. I'll be discussing concepts and reflecting on how ideas are processed when thinking about making marks with light . . . and not simply describing the syntax and processes used in the construction of photographic images. As I wrote in the beginning of this book, to paraphrase Mark Twain, it hardly matters that your technique is perfect if your imagination is out of focus.

The last chapter in this book could be considered, in a sense, the first chapter in my new book, *The Book of Photographic Alternatives* . . . perhaps. With that optimistic mind-set, I'm going to test drive a few ideas. I've invested the past 30-plus years of my life, at both Harvard University and The Art Institute of Boston, doing what I love. I have been guided by a collection of concepts pertaining to visual literacy, that I first addressed in my graduate thesis at R.I.S.D. in 1971. These were the core truths of my thesis . . .

Figure 23–1

Anselm Kiefer, *Heavy Cloud*, 1985—lead, shellac on photo

When asked the question about whom my favorite artist is, the first person I mention is Anselm Kiefer. In the 1970s, he created a series of landscapes that were melancholic metaphors for both Germany and its recent history. In some respects, they were similar to the emotional-, and color-, neutral symbolic landscapes of the 19th century German painter, Casper David Friedrich. In the 1980s, Kiefer began adding physical elements to some of this work, as in this altered photograph with lead.

(Courtesy of The Metropolitan Museum of Art)

Figure 23–2

Christopher James, *Minor White at M.I.T.*, 1971—photograph with special enamel zone paints
One of the things that I enjoyed most, after finishing my graduate studies at R.I.S.D., was to go to Cambridge and argue with Minor White about photography. For me, it was a little like being able to go and visit Stieglitz . . . I knew I would get hammered but I learned a lot. Minor didn't like my work very much . . . even after I showed him my special "zone" paints.
(Courtesy of the author)

Core Truths of Creativity & Learning

Truth 1 The things that you do best in your life you teach yourself.

Truth 2 Play, and the spirit of play, is the only consistently perfect way to learn anything. Every little bear in the woods knows this is true.

Truth 3 The industrial revolution's assessment paradigm does not apply to the arts (with the exception of the bottom-line driven popular music industry) or to arts education.

Truth 4 The history of humanity is known only through the art it leaves behind. Think about it, when was the last time an archeologist unearthed a political speech?

Truth 5 Don't ever be frightened by anyone who possesses a rich imagination . . . this includes yourself of course.

Truth 6 The single greatest gift a mentor can offer to a student is the gift of seeing and that includes respecting what that student's eyes see. Most of this gift will be forever cherished.

My intention is to talk about alternative ways of making and thinking about photographic images. I am interested in how to inspire you and others . . . perhaps your own students, with conceptual ideas that address the creative process individual rather the institution that houses that person. The final section of this chapter is based on an essay titled Visual Literacy: Revolution, Arts, & Mirrors and it deals with a few thoughts that I've been tossing around for some time.

I believe that it is difficult to be creative if you are afraid to fail and that you will never learn to sing if you are afraid to hum. This principle applies to both success in the arts and success in the "art-world"—and, yes, these are truly two separate concerns. In this section I will try to provide some important issues to consider, by those who teach and learn. Along the way I will show and tell in areas such as Lazertran, Solarplates, image transfer, etchings, and more. I'll begin the chapter with one of the best examples that I have left to offer you . . . the toy plastic camera.

THE PLASTIC CAMERA

This section covers a little history of the plastic camera beginning with The Great Wall Plastic Factory in Kowloon in the 1950s, and describes the attributes and varieties associated of this great toy. The primary reason for plastic camera to be in this book, as it really isn't an alternative process, is to make a point about the value of play in art. A good deal of this writing examines why you might want to use a cheap toy camera and how it has become an integral element of my teaching and work as an artist. Some instructions are also provided on how to modify the toy camera so that you can get the most from the experience with the minimum amount of frustration. It is also a nice medium-format negative to look at, scan, and use to make little contact prints.

A LITTLE HISTORY

Once upon a time . . . there was a novelty manufacturer in Kowloon, Hong Kong, called The Great Wall Plastic Factory. Their contribution to the history of photography was molding several pieces of plastic into a Diana camera that made nifty looking images. The Diana, with mandatory taping of all the seams, and a few other modifications, became the camera of choice for photographers seeking alternatives when making images that expressed what they saw, rather than living with the optical perfection of modern photographic equipment, i.e., adult cameras. For many photographers, this camera represented a perfect tool with which to address that old "mirrors and windows" conflict that has been raging for the last century . . . the "mirror," where the image is an expression of the artist, and the "window," where the image defined the information within the photograph.

Beginning with its development in the late 1950s, and early sixties, The Great Wall Plastic Factory made and sold the Diana, and the Diana F (*with a built-in flash*), for about $2.25 apiece. Shutter speeds were tenaciously capricious but if you were really curious you could calibrate and test your camera's shutter and find that its speed ranged between 1/15 to 1/250 of a second. Apertures were equally unpredictable but most cameras featured apertures that fell between ƒ4.5 to ƒ16 . . . not too bad for spring loaded shutter that got slower over time.

Focus was another whimsical characteristic and it was essential that you knew just how out of line your camera's viewfinder was in order to capture what you

Figure 23–3

Holly Roberts, *Small Wolf w Forest*, 2000

I have been a big fan of Holly Roberts's work since the first moment I saw one of her painted photographs. Holly begins her work by preparing a panel with acrylic paint. Then she collages digital prints and varnishes the surface. The final stage is to paint with oils, allowing the push and pull of the paint, and painting, to create an enigmatic, compelling, and mysterious work of art. *(Courtesy of the artist)*

Figure 23–4

Christopher James, *Market*, Cairo, Egypt—1992—plastic camera

This image was shot in an open-air market, in Cairo, with a plastic, and modified, Diana camera. It is part of a series dealing with the final moments of this angel-like chicken's life. An inter-negative was generated on a piece of SO-132 film (sadly, no longer made) and used to make this print. *(Courtesy of the author)*

Figure 23–5

Lucy Soutter, *Dog Run*, Hyde Park, London—1988

Lucy, now a respected critic and writer in London, created this whimsical diptych of taking the dogs out for run while a student of mine at Harvard. One of the great things about the plastic camera is its predilection for illustrating, in its frames, the moment-to-moment simplicity of memories.
(Courtesy of the artist)

wanted on film. Many plastic camera shooters carry a bag full of cameras, each with the specific camera's idiosyncrasies scratched into the body for identification. Shooting with them requires something akin to a sniper accounting for wind and distance. Eventually, desiring the plastic lens, but tired of the bag of cameras, I had one of my Dianas fitted with a Graflex shutter and the least scratched single element plastic lens in the bag.

In the years since The Great Wall Plastic Factory created the Diana, the plastic camera has re-emerged with nearly the same shape and parts but with a different name attached to its body. Some, like the unpredictable Diana, are considered treasures and sell for premium collector dollars on eBay. Other plastic camera types held together for a very short time and were shunned due to chronic failures or, ironically, too much perfection in the plastic lens. Among the cameras that have fit the prerequisites of the plastic toy camera are: Anny, Arrow, Arrow Flash, Asiana, Banner, Debonair, Diana, Diana Deluxe, Diana F, Dionne F2, Dories, Flocon RF, Hi-Flash, Holga, Lina, Lina S, MegoMatic, Panax, Photon 120, Raliegh, Rover,

Shakey, Stellar, Sun Pet 120, TraceFlex, Tru-View, Valiant, and Windsor. Of these, the most commonly found these days is the Holga.

The Holga is occasionally too well made and predictable for me to feel emotionally connected to it. Basically, in order to be considered a true and worthy toy camera, the following qualities have to be present; a mysterious shutter speed, minimal aperture control, no focusing control, a romantic interpretation of subject and light, light leaks, the potential for the dreaded fat roll and other disasters, and infinite charismatic charm. There is a certain Zen-like peace attached to the act of making pictures and not knowing if they will come out. Read Eugene Herigel's *Zen and the Art of Archery*, 1953, for an explanation of this point. This is the book that was a detour on the road map for the abstract expressionist painters of the late 1940s and 1950s.

Toy Camera Philosophy

Throughout the 13 years that I taught at the Carpenter Center for Visual Arts at Harvard University, and for the last 15 years at The Art Institute of Boston at Lesley University, I've worked on eliminating the myth of "great equipment equals great photography." My intent has been to create an attitude in my students about image making that has, at its core, the love of craft, image, and printmaking married to the phenomenon of play; the one truly universal learning process that all living things with faces enjoy and share in common. I wanted to instill in my students several salient and critical truths regarding learning. These are closely tied to the beliefs about creativity that I articulated at the beginning of my career—and the beginning of this chapter.

Learning Truth 1 You've got to love doing something before you will invest your time and resources learning to do it well.

Learning Truth 2 Almost everything you do really well in your life, outside of such natural gifts like breathing and digesting, you will teach yourself.

Learning Truth 3 Play is the most effective and persuasive method to teach anyone anything. To paraphrase Aristotle, ". . . play and introspection are the only two human pursuits that are engaged in just for the hell of it."

With that premise in mind, at the beginning of each semester or workshop, I purchase several dozen plastic toy cameras and make a gift of them to each student. Initially, the cameras were the classic Dianas, then Banners and Dories. I would also provide a roll of black gaffer's tape to ensure a light-tight toy, although Holga has almost eliminated this need, and a couple of rolls of 400 ASA 120 mm film per student. Ilford has a nice 3200 ASA speed film, which is terrific for the low light, plastic camera, experience. In the past few years the Holga has improved and now sports foam pads behind the film spools (*preventing the dreaded fat roll*) and a push–pull lever to switch between regular and time exposure. It's getting close to being too good.

I would ask my students, as I have every foundation class, to put away their sophisticated gear and their perception that good equipment could mask, and make up for, any shortcomings in technique and creativity. I

Figure 23–6

Jonathan Bailey, *Playa del Carmen*, 1984

Jonathan is one of the champions of plastic camera simplicity and elegance . . . as this image well represents.

(Courtesy of the artist)

offered them the opportunity to experience, with their new "toys," several significant things that I call the Five Plastic Virtues.

The Five Plastic Virtues
Plastic Virtue #1 — The True Memory

The plastic camera is an image-making tool that records life the way it is remembered rather than the way a conventional lens, far more perfect than the human eye, renders it.

Plastic Virtue #2 — The Element of Gesture

Gesture is a creative device and a key element of expression in all of the arts. Unfortunately, due to the technically dependent nature of the medium, photographers have traditionally been unable to share this characteristic . . . unless something goes wrong and the artist is lucky, or has the know-how and experience to translate the accident into a creative option. Gesture is a difficult thing to locate in a photograph and an even more difficult treasure to access in one that is made with digital tools. In the alternative process arena, with all of the hand-applied emulsions, gesture does become part of the photographic equation.

Figure 23–7
Christopher James, *Morning*, Calcutta, India, 1994
Somehow, trying to describe that morning in Calcutta with anything other than a single plastic element toy camera would have been inaccurate. An adult camera lens, regardless of its perfection, would not have seen what I was feeling . . . if you know what I mean.
(Courtesy of the author)

Plastic Virtue #3 — The Contentment of Being Anonymous

The nice thing about using a "toy" to make your art is that only those with similar experiences will take you seriously. In this, you may be a little bit like Jacques-Henri Lartigue, who was able to produce images of great energy and beauty in part because he was a 9-year-old child and no one felt threatened by his camera or his interest in making images with it. A beginning student can move about freely, encountering curiosity rather than suspicion . . . even in this odd paranoid era of political fear mongering.

In my own experience, shooting in many different cultures and countries with nothing but my trusty and indestructible Dianas (*the crème de la crème of cheap photographic equipment*), I have been able to photograph in places where "real grown-up" cameras are forbidden or unwelcome. People assume that I am not quite "all there" pointing a child's toy wrapped in black tape at the subject of my intentions. As an aside, the confessionals in the Vatican (*where you are not allowed to photograph*) make exceptional "changing bags" for switching film or salvaging the occasional "fat roll."

Plastic Virtue #4 — The Pleasure of Simplicity and Play

A plastic camera has few qualifying controls and therefore eliminates the problem of doing something wrong . . . a great relief to a beginner. The cameras are inexpensive (*Holgas sell for around $20.00 although I recently saw that the Sundance catalogue is selling them for $75.00 because they are now so chic. The camera is accompanied by a useless roll of black tape*) and incredibly simple. There are two aperture settings, sun and sun, or cloud with lightning bolt, which doubles as a hot shoe setting. There are also four focus options: a contemporary lonely single person (*you'll be shooting in this setting most of the time*), a 1950s Disney-definition of the perfect nuclear family, an academic committee, and the mountain range of your choice. The camera can be dismantled, modified in an infinite number of ways, and rebuilt to allow you to achieve specific image-making goals.

Plastic Virtue #5 — Plastic Inspiration

Due to the simplicity of these cameras, they can be thought of as tools rather than machines, and their output as "gifts" rather than life and death negatives. The great thing about the play/learning duality is that almost everyone, from beginning student to experienced photographer, learns to love the process of image making while exploring the techniques that are traditional and essential to the medium. Once a student is in love with the process, much like falling for a cuisine or a culture, the student will be eager to digest the nuances and beauty of that process's language.

As for the argument that the plastic camera is a gimmick, and that it does not teach a person how to be a photographer, I ask critics to remember that photography is simply making marks with light. I would also pose this question . . . *Where is the greater value to a young artist: learning through positive play, mistakes, and failures or learning using technically predictable tools and assignments that may not allow for fortuitous mistakes and interesting failures?* To me, the indelible

Figure 23–8

Rebecca Welsh, *Hydrangea*, 2007—digital plastic bag camera

In the last few years, my wife Rebecca has been working hard to humanize the syntax of digital photography . . . not a simple task considering the noun - verb relationship that defines digital imaging. An issue that is most relevant to her work is the recording of gesture and emotional light. One of her solutions . . . a simple plastic zip-lock bag.

(Courtesy of the artist)

benefit of process is in the play and the love of making images that are unexpected and personal. The philosophical difference . . . the gift of a lifetime versus the information of the moment.

The plastic camera is one of the best solutions to the problem of creative lethargy. The expense and replacement costs are minimal, and thus it also addresses concerns of equal quality equipment being available to all students by putting the same camera and technology in each student's hands. It also generates a willingness to play, within a technology-based learning process. Virtually every level of student from grade school to graduate school begins to think of the camera as a toy to create images that express perceptions that are as diverse as the individuals who make them. Best of all,

this "toy" will mold a person's affection for seeing and photography for life . . . rare achievements for any learning process.

PLASTIC TIPS

The Lens Cap is a Good Frisbee . . . Throw It

Throw away the lens cap immediately. You are using a single element plastic lens and it doesn't need protection.

The Viewfinder & Lens Are Only Remotely Connected

The viewfinder and the lens are two separate parts that are only remotely working together . . . both point in the same direction.

Shutters Are Meant to be Taken Apart

If you want a very low-tech solution to the shutter speed
issue you may opt to remove the entire shutter mechanism
from the camera and use the lens cap as a shutter. Take it off
the lens and you expose the film . . . put it back and you stop
the exposure. I recommend this technique for very low light
situations where you might want to illuminate your subject
with multiple test "pops" from a hand-held strobe. By the
way, it takes 75 pops to make a decent negative of a face in a
totally dark environment. The new Holgas have a time/bulb
setting lever that makes this all pretty elementary.

Tape Your Holes

To eliminate the only light leak problem that the
Holga seems to offer, remove the camera back, look
inside the main camera compartment and turn the
camera upside down. You will see two small holes on
the inside on the geometric shape lens housing that
serves as a support for the viewer and hot-shoe set up.
Take two small pieces of black gaffer's tape and put it
over these two holes.

To keep the film from fogging on a sunny day:
place a piece of black gaffer's tape over the red,
acetate frame counter window, on the back of the
camera, during normal use.

To keep the camera from opening accidentally:
tape up the silver, camera back, sliding bar releases . . .
especially if you're using the designer strap that comes
with the camera. If you are running with your camera
(*because, say, the Swiss Guards at the Vatican don't
want you to take pictures*), the bars are likely to slide
upward and cause the back of your camera to fall off.

The Dreaded Fat Roll

A "*dreaded fat roll*" situation is when your plastic take
up spool (also referred to as the "free gift") on the right
inside of your camera doesn't roll the exposed film
tightly enough. This means that it is increasingly difficult for you to turn the advance winder. The new Holgas
have foam pads in the camera, behind the plastic spools,
to prevent this problem but I would advise carrying
some tin foil with you, to wrap the film in, just in case.

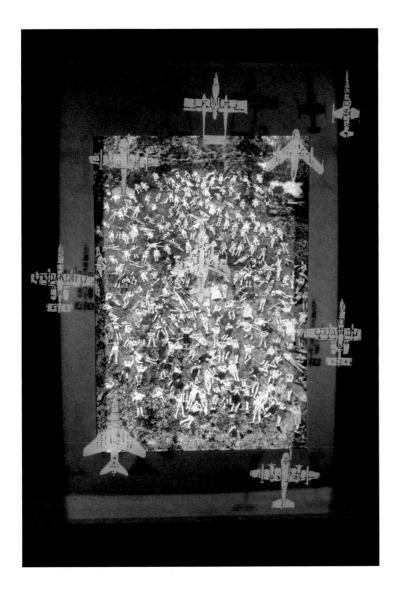

Figure 23–11

Rosemary LeBeau, *I Dream Awake . . . I Dream of Falling Dolls—1998* (24" x 36" hand-colored laser transfer, glass encased with sand-blasted airplanes on glass)

This extraordinary piece really needs to be seen in person . . . and lifted. Like many of Rose's works it begins with a found image that is laser copied and transferred to a substrate. Rose then hand colors and selectively edits within the imagery to discover qualities that were not initially evident. To complete the piece, Rose placed the image in a box and sealed it with thick glass that she sandblasted airplane icons upon.
(Courtesy of the artist)

If you have an older model Holga and want to avoid the fat roll problem, take the end flap from your film box and fold it over itself about 2 to 3 times (*about 2 mm*) and slip it under the plastic spools before closing the camera back on a new roll of film. This will create tension on the spools and should eliminate the fat roll predicament. Be sure that you put a little finger tension on the unexposed roll when advancing the first few turns into the camera (*up to the first manufacturer's text on the backing paper*) . . . this gives the film the right idea.

Avoid Low Light

To prevent thin exposures: shoot in the brightest light you can find because this camera gives traditional HP-5 or T-Max an infrared look. Avoid low light unless you have a modified shutter for long "bulb"–like exposures, are using a strobe attachment, or shooting 120 mm, 3200 ASA, film.

On that note, processing plastic camera film is a great opportunity to experience the graphic potential of "pushing" your film in development. You will likely get blown-out highlights and a lot of grain and contrast but if you're not sure that you had enough light to work with, it is more prudent to extend the development time 10%—15% rather than having nothing on the negative.

Finally, lighten up a little . . . this is a toy you're working with. If you approach the plastic camera with the proper attitude, it will reward you with all of those great feelings you had when you first decided that being a photographer was a perfect way to spend your life.

IMAGE TRANSFER PROCESSES

One of tools that I enjoy using quite a lot is the color copier. Like a scanner, it's quite like a very large and expensive plastic camera . . . great for playing and dis-covery with few expectations for image perfection.

How a Color Laser Copier Works

When you make a copy on a color laser copier the machine assembles four colors—yellow, cyan, magenta, and black (CMYK) – to form the final image. The photo-conductor creates "charge images" using blue, red, green, and white illumination in successive order and then uses those colored images to form image patterns of yellow, cyan, magenta, and black toner particles. These toner particles are then superimposed to form the final image. The copying entails a stage called "*fusing.*" This fusing process permanently bonds the thermographically sensi-tive toner to the paper. When the loose toner image on the copied paper reaches the fuser unit, then the image made of toner particles is permanently fused to the paper by means of heat, roller pressure, and silicone oil.

Color copiers are part of an ever-expanding family of contemporary electronic imaging systems that are adding to the myriad options we have as visual artists. Laser copies from these machines are capable of producing a wide variety of output yielding both positive and negative imagery that can be used in your work. The potential of this technology is seemingly unlimited . . . as digital com-patibility improves, and home computer and printer capabilities, become more cost-accessible. The film and paper images produced by these disparate sources can be utilized as intermediate and final stages (*and as appropriated additions*) in the translation of your cre-ative process. A few of the examples of this might include the manipulation of existing imagery, fabric transfers, montage, collage, drawing, sculpture, digital morphing, and giant modular murals.

Using the copier to create CMYK (*cyan, magenta, yellow and black*) separated negatives and/or masks for gum bichromate is particularly effective and cost efficient. Copiers also allow you, in these post modern times, to appropriate and utilize almost anything in print as long as you alter the original concept, form, or meaning in the process of expressing yourself. As a rule, copyright problems occur when there has been lit-tle effort to create a personal perspective or reinterpre-tation on an appropriated image. Appropriated work that is derivative, that is, work that is *derived* from another source and that expresses a *different intention* in an original manner, appears to avoid copyright infringement issues.

" © "—Copyright

Copyright (©) is a symbol that stands for a constitutionally mandated law protecting original creations by artists, authors, and anyone else who converts an original idea into a tangible form. Intellectual property reflects a different bundle of ideas and deals with issues that are the products of the mind and intellect. Oddly, (he says with a touch of sarcasm) this concept is not entirely understood by anyone and is the matter of quite of few controversial encounters in the courts.

In these post-modernist* times, when the value of that movement's stature has been impaired due to its over-inflated language, it is often difficult to differentiate between an original idea and the expression of that idea. Under copyright law, only the tangible expression of an idea is protected. Regardless, conceptualization and appropriation are non-contact sports and it is quite common to find images from contemporary sources incorporated into the work of active artists. In collage, digital montage, and interdisciplinary works of art, there is always a risk of infringement, but it can be argued that fair use, parody, commentary, and reinterpretation do not constitute a violation. It is my understanding that as long as the appropriated imagery is altered in an original way, and sufficiently expresses an artist's original intent, then that is not considered an infringement on copyright. Making an acrylic lift of a portion of a reproduced image in your work may well be free of litigation issues, unless you happen to become rich and famous. If you feel clarification is needed, I recommend that you click on Boston arts lawyer Drew Epstein's informative Web site at www.photolaw.net. Drew is a specialist in photographic and artistic copyright law and a nice guy as well.

One of the most conventional, versatile, and graphically interesting options, involves breaking down the thermographic dyes on the copy with a solvent and transferring it to the paper, or fabric, of your choice. For many artists influenced by the work of people such as Robert Rauschenberg, this transfer stage is a beginning of a new way to express oneself. The following techniques are a few of the ways that you can transfer laser copy images. Later in this chapter, we'll discuss an equally interesting transfer system using digital prints.

At the Copy Store

Many commercial copy establishments are open 24 hours a day . . . especially those adjacent to a college campus. Consider going for a first visit in the early morning hours, say around 3:00 a.m. The students who generally work those late shifts are bored out of their minds and often relish the opportunity to play with you and your ideas with their copy machines. Make friends with these people because they will be the ones to help you when you finally figure out what you want to achieve in laser copy form. Often, once a level of trust has been established, you may actually be allowed to operate the copiers without supervision, simply paying for what you produce when your work is done. Another option, of course, is to get a part time job in a copy shop and work the late shift.

In any event, there are a few things to keep in mind when working in this genre. When ordering copies, ask that your copy be printed in "mirror mode" so that when you flip it over to transfer to another paper, the image will be "right-reading." When your intention is to transfer the laser copy image, ask that it be intentionally overexposed. Always have your black and white images copied as if they were in full color C-M-Y-K mode. This request adds additional layers of dye to your paper that will make for a more saturated transfer since there is more toner on the copy.

Materials You Will Need

- A quality substrate: paper such as Arches, Lana, Fabriano, Rives BFK, or Arches' Platine or a fabric such as canvas, silk, or cotton.

- A piece of Plexiglas® that is larger than the paper or fabric that you are working on.

- A cheap paintbrush or woodblock printing brayer.

---

* The term Post-modernism originally described the practice of appropriating an architectural style from the past in the design considerations of contemporary building. . . Doric columns on a ranch houses, for instance. This term has come to represent work that exhibits a reference to, or inclusion of, evidence of the culture that it originates from. For even more confusion on this pressing critical matter, find a current MFA (Master of Fine Arts) candidate and ask for an explanation of the debate surrounding Modernism and Post-modernism theory.

Figure 23–13

Donna Talman, *Presence #12*—1998—solvent laser copy transfer, batik wax and wood

For the past several years, Donna has been intensively exploring alternative photo processes and the possibilities of image transformation. She is less drawn to objective reality, what the camera is designed for, and more interested in the psychological, emotional, and spiritual aspects of existence. Her approach is to transform images in a way that combines reality with these other, less recordable, elements. Donna created this compelling montage by solvent transferring laser copy images and incorporating batik wax, resists, and wood in the transfer process.
(Courtesy of the artist)

- Several copies of an image; high-quality color or black and white laser copies.

- Tape, scissors, PO Blender pens for smoothing color, and assorted art toys.

- A commercial solvent such as Kleen Strip®, oil of wintergreen, or citric acid, all of which are easy to locate.

Be really careful with paint strippers like Kleen Strip®. They work very well but the fumes are horrendous and they eat most surfaces they come into contact with - including your skin, the paper cup you put the solvent into, and your desktop. An excellent solvent is Duracryl®, an automotive painting solvent. This product works very, very well and is great if you can find it. Check out automotive supply businesses or body shops.

Solvent Transfer Technique

First, go outside. If you do not heed this advice and have a long working session with the solvents, you will likely experience a distinct lack of well-being. Be rational and intelligent . . . don't subject yourself to solvent fumes without adequate ventilation. Begin the process by placing your paper on a hard and clean surface such as the piece of Plexiglas® because that material will stand up to the solvents and save your table surface.

On a light table or window, register the copies and tape them together at the top. Lay them face down on the paper that you are transferring to and tape the registered set on the receptor paper. This allows you to check on your progress while you are working, without losing your registration. To facilitate this registration, do this: take each of the copies (*3 or 4 will be fine*) and trim each of them at the top so that when they are registered, each piece of paper will be slightly different from the others in the group but still in perfect registration where it matters . . . in the image portion. This technique will allow you to make multiple transfers of the same image in registration on the paper by simply ripping off a used copy and flipping down the next one in the pack. When the copies are registered and taped together, tape the corners down so that the copies and final print paper stay in one place. Then "*prime*" the receptor paper with a coating of the solvent.

Next, flip the first laser copy face down on the "primed" receptor paper. Doing this means that your print is now reading backwards, which is why you ask for the "mirror setting" when getting your copies made. Dip your brush in the solvent and quickly coat the back of the first copy. Now begin to burnish the laser copy as if you are pressing the copy's image into the receptor. You may use a woodblock brayer, a stubby brush, or a metal or wooden spoon for this step, although the spoon may show lines. You may add more solvent to the back of the first copy if necessary and if you don't get the density you are looking for all you have to do is remove the first copy page and flip the next one down to repeat the process.

There is no need to coat the base paper a second time and doing so will likely mess up your first transfer.

Think about working in a grid pattern or in small areas, in sequence, rather than as a single transfer operation. You will see the image as you work and when the first sheet is completely painted, lift it up very slowly and check your densities. If you are satisfied, then you are done. If not, tear the copy that you have been working on away from the registered stack and flip the second copy in the set down on the receptor paper. Repeat this process until you are happy. Color transfers almost always take several sheets to give the saturation you will likely be looking for. Black and white transfers take fewer sheets but tend to get "gooey" as you lift the copies off the paper. Remember to lift the donor copy slowly from the base paper that you are transferring on.

To complete and fine-tune your transfer, you can use P-O blender pens on the finished print to smooth any rough areas or flaws. These blender pens can be found in most art supply establishment and are common tools for graphic designers and illustrators. P-O Blender pens are filled with a clear solvent and come in a variety of tip widths. They are less messy and easier to work with than liquid solvent due to the small amount used during a work session. The working life of each pen is relatively short so it is a good idea to purchase them a dozen at a time.

I have used citric acid (*all natural Citra-Solv®*) and oil of wintergreen in place of the more toxic commercial solvents and have been quite pleased with the results. Oil of wintergreen seems to work best but leaves an everlasting impression on the audience whenever the work is displayed indoors. My former student Rose Lebeau uses a product called Duracryl® that is common in automobile painting shops.

Note: You should be aware that in many states it is illegal to dispose of used solvents and thinners. Please read all safety warnings and dispose of the solvents in an environmentally safe fashion.

The Varneytype Transfer Process

An interesting thing happened when one of my workshop students, Frank Varney, got frustrated with his work and decided to play with transfers and cyanotype together. He was in a workshop class with Rose LeBeau, whose husband, Bill, worked with an automotive and silkscreen solvent called Duracryl®. Rose offered Frank some of the Duracryl® and he accepted. Still unhappy with his transfers even though they had been greatly improved, he decided to make a cyanotype print on top of the Duracryl®–transfer and discovered that the Duracryl® transfer *repelled* the cyanotype emulsion. This same effect can be realized on top of both lithographic prints and etchings, as well.

Frank got inspired and began making Duracryl® transfers on printmaking paper. He then coated the transferred image with a cyanotype solution and using a straw, blew the cyanotype emulsion away from the Duracryl® image before it had had a chance to set up and dry. After the cyanotype was exposed and washed, he had a nice dimensionally layered piece with the cyanotype image lying behind colored Duracryl® transfers.

Water/Dry Mount Process

Take a piece of quality watercolor or printmaking paper and soak it in warm water, or check out the Cat Carrier Humidity Box in the Argyrotype chapter for a method for making your paper damp without making it soaking wet.

Place your laser copy face down on the damp paper and put both pieces into a hot (250°F–300°F) dry mount press for 1 to 3 minutes. Most art/photography departments will not enjoy the fact of you putting wet paper and thermographic dyes in their dry mount presses. Be sure to ask first and perhaps purchase your own base pad and safety papers, so that the press is not compromised for those who will follow you. The image will often transfer well and will occasionally provide a very intense color field. In this method, the colors seem to separate and transfer in reverse of the order that they are printed so the time in the press becomes a factor. The sequence order seems to be black, red, orange, yellow, blue/green. Hot press papers work best because transfer bases but don't automatically avoid heavily textured or cold press papers as they often add a different quality to the work.

Transfers to Fabric

Another transfer option using a dry mount press or an iron instead of a solvent to move the image employs the fabric transfer films and positives that you can

Figure 23–14

Joy Christiansen, *The Dialogue*, 2003— two wingback chairs, Epson iron-on transfer on upholstery with embroidered text, 72" x 48" x 36"
This installation piece consists of two Victorian chairs facing each other as if joined in conversation . . . or battle. Conversations occur within the embroidered text that is embedded in chair's fabric. The text and transferred images of the figure succeed in bringing the chairs to life, such as a memory of what may have occurred in the past.
(Courtesy of the artist)

Figure 23–15

Brenda Kleinfelder, *Musings From the Gatherings—1998* (*20 x 20, laser transfer on fabric and miscellaneous media, hand-sewn*)
Brenda Kleinfelder, made a portfolio of image transfer and hand-sewn works, of her neighbors, while working as a long-line fisher-man in Alaska. These fabric pieces are mostly whimsical in nature but nicely illustrate the strength of the subjects who brave the weather for her photographs and performance works.
(Courtesy of the artist)

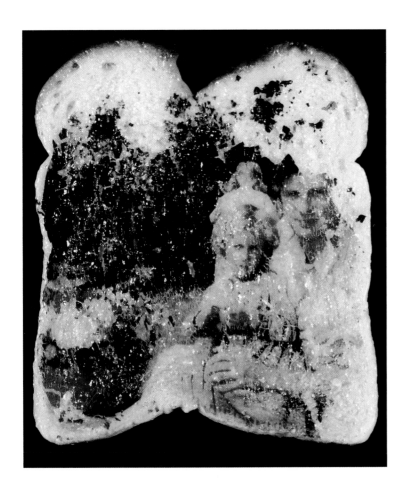

Figure 23–16

Caroline Reeves, *Family Portrait—1999 (Lazertran on slices of toast)*

This is a Lazertran transfer on breakfast toast from Caroline's family portrait series. Caroline made this series while participating in a semester residency, away from her college in England, at The Art Institute of Boston.

(Courtesy of the artist)

have made in the same laser copy establishments or at home on your desktop printer. Epson, for instance, makes heat transfer sheets specifically for its printers. These transfers can be combined with many of the alternative processes on fabrics (*cyanotype, Van Dyke, etc.*) for some amazing effects. Because fabric is the base material for both the heat transfer and the alternative process, you may begin to think about such things as sewing, fabric montage, clothing, murals, and bed linens.

Recently, I was looking through the latest edition of *The Fiberarts Design Book*. In years past, this book was dedicated to traditional fiber crafts but in the last few years, according to its editor, more and more fiber artists are employing photography, the digital imaging, digital transfers (*see Lazertran, this page*), alternative processes, and laser transfer systems with their fiber arts. This, I believe, is the shape of things to come and I am hoping that you can get a feel for this new vision

from the examples in the book. Again, experiment a lot and learn what you can do to make the copier, and associated transfer processes, work for your intentions and personal vision.

LAZERTRAN TRANSFER PROCESSES

Lazertran Transfer Papers for Artists

The Lazertran Transfer process is a relatively new variation on color laser transfer and one that enables you to transfer images onto nearly every surface imaginable. Caroline Reeves, a former English student of mine at The Art Institute of Boston, made wonderfully comical transfers of her family on toast. She made an effort to transfer her cousins onto a fried egg but that proved to be one of the few surfaces that was problematic for the material. The Lazertran process is relatively simple and with a little practice you will be able to transfer laser copy images on most papers, ceramics, glass, wood, plastics, and assorted foods.

Laser copy images are essentially transparent and can be overlaid repeatedly, allowing one image to be seen through another. This layering allows the creation of multiple and modular image construction. By utilizing the "tileing" ability of most high-end copiers (*where mural size images can be proportioned from smaller ones*), you can create large pieces by having a single, or montaged, image made to virtually any size that you desire. Lazertran makes a product called *Lazertran Silk*, which is a simple iron on transfer paper that can be used with most transparent fabrics and doesn't create an artificial stiffness in the transferred image. This has the look and feel of an old process used by Catherine Jansen called Sharpography.

Using Water-Based Adhesive Lazertran for Paper or Canvas

All Lazertran papers have been specially developed for use with color photocopiers and are manufactured by Tullis Russel Brittains in accordance with ISO 9001 quality standards. Lazertran is a "water slide" paper that allows the transfer of color images onto almost any surface including glass, paper, canvas, ceramic, Perspex® (*a high-quality acrylic material*), metal, plaster, wood, stone, and vacuum-formed plastics. Because the transfer is transparent, these images can be laid on one another for multiple image impressions. These are the basic steps for canvas and paper. Other substrates and information on Lazertran Silk and Lazertran Etch will follow.

Step 1   Make a color laser copy on the specific Lazertran paper by removing the protective tissue and running the transfer paper through the copier so that the image is printed on the shiny side of the paper.

Step 2   In the studio, stretch a piece of canvas or pin down a piece of paper so that the surface you intend to transfer on is flat. Then, coat the paper's surface with an acrylic matte polymer emulsion or, if using canvas, with an acrylic primer. Allow the coating to dry thoroughly. While the surface is drying, cut the copied image on the Lazertran paper to the required size. Remove the borders and trim as necessary.

Figure 23–17

Margret Hall, *Self in Red*, **2006—Lazertran on canvas/mixed media**
Maggie made this large piece during her Foundation Seminar at The Art Institute of Boston. Maggie relates that the gist of this Lazertran piece is that no one's straight, everyone's tangled. It's also about the little pieces or our past and our present that mesh together to lead us to the future. The threads are most often tangled and hard to read, but like any good twine, once they are there they will never break.
(Courtesy of the artist)

Step 3   The next step is to immerse the Lazertran image in a bath of warm water and allow it to soak for 1 minute. It will curl naturally so don't be alarmed.

Step 4   Apply a thin coat of the polymer emulsion with a short nap paint roller (for smooth surfaces) to the specific area you wish to transfer to. These paint rollers can be large or very small, as those used for painting trim.

Step 5   Carefully remove the Lazertran from the warm water and lay it face down on a sheet of newsprint. Place your hand flat on the backing and partly slide the image off. Then flip the image over and position it face up on the surface you are transferring to. Gently slide the backing paper off from underneath.

Step 6 Using a rubber wood block brayer, gently roll over the surface, removing any bubbles until the transfer is laying flat. When the image is dry (after a few hours), apply another coat of co-polymer or matte acrylic medium to protect the image. Additional images may then be applied using the same technique. Lazertran can be applied over acrylic paint and oil and acrylic can be applied over the Lazertran surface.

Fixing a Lazertran to Paper, Wood, Stone, and Plastic with Turpentine

Follow the steps listed above until you get to the part where you lift the Lazertran paper from the water and lay it on the newsprint. At that point, take a brush and coat the surface that you are applying to (the ceramic, glass, stone, wood) with a generous coating of turpentine. Now, lay the transfer paper, face down, and work the transfer into the surface. For a transfer onto paper, carefully roll the transfer into the paper substrate and leave it for 8 hours. The transfer will melt and become part of the paper. You can assist the integration of the transfer into the pores and crevices of materials like stone, wood, and toast by spraying a fine mist of turpentine onto the material.

Lazertran Silk

Lazertran Silk is used to transfer images onto sheer Habuti type silk and also as a fast etch resist. Keep in mind that it is difficult to transfer onto open weave silks such as Organza, or Chiffon, as the toners only adhere to the weave and fall off the holes—leaving a ghost of the image. Here is a rough idea of the steps to make this technique work.

Step 1 Gather the images you want to transfer onto silk and head to your local laser copy center. When you are ready to copy, have your images reproduced on the Lazertran Silk transfer paper and return to your studio or workspace. Set up an ironing board, plug in your steam iron, and set it to the "silk" setting, without steam.

Step 2 Iron your silk flat on a silk fabric setting.

Step 3 Set the iron hot enough for the toners to stick to the silk.

Step 4 Lay your silk over your image and iron until the silk is stuck to the image.

Step 5 Without pulling at the paper, place the silk, with the Lazertran paper attached, in clean warm water, paper side down, and leave until the paper falls off.

Step 6 Lift the silk carefully from the water and lay the image face down. Then, lightly iron with a cool iron until dry.

Step 7 When dry, turn the silk over, image side up, and place a sheet of silicon baking parchment over the image.

Step 8 Iron through the baking parchment with a hot iron and then allow it to cool. When cool peel off the parchment. This method produces a beautiful result and can be rinsed in warm water but will not stand up to a vigorous wash.

Lazertran Silk: Temporary Tattoos

Step 1 Copy onto the Lazertran Silk transfer paper in mirror or reverse view.

Step 2 Apply a thin coat of Spirit gum (the adhesive used in the theatre for false beards) over the image and apply it to the skin.

Step 3 Press well until stuck then wet the backing paper.

Step 4 Keep wetting until the backing paper slides off.

Step 5 Go and be dangerous-looking.

Step 6 Return home. Your temporary tattoo can be removed in a hot shower or by using makeup remover.

Lazertran Silk: On Ceramic and Other Non–Absorbent Surfaces

Step 1 Have your image printed in reverse using a laser copier machine.

Step 2   Condition white polymer clay according to brand guidelines until it can be easily worked. Smooth, or roll, clay out to a flattened shape of desired size.

Step 3   Cut, or tear out, your image from sheet of Lazertran Silk and place it, image facing down, on the flattened surface of the polymer clay. It is important to have the image fully touching the surface of the clay at every point to avoid an incomplete transfer. Smooth the image down firmly into the clay.

Step 4   Allow the Lazertran image to stay in contact with the polymer Clay for about 30 minutes.

Step 5   Place the clay with the Lazertran Silk image attached into a bowl of water. Leave for about 2 minutes.

Step 6   Swish the water and the paper backing will float off the polymer clay leaving the full image attached to the clay.

Step 7   Allow the clay and image time to fully dry.

Step 8   Bake the clay in your oven at a temperature and time directed by individual manufacturer.

Step 9   Cool and seal with acrylic gloss medium or polymer clay varnish if desired.

🔧 **Note: If you wish to make an image transfer onto a rounded or domed surface, leave the clay with the image on for a few hours then you can shape the piece without the colors cracking.**

Lazertran Etch as an Etch Resist for Printmaking

Lazertran makes a product called Lazertran Etch, which, when using a color copier, is capable of replacing most existing photographic etching systems. Your image is copied onto Lazertran Etch as a negative and affixed to a metal etching plate using an iron. The plate is aquatint-compatible.

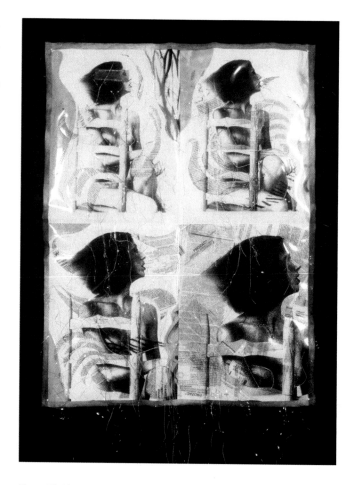

Figure 23–18

Patty Kennedy—*Zafred, Matter Over Mind—1995*—laser transfer on acetate and silk with text

This artist's quilt was made by making transfers to acetate and embellishing the concept with additional elements such as silk strands and text. *(Courtesy of the artist)*

Lazertran has recently discovered that Isopropyl Alcohol, available from the pharmacy, can be substituted for real turpentine in their etching process. This may suit many printmakers as the smell is more tolerable and the product, which is basically rubbing alcohol, is far less toxic than turpentine. Use in a well-ventilated room and follow the warnings on both the turpentine and the alcohol containers. Another reason for using isopropyl alcohol is that some new types of toners dissolve in real turpentine so alcohol has to be used to remove the decal after baking it onto your plate.

Note: Some printmakers of late have been having trouble with bubbling. This can be due to the toners not being fused properly during printing. If fusion of the powdered toners is not complete then as they turn from dust to liquid tiny air bubbles are released under the decal. To avoid this, after printing your image, and before soaking it in water, just pop it into a hot domestic oven for several seconds or until the black toners go very shiny. You can also run a hot air gun (paint-stripper) over the image until the toners go shiny. This will help enormously with this problem.

Step 1 Copy image in black & white, in a negative rendition, using a color photocopier, onto a sheet of Lazertran and then cut the image to the size of plate. Bump up the density of the toners to get good solid blacks. You may have to work with the image in Photoshop first, invert it and print the negative version out for the copier.

Step 2 Soak the Lazertran copy in water and then place the decal image side down onto the metal plate. Wash off any gum from the decal and using a soft rubber squeegee to expel all air bubbles, creases, and moisture.

Step 3 Put the plate on the bottom rack of a domestic oven at a very low temperature to remove any moisture. By low I mean the lowest temperature the oven will permit. Leave it there for at least 1 hour or longer. Increase the temperature slowly over the next hour and a half until the decal melts and becomes tacky. This can occur within a range of temperatures depending on how long the plate has been left in the oven.

Step 4 After cooling the plate, place it in a bath of pure turpentine until the decal washes away leaving only the toners on the plate. You can use a soft brush to help remove the decal and you will feel the clean metal (no longer slimy) when it is ready. This takes about 15 minutes.

Step 5 If you are using isopropyl alcohol to remove the decal then do not use a bath but pour a little of the alcohol onto the plate. Leave it for a short time and then wipe it away with a non-abrasive cloth or paper. Repeat this step until the decal is gone and you are back to the metal. This will take some time and quite a few applications of the alcohol. Be sure to remove all of the decal, as any residual decal will block the plate from etching. Wash with hot water and washing up liquid.

Step 6 Carefully wash the plate and any melted decal in warm soapy water.

Step 7 The toners are then removed with acetone, wintergreen oil or alternatively heat until the toners melt and wipe off. Finish with metal polish.

Step 8 You are now ready to etch. An aquatint can be applied at this point. This method can also be used on glass and metal if you want a full colour image and wish to remove the decal

SOLARPLATES

For those who are interested in integrating traditional printmaking techniques with their images, or in placing images on steel surfaces, there is a terrific product distributed by Dan Welden's company, Hampton Editions, Ltd., that goes by the name of Solarplate. The Solarplate technology is enticing because it is both a safe and uncomplicated introduction into graphic and photographic arts plate making. Solarplates are made of steel and are manufactured with a UV light-sensitive polymer emulsion that is only affected by light and water. Using Solarplates is simple and an acid-free alternative to etching or embossed relief printing and can be employed easily by anyone familiar with the basic working processes of a printmaking studio and photographic lab. Solarplates come ready to use in precut sizes ranging from 5" x 7" to 18" x 24", with well-written instructions for their use.

Figure 23–19

Dennis Olsen, *Scudo*, 2005 Porcelain w/Solarplate Impression

Dennis, who is the president of the Santa Reparta International School of Art in Florence, Italy, makes his porcelain tablets by using very thin layers of clay into which he presses exposed and processed Solarplates. The bone china pieces were first made in plasteline using his normal method of pressing Solarplates into the surface. They were then cast in plaster and slip cast in bone china.

(Courtesy of the artist)

As with other contact-based exposure procedures, all you will need is a positive or negative film, glass plate, cliché verre, acetate, or photogram stuff. Any areas of the plate that are blocked from UV exposure by the transparency will remain water-soluble. All areas that have been affected by the UV light will harden and will not wash out during the water development. The exposure and development principles here are very consistent with the way you would be thinking about a gum bichromate exposure. The difference being that if you intend to take the print to the traditional intaglio printmaking stage on a press, you use a film positive, rather than a negative, to make your exposure.

Exposing a Solarplate with a positive transparency, followed by water development, results in a negative *intaglio* plate that is recognized by its etched depressions that will accept ink for printing on paper. The word *intaglio* comes from the Italian *intagliare* meaning "to carve out or cut into." The original, unbitten plate surface that is wiped clear of ink with a cheesecloth, after inking, will be higher than the ink-filled etched grooves (*that will escape the wiping*) and will print as highlights (*no ink = no impression = highlight*). If you were to expose a positive image in a right reading state to a plate and etch it, it would end up on a developed plate as a negative image reading backwards. This negative, backwards-reading image would then be inked, wiped, and printed, resulting in a positive right-reading image on paper. You may, of course, elect to make the plate as individual statement without extending the process to a press. A transparent negative will result in a positive relief image of your negative. This type of plate can be inked and shown as a powerful ink and metal statement and will have a look that is conceptually in the same neighborhood as Naomi Savage's wonderful inked metal plates.

You are not restricted to using photographically based imagery. Artwork for transfer to the plate can be made on a great variety of surfaces, such as hand-painted or digitally derived acetates. You can also work on a variety of transparent surfaces with many different materials, such as paint, ink, litho crayons, and photogram objects, and using Solarplates would be an ideal time to mix your media a little. Consider using a contact transparency and laying acetate with text on top of it prior to the exposure. Remember to think about the way this text will read at whatever point you decide to stop the process. Once you have determined what you will lay on the Solarplate's UV-sensitive polymer emulsion, begin to set up the plate for exposure by making a layered sandwich, starting from the top to bottom. (*Use a contact-printing frame if you have one large enough for the plate and film that you are using. If not, use a sheet of clean glass to compress the transparency to the plate.*)

Materials You Will Need

- Your transparent film, artwork, acetate or photogram objects. Be sure that you determine how it will be rendered once the development is done. The normal placement is emulsion to emulsion.

- The Solarplate, UV-sensitive plate, polymer emulsion side up

- A piece of compressed rubber, or bubble wrap, to lay the plate on

- A hard flat surface, such as a board, for moving the work around between the lab and your exposure area

- A set of clamps to hold everything together

Once you are ready with this layered set-up, move into the sunlight and expose the Solarplate for between 2 and 12 minutes in direct sun. This is obviously an average exposure recommendation and you will likely experience an assortment of correct exposures at different times of the day and year. Different transparent materials will always require a test of some kind in order to be sure. **Always buy a few small plates to use as tests before committing an 18" x 24" plate to the sun.** Once the exposure is complete, move the plate to a tray of 68°F water. The water development is used to "*etch*" the polymer plate rather than using a more traditional acid bath for the same purpose. The longer you develop the Solarplate in water, the deeper the intaglio cut in the polymer.

Once your Solarplates are ready for "etching," take a very soft nylon vegetable scrubbing brush and gently scrub the emulsion while you pour temperate water on the surface. During this washing-out stage you will begin to see the image emerge on the plate. You will also see a milky residue in the wash—which will remind you that you should be wearing latex gloves while you're doing this task. After the development, blot the plate with paper towels, and blow-dry the surface with a hairdryer. Then, take the plate and return to the sunlight for a post exposure (*hardening*) of between 5 and 10 minutes. After that, you can do what you want with the plate, from inking to painting to intaglio printing. Be careful to use only oil-based inks (as you would with most traditional etching techniques) because the Solarplate emulsion is affected by water.

Double–Exposure Technique with an Aquatint Screen

If you decide to take your Solarplate into the traditional intaglio process, then there is the possibility of the polymer emulsion wearing away or washing out. The solution to this is a double exposure on the plate with an aquatint screen. This step allows you to retain extensive areas of deep black in the intaglio image because you are supplying a screened texture to the plate and image. The double-exposure technique eliminates the problem of the polymer washing away . . . a situation that would create large open areas that could not hold the ink during a "wipe." This is what printmakers call an "open-bite" in the traditional etching process. By manipulating exposure times, you can vary the depth and richness of blacks in your image, and eliminate problems that are associated with deep grooves holding too much ink, a situation that causes ink-bleed during printing. Here's how to make a double exposure with an aquatint screen, a product that you can easily obtain at a decent art, graphic arts, or print-making supply retailer.

Figure 23–20

Dan Welden, *Denver Moment*, 2005—created at "Open Press" in Denver in collaboration with master printer Mark Lunning in 2005

Denver Moment was created with two separate images. The first was drawn with Stabilo 8046 pencil on thick glass, which was grained with 220 carborundum grit. The Solarplate was exposed through the glass for approximately 1.5 minutes in the sun. In order to hold the dark tones, an aquatint screen was also exposed separately to the same plate for the same time. The second plate was created by painting directly on the Solarplate with etching ink. It was exposed for 2 minutes in the sun. The ink was removed and the plate processed with water. In order to give the plate a strong relief, it was washed for about 7–10 minutes. Both plates were printed on Hahnemühle Copperplate 300 gram, intaglio first, relief second. *(Courtesy of the artist)*

Step 1   Make some test strips so that you can adjust separate exposure times for both the image and the screen.

Step 2   Next, expose the Solarplate with the *aquatint* screen for 1 minute. You will notice that the aquatint screen has both a shiny surface and a less shiny, semi-matte surface. The semi-matte surface is the emulsion side and it must be placed face to face with the plate surface for the first exposure.

Step 3   Remove the aquatint screen and place your positive transparency on the plate for 1 minute. This time may need to be adjusted depending on the quality and density of the positive film that you are using. When you have completed the second exposure, remove the positive transparency and proceed to develop your plate in water. Dry and post-expose the plate as defined in the instructions, and then print.

Step 4   To increase the richness of blacks, darken your image, and retain more detail, just reduce the exposure times. Conversely, if you experience problems with the etched grooves in the plate holding too much ink, then too much polymer is washing away; to lighten your image, try increasing exposure times.

Trouble Shooting

◆ If the plate won't clear enough to show a defined image, you have likely overexposed the plate or your washing time is incomplete.

◆ If the plate is sticky following development, then it is likely that your post-exposure time was omitted or was too brief.

◆ If your image is blurry, the contact of the negative emulsion to the plate emulsion was too light. Consider using a heavier piece of glass for compression of the art to the plate.

◆ If you have abnormal spots, try heavier weight acetate or dust the emulsion side of the acetate, prior to laying it down, with a fine dusting of baby powder. A fine mist of talc on the film is also a solution for Newton's Rings.

◆ If you have black spots, go back and clean the glass or transparency a little better for the next exposure attempt.

◆ If your plate shows water spots, then take more care in blotting and drying the plate immediately after it has been through the water development.

◆ Above all, treat this material as an invitation to really cut loose with some interdisciplinary thinking about your work.

Figure 23–21
Dennis Olsen, *Substrate 2—Solarplate*
This piece by Dennis Olsen was created using a Solarplate, a UV-sensitive, water-developed, polymer on steel. For continuing the translation to an intaglio stage, it might be necessary to make a partial exposure with a stochastic screen.
(Courtesy of the artist and Hampton Editions / Solarplate)

PHOTO-RESISTS

Photo-resist on metal is compatible with both Solarplate and gum bichromate because both use water as the vehicle for developing out the image. The purpose of traditional photo-resists is to provide the artist with a light-sensitive coated plate (*metal, glass, ceramic, etc.*) that can be exposed to UV light and developed so that the un-exposed and un-hardened resist washes away. During exposure, light enters the clear portions of the negative, or positive, film and hardens that resist. Simultaneously, the dense portions of the transparency prevent light from hardening the resist and these portions wash away in development. When development and subsequent etch are complete, the result is a polymer, i.e., *Solarplate*, or intaglio metal relief of the photograph in either a positive or a negative, depending on the type of transparency used during the exposure.

At this point in the process, the resist that remains on the plate after development is additionally UV heat hardened, making it more acid resistant. The areas of the plate without the resist are susceptible to the acid and are etched by the acid to create an intaglio-etched plate. This metallic photographic relief is then cleaned with a solvent and either considered a unique object by itself, or regarded as a plate that can be inked, wiped, and printed on paper with an etching press.

A Simple Photo–Resist Formula for Intaglio

The following is a simple formula, for creating a resist, for an etching plate, using fish-glue, albumen, ammonium dichromate, and water. You will need:

◆ 30 ml fresh albumen (egg white)

◆ 45 prepared fish glue

◆ 6 g ammonium dichromate

◆ Distilled water

Step 1 Put 30 ml of fresh egg white (albumen) in a mixing bowl, add 30 ml of distilled water, and beat it well. You may use powdered albumen but because this formula requires only a single egg's albumen (approximately 30 ml) it really isn't worth the trouble to go get the powdered variety.

Step 2 In another bowl, mix 45 ml of prepared fish-glue (*LePage's or photo engraving glue*) thoroughly with 30 ml of distilled water. Slowly pour the egg mixture from Step #1 into the glue mixture, stirring slowly.

Step 3 Mix 6 g of ammonium dichromate with 30 ml of distilled water. Under normal room light, add the ammonium dichromate solution to the glue-egg colloid so that it becomes light sensitive.

Step 4 Then add 30 ml of distilled water, more or less, to the solution. The amount of water you add depends upon how thin or thick you want the quality of the emulsion. You can also increase the sensitivity of the emulsion by adding more of the ammonium dichromate. Before the plate is exposed it is a good idea to "bake it" with a hairdryer set on a hot setting. This step ensures the best chance of the resist adhering to the plate through the development stage. Just blow-dry for a few minutes; don't put the plate in the oven because excessive time and heat will fog the emulsion.

Step 5 In low-level light, pour the colloid resist on your plate and rotate the plate in the air, emulsion side up, to ensure an even coating. You may want to use a brush for the coating but the pour and rotate method seems to provide a smoother surface.

Step 6 Once the plate's surface has dried, you may take a transparency (*a positive or negative*) and place it in contact with the sensitized emulsion. Remember, your decision as to whether you will use a positive or negative transparency is dependent on the stages that the plate will go through and where you want to end the process. Lay a thick piece of glass on the transparency and sensitized plate to ensure a firm pressure between the film and the plate and expose this "sandwich" to UV light. You may use either an exposure unit or the sun and you should definitely make exposure tests before committing your prepared plate to the UV light.

Step 7 Once the exposure is done, move to the lab for development. This stage is done easily in a bath of slightly warm water and continues, with gentle movement of the water, until the unexposed portions of the plate begin to fall away from the plate. The look here is quite similar to the way a gum bichromate print clears. Once you are content with the development, gently remove the plate from the water, blow-dry it, and place it on a hotplate to re-harden the resist that is left. Continue until the resist that remains turns a deep brown. Once that happens, take the plate from the hotplate and let it cool before etching it with acid.

Acid Etch Formulas

As a point of interest, you might want to know about several acids used in *traditional* printmaking when making an intaglio-etched plate. Nitric acid, in concentrations of 1:4 (*for deep bites*) to 1:12 (*for aquatinting and fine line bites*) is most often used on zinc or copper plates. A second type of acid etch bath, called a Dutch Mordant, is generally used on copper and is made by combining 10% hydrochloric acid, 2% potassium chlorate, and 88% water. A third type of acid etch is ferric chloride, normally purchased in a prepared solution and described in more detail in the photo-resist section of this chapter. I specifically mention these formulas as the acid baths that you would most commonly find in a traditional printmaking studio. *However, they are not appropriate to etch the steel that serves as a support for the Solarplate emulsion.*

There is enough to say about the subject of photo-resists and print-making to justify a completely new book. Here, I am briefly touching on a simple bichromate-based resist that can be applied to a metal plate and then acid etched following exposure. If this process instills a great curiosity in you about this area of image making, an abundance of other reference material awaits. Please take a workshop or a class as well; don't try to teach yourself about these techniques and materials.

Etching

Put on a pair of rubber gloves and make sure the etching area is well ventilated. If you have never worked with an acid etching bath then it would imperative to talk with a printmaker about acids and options in plate biting. *Remember to never add water to acid.* For this chapter I tell you how to use *ferric chloride* as your etching solution because it is one of the safer acid etch options. Rather than make this bath yourself (*because the process is rather tedious*), I advise going to an art, printmaker, or chemical supply and buying a prepared ferric chloride etching solution. This will work on several types of metal including the zinc that you are using.

Heat the ferric chloride to 100°F using a tray-within-a-tray method where a larger tray with very hot water is holding an inner tray holding the acid and plate. Immerse your plate and remember, the hotter the acid, the faster the etching action. Use a feather, or fan brush without a metal ferrule, to whisk away at the areas of the plate that are being etched and be gentle with the plate's resist emulsion.

Ferric chloride is a slow etch process and you may be feathering the plate for 30 to 60 minutes. Unlike nitric acid, there is no evident "action" bubbling in a bite with ferric chloride. If you want to have bubbles, which will accelerate the etching energy, add about 30 ml of hydrochloric acid to every 750 ml of ferric chloride developer solution. One additional piece of information regarding ferric chloride: unlike other etching solutions, ferric chloride turns the etched parts of the plate black during the etch. This black washes away with water and allows you to monitor the progress of your bite. Once the etching stage is done, you may remove the resist, using water or solvents. What you will have is an intaglio plate that can be inked, printed, used for embossing, and so on. It's up to you to decide where to go and what to do next. My advice would be to take an Introduction to Intaglio workshop or class and find out if it rings your bells.

THE MORDANÇAGE PROCESS

A Really Quick Overview

In this very brief section, you will be introduced to an often stunning, mercurial, and chemically driven post-print manipulation technique called the Mordançage Process. Unfortunately, the process requires a real darkroom as well as the great outdoors or a superior ventilation system. I provide you with a little information regarding its beginning and then describe the materials and procedures you will follow to learn its many idiosyncrasies. I expect you'll find this process quite seductive, but don't let that distract you from the fact that the chemistry required to perform this technique is not compatible with your skin or respiratory system. Be vigilant with safety precautions, wear gloves and a dual-filter respirator, and make every effort to work outdoors with the wind at your back.

The Process

The Mordançage process appears to have made its formal debut in L. P. Clerc's book, *La Technique Photographique** in a chapter entitled "Generalities sur les visages par teinture sur mordançage," in which Clerc refers to R. Namias's use of mordants of various metallic ferrocyanides. This process is quite lovely

Figure 23–22

Jean Pierre Sudre, *Insects—1979—Mordançage*

Jean Pierre Sudre was, and will always be, the acknowledged master of the Mordançage process. This is a perfect example of his technique and sensitivity to subject and process.

(Courtesy of Claudine Sudre)

(when it works) but it is unfortunately rife with bad vapors and chemistry. The other problem is that it requires a traditional darkroom and chemistry and silver gelatin paper . . . all of which will be more difficult to find with the passing of time. Although the mordançage process had an early photographic history, it was not until Jean Pierre Sudre adopted and refined it as his own that the technique received much recognition. Little was known about the technique and for years it was practiced only by people who went to Sudre's home in France to study with him. One of those travelers was my friend Craig Stevens and the chemistry in these notes are adapted from those given to me by Craig. Here's the basic overview and please, if you take a workshop with me someday, don't ask me to demonstrate.

Figure 23–23

Elizabeth Opalenik, *Windswept,* 1993—mordançage

Elizabeth learned the mordançage process directly from Sudre and has been one of the leading practitioners of the technique. Starting with a high contrast gelatin silver print, the photographic silver emulsion is chemically lifted, removed, or rearranged in the shadow areas. Elizabeth recently published her monograph, *Poetic Grace.*

Mordançage Chemistry: To Make 1 Liter of Mordançage Solution

- 750 ml distilled water in a plastic beaker
- 10 g copper chloride (stir this into solution)
- 50 ml glacial acetic acid (*always add acid to water)*
- 25 ml to 35 ml of 30%-35% (110 vol.) hydrogen peroxide
- Add water to make 1 liter of working solution

30% Hydrogen Peroxide

This is not the 3% drugstore version you use for cuts. If you can't find the strong 30% hydrogen peroxide (H_2O_2) you will have to buy the 12% to 18% liquid solution that is available in hair and beauty salons. If you are using the 12% or 18 % concentrations, substitute as follows:

- 18%: 50 ml instead of the 25 ml with the 30% to 35% concentration
- 12%: 75 ml instead of the 25 ml with the 30% to 35% concentration

Note: Be sure to ask for the clear formula of hydrogen peroxide. Many salons sell the "crème" version.

Warning: Before you go any further, it is imperative that you put on a pair of surgical quality latex gloves and a dual-filter respirator. You should also be outdoors with the wind blowing at your back.

Step 1 Begin with a washed and wet fiber-based print. Brovira is the paper Sudre used, but Ilford Warmtone works as well. Warm tone quality papers appear to work better than others and few papers work anymore.

Step 2 Using tongs, immerse the print in the mordançage solution for 3 minutes or until the image has bleached out. It will turn yellow at first and then the image will begin to etch away. You may subjectively determine at what point you will stop this step because every choice you make from this point on will result in a unique final print.

Step 3 Remove the bleached print from the mordançage solution and immerse it in a tray of clean water. Wash the print for 15 minutes and replace the volume with fresh water every 3 to 5 minutes.

Step 4 After the washing stage, redevelop the print in a 1:5 to 1:10 solution of Dektol or any very dilute toner, for example, Kodak Sepia (*sodium sulfide*) Toner Part B, or Polytoner. The degree of dilution of the redevelopment chemistry will have a pronounced effect on the colors that come up in the print.

Step 5 When the redevelopment is complete, rinse the print briefly in a paper stop bath solution.

Step 6 **Depouillment** (Gelatin Removal)—Remove the print from the stop bath and lay it on a firm piece of Plexiglas®. Begin to rinse it with a strong spray of water. Wipe away loosened gelatin (*parts of the image*) with cotton swabs or an assortment of brushes of different sizes and degrees of stiffness. The original print exposure will determine what areas of the print will lose gelatin. During this stage you will begin to see a varied display of effects. Some will be as pronounced as a solarized image while others will be more delicate. The degree will be based on the original image and its densities. You will see a bas-relief like effect and portions of the original paper base will be evident to you. When the gelatin removal is complete, immerse your printed image in a 1:5 to 1:10 Dektol, or any exhausted developer solution, for 3 minutes or until you see the image in the way you want it realized.

Step 7 **Oxidation**—Remove the print from the Dektol developer, roll it flat on a hard surface with a rubber woodblock brayer print side down, on a paper towel. Turn the print over, place it on fresh paper towels and allow it to oxidize and dry. Keep in mind that paper towels are white because they are bleached to be that color. If you leave any photographic print face down on a wet paper towel, it will eventually show an imprint of the towel's texture.

Step 8 If you want to stop the process at any time the print may be briefly immersed in a paper stop bath, washed for 30 minutes, and screen dried. Re-developed prints can also be re-toned to further alter the coloration. Play with the process but be careful and do not attempt to experiment with this procedure unless you are outside or have extraordinarily good ventilation. Do not play with, drink, bathe in, fool around with, or splash the mordançage solution.

VISUAL LITERACY: REVOLUTION, ARTS, & MIRRORS

You've arrived at an interesting point. I've nearly exhausted the menu of photographic processes that I had planned to include and have incorporated about as many images as the publisher will allow. The book is significantly larger in text, content, and imagery than the first edition but there are still a few things I need to say about visual literacy, arts education, and where alternative processes fit in the grand design. This may seem out of context for a book dealing with alternative processes but it actually couldn't be more relevant. With digital imaging hosting the new "mushy democracy" of photographic expression; one in which the equipment finds the faces, exposes for neutral feeling, and then makes the perfect print, there is a (forgive the theater in the next word) *hunger* for the accident, the raw imperfect light and texture of life. Alternative process image making grows ever stronger in this environment and perhaps that is why you are reading this page.

Photography is the one universal form of expression in which people of all cultures happily participate. (*I will assume you realize I am making a point and not ignoring the popularity of singing, dancing, and romance.*) When questioned about the order that things are rescued when fleeing a burning house, respondents say children, pets, and family photographs. I recall sitting in a theater and watching *Schindler's List;* in the scene where the audience gets its first visual sense of the concentration camps and of the people being stripped of their possessions, the camera pans from one pile of belongings to the next . . . shoes, glasses, and the like. The audience was still and silent until the camera paused on a pile of family photographs . . . then I remember a collective gasp taking the air from the room.

My students' generation is the most visually sophisticated in history; they arrive from high school with a visual vocabulary that dwarfs that of their parents' generation. They may not know all of the buzz-words and art-speak . . . yet . . . but the ease of their visual expression is stunning. So many times I've finished running a critique seminar and thought how amazing it would have been to have the operant visual conditioning they have

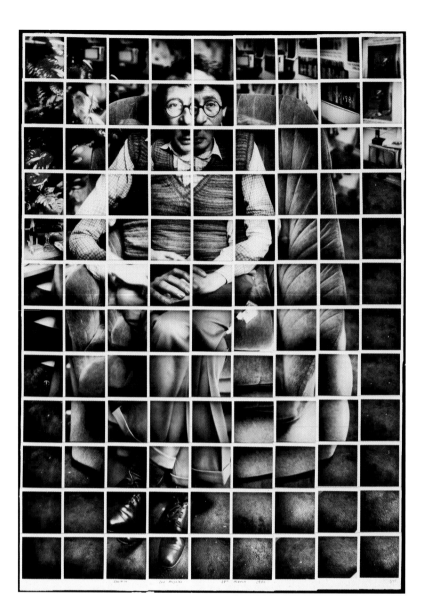

Figure 23–24

David Hockney, *Kasmin*, Los Angeles, 28 March, 1982—composite Polaroid

Arguably, David Hockney is the best-known British artist of his generation. His career has incorporated the disciplines of painting, printmaking, papermaking, photography, and theater set design. In the 1980s, he began working with the concept of photomontage and cubism and this piece is an example of that period in his creative life. *(Courtesy of the artist, © David Hockney)*

been raised on when I earned my degrees at Massachusetts College of Art and R.I.S.D. That's when I begin to think about how they see. With machines and popular media defining what "good" and "art" mean, the best place to begin is to tell you what I believe.

To me, visual literacy is the ability to see. More specifically, it is the capacity to interpret, associate, and communicate signs, symbols, codes, signals, metaphors, and marks. A visually literate person is able to draw on a knowledge base that includes cultural and art history, criticism, and semiotics, which is the study of how meaning is established and understood. Don't get frightened off here. I won't be going on an academic romp through the often incomprehensible, and political, mine-field of

semiotic theory; I promise not to beat on you with important life issues such as modalities, representation, paradigms, and syntagmatic analysis. What was that joke in Daniel Chandler's, *Semiotics for Beginners*? . . . "What do you get if you cross a semiotician with a member of the Mafia? . . . An offer you can't understand."

Visual Literacy means different things to different people. In my personal context, the issues related to visual literacy that are relevant to our programs at The Art Institute of Boston are not always in harmony with those in other programs at our parent institution, Lesley University. If you dissected our respective paradigms with the same academic scalpel we would bleed the same color blood, but our types would differ, as would our methods of assess-

Figure 23–25

Jon Laurence, *Waistline,* **2006**

Art Institute of Boston student Jon Laurence is as eclectic in his creative interests as anyone I've ever taught. This piece, part of a series dealing with graphic reinterpretations of cinema is from work done in 2006. The syntax included digital inkjet print mounted with gel medium on Luan. The surface work included washes of thinned out gel medium mixed with acrylic paint that was hand rubbed onto the surface. Each wash of gel and acrylic was followed by hand sanding with assorted grits of sandpaper.

(Courtesy of the artist)

ment. But if we can put aside the specifics for long enough, we begin to recognize that what we all do as educators coalesces into a mission with the same goals . . . to allay the fear of imagination, especially of those that possess a good one, and to inspire the creative process.

Creativity is as important to me as language, and it's difficult to be creative if you are afraid to fail—just as it's impossible to sing if you are afraid to hum. Nurturing creativity is one of the very few gifts that a parent or teacher can give a child that will continue to evolve over the child's lifetime. The mentors who remain in me are the ones who offered the gift of how to teach myself to see.

I'm reminded of a story I heard recently that makes the point about how confidence and imagination are nurtured. In a first grade classroom, the teacher passes out a piece of paper to each of her students and tells them to draw a picture . . . this is the 15-minute portion of the day that is scheduled for creativity. A 6-year old girl begins to draw and the teacher comes by her desk and asks what her picture is of. The girl replies that she is drawing a picture of God.

"Well, the teacher responds, you can't draw a picture of God because no one knows what God looks like."

The girl thought about this for a heartbeat and then, looking up from her drawing, replied, "Well, they will in a minute."

Bauhaus . . . is a very, very, very, fine house . . .

Walter Gropius, one of the founders of the Bauhaus (1918), admired the medieval guilds, "The Bauhatten," that had created the great cathedrals in his native Germany. Gropius sought to emulate that model while creating a cultural synthesis and reconciliation between the atelier, modern art, and the goals of the industrial revolution. His goal was to develop a curriculum that was essentially a "foundation" program, in which students were expected to become visually literate through the study of drawing, design, color, and form. Essentially, this model's approach to learning, and intent, was to solidify, and unify, art, craft, and technology. This is, as you know if you have experienced it, the traditional structure in most accredited art schools today and has been for nearly a century.

The problem with this Bauhausian design is that the majority of "good" art programs are dedicated to promoting *individualism* while simultaneously turning out students who have been forced to learn most of their required subjects in a repetitive, cookie-cutter, curriculum that is evaluated through standardized assessment. This is a significant disconnect.

Figure 23–26

Luis Gonzalez Palma, *Como un Secreto se Seduce a Si Mismo*—Kodalith, gold leaf, red paper, all embedded in resin, 40" x 50"

Luis is well known for his powerful images of Guatemala's Mayan Indians. This work represents the concept of absence . . . where the fragility of the physical object is a link to a secret world of dislocated objects that serve as a metaphor of internal drama and the loss of oneself faced by oneself. Images that show situations such as those in this series generate a desire to know what is not present.

The Industrial Revolution and Arts Education

Our present educational system for teaching the arts is predicated on assessment models and values established during the Industrial Revolution in the 19th century. Nothing defined that revolution more than the assembly line . . . and the method of assessing a line's success was dependent on reaching specific levels of performance, volume, and generic consistency, from one object to the next, as it rolled through to the consumer and society. There was nothing subjective about it. If there were no inconsistencies, if the workers performed their tasks in the prescribed manner, the line could go faster. Without change, increasing the speed of the line meant greater production, which equated to employment for all, and greater profit for the machine. As efficiency led to greater and greater profits, people decided it was logical to apply what worked in the factories to other areas of society.

Education was presented as a standardized package and the guaranteed path to employment, success, and a better life, as long as the line kept moving. The school was the factory, the children were the products, and they were assessed by assigning grades indicating success, failure, or an in-between, at defined intervals. If the product failed, it meant a failure to meet the standard and a return to the beginning of the line, where they could be made again.

It was a fairly simple task to assess and quantify success in mathematics, science, English, and the like, where learning through repetition was the norm. However, when it came to subjects involving the creative process, and imagination, there was a problem applying this assembly line paradigm. Grades still had to be given but because it was impossible to successfully mandate competency levels of creativity another significant disconnect occurred. Like assessing an obese child in a gym class rope-climbing test, the standards for competency were based on things that the school could not influence.

One additional glitch in the system was that the industrial model mandated a connection between the education of the child and that child's eventual ability to be employable. The theory was that a literate and productive work force would make the line move faster and better and that all in society would benefit. Unfortunately, it was clear that not a lot of artists, musicians, writers, or dancers making a living in art factories. Because of this, it was assumed that these subjects couldn't be important if immediate employment

Figure 23–27
Shoshannah White, *Straw Field*, **2006–2007—encaustic on photo**
Maine artist Shoshannah created this beautiful work by applying encaustic wax painting techniques to the surface of her photograph. The encaustic process involves painting with heated beeswax to which colored pigments are added. Encaustic painting has been practiced for eons and examples of it, from Greece, date back to 5ᵗʰ century BCE.
(Courtesy of the artist)

Figure 23–28
Ashley Haley, *Tower of Babel*, **2007—montage**
Ashley wrote, "I looked for characteristics in the human form to recreate a flux in time that occurred during the conversation that occurred when making the image. I avoided using archival methods of altering the prints to distance myself from the holier than thou fiber print essence. For materials I used: Colombian coffee, tea, household bleach, candle wax, printmaking inks, acrylic paint, sandpaper, black cat India ink, brown henna and spot toner. The torn/ cut prints where then glued together with craft glue and masking tape, scratches where created using razors blades and my fingernails.
(Courtesy of the artist)

and success were not available to all. Whoever heard of someone working hard and becoming vice president of art?

But you can't argue with success and you couldn't stop the line. We became so efficient at getting everyone into higher education that we have determined—in the same way that Susan Sontag reasoned that photographs had become meaningless due to their sheer numbers—that the high school diploma, and undergraduate degree, are of diminished value simply because everyone had one. I'm going to try and close the circle now.

Mirrors and Windows

Many years ago I was sitting in a lecture hall at Wellesley College listening to John Szarkowski; then curator and *Photography Tsar* of The Museum of Modern Art. He spoke of the valueless-ness of photographs and how there were now more of them in the world than bricks. This lecture reinforced Szarkowski's opinion that there were two types of photographers in the world and they were represented by the metaphors of *windows* and *mirrors*.

The "mirrors" photographers took images that were, for better or worse, describing their personal sensibilities and this was the meaning and intent of their photographs. They were their own context. The "windows" photographers made pictures that described information. Their images documented facts as well as commenting on the "system" of making photographs.

Robert Hughes (read everything by him you can find) wrote, in a 1978 *Time* essay, "Everything that happened, one might suppose, happened before a camera; there has never been anything like the sheer bulk of visual documentation left as the residue of a popular-photography culture. People and events seem ghostly unless they have been verified by a camera. Wars, elections, riots,

CHAPTER 23 LIGHT MARKING: PHOTOGRAPHIC ALTERNATIVES

539

Figure 23–29

Elena Baca, *Espejismo—1998—20" x 64" gum-oil on paper and wood*

Graduate of the rigorous MFA program at the University of New Mexico, Elena works in a variety of media. This example is in gumoil and wood.

(Courtesy of the artist)

disasters, communal ecstasies, the speeches of politicians and their deaths—all are eaten up by the omnivorous lens, as photography (through journalism) defines the terms of our fictitious intimacy with the world. This intimacy means a ravenous consumption, rather than contemplation, of images."

In 1978, Szarkowski cynically insisted that most issues of importance couldn't be photographed. This may be compatible with Salman Rushdie's sentiment from *Midnight's Children*, "*Most of what matters in your life takes place in your absence.*" From Szarkowski's *window* view, that perception was not a surprise.

Szarkowki's world of more photos than bricks has been superceded; we are presently swimming in the limitless sea of digital photography, where everyone makes, from a 19th century critical perspective, "good" pictures. If Hughes was concerned about volume leading to ravenous consumption rather than contemplation, and Szarkowski was cynically insisting that issues of importance in life cannot be photographed, then the sheer volume of digitally made images, stored in increasingly huge, and easily edited, archiving systems . . . is an issue destined to grow larger. It seems that the choices are more clarified than ever.

The long-running show of silver-based gelatin films and paper is coming to an inevitable end. (This image making system will probably be designated an *official* alternative process in the next few years but since it is not yet on life-support I have refrained from including it as a chapter.) The people who loved photography for its accidents, expression, and unpredictability are moving in droves to alternative process image making. This transition is not at all unlike the artistic tsunami that swept through the contemporary painting world in the late 1950s and early 1960s and it is healthy for the genre. I saw these changes coming a few decades ago when I first began offering alternative processes classes at Harvard. Many of my former students from that time are in this book and have made a life for themselves in the medium. It is clear to me that photography is now a part of every visual discipline in some way or other and if it is to have a place of its own, as an art form, that place may be the realm of handmade photo-sensitive imagery.

The Future of Photography Is in Its Past

A few pages back, I stated that visual literacy is the capacity to interpret, associate, and communicate signs, symbols, codes, and marks. And for a contemporary digital photographer, being immersed in the history, criticism and semiotics of the medium could lead to being in perfect harmony with the "windows" definition ushered into our language by Szarkowski. In fact, they seem made for one another; digital photography might well be a marriage of Donald Norman's "*information appliance*" and Szarkowski's *windows* where the image is as much about the information as it is about the system of delivering the content.

Figure 23–30
Takashi Suzuki, *Three Elvis*, 1993—image transfer
Art Institute of Boston graduate Takashi Suzuki once did a year-long project where he took a single photograph of everything he ate for the entire year.
(Courtesy of the artist)

Figure 23–31
Joy Goldkind, *Ruth at 80*—bromoil
"Ruth at 80 was my first attempt at Bromoil. The image was made at my aunt's 80th birthday party. Seeing her standing there I thought how wonderful she looked at 80."
(Courtesy of the artist)

Figure 23–32
Peter Liepke, *Fair Ride*, 2006—gum bichromate over ink-jet
This piece is a 3-coat gum bichromate print (with C-M-Y washes) printed with a waxed digital paper negative in registration over an initial very light Epson ink-jet print on Fabriano watercolor paper. The initial image is printed just for highlights, so it's quite faint. Peter then pumps up the mid-tones and shadows with different layers and washes of gum bichromate.
(Courtesy of the artist)

But from the "mirrors" perspective, visual literacy emphasizes the *light-marking* . . . the *photo-graphis*. In alternative process printmaking, the hand and the eye are equal partners in the art and crafting of the image. The print itself is a sign, a symbol, and a mark . . . perhaps even a metaphor for the process of making the print.

Obviously, there are no absolutes in this discussion. Creative issues arise in every form of expression. I know many digital artists who are deeply involved in their art

and the very relevant issues of visual literacy that can be explored quite well within their discipline. In fact, the addition of digital technology to the Bauhaus recipe would, I think, be an ingredient that Gropius would have greatly approved of.

That said, I nonetheless believe the future of photography as a distinctive medium is to be found in its past. Contemporary alternative process artists are, as Lyle Rexer coined well, the antiquarian avant-garde. France Scully Osterman and her husband, Mark Osterman, call

542

Figure 23–33
Gene Laughter, *End of Summer*, 2003— Bromoil
Gene wrote, "*In my photographic art I am not striving for pin-point sharpness or to document a moment in time or a particular place. Rather I seek to portray my emotions and feelings about the subject. Reality is not my objective. Bromoil, being a control process, and utilizing brush applied pigments, allows me to take the image another layer away from a strictly photographic image and to experiment with the surreal rather than the real.*"
(*Courtesy of the artist*)

this approach to photography "photo-humanism" and those who embrace it "photo-humanists." It's all about the human reference in both the *vision* and *crafting* of photographic imagery. The light-marking art they produce, and how they define their creative process, is flourishing as a language without compromise, or conditions . . . one that is not tied to a syntax-dependent feast (as perfect as it is) of 1's and 0's that is only a solar flare away from erasing its history.

Safety Considerations and Data for Chemicals Used in This Book

CHEMICALS & MATERIAL SAFETY DATA SHEETS (MSDS)

Vermont SIRI Index

www2.hazard.com/msds/index.php

This is a free site for 180,000 Material Safety Data Sheets (MSDS) AND CAS #'S

www.webelements.com

This site has information regarding the Periodic Table of Elements.

A FEW BASIC CHEMISTRY DEFINITIONS

ACIDS: Acids are compounded solutions with a **pH of less than 7**. Acids neutralize alkalis such as developers. An acid will turn a blue litmus paper a pink-red. Acids are compounds containing hydrogen that can be replaced by a metal to form a salt, that is, the metal sodium will replace the hydrogen atom in hydrochloric acid to form the salt, sodium chloride. Acid strength affects two of the most common functions: imparting a sour taste and creating an acid environment to limit microbial growth.

ALKALIS: Alkalis are compounded solutions with a **pH greater than 7**. Alkalis are the assorted soluble metallic hydroxides that neutralize acids to form salts. An alkali can also be a compounded salt. An alkali functions as an accelerator in photographic developing formulas (*generally potassium and sodium hydroxide*). Alkalis turn red litmus paper blue. Examples of alkalis are sodium carbonate, and borax.

ANHYDROUS: Meaning a solid substance without water or crystallization

BASE: Bases are the chemical opposite of acids and react with acids to produce water and salts (*or their solutions*). Some general properties of bases include: bitter taste, slick texture (like soap and water), reacts violently with acids, caustic to organic matter, turns red litmus paper blue.

BUFFER: Weak acid(s) or base(s) dissolved in water that hold the pH near to a constant value when acid or base are added. Buffering is the ability of a weak acid/salt combination, such as citric acid and sodium citrate, to control the amount of free hydrogen ions. When certain

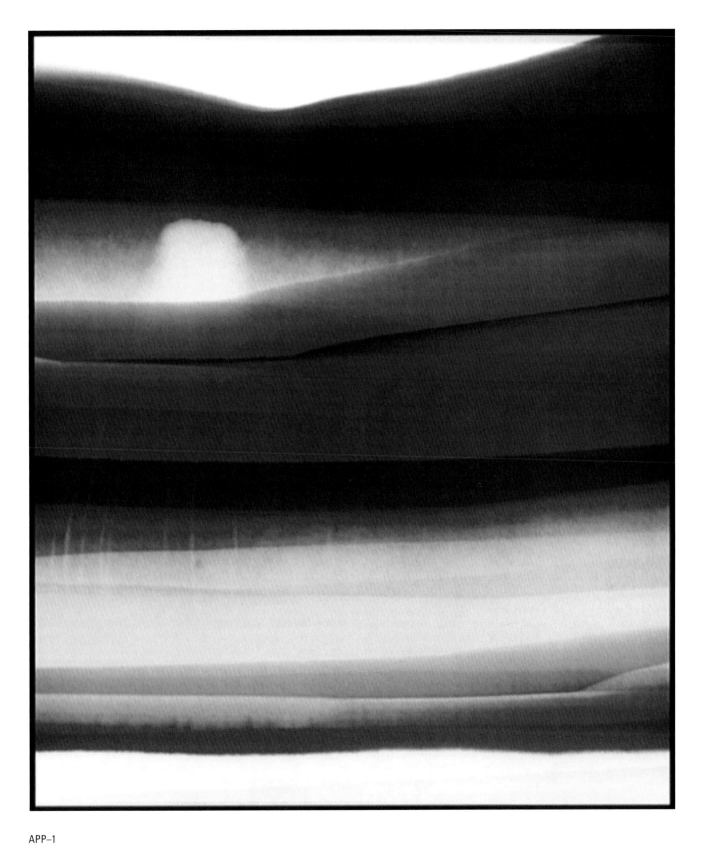

APP–1

Christopher James, Solargraph #30, 1970

I made this Solargraph in graduate school at RISD when it had become crystal clear to me that I had to make images that were mine, and not ones that were dictated by academic paradigms regarding what a photograph was, or how it was made. This was the beginning of my life making marks with light and creating alternative imagery.

(Courtesy of the author)

amounts of acid or base are added, the system resists changes in pH. Citric acid has the widest effective buffer range—from pH 2.5 to 6.5. Tartaric acid can only be used for buffering between pH 3.0 and 4.5.

DELIQUESCENT: A deliquescent chemical is one that readily absorbs moisture from the air. Salts are a prime example.

pH: "pH" designates a numerical value assigned to an aqueous solution to indicate that it is either acidic or alkaline. It represents a chemical symbol for the logarithm of the reciprocal of the *hydrogen* ion concentration in gram atoms per liter—got that?

SALT: A salt is formed when an acid and a base are mixed and the acid releases H+ ions while the base releases OH⁻ ions. This process is called hydrolysis. This action creates an ionic compound. The pH of the salt depends on the strengths of the original acids and bases:

Acid	Base	Salt	pH
strong	strong		pH = 7
weak	strong		pH > 7
strong	weak		pH < 7
weak	weak		depends on which is stronger

SATURATED SOLUTION: Definition of a solution that cannot accept any more solid (solute), at a given temperature, without leaving sediment in the solution.

SOLUBILITY: The maximum weight of a substance that will dissolve completely in a given volume of solvent and a specific temperature.

SURFACTANT: An agent, such as Tween, that reduces the surface tension of a liquid enabling it to more easily penetrate a paper substrate.

HOW CHEMICALS CAN AFFECT THE BODY

- **Breathing**: Airborne chemical matter and vapors in the form of gases can enter the body through your nose and mouth. Work in a well-ventilated environment, preferably outdoors or using ventilation that will not pull the vapors past your face on their way to an exhaust fan. Paper painter's masks offer only a modest protection against chemicals and practically none against harmful fumes.

- **Ingestion**: It is a bad idea to eat while working in the lab, or with chemistry, because you are quite likely going to ingest this same chemistry. Eat somewhere else.

- **Absorption**: Chemistry can enter the body through the skin and get into the bloodstream. Open cuts or healing wounds on your skin can be an avenue for absorption as well. Wear barrier gloves and a mask when mixing chemistry. Gloves may present a number of problems. Commonly available types are made from a variety of materials not all of which provide an adequate barrier from specific chemicals. Gloves made of nitrile, available from laboratory and chemical supply houses, work well for most chemicals that you will use in alternative process. Except for mild chemical usage, avoid latex or kitchen gloves, because these are susceptible to chemical reactions and are often clumsy.

Protecting Yourself

The key to chemical safety is controlling the degree of exposure to the hazards encountered in the mixing and use of all chemistry. Ingestion and absorption are easy to protect against in a working lab; it's simply common sense. However, if you are working in a home lab, and you have children or pets, it is imperative that you store your chemistry in a safe and secure place. Prohibit any eating, drinking, and splashing in the toning area. Prevent skin absorption by keeping chemicals from contacting the skin or eyes. If you have sensitive skin, or your skin has cuts, or abrasions, protect it with some type of separation such as tongs, splash goggles, and nitrile gloves. Safety goggles are essential when mixing powdered chemistry, because eyes will readily absorb and pass contaminants along to the rest of the body. Be extra cautious if you wear contact lenses to prevent the powders and chemical fumes from getting between your contact lenses and your eyes.

FIRST AID

First Aid for Ingestion of Acids and Alkalis

Curiously, the signs and symptoms for ingestion of acids and alkalis are quite similar, as are the recommendations for treatment. In the past, if an acid was swallowed, the immediate response was to neutralize the acid with an alkali drink, i.e. sodium bicarbonate, several glasses of milk or milk of magnesia, or 8 to 12 antacids. If an alkali was not at hand, then the response was to force the victim to rinse the mouth area repeatedly.

Symptoms and signs associated with significant alkali-induced tissue injury include pain in the mouth and throat, drooling, pain on swallowing, vomiting, abdominal pain and haematemesis . . . a nice way to say vomiting blood. If the larynx is involved, local edema may produce respiratory distress and a hoarse voice. Veterinarians recommend giving a solution of 1 part vinegar to 4 parts water. Rinse the mouth with water or saline solution and call for medical assistance in either acid or alakali events.

There is disagreement over the effectiveness of having the victim drink large quantities of water. My friend, Dr. Jacek Mostwin, at Johns Hopkins, says that the water simply makes the injury spread and that acid or alkali ingestion is not really a first aid situationat all . . . you need professionals right away. One thing is for sure . . . **DO NOT INDUCE VOMITING**. This is especially true for hydrofluoric acid ingestion.

That said, here are the basic immediate first aid recommendations for both acid and alkali ingestion:

- Do NOT induce vomiting.
- Do NOT attempt neutralization.
- Do NOT give oral fluids.
- Do NOT give activated charcoal (for alkali).
- DO rinse the mouth with saline or water for acid.
- DO remove visible material from mouth with water or saline (for alkali).
- DO call 911 and request immediate medical assistance.

First Aid for Skin Contact

If an acid or corrosive chemical is splashed on the skin, immediately proceed to the nearest sink, or emergency shower, and flush affected area for at least 15 minutes. If the chemical is on your clothing, remove all contaminated clothing.

If a chemical splashes in the eye the immediate response is to flush the eye repeatedly with warm water or first aid saline solution eyewash. If an acid, make a very dilute solution of sodium bicarbonate and use that as well. If an alkali, repeatedly flush with water, or saline solution, and rinse with a very dilute solution of boric acid. In all cases, call for professional medical help.

When to Seek Emergency Medical Assistance:

1. The victim has signs of shock, such as fainting, pale complexion or breathing in a notably shallow manner.

2. The chemical burn penetrated through the first layer of skin, and the resulting second-degree burn covers an area more than 2 to 3 inches in diameter.

3. The chemical burn occurred on the eye, hands, feet, face, groin or buttocks, or over a major joint.

If you're unsure whether a substance is toxic, call the poison control center at (800) 222-1222. If you seek emergency assistance, bring the chemical container or a complete description of the substance with you for identification.

CHEMISTRY & SAFETY

- Do not place an exhaust vent above your face. If you are building a darkroom, install the exhaust in the floor or, better yet, do as we do at The Art Institute of Boston: build your ventilation system into the sink itself so that the fumes are vented before reaching the student's face. Having an exhaust above your face just pulls all of the fumes past your eyes, nose, and mouth on their way to the vents. The fan and exhaust capacity should be able to completely exchange the air in the room every 3 to 6 minutes. Consult with an air quality company for the specifics that will be best for your space.

- Prevent chemical material from becoming airborne through careful handling and mixing of liquids and powders. Work slowly and don't splash.

- Cover trays and tanks when not in use to prevent vapors from filling your working space. Sheets of Plexiglas work well. Label each sheet with the chemical that it covers so that it is always used for the same chemicals.

- When mixing: **always add acid to water; never add water to acid**. In this way, which is the only way, heat produced by the acids will not cause a splattering acidic liquid eruption.

- When weighing chemicals on digital gram scales, never place raw chemicals on the weighing platform of the scale. Always place a weighing paper or a plastic/paper cup on the scale to hold the chemistry. Always weigh the paper or cup, before depositing the chemical, and re-calibrate your scale to zero by pressing "TARE" so that the chemical weight will be the only thing being weighed.

- Prior to working with any chemical that you are not familiar with, be sure to read the chemical's MSDS data sheet to understand that particular chemical's traits and how to deal with it in the event of an accident or emergency. Mix chemistry in glass or plastic containers - never metal.

- Always wear gloves and safety glasses when weighing and mixing chemistry.

- Always use a plastic funnel to prevent spilling and splashing when transferring chemistry, solids or solutions.

- Always clean all utensils and equipment that have been in contact with chemistry.

- Always keep your mixed chemistry in labeled and sealed containers.

- Never keep your chemistry in a location that will be accessible to children, pets, and guests. In other words, do not store your chemistry in your home refrigerator, whether it is labeled or not. If your chemistry needs to be refrigerated buy a small dorm-type unit for your lab and lock it.

- Always mix chemical formulas in the order that the components are listed. There are exceptions to this but those exceptions should be noted along with the ingredients in the formulas.

- Always have 911 or poison control numbers posted in your lab.

- As an artist, your eyes are your life. You must have an eyewash kit in your lab.

Note: Please be aware that all chemicals are hazardous in one form or another and any concerns you may have regarding their use and dangers can be found by accessing MSDS Web sites or by requesting MSDS data sheets from the companies that supply you with chemistry. If you intend to use any of these chemicals in a class situation it is imperative that you have MSDS data sheets on hand in the event of an emergency.

Dichromates: Safety and Disposal

Dichromates—ammonium, potassium, and sodium versions are potentially hazardous chemicals and care should be taken in both their use and disposal. Be very careful to avoid breathing a dichromate dust, because it is toxic, and allowing the chemical to come in contact with your skin. Do not touch your skin, mouth, or eyes when working with any dichromate, and if you experience a problem (burning, coughing, difficulty breathing, vomiting, cramps, blurred vision, etc.), flush the problematic area with lots of water for 15 minutes and seek immediate medical attention. If a dichromate spills on your clothing, remove that article of clothing and wash it well before putting it back on. Wear gloves when working with this chemical. Be especially careful around high heat sources because this chemical's reaction to heat can be quite intense as it decomposes.

Proper disposal of dichromate solutions is important. As a rule, never throw loose and dry dichromate/bichromate orange crystals in the trash. Very small amounts of solution can be disposed of by dilution with copious amounts of water and flushed away. Larger volumes of dichromate are a different matter. One method is to add used developer to a dichromate solution. Another is to make the solution alkaline by adding baking soda to the solution until it becomes alkaline. This change can be detected by using litmus paper. Once the solution is alkaline, pour it through several layers of coffee filters. The liquid will be free of the chromium and flushing of the liquid can take place. The sludge in the coffee filters *must* be disposed of by a hazardous waste facility. Check local college photo lab managers to get the names of these facilities.

CHEMICAL ABSTRACT SERVICE REGISTRY (CAS)

The numbers following each chemical's name are part of a worldwide indexing system called Chemical Abstracts Services Registry (**CAS**). It is used here to ensure that everyone using a chemical is dealing with the same one when describing it for any purpose. The CAS numbers for these, and other chemicals on earth can be found at various sites that offer CAS numbers.

CHEMICALS

Acetic Acid CAS #64-19-7

Acetic acid is a clear fluid and has a pungent vinegar like odor to it. This chemical is used in 20% to 28% dilutions for photographic purposes although a 33% solution is called for in calotype (stronger if the ambient temperature is hot). At 28% it is primarily used as a stop bath and found in hardening fixer bath. It can also be used as a solvent of gelatin and collodion. To prepare a photo grade solution take 3 parts glacial acetic acid and dilute it with 8 parts water. A 5% variation is used to make pickles. I have heard that a weak dilution is also used for treating sunburn but I wouldn't recommend this idea without medical advice. In high concentrations, both its vapors and solution are corrosive and unpleasant for the skin and respiratory system. In low concentrations it will make your eyes sting and may cause an allergic reaction on your skin. Vinegar is a 5% acetic acid. If you spill acetic acid on your skin, wash well with clean water. Do not drink acetic acid at any level stronger than vinegar. If somehow you ingest a strong concentration, take milk of magnesia and seek medical attention. Acetic acid is incompatible with strong oxidizers (*meaning that it will generate heat*), carbonates, hydroxides and strong alkalis (a *violent reaction*). *Never* expose acetic acid to sodium peroxide or nitric acid because it will produce a potential explosion. Dilute well before disposing. Store above 63°F to prevent it from solidifying.

Note: Glacial acetic acid refers to very strong concentrated acetic acid, usually between 80 % to 99 %, with a pH of 2.4. At this concentration it is highly corrosive and a severe poison.

Alum (Ammonium Alum, Ammonia Aluminum Sulfate) CAS #7784-26-1

This component is often found as a hardener for fixing baths and gelatin, hypo-alum toner, and clearing baths. Its fumes will cause distress to your respiratory and intestinal tract and contact will cause itching and reddening to

your skin. If it is ingested, do not induce vomiting. Take normal safety precautions with gloves, goggles, and respirator.

Ammonia CAS #7664-41-7

Ammonia is a corrosive gaseous fluid that can cause severe burning reactions to the respiratory system, eyes and tissue. It is normally used in solution as ammonium hydroxide. High degrees of exposure can cause fatal reactions, including death. Be cautious when using this chemical. There is a very strong odor associated with it and a dual-filter respirator is advised. Be especially careful of getting this chemical in your eyes, because even the slightest amount will cause severe problems—even with immediate first aid treatment and wash.

Note: Never mix ammonia with silver nitrate or gold because it forms explosive azides.

Ammonium Carbonate CAS #506-87-6

This chemical presents itself as a fine, white crystal with a hint of ammonia in its odor. It is found most often as an accelerator in warm tone developers and is not particularly dangerous. Vapors may cause respiratory distress and contact with eyes, mucous membranes, and skin will result in redness and irritation. It should be kept at a good distance from acids and strong alkalis. Use normal safety precautions.

Ammonium Chloride (Sal-Ammoniac) CAS #12125-02-9

Ammonium chloride is a white crystal/powder used as an accelerator in sodium thiosulfate fixing baths. It is also employed in salted albumen papers. This chemical is troublesome for the eyes and your respiratory system. It is important to know that heating this chemical will cause a wispy smoke that is very unpleasant. (*hydrochloric acid and ammonia*). Ammonium chloride will cause respiratory distress if inhaled. It is not compatible with acid concentrates, potassium chlorate, and ammonium nitrate. Wear a respirator, safety glasses, and gloves when mixing.

Ammonium Citrate CAS #12125-02-9

This chemical is a moderately safe one to work with. Inhalation of the powder will cause respiratory distress and is particularly problematic if it gets into your eyes causing redness and pain. Be careful not to inhale, ingest, or rub this chemical on your skin. If you experience a bad reaction to ammonium citrate on your skin or in your eyes, flush well with water and seek medical attention.

Ammonium Dichromate (Also Bichromate) CAS #7789-09-5

This chemical is used in sensitizers for a number of non-silver and alternative processes (*gum bichromate and carbon printing*) and behaves in much the same manner as potassium dichromate except that it is more aggressive and becomes saturated at 25% vs. 13%. Its crystals are orange in color and a strong irritant for literally every part of your being. It can cause ulcerations on the skin, and if inhaled, significant respiratory distress—especially in mucous membranes. Ammonium dichromate is flammable.

Ammonium Ferric Oxalate CAS #14221-47-7
(Ammonium iron(III) oxalate trihydrate)
Like all oxalates, this chemical will be toxic to your health and *highly corrosive* to skin, eyes, tissue, and respiratory system. This chemical can be absorbed in the body by breathing or ingesting and can cause havoc with your kidneys. Be very careful around any oxalate. Wear Nitrile gloves, a dual-filter respirator and safety glasses. Also, never work with any oxalate without adequate ventilation. Do not breath the fumes of any oxalate because its fumes can be absorbed through the lungs. If you spill an oxalate on your clothing, forget modesty; remove the clothing and wash it well with plenty of water. Do not mix any oxalate with a strong concentrated acid or oxidizer and do not dispose of it in any place but a hazardous waste facility. Most college photography labs have contracts with chemical disposal services and you should contact them for assistance if you need to get rid of dangerous chemistry.

Ammonium Hydroxide (30% Ammonia) CAS #1336-21-6

This chemical, also known as *ammonia water*, is often found in developing and toning solutions as an accelerator. Essentially, it is an aggressive form of ammonia and water used in the Mordançage process. A 5% solution is the equivalent of household ammonia. Always work with good ventilation and wear gloves.

Ammonium Thiocyanate CAS #1762-95-4

Also known as ammonium sulphocyanide, ammonium thiocyanate is a component of gold-thiocyanate toning in POP and appears as a colorless, deliquescent (readily absorbs water) crystal with a slight odor of ammonia. It is incompatible with chlorates, oxidizing agents, peroxides, and strong acids where contact will liberate a toxic hydrogen cyanide. Inhalation will cause respiratory distress and all normal safety precautions should be adhered to when using the chemical.

Ammonium Thiosulfate (Rapid Fixer) CAS #1183-18-8

This chemical, when substituted for sodium thiosulfate, is used as a fixing salt in many high-speed fixers, i.e., rapid fixer. In terms of fixing speed, it is much faster than sodium thiosulfate. Ammonium thiosulfate is a colorless crystalline salt. Extended contact, as all photographers know, will cause skin irritations. Decomposition or heating of this chemical will release a highly toxic sulfur dioxide gas. Keep it away from cyanotype chemistry. Use tongs when working with this chemical and wear gloves and a respirator when mixing.

Borax (Sodium Tetraborate) CAS #1303-96-4

Borax is often used as a weak alkali accelerator in developers and in some hardening fixing baths. It is also used to make a gold toner more alkaline and allows for a faster rate of gold deposit. Employed as a laundering agent, borax is the same chemical you will find in the supermarket. Its use has a moderate health risk and normal safety precautions should be adhered to when using it. If you ingest or breathe large quantities of it, wash the exposed area well and seek medical attention if symptoms persist, i.e., difficulty breathing, irritation, muscular spasms, itching, or pain.

Boric Acid CAS #10043-35-3

This chemical is used in hardening fixers containing potash alum and acetic acid. It extends the life of fixers and can be found in some buffered fine-grain developers.

Cesium Chloropalladite

Cesium is a double salt built on an alkaline metal compound. Cesium sits at the lower end of Group 1 on the periodic table and is a very heavy metal used in the Ziatype process (*for the brown coloration*). This chemical, found in certain non-silver processes, is an irritant to the skin, eyes, and respiratory system. Seek medical attention if physical distress accompanies its use.

Chrome Alum (Potassium Sulfate) CAS #7778-99-0

Chrome alum appears as a deep red/purple granule and has no odor. It is sometimes employed as a hardening agent for gelatin and has a moderate health risk associated with its use. It is incompatible with aluminum and magnesium and will cause respiratory distress if inhaled. Do not touch your skin, eyes, or mucous membranes while using it, and flush any infected area with copious amounts of water. Seek medical attention if symptoms persist.

Citric Acid (2-Hydroxypropane) CAS #77-92-9

Since we use a great deal of this acid in alternative process work I have a little more to say about it than others. Citric acid is very useful as a first rinse bath in iron processes in that it lessens the chance of your print developing iron stains. EDTA performs a similar chore as a chelate. Citric Acid is the most common food acidulant (*an acid combined with a food product to flavor or preserve*) is citric acid. This acid was initially extracted from lemons or other citrus fruit but today it is manufactured through a sucrose fermentation technique and recovered by precipitation, evaporation, or crystallization. It is available in two forms: monohydrate or anhydrous (approximately 8.6% moisture), and is sometimes available as a solution. The product obtained by fermentation is identical to organic citric acid.

We work with citric acid in a white powder form and it is colorless upon dilution. It is also odorless with a strong acidic flavor. One gram is soluble in 0.5 ml water. The pH of a 1% solution of the monohydrate is 2.3 and of a 1% solution of the anhydrous form is 2.2. The Food and Drug Administration recognizes citric acid as safe.

Citric acid aids in the preservation of texture, color, aroma and vitamin content of food products and is particularly useful as a chelant. Citric acid is the preferred acidulant to ensure optimum gel formation in pectin products. This chemical is commonly used in toners, as a

clearing bath for some alternative processes, and is one of the options to hydrochloric acid in platinum/palladium clearing. Citric acid is also used to transfer photomechanical ink images (*Rauschenberg used it*) via saturation and rubbing the image on a clean piece of paper. It is not dangerous to work with but can cause irritations to eyes, skin, and respiratory system if handled in a cavalier manner. However, do not mix citric acid with metallic nitrates because the reaction may be explosive. It is also incompatible with carbonates, copper, aluminum, and zinc.

Collodion

Collodion is a viscous fluid that is used in photographic practice as a salted binder for sensitizing wet plate, ferrotype, and Ambrotype glass plates. It is not particularly dangerous but is highly flammable and precautions should be made when working with the material. Although it is possible to make collodion at home with nitrated cotton, ether, and alcohol, I strongly advise that you do not do so. Instead, purchase a prepared plain collodion.

When using collodion be sure to have adequate ventilation, wear gloves, and wear a respirator if airborne concentrations are high. Collodion vapors can exist quite a distance from the actual material and you must be sure that any ignition source is off before use. Keep the collodion away from strong acids and oxidizers and take general lab safety precautions when using it.

Copper Chloride CAS #10125-13-0

Copper chloride appears as a blue/green crystal and is used in many toners, bleaches (*Mordançage*), and intensifiers. This chemical is a strong oxidizing agent and presents a significant health hazard if used casually. Avoid light, air, and moisture in storage. Toxic fumes are harmful if breathed and its dust must be avoided. Always wear a dual-filter respirator, gloves, and goggles when mixing or using. Copper chloride is incompatible with potassium, sodium, oxidizers, and strong acids that may result in the release of toxic chloride vapors. Overexposure will result in a host of problems, including respiratory distress, chills, burning sensations in the intestinal tract, headache, and so on. Be very careful when using this chemical and seek immediate medical attention if in distress.

Copper Nitrate CAS #10402-29-6

Be careful around this chemical because it is harmful to your body. Prolonged or intense contact will cause chills, gastrointestinal problems, and pain. Avoid contact with the skin, breathing or ingestion. Irritations of many sorts, and burns, are common if precaution is not taken in the use of this chemical. Like all nitrates, you must be vigilant when using it and adhere to all safety precautions; gloves, goggles, and a respirator. Seek immediate medical attention if in distress.

Copper Sulfate CAS #7758-98-7

Copper sulfate appears as a blue/translucent crystal or powder. This chemical is used in toners (*copper*), bleaches, and intensifiers. Not a great deal is known about this chemical other than it is a moderately toxic one and all precautions should be taken in its use and handling. Wear gloves and a respirator for mixing or prolonged use and do not touch your eyes or mouth when using it.

EDTA

Disodium EDTA (Disodium Salt Dihydrate) CAS #6381-92-6

Also known as Ethylenediamine Tetracetic Acid, Disodium Salt. Used as a first clearing bath for Pt / Pd. It may irritate the skin, eyes, and respiratory system. This chemical is more of an irritant than a danger and should be handled in a similar manner as its sibling tetrasodium EDTA.

Tetrasodium EDTA (Tetrasodium Salt Dihydrate) CAS #10378-23-1

Repeat after me . . . *ethylenediamine tetraacetic acid tetrasodium salt dihydrate* is a chemical recently employed as an alternative to hydrochloric or citric acid in some clearing baths. It is relatively safe to use and is commonly found as a preservative in some foods and in agricultural uses. It may irritate the skin, eyes, and respiratory system. EDTA is generally purchased in a white crystal form and can cause minor problems if you are too casual when using it.

EDTA is commonly found as a preservative in processed foods, in cosmetics to improve stability, as a detergent in the dairy industry to clean bottles, as a treatment for mercury poisoning, and in soft drinks containing ascorbic acid and sodium benzoate (most all of them) to reduce the formation of the carcinogenic benzene. It can also be used in the recovery of used lead acid batteries and is found in cleaning compounds, detergents, and in photography as an oxidizing agent.

Ferric Ammonium Citrate CAS #1185-57-5

Ferric ammonium citrate is also known as *iron ammonium citrate, ammonium ferric citrate, iron citrate, and ammonium iron(III) citrate*. It presents itself as a green, or brown, scale crystal / powder, has a somewhat undetermined structure, and is prepared by treating ferric hydroxide with hydrated citric acid (75%), iron (16%), and ammonia (7.5%). This chemical is commonly found in iron supplements, cyanotype formulas, iron toners, other non-silver formulas and functions as a sensitizer. It is not particularly toxic but you must still exercise care in its handling, storage, and use. It may be the cause of eye and skin irritations if precautions are ignored. If you notice that your urine is pink then you have absorbed or inhaled far too much of this chemical. Seek medical attention.

Ferric Citrate CAS #2338-05-8

Ferric Citrate is a brownish red powder in a 17% iron state. There is a purified variation of this chemical but it is not what you are looking for in alt pro work. Ferric citrate is light sensitive and is used, for our purposes, primarily as an ingredient in preparing a Van Dyke Part C Contrast Control alternative to be mixed with the tradition Van Dyke Part C. (See the Van Dyke chapter.) It is not particularly toxic but you must still exercise care in its handling, storage, and use. It may be the cause of eye and skin irritations if precautions are ignored.

Ferric Oxalate (Ferric Ammonium Oxalate) CAS #2944-67-4

Platinum and kallitype printers use ferric oxalate as the light sensitive ingredient in their sensitizers. It is an oxalic acid salt and is toxic. The body can deal with it in small quantities. Ferric oxalate is a weakly bound chemical and will quickly decay to ferrous oxalate and then to oxalic acid and ferric oxide (rust). Please see the potassium oxalate entry for more information.

Ferric oxalate is a green/transparent crystal and is light sensitive. All oxalates are toxic and you should avoid breathing, touching, or ingesting them. They are corrosive to all parts of your body and can cause ulcerations on the skin. Severe kidney damage can be the result of large amounts of absorption or breathing fumes. Wear latex or Nitrile gloves, respirator, and eye protection when working with oxalates. If you happen to spill ferric oxalate on your skin, wash it well with clean water. If you spill it on your clothing remove that clothing and wash it well. If it is ingested, immediately administer magnesia, administer an emetic (*a medicine that causes vomiting*), and call a doctor. Be extra cautious when using any oxalate because it is a most serious health hazard if used in a casual manner.

EDTA is a chelate that will dissolve ferric oxalate . . . an important thing to know when you need to use it as a clearing bath.

Ferrous Sulfate CAS #7782-63-0

This is used in stain removing and clearing baths. If you have taken in too much of this chemical through breathing, touching, or tasting, you will have an acidic and sour taste in your mouth. It does not keep well in solution. This chemical can cause itching, burning in the eyes, breathing difficulty, and general ill health. Be diligent in its use and follow all safety precautions. Seek immediate medical attention if you find yourself in discomfort or distress when using this chemical.

Formalin/Formaldehyde CAS #50-00-0

Formalin/Formaldehyde, a 37% concentration of formaldehyde gas in water with additional component of methyl alcohol, is employed as a hardener and preservative in photography. Formalin is used as a tanning and hardening agent of gelatin in gum bichromate and other processes where sizing/hardening is required. This chemical is highly toxic and unhealthy to the body if safety precautions are not used. Do not breathe the fumes (*which are very strong*) and work only in very well ventilated environments, such as outdoors with the wind at your back. Be cautious of formalin prepared papers indoors, after they are dry, because they will continue to outgas for a day or so and be dangerous to your respiratory system. Fumes from formalin will attack your mucous membranes of eyes, nose, and throat. This

chemical is a carcinogen and you must take it very seriously. If somehow this chemical is ingested, seek immediate medical attention: You will see the following . . . coughing and respiratory distress that persists, violent vomiting, headache, severe abdominal pain, weak pulse, burns, blurred vision, sudden change in skin color to white. In other words, take this seriously.

See Glyoxal below.

Gallic Acid CAS #149-91-7

Gallic acid appears as a white/pale yellow crystal and is used as a component in cyanotype toning and in Talbot's original calotype process. It does not present a significant health hazard but is incompatible with ferric salts, silver salts, alkalis, ammonia, chlorates, and strong oxidizing agents. Over-exposure will cause moderate discomfort and should be treated with respect regardless of its low toxicity.

Glyoxal CAS #107-22-2

This chemical is recommended as a substitute for formalin as a hardening agent for gelatin in sizing for the gum bichromate process. It is a variation, in terms of reactivity and toxicity, to formalin but insufficient evidence has been offered by the scientific community to allow you to treat it casually. Glyoxal should never be mixed with sodium hydroxide or nitric acid and if heated in an enclosed container it is explosive. It is also corrosive to all metals. Glyoxal should be used in well-ventilated environments (such as outdoors) and all precautions should be taken to prevent ingestion, contact with the skin and breathing its fumes. Note: just because glyoxal doesn't have an offensive odor like formaldehyde, does not indicate that it is safer and that you can relax using it. Treat glyoxal with the same respect you would formalin.

Gold Chloride CAS #16903-35-8

Gold chloride is also known as *chloroauric acid, gold trichloride acid and hydrogen tetrachloroaurate(III)*. Gold chloride is generally used in dilutions of 1%, 5%, and 8% for purposes of toning in a number of processes. Gold chloride is also a primary component in Ziatype printing and will raise the contrast of the print when added to the formula. Gold chloride is a strong irritant and can cause significant skin and respiratory allergies if you are casual with it. Pay heed to all normal precautions when using this chemical.

Gum Arabic CAS #9000-01-5

Gum arabic, or gum acacia, can be traced back in time to 2650 B.C.E. where it was harvested from the sap of various species of Acacia trees in Nigeria, Cameroon, Chad, Mali, and the Sudan. The Acacia trees grow primarily in the sub-Saharan (Sahel) areas of Africa and the Sudanese variety is considered the premium grade. In gum printing, the dichromate is added to the gum to create the liquid foundation of the gum sensitizer. Gum arabic comes in a variety of grades (tints) from colorless to dark brown. On exposure to light, the gum and the ammonium dichromate solution will harden in proportion to the exposure of UV light.

Hydrogen Peroxide (3%) CAS #7722-84-1

Hydrogen Peroxide is a colorless and not very stable liquid used primarily as a bleaching agent, as an antiseptic and as an oxidizing accelerator in the cyanotype process. You do not have to be enormously concerned with this chemical when purchased in its 3% over-the-counter form. In dentistry applications it is often mixed with water and used to clean wounds inside the mouth.

Hydrogen Peroxide (28%—33%)

In this strong concentration, used primarily for Mordançage bleaching and in beauty parlors to alter hair color. Hydrogen peroxide is a health hazard. Wear appropriate protection, do not breathe the fumes, and flush exposed areas well with water if you experience problems after contact. If you work in a beauty salon, please wear appropriate protective clothing, gloves and breathing apparatus . . . this stuff is not good for you and may, under some circumstances, lead to pulmonary edema . . . also known as high altitude sickness, where fluid accumulates in the lungs.

Hydrogen tetrachloroaurate(III) trihydrate CAS #27988-77-8

Used in the sensitizer for Chrysotype–Version S. Also known as gold(III) chloride hydrate and hydochloroauric acid. In early literature it was called gold chloride. This chemical is corrosive and can be destructive to your mucous membranes. Take appropriate safety and working measures when using this chemical.

Kodak Hypo Clearing Bath

This solution is used to accelerate the neutralization of fixer and therefore cut the wash times for films and papers. Two formulas for hypo clearing baths are:

Formula #1: 750 ml of water, 200 g sodium sulfite (anhydrous), 50 g sodium bisulfite, and water to make 1 liter.

Formula #2: 125 ml hydrogen peroxide, 10 ml ammonia solution, and water to make 1 liter.

Other formulas include sodium sulfite, EDTA, sodium citrate, and sodium metabisulfite. Hypo clearing agents can be mild irritants to the body in concentrated solutions for lengthy exposure.

Lead Acetate CAS #301-04-2

This chemical is used as a toner. Lead acetate is a possible carcinogen, and like other lead products, is toxic. It can be a problem for your body and can be absorbed by breathing its fumes. It is a poison if ingested and can cause brain damage. Fumes are released when it is heated. Be cautious in all safety respects when using this chemical.

Lithium Palladium Chloride/Lithium Chloropalladite

Lithium Palladium Chloride/Lithium Chloropalladite is a double salt built on an alkaline metal compound (*lithium*) which is a lightweight alkali sitting atop the periodic table. It is used in the Ziatype process and results in a cool black value. Do not drink it or play with it. Lithium is a primary component in medicating manic depression and high incidences of exposure can have adverse effects on the nervous system.

Mercuric Chloride CAS #7487-94-7

Also known as mercury(II) chloride was used as a photographic intensifier to produce positive pictures in the collodion process of the 1800s. When applied to a negative, the mercury(II) chloride whitens and thickens the image, thereby increasing the opacity of the shadows and creating the illusion of a positive image (*Towler, 1864*).

Mercuric chloride is toxic, white, and a soluble salt of mercury (at 6%). It has been used in disinfectant, as a fungicide, as a treatment for syphilis before antibiotics, and in photographic fixers. It's also odorless, colorless, and really dangerous, which is why I'm letting you know about it here. Take all safety precautions when working with this chemical.

Methyl Alcohol (Wood Spirit) CAS #67-56-1

This is a poison. It can be readily absorbed by breathing and through the skin and is considered very dangerous to the central nervous system. It can cause blindness. Use all safety precautions against exposure when using methyl alcohol. If methyl alcohol is swallowed, administer an emetic (a medicine that induces vomiting) and bicarbonate of soda (1 tsp. in a cup of water) and call a doctor.

Muriatic Acid (Hydrochloric Acid) CAS #7647-01-0

Muriatic, or hydrochloric, acid is a clear, colorless, irritating vaporous, poison that was used as a primary clearing bath with Pt / Pd and as a tray cleaner . . . among other uses. It can be purchased at hardware stores and pool supplies and is often used by masons for cleaning bricks. Be respectful of this chemical and take precautions while using it.

Nitric Acid CAS #7679-37-2

Nitric acid is a colorless liquid and will make its appearance known as soon as you unscrew the top to its bottle; a chemical vaporous smoke will appear like an evil genie from the bottle. It is used in some cyanotype toning formulas as a preservative in Pyro developers and as a component in bleach. Nitric acid is highly corrosive to most anything it comes in contact with, including your body. At present, there is really no safe way to use this chemical in regards to ventilation except for a professional chemical hood. Nitric acid is a very aggressive oxidizer and will react violently with a vast range of metals, acids, solvents, and other things found in the lab or home. Although I like using it in cyanotype toning I am not sure if the resulting color is actually worth the risk. If you are a teacher, you mix the formula. Also, be careful of the cap on the glass bottle that the acid is stored in. If it is an old fashioned plastic cap, there is a good chance that the acid

will destroy the cap's integrity in time. Be hyper-careful in its use and storage. If this chemical is spilled on skin, wipe off what you can, immerse the relevant skin areas in water, and then cover the area with a paste of water and baking soda. Go to a hospital and seek immediate medical attention. If you spill it on your clothing, forget modesty and immediately remove your clothes. If nitric acid is ever swallowed, administer a small amount of soap softened in water, milk, or raw egg. You can also force the patient to drink a small amount of magnesia or plaster softened in water. Go to a hospital or call 911.

Oxalic Acid (Ethanedioic Acid) CAS #144-62-7

Oxalic acid is translucent and odorless. This chemical is used in blue toners and as a preservative in certain Pyro formulas. It is found in all leafy green vegetables but is highly toxic in strong concentrations and you must use all safety precautions in its use and storage. Oxalic acid is corrosive to tissue and removes calcium from the blood which may result in kidney damage. It is incompatible with alkalis, silver, and oxidizing agents. Take normal safety precautions when using this chemical.

Palladium Chloride CAS #7647-10-1

Palladium chloride is dark brown and without odor. This chemical is found primarily in palladium printing and in certain other non-silver processes and is an irritant to the skin, eyes, and respiratory system. Palladium chloride is moderately toxic. It is often associated with manic depression altering medication. High doses can cause problems with central nervous system functions. Be cautious of contact with the skin, ingestion, and breathing fumes. Use normal precautions in its use and handling.

Potassium Bromide CAS #7758-02-3

Potassium bromide appears as white crystal and is without odor. This chemical is often used as a restrainer in bleachers and developers. It is also widely used in intensification, reducing, toning and many other photographic formulas. It is mildly irritating to the tissues of your body and can sometimes cause skin problems. It is a mutagen and extreme exposures can result in depression of the central nervous system. Potassium bromide is incompatible with strong oxidizers and acids. Use all safety precautions.

Potassium Chloroplatinite CAS #10025-99-7

This chemical is found in toners, intensifiers, and is the primary ingredient in platinum printing. This chemical is highly corrosive to human tissue and can cause severely adverse reactions to extreme or long-term exposure. This chemical is a poison and should be used and handled with all safety precautions.

Potassium Dichromate CAS #7778-50-9

Potassium dichromate (bichromate) is a beautiful orange crystal and is used as a principal sensitizer in the gum bichromate processes, and as a contrast boost additive in many non-silver processes. It is also a bleaching agent. It is most often used as a saturated solution or diluted for use as a contrast additive to wash-development baths or sensitizer. It is highly toxic, corrosive, and can enter the body through absorption, ingestion, and breathing. It can cause extreme allergic reactions and is a powerful irritant to human tissues and internal systems. It is a carcinogen and must be handled with care. It is incompatible with any combustible, organic, or oxidizable material. It is extremely destructive to tissue and respiratory systems and may cause distress. If this chemical is spilled on clothing, remove the clothing immediately. Do not be the least bit casual when using this chemical and seek immediate medical attention if you experience discomfort in breathing, burning, or dizziness.

(See Dichromate Safety and Disposal under Ammonium Dichromate)

Potassium Ferricyanide CAS #13746-66-2

Potassium ferricyanide is an orange-red crystal and has no odor. It is also called *"Red Prussiate of Potash"* and is used in reducers, bleaches, toners and many alternative and non-silver processes, specifically iron based. Ruby red in color, potassium ferricyanide is a low toxicity level chemical. It is the Part A (*bleaching agent*) of sepia toner and one of the primary ingredients in cyanotype. Potassium ferricyanide is poisonous in high concentrations. Take all necessary precautions in its use and handling. Do not expose it to acids, because it may release a cyanide gas (*hydrocyanic acid*). If potassium ferricyanide is swallowed, administer a tablespoon of 3% hydrogen peroxide. Have the patient inhale ammonia fumes, provide artificial respiration if necessary, and call a doctor. Potassium ferricyanide is incompatible with extreme heat and can release fumes of cyanide and oxides of nitrogen. It is also incompatible with ammonia. Use standard safety precautions when using this chemical.

Potassium Iodide CAS #7681-11-0

Potassium Iodide, also known as potassium salt, is a white odorless chemical used as a salting agent in the first stage of the Calotype and is responsible, in combination with silver nitrate, for the silver iodide compound. It is not a particularly hazardous chemical but you should take normal safety precautions when using it. Avoid breathing, ingesting, or placing potassium iodide in direct contact with your skin. If you get any in your eyes or on your skin, flush the area with clean water for 15 minutes. Seek medical attention if irritation or a rash persists.

Potassium Metabisulfite CAS #16731-55-8

Potassium metabisulfite is a white crystalline powder with a pungent sulfur odor. The main use for the chemical is as an antioxidant or chemical sterilant. It is a sulfite and is chemically very similar to sodium metabisulfite, with which it is sometimes used interchangeably. Potassium metabisulfite is used as a clearing agent in the gum bichromate process.

Potassium Oxalate CAS #583-52-8

The oxalates are the only salts that are poisonous but they are not always bad for you or the environment. Oxalic acid is commonly found in nature, i.e., in green leafy vegetables, and is responsible for the bitter taste. Too much of it is not good for you . . . 10 pounds of spinach in one sitting is a lethal dose of oxalic acid. In small quantities the human body deals with the oxalates quite handily as the body produces natural chelates that render them harmless. The most commonly used developers such as ammonium citrate; potassium oxalate, sodium acetate, and sodium citrate are quite harmless and can be disposed of in a municipal sewage system if well diluted.

Potassium oxalate is transparent, odorless, used in toners, and as one of the developer options for platinum/palladium. Like all oxalates, this chemical in a concentrated form is toxic and corrosive to human tissue. Unsafe exposure is foolhardy because this chemical can cause significant problems for all parts of your body. It is incompatible with strong acids and oxidizers. Use all safety precautions, including Nitrile gloves, respirator, and safety glasses. Seek immediate medical attention if you experience distress when using it. Signs and symptoms of distress are: nervousness, cramps, depression, corrosive action on the mucous membranes, redness of the skin, blurred vision, burns, and pain.

Potassium Sodium Tartrate (Rochelle Salt) CAS #304-59-6

Potassium sodium tartrate is a double salt first prepared in La Rochelle, France, in 1675. As a result the salt is known as Rochelle salt and is used in alternative processes in the Kallitype. Rochelle salt can be made from common household goods: cream of tartar and baking powder.

Pyrogallic Acid CAS #87-66-1

This chemical, principally used as a high-octane developer for "*pyromaniacs*" enters the body through absorption. It may cause respiratory and gastrointestinal problems. Avoid the chemical's dust or breathing its fumes. Use appropriate safety precautions.

Silver Nitrate CAS #7161-88-8

Silver nitrate appears as a colorless and odorless crystal and discolors on exposure to light. Silver nitrate is highly corrosive. This chemical can cause severe skin and eye problems and is particularly destructive to mucous membranes and the upper respiratory tract. It is the primary silver salt found in photographic emulsions, alternative processes (i.e., van dyke, salted paper, kallitype, albumen, calotype, etc.) and intensifiers. Silver nitrate will discolor your skin, is a caustic substance, and may cause blindness if it gets into your eyes. If you get silver nitrate on your skin you may experience redness and eventual henna like brown stain that will last for several days. On exposure, wash the area well with repeated rinses of water. Rubbing the area of exposure with sodium chloride (*table salt*) will help lessen the damage to a degree and with stain removal.

   This is more serious . . . If you get silver nitrate in your eyes, immediately flush with copious amounts of water, or saline solution, and continue doing so while medical attention is summoned. If you get a bad silver nitrate stain on anything but your eyes, you can eliminate the black stain by washing the area with a solution of 2 teaspoons of sodium bisulfite in a quart of water. Be cautious of the sulfur dioxide gas that will be created by this act of cleansing. If you happen to ingest silver nitrate, you will experience great distress, burning, shock, and coma. **Do not induce vomiting**. Force-feed strong salted water concentrations.

   Silver nitrate is a very strong oxidizer. It will combust and explode if allowed to come into contact with any ammonia compounds, i.e., ammonium hydroxide (*the strong concentration of ammonia used in mordançage*). Never mix silver nitrate solutions with metals such as aluminum or zinc. Use extreme safety precautions especially by wearing gloves, respirator, and goggles or safety glasses when working with this chemical.

Sodium Acetate CAS #127-09-3

Sodium acetate is the sodium salt of acetic acid. Its pH rests between 7.5 and 9.5. It is an inexpensive chemical produced in industrial quantities for a wide range of uses. As the conjugate base of acetic acid, it is a relatively strong base. Sodium acetate is used as one of several developer options for platinum/palladium is not particularly toxic. Sodium acetate is often found in toners such as gold and is employed as a buffer in acidic solutions. It should be used and handled with respect. Use normal safety precautions.

Sodium Bisulfate CAS #7681-38-1

Sodium bisulfate appears as a white crystal and is odorless. It is used as an acid rinse and in combination with acetic acid, as a stop bath. It can also be used in conjunction with sodium chloride to make a hydrochloric acid substitute. It presents a low health risk but normal safety precautions should be adhered to when using it.

Sodium Bisulfite CAS #7631-90-5

Sodium bisulfite is a coarse, white granule and has a strong odor of sulfur. It is used as a preservative in fixing baths and for removing stains from gum bichromate and POP processes. It can be substituted for sodium metabisulfite. It is a strong irritant to the respiratory system and can cause irritation to the skin, eyes, and mucous tissue. Take normal safety precautions when using this chemical.

Sodium Carbonate (Anhydrous) CAS #497-19-8

Sodium carbonate appears as a white odorless granule. This chemical is also called *soda ash*, and *hydro-sodium*, and is used as a primary alkali accelerator in developers. It is also used in cyanotype toning and works as a reducer and bleach on iron prints. It is an irritant to eyes, tissue, and the respiratory system. Sodium carbonate can release a gas when mixed with acid, stop, or fixing baths. It reacts violently with acids and caution should be taken. Kodak Balanced Alkali (Kodalk) can be used as a replacement for sodium carbonate. Use with care regardless of the low risk.

Sodium Chloride (Kosher Salt) CAS #7647-14-5

Sodium chloride appears as a white odorless crystal and has a very low health risk associated with it. It is used primarily in salting gelatin for albumen and salted paper printing, as a fixing agent, as an additive to first rinse washes, and when mixed with water, a wonderful substance to go scuba diving in. It is also good to keep on hand in the lab for when you order out for pizza. Note: do not buy ordinary table salt and think that it is pure sodium chloride. More than likely, it is loaded with additives. Buy kosher salt or sodium chloride from a chemical supply. Use caution not to rub it in your eyes and flush overexposed areas with water to rinse it clean.

Sodium Citrate (Tri-Sodium Citrate) CAS #68-04-2

Add baking soda to citric acid and you'll get sodium citrate. Sodium citrate appears as a fine white odorless granule and is incompatible with strong oxidizers. A common use of this chemical is as a primary ingredient in Salted Paper gelatin salted emulsion and Kallitype developer. This chemical has a low health risk but can cause mild irritations to the eyes, tissues, and respiratory system. Sodium citrate is used in ice cream to keep the fat globules from sticking together and as a buffering agent. Sodium citrate attaches to calcium ions in water. Compounds with similar functions are sodium carbonate, EDTA, and phosphoric acid.

Sodium Gold Chloride CAS #13874-02-7

Sodium Palladium Chloride (*see Potassium Chloroplatinite*)

This chemical can cause severe allergic reactions and is an irritant to human tissue. Do not allow it to get into contact with your skin, do not ingest, or breathe its fumes. Use proper safety precautions at all times.

Sodium Potassium Tartrate CAS #304-59-6

Also known as *Rochelle salt*. It is used in some toners, sensitizers, and as a developing component in Kallitype. There are no health hazards associated with this chemical.

Sodium Metabisulfite CAS #7681-57-4

Used as a clearing aid in the gum bichromate process. It may act as an irritant to eyes and skin but is generally considered safe.

Sodium Selenite CAS #10102-18-8

(*See Kodak Selenium Toner*) Refer to selenium for safety concerns.

Sodium Sulfite CAS #7757-83-7

Sodium sulfite appears as a white odorless crystal. This chemical is used extensively in alternative process wet work as a clearing agent for albumen, Ziatype, and chrysotype, as a preservative in many developers, and as a clearing bath for some films such as Polaroid Type 55 Positive/Negative. It is also used as a primary component in fixing baths and presents a very mild health risk. It can be an irritant to eyes and tissue and will release a sulfur dioxide gas if heated. Use general safety precautions in use and handling. It can be substituted for sodium bisulfite.

Sodium Tetraborate CAS #1303-96-4

(*See Borax*)

Sodium tetrachloroaurate(III) dihydrate CAS #13874-02-7

This chemical is used in the Part B solution of the New Chrysotype sensitizer formula and is also known as sodium chloroaurate and sodium gold chloride. Very precious in regards to use with a g cost of $82.00. It is corrosive and can be destructive to your mucous membranes.

Tale appropriate precautions when working with this chemical as it may also cause allergic skin reactions.

Sodium Thiosulfate (Hypo/Fixer) CAS #7772-98-7

Sodium thiosulfate is a colorless and odorless crystal. Sodium Thiosulfate is also known as sodium hyposulfate, "hypo," and incorrectly referred to as hyposulfate of soda since Herschel's discovery of it in 1819. It is used in a vast variety of dilutions depending upon what process you are using it for, and is one of the very few substances that is capable of dissolving silver bromide. Contact with the skin is not dangerous but it can decompose through the action of aging or heat and form a sulfur dioxide gas that is toxic. Be careful not to let this chemical come into contact with your eyes and don't use it as a fragrance behind the ears as one of my students once did.

Sodium Tungstate CAS #53125-86-3

This chemical, according to MSDS data I have read, is one that is being tested for human mutations in the reproductive cycle. It is a primary component in the Ziatype formula system and will lower contrast in that process. It is supposedly not highly toxic, but it will cause general irritation of eyes, tissues, and respiratory system if safety precautions are not adhered to.

Sulfamic Acid CAS #5329-14-6

Sulfamic acid appears as a white and odorless crystal. Sulfamic acid is used as a contrast control in the argyrotype process and employed as an acidifier in ammonium thiosulfate fixing baths. This chemical is corrosive to tissue, eyes, and the respiratory system. It is highly and violently reactive when hot and in combination with nitrates and nitrites. If this sounds like a bomb recipe then you will take great care not to fool around with this chemical near an open heat source. Take great care in using this chemical with gloves, safety glasses, and a respirator.

Tannic Acid CAS #1401-55-4

Tannic acid is a yellow/tan powder and may not, depending on your sensibilities, have an offensive odor. Personally, I rather like it and think it smells like instant iced tea mix. This chemical is a tanning agent and is often used in the toning of cyanotypes. It is a strong oxidizer of metals and chronic exposure is harmful to the liver. It is found in grapes, tea, and cat urine. It can be irritating to the mucous membranes and general caution should be taken when using it. It is incompatible with albumen, gelatin, salts of metals, and strong oxidizers. There is a low health risk with tannic acid but be cautious of the powder's dust and seek fresh air if you experience discomfort.

Tartaric Acid CAS #87-69-4

Tartaric acid is a white, crystalline powder with a strong fruit acid flavor, approximately 10% stronger than citric acid can be manufactured synthetically or recovered from natural sources. It is highly soluble in water, but only slightly hydroscopic. This acid gives apples their sour flavor. It is only mildly toxic and general safety precautions should be used in its handling and use. Tartaric acid is used in several formulas in order to prevent the highlights from getting muddy. It is not used for making tartar sauce . . . and I will not relate the story that goes along with that warning.

3,3' Thiodipropanoic Acid CAS #111-17-1

This chemical, with sodium carbonate and water, is the ligand in the S version of the new Chrysotype. It can be purchased reasonably from the Alfa Aesar company (see Appendix F). It is a skin, eye, and respiratory irritant.

Tri-Sodium Phosphate CAS #7601-54-9

Tri-sodium phosphate is white, odorless, solid, and strongly alkaline. It is commonly found in photographic developers, water softeners, scouring powders, laundry soaps, and dishwashing compounds. In an alternative process application, it works as a yellow toner for cyanotypes.

Tween 20 CAS #9005-64-5

This inexpensive surfactant that may be added to sensitizers, specifically iron-based processes, and it helps in getting the sensitizer into the paper fibers. Can be an eye irritant.

Vinegar

Vinegar strength commonly is measured in "grains." In the United States, this refers to the percentage of acid times 10. For example, 100-grain vinegar contains 10% acetic acid, 90% water. Distilled vinegar strength ranges from 50 to 300 grains. Specialty vinegars range from 40 to 100 grains.

The color of distilled vinegar ranges from a straw color to water white. Most vinegar is 5%.

READER RESPONSIBILITY

I have placed warnings and considerations throughout the text to alert you to possible chemical and health concerns. For a complete overview of all chemicals in use, and their individual MSDS documentation, please refer to the previous chemical descriptions or to the chemical research sites that have been provided. These sites have connections and links to many MSDS databases and each of these databases have MSDS sheets for individual distributors of that chemical. If you have a question about a particular chemical, it is your responsibility find out about that chemical before using it. It is completely the responsibility of the reader to take prudent and appropriate caution when using chemistry of any kind.

A SIMPLE TEST FOR RESIDUAL HYPO/FIXER

A simple test to be sure that all of the sodium thiosulfate/fixer/hypo is removed from your print is to make the following solution. 750 ml of water, 125 ml of 28% acetic acid, 7.5 g of silver nitrate and cold water to make a liter of solution. Place a drop of it in the center of a piece of photographic paper that has experienced the same development, fixing, and washing as the prints you want to keep. After several minutes, rinse the paper with a salt water solution and examine it for a stain in the drop location. Any color deeper than a very light tan stain indicates the presence of hypo. This means that you should wash your prints longer. Store the solution in a dropper bottle and use it when you are concerned about the success of your washing technique.

A SIMPLE TEST FOR RESIDUAL SILVER USING SODIUM SULFIDE

One way of determining whether or not you have fixed your print long enough is to give it a simple sodium sulfide drop test. Mix up a 10% solution of sodium sulfide (*10 g of sodium sulfide with 100 ml of distilled water*) and place a drop of it on a light area of your image. If the drop of sodium sulfide turns brown, this means that you still have residual silver salts in your paper and that additional fixing time is necessary.

Small Volume Conversion Table

DRY MEASURE

1 pound = 453.6 grams

16 ounces = 453.6 grams

1 pound = 16 ounces

16 ounces = 7000 grains

1 ounce = 28.35 grams

1 ounce = 437.5 grains

1 gram = 0.03527 ounce

1 gram = 15.43 grains

10 grams = 154 grains

1 grain = 0.0648 grams

10 grains = .648 grams

7 g sugar = 1 tablespoon

10 grams = 154 grains

10 grains = .648 grams

100 grains = 6.48 grams

1 gram = weight of 1 ml / 1 cc water

1 nickel = 5 grams

1000 g = 2.2 pounds

- To change ounces to grams: multiply ($\times$) ounces by 28.35
- To change grams to ounces: divide ($\div$) grams by 28.35
- To change pounds to grams: multiply ($\times$) by 453.6
- To change grains to grams: multiply ($\times$) grains by 0.0648
- To change grams to grains: divide ($\div$) grams by 0.0648
- To change grams to milligrams: multiply ($\times$) grams by 1000
- To change milligrams to grams: divide ($\div$) milligrams by 1000

LIQUID MEASURE

1 gallon = 4 quarts or 128 fluid ounces (fl oz)

1 gallon = 3.785 liters or 3785 milliliters (ml)

1 quart = 32 fl oz

1 quart = 946 ml

1 liter = 1000 ml

1 liter = 33.81 fl. oz.

1 cup = 240 ml

4 cups = 950 ml

1 pint = 16 fl oz

1 pint = 473.12 ml

1 fluid oz. = 29.57 ml (USA)

1 fluid oz. = 28.41 ml (GB)

1 fluid oz. = 8 fluid dram

1 Tbs = 15 ml / 15 cc

3 Tsp = 1 tablespoon (Tbs.)

1 Tsp = 5 ml / 5 cc

1 dram = 3.697 ml

1 ml = 1 cc   (*cubic centimeters - c. cm.*)

1 cc = 1 ml

1 ml of water = 1 gram (dry weight)

100 ml = 3.38 fl oz.

20 drops = 1 ml / 1 cc / 20 minums

(*use a plastic dropper for consistency*)

1 drop = .067 ml / 1 minum

Ounces & Milliliter Conversions

- To change ounces to milliliters: multiply (×) ounces by 29.57

- To change milliliters to ounces: divide (÷) milliliters by 29.57

Making a Saturated Solution

A saturated solution is one where a specific chemical is added to a volume of water until no more of that chemical will dissolve and where sediment remains in the liquid solution. An example of seeking a saturated solution is where you are mixing up potassium, or ammonium, dichromate to use as an ingredient in a gum bichromate sensitizer. Dichromates are used in a saturated solution in gum printing. Ammonium dichromate is *saturated* at around 25% to 30% and potassium dichromate at 10% to 13%. If you had 100 g of potassium dichromate and you stirred that chemical into 1000 ml of water you would begin to see evidence of saturation in that 10% solution.

TEMPERATURE CONVERSIONS

To Convert Fahrenheit (°F) into Centigrade (°C):

1. Subtract (−) 32 from °F temperature

2. Multiply (×) that number by 5

3. Divide (÷) by this number by 9 to get the °C conversion.

Example: 100°F, minus 32 = 68, times 5 = 340, divided by 9 = 38°C
Equals: *37.77 °C*

To Convert Centigrade into Fahrenheit

1. Multiply (×) Centigrade temperature by 9

2. Divide (÷) that number by 5

3. Add 32 to that number and get the °F conversion.

Example: 38°C, multiply by 9 = 342, divide by 5 = 68.4, add 32 = 100°F
Equals: *100.4°F*

HOW TO FIGURE PERCENTAGES

Percentage (%) is a term applied to expressing the concentration of a given solution where a specific chemical weight has been stirred into a specific volume of liquid. It defines the number of parts in a particular compound when added to 100 parts of a solution. In other words, if you needed to make a 10% solution of potassium dichromate you would simply add 10 grams of potassium dichromate to water until you had a total liquid volume of 100 ml. This is called percent weight per volume (**% w / v**).

Percentages Can Be Expressed in Three Different Ways

- **% w / v** (*percent weight per volume*): This is used when combining a solid with a liquid.

- **% v / v** (*percent volume per volume*): This is used when combining two liquids together. For instance, a 30% solution of hydrogen peroxide would comprise 30 ml of hydrogen peroxide in 100 ml of water.

- **% w / w** (*percent weight per weight*): Seldom used as a measurement, this refers to grams of a given compound per 100 grams of a given solution. *As 1 ml of water has a weight of 1 gram it is not uncommon for grams and ml's to replace one another.*

Figuring a Percentage for a Solution

Here's a quick elementary reference for you to use if you need to make a liter of 15% solution of sodium thiosulfate. Multiply 1000 by 0.15 and you will get 150. Mix 150 grams of sodium thiosulfate into the liter of water for the solution.

If you need to make a liter of 3% solution of sodium thiosulfate multiply 1000 by 0.03 and you will get 30. Mix 30 grams of sodium thiosulfate into the liter of water for the solution.

Light & Exposure Options

LIGHT & EXPOSURE OPTIONS

Sun

What can I say? It's free, exceptionally pleasant to sit around under with friends while making prints; it provides a nice overall exposure but tends to be a bit contrasty in direct sun. It also has a terrific ambience factor. Van Dyke is an exceptionally fast process, compared to a cyanotype, and so you need to be somewhat restrained in your exposure. I recommend a combination of shade and sun for both contrast and highlight information. Personally, I prefer the sun as my light source for exposures due to the slight contrast boost and ambience factor it provides.

1000-Watt Metal Halide Light Source

If you really want to simplify the whole process then you can purchase a 1000-Watt metal halide light source and use that. An example would be the 1000-Watt Metal Halide Maximizer Grow Light System from www.hydroponics.net. The set up includes a bulb, ballast, reflector, and socket assembly. The Maximizer reflector is constructed of brushed aluminum with a bright white finish on the inside. The reflector measures 21" long × 17" wide × 7-1/2" tall. The Maximizer reflector has a unique adjustable light pattern to customize the spread of light. The average exposure time with an average Van Dyke negative will be 8–12 minutes.

Metal halides emulate mid-day summer sunlight and contain all the wavelengths of the visible spectrum. To plants this means quality simulated sunlight and photosynthesis at a level much higher than that which fluorescent lamps can achieve. The unit runs about $250. And is more than adequate for your UV needs.

The downside of the 1000-Watt metal halide light source is that while it is remarkably efficient in separating the darker values in a Van Dyke image it has a very narrow range when interpreting highlight details. The upside is that it is faster than a traditional UV exposure unit.

HID (High Intensity Discharge)

You have seen these types of light attached to oncoming traffic on the road at night . . . an eerie blue glow and very bright. Briefly, HID light sources are easy to use, not terribly expensive when compared to some other options, and are a good source of light with decent exposure speed. HID units, large enough to cover a 30" width, are at least a stop faster than a similarly sized UV printer. The only possible drawbacks to using them would be their need to be left on because the warm up time is significant depending upon the size of the unit. They also pump out a great deal of heat and this is not pleasant in the lab during the summer, on a humid day, when it's raining outside.

UV Exposure Unit

These manufactured "pizza oven" (*because they have a hinged flap door in the front for loading the contact printing frames*) like exposure units are moderately expensive but so consistent and dependable that for a serious alt pro artist, or a college lab, they are ideal. My favorite unit is made by Jon Edwards at **www.eepjon.com/uv** and I have a bank of 4 at The Art Institute of Boston and a couple in my studio. Because of their dependability, and consistent exposure, these units are very important for those who do not live in perfect climates.

Jon's UV exposure unit uses BL black light (UV) tubes that are rated at 7,500 hours life, while most light bulbs are rated at only 1,000 hours. After 2000–3000 hours of use, there will be about 12% reduction in intensity at these times. One year of 8-hour work days equals 2080 hours; so estimating your total "on" time for an average day and the number of days per year you print will give you a bench mark for when you need to change your tubes. Two thousand hours would be about 5–10 years' use for most photographers who use their light source once or twice a week.

They are designated as: F15T8/BL preheat (11 × 14 and 14 × 16) or F20T12/BL preheat (18 × 20 for the standard units. Some lighting supply houses may have them or can order them. (See Appendix F.)

Building a UV Light Source from Kits (www.eepjon.com)

Jon Edwards retails a UV Light Source Kit and these are available for 8, 12, or 16 black light fluorescent lamp option. The kits are a different design than the UV light sources shown on the web site, and do not have an off-on switch or GFIC, but they have functionally the same UV output. The units are designed to start and stop with a GRAlab timer. Each fluorescent lamp and ballast is tested and includes all the parts to assemble your light source except for the white paint (optional), yellow carpenter's glue, black PVC electrical tape, and Band-Aids for your cuts and scrapes. Brass-plated piano hinge for the door to finish out your light source is included. The 4" fan opening and the air-cooling slots will be cut for you. So, all you all you have to do is drill ¼" wire feed-through holes for the ballast wires, then assemble your light source. The ¾" plywood is cabinet grade material that is cut to size and is the same material used for the assembled light sources shown on this web site. Complete step-by-step instructions included.

A SIMPLE ULTRAVIOLET UV EXPOSURE UNIT

When snow, sleet, freezing rain, or dead of night is preventing you from making your alternative process exposures it's nice to have an ultraviolet (UV) exposure unit. These units can be purchased from several companies but generally cost between $800 and $1200. for a decent one. They are a bit slower than summer sunlight and will yield values that exhibit a little less contrast. They have the advantage of being a convenient, controlled, and constant source of light. Here are some instructions for making an inexpensive UV exposure unit without having to call an electrician or worry about electrocuting yourself.

Materials Needed

- A footlocker. The kind you used to take to camp with a removable shelf that sat on an inside rail for socks and special stuff. Check out an army and navy store, or a discount superstore.

- A piece of ½" plywood slightly smaller than the inside of your footlocker's inner dimensions.

- A can of silver-metallic spray paint.

- As many under-cabinet fluorescent light units as you can put in the trunk. These can be purchased at a hardware store.

- Same length replacement UV tubes for each of the under-cabinet units (*General Electric F15T8-BL or equivalent*).

- A 4" × 4" axial fan (*woodstove store*) to push heat out during exposure.

- A coping saw.

- A bottle of woodworker's yellow glue.

- A couple of nonsurge powerstrips for plugging all the cords from the under-cabinet units, your timer, and fan.

- A piece of ¼" glass cut to the same size as the flat shelf insert you will take out of the footlocker. This glass will be the shelf you'll be laying your contact print frame on during exposures.

How to Make It

Step 1 Cut a piece of plywood, which will fit, and sit snugly, on the bottom of your footlocker.

Step 2 Go outside and spray the inside of your footlocker and the plywood you have just cut with a silver metallic, or white, reflective paint.

Step 3 Take each of your new under-cabinet light fixtures and remove the standard bulbs that came with them. Take a close look at the unit and you'll notice that each end has a bi-pin holder that the pins of the fluorescent tubes twist into. Notice also that there is a base to that unit that holds the tube. Those two landmarks indicate the dimensional limits of your next step.

Step 4 Take your coping saw and cut away the back panel of each under-cabinet unit down to the part that holds the bulb and the bi-pin holder.

Step 5 On the piece of cut plywood, lay out the recently cut under-cabinet fixtures adjacent to one another. Mark their locations, this is where they will be glued to keep them in place.

Step 6 Cut a square 4" × 4" fan hole in the bottom of the footlocker for the fan unit. These units were once used to cool big computers and now are sold in woodstove stores as a way of blowing warm air from one room to another. Make sure the fan, when installed, will be blowing out. Be sure to figure out a way to get the power cord from this fan to the powerstrip.

Step 7 Cut a hole big enough for the fixture power cords to exit the footlocker and be plugged into the powerstrip. Use the black tape to wrap these cords together for a neat appearance.

Step 8 Glue the modified under-cabinet fixture units to their assigned locations on the plywood sheet and lay the board and units in bottom of the footlocker.

Step 9 Run the under-cabinet and fan power cords out of the trunk and plug them into the powerstrips. Plug in your timer and then plug in the power strip(s) to an outlet.

Step 10 Take your sheet of glass and lay it on the molding that used to hold the thin shelf that you removed earlier.

Step 11 Close the lid of the footlocker to protect your eyes from the UV light.

Step 12 Turn on the power and see if it works, but never look directly at the light.

If everything was done correctly, your new exposure unit should be ready for use. Make a quick coating of something like POP or cyanotype, drop it into a contact frame with a simple high contrast negative (*success is important for your psyche here*), and make an exposure. If you feel that the light source is too far away from your glass shelf, simply raise the plywood base off the bottom of the footlocker. Congratulations; you have just made a perfectly usable exposure unit at a fraction of what it would cost pre-made.

An Alternative Process Working Space

Setting up an alternative working space is relatively simple and requires only small and inexpensive adjustments to your home, apartment, or classroom. With the exception of some of a few lab-dependent processes, such as wet collodion, nearly all alternative process work can be done in an environment that requires very little modification. Due to the relative light insensitivity of most alternative process sensitizers, a darkroom is unnecessary. I have conducted alternative process demonstrations in motel conference rooms, on back porches, offices, garages, closets, kitchens, beaches, riverbanks, in the street, and in the backs of vans in parking lots in Oklahoma. Literally any place where I am out of UV, very bright, or long-term fluorescent, light and have access to water, will work.

My lab at home is a separate addition to the studio. The space is broken up into wet and dry areas. The dry consists of an office with digital printers, light tables, and a book & slide library. This room has a full wall-size glass sliding door, windows, and track lighting for illumination. If you put the lighting on a dimmer switch you can control the illumination easily. The inner part of the space is a wet lab with a 12" × 40" × 15' fiber-glassed marine plywood sink and two faucets. The sink has duckboard slats to keep trays off of the bottom of the sink. My ventilation is above sink level and if I were building the space again I would put the outflow vents at sink or floor level.

In the first edition of this book, I had an enlarger in the lab but those days are gone and now I make my negatives in large-format cameras or enlarge them digitally and make digital versions using Pictorico OHP film. When I need to make a print from one of my elderly negatives I simply get it scanned at 4000 dpi, clean it up in Photoshop, and print it out on inkjet film. There is a safelight in the wet lab but, more often than not, I simply keep the door open to the office area and work with the ambient light available. In fact, I recently added a casement window to the darkroom and simply lower the blinds when working in the middle of the day. At night, I keep the window open and get fresh air.

You can be relatively comfortable working in any low light area. If you want to test it, simply coat a piece of paper with your process of choice and when it is dry, put a few small opaque objects (like quarters) on the sensitized surface and remove one of them every few minutes. Process the paper normally and if you can see any evidence of a the quarter's circular shape, check the notation for the time and that will tell you how long you can work under that illumination before your print will be affected by it.

You will also need a clean and dry table, or counter, to work on. This is essential; moisture or chemical contamination will play havoc with your coating process. This recommendation seems obvious but it is important to pay heed to it because a dirty working environment will always punish your printing efforts eventually. I recommend laying down fresh brown butcher's paper on your counters before working. You know that the surface is clean and clean-up is very simple.

For washing and processing, all you need is a selection of appropriately sized trays and a sink with running water. For drying prints, I have always used a clothesline and clothespins. This eliminates any chance of chemical and residual contamination from prints that have gone before.

If you are living in a rented apartment, a bathroom makes a fine lab because it generally has working plumbing and exhaust ventilation. The best part is the big washing tank called a bathtub. In my student days, I installed a large piece of plywood, with a plastic laminate, on the wall next to the bathtub and attached it with door hinges. I cut a "mail slot" into the end of the board and attached the hinges to its long edge. The board was then attached to the wall so that it could be lifted up and locked against the wall's surface should anyone wish to use the tub for a bath. The board, for working sessions, could be released from the lock position and swung down so that it lay on top of the tub's rim. In that position, it worked as a shelf and a direct deposit slot for the prints into the tub water for holding and washing.

Ventilation is, of course, important. Any chemical mixing, or usage, should only take place where there is adequate inflow and outflow of air. Simply because a chemical lacks an offensive odor does not mean that it's safe to breathe. Be aware that an exhaust fan above your head is only drawing the chemical fumes into your face as they go to the exhaust. At The Art Institute of Boston we have installed our exhaust system in the side-walls of the sinks. If you are going to install a fan specifically for a working space, try to place it lower than where your face will be. In the meantime, use common sense whenever you work with chemicals. This means that you check out the MSDS sheet on a chemical you are unfamiliar with and if that chemical is hazardous, you wear Nitrile gloves when working with it. If necessary, wear a dual filtered respirator and lab apron. If you are working with glyoxal or formalin, do so outdoors. Don't forget to dry recently glyoxal hardened papers outdoors as well as the paper off gasses for 24–48 hours.

There are a few tools and materials that you will have to have in your alt pro working space. Here's a partial list of the most important:

- A well-made contact printing frame
- A great sense of humor
- A selection of hake brushes
- A large ruler for ripping paper and a small one for measuring

- A digital gram scale
- A roll of transparent tape
- Tape for labels and sealing bottles
- A hairdryer
- A set of very clean trays
- A thermometer
- Pencils, Sharpies, and a notebook
- A box of chemical or coffee filters
- An ample supply of distilled water
- An electric teakettle for boiling water
- A hand held blender wand for albumen
- A selection of measuring beakers that can measure 5–10 ml and up
- Beakers that can handle 1–2 liter capacity
- A large sheet of plate glass or white Lucite for coating
- A selection of 11" × 14" Lucite sheets for mating carbon
- A hand-held wand blender for albumen
- Clothesline and wooden spring loaded clothespins
- Dark glass bottles with eyedropper caps for sensitizers
- A selection of clean dark brown plastic bottles for mixed chemicals
- A UV light source for winter and night
- A wet area that can hold the trays for your processes
- A secure chemical storage area especially if children are present
- A selection of high-quality paper to work on
- Your negatives

Finally, look around your space and discuss what you want to do to make a working space with those who live with you. Assure them that the adjustments are minor and without a great deal of expense. Be careful with your chemistry. Don't set up a lab in the kitchen. Label and date anything you mix and store it out of harm's way. Cover your working surfaces with paper that can be thrown away after your printing sessions. Put yellow curtains up on windows, hang Christmas lights for a festive atmosphere, clean up after yourself, and have a great time.

Alternative Process Shopping List

OK	ORDER	CHEMISTRY / BOSTICK & SULLIVAN	UNIT COST	TOTAL
——	———	CYANOTYPE KIT—A & B SOLUTION—250 ml	———	———
——	———	FERRIC AMMONIUM CITRATE—Cyanotype Part A—500 grams	———	———
——	———	POTASSIUM FERRICYANIDE—Cyanotype Part B—250 grams	———	———
——	———	VAN DYKE KIT—100 ml	———	———
——	———	PALLADIUM KIT—(wet pack)—25 ml	———	———
——	———	PALLADIUM KIT—(dry pack)—25 ml	———	———
——	———	ARGYROTYPE KIT—(Ware Formula)—100 ml	———	———
——	———	ZIATYPE KIT—100 ml Kit	———	———
——	———	FERRIC OXALATE SOLUTION #1—27%—(for Pt / Pd printing) 25ML	———	
——	———	FERRIC OXALATE SOLUTION #2—(for Pd printing) 25ML	———	———
——	———	SODIUM CHLOROPALLADITE #3—(Pd Printing)—25 ml	———	———
——	———	Na2 PLATINUM / PALLADIUM KIT—(*makes 35 8 × 10 prints*)	———	———
——	———	KALLITYPE KIT, w/black developer—25 ml	———	———
——	———	FERRIC OXALATE SOLUTION 20% (Part B—Kallitype)—100 ml	———	———
——	———	SILVER NITRATE 10% SOLUTION—(Kallitype A—100 ml	———	———
——	———	SILVER NITRATE—DRY (30 gram pack only for shipping) salt & albumen	———	———
——	———	FERRIC CITRATE (Contrast control for VDB)—grams	———	———
——	———	BLACK KALLITYPE DEVELOPER (Sodium Acetate)—1 liter	———	———
——	———	AMMONIUM CITRATE DEVELOPER (Pt/Pd & Kallitype)—1 liter	———	———
——	———	AMMONIUM CITRATE DIBASIC (Pt/Pd mix 250 to 1 liter)— 250 grams	———	———
——	———	GOLD / AMMONIUM THIOCYANATE POP TONING KIT—500 ml	———	———
——	———	AMMONIUM THIOCYANATE—25 gr (for POP toner)	———	———
——	———	GOLD CHLORIDE 1%—100 ml (for POP toner)	———	———
——	———	TARTARIC ACID—Kallitype and POP toning—50 grams	———	———
——	———	PLATINUM TONING KIT FOR POP	———	———
——	———	SODIUM FERRIC OXALATE—(SFO for Ziatype printing)—25ML	———	———

— ——— AMMONIUM FERRIC OXALATE—(AFO for Ziatype printing)—50ML ——— ———

— ——— LITHIUM PALLADIUM SOLUTION #3—(LiPd for Ziatype)—25 ml ——— ———

— ——— SODIUM SULFITE (Ziatype & Polaroid clearing baths) (1 lb) ——— ———

— ——— GOLD CHLORIDE 5%   (Kallitype toning & Ziatype)—25 ml ——— ———

— ——— EDTA—DISODIUM—1000 grams (first EDTA bath Pt/Pd) ——— ———

— ——— EDTA—TETRASODIUM—1000 grams (2nd & 3rd EDTA baths Pt/Pd) ——— ———

— ——— CITRIC ACID   (Ziatype clearing—argyrotype toner, etc.)—300 grams ——— ———

— ——— SODIUM ACETATE   (Salt toner / Kallitype developer)—250 grams ——— ———

— ——— SODIUM THIOSULFATE—(all purpose fixer)—2000 grams ——— ———

— ——— SODIUM CHLORIDE 250. grams ——— ———

— ——— GUM ARABIC—(1000 ml bottle) ——— ———

— ——— GELATIN (250 bloom) 1 lb ——— ———

— ——— GALLIC ACID—for Cyanotype toning & Calotype process ——— ———

— ——— GLYOXAL 500 ML—gelatin hardening for gum bichromate ——— ———

— ——— POTASSIUM CHLOROPLATINITE (20%)—for Platinum #3—25 ml ——— ———

— ——— POTASSIUM DICHROMATE—gum bichromate sensitizer—150 grams ——— ———

— ——— POTASSIUM METABISULFITE   (Gum Clearing 1%—Carbon Clearing 2–5%—100 grams) ——— ———

— ——— POTASSIUM IODIDE—(Bayard's Direct Positive—4% solution) 100 g ——— ———

— ——— SODIUM CITRATE—Salting formula #1—500 grams ——— ———

— ——— AMMONIUM CHLORIDE—Salting #1 & Bayard Direct Pos. formulas—500 grams ——— ———

— ——— SODIUM CARBONATE—cyanotype toning—100 grams ——— ———

— ——— SODIUM BICARBONATE—Bayard Direct Fix Additive—50 grams ——— ———

— ——— CALCIUM CARBONATE—with alcohol, glass cleaning for wet collodion—100 grams ——— ———

— ——— SODIUM BORATE / BORAX—100 grams—For gold / borax salt toner ——— ———

— ——— TANNIC ACID—cyanotype toning—100 grams ——— ———

— ——— DROPPER BOTTLES 28 & 56 ml. (dark brown glass with dropper) ——— ———

— ——— ACETIC ACID—28%–33% used in calotype process ——— ———

— ——— COLLODION—wet plate—500 ml ——— ———

— ——— pH TESTING STRIPS ——— ———

PAPER

— ——— BERGGER COT 320 PAPER   (20 × 24—)—p / 25 sheets (excellent for most processes) ——— ———

— ——— BUXTON Paper (240 g 22 × 30 at 13.00 p/sh) NY Central Art Supply ——— ———

— ——— CRANES PLATINOTYPE PAPER—(white 23. × 29)—50 sheets ——— ———

— ——— SOMERSET SATIN WHITE, (22 × 30, 250 g, (best for albumen and Van Dyke) ——— ———

— ——— LANAQUARELLE—(300# & 140#—11 × 15—22 × 30, hot or cold press) ——— ———

— ——— CENTENNIAL POP—(8 × 10, 50 Sheets) ——— ———

— ——— CENTENNIAL POP PAPER (11 × 14, 50 Sheets) ——— ———

— ——— ARCHES 88, (22 × 30, 300 gsm, good for albumen) ——— ———

— ——— CRANES 8111S STATIONARY—Bayard's Direct Positive ——— ———

CARBON TISSUE

—— ———— BOSTICK & SULLIVAN CARBON TISSUE 36 × 36 (SKU#: CTSQ18)—76.00

PHOTO AND DIGITAL SUPPLIES

—— ———— PICTORICO OHP INK JET FILM—packages in various sizes

—— ———— PICTORICO TPS Ultra Premium INK JET FILM—13" roll

—— ———— POLARIOD TYPE 55 4 × 5 FILM

—— ———— MACO BLACK MAGIC LIQUID EMULSION (normal grade)

—— ———— MACO BLACK MAGIC LIQUID HARDENER (1 capfull to a liter of developer)

—— ———— MACO BLACK MAGIC PHOTO GELATIN (250 ml)

BLUEPRINTSONFABRIC.COM / 800-631-3369

—— ———— 90" × 3 yds PRE-COATED CYANOTYPE FABRIC

—— ———— 90" × 6 yds PRE-COATED CYANOTYPE FABRIC

—— ———— 108" × 108" PRE-COATED CYANOTYPE FABRIC

—— ———— 90" × 6 yds PRE-COATED CYANOTYPE FABRIC—RAW SILK

ART SUPPLIES

—— ———— HAKE BRUSHES—1.5" (Jerry's Artarama)

—— ———— CLEAR ACETATE SHEETS—8 × 10 25 or 50 sheet pad

—— ———— DORLANDS ART WAX—4 OZ

—— ———— WINDSOR NEWTON WATERCOLORS: Lamp black, Cobalt Blue, Cad. Red, Naples Yellow, Davy's Gray, Oxide of Chromium White, Yellow Ochre, Ventian Red, Raw Sienna, Sepia

—— ———— KRYSTAL SEAL 11 × 14 envelopes, etc.—carbon process (Jerry's Artarama)

—— ———— PREMIUM PHOTO MICROPORE LUSTER (carbon support—www.premierart.info)

—— ———— Blotter Paper

SUPERMARKET

—— ———— DISTILLED WATER—gallon bottles

—— ———— RUBBING ALCOHOL (70%)—carbon sensitizeradditive

—— ———— HOUSEHOLD AMMONIA (quart)

—— ———— KNOX GELATIN (small box 4—7 gr packets per box)

—— ———— HYDROGEN PEROXIDE—3%—1 quart

—— ———— BOX OF MORTON'S KOSHER SALT—sodium chloride

—— ———— TAPIOCA STARCH—Zimmerman matte albumen solution

—— ———— EGGS (3 dozen large for albumen)

CLASSROOM SET-UP NEEDS

—— ———— new 1 liter, wide mouth, bottles

—— ———— 1 hose and outside spigot

—— ———— 1 very clean 39-gallon plastic trash barrel

—— ———— 4 × 5 Polaroid backs

—— ———— 4 × 5 pin hole cameras

—— ———— 8 × 10 / 11 × 14 contact printing frames

___ _____ clothes line and pins
___ _____ 200 push pins
___ _____ folding tables (3–4)
___ _____ chairs for the class

_____ _____
_____ _____
_____ _____
_____ _____

Resources & Internet Sites

CHRISTOPHER JAMES: http://www. christopherjames-studio.com

CHEMISTRY, PAPER, LAB GEAR, GREAT SITES, REFERENCES & MORE

MSDS Search Site

Vermont SIRI Index

http://www2.hazard.com/msds/index.php

This is a free site for 180,000 Material Safety Data Sheets (MSDS).

Material Safety Data Sheets for all chemicals can be found and linked to the manufacturer at this Web site. If you have any questions or concerns regarding a chemical, you should consult this site before you buy. If you are having a health issue due to ingestion, eye contact, skin contact, or respiratory problems you should seek immediate medical attention. All educational or business, institutions that use chemistry are required to have MSDS data for all chemicals in use on site . . . this is the law.

Acros Organics

711 Forbes Avanue, Pittsburgh, PA 15219

Tel: (800) 227-6701—within United States only

Fax: (800) 248-3079—within United States only

Web site: http://www.acros.com

Chemicals and scientific gear

APP – 2

Jacqui Mahan, Self as Kid, 2003

Jacqui graduated from the Art Institute of Boston a few years ago and is now the art powerhouse of Ohio with her hugely successful Mahan Gallery in Columbus. This self-portrait explains a lot.

(Courtesy of the artist)

Alfa Aesar

Alfa Aesar

26 Parkridge Road

Ward Hill, MA 01835

E-mail: info@alfa.com

Web site: http://www.alfa.com

A leading supplier of hard-to-find high-purity chemistry such as the ingredients needed for Chrysotypes. Recommended by a lot of serious alt pro people.

Alternative Photography.com

http://www.alternativephotography.com

(Malin Fabbri—Editor / Owner / Director)

This site, operated by Malin Fabbri, is a lot of fun to roam around in. There is a lot of work to look at from subscribers who join the site as well as a good deal of technical information. Like Wikepedia, not all of the information is entirely accurate, but that free form of editorial control is what makes the site so attractive. This is also a good place to download a free digital curve to experiment with when making your own digital negatives.

Altphotosource

(Moved to Europe 2007 . . . no more USA orders)

Web site: http://www.altphotosource.com

E-mail: sales@altphotosource.com

Ready to use, Wet Plate Collodion Kits for both positive and negative images (ambrotypes, Ferrotypes/Tintypes and Negatives for POP) and individual chemicals. Black glass, clear glass, tin and aluminum for making wet plate collodion and dry plate emulsion.

Alternative Process Newsgroup & Battleground

http://www.usask.ca/lists/alt-photo-process-l/

Have fun searching the archives and try keeping your head on straight when, and if, you decide to participate in the real-time jousting. It takes true grit, and immeasurable patience, to hang out in this newsgroup.

Analog Photographers Group

http://www.apug.org—Analog Photographers Group

Andrew Cahan Bookseller, Ltd.

(919) 968-3517

Web site: http://www.cahanbooks.com

E-mail: acahan@cahanbooks.com

Andrew and Robin Cahan are extremely knowledgeable specialists in photographic literature and are invaluable as a resource if you are seeking an out-of-print book. Best of all, they are really nice people.

Aristo Grid Lamp Products, Inc.

400 Captain Neville Drive

Waterbury, CT 06705

Tel: (203) 575-3425

Fax: (203) 575-3456

Send mail to: sales@aristogrid.com

Web site: http://www.aristogrid.com

This is a manufacturer of high-end UV printers for those of you who have winter in your lives.

Artcraft Chemicals Inc.

PO Box 583, Schenectady, NY 12301

Tel: (800) 682 1730 - within U.S.A only

E-mail: through Web site

Web site: http://www.artcraftchemicals.com

Mike Jacobson is Artcraft. It's a one-man business and it's a great business. Photographic chemicals for Argyrotype, Ware Cyanotype process and the Ware print-out platinum/palladium processes at reasonable prices. Will also make kits to order.

Artspace

http://www.artspace.org.au

As We May Think

By Vannevar Bush

The Atlantic Monthly | July 1945

Web site: http://www.theatlantic.com/doc/194507/bush

Bad At Sports

http://www.badatsports.com - brave new world Web site

Big Red & Shiny

http://www.bigredandshiny.com

This site, featuring Matt Nash and Jason Dean, has over 80 participating artists and non-profit status. They are up to Issue #66 as I write this and just dipping into the catalogue of what's been on this site is an education in itself. Here's the first third of their Mission Statement: Big RED & Shiny seeks to be a forum for criticism, discussion and promotion of the Boston arts scene. To this end we will provide reviews of exhibitions and events, articles examining the larger scope of Boston arts, and news that is up-to-the-minute and helpful to Boston artists and those interested in the arts. Join today!

B & H Photo

Web site: http://www.photovideo.com

APP – 3

Harvey Loves Harvey illustration

Since 1992, Matthew Nash (who teaches at The Art Institute of Boston) and Jason Dean have collaborated under the name "Harvey Loves Harvey." They write, "We have set out to explore the themes of communication, friendship, artistic intent and identity through our work. In fifteen years of collaboration, we have never lived in the same city, and the tools of communication have become the both subject and the subtext of our work, as we seek forms of communication that can accommodate two artists as a single voice."
(Courtesy of the artists)

This is a huge company that deals with all things photographic and video. Volume sales on the internet translate into excellent prices for your supplies.

Blueprints On Fabric

20504 81st. Ave. SW, Vashon Island, WA 98070

Tel: (800) 631-3369—within United States only

(206) 463-3369—for international callers

E-mail: linda@blueprintsonfabric.com

http://www.blueprintsonfabric.com

Linda Stemer is a great friend and one of the really good people in the alt pro industry. Pre-coated 100% natural fiber cotton and silk fabric for cyanotype, pieces and yardage, T-shirts and scarves. Pre-washed, hand-treated, and individually packaged in a UV protective bag.

Bostick & Sullivan Inc

PO Box 16639, Santa Fe, NM 87506-6639

Tel: (505) 474-0890

Fax: (505) 474-2857

E-mail: rderinfo@earthlink.net

Web site: http://www.bostick-sullivan.com

Dick Sullivan and his wife Melody Bostick founded this long respected business in the early 1980s. Their sons are now involved and the enterprise is healthier than ever. Kevin Sullivan is starting a digital contact negative service as I write this and the first results look outstanding. These are also great people on every level and a joy to deal with. I've been doing business with them for over 25 years. B & S has chemicals for every process, tons of kits, paper, contact frames, everything for the alt pro lab. Dick is also just starting his carbon tissue manufacturing so if that is a process you want to do, then this is the place to call. They also sell a lot of books.

Bulb Direct

(716) 385-3540

Web site: http://www.bulbdirect.com

This supplier has thousands of different bulbs for all of your UV needs.

Byron Weston Paper Company (Division of Cranes Paper)

Distributor: Butler & Dearden Paper Service

80 Shrewsbury Street

P. O. Box 1069

Boylston, Massachusetts 01505

Telephone: (800) 634-7070 or (508) 869-9000

APP – 4
**Marie-Susanne Langille,
Monsterhands, 2004 - Pt/Pd**
(Courtesy of the artist)

Fax: (508) 869-0211

E-mail: sales@butlerdearden.com

Web site: http://www.butlerdearden.com

Contact: John Zokowski

jzokowski@butlerdearden.com

Weston Diploma Parchment is produced by the Byron Weston Paper Co. (a division of Crane Paper) in Boylston, MA. The paper is warm-white 100% rag denim, 177 GSM, no brighteners, no buffering, is rosin alum sized, and a pH in the good neighborhood of 5.5 to 7.5. It has also been manufactured for more than 50 years so the track record is strong. As well, it appears that this paper is excellent for several processes such as PT/PD, Cyanotype, and Kallitype.

Cachet

(714) 332-7070

Web site: http://www.onecachet.com

Cachet makes a wide assortment of films (Maco Genius) and emulsions for hand application. Most important in the latter offering is Maco Black Magic Photo Emulsion (variable contrast and hard contrast liquid emulsion) Maco Black Magic Photo Gelatin, and Maco Black Magic Liquid Hardener. Of all the commercial grade emulsions, theirs is the best.

Calumet Photographic

890 Supreme Drive, Bensenville, IL 60106

Tel: (708) 860-7458 or (800) 225-8638—within United States only

E-mail: custserv@calumetphoto.com

Web site: http://www.calumetphoto.com

Camera and darkroom supplies and gelatin and glass filters. Also kits for argyrotype and cyanotype II and cyanotype chemicals. Can ship internationally, although buyer is responsible for charges.

Carbon Printing Forum

http://www.carbonprinting.com—a great forum dedicated to carbon printing

Chicago Albumen Works

P.O. Box 805

174 Front Street

Housatonic, Massachusetts 01236

Phone: (413) 274-6901

Fax: (413) 274-6934

http://www.albumenworks.com

The Chicago Albumen Works provides a wide range of traditional and digital services for institutional and corporate photograph collections. Founded in Chicago in 1976, the firm moved to the Berkshire Hills of western Massachusetts in 1982. This is the distributor for the Centennial™ gelatin-chloride Printing-Out Paper (P.O.P.) and related chemistry for working photographers. Their facilities are located in a renovated textile mill on the banks of the Housatonic River.

Correspondence of William Henry Fox Talbot Project

http://foxtalbot.dmu.ac.uk/

The Correspondence of William Henry Fox Talbot Project has prepared a comprehensive edition of the nearly 10,000 letters to and from Talbot (1800-1877), the Wiltshire polymath best known for his invention of photography. Draft transcriptions of nearly all the letters were posted by September 2003 and these are now being further annotated and edited.

The conception and editorial foundations of the project took place at the University of Glasgow between 1999 and 2004. Additional development and hosting is now undertaken by Knowledge Media Design, De Montfort University. The Correspondence editor is Professor Larry Schaaf.

Daniel Smith:

(800) 426-6740

E-mail: dsartmatrl@aol.com

Web site: http://www.danielsmith.com

This is a great art supply store with everything you will need in the way of artist's materials.

D.F. Goldsmith Chemical & Metal Corporation

909 Pitner Avenue, Evanston, IL 60202

Tel: (708) 868-7800

E-mail: goldchem@aol.com

Web site: http://www.dfgoldsmith.com

Precious metals, such as silver nitrate and gold chloride

Information confirmed December 2005

Digital Art Supplies

9596B Chesapeake Drive, San Diego, CA 92123

E-mail: ineedhelp@digitalartsupplies.net

Web site: http://www.digitalartsupplies.com

This is my favorite digital supply Web site and they are a delight to work with. Dave Schaffer helped out tremendously when I was testing products for the book and was always great to deal with. You can get ink-jet papers, printer inks, profiles, Printshield, and a host of other products.

George Eastman House

http://www.geh.org

Graphic Chemical & Ink Company

http://www.graphicchemical.com

powdered asphaltum for Heliography

eBay

http://www.ebay.com

Whenever I need a contact printing frame, a Polaroid back, a dye transfer registration unit, a lens . . . it doesn't matter really . . . I know I'll find it on eBay.

Edwards Engineered Products

(512) 267-4274

E-mail: eepjon@aol.com

Web site: http://www.eepjon.com

Jon Edwards makes superbly constructed and fine-quality actinic light (UV) exposure units . . . both the pizza oven variety and the vacuum type. I can't say enough good things about Jon and his products and have purchased his units for my labs at The Art Institute of Boston and for my own studio. Edwards also makes and sells glass coating rods and tray agitation systems.

France Scully Osterman & Mark Osterman Studio

Web site: http://www.collodion.org/

You would be hard-pressed to find two nicer and more knowledgeable people than France Scully Osterman and Mark Osterman. This is their site devoted to wet collodion and gelatin dry plate photography. It is also a way to find out when you can take one of their workshops.

Frank Van Riper / Camera Works / The Washington Post

http://www.washingtonpost.com/wp-srv/photo/essays/vanRiper/

Freestyle Sales Company

5124 Sunset Blvd., Los Angeles, Ca 90027

Tel: (800) 292-6137 E-mail: via Web site

Web site: http://www.freestylephoto.biz

APP – 5

Jon Edwards's UV Units

Jon's mechanical UV "pizza box" exposure units are perfect in all ways. I've been working with them for years and they would be the first ones I would recommend if you asked about filling out your alt pro lab. Jon also sells kits and plans if you're handy.

(Courtesy of the artist)

Ready-made kits and chemicals. Their catalogue is huge and they supply most everything you might want that is photographic. They have discount films in many different sizes and styles including esoteric stuff like x-ray, Aristo Ortholith (20 × 24 and rolls), lith film 4" × 5" to 20" × 24" in roll form, and aerial duplicating film. This is one of a few places that you can buy plastic cameras and they have a Web page set up just for those who find the plastic camera a religious experience. You may also find Polaroid 4" × 5" backs here for use in the pinhole cameras below. This is the hardware store of photography.

Hahnemühle Fine Art paper

http://www.hahnemuehle.com

Few companies can look back proudly on having such a long and diligent tradition as Hahnemühle's. Since 1584, this papermaker has been creating unique and beautiful papers. This is my second favorite paper, after Museo II, for digital inkjet printing with pigment based inks.

InkAID

Site: http://www.inkaid.com

If you have been thinking about running thin and flat objects through your ink-jet printer, just to see if it was possible to print on them, there is a product that you can consider using. It's called InkAID. InkAID is essentially a liquid coating that is applied to a thin substrate to prepare it for accepting your attempt at making an inkjet print on it. Among the surfaces you might consider; aluminum, thin sheets of wood laminate, exotic hand-made papers, acrylic sheets, and any flat thing that you can hand feed and run through your printer. I would not recommend deli sliced meat products. I do, however, recommend that you go to eBay and purchase a very used printer to work with if you are thinking of using substrates that might damage the machine. InkAid is quite simple to use. Stir it ... brush it on ... let it dry ... and print. The surfaces are water-resistant and can be reworked with subsequent printings, over-painting, or distressing.

Ink-Jet Fabrics

http://www.inkjetfabrics.com—Web site for ink-jet on fabrics

Jerry's Artarama

Web site: http://www.jerrysartarama.com

This is a terrific Internet site for hard-to-find hake brushes, Krystal Seal envelopes for carbon printing, and all at discount prices.

Kageno Kids

Web site: http://www.kageno.org

http://www.kagenokids.org

This is, along with Zana Briski's Kids with Cameras, on of the most optimistic and positive art sites you can visit. Jane Hinds Bidaut does a lot of work with this group and you can see some of the results in the book. Kageno, in the Kenyan dialect means "a place of hope." This is a multi-faceted community development project in Kenya that transforms communities suffering from inhumane poverty into places of hope and opportunity. Making art is part of this process. Get involved!

Kids With Cameras

http://www.kids-with-cameras.org/home/

Zana Briski & Ross Kaufman (*Born Into Brothels*)

Kids with Cameras

341 Lafayette Street

Suite 4407

New York, NY 10012

Stephen Keen Contact printing Frames

Web site:

http://www.stephenkeenphotography.citymax.com/page/page/1655355.htm

Stephen Keen e-mail: stephen.keen@comcast.net

(801) 232-6906

(801) 467-8026

Stephen makes some of the most beautiful contact printing frames I've ever used. I own several and they are suitable as heirlooms.

Lazertran Ltd.

US Information

1501 W. Copans Road, Suite 100

Pompano Beach

Florida 333064

E-mail lazertran@d2fi.com

Web site: http://www.lazertran.com

More e-mail: mic@lazertran.com

This is a great company to deal with and they have one of the most interesting new materials to play with that I have seen in a long time. My students love their product. They are dedicated to the transfer of laser copy images, decals, and to a variety of materials, from etching plates to silk to toast.

Lensless Camera Company

Lensless Camera Mfg. Co.

904 Thorne Drive

Fernley NV 89408

(775) 575-5189

info@pinholecamera.com

This company makes really well made pinhole cameras in a vast assortment sizes and of traditional and exotic woods. Sizes range from 4" × 4" to 11" × 14" and each camera, like the Great Basin Contact Frame, makes you feel very nice while you're working. I've been using these cameras for several years, in non-silver and alternative workshops, in combination with Polaroid Type 55 Positive / Negative Film and 4" × 5" Polaroid backs.

Legacy Photo Project / The Great Picture Project

Web site: www.legacyphotoproject.com/index2.php

Everything you want to know about the world's largest pinhole camera.

Robert Leggat Photo History Site

http://www.rleggat.com/photohistory/

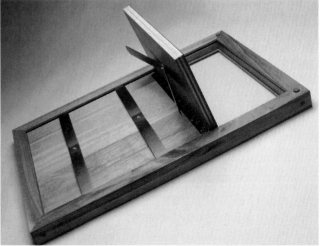

APP – 6

Steve Keen Contact Frames

Steve Keen makes beautiful frames. Not only are they finely crafted; they are also indestructible and envy producing when you demonstrate with them.
(Courtesy of the artist)

Light Impressions

(800) 828-6216

Web site: http://www.lightimpressionsdirect.com

In my opinion, they are the best source for all, exhibition, archival storage and handling, shipping, and cataloging of photographic materials and images. They also custom cut mats for exhibition and have a complete framing supply.

Luminous Lint

http://www.luminous-lint.com—Fine Art Photography

MIS Associates, Inc.

(248) 814-9398

Web site: http://www.missupply.com

MIS is a company that manufactures and distributes archival inks and papers for archival ink-jet, Iris, laser, and digital printmakers. They have an excellent Web site and a fine collection of archival rag papers.

Modern Postcard

(800) 959-8365

Web site: http://www.modernpostcard.com

This is the company of choice for many "starving" artists as it makes a nice card, sometimes dependent on what is scanned in with your card, at a very reasonable price—$100. or so will give you 500 copies. They have a very thorough Web site and provide all of the instructions and links to permit you to prepare and submit digital files. Get your art printed and sneak it into the postcard racks at the Museum of Modern Art and the Whitney. You won't get a royalty, but it's fun to see how many of your cards sell.

Mostly Metals

http://www.mostlymetals.com

http://orders@mostlymetals.com

This business is highly recommended if you're looking for rare and difficult to find metal salts.

National Media Museum

Web site: http://www.nationalmediamuseum.org.uk

The National Media Museum is part of the NMSI Museums Group (National Museum of Science and Industry) that also includes the Science Museum (based in London and at Wroughton in Wiltshire) and the National Railway Museum (based in York and at Shildon in County Durham). The Photography Collection is one of the finest and most extensive anywhere in the world. It is best

APP – 7

Christopher James, Lucy, Boston, 2004—pinhole, gold toned salted paper print

(Courtesy of the artist)

regarded as a collection of collections, encompassing not only that of the Science Museum, but other world-class collections such as The Royal Photographic Society Collection, the Kodak Museum and the Daily Herald Archive.

New York Central Art Supply

(800) 950-6111

Web site: http://www.nycentralart.com

Considered "THE" artist's supply store. They have 2 large catalogues and deal in exotic papers from all over the world. They are the dealer for the hard to find Buxton that is the crème de la crème of alt pro papers. They also have literally every thing one could ask for in the way of artist's supplies.

Niépce

http://www.nicephore-niepce.com—Niépce/Photo History site

Ohaus

Web site: http://www.ohaus.com

Ohaus manufactures and sells a wide variety of lab equipment and is well known for their gram scales.

Pearl Paint

(800) 451-PEARL

Web site: http://www.pearlpaint.com

This is another great art supply store with stores in many urban areas. In New York, Philadelphia, and Boston they have several floors of merchandise and I strongly advise leaving your credit card at home.

Dan Pelland Hand Made Contact Printing Frames

Daniel Pelland e-mail: dan@pellandphoto.com

http://www.pellandphoto.com/

For practitioners of traditional and alternative photographic processes. Made from the finest materials—native American Cherry, Birch and Oak. Solid brass fittings. Dan makes a beautiful frame.

Periodic Table

Just in case you can't remember it clearly from junior high.

http://www.webelements.com/

Photo Eye

(800) 227-6941

Photo-Eye Gallery

376 Garcia Street, Suite A

Santa Fe, NM 87501 USA

Web site: http://www.photoeye.com

Photo Eye This book dealer has just about everything in the way of photographic text . . . new, old, signed, and rare. The book part is run by the extremely knowledgeable Darius Himes. They put out a large, full-color, catalogue several times a year. They also have a wonderful gallery.

Photographers Formulary

PO Box 950, Condon, MT 59826

Tel: (406) 754-2891 or (800) 922 5255—within United States only

Fax: (406) 754 2896

E-mail: formulary@blackfoot.net

http://www.photoformulary.com

Bud and Lynn Wilson run this excellent business in the heart of Montana. They also run workshops where you can study with many of the best in the business. Chemistry is sold in bulk, as well as in kit form. All kits come with instruction sheets on storage and use.

Pictorico

Web site: www.pictorico.com

Pictorico makes the excellent OHP ink-jet film that I've been using for the past few years to make my digital contact negatives. Their Ultra Premium ink-jet film (rolls only at the moment) is even better and allows you to take nearly any source and transform it into a very adequate

APP – 8

Dan Pelland Contact Printing Frame

Like Steve Keen, Dan Pelland is another craftsman who is making beautiful handmade contact printing frames.

(Courtesy of the artist)

ink-jet contact negative film within minutes of scanning. This is the future and Pictorico will likely be a leader in it.

Pinhole Resource

(505) 536-9942

Web site: http://www.pinholeresource.com

E-mail: pinhole@gilanet.com

This is Eric Renner and Nancy Spencer's enterprise. This is one of the very best resources for pinhole photography in existence. They distribute both inexpensive and very expensive cameras, zone plates, and assorted books and pinhole paraphernalia. One-stop expert advice and shopping and home of the Leonardo Pinhole Camera, a beautifully made custom pinhole in assorted formats. Pinhole Resource is a non-profit public institutional archive for pinhole photography. Keep an eye open for Eric Renner's new pinhole book.

Premier Imaging Products

Web site: http://www.premierimagingproducts.com

This company makes the Professional Premium Micropore Luster, 10.4 mil transfer paper that works so well for carbon printing transfer support. They also produce Eco Shield and Print Shield for protecting digital prints and a large variety of digital printing products.

Real Time Arts

http://www.realtimearts.net—new media site

Rockland Colloid

PO Box 376, Piermont, NY 10968

Tel: (845) 359-5559

Fax: (845) 365-6663

E-mail: info@rockaloid.com

Web site: http://www.rockaloid.com

Liquid light emulsion, projection-speed emulsion for canvas and wood, toners, and sensitizers. Cyanotype kit.

Ruscombe Paper Mill

Bingham / Rustige

4, cours Pey-Berland

33460 Margaux, France

Tel: 0033 (0)5 57 88 73 77

Fax: 0033 (0)5 57 88 73 92

E-mail: info@ruscombepaper.com

Ruscombe makes one of the most beautiful alt pro papers in the world, Buxton. The business was founded by Christopher Bingham, a chartered engineer, with extensive manufacturing experience across a wide range of industries, including the papermaking sector. He is assisted by his wife, Jane, and a number of local people who carry out the papermaking. The sales and manufacturing business is jointly owned by Christopher Bingham and Martin Rustige, the proprietor of Anton Glaser in Stuttgart, Germany.

Science & Society Picture Library

Web site: http://www.scienceandsociety.co.uk

Science & Society Picture Library represents the collections of the Science Museum, the National Railway Museum and the National Museum of Photography, Film & Television—as well as a variety of related collections. There also are archives from The Royal Photographic Society.

Siderotype.com

http://www.siderotype.com/

This site is dedicated to the Chrysotype, a wonderful, flexible, and archival process developed by my friend Mike Ware. This site explains the reasons for learning the technique, sells Mike's books, and offers custom printing services.

Silverprint, Ltd.

0171 620-0844 (in London)

Web site: http://www.silverprint.co.uk

The distributor of most everything one needs to work in the non-silver and alternative process mode, Silverprint carries everything: paper, film, chemistry, equipment, Argyrotype kits, and storage materials. They distribute an exceptionally fine liquid emulsion that is highly recommended. Silverprint also markets Centennial POP paper.

Solarplate

(631) 725-3990

Web site: http://www.solarplate.com

This company, owned and run by Dan Welden, makes an excellent prepared polymer emulsion steel plates that are UV-sensitive and water-developed. If you are planning on going to press, they also sell half tone screens.

Spectrum Chemical Corp.

14422 S San Pedro Street, Gardena, CA 90248-2027

New Jersey Office:

755 Jersey Ave., New Brunswick, NJ 08901-3605

Telephone: (800) 813-1514 (Toll Free United States)

(310) 516-8000 (Internationally)

E-mail: sales@spectrumchemical.com

Web site: http://www.spectrumchemical.com

Spectrum is a multi-national corporation and supplies chemicals and lab products.

APP – 9

2007 Zero Image Line

Plain and simple, Zernike Au's cameras are nothing less than works of art and they are supremely functional as well. The cover of this book was created with his 4 x 5 zone plate… thanks Zernike!

(Courtesy of the artist)

Tim Whelan Photographic Books

Timothy Whelan Fine Photographic Books & Prints

25 Main St

P.O. Box 471

Rockport, ME 04856

T: (207) 236-4795

E-mail: photobks@midcoast.com

Tim is as nice a person as you could ever hope to meet, and he can get you any book, new or out of print, and will do so with pleasure. You will find Tim a complete delight and one of the most knowledgeable people in the world when it comes to photographic books.

Turbulence.Org

http://www.turbulence.org—another brave new world site

Ultra Fine On Line

Web Site: **www.ultrafineonline.com**

This is the site to go to when you need transfer support paper for the carbon process. Look for Professional Grade Photo Quality Luster, 10.2 mil. The paper works beautifully but may leave you unsatisfied when it dries as it looks a lot like ink-jet paper. Still, it is the very best paper to try when you are learning the process.

Unblinking Eye

http://www.unblinkingeye.com—a great alt pro photo site

Mike Ware

Web site: http://www.mikeware.co.uk/mikeware/main.html

Mike Ware has forgotten more about alternative processes than most people know after years of working in the genre. What this means is that he knows just about everything that is worth knowing about photographic history and, specifically, iron-, gold-, palladium-, and platinum-based processes. This site is a lot of fun to meander around in and should be enjoyed.

Wilcox Watercolor Site

http://www.handprint.com/HP/WCL/waterfs.html —Wilcox Watercolor Site

Without Lenses

http://www.withoutlenses.com—pinhole camera magazine site

Zero Image

Web site: http://www.zeroimage.com

E-mail: zerinke@zeroimage.com

This is the world-renowned enterprise belonging to a gentleman by the name of Zernike Au. He crafts beautifully made pinhole cameras out of fine woods and brass fittings and adds important parts such as metal pressure tabs to ensure that the roll film has adequate tension during winding—an important consideration to prevent the dreaded "fat roll." Without question, Zero Image pinholes are works of art.

WORKSHOPS

NOTE: **These are the workshops that I teach at yearly or every other year. I offer Intro to Alternative Processes and Advanced Alternative Process. If you want to take a weeklong workshop with me get in touch with these organizations and reserve a spot for the next class.**

The Maine Photographic Workshops/Maine Media Workshops

Web site: http://www.theworkshops.com

Founded by David Lyman over 35 years ago, the Maine Media Workshops continues to prosper under the new leadership of Charles Altschul, Joyce Tennyson, and Program Director Elizabeth Greenberg. I've been teaching intro and advanced alternative process workshops there for a few weeks each summer for over 33 years and it is still one of my favorite places to be.

The Santa Fe Workshops

Web site: http://santafeworkshops.com/

This is an excellent business owned and run extremely well by my friend Reid Callanan and is one of the best workshops in the world. For over a decade, they have been dedicated to digital imaging, but lately they have opened up to alternative processes and I've been teaching intro and advanced workshops there every summer. Sign up early.

Center for Photography at Woodstock

Web site: http://www.cpw.org

Founded by Colleen and Kathleen Kenyon, back when we were young, this charming workshop, in the charming village of Woodstock (not actually where the 1969 concert was held . . . that was 40 miles away in Bethel) continues to be a gentle reminder of quieter times. I teach there every other year and am always impressed that we manage to accomplish so much in the available space and driveway. Always packed with big name instructors, they are doing everything right.

Anderson Ranch Center for the Arts

Web site: http://www.andersonranch.org

Located in Snowmass, and a short jog to Aspen, this venue is as lovely a location as you could hope for. I teach intro and advanced workshops here every other year and totally enjoy myself as all of the arts are represented every week of the summer. Jim Baker was the director for quite a while before moving to Maine and now the operation is directed by former Boston resident Hunter O'Hanian.

A FEW ARTIST SITES

http://www.binaalteraimaging.com (Bina Altera)

http://www.czaphotography.com (Christina Z Anderson)

http://http://www.dickarentz.com/ (Dick Arentz)

http://www.jobabcock.com (Jo Babcock)

http://www.elenabaca.com/ (Elena Baca)

http://www.jonathanbailey.com (Jonathan Bailey)

http://www.matthewbelanger.com (Matt Belanger)

http://www.jaynehindsbidaut.com (Jayne Hinds Bidaut)

http://www.joeboyleart.com/ (Joe Boyle)

http://www.nancybreslin.com (Nancy Breslin)

http://www.jerryburchfield.com (Jerry Burchfield)

http://www.danburkholder.com (Dan Burkholder)

http://www.missconceptions.net/ (xtine Burrough)

http://www.johnpaulcaponigro.com/ (John Paul Caponigro)

http://www.keithcarterphotographs.com (Keith Carter)

http://www.joychristiansen.com/ (Joy Christiansen)

http://www.edelmangallery.com/connor (Linda Connor)

http://www.hainesgallery.com (Binh Dahn)

http://pathetica.net/ (Dan Estabrook)

http://www.marigardner.com (Mari Gardner)

http://www.absolutearts.com/portfolios/d/danutagibka/ (Danuta Gibka)

http://www.jessicatoddharper.com (Jessica Todd Harper)

http://www.brentonhamiltonstudio.net (Brenton Hamilton)

http://www.cigharvey.com/ (Cig Harvey)

http://www.gracehuang.com (Grace Huang)

http://www.christopherjames-studio.com (Christopher James)

http://www.catherinejansen.com/ (Catherine Jansen)

http://www.michaelkenna.net/ (Michael Kenna)

http://www.davidmichaelkennedy.com/ (David Michael Kennedy)

http://www.studiocyberia.com/ (Mark Kessell)

http://www.hands-on-pictures.com (Terry King)

http://www.lesleykrane.com (Lesley Krane)

http://www.cvknowlton.com/ (Charlene Knowlton)

http://www.jonathanlaurence.com (Jonathan Laurence)

http://www.peterliepke.com (Peter Liepke)

http://www.absolutearts.com/portfolios/c/carmen/ (Carmen Lizardo)

http://www.livick.com/ (Steven Livick)

http://www.marthamadigan.com (Martha Madigan)

http://www.ronniemaher.com (Ronnie Maher)

http://malde.sewanee.edu/ (Pradip Malde)

http://www.galina.no (Galina Manikova)

http://www.gagosian.com/artists/sally-mann/ (Sally Mann)

http://www.scottmcmahonphoto.com (Scott McMahon)

http://www.xs4all.nl/~moroux/ (Philippe Moroux)

http://www.zonezero.com (Pedro Meyer)

http://www.colleenmullins.net (Colleen Mullins)

http://www.bigredandshiny.com (Matt Nash)

http://www.harveylovesharvey.com (Matt Nash & Jason Dean)

http://www.beanettles.com (Bea Nettles)

http://www.bmpalm.com (Brian Palm)

http://www.gonzalezpalma.com/ (Luis Gonzale Palma)

http://www.oliviaparker.com (Olivia Parker)

http://www.pinchbeckphoto.com/ (Chris Pinchbeck)

http://www.douglasprince.com/ (Doug Prince)

http://pinholeresource.com/ (Eric Renner)

http://www.hollyrobertsstudio.com/ (Holly Roberts)

http://www.centurydarkroom.com (Mike Robinson)

http://www.ernestineruben.com/ (Ernestine Ruben)

http://www.marilynruseckas.com/ (Marilyn Ruseckas)

http://www.indulgencepress.com (W.H. Shilling)

http://www.leahsobsey.com (Leah Sobsey)

http://www.artropia.co.uk/surprise/gallery/lucy.html (Lucy Soutter)

http://www.jerryspagnoli.com (Jerry Spagnoli)

http://www.alchemy-studio.net (Panero-Smith & Hajicek)

http://www.lauriesnyder.com (Laurie Snyder)

http://pinholeresource.com/ (Nancy Spencer)

http://www.bostick-sullivan.com (Dick Sullivan)

http://www.er3.com/donna/ (Donna Hamil Talmin)

http://www.uelsmann.net/ (Jerry Uelsmann)

http://got.net/%7Ervail/recent/recent.html (Roger Vail)

http://www.mikeware.co.uk/ (Mike Ware)

http://www.shoshannahwhite.com (Shoshannah White)

http://www.lisawiltse.com (Lisa Wiltse)

http://www.rachelwoodburn.com (Rachel Woodburn)

http://www.savedge.com/ (Willie Anne Wright)

APP – 10

Dan Estabrook, Portrait of the Artist for JPW, 1991—montage

When Dan was a student of mine at Harvard, he was listening to me one day as I was offering up some observations about a Joel Peter Witkin show that I had just attended. In response, Dan went off and made this piece for me . . . thanks Dan!
(Courtesy of the artist)

Selected Bibliography: Alternative Processes.

CONTEMPORARY BIBLIOGRAPHY

Stephen Anchell, *The Darkroom Cookbook* (Boston: Focal Press, 1994).

Jan Arnow, *Handbook of Alternative Photographic Processes* (New York: Van Nostrand Reinholt Co., 1982).

Dick Arentz, *Platinum & Palladium Printing: Second Edition* (Focal Press, Elsevier, 2005).

Dick Arentz, *Outline for Platinum / Palladium Printing* (self-published 3rd edition, 1998).

Janet Ashford & John Odam, *Start With a Scan* (Berkeley, CA: Peachpit Press, 1996).

Geoffrey Batchen, *Burning With Desire* (Cambridge, MA, The MIT Press, 1999).

John Barnier, ed. *Coming Into Focus* (San Francisco, CA: Chronicle Books, 2000).

Bill Bryson, *A Short History of Nearly Everything* (New York: Broadway Books, 2003).

Buckland, Gail, *Fox Talbot and the Invention of Photography* (Boston, Godine, 1980).

Peter C. Bunnell, ed. *Non-Silver Printing Processes* (New York: Arno Press, 1973).

Peter Bunnell, ed., *A Photographic Vision: Pictorial Photography, 1889–1923* (Salt Lake City, Peregrine Smith, 1980).

Dan Burkholder, *Making Digital Negatives for Contact Printing* (San Antonio, TX: Bladed Iris Press, 1998).

Vannevar Bush, *As We May Think* (The Atlantic, 1945).

Max Byrd, *Shooting the Sun* (Bantam/Random House, 2004).

Charles Caffin, *Photography as a Fine Art, the Achievement and Possibilities of Photographic Art in America*, 1901 (Reprint, with introduction by Thomas F. Barrow, Dobbs Ferry, NY, Morgan & Morgan, 1971).

John Paul Caponigro, *Adobe Photoshop Master Class* (San Jose, CA: Adobe Press, 2000).

John Paul Caponigro, *Adobe Photoshop Master Class: John Paul Caponigro, 2nd Edition* (Adobe Press; 2 edition (2003).

Cassell's Cyclopedia of Photography, ed. by B. E. Jones (New York: Arno Press, 1973).

Nancy Clark, *Ventilation* (New York: Lyons & Burford, 1990).

Brian Coe and Mark Haworth-Booth, *A Guide to Early Photographic Processes* (London: Victoria & Albert Museum, 1983).

Athel Cornish-Bowden, "Elizabeth Fulhame and the Discovery of Catalysis 100 Years Before Buchner," *Journal of Bioscience*, 23 (1998), pp. 87–92.

APP – 11

Jill Skupin Burkholder, *Man With Baseballs*, 2001 – bromoil
This image, from the State Fair of Texas in Dallas, is made with the bromoil process. Jill writes, "I have a strange reaction to this image. Maybe because it's just the torso, it makes me think of the statue "David" which throws me into an antiquity state of mind. The carnival barker seems more like a Greek hero to me, ready to battle the dark forces." *(Courtesy of the artist)*

William Crawford, *The Keepers of Light* (Dobbs Ferry, NY: Morgan & Morgan, 1979).

George DeWolfe, *George DeWolfe's Fine Digital Photography Workshop* (McGraw-Hill Osborne Media; 1st edition (April 25, 2006).

Robert Doty, *Photo-Secession: Stieglitz and the Fine Art Movement in Photography* (New York, Dover Publications, 1978).

George Eaton, *Photographic Chemistry*, Dobbs Ferry, NY: Morgan & Morgan, 1999).

Dan Estabrook, 3-D Gum Printing Worksheet and e-mail reply to Anthotype question (1998).

Howard Etkin & Carson Graves, *Toning Safety* Ilford Photo Instructor Newsletter, 1997.

Richard Farber, *Historic Photographic Processes* (New York: Allworth Press, 1998).

Galassi, Peter, *Before Photography—Painting and the Invention of Photography*, New York, The Museum of Modern Art, 1981.

Arnold Gassan, A *Chronology of Photography* (Athens, OH: Handbook Company, 1972).

Arnold Gassan, *Handbook for Contemporary Photography*, 4th ed. (Rochester, NY: Light Impressions, 4th edition, 1977).

Helmut Gernsheim, *The Origins of Photography* (New York, Thames and Hudson, 1982).

Allan Goodman, *Elegant Images: Instructions and Troubleshooting Guide for Platinum and Palladium Photoprinting* (Delaware, MD: Elegant Images, 1976).

Christopher Grey, *Photographer's Guide to Polaroid Transfers* (Buffalo, NY: Amherst Media, 1999).

Sarah Greenough, *On the Art of Fixing a Shadow: 150 Years of Photography* Boston: Bulfinch Press, 1989).

Betty Hahn, *Photography or Maybe Not* (Albuquerque: University of New Mexico Press, 1995).

John Hammond, *The Camera Obscura: A Chronicle* (Bristol, England: Adam Hilger Ltd., 1981).

Margaret Harker, *The Linked Ring: The Secession Movement in Photography in Britain, 1892–1910* (London, Heineman, 1979).

Barbara Hewitt, *Blueprints of Fabric: Innovative Uses for Cyanotype* (Loveland, CO: Interweave Press, 1995).

Wolfgang Hesse, *Hermann Krone. Historisches Lehmuseum fur Photographie, 1998* (Dresden: Kupferstich-Kabinett der Staatlichen Kunstsammlungen Dresden, Technishe Universitat, 1998) Dresden.

Ann Hoy, *Fabrications* (New York: Abbeville Press, 1987).

Robert Hughes, "Mirrors and Windows," *Time*, August 7, 1978.

Christopher James, *The Book of Alternative Photographic Processes: 1st Edition* (Albany, NY: Delmar Thomson Learning, 2002).

Ross King, *Brunelleschi's Dome: How a Renaissance Genius Reinvented Architecture* (Penguin, 2001).

Ross King, *Michelangelo and The Pope's Ceiling* (Pimlico, 2006), New Edition.

Jaromir Kosar, *Light Sensitive Systems: Chemistry and Application of Non Silver Halide Photographic Processes* (New York: John Wiley and Sons, 1965).

Steven Levy, *Insanely Great* (New York: Penguin Books, 1994).

The Merck Index, *Encyclopedia of Chemicals and Drugs* (Whitehouse Station, NJ: Merck & Co., 1968).

Luis Nadeau, *History and Practice of Platinum Printing* (New Brunswick, Canada: Atelier Luis Nadeau, 1994).

Luis Nadeau, *Encyclopedia of Printing, Photographic & Photomechanical Processes* (New Brunswick, Canada: Atelier Luis Nadeau, 1989).

Luis Nadeau, *Gum Dichromate* (New Brunswick, Canada: Atelier Luis Nadeau, 1987.

Bea Nettles, *Breaking the Rules: A Photo media Cookbook* (Rochester, NY: Inky Press Productions, 1977; expanded 3rd edition Urbana, IL, 1992).

Beumont Newhall, *The History of Photography* (New York: Museum of Modern Art, 1982).

Beaumont Newhall, *The Art and Science of Photography*, Edited by Beaumont Newhall, (Watkins Glen, NY: Century House, Watkins Glen, NY, 1956.

Lynn Picknett and Clive Prince, *Turin Shroud: In Whose Image? The Truth Behind the Centuries-Long Conspiracy of Silence* (Amherst, MA: Acacia Press, 1994).

James Reilly, *The Albumen and Salted Paper Book - The History and Practice of Photographic Printing 1840–1895*, Light Impressions, (Rochester, NY: Light Impressions, 1980).

Martin Reed and Sarah Jones, *Silver Gelatin: A Users Guide to Liquid Emulsions* (New York: Amphoto, 1996).

Eric Renner and Nancy Spencer, *Pinhole Photography* (Focal Press, Stoneham, MA: Focal Press, 1994.

Lyle Rexer, *Antiquarian Avant-Garde: The New Wave in Old Process Photography* New York: Harry N. Abrams, 2002).

Nancy Rexroth, *The Platinotype 1977* Missoula, MT: Formulary Press / Violet Press, 1977).

John Ross, Clare Romano, and Tim Ross, *The Complete Printmaker* New York: Collier Macmillan Publishers, The Free Press, 1990).

John Rudiak, "The Platinotype," *View Camera*, January/February 1994.

John Rudiak, "Creating a Platinotype," *View Camera*, July/August 1994.

Salman Rushdie, Random House, *Midnight's Children* (New York: Random House, 1981).

David Scopick, *The Gum Bichromate Book* (Rochester, NY: Light Impressions, 1987).

Larry Schaaf and Hans Kraus (contributors), *Sun Gardens: Victorian Photograms by Anna Atkins* (New York: Aperture, 1985). [This book is based on Anna Atkins' 10-year, 3-volume collection entitled *British Algae: Cyanotype Impressions*, privately printed (1843–1853).]

Larry Schaaf, *Out of the Shadows: Herschel, Talbot, and the Invention of Photography* (New Haven, CT: Yale University Press, 1992).

Larry J Schaaf, 'The Talbot Collection: National Museum of American History," *History of Photography*, 24:1 (Spring 2000), pp. 7–15.

Larry Schaaf (editor), *The Correspondence of William Henry Fox Talbot,* Project has prepared a comprehensive edition of the nearly 10,000 letters to and from Talbot (1800–1877), in association with De Montfort University, Leicester, web site; www.foxtalbot.dmu.ac.uk/.

Susan Shaw and Monona Rossol (contributors), *Overexposure: Health Hazards in Photography* (New York: Allworth Press, 1991).

Thomas Shillea, *Instruction Manual for the Platinum Printing Process* (1986).

Jim Schull, The *Hole Thing: A Manual of Pinhole Photography* (Dobbs Ferry, NY: Morgan & Morgan, 1974).

Judy Seigel, Ed., *"Post Factory Photography"* - Issues 1, 2, 3, 4, 5, 6, 7, and 8, New York: Post Factory Press, 1998—2000.

Jerry Spagnoli, *Daguerreotypes: 1995–2004,* (Steidl Publishing, Göttingen, Germany: Steidl Publishing, 2006.

D. A. Spencer, *Ed., Focal Encyclopedia of Photography* (London & New York: Focal Press, Ltd., 1973).

Dick Stevens, *Making Kallitypes—A Definitive Guide* (Stoneham, MA: Butterworth & Heinemann, 1990).

Craig Stevens, *a Mordançage Process Worksheet . . . from Jean Paul Sudre notes, 1998.*

Dick Sullivan, *Lab Notes* (Van Nuys, CA: Bostick & Sullivan, 1982).

Dick Sullivan and Carl Weese, *The New Platinum Print* (Santa Fe, NM: Working Pictures Press Book, 1998).

John Szarkowski, *Looking at Photographs* (New York: Museum of Modern Art, 1973).

George Tice, "Processes: Palladium & Platinum," *Modern Photography* (March 1971).

Hollis Todd and Richard Zakia, *Photographic Sensitometry* (Dobbs Ferry, NY: Morgan & Morgan, 1969).

Alan Trachtenberg, ed. *Classic Essays on Photography* (New Haven, CT: Leete's Island Books, 1980).

Sarah Van Keuren, *A Non-Silver Manual, self-published notes for students at the University of the Arts in Philadelphia, 1999–2006.*

Kent Wade, *Alternative Photographic Processes* (Dobbs Ferry, NY: Morgan and Morgan, 1978).

Dr. Michael Ware, "The Argyrotype," *British Journal of Photography*, 139:6824 (13 June 1991), pp. 17–19.

Dr. Michael Ware, *Cyanotype: The History, Science & Art of Photographic Printing in Prussian Blue* (London: Science Museum & National Museum of Photography, Film & Television, 1999).

Mike Ware and Pradip Malde, *A Contemporary Method for Making Photographic Prints in Platinum & Palladium* (1988).

Dr. Michael Ware, *Mechanisms of Image Deterioration in Early Photographs—the sensitivity to light of W.H.F. Talbot's halide-fixed images 1834–1844* (London: Science Museum and National Museum of Photography, Film & Television, 1994).

Dr. Michael Ware, *Gold in Photography: The History and Art of Chrysotype* (Abergavenny: ffotoffilm publishing, 2006).

Dr. Michael Mike, *The Chrysotype Manual: The Science and Practice of Photographic Printing in Gold* (Abergavenny: ffotoffilm publishing 2006).

Dr. Michael Ware, "An Investigation of Platinum and Palladium Printing," *Journal of Photographic Science*, 34 (1986), 13–25.

Dr. Michael Ware, 'The Eighth Metal: The Rise of the Platinotype Process', in *Photography 1900, The Edinburgh Symposium*, 99–111, (National Museums of Scotland and National Galleries of Scotland, 1994).

Dr. Michael Ware, "Photographic Printing in Colloidal Gold," *Journal of Photographic Science*, 42:5 (1994), 157–161, (1994).

Bruce Warren, *Photography* (New York: Delmar Publishers, 1993).

Randall Webb and Martin Reed, *Spirits of Salts* (London: Argentum, an imprint of Aurum Press, 1999).

Mike Wooldridge and Linda Wooldridge, *Teach Yourself VISUALLY Photoshop CS2* (2005).

Lee Witkin and Barbara London, *The Photograph Collector's Guide* (Boston: New York Graphics Society, 1979).

EARLY & HISTORICAL BIBLIOGRAPHY

Aristotle, *Problems*, I. Books I–XXI, with English translation by W. S. Hett (London: William Heinemann Ltd., 1936).

W. de W. Abney and Lyonel Clark, *Platinotype* (London: Sampson Low, Marston and Co., 1895).

W. de W. Abney and Lyonel Clark, *Platinotype* (New York: Scovill & Adams of New York, 1898).

W. de W. Abney, *Instruction in Photography* (London, England, Piper and Carter, 1886).

Leon Battista Alberti, *On Painting*, translated by Cecil Grayson (London: Phaidon Press Ltd., 1972).

Count Francesco Algorotti, *Essays on Painting* (London: Davis & Reymers, 1764).

Paul Anderson, *Pictorial Photography, Its Principals and Practice* (New York: J.B. Lippincot, 1917; (republished as *The Technique of Pictorial Photography*, 1939).

Paul Anderson, *Handbook of Photography* (New York: Whittlesey House, 1939).

Anna Atkins, *British Algae: Cyanotype Impressions*, Halstead Place, Sevenoaks, 3 volumes, privately printed (1843–1853). A dozen copies are known to exist. The first volume of images was issued in October 1843 (prior to Talbot's *The Pencil of Nature*). See: L. J. Schaaf and H. P. Kraus, *Sun Gardens— Victorian photograms by Anna Atkins* (New York: Aperture Books, (1985).

George E. Brown, F.I.C., *Ferric & Heliographic Processes* (London: Dawbarn and Ward, Ltd., 1900).

Rev. W. H. Burbank, *Photographic Printing Methods* (New York, Scovill & Adams Co., 1891).

Lyonel Clark, *Platinum Toning: Introducing Directions for the Production of the Sensitive Paper* (New York: E & H T Anthony and Co., 1890).

L. P. Clerc, *The Technique of Photography* (Bath, England, Henry Greenwood & Company, 1930, and New York: Pitman & Sons, 1930).

Peter Henry Emerson, *Life and Landscape on the Norfolk Broads* (London: Sampson Low, Marston, Searle, & Rivington, 1886).

Peter Henry Emerson, *Naturalistic Photography for Students of the Art* (London: Sampson Low, Marston, Searle & Rivington, 1889).

Peter Henry Emerson, *The Death of Naturalistic Photography* (London: self-published, 1890).

Frank R. Fraprie and Walter E. Woodbury, *Photographic Amusements: Including tricks and Unusual or Novel Effects Obtainable with the Camera* (Boston: American Photographic Publishing, 1931).

Frank R. Fraprie and Florence O'Connor, *Photographic Amusements: Including tricks and Unusual or Novel Effects Obtainable with the Camera* (Boston: American Photographic Publishing, 1937).

Elizabeth Fulhame, *An Essay on Combustion, With a View to a New Art of Dying and Painting, wherein the Phlogistic and Antiphlogistic Hypotheses are proved Erroneous* (London: self-published in 1794).

W. Jerome Harrison, *Scoville Photographic Series, A History of Photography* (New York: Scoville Mfg. Company, 1887).

W. Jerome Harrison, *The Chemistry of Photography* (Scoville & Adams Company New York, 1892).

J. F. W. Herschel, "On the Action of Light in Determining the precipitation of Muriate of Platinum by Lime-Water," London and Edinburgh Philosophical magazine and Journal of Science, Vol. I, July 1832.

J. F. W. Herschel, "On the Action of the Rays of the Solar Spectrum on Vegetable Colours and on Some New Photographic Processes," *Philosophical Transactions of the Royal Society*, 202 (1842).

Margaret Herschel, *Memoir and Correspondence of Caroline Herschel* (New York: Appleton & Co., 1876).

Ibn al-Haitam, *On the Form of an Eclipse*, c. 1038. This document can be found at the India Office Library in London.

Robert Hunt, *Researches on Light* (London: Longman, Brown Green and Longmans, 1844; reprinted Arno Press, New York, 1973).

Bernard E. Jones (editor), *Cassell's Cyclopaedia of Photography* (London, Cassell and Co., 1911).

Edward MacCurdy, *The Notebooks of Leonardo da Vinci* (New York: Reynal & Hitchcock, 1938).

C. B. Neblette, *Photography: its Materials and Processes* (New York: Van Nostrand Co., 1927).

Isidore Niépce (son of Joseph Nicéphore Niépce), *History of the discovery improperly called daguerreotype* (Paris: Astier, 1841).

G. Pizzighelli and Baron A Hübl, *Platinotype* (London, Harrison and Sons, 1886).

Karl Wilhelm Scheele, *Chemical Observations and Experiments on Air and Fire* (1777).

R. S. Schultze, *"Rediscovery and Description of original material on the Photographic Researches of Sir F.W. John Herschel, 1939–1944,"* Journal of Photographic Science, Vol 13, (1965).

Jean Senebier, *Mémoires physico-chimiques sur l'influence de la lumière solaire* (Genève 1782), vol. III.

Henry Snelling, *The History and Practice of the Art of Photography.* Published by G. P. Putnam, 155 Broadway, 1849.

Mary Somerville, *On the Action of Rays of the Spectrum on Vegetable Juices,* Philosophical Transactions of the Royal Society, Vol. 136, 1846.

Thomas Sutton & John Worden, *The Encyclopedia of Photography* (London: Sampson Low & Son, 1858).

William Henry Fox Talbot, *Calotype Photogenic Drawing,* Communique to the Royal Society, London, June 10, 1841.

William Henry Fox Talbot, *The Pencil of Nature* (London: Longman, Brown Green & Longmans, 1844).

William Henry Fox Talbot, Fine Arts / Royal Society, Letter sent to the Royal Society on February 20, 1839, clarifying the specifics in the production of Photogenic Drawings.

William Henry Fox Talbot, Photogenic Drawing details, *The Literary Gazette*, London, February 22, 1839.

Norman Tiphaigne de la Roche, *Giphantie* (Paris, 1760).

John A. Tennant, ed., *The Photominiature #47* (London, Dawbarn and Ward, 1903).

John Tennant. *The Photo-Miniature*, #10 (London, Dawbarn and Ward, January 1900).

John Tennant. *The Photo-Miniature*, #69 (London, Dawbarn and Ward, December 1904).

John Towler, *The Silver Sunbeam* (New York: Joseph H. Ladd, 1864).

E. J. Wall and Franklin I. Jordan, *Photographic Facts and Formulas* (Boston: American Photographic Publishing Co., 1947).

H. Snowden Ward, *Figures, Facts and Formulae of Photography* (London, Dawbarn and Ward, 1903).

W. A. Watts, *The Photographic Reference Book* London: Iliffe and Son, 1896).

Thomas Wedgewood and Sir Humphry Davy, *An Account of a method of Copying paintings Upon Glass and Making Profiles by the Agency of Light Upon Nitrate of Silver* (1802).

APP – 12

Etienne Carjat (1828–1906), *Portrait of Charles Baudelaire (1821–1867),* c. 1863, Woodburytype plate from Galerie Contemporaine, Paris, 1878
Charles Baudelaire (1821–1867), the subject of this image, was a man of deep moods and un-relenting despair whose poetry centered upon the inseparable connection between beauty and the inevitable corruption of that beauty. Baudelaire wrote about his first impressions of photography in less than glowing terms, implying that society was squalid and narcissistic in its rush to gaze upon trivial images of itself rendered on scraps of metal. He also wrote, in a critique of an exhibition in 1859, "If photography is allowed to supplement art in some of its functions, it will soon have supplanted or corrupted it altogether . . . " And that, my friends, is about as positive a statement as Baudelaire ever made.
(Courtesy of The George Eastman House, Rochester, NY)